Directory *of* Specialized American Bookdealers

1987-1988

Directory *of* Specialized American Bookdealers

1987-1988

Prepared by the staff of *American Book Collector*

New York: The Moretus Press, Inc.

R0105182434

Table of Contents

How To Use This Directory

Use this third edition of *Directory of Specialized American Bookdealers* as you would any good reference book. It contains a wealth of information about nearly 3,000 rare, antiquarian, used, and out-of-print bookdealers in the United States and Canada.

The *Directory* is divided into four sections. The key section is the first, the *Main, or Geographical,* section. Here are listed, alphabetically by state and then alphabetically by city and within each city, the name, address, telephone number, proprietors, and specialties of each bookdealer. In addition, most dealers have provided information about their hours (if they keep an open shop) or whether they prefer to be contacted soley by mail or will meet visitors by appointment.

The *Specialties* section contains 525 book specialties, some broad (such as "Americana") and some quite narrow (such as "Adirondacks"). Each dealer who has listed a particular specialty in the main section will be found under that specialty in this section. To find the street address and telephone number of that dealer, you can easily check it in the main section.

In the *Alphabetical Index* we have provided a complete alphabetical listing of all the dealers included in the *Directory.*

And, finally, there is the *"Who's Who"* section. Here is a complete index to the names of all the proprietors of the firms listed in the *Directory.*

Many dealers represented in this *Directory* have chosen to expand on their listings by providing display advertisements, and these have been placed throughout the book.

As with any refernce book, knowledge of the assumptions that the *Directory*'s compilers have made will help you use the *Directory* more efficiently.

"Out-of-Print" and "Uused" Books. This is what the bookdealers listed in this *Directory* stock: we thus have not provided categories for these kinds of books. It is the "general" bookdealer who carries a wide variety of books.

Search Services. Most bookdealers will search for a book that a collector wants. Thus we have listed "search services" *only* when that is the sole activity that a dealer engages in.

Shop Hours and "By Appointment Only." Sharply increasing store rents have forced many dealers out of what were once highly bookish districts as Fourth Avenue in New York City and Westwood Boulevard in Los Angeles. The decline of these districts, while lamentable, has led to two related phenomena: the dispersion of the open shops around the major cities and the rise of the "non-store bookstore."

The breaking up of bookish districts in our major cities by increasing shop rents has led many dealers who thrive on daily customer contact (both to sell and to buy books) to remove their businesses to less expensive parts of these cities or areas not generally thought of as bookish. Knowledgable visitors and residents alike consider the slight change in their normal routine that travelling to, say, Brooklyn or Cambridge from Manhattan or Boston presents well worth it when they find the dealers there eager to provide hard-to-find books.

Where we have shown shop hours it means that the bookdealer is on the premises at that time and welcomes buyers without the need to call ahead. Dealers that list themselves "by appointment only'' are either in non-retail premises (such as urban apartments or suburban homes), but they too are eager to receive visitors. Do not be put off by the ''by apppintment only'' notation concerning hours.

Acknowledgments

The making of this *Directory* was no solitary effort. Many diverse hands have had a part in its compilation, production, and distribution. *Aleena O. Pederson* has been the invaluable steadying force in seeing that information was correctly entered in the computer and that questions about its publication date were answered truthfully. *Ed Shencker* saved our bacon when our homebrew database froze up as tight as an arctic icepack. Finally, the apolmb with which *Mark and Larry Murphy* handled our page makeup and typesetting was remarkable.

A Reminder About All Directories —And Certainly This One

No directory of any group of small businesses, and certainly no directory of the group of small businessses that comprise the antiquarian book trade, is error-free or absolutely current at the time it is published. But you have in your hands a directory that is far more up-to-date and valuable than any similar reference book because of the comparatively short time between information gathering and publication.

Nevertheless, we add this *caveat*: while this *Directory* is by far the most extensive book of its kind available today, it was produced by human beings with the aid of computers, which implies the possibility of error. If you find an error, know of anyone who ought to be included in future editions, or if you have any suggestions about any aspect of this book for future editions, by all means let us hear them. We have done our best but, alas, we cannot be responsible for errors shown here beyond making a correction in our files for the next edition.

Main Section
(Geographical)

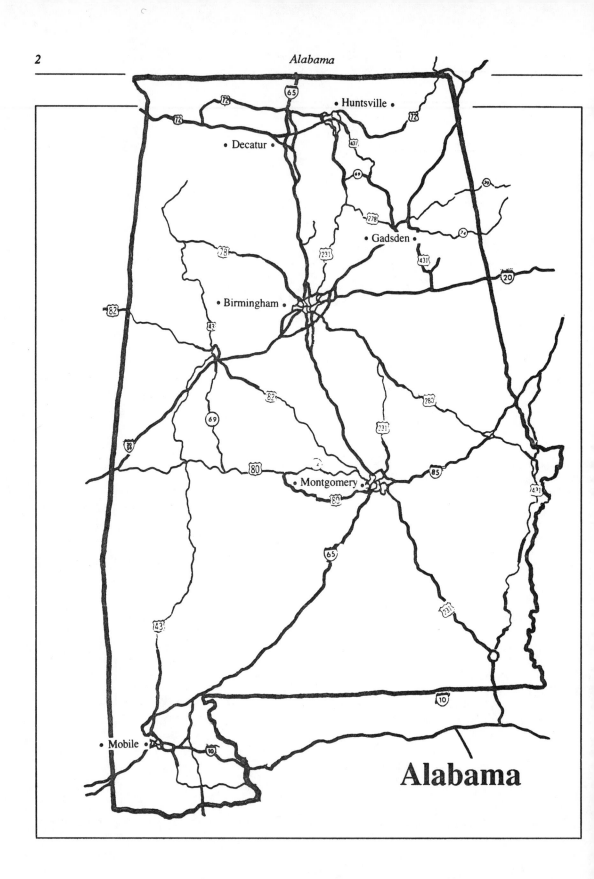

Alabama

Cather & Brown
P. O. Box 313
Birmingham, Ala. 35201
(205) 591-7284
By appointment only
Catalogues issued
*Alabama; Civil War &
Confederacy; Americana; Southern
Americana*

Reed Books
P. O. Box 55893
Birmingham, Ala. 35255
Jim Reed
Search Service, Without Stock

Sessions Book Sales
P. O. Box 9593
Birmingham, Ala. 35220
(205) 853-4688
By appointment only
Catalogues issued
Lewe H. Sessions
*Conservative Literature & Authors;
Radical Poltics & Literature;
Espionage; Conspiracies &
Conspiracy Theory*

Linda Ivey
Route 4, Box 144
Brewton, Ala. 36426
(205) 867-7309
By appointment only
Catalogues issued
Linda Ivey, John Robinette
Americana; Southern Americana

Book & Art Shop
210 North Foster Street
Dothan, Ala. 36303
(205) 792-9812
9:30-5 Mon-Sat
Children's Books; General

R E Publications
902 Morphy Avenue
Fairhope, Ala. 36532
(205) 928-8637
3-10 Tues-Sat
Catalogues issued
R. E. Rhoades, Phyllis Rhoades,
Jimmy Saloom
*Civil War & Confederacy;
Alabama; Local History; Lafcadio
Hearn; Naval & Nautical; Marine
& Maritime*

Gary Wayner
Route 3, Box 18
Fort Payne, Ala. 35967-8501
(205) 845-5866
By appointment only
Catalogues issued
Gary Wayner
*Botany; Gardening & Horticulture;
Natural History; Scholarly Books;
Sporting; Rare Books*

Alec R. Allenson, Inc.
P. O. Box 447
Geneva, Ala. 36340
By mail only
Catalogues issued

Robert D. Allenson
*Religion & Religous History; Bible
& Bible Studies; Bibliography*

David L. Stone
515 Jordan Lane, Box 11009
Huntsville, Ala. 35805
(205) 895-9992
10-6 Tues-Sat
David L. Stone
General

Far Corners Book Search
2000 Dauphin Street (Termite Hall)
Mobile, Ala. 36606
(205) 479-2937
By mail only
Adelaide M. Trigg
General

The Bookmonger
1 North Goldthwaite Street
Montgomery, Ala. 36104
(205) 834-5238
10-5 Mon-Sat
Julian Godwin
Regional Americana

Red House Books
3774 Atlanta Highway
Montgomery, Ala. 36109-3624
(205) 272-2510
10-6 Mon-Sat
Margaret Jackson
General

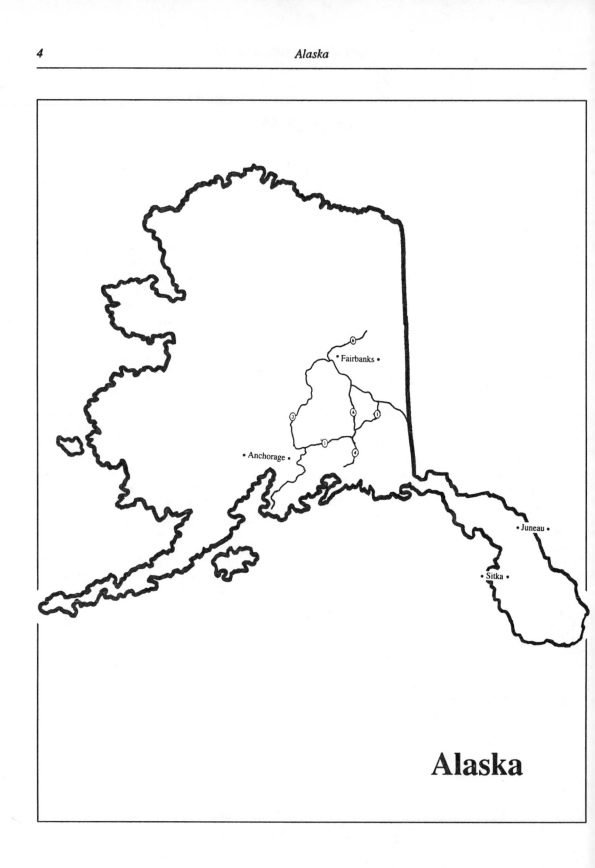

Alaska

Alaska

Herb Hilscher
2224 Foraker Drive
Anchorage, Alk. 99517
(907) 243-4383
By mail only
Herb Hilscher
Alaska

Martin's Books
3rd & Lacey Streets (northwest
building), suite 115
Fairbanks, Alk. 99701
(907) 456-2240
11-5:30 Mon-Fri
Marie Martin, Kenneth Martin
*Alaska; Arctica & Antarctica;
Birds & Ornithology; Fishing &*

Angling; Mining & Metallurgy

Compass Rose
P. O. Box 2431
Sitka, Alk. 99835
(907) 747-8430
9-6 Mon-Sat
Catalogues issued
Phillip Sax
*Naval & Nautical; Marine &
Maritime; Sailing & Yachting;
Ships & The Sea*

The Observatory
P. O. Box 1770, 202 Katlian Street
Sitka, Alk. 99835
(907) 747-3033

10-5:30 Mon-Sat (Summers), else
1-5 Mon-Sat
Catalogues issued
Dee Longenbaugh
*Arctica & Antarctica; Alaska; Voy-
ages, Travels, & Exploration;
Maps, Atlases, & Cartography*

Old Harbor Books
201 Lincoln Street, Box 1827
Sitka, Alk. 99835
(907) 747-8808
10-6 Mon-Fri, 10-5 Sat
Don Muller
*Alaska; Arctica & Antarctica; Voy-
ages, Travels, & Exploration*

Alberta

Robert C. Scace
P. O. Box 7156, Stn. E
Calgary, Alt. T3C 3M1
(403) 246-8303
Catalogues issued
Robert C. Scace
*Canada & Canadiana; Conserva-
tion*

Tom Williams
P. O. Box 4126, Stn. C
Calgary, Alt. T2T 5M9
(403) 264-0184
By appointment only
Catalogues issued
Tom Williams
Arctica & Antarctica; Canada &

*Canadiana; Mountaineering; Petro-
leum; Natural History; Voyages,
Travels, & Exploration*

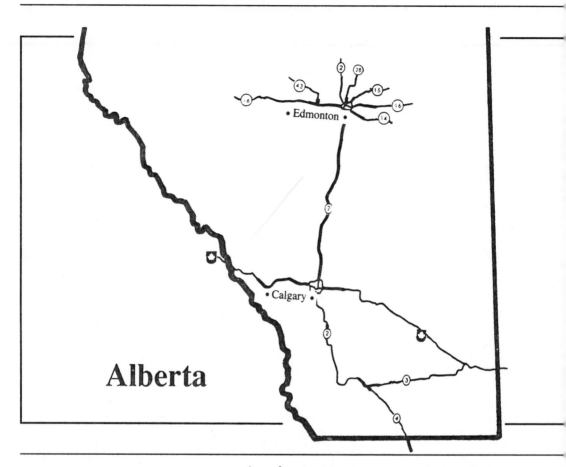

Arizona

David Eshner
8 Brewery Gulch, Box 353
Bisbee, Ariz. 85603
(602) 432-4249
8-5 Mon-Sat, 9-2 Sun
Catalogues issued
David Eshner
Latin America; Central America;
Mexico; Southwestern Americana;
Spanish Books & Literature; Indi-
ans & Eskimos

John W. Kuehn
P. O. Box 73, Brewery Gulch
Bisbee, Ariz. 85603
(602) 432-4249

9-5 Mon-Sat, 10-3 Sun
Catalogues issued
John W. Kuehn
Arizona; Western Americana;
Mexico

Caddo Book Sales
P. O. Box 71
Cartaro, Ariz. 85652
(602) 297-3045
By appointment only
Catalogues issued
Irene Werner
Western Americana; Art; Illus-
trated Books

Russ Todd Books
Star Route 2, Box 872-F
Cave Creek, Ariz. 85331
(602) 585-0070
By appointment only
Catalogues issued
Russ Todd
Western Americana; Modern Firs
Editions; Photography; Outlaws &
Rangers; Southwestern Americana
Collection Development

Donald E. Hahn
P. O. Box 1004, 512 West Gila
Cottonwood, Ariz. 86326
(602) 634-5016

By appointment only
Catalogues issued
Donald E. Hahn
*Natural History; Fish &
Ichthyology; Herpetology;
Mammalogy; Paleontology;
Entomology*

Duck's Books
1800 South Milton
Flagstaff, Ariz. 86001
(602) 779-5365
10:30-7:30 daily
John C. Duck, Bonita B. Duck
Western Americana

Ruth I. Kern
P. O. Box 5130
Glendale, Ariz. 85311
(602) 938-0975
By appointment only
Ruth Kern
*Voyages, Travels, & Exploration;
Women; Church History; Chil-
dren's Books; Ships & The Sea;
Fires & Firefighting*

J. & L. Books
158 West Main Street
Mesa, Ariz. 85201
(602) 964-0381
8-5 Mon-Sat
J. H. Schrooten
General

Collector's Books
P. O. Box 10159
Phoenix, Ariz. 85064
(602) 941-8496
By mail only
Catalogues issued
Tom Torbert
*Fishing & Angling; Big Game Hunt-
ing; Hunting; Guns & Weapons*

Harold J. Mason, Inc.
P. O. Box 32363
Phoenix, Ariz. 85064
(602) 956-6269

By mail only
Catalogues issued
Harold J. Mason
*Business & Business History;
Humanities; Back Issue Period-
icals; Political, Social, & Cultural
History; Social Sciences; Stock
Market & Wall Street*

North Mountain Books
746 East Dunlap Avenue
Phoenix, Ariz. 85020
(602) 997-1643
10-6 Mon-Fri, 11-4 Sat
Lawrence W. Jerome
*Science; Technical; Scholarly
Books*

Bonita Porter
2011 West Bethany Home Road,
Box 1765
Phoenix, Ariz. 85015
(602) 242-9442
9:30-5:30 Tues-Sat
Catalogues issued
Bonita Porter, Paul Porter
*Regional Americana; First Edi-
tions; Prints; Art, Western*

Cow Country Books
P. O. Box 2391
Prescott, Ariz. 86303
By mail only
John W. Gould, Margaret Gould
*Cattle & Range Industry; Western
Americana; Arizona*

Guidon Books
7117 Main Street
Scottsdale, Ariz. 85251
(602) 945-8811
10-5 Mon-Sat
Aaron L. Cohen, Ruth K. Cohen
*Civil War & Confederacy; West-
ern Americana; Art, Western*

Natural History Books
P. O. Box 67
Scottsdale, Ariz. 85252

(602) 948-2536
By mail only
Catalogues issued
William R. Hecht
*Natural History; Falconry;
Americana; Southern Americana*

Scottsdale Bookseller
7136 Main Street
Scottsdale, Ariz. 85251
(602) 946-0022
9:30-5:30 Mon-Sat
Catalogues issued
Wendy Moss, Russ Todd
*Western Americana; Art, Books
about; Art, Western*

Ruby D. Kaufman
518 East Loma Vista Drive
Tempe, Ariz. 85282
(602) 968-9517
By appointment only
Catalogues issued
Ruby D. Kaufman
*Children's Books; Illustrated
Books; Art*

Old Town Books
10 West 7th Street
Tempe, Ariz. 85281
(602) 968-9881
10-5 Mon-Sat
Greg Johnson
*Western Americana; Fishing &
Angling; Hunting; General*

Those Were The Days!
516 South Mill Avenue
Tempe, Ariz. 85281
(602) 967-4729
9:30-5:30 Mon-Sat (Thurs to 9),
12-5 Sun
Antiques

Rosetree Inn Books
P. O. Box 7
Tombstone, Ariz. 85638
(602) 457-3326
9-5 daily

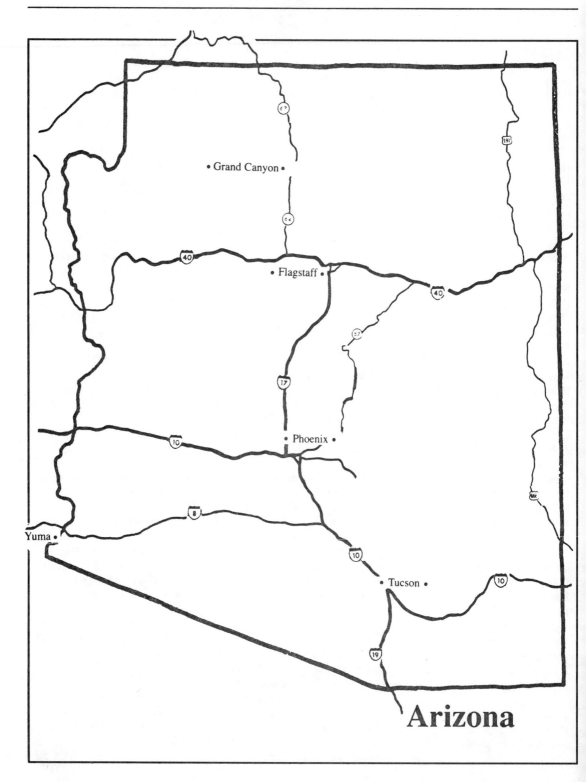

Arizona

Catalogues issued
Burton Devere
Indians & Eskimos; Regional Americana; Outlaws & Rangers

Baseball Books Only
5672 East Scarlett Street
Tucson, Ariz. 85711
(602) 747-5394
By mail only
J. C. Percell
Collection Development; Sporting

A Booklover's Shop
P. O. Box 43607
Tucson, Ariz. 85733
By mail only
Robert Hershoff
Catholica; Southwestern Americana; Local History

Bookmans
1950 East Grant Road

Tucson, Ariz. 85719
(602) 325-5767
10-9 Mon-Sat, 1-5 Sun
Robert Schlesinger, Robert Hershoff
Arizona; Computers; Southwestern Americana; Cooking

The Book Stop
2504 North Campbell
Tucson, Ariz. 85719
(602) 326-6661
10 a.m.-11 p.m. daily
Laurie Allen
Regional Americana; Scholarly Books

Rodney G. Engard
3932 East 1st Street
Tucson, Ariz. 85711
(602) 881-8523
By mail only
Rodney G. Engard

Botany; Natural History; Anthropology; Cactus & Succulents; Zoology; Art

Janus Books
P. O. Box 40787-ABC
Tucson, Ariz. 85717
(602) 881-8192
By appointment only
Catalogues issued
Michael S. Greenbaum
Mystery & Detective Fiction; Sherlock Holmes & A. C. Doyle

Morgan Park Trading Company
1555 Arcadia Street
Tucson, Ariz. 85712
By appointment only
Beverley Furlow
Mystery

Arkansas

B. Caldwell
609 Crittenden
Arkadelphia, Ark. 71923
(501) 246-5871
12-5 Tues-Sat
Bill Caldwell
Children's Books; Southwestern Americana; General

H. H. Wilson
Route 1, Box 285
Bull Shoals, Ark. 72619
(501) 445-4724
8 a.m.-10 p.m. Mon-Sun
Catalogues issued
Sarah Wilson
Science Fiction; Children's Books;

Americana; Antiques; Cookbooks; Alaska

Books 'n Bytes
405 North Newton
El Dorado, Ark. 71730
(501) 862-0972
9-8 Mon-Sat
James Goolsby
Science Fiction; Mystery & Detective Fiction; Children's Books

Jan-Er and Company
11 Hilton
Eureka Springs, Ark. 72632
By mail only

Catalogues issued
John C. Parkhurst
Farming, Ranching, & Livestock; Gardening & Horticulture; Holistic Health & Nutrition; Health; Herbology & Herbs

Dickson Street Books
318 West Dickson Street
Fayetteville, Ark. 72701
(501) 442-8182
11-9 Mon-Sat
Catalogues issued
C. O'Donnell, D. Choffel
Arkansas; Poetry; Ireland & The Irish; Literature; History

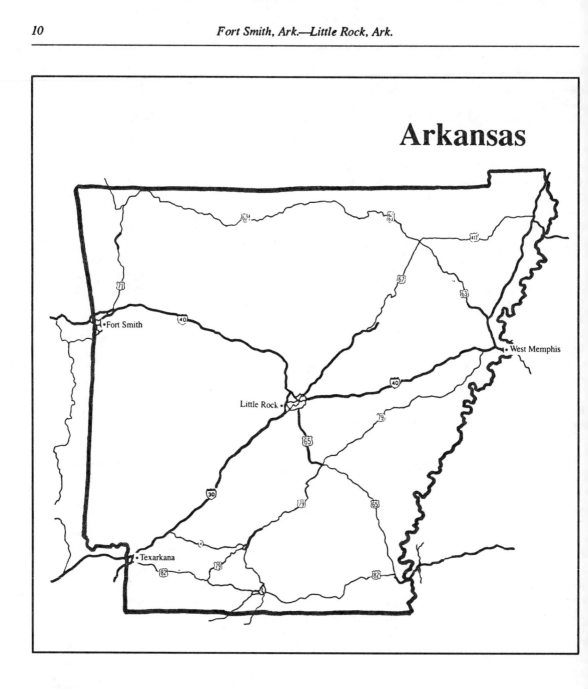

Arkansas

Book Nook
520 B North Greenwook
Fort Smith, Ark. 72901
(501) 783-0277
10-5 Mon-Sat
Mayrene Nelms
New Paperbacks; General

Yesterday's Books, Etc.
211 Woodbine Street
Hot Springs, Ark. 71901
(501) 624-6300
9:30-4 Mon-Wed, Fri, & Sat
Catalogues issued
Rose Edwards

*Arkansas; Americana; Cookbooks;
General*

Thomas H. Harris
22 Tallyho Lane
Little Rock, Ark. 72207
(501) 224-5521

By appointment only
Thomas H. Harris
Sets; Bindings, Fine & Rare; Color Plate Books

Appletree Books
Route 1, Box 361
Williford, Ark. 72482
(501) 966-4666
By appointment only
Catalogues issued

Margaret M. Hudspith
History; Biography & Autobiography; Cooking; Gardening & Horticulture; Crafts & Hobbies; Philately & Philatelic Literature

British Columbia

Thunderbird Books
P. O. Box 1270
Aldergrove, B.C. V0X 1A0
(604) 856-5179
By appointment only
Catalogues issued
Mary Bell, Bill Bell
*Aviation & Aeronautics; Marine
& Maritime; Militaria; Fishing &
Angling; Arctica & Antarctica;
Canada & Canadiana*

Donaldson & Company
P. O. Box 910
Nanaimo, B.C. V9R 5N2
(604) 758-1375
By mail only
Catalogues issued
Morris Donaldson, Patricia
Donaldson
Canadian Literature

Academic Books
P. O. Box 86-365
North Vancouver, B.C. V7L 4K6
(604) 980-1810
By appointment only
Catalogues issued
B. Rowell
*Canada & Canadiana; Arctica &
Antarctica; Pacific Region;
Americana; Voyages, Travels, &
Exploration; Back Issue
Periodicals*

Stephen C. Lunsford
P. O. Box 86773
North Vancouver, B.C.
(604) 681-6537
10-5:30 Tues-Sat
Catalogues issued
Stephen C. Lunsford

*Indians & Eskimos; Pacific
Region; Americana; Overland
Narratives; Arctica & Antarctica;
Canada & Canadiana*

Pacific Books
1135 Lansdale Avenue
North Vancouver, B.C. V7M 2H4
(604) 980-2121
9-5:30 Mon-Sat, 12-5 Sun
George Carroll
Art; Architecture; Music

Bill Ellis
P. O. Box 436
Queen Charlotte City, B.C. V0T
1S0
(604) 559-4681
By appointment only
Bill Ellis
Indians & Eskimos; Local History

Venkatesa Books
P. O. Box 524
Tofino, B.C.
(604) 725-4218
By appointment only
Catalogues issued
C. J. Hinke
*Children's Books; Color Plate
Books; Appraisals & Appraisal
Services; Authors; Author
Collections; First Editions*

E. R. Bowes
319 West Hastings Street
Vancouver, B.C. V6B 2H6
(604) 688-5227
10-6 Mon-Sat
Catalogues issued
Ed Bowes
Arctica & Antarctica; Canada &

*Canadiana; Voyages, Travels, &
Exploration; Illustrated Books*

William Hoffer
58-60 Powell Street
Vancouver, B.C. V6A 1E7
(604) 683-3022
9:30-5 daily
Catalogues issued
William Hoffer, Capria Munro
*Literature In English Translation;
Literature; Pacific Region; Poetry;
Voyages, Travels, & Exploration;
Rare Books*

MacLeod's Books
455 West Pender Street
Vancouver, B.C. V6B 1V2
(604) 681-7654
10-5:30 Mon-Sat, 12-5 Sun
Don Stewart
*Canada & Canadiana; Literature;
History; General*

Charles H. Tupper
756 Davie Street
Vancouver, B.C. V6Z 1B5
(604) 683-2014
11-6 Mon-Sat
C. H. Tupper
Marine & Maritime; Art; General

The Haunted Bookshop
13 Market Square, 560 Johnson
Victoria, B.C. V8W 3C6
(604) 382-1427
10-5 Mon-Sat
Catalogues issued
Marina Gerwing
*Literature; Canada & Canadiana;
Children's Books; Rare Books;
General*

California

In addition to the state map of California on page 14, we have also included city street maps or metropolitan area maps of Los Angeles, San Diego, San Francisco, and Santa Barbara, which occur facing or following the page where these cities are first mentioned..

Trophy Room Books
P. O. Box 3041
Agoura, Calif. 91301
(818) 889-2469
By appointment only
Catalogues issued
Ellen Enzler-Herring
Big Game Hunting; Voyages, Travels, & Exploration; Asia; Africa

Richard Persoff
P. O. Box 2918
Alameda, Calif. 94501
(415) 521-9588
By mail only
Richard Persoff
Travel; Mining & Metallurgy; Ships & The Sea; Desert; Western Americana; Natural History

The Ross Valley Book Co.
1407 Solano Avenue
Albany, Calif. 94706
(415) 526-6400
10-6 Tues-Sat
Catalogues issued
Robert L. Hawley
Western Americana; Latin America; South America

Robert Allen
P. O. Box 582
Altadena, Calif. 91001
(818) 794-4210
By appointment only
Catalogues issued
Robert Allen, Priscilla B. Allen

18th Century Literature; Children's Books; California

Joseph Cavallo
P. O. Box 74
Altadena, Calif. 91001
(818) 797-9527
By appointment only
Catalogues issued
Joseph Cavallo, Sherry Cavallo
Americana; Western Americana

Book Baron
12365 Magnolia Avenue
Anaheim, Calif. 92804
(714) 527-7022
10-6 Mon-Sat, 12-5 Sun
Catalogues issued
Bob Weinstein
Science Fiction; First Editions; General; Mystery & Detective Fiction

The Book-Bind
901 North Euclid
Anaheim, Calif. 92801
(714) 535-4385
By appointment only
Catalogues issued
V. Gramlich
Military; Military History; Modern First Editions; Americana; Western Americana; Music

House Of Books
1758 Gardenaire Lane
Anaheim, Calif. 92804
(714) 778-6406

By appointment only
Catalogues issued
Marilyn Bennett, W. O Bennett
Scotland & The Scotish; Ireland & The Irish; Wales & The Welsh

Gail Klemm
P. O. Box 518
Apple Valley, Calif. 92307
(619) 242-5921
By appointment only
Catalogues issued
Gail Klemm
Children's Books; Illustrated Books; Americana; Typography & Type Specimens; Collection Development; Original Art For Illustration

Rare Oriental Book Company
P. O. Box 1599
Aptos, Calif. 95001
(408) 724-4911
By appointment only
Catalogues issued
Jerrold G. Stanoff
Japan; China; Art; Woodcut Books; The Orient & Orientalia; Lafcadio Hearn

Tin Can Mailman
100 "H" Street
Arcata, Calif. 95521
(707) 922-1307
10:30-6 Mon-Sat
Catalogues issued
William Mauck, Leslie Mauck
Australia & New Zealand

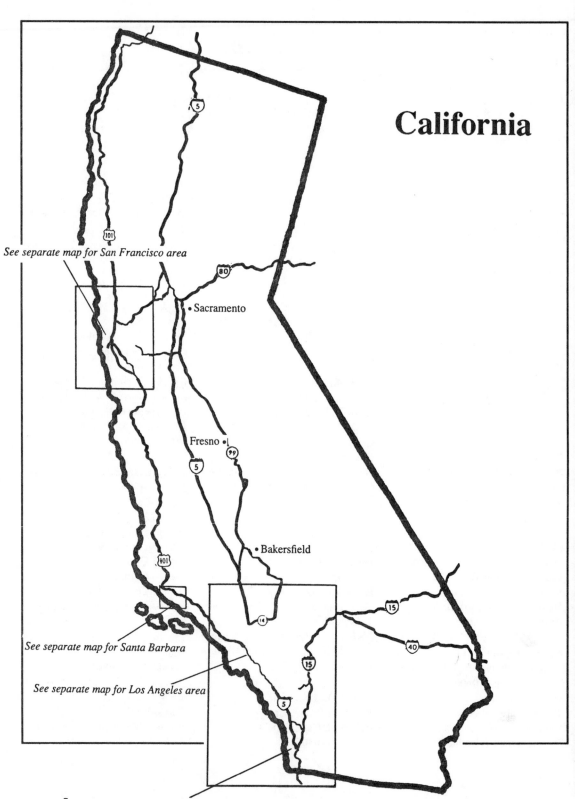

California

See separate map for San Francisco area

• Sacramento

Fresno •

• Bakersfield

See separate map for Santa Barbara

See separate map for Los Angeles area

See separate map for San Diego

W. R. Slater
509 Malibu Court
Bakersfield, Calif. 93309
(805) 322-9492
By appointment only
Catalogues issued
Bill Slater, Kathleen Slater
Science Fiction; Fantasy; Pulps;
Back Issue Magazines

Carpenter Books
P. O. Box 5060
Balboa Island, Calif. 92662
By mail only
Stuart Robinson
California; Western Americana;
Botany; Desert; 18th Century
Literature

Jack Ray
12706 East Farnell
Baldwin Park, Calif. 91706
(213) 337-8103
By mail only
Jack Ray
Automotive; Fiction; Cinema &
Film; Literature; Americana

Seashell Treasures
1701 Hyland Street
Bayside, Calif. 95524
(717) 822-1024
By appointment only
Catalogues issued
Steven J. Long, M. Sally Long
Marine Biology

Anacapa Books
3090 Claremont Avenue
Berkeley, Calif. 94705
(415) 654-3517
9-3 Mon-Fri
Catalogues issued
David S. Wirshup, Jane Willsea
Modern First Editions; Poetry;
Ephemera; Fiction

Bibliomania
2556 Telegraph Avenue

Berkeley, Calif. 94704
(415) 848-1178
12-6 Mon-Sat, 12-4 Sun
Catalogues issued
Daryl Van Fleet, Martha Burke
Literature; Military History;
General

Black Oak Books, Inc.
1491 Shattuck Avenue
Berkeley, Calif. 94709
(415) 486-0698
10-10 Mon-Sun
Bob Brown, Bob Baldock, Don
Pretari
Scholarly Books; Greek & Roman
Classics; Art; Cooking;
Photography; Literature

Carol Docheff
1605 Spruce Street
Berkeley, Calif. 94709
(415) 841-0770
By appointment only
Catalogues issued
Carol Docheff
Children's Books; Illustrated
Books; Black Literature & Studies;
Juveniles; Original Art For
Illustration; Juveniles

Peter R. Feltus
P. O. Box 5339
Berkeley, Calif. 94705
(415) 658-9627
By appointment only
Catalogues issued
Peter R. Feltus
Middle East; Arab World; North
Africa; Travel Guides &
Baedekers; Philately & Philatelic
Literature

Household Words
P. O. Box 7231
Berkeley, Calif. 94707
(415) 524-8859
By mail only
Catalogues issued

Harry J. Caughren, Christine
Caughren
Cooking; Beverages; Bibliography;
Wines; Ephemera

Invisible Bookman
97 Franciscan Way
Berkeley, Calif. 94707
(415) 524-7823
By mail only
Louis Laub, Virginia Malbin
Modern First Editions; Black
Literature & Studies; Poetry; Rare
Books

Ian Jackson
P. O. Box 9075
Berkeley, Calif. 94709
(415) 548-1431
By mail only
Catalogues issued
Ian Jackson
Botany; Gardening & Horticulture

Louis Laub & Associates
P. O. Box 9656
Berkeley, Calif. 94709-0656
(415) 524-7668
By mail only
Louis Laub
Appraisals & Appraisal Services

J. B. Muns
1162 Shattuck Avenue
Berkeley, Calif. 94707
(415) 525-2420
By mail only
Catalogues issued
J. B. Muns
Art; Architecture; Photography;
Music; Autographs & Autograph
Material

Sand Dollar Books
P. O. Box 7400, Landscape Stn.
Berkeley, Calif. 94708
(415) 527-1931
By appointment only
Victoria Shoemaker, Jack

Sheomaker
Modern First Editions; Poetry;
Dance; Autographs & Autograph
Material; Appraisals & Appraisal
Services

Serendipity Books, Inc.
1201 University Avenue
Berkeley, Calif. 94702
(415) 841-7455
9-5 Mon-Sat
Peter Howard
Modern First Editions; Poetry;
Press Books & Fine Printing;
Black Literature & Studies; Author
Collections; Appraisals &
Appraisal Services

Toad Hall
P. O. Box 902
Berkeley, Calif. 94701
(415) 843-0383
By mail only
Catalogues issued
Judith A. Baker
Gardening & Horticulture;
Children's Books

Harry A. Levinson
P. O. Box 534
Beverly Hills, Calif. 90213
(213) 276-9311
By appointment only
Catalogues issued
Harry Levinson
STC & Wing Books; Incunabula;
Medieval Manuscripts; Medicine
& Science; Illustrated Books;
Bibliography

The Scriptorium
427 North Canon Drive
Beverly Hills, Calif. 90210
(213) 275-6060
11-6 Tues-Sat
Charles W. Sachs
Autographs & Autograph Material;
Manuscripts; Documents;
Appraisals & Appraisal Services

Singer Communications Inc.
P. O. Box 6538
Buena Park, Calif. 90622-6538
(714) 527-5650
8-4:30 daily
Catalogues issued
Natalie Carlton, Kurt Singer
Gothics & Romantic Novels; Crafts
& Hobbies; Autographs
Autograph Material

Burbank Book Castle
144 South Golden Mall
Burbank, Calif. 91502
(818) 845-1563
By mail only
Catalogues issued
Chris Nickle, Paul Hunt
European History; Literature In
English Translation; Women;
Radical Poltics & Literature

Harold B. Diamond
P. O. Box 1193
Burbank, Calif. 91507
(818) 846-0342
By appointment only
Catalogues issued
Harold Diamond
Shakespeare; Literary Criticism;
Literature; Latin America; Social
Sciences; Art

Paul Hunt
P. O. Box 10907
Burbank, Calif. 91510
By mail only
Catalogues issued
Paul Hunt
Military History; World Wars;
Vietnam War & Literature;
Military

Vernon Howard
733 Plymouth Way
Burlingame, Calif. 94010
(415) 347-5620
Mornings daily, 1-5:30 Sat
Catalogues issued

Vernon Howard
Mountaineering; Western
Americana; Literary Criticism;
Voyages, Travels, & Exploration;
General

Peninsula Booksearch
P. O. Box 1305
Burlingame, Calif. 94011-1305
By mail only
Terry Nagel, James Nagel
Search Service, With Stock

William H. Hessel
P. O. Box 824
Calimesa, Calif. 92320
(714) 795-9150
By mail only
William H. Hessel
Rare Books

Taylor Coffman
1441 Astor Avenue
Cambria, Calif. 93428
(805) 927-4343
By mail only
Taylor Coffman
American History; Western
Americana; California; Decorative
Arts

John Carlton
4550 8 Mile Road, Box 865
Camino, Calif. 95709
(916) 644-1091
9:30-4:30 Mon-Fri
Catalogues issued
John Carlton
Early & Collectible Paperbacks;
Trade Catalogues; Automotive; Art
History & Reference

Campbell Book Shoppe
428 East Campbell Avenue
Campbell, Calif. 95008
(408) 374-3880
10:30-5 Mon-Sat, 12-5 Sun
California; Poetry; Children's
Books; Science Fiction

Aide
962 Greenlake Court
Cardiff, Calif. 92007
(619) 753-3392
By mail only
Ted Rogers
Religion & Religious History;
Metaphysics; Occult & Magic

Bookpost
962 Greenlake Court
Cardiff, Calif. 92007
(619) 753-3392
By mail only
Ted Rogers
Religion & Religious History;
Metaphysics; Eastern Religions

James Hansen
3514 Highland
Carlsbad, Calif. 92008
(619) 729-3383
By appointment only
Catalogues issued
James Hansen
Modern First Editions; Author
Collections; Illustrated Books;
Back Issue Periodicals; California

The Fantasy Connection
P. O. Box 676
Carmichael, Calif. 95609
(916) 393-8269
By appointment only
Catalogues issued
Dale Johnson
Fantasy; Science Fiction; Horror

Richard Gilbo
P. O. Box 12
Carpinteria, Calif. 93013
(805) 684-2892
By appointment only
Catalogues issued
Richard Gilbo
Americana; Black Literature &
Studies; Literature

Don Discher
4830 Audrey Drive
Castro Valley, Calif. 94546
(415) 537-5218
By mail only
Catalogues issued
Don Discher
Mystery & Detective Fiction;
Reference; Science Fiction;
Adventure

Associated Students Bookstore
California State University
Chico, Calif. 95929
(916) 895-6044
7:15-7 Mon-Thurs, 7:45-5 Fri, 11-
5 Sat
Lou Bentley, Bob Paolone
New Books; Juveniles; Reference;
Cookbooks; Computers; Education

John R. Butterworth
742 West 11th Street
Claremont, Calif. 91711
(714) 626-0763
By appointment only
Catalogues issued
John R. Butterworth, Mrs. John
R. Butterworth
Modern First Editions; Author
Collections

Huntley Bookstore
8th at Dartmouth
Claremont, Calif. 91711
(714) 621-8168
8:30-5:30 Mon-Fri, 10-5 Sat
C. Gilmore
Philosophy; Greek & Roman
Classics; Literature; Political
Science & Theory; Religion &
Religious History

Christophe Stickel
205 Village Lane
Colma, Calif. 94015
(415) 755-4483
By appointment only
Catalogues issued

Christophe Stickel
Books about Books; Western
Americana; Press Books & Fine
Printing; Autographs & Autograph
Material; John Muir

Mil-Air Photos & Books
901 West Alondra Boulevard (D10,
M9, Q5)
Compton, Calif. 90650
(213) 632-8081
12-5 Mon-Fri, 10-5 Sat
Catalogues issued
Harold N. Miller
Aviation & Aeronautics;
Autographs & Autograph Material;
Civil War & Confederacy;
Militaria; Marine & Maritime;
Zeppelins & Dirigibles

Liberty Quill Arts
P. O. Box 272
Concord, Calif. 94522
(415) 685-2484
By appointment only
Catalogues issued
Kathleen Mero
Americana; Military

Dorth Foster
25079 Ohio Avenue
Corning, Calif. 96021
(916) 824-2614
10-5 Sat & Sun
Dorth Foster, Henrietta M. Foster
Rare Books

The Memory Box
519 Jasmine Avenue
Corona Del Mar, Calif. 92625
(714) 644-1053
By mail only
Sandy Freeman
Calligraphy; Children's Books;
Ephemera; Graphic Arts;
Illustrated Books; Prints

Richard Glassman
15 First Street

Corte Madera, Calif. 94925
(415) 924-0410
Sat afternoons
Richard Glassman
Modern Library Publishing
Company; Biography &
Autobiography; Natural History;
History; Needlework; Children's
Books

Eeyore Books
P. O. Box 477
Cotati, Calif. 94928
(707) 795-8301
10-9 Mon-Fri, 10-6 Sat, 12-5 Sun
Lote Thistlethwaite
General

George Frederick Kolbe
P. O. Drawer 3100
Crestline, Calif. 92325
(714) 338-6527
By appointment only
Catalogues issued
George F. Kolbe
Numismatics

Sal Noto
21995 McClellan Road
Cupertino, Calif. 95014
(408) 253-7864
By mail only
Sal Noto
Jack London; California

Beaver Books
P. O. Box 974
Daly City, Calif. 94017
(415) 584-1302
By mail only
Catalogues issued
E. L. Weber
Fur Trade

Town & Gown Book Company
P. O. Box 190
Dutch Flat, Calif. 95714-0190
(916) 389-2363
By appointment only

Nicolaas Pansegrouw
Literature; Social Sciences;
History; Law; Women

Bible CommentaryHouse
P. O. Box 2485
El Cajon, Calif. 92021
(619) 440-5871
By mail only
Catalogues issued
Arnold D. Ehlert
Bible & Bible Studies; Church
History

50,000 Books, Inc.
116 East Main Street
El Cajon, Calif. 92020
(714) 444-6191
10-7 Mon-Sat (to 5:30 Sat), 11-4
Sun
Tom Chambers
Metaphysics; Art; New
Paperbacks; Literature;
Psychiatry, Psychology, &
Psychoanalysis; Science Fiction

New Steamship Consultants
P. O. Box 1721
El Cajon, Calif. 92022
By appointment only
Catalogues issued
Alan Taksler
Natural History; Ephemera

Info 21 Booksellers
P. O. Box 12
El Cerrito, Calif. 94530-0012
(415) 527-2840
Scholarly Books; Back Issue
Periodicals

Graeme Vanderstoel
P. O. Box 599
El Cerrito, Calif. 94530
(415) 527-2882
By mail only
Catalogues issued
Graeme Vanderstoel, Eve
Vanderstoel

Africa; Asia; The Orient &
Orientalia; Australia & New
Zealand; Jazz; Art

Shuey Book Search
8886 Sharkey Avenue
Elk Grove, Calif. 95624
(916) 685-3044
By mail only
Catalogues issued
C. R. Shuey
General

Ten O'Clock Books
8786 Cling Court
Elk Grove, Calif. 95624-1837
(916) 685-8219
By mail only
Catalogues issued
J. A. Grenzeback
Spanish Books & Literature;
Literature In English Translation

P. F. Mullins
109 Beechtree Drive
Encinitas, Calif. 92024
(619) 436-7810
By appointment only
Catalogues issued
Paul F. Mullins, Roslyn Mullins
Literature; First Editions; John
Steinbeck; Authors; Black
Literature & Studies; General

Books & The Collector Art
P. O. Box 589
Encino, Calif. 91316
(818) 981-6453
By appointment only
Catalogues issued
Alexander A. Dzilvelis
Press Books & Fine Printing;
Original Art For Illustration; Art,
Western; Art; Books about Books

American Fragments
P. O. Box 271369
Escondido, Calif. 92027
By mail only

Catalogues issued
Jim Landce
Children's Books; Color Plate Books; Illustrated Books; Maps, Atlases, & Cartography; Natural History; Prints

Book Nook
636 North Broadway
Escondido, Calif. 92025-1802
(619) 746-9797
10-4:30 Mon-Sat
Laura Weiss
Metaphysics; Technical; Cooking; Collecting & Collectibles; General

Bookfinder
2035 Everding Street
Eureka, Calif. 95501
(707) 445-0507
By mail only
Catalogues issued
Elizabeth Van Treuren
General

Ferndale Books 405 Main Street, Box 1034
Ferndale, Calif. 95536
(707) 786-9135
10-5 daily
Catalogues issued
Carlos E. Benemann, Marilyn F. Benemann
Latin America; Geography; Geology; Archaeology; California

Ron Graham
8167 Park Avenue
Forestville, Calif. 95436
(707) 887-2856
By appointment only
Ron Graham
Music; Cartoons & Caricature; Poetry

Terence M. Knaus
21601 Foster Lane
Fort Bragg, Calif. 95437
(707) 964-0681

By appointment only
Terence M. Knaus
Ireland & The Irish; Fiction; History; Gardening & Horticulture; Religion & Religious History

Oliver Oriole
P. O. Box 7355
Fremont, Calif. 94537-7355
(415) 794-5739
By appointment only
Catalogues issued
Dick Lamoureux
General

American Book Store
608 East Olive
Fresno, Calif. 93728
(209) 264-2648
10-5 Mon-Sat
Catalogues issued
Marilyn Affeldt
Americana; Religion & Religious History; Science; Technical; History

Monroe Books
809 East Olive
Fresno, Calif. 93728
(209) 441-1282
10-5 Tues-Sat
Catalogues issued
John M. Perz, Jack M. Perz
Western Americana; Fiction; California; First Editions

William T. Richert
3831 North Van Ness Boulevard
Fresno, Calif. 93704
(209) 454-8794
2-5:30 daily
William Richert
Authors

R. Sorsky
3845 North Blackstone
Fresno, Calif. 93726
(209) 227-2901

9:30-5:30 Mon-Fri
Catalogues issued
R. Sorsky
Forestry

Aladdin Books
122 West Commonwealth Avenue
Fullerton, Calif. 92632
(714) 738-6115
10-6 Mon-Fri, 10-5 Sat
John T. Cannon
Modern First Editions; Science Fiction; Mystery & Detective Fiction; Cinema & Film; Conjuring & Magic

Book Cellar
124 Orangefair Mall
Fullerton, Calif. 92632
(714) 879-9420
10-9 Mon-Fri, 10-6 Sat & Sun
Catalogues issued
David Cormany
Food & Drink; Literature; Americana; Art; Architecture; Photography

Book Harbor
201 North Harbor Boulevard
Fullerton, Calif. 92632
(714) 738-1941
11-6 Mon-Fri, 10-5 Sat, 12-5 Sun
Al Ralston
First Editions; Philosophy; Metaphysics; Cooking; Transportation; Heritage Press

Lorson's Books & Prints
305 North Harbor Boulevard, No. A-9
Fullerton, Calif. 92632
(714) 526-2523
10-5:30 Mon-Sat
Catalogues issued
James Lorson, Joan Lorson
Miniature Books; Americana; Bibliography; Press Books & Fine Printing; First Editions; General

Ra lston Popular Fiction
P. O. Box 4174
Fullerton, Calif. 92634
(714) 990-0432
By appointment only
Catalogues issued
Al Ralston
Fiction; Science Fiction; Modern
First Editions; Children's Books;
Western Books

Brannan Books
P. O. Box 475
Garberville, Calif. 95440
(707) 923-3552
By appointment only
Catalogues issued
Paul Brannan
Art; The Orient & Orientalia

Orange Cat Goes To Market
442 Church Street
Garberville, Calif. 95440
(707) 923-9960
9-6 Mon-Sat
Catalogues issued
Kathy Epling
Parenting & Child Care; Botany;
Children's Books; Cooking;
Gardening & Horticulture; Pacific
Region

Fantasy Illustrated
12531 Harbor Boulevard
Garden Grove, Calif. 92640
(714) 537-0087
12-6 Mon-Fri, 11-5 Sat, 12-4 Sun
Catalogues issued
Dave Smith
Comic Books; Pulps; Early &
Collectible Paperbacks; Disneyana

Talisman Press
P. O. Box 455
Georgetown, Calif. 95634
(916) 333-4486
10-5 daily
Catalogues issued
Robert Greenwood, Newton Baird

California; Western Americana;
20th Century Literature;
Literature; Photography;
Stereoviews

Jack London Bookstore
P. O. Box 337
Glen Ellen, Calif. 95442
(707) 996-2888
10-5 Mon-Sun
Winnie Kingman, Russ Kingman
Jack London; First Editions;
Alaska; Hawaii; Western
Americana; 19th Century
Literature

Aviation Book Company
1640 Victory Boulevard
Glendale, Calif. 91201
(213) 240-1771
8-4:30 Mon-Fri, 8-12 Sat
Catalogues issued
Walt Winner, Dick Harker
Aviation & Aeronautics; Zeppelins
& Dirigibles

Arthur H. Clark Company
P. O. Box 230
Glendale, Calif. 91209
(213) 254-1600
8:15-4:45 daily
Catalogues issued
Robert A. Clark, Arthur H. Clark
Western Americana

Roy A. Squires
1745 Kenneth Road
Glendale, Calif. 91201
(818) 242-4818
By mail only
Catalogues issued
Roy A. Squires
Science Fiction; Fantasy

Wayne G. Kostman
P. O. Box 393
Glendora, Calif. 91740
(818) 963-1755
By appointment only

Wayne G. Kostman
Voyages, Travels, & Exploration;
German Books & Literature;
Manuscripts; Voyages, Travels, &
Exploration

Bud Plant, Inc.
P. O. Box 1886
Grass Valley, Calif. 95945
(916) 273-9588
8-5 Mon-Fri
Catalogues issued
"JW" Chapman, Steve Bond, Dana
Ringlein
Comic Books; Fantasy; Cinema
& Film; Illustrated Books; Back
Issue Periodicals; Science Fiction

Jon Aldrich Aero
P. O. Box 706
Groveland, Calif. 95321
(209) 962-6121
By mail only
Catalogues issued
Jon Aldrich
Aviation & Aeronautics;
Ephemera; Documents;
Autographs & Autograph Material

Avalon Book Store
18565 Mission Boulevard
Hayward, Calif. 94544
(415) 278-2741
10-6 daily
James C. Bryan
Regional Americana; Science
Fiction; Indians & Eskimos;
Antiques; Fantasy; Birds &
Ornithology

Angriff Press
P. O. Box 2706
Hollywood, Calif. 90028
(213) 233-9848
8-5 daily
Catalogues issued
William Morrison
Political Science & Theory;

Political, Social, & Cultural History

Baroque Book Store
1643 North Las Palmas Avenue
Hollywood, Calif. 90028
(213) 466-1880
10-4:15 daily
Sheldon Stedolsky
Modern First Editions

Book City Collectibles
6625 Hollywood Boulevard
Hollywood, Calif. 90028
(213) 466-0120
10-10 Mon-Sat, 10-8 Sun
Catalogues issued
Marci Siegel, Rose Feick, Mitch Siegel
Cinema & Film; Rock 'n Roll; Autographs & Autograph Material; Photography; Movie & Fan Magazines; Ephemera

Cherokee Book Shop
6608 Hollywood Boulevard
Hollywood, Calif. 90028
(213) 463-6090
10-4:30 Mon-Fri, 10-5 Sat
Gene Bowm
Bindings, Fine & Rare; First Editions; Children's Books; Illustrated Books; Militaria; Prints

Cinema Collectors
1507 Wilcox Avenue
Hollywood, Calif. 90028
(213) 461-6516
11-7 Sun-Wed, 11-10 Thur-Fri, 10-7 Sat
Catalogues issued
Cinema & Film; Pulps; Posters; Poetry; Ephemera

Larry Edmunds Bookshop
6658 Hollywood Boulevard
Hollywood, Calif. 90028
(213) 463-3273
10-6 Mon-Sat

Catalogues issued
Cinema & Film; Theatre; Television & Radio

Hollywood Book City
6627 Hollywood Boulevard
Hollywood, Calif. 90028
(213) 466-1049
10-10 Mon-Sat, 10-8 Sun
Alan Siegel, Frances Siegel, Teri Hannemann
Cinema & Film; Art; Photography; Ilustrated Books; Rare Books; General

Hollywood Book Service
1654 Cherokee Avenue
Hollywood, Calif. 90028
(213) 464-4164
12-5 Mon-Fri, 12-3 Sat
Helen Hall
Political Science & Theory; Cinema & Film

Sun Dance Books
1520 North Crescent Heights
Hollywood, Calif. 90046
(213) 654-2383
By appointment only
Allan Adrian
Political, Social, & Cultural History; Fantasy; Gambling

Biblioctopus
Idyllwild, Calif. 92349
(714) 659-5188
By mail only
Catalogues issued
Mark Hime, Melissa A. Hime
First Editions; Mystery & Detective Fiction; Fiction; Literature; Manuscripts; Science Fiction

Merlin's Bookshop
6543 Pardall Road
Isla Vista, Calif. 93117
(805) 968-7946
12-7 Tues-Sat
Catalogues issued

Merlin D. Schwegman
Science Fiction; Mathematics; Biography & Autobiography; American Colonies & the Revolution; Engineering; Physics

Anne M. Ellis Sales
P. O. Box 854
Kentfield, Calif. 94914
(415) 461-9053
By appointment only
Anne M. Ellis
Sheet Music

Thelema Publications
P. O. Box 1293
King Beach, Calif. 95719
(916) 546-2160
By mail only
Catalogues issued
Mrs. H. P. Smith
Occult & Magic; First Editions; Collection Development; Religion & Religious History; Author Collections; Rare Books

John Cole's Book Shop
780 Prospect, Box 1132
La Jolla, Calif. 92038
(619) 454-4766
9:30-5:30 Mon-Sat
Barbara Cole
Art; Mexico; Children's Books; Travel

Laurence McGilvery
P. O. Box 852
La Jolla, Calif. 92038-0852
(619) 454-4443
By appointment only
Catalogues issued
Laurence McGilvery, Geraldine McGilvery
Art; Appraisals & Appraisal Services; Art Catalogues, Periodicals, & Books; Fine Arts; Avant Garde, Experimental, & Modern Art; Back Issue Periodicals

The White Rabbit
7777 Girard Avenue
La Jolla, Calif. 92037
(619) 454-3518
9-5:30 Mon-Sat
Catalogues issued
Louise Howton
Children's Books

Book Stop
3369 Mount Diablo Boulevard
Lafayette, Calif. 94549
(415) 284-2665
12-6 Tues-Sat
Catalogues issued
Milan Gilmore
General

Carlton Lowenberg
737 St. Mary's Road
Lafayette, Calif. 94549
(415) 284-4988
By mail only
Carlton Lowenberg
Emily Dickinson; Massachusetts;
Education

Buccaneer Books, Inc.
P. O. Box 518
Laguna Beach, Calif. 92652
(714) 494-4243
12-5 daily
Catalogues issued
Ruth Adams, J. C. Vincent
Search Service, With Stock

Marchioness Books
P. O. Box 1744
Laguna Beach, Calif. 92652
(714) 497-3011
By appointment only
Catalogues issued
Isabel Smith
California; Mexico; Latin America

Mary Mackensen
1616 Circa del Lago, C.102
Lake San Marcos, Calif. 92069
(619) 471-9518

9-5 Mon-Fri
Mary Mackensen
General

Lemon Grove Books
7905 Broadway
Lemon Grove, Calif. 92045
(619) 463-2503
William R. Burgett
Americana; Science Fiction;
Literature; Art; Rare Books

Associated Book Service
P. O. Box 7764
Long Beach, Calif. 90807
(213) 422-0059
Catalogues issued
Bill Lorenz, Edna Lorenz
California; Southwestern
Americana; Books about Books;
Desert; Mexico

Bargain Bookshop
3325 South Street
Long Beach, Calif. 90805
(213) 531-6909
12-6 Tues-Sat
Dolores Martin
Americana; Book Trade &
Catalogues; Children's Books;
Antiques; Color Plate Books;
Books about Books

The Folk Motif
2752 East Broadway
Long Beach, Calif. 90803
(213) 439-7380
9-5 Tues-Fri, 10-4 Sat
Catalogues issued
Marge Galicki
Folk Ar

Rodden's Bookshop
500 East Broadway
Long Beach, Calif. 90802
(213) 432-5896
9-5 Mon-Sat
Viola McDonald, Lillian Wilkins,
Cecil Antone

Science Fiction; Comic Books;
Back Issue Magazines; Geography;
General

World Wide Hunting Books
P. O. Box 3095
Long Beach, Calif. 90803
(213) 430-3693
By mail only
Catalogues issued
Ludo J. Wurfbain
Big Game Hunting

The Book Nest
366 2nd Street
Los Altos, Calif. 94022
(415) 948-4724
10-5:30 Tues-Sat
Edwin Schmitz
John Steinbeck

Sylvia Asendorf
14510 Manuella Road
Los Altos Hills, Calif. 94022
(415) 948-8903
By appointment only
Sylvia Asendorf
Children's Books; Illustrated
Books; Modern First Editions;
General

Abbey Books
P. O. Box 64384
Los Angeles, Calif. 90064
Catalogues issued
Gideon Berman, David Berman
Voyages, Travels, & Exploration;
The Orient & Orientalia; Western
Americana; Civil War &
Confederacy; Military History;
General

Art Catalogues
625 North Almont Drive
Los Angeles, Calif. 90069
(213) 274-0160
10-5 Tues-Sat
Catalogues issued
Dagny Corcoran

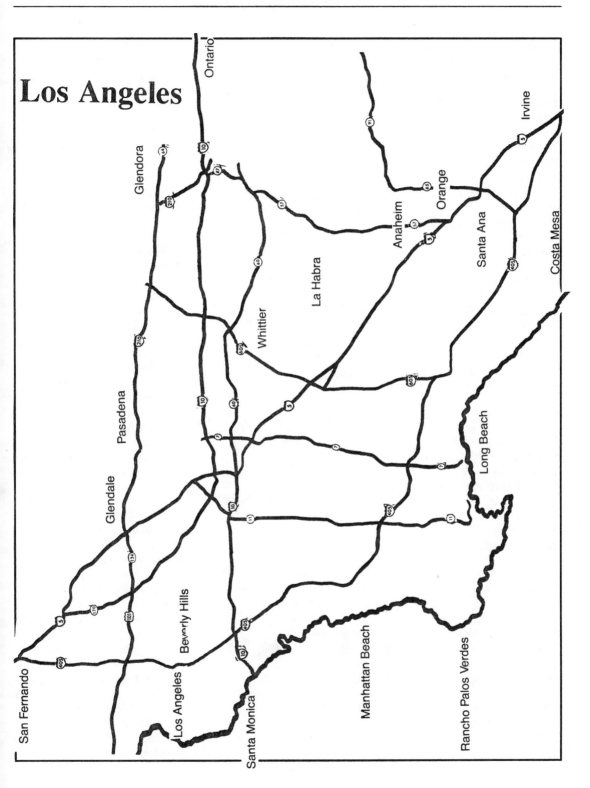

Los Angeles

*Art Catalogues, Periodicals, &
Books; Art; Photography;
Architecture*

Messrs. Berkelouw
830 North Highland Avenue
Los Angeles, Calif. 90038
(213) 466-3321
10-5 Mon-Sat
Catalogues issued
Henry Berkelouw, Isidor
Berkelouw
*Pacific Region; Africa; Asia;
English Literature; Whaling;
General*

David Berman
P. O. Box 64574
Los Angeles, Calif. 90064
(213) 470-2296
Catalogues issued
David Berman
*Golf; Archery; Military; History;
Natural History; Big Game
Hunting*

The Book Barrel
6937 La Tijera Boulevard
Los Angeles, Calif. 90045
(213) 641-6889
11-5 Tues-Fri, 10-5 Sat
George Thomson
General

Caravan Book Store
550 South Grand Avenue
Los Angeles, Calif. 90071
(213) 626-9944
10:30-6 Mon-Fri, 11-5 Sat
Lillian E. Bernstein, Leonard
Bernstein
*California; Cooking; Bindings,
Fine & Rare; Rare Books; Aviation
& Aeronautics; Ships & The Sea*

Chapman & Berryman
2377 Teviot Street
Los Angeles, Calif. 90039
(213) 667-2430

By mail only
Catalogues issued
David Chapman
*Pacific Region; Hawaii; Australia
& New Zealand; Ephemera*

Grayson D. Cook
367 West Avenue 42
Los Angeles, Calif. 90065
(213) 227-8899
By mail only
Catalogues issued
Grayson D. Cook
*Western Americana; Cinema &
Film; Modern First Editions;
Metaphysics; Science Fiction*

William & Victoria Dailey
8216 Melrose Avenue, Box 69160
Los Angeles, Calif. 90069
(213) 658-8515
10-6 Tues-Fri, 11-5 Sat
Catalogues issued
William Dailey, Victoria Dailey
*Rare Books; Prints; Art; Press
Books & Fine Printing; Illustrated
Books; History of Medicine &
Science*

Dawson's Book Shop
535 North Larchmont Boulevard
Los Angeles, Calif. 90004
(213) 469-2186
9-5 Mon-Sat
Catalogues issued
Glen Dawson, Muir Dawson
*Western Americana; Books about
Books; Miniature Books;
Mountaineering; Printing &
Printing History*

Gene De Chene
11556 Santa Monica
Los Angeles, Calif. 90025
(213) 477-8734
10-6 Mon-Sat
Gene De Chene, Diana De Chene
General

May Ellam
1007 North Avenue 51
Los Angeles, Calif. 90042
(213) 255-5991
By appointment only
Catalogues issued
May Ellam
Children's Books; Illustrated Books

Frontier Pioneer Books
6014 Burwood Avenue
Los Angeles, Calif. 90042-1206
(213) 256-2321
10-5:30 Mon-Fri, 10-5 Sat
Catalogues issued
Philip O. Davidson, Mary A.
Davidson
*Arctica & Antarctica; Canada &
Canadiana; Cooking; Children's
Books; General*

George Sand Books
9011 Melrose Avenue
Los Angeles, Calif. 90069
(213) 858-1648
11 a.m.-midnight Mon-Sat, 4 p.m.-
midnight Sun
*Literature; Biography &
Autobiography; Cinema & Film;
Little Magazines & Literary Small
Presses; Performing Arts; Poetry*

Bennett Gilbert
P. O. Box 46056
Los Angeles, Calif. 90046
(213) 876-8677
By appointment only
Catalogues issued
Bennett Gilbert
*Early Printed Books; Philosophy;
Religion & Religious History;
Science; History; Humanism*

Golden Legend, Inc.
7615 Sunset Boulevard
Los Angeles, Calif. 90046
(213) 850-5520
10-5:30 Mon-Sat
Catalogues issued

Gordon Hollis
Dance; Theatre; Literature;
Illustrated Books; Prints

Bernard Hamel
10977 Santa Monica Boulevard
Los Angeles, Calif. 90025
(213) 475-0453
10-6 Mon-Sat
Catalogues issued
Bernard Hamel
Spanish Books & Literature

Doris Harris
5410 Wilshire Boulevard
Los Angeles, Calif. 90036
(213) 939-4500
10-12 & 2-4 Mon-Fri
Catalogues issued
Doris Harris
Autographs & Autograph Material;
Documents; Manuscripts;
Presidents; Association Copies;
Overland Narratives

Heritage Bookshop
8540 Melrose Avenue
Los Angeles, Calif. 90069
(213) 659-5738
9:30-5:30 Mon-Fri, 10-4:30 Sat
Catalogues issued
Ben Weinstein, Louis Weinstein
First Editions; Rare Books; Press
Books & Fine Printing; Illustrated
Books; Bindings, Fine & Rare;
Voyages, Travels, & Exploration

George Houle
7260 Beverly Boulevard
Los Angeles, Calif. 90036
(213) 937-5858
10-6 Mon-Fri, 11-4 Sat
Catalogues issued
George Houle
Autographs & Autograph Material;
Antiques; Art; First Editions; Press
Books & Fine Printing; Western
Americana

Hyman & Sons
2341 Westwood Boulevard, suites
2 & 3
Los Angeles, Calif. 90064
(213) 474-8023
9:30-3:30 Mon-Sun
Catalogues issued
Virginia L. Blackburn, Paul S.
Hyman
Egypt & Egyptology; Archaeology;
Greece, Turkey & Cyprus

Jensen & Walker
8802 Ashcroft Avenue
Los Angeles, Calif. 90048
(213) 273-8696
By appointment only
K. H. Walker
Art; Architecture; Illustrated Books

Sam: Johnson's Bookshop
11552 Santa Monica Boulevard
Los Angeles, Calif. 90025
(213) 477-9247
11-6 Mon-Sat
Robert E. Klein, Lawrence D.
Myers
Scholarly Books; Literature;
General

Elliot M. Katt
8568 Melrose Avenue
Los Angeles, Calif. 90069
(213) 652-5178
11-6 Mon-Sat
Catalogues issued
Elliot M. Katt
Performing Arts; Civil War &
Confederacy; Circus & Carnival;
Music; Dance; Opera

Samuel W. Katz
10845 Lindbrook Drive, No. 6
Los Angeles, Calif. 90024
(213) 208-7934
By appointment only
Samuel W. Katz
Mexico; Latin America; Medicine
& Science; Illustrated Books;

Illuminated Manuscripts; Rare
Books

Jay Kieffer
430 South Burnside Avenue, No.
12-L
Los Angeles, Calif. 90036
(213) 938-4627
General

Barry R. Levin
2265 Westwood Boulevard, No.
669
Los Angeles, Calif. 90064
(213) 474-5611
By appointment only
Catalogues issued
Barry R. Levin, Sally Ann Levin
Science Fiction; Fantasy; Horror;
anuscripts; Limited & Signed
Editions

McCullough Associates
2627 North Beachwood Drive
Los Angeles, Calif. 90068
(213) 462-4598
By mail only
Catalogues issued
Larry McCullough
Military; History; Political Science
& Theory; Philosophy; Foreign
Affairs; Marine & Maritime

Needham Book Finders
P. O. Box 491040
Los Angeles, Calif. 90049
(213) 475-9553
By mail only
Catalogues issued
Search Service, Without Stock

John D. Nomland
404 South Benton Way
Los Angeles, Calif. 90057
(213) 389-9745
By appointment only
John Nomland

Mexico; Poetry; 20th Century Literature

Pettler & Lieberman
2345 Westwood Boulevard, No. 3
Los Angeles, Calif. 90064
(213) 474-2479
12-6 Wed-Sat
Catalogues issued
Robert Pettler
Modern First Editions; Mystery & Detective Fiction

Scholarly Bookfinders
415 West Avenue 42
Los Angeles, Calif. 90065
(213) 223-8257
By mail only
Catalogues issued
Norma Almquist
Literature In English Translation; Travel

Sisterhood Bookstore
1351 Westwood Boulevard
Los Angeles, Calif. 90024
(213) 477-7300
By mail only
Catalogues issued
Simone Wallace
Women; Gay & Lesbian Literature; Posters; Jewelry

Monroe Stahr
166 South Sycamore Avenue
Los Angeles, Calif. 90036
(213) 931-9919
By appointment only
Catalogues issued
Tom Rusch
Hollywood; Modern First Editions; Mystery & Detective Fiction

Sylvester & Orphanos
2484 Cheremoya Avenue, Box 2567
Los Angeles, Calif. 90078
(213) 461-1194
By mail only

Catalogues issued
Ralph Sylvester, Stathis Orphanos
Modern First Editions; Literature; Press Books & Fine Printing; Collection Development; Poetry; Mystery & Detective Fiction

Tolliver's Books
1634 South Stearns Drive
Los Angeles, Calif. 90035
(213) 939-6054
12-4 Sat & Sun
Catalogues issued
James D. Tolliver, Jr.
Birds & Ornithology; Herpetology; Fish & Ichthyology; Mammalogy; Mexico; Science

Manuel Urrizola
136 South Virgil Avenue, No. 139
Los Angeles, Calif. 90004
(213) 487-3228
By appointment only
Catalogues issued
Manuel Urrizola
Maps, Atlases, & Cartography; Rare Books

Wall Street Books
P. O. Box 24A06
Los Angeles, Calif. 90024
(213) 476-6732
By mail only
Catalogues issued
R. G. Klein
Stock Market & Wall Street

West Los Angeles Book Center
1650 Sawtelle Boulevard
Los Angeles, Calif. 90025
(213) 473-4442
12-7 Mon-Fri, 12-6 Sat, 1-5 Sun
Catalogues issued
Kenneth M. Hyre
Art; First Editions; General; Literature; Poetry; Science Fiction

Zeitlin Periodicals Co.
817 South La Brea Avenue

Los Angeles, Calif. 90036
(213) 933-7175
8:30-5 Mon-Fri
Catalogues issued
Stanley Zeitlin
Back Issue Periodicals; Reprints

Zeitlin & Ver Brugge
815 North La Cienega Boulevard
Los Angeles, Calif. 90069
(213) 655-7581
10-5 Mon-Sat
Catalogues issued
Jacob Zeitlin, Jeff Weber, Paul Naiditch
History of Medicine & Science; Press Books & Fine Printing; California; Art; Horology (Clocks); Fore-Edge Paintings

Lady At The Lake
P. O. Box 678
Lower Lake, Calif. 95457
(707) 994-5254
By mail only
Edith Dexter
General

Book Connection
P. O. Box 486
Mariposa, Calif. 95338
(209) 966-2877
10-5:30 daily
Pat Wallesir
General; New Paperbacks

The Joyce Book Shops
P. O. Box 310
Martinez, Calif. 94553
(415) 228-4462
By mail only
Everett V. Cunningham
Foreign Languages; Fiction; Religion & Religious History; General

Isabel Vogt
15980 McElroy Road
Meadow Vista, Calif. 95722

(916) 878-1752
By mail only
Isabel Vogt
*Fiction; Natural History;
Biography & Autobiography;
Americana, States; Political,
Social, & Cultural History;
Military*

James G. Leishman
P. O. Box A
Menlo Park, Calif. 94026-1201
(415) 327-3043
Catalogues issued
James G. Leishman, Harry W.
Becker
*Geology; Appraisals & Appraisal
Services; Paleontologyi; Mining &
Mentallurgy*

Mitch's Archives
155 Yale Road
Menlo Park, Calif. 91608
By mail only
Catalogues issued
*Ephemera; Autographs &
Autograph Material; Americana,
States; Documents; Overland
Narratives*

Wessex Books & Records
558 Santa Cruz Avenue
Menlo Park, Calif. 94025
(415) 321-1333
11-6 Mon-Sat, 12-5 Sun
Tom Hayden
*Fiction; Modern First Editions;
Foreign Languages; Literature;
University Press Books; Scholarly
Books*

Ethnographic Arts Publications
1040 Erica Road
Mill Valley, Calif. 94941
(415) 383-2998
By appointment only
Catalogues issued
Arnold M. Rogoff
Indians & Eskimos; Art, African;

*Primitive & Pre-Columbian
Culture; Latin America; Art*

Carol Lambert
10201 Kester Avenue
Mission Hills, Calif. 91345
(818) 892-4628
By mail only
Carol Lambert
General

Yesterday's Books
2717-E Coffee Road
Modesto, Calif. 95355
(209) 521-9623
10-6 Mon-Sat
Laurence Dorman, Kathleen
Dorman
*Bible & Bible Studies; Religion &
Religious History*

This Old House Bookshop
5399 West Holt
Montclair, Calif. 91763
(714) 624-5144
Daily
Thomas Guthormsen
*Cooking; Crafts & Hobbies;
Literature; Religion & Religious
History; Scholarly Books; Modern
First Editions*

The Book End
245 Pearl Street
Monterey, Calif. 93940
(408) 373-4046
10:30-5:30 Mon-Sat, 12-4 Sun
Sylvia Anderson
*Foreign Languages; Children's
Books; Biography &
Autobiography; Literature*

Old Monterey Book Company
136 Bonifacio Street
Monterey, Calif. 93940
(408) 372-3111
11:30-5:30 Tues-Sat
Cecil M. Wahle

*First Editions; John Steinbeck;
Rare Books*

Booksville
2626 Honolulu Avenue
Montrose, Calif. 91020
(818) 248-9149
9:30-7 Mon-Sun
Shirley McCormick
General

Sleepy Hollow Books
1455 Camino Peral
Moraga, Calif. 94556
(415) 376-9235
By appointment only
Catalogues issued
Richard G. Allen, Elizabeth Allen
*Western Americana; Limited
Editions Club; Press Books & Fine
Printing; Books about Books;
Sherlock Holmes & A. C. Doyle;
Mystery & Detective Fiction*

Sagebrush Press
P. O. Box 87
Morongo Valley, Calif. 92256
(619) 363-7398
By appointment only
Catalogues issued
Dan Cronkhite, Janet Cronkhite
Western Americana

Mt. Eden Books & Bindery
P. O. Box 421
Mount Eden, Calif. 94557
(415) 782-7723
By appointment only
Catalogues issued
Jerome Pressler
*Geography; Geology; Mining &
Metallurgy; Petroleum;
Paleontology; Maps, Atlases, &
Cartography*

Books Unlimited
1127 Highland Avenue
National City, Calif. 92050
(619) 477-1717

10-6 Mon-Sat
Janet Richards
Children's Books; Cooking;
Dictionaries; Medicine & Science;
Marine & Maritime; Technology

Mainly Mysteries
P. O. Box 15398
North Hollywood, Calif. 91615
(213) 875-0557
By mail only
Catalogues issued
Sol Grossman, Patty Grossman
Mystery & Detective Fiction

Sharp's Bookstore
5041 Lankershim Boulevard
North Hollywood, Calif. 91601
(818) 762-7595
9-6 Mon-Fri, 10-5 Sat
Johnny Ching
Genealogy; Religion & Religious
History; Occult & Magic;
American History

Valley Book City
5249 Lankershim Boulevard
North Hollywood, Calif. 91601
(818) 985-6911
11-7 Mon-Sun
Mark Marlow
Art; Science Fiction; Cinema &
Film; Metaphysics; Photography;
Biography & Autobiography

Wilshire Book Company
12015 Sherman Road
North Hollywood, Calif. 91605
(213) 875-1711
8:30-5 Mon-Fri
Catalogues issued
Melvin Powers, Frieda Freedman
Income Opportunities; Horses &
Horse Sports; Gambling; Games
& Pastimes

Herb Yellin
19073 Los Alimos Street
Northridge, Calif. 91324

(213) 363-6621
By mail only
Catalogues issued
Herb Yellin
Modern First Editions; First
Editions; Science Fiction; Poetry;
Press Books & Fine Printing

Archaeologia
707 Carlston Avenue
Oakland, Calif. 94610
(415) 832-1405
9-5 Mon-Fri
Catalogues issued
Arthur Richter, Andrew Gordon
Archaeology

Bibliomania
1539 San Pablo Avenue
Oakland, Calif. 94612
11-5 Mon-Sat
Daryl Van Fleet
Literature; Military History;
General

Gull Book Shop
1547 San Pablo Avenue
Oakland, Calif. 94612
(415) 836-9141
11-4 daily
Everett V. Cunningham
Foreign Languages; Fiction;
Religion & Religious History;
General

Gull Books & Print Gallery
1551 San Pedro Avenue
Oakland, Calif. 94606
(415) 836-9142
10-5 Mon-Sat
Everett V. Cunningham
Literature; Art; Black Literature
& Studies; Avant Garde,
Experimental, & Modern Art;
General

Holmes Book Company
274 14th Street
Oakland, Calif. 94612

(415) 893-6860
9:30-5:30 Mon-Sat (Wed to 7),
11-5 Sun
Catalogues issued
California; Western Americana;
New Books; First Editions; Rare
Books

The Mermaid Books & Records
4236-A Piedmont Avenue
Oakland, Calif. 94611
(415) 232-4447
By appointment only
Catalogues issued
Martin Neil, Bonnie Lucas
Travel Guides & Baedekers;
Modern First Editions; Mystery
& Detective Fiction; Phonograph
Records

Robert Perata
3170 Robinson Drive
Oakland, Calif. 94602
(415) 482-0101
By appointment only
Catalogues issued
Robert Perata
Illustrated Books; Press Books &
Fine Printing; Bindings, Fine &
Rare; Western Americana;
Ephemera

Bookmine
1015 2nd Street
Old Sacramento, Calif. 95815
(916) 441-4609
11-5 daily
Catalogues issued
Steve Mayer, Marie Mayer
Americana; Mining & Metallurgy;
Geology; Railroads; Children's
Books; Medical & Medicine

Book Carnival
870 North Tustin
Orange, Calif. 92667
(714) 538-3210
11-6 Mon-Thurs, 11-7 Fri, 10-5
Sat

Ed Thomas
Mystery & Detective Fiction;
Science Fiction; Fantasy;
Adventure

The Book Sail
1186 North Tustin
Orange, Calif. 92667
(714) 997-9511
By mail only
Catalogues issued
John McLaughlin
Political, Social, & Cultural
History; Bindings, Fine & Rare;
Modern First Editions; Rare Books

Kenneth L. Wolf
P. O. Box 2643
Orcutt, Calif. 93455
(805) 928-8024
Catalogues issued
Kenneth L. Wolf
General

Wayne Pierce
4400 Pine Cluster
Oroville, Calif. 95965
(916) 533-2131
Catalogues issued
Wayne Pierce
Children's Books; Fiction; Western
Books; Sporting

Valerie Kraft
41-617 Armanac Court, Box 1537
Palm Desert, Calif. 92261
(619) 340-4674
By appointment only
Catalogues issued
Valerie Kraft
Rare Books; First Editions; Art;
Children's Books; Sporting; Prints

Buckabest Books & Bindery
247 Fulton Street
Palo Alto, Calif. 94301
(415) 325-2965
By appointment only
M. Simmons

Performing Arts; Appraisals &
Appraisal Services; Conservation;
General

Chimera Books
405 Kipling
Palo Alto, Calif. 94301
(415) 329-9217
10-8 Mon-Fri, 10:30-6:30 Sat, 12-
5 Sun
Walter Martin
Scholarly Books; Literature; Greek
& Roman Classics; Philosophy;
Cooking

R. & G. Desmarais
907 Cowper Street
Palo Alto, Calif. 94301
(415) 328-4388
By appointment only
Catalogues issued
Rebecca B. Desmarais, Gilles
Desmarais
Literature; First Editions; Press
Books & Fine Printing; Autographs
& Autograph Material

Jim Pollock
P. O. Box 60152
Palo Alto, Calif. 94306
(415) 969-2400
By appointment only
James W. Pollock
Art; Photography; Voyages,
Travels, & Exploration; Erotica;
Boxing; Herpetology

The Printers' Shop
4047 Transport Street
Palo Alto, Calif. 94303
(415) 494-6802
9-5 Mon-Fri
Catalogues issued
Frederica Postman
Press Books & Fine Printing;
Printing & Printing History; Books
about Books; Typography & Type
Specimens; Graphic Arts

John P. Slattery
352 Stanford Avenue
Palo Alto, Calif. 94306
(415) 323-9775
By mail only
Catalogues issued
John Slattery, Madeleine Slattery
Russia & Slavic Countries

Starratt Enterprises
3669 Middlefield Road
Palo Alto, Calif. 94303
(415) 493-3185
By appointment only
Catalogues issued
Jan Starratt
Juveniles; Original Art For
Illustration

Szwede Slavic Books
P. O. Box 1214
Palo Alto, Calif. 94302-1214
(415) 327-5590
10-5 Tues-Sat
Catalogues issued
Russia & Slavic Countries

The Theater Bookshop
P. O. Box 837
Palo Alto, Calif. 94302
(415) 494-6004
By appointment only
Catalogues issued
Sonja Levinger, Liz Christopher
Performing Arts; Theatre;
Puppetry & Marionettes; Circus
& Carnival

William P. Wreden
206 Hamilton Avenue, Box 56
Palo Alto, Calif. 94302-0056
(415) 325-6851
10-5 Tue-Sat
Catalogues issued
William P. Wreden, Jr., William
P. Wreden, John Prior
Rare Books; English Literature;
American Literature; Western

Americana; Press Books & Fine Printing; Trade Catalogues

The Book Company
1328 North Lake Avenue
Pasadena, Calif. 91104
(818) 798-4630
10-6 Mon-Sat, 12-6 Sun
Mark Sailor
General

M. Gordon
1185 Michillinda
Pasadena, Calif. 91107
(818) 351-8525
By mail only
M. Gordon
Theatre; Fiction; Biography & Autobiography; History; Science Fiction

Joseph Holden
P. O. Box 50012
Pasadena, Calif. 91105
(818) 796-3703
By mail only
Joseph Holden
Photography; Photographically Illustrated Books

Maynard's Book Service
P. O. Box 40759, Washington Stn.
Pasadena, Calif. 91104
(818) 797-3146
Lou Maynard
Anthropology; Archaeology; History; Art

Mitchell Books
1395 East Washington Boulevard
Pasadena, Calif. 91104
(213) 798-4438
11-5:30 Tues-Sat
Catalogues issued
John Mitchell
Mystery & Detective Fiction; Modern First Editions

The Oriental Book Store
1713 East Colorado Boulevard
Pasadena, Calif. 91106
(518) 799-5774
3:30-5:30 Mon-Fri, 11-5:30 Sat
Frank Mosher
Middle East; The Orient & Orientalia; Pacific Region; Asians In America; Southeast Asia; Remainders

Prufrock Books
531 South Marengo
Pasadena, Calif. 91101
(818) 795-3558
By appointment only
Catalogues issued
Robert L. Wilkerson
Architecture; Art; Black Literature & Studies; Women; Western Americana; Crafts & Hobbies

Armenian Coins & Books
8511 Beverly Park Place
Pico Rivera, Calif. 90660
(213) 695-0380
By appointment only
Catalogues issued
Y. T. Nercessian
Numismatics; Rare Books; Manuscripts

William J. B. Burger
P. O. Box 832
Pine Grove, Calif. 95665
(209) 296-7970
By appointment only
Catalogues issued
William Burger
Western Americana; California; Paintings; Prints; Manuscripts; Autographs & Autograph Material

Fred W. Smith
1010 Hook Avenue
Pleasant Hill, Calif. 94523
(415) 935-7191
By mail only
Fred W. Smith, W. K. Flaherty,

P. W. Smith
Author Collections; Modern First Editions; Jack London; Southern Americana; Music

Day's Arms & Antiques
P. O. Box 1846
Quincy, Calif. 95971
(916) 283-3291
10:30-5:30 Mon-Sat
Pat Day, Rod Day
Western Americana

Acoma Books
P. O. Box 4
Ramona, Calif. 92065
(619) 789-1288
By mail only
Catalogues issued
Robert E. Neutrelle, S. Dale Neutrelle
Indians & Eskimos; Appraisals & Appraisal Services; Archaeology; Central America; Publishing History

R. M. Ryan
P. O. Box 895
Rancho Mirage, Calif. 92270
(619) 346-2965
By mail only
Catalogues issued
R. M. Ryan
Music

Lance Bowling
2625 Colt Road
Rancho Palos Verdes, Calif. 90274
(213) 427-1494
By appointment only
Lance Bowling
Americana; Cooking; Documents; Ephemera; Reference; Music

Robert Loren Link
1855 Wisconsin Avenue
Redding, Calif. 96001
(916) 243-8125
By appointment only

Catalogues issued
Robert Loren Link, Charles
Lenteria
*Modern First Editions; 20th
Century Literature; English
Literature; Press Books & Fine
Printing*

Libros Latinos
P. O. Box 1103
Redlands, Calif. 92373
(714) 793-8423
By appointment only
Catalogues issued
Alfonso Vijil
*Indians & Eskimos; Archaeology;
Art; Caribbean; Latin America;
Central America*

The Silver Door
P. O. Box 3208
Redondo Beach, Calif. 90277
(213) 379-6005
By appointment only
Catalogues issued
Karen La Porte
*Mystery & Detective Fiction;
Criminology; Espionage;
Adventure*

Grand Canyon Book Search
P. O. Box 3867
Redwood City, Calif. 94064
(415) 364-4648
By mail only
Richard Quartaroli
*Local History; Colorado;
Southwestern Americana*

Allen C. Ross
896 Jefferson Avenue
Redwood City, Calif. 94063
(415) 964-1401
By appointment only
Catalogues issued
Allen Ross
*English Literature; 19th Century
Literature; 20th Century*

*Literature; Americana; Western
Americana; Modern First Editions*

Bookie Joint
7246 Reseda Boulevard
Reseda, Calif. 91335
(213) 343-1055
11:30-6 Mon-Fri, 10:30-5:30 Sat
Jerry Blaz, Rose S. Blaz
*Judaica & Hebrica; Literature;
Scholarly Books; Science Fiction;
Mystery & Detective Fiction; Back
Issue Magazines*

Rails Remembered
P. O. Box 464
Rosemead, Calif. 91770
(213) 572-0419
By mail only
Catalogues issued
Robert O. Greenawalt
*Antique Stocks & Bonds;
Railroads; Mining & Metallurgy*

Argus Book Center
1714 Capitol Avenue
Sacramento, Calif. 95814
(916) 443-2223
10-5 Mon-Sat (Tues to 9)
Bill Ewald, Don Conner, Sheri
Plummer-Raphel
*Western Americana; Mining &
Metallurgy; Natural History;
Aviation & Aeronautics; Trades;
Ephemera*

Barnstormer Books
1714 Capitol Avenue (rear)
Sacramento, Calif. 95814
(916) 677-8823
10-5 Mon-Sat (Tues to 9)
Catalogues issued
Sheri Plummer-Raphal
*Aviation & Aeronautics; Jazz;
Music*

Black Swan Books
P. O. Box 22028
Sacramento, Calif. 95822

(916) 441-2156
By mail only
Catalogues issued
Charles Vercoutere
*Gardening & Horticulture;
Agriculture; Natural History;
Travel; Art; World's Fairs*

Vernon & Zona Braun
9004 Rosewood Drive
Sacramento, Calif. 95826
(916) 363-3862
8-5 daily
Vernon Braun, Zona Braun, John
Braun
*Western Americana; Local History;
Natural History; Voyages, Travels,
& Exploration; Ephemera;
Photography*

Barry Cassidy
2003 "T" Street
Sacramento, Calif. 95814
(916) 456-6307
9:30-4 Mon-Sat
Catalogues issued
Barry Cassidy
*Books about Books; California;
Association Copies; Literature;
Press Books & Fine Printing;
Western Americana*

Chloe's Books
P. O. Box 255673
Sacramento, Calif. 95865
(916) 488-3892
By mail only
Catalogues issued
Philip Ciapponi
*First Editions; Modern First
Editions; Literature; Poetry; Press
Books & Fine Printing; Little
Magazines & Literary Small
Presses*

Churchilliana Company
4629 Sunset Drive
Sacramento, Calif. 95822
(916) 488-7053

By appointment only
Eleanor Dalton Newfield
Sir Winston Churchill

Time Tested Books
1114 21st Street
Sacramento, Calif. 95814-4208
(916) 447-5676
11-5:30 Mon-Fri, 10-4 Sat
California; Children's Books;
Illustrated Books

The Book Attic
555 West Base Line
San Bernardino, Calif. 92410
(714) 888-2626
12-5:30 Wed-Fri, 10-3:30 Sat
Catalogues issued
Richard D. Thompson, Kathy
Thompson
California; Western Americana

Arthur Meyerfeld
1830 Eaton Avenue
San Carlos, Calif. 94070
(415) 593-7179
Arthur Meyerfeld
General

Out-Of-State Book Service
P. O. Box 3253-B
San Clemente, Calif. 92672
(714) 492-2976
By mail only
Ann Spigler
General

Charles E. Wyatt
P. O. Box 178623
San Deigo, Calif. 92177
(619) 275-5630
By appointment only
Catalogues issued
Charles E. Wyatt
Arthurian Legend; Science Fiction;
Literature; Fantasy

Alcala Books
P. O. Box 22503

San Diego, Calif. 92122
(619) 453-5473
By mail only
Catalogues issued
Alfred Bauer
Criminology; Medical & Medicine;
American Literature; Astronomy;
Literary Criticism

Bargain Book Store
1053 Eighth Avenue
San Diego, Calif. 92101
(619) 234-5380
10-5 Mon-Sat
Jim Lindstrom, Nancy Lindstrom
Modern First Editions;
Southwestern Americana; Stock
Market & Wall Street; Art;
Architecture

Blue Lantern Books
P. O. Box 8009
San Diego, Calif. 92102
(619) 235-6751
By mail only
Catalogues issued
Harold Darling, Benjamin Darling
Cinema & Film; Children's Books;
Illustrated Books; Mystery &
Detective Fiction; General

Rosalie C. Davidson
6315 Connie Drive
San Diego, Calif. 92115
(619) 582-0894
By appointment only
Catalogues issued
Rosalie C. Davidson
California; Southwestern
Americana; Natural History;
Mexico

J. & J. House
632 Broadway
San Diego, Calif. 92101-5402
(619) 265-1113
10-5:30 Mon-Sat
Catalogues issued
J. G. House

Philosophy; Voyages, Travels, &
Exploration; Press Books & Fine
Printing; Natural History; Color
Plate Books

Margaret Mannatt
P. O. Box 16243
San Diego, Calif. 92116
By appointment only
Catalogues issued
Margaret Mannatt
Theatre; Children's Books;
Illustrated Books; Science Fiction;
Mystery & Detective Fiction;
Modern First Editions

Oasis Books
P. O. Box 171067
San Diego, Calif. 92117
(619) 272-0384
By appointment only
Catalogues issued
Michael J. Fenelon, Dolly Fenelon
Medical & Medicine; Science;
Psychiatry, Psychology, &
Psychoanalysis; Technology;
Computers; Medicine & Science

"Otento" Books
3817 Fifth Avenue
San Diego, Calif. 92103
(619) 296-1424
11-5 Mon-Sat
Robert J. Gelink
Bindings, Fine & Rare; Voyages,
Travels, & Exploration; Appraisals
& Appraisal Services; General

J. Parmer
7644 Forrestal Road
San Diego, Calif. 92120
(619) 287-0693
By appointment only
Catalogues issued
Jean Parmer, Jerry Parmer
Voyages, Travels, & Exploration;
Western Americana; Arctica &
Antarctica

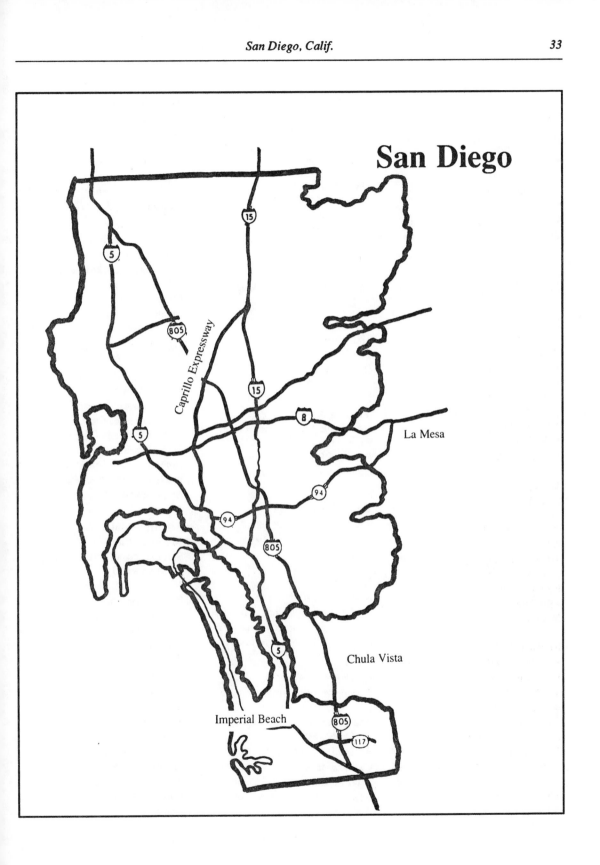

San Diego

Peri Lithon Books
5372 Van Nuys Court, Box 9996
San Diego, Calif. 92109
(619) 488-6904
By mail only
Catalogues issued
John Sinkankas, Marjorie J.
Sinkankas
Geology; Mining & Metallurgy;
Jewelry; Minerology & Gemology

Jack Qualman
5491 Mantua Court
San Diego, Calif. 92124
(619) 279-8633
By mail only
Catalogues issued
Jack Qualman, Michael Qualman
Poetry; Antiques; Business &
Business History

John Roby
3703 Nassau Drive
San Diego, Calif. 92115
(619) 583-4264
By appointment only
Catalogues issued
John Roby
Aviation & Aeronautics;
Technology

Univelt, Inc.
P. O. Box 28130
San Diego, Calif. 92128
(619) 746-4005
8:30-5 daily
Catalogues issued
H. Jacobs, R. H. Jacobs
Technology; Reference; History;
Astronomy; Aviation &
Aeronautics; Technical

Wahrenbrock's Books
726 Broadway
San Diego, Calif. 92101
(619) 232-0132
9:30-5 Mon-Sat
Catalogues issued
C. A. Valverde, Jan Tonnesen

California; Autographs &
Autograph Material; Latin
America; Rare Books; Sets;
Voyages, Travels, & Exploration

Wizard's Bookshelf
P. O. Box 6600
San Diego, Calif. 92106
(619) 235-0340
10-6 daily
Catalogues issued
Richard Robb
Philosophy; Occult & Magic

Words & Music
3806 4th Avenue
San Diego, Calif. 92103
(619) 298-4011
10-6 Mon-Sat (Fri & Sat to 8),
11-5 Sun
Victor Margolis
Cookbooks; Art; Architecture;
Biography & Autobiography;
Political Science & Theory;
Cartoons & Caricature

Yesterday's Books
2859 University Avenue
San Diego, Calif. 92104
(619) 298-4503
11-5:30 Mon-Fri, 11-4:30 Sat
Ken Baker
Americana; Religion & Religious
History; Metaphysics; Psychiatry,
Psychology, & Psychoanalysis;
Ships & The Sea; Aviation &
Aeronautics

San Fernando Books
P. O. Box 447
San Fernando, Calif. 91341
(818) 362-2173
By mail only
Catalogues issued
Emil N. Eusanio
Numismatics; Treasure Hunting;
Antiques

Aardvark Books
237 Church Street
San Francisco, Calif. 94114
(415) 552-6733
10:30-10:30 Mon-Sun
John Hadreas
Medicine & Science; Modern First
Editions; Art; Rare Books

Academy Library
2245 Larkin Street
San Francisco, Calif. 94109
(415) 558-3191
By mail only
Catalogues issued
John K. Addison
Metaphysics; Philosophy; Religion
& Religious History

Acorn Books
510 O'Farrell Street
San Francisco, Calif. 94102
(415) 563-1736
11-7 Mon-Sat
Joel Chapman, Frank Reiss
Western Americana; Railroads;
Art; Literature

Albatross Book Company
166 Eddy Street
San Francisco, Calif. 94102
(415) 885-6501
10-6 Mon-Fri, 11-6 Sat
Rose H. Sharp, George F.
Wilkinson
Western Americana; First Editions;
Technical; Press Books & Fine
Printing; General

Antiquus Bibliopole
4147 24th Street
San Francisco, Calif. 94114
(415) 285-2322
11-5 Wed-Sat
Pauline Grosch
Americana; Literature; Modern
First Editions; Cooking; Children's
Books

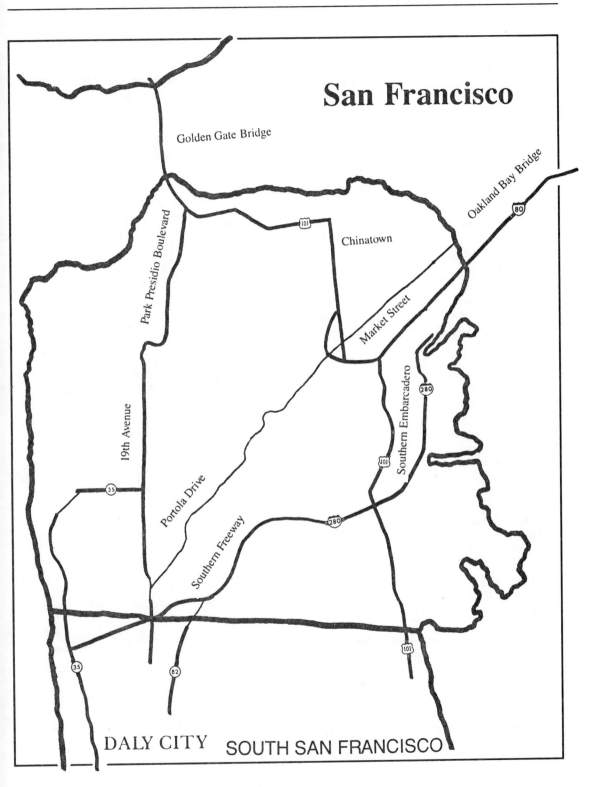

San Francisco

Golden Gate Bridge

Park Presidio Boulevard

Oakland Bay Bridge

Chinatown

Market Street

19th Avenue

Portola Drive

Southern Embarcadero

Southern Freeway

DALY CITY   SOUTH SAN FRANCISCO

W. Graham Arader III
560 Sutter Street, No. 201
San Francisco, Calif. 94102
(415) 788-5115
9-5 Mon-Fri
Catalogues issued
David Howard
*Prints; Maps, Atlases, &
Cartography; Natural History*

Argonaut Book Shop
786-792 Sutter Street
San Francisco, Calif. 94109
(415) 474-9067
9-5 Mon-Fri, 9-4 Sat
Catalogues issued
Robert D. Haines, Jr.
*Western Americana; California;
Press Books & Fine Printing;
Voyages, Travels, & Exploration;
Rare Books*

Alan S. Bamberger
2510 Bush Street
San Francisco, Calif. 94115
(415) 931-7875
By appointment only
Catalogues issued
Alan S. Bamberger
*Art; Architecture; Decorative Arts;
Design; Fine Arts; Photography*

Bibliofile Book Search
1346 20th Avenue
San Francisco, Calif. 94122
(415) 731-0862
By appointment only
Catalogues issued
John T. Selawsky, Pamela W.
Webster
*Fiction; Poetry; Art; Architecture;
Religion & Religious History;
Philosophy*

Bolerium Books
2141 Mission Street (3rd floor)
San Francisco, Calif. 94110
(415) 863-6353
12-6 Fri & Sat

Catalogues issued
John Durham, Jesse Judnick,
Michael Hackenberg
*Greek & Roman Classics; Women;
Industry; Linguistics; Religion &
Religious History; Philosophy*

Books America
P. O. Box 4006
San Francisco, Calif. 94101
By mail only
Catalogues issued
Karl Matsushita
Immigration; Social Sciences

Books & Co. Book Shop
1220 Polk
San Francisco, Calif. 94101
(415) 441-2929
10-9 Mon-Fri, 1209 Sat & Sun
Keith Clarey, Gary Swartzburg
*Art, Books about; Cookbooks;
Remainders; General*

The Bookstall
708 Sutter Street
San Francisco, Calif. 94109
(415) 673-5446
11-5:30 Mon-Sat
Catalogues issued
Henry Moises, Louise Moises
*Children's Books; Illustrated
Books; L. Frank Baum & Oziana;
Mountaineering; History of
Medicine & Science; Mathematics*

The Brick Row Book Shop
278 Post Street, room 303
San Francisco, Calif. 94108
(415) 398-0414
9:30-5:30 Mon-Fri, 11-4 Sat
Catalogues issued
John Crichton, Matt Lowman
*English Literature; American
Literature; Books about Books;
Bibliography; Press Books & Fine
Printing; Americana*

K. Buck
P. O. Box 11155
San Francisco, Calif. 94101
By mail only
K. E. Buck
*Natural History; Illustrated Books;
Printing & Printing History;
Architecture; Woodcut Books*

Califia
2266 Union Street
San Francisco, Calif. 94123
(415) 346-9740
11-6 Tues-Sat
Catalogues issued
Edwina Evers
*Press Books & Fine Printing;
Illustrated Books; Children's
Books; Art*

City Lights Bookstore
261 Columbus Avenue
San Francisco, Calif. 94133
(415) 362-8193
10 a.m.-midnight daily
Richard Berman, Nancy Peters,
Robert Sharrard
*New Paperbacks; Poetry; Jazz;
Literary Criticism; Cinema &
Film; Theatre*

Louis Collins
1083 Mission Street
San Francisco, Calif. 94103
(415) 431-5134
By appointment only
Catalogues issued
Louis Collins
*Anthropology; Indians & Eskimos;
cholarly Books; Modern First
Editions*

Columbus Books
540 Broadway
San Francisco, Calif. 94101
(415) 986-3872
General

Fantasy, Etc.
808 Larkin Street
San Francisco, Calif. 94109
(415) 441-7617
11-7 Mon-Sat, 12-6 Sun
Charles Cockey
Science Fiction; Mystery &
Detective Fiction; Militaria;
Horror; First Editions

Fields Bookstore
1419 Polk Street
San Francisco, Calif. 94109
(415) 673-2027
11-6 Tues-Sat
Catalogues issued
Richard Hackney, Ruth Cooke,
Greg Bracken
Psychiatry, Psychology, &
Psychoanalysis; Religion &
Religious History; Occult &
Magic; Myths & Mythology;
Alchemy & Hermetics

Green Apple Books
506 Clement Street
San Francisco, Calif. 94101
(415) 387-2272
10-10 Mon-Thurs & Sun, 10 a.m.-
midnight Fri & Sat
Paula Rodman
Remainders; Mystery & Detective
Fiction; Science Fiction; Fine Arts;
Metaphysics; General

Hall, McCormick & Darling
P. O. Box 11363
San Francisco, Calif. 94101
By mail only
Catalogues issued
Modern First Editions; Women;
Western Americana; Book Trade
& Catalogues

Austin Hills
490 Post Street, suite 1049
San Francisco, Calif. 94102
(415) 390-0480
By appointment only

Austin D. Hills
Americana, States; Pacific Region

The Holmes Book Company
22 Third Street
San Francisco, Calif. 94103
(415) 362-3283
9-5:15 Mon-Sat
Catalogues issued
David Lemmo
Americana; Western Americana;
alifornia; Scholarly Books;
General

In & Out Of Print #1
401-A Judah
San Francisco, Calif. 94101
(415) 665-1118
10 a.m.-midnight daily
James Noonan, Ken Thompson
Science Fiction; Mystery &
Detective Fiction; Children's
Books; Military History; Art;
Performing Arts

In & Out Of Print #2
443 Clement Street
San Francisco, Calif. 94118
10 a.m.-midnight
Rowena Henry
Science Fiction; Mystery &
Detective Fiction; Children's
Books; Military History; Art;
Performing Arts

Lake Law Books
142 McAllister Street
San Francisco, Calif. 94102
(415) 863-2900
9-5 Mon-Fri
Catalogues issued
William Yeago
Law; Appraisals & Appraisal
Services

Limelight Bookstore
1803 Market Street
San Francisco, Calif. 94103
(415) 864-2265

11-6 Mon-Sat
Roy Johnson
Cinema & Film; Theatre

Maelstrom
572 Valencia
San Francisco, Calif. 94110
(415) 863-9933
11-6 Mon-Sat
Chris Bogosian
Literature In English Translation;
Literature; General; Art

The Magazine
731 Larkin Street
San Francisco, Calif. 94109
(415) 441-7737
12-7 Mon-Sat
Robert Mariardi
Ephemera; Back Issue Magazines;
Back Issue Periodicals; Pacific
Region; Sporting

Manning's Fine Books
1255 Post Street
San Francisco, Calif. 94109
(415) 621-3565
By appointment only
Catalogues issued
Kathleen Manning
Photography; Illustrated Books;
California; Maps, Atlases, &
Cartography

McDonald's Book Shop
48 Turk
San Francisco, Calif. 94101
(415) 673-2235
10-6 Mon, Tues & Thurs; 10:30-
6:45 Wed, Fri, & Sat
Itzhak Volansky
Back Issue Periodicals; General

Meyer Boswell Books
982 Hayes Street
San Francisco, Calif. 94117
(415) 346-1839
9-5 Mon-Fri
Catalogues issued

Jordan D. Luttrell
Law; Famous Trials

Jeremy Norman & Co., Inc.
442 Post Street
San Francisco, Calif. 94102
(415) 781-6402
10-6 Mon-Fri
Catalogues issued
Jeremy Norman, Ann Kidd
*Medicine & Science; Natural
History; Rare Books; Voyages,
Travels, & Exploration; Business
& Business History*

Old Book Shop
1104 Sutter Street
San Francisco, Calif. 94109
(415) 776-3417
11:30-4:30 Tues-Sat
Sidney Engelbert
*General; California; Prints; Maps,
Atlases, & Cartography*

Ken Prag
1676 Market Street (Grand Central
Street)
San Francisco, Calif. 94102
(415) 566-6400
Catalogues issued
Ken Prag
*Documents; Postcards; Ephemera;
Railroads; Mining & Metallurgy;
Photography*

Bernard M. Rosenthal, Inc
251 Post Street
San Francisco, Calif. 94108
(415) 982-2219
By appointment only
Catalogues issued
Bernard Rosenthal, Ruth Rosenthal
*Bibliography; Middle Ages;
Renaissance; Scholarly Books*

John Scopazzi
278 Post Street
San Francisco, Calif. 94108
(415) 362-5708

10:30-5 daily
Catalogues issued
John Scopazzi
*Press Books & Fine Printing;
Color Plate Books; Voyages,
Travels, & Exploration; Illustrated
Books; Bindings, Fine & Rare; Art*

Second Front Books
4079 19th Avenue
San Francisco, Calif. 94132
(415) 584-1692
10-5 Mon-Sat
Michael Witter
*Natural History; Mathematics;
Psychiatry, Psychology, &
Psychoanalysis; Archaeology;
Medicine & Science*

Seven Roads
2611 Lake Street
San Francisco, Calif. 94121
(415) 751-7427
By appointment only
Catalogues issued
Robert B. Stitt, Olympia T. Stitt
Music

K. Starosciak
117 Wilmot Street
San Francisco, Calif. 94115
(415) 346-0650
By appointment only
Catalogues issued
K. Starosciak
*Architecture; Art; Books about
Books; Antiques; Textiles; First
Editions*

Sunset Book Store
2161 Irving Street
San Francisco, Calif. 94122
(415) 664-3644
Carol Savoy
*Art; Psychiatry, Psychology, &
Psychoanalysis; Cooking; Music*

Jeffrey Thomas
49 Geary Street, suite 230

San Francisco, Calif. 94108
(415) 956-3272
9-5 Mon-Fri
Catalogues issued
Jeffrey Thomas
*Literature; Press Books & Fine
Printing; Illustrated Books;
Americana; California; Voyages,
Travels, & Exploration*

Toy Boat Books
P. O. Box 27478
San Francisco, Calif. 94127
(415) 661-1633
By appointment only
Catalogues issued
James T. Friedman
*Children's Books; L. Frank Baum
& Oziana; Edgar Rice Burroughs;
Series Books For Boys & Girls;
Disneyana*

Transition Books
209 Post Street, suite 614
San Francisco, Calif. 94108
(415) 391-5161
12-5:30 Tues-Sat
Catalogues issued
Richard Q. Praeger, Roger Wicker
*Avant Garde, Experimental, &
Modern Art; Original Art For
Illustration; Literature; Modern
First Editions; Photography;
Architecture*

Alan Wofsy Fine Arts
401 China Basin Street
San Francisco, Calif. 94107
(415) 986-3030
By appointment only
Catalogues issued
Alan Wofsy
*Art; Graphic Arts; Bibliography;
Architecture; Autographs &
Autograph Material*

Yerba Buena Books
882 Bush Street
San Francisco, Calif. 94108

(415) 474-2788
10:30-5 Mon-Sat
Jennifer S. Larson
California; Books about Books;
Prints; Press Books & Fine
Printing; Voyages, Travels, &
Exploration

Marian L. Gore
P. O. Box 433
San Gabriel, Calif. 91778
(818) 287-2946
By appointment only
Catalogues issued
Marian Gore
Cooking; Cookbooks; Beverages;
Wines; Hotels & Inns

Stephen Doi
1714 Grizilo Drive
San Jose, Calif. 95124
(408) 265-8351
By appointment only
Catalogues issued
Stephen Doi
Immigration; Asians In America

A. S. Fischler
P. O. Box 556
San Jose, Calif. 95106-0556
(408) 297-7090
By appointment only
Catalogues issued
Al Fischler
Press Books & Fine Printing; First
Editions; California; Western
Books; Western Americana

Lincoln Avenue Books
2194 Lincoln Avenue
San Jose, Calif. 95125
(408) 448-0373
10-5 Tues-Sat
Joyce Link
Fashion; Textiles

Perry's Antiques & Books
1863 West San Carlos
San Jose, Calif. 95128

(408) 286-0426
10-5 Tues-Sat
Catalogues issued
Frank Perry
Edgar Rice Burroughs; Jack
London; Occult & Magic;
Biography & Autobiography;
mericana; Business & Business
History

Byron Walker
P. O. Box 3186
San Leandro, Calif. 94578
(415) 352-1854
By appointment only
Catalogues issued
Byron Walker
Occult & Magic; Gambling

Novel Experience
778 Marsh Street
San Luis Obispo, Calif. 93401
(805) 544-1549
2-5 Tues-Sat
Jo Mott
Literature

Phoenix Books
1127-A Broad Street
San Luis Obispo, Calif. 93401
(805) 543-3591
10-5:30 Mon-Sun
Bruce W. Miller III
Art; Science Fiction; Fine Arts;
Scholarly Books

Charles Annegan
P. O. Box 1304
San Marcos, Calif. 92069
(619) 941-4055
By appointment only
Catalogues issued
Charles Annegan
Civil War & Confederacy; Western
Americana; American Colonies &
the Revolution; Business &
Business History; Fashion;
Ephemera

Bill Carroll
P. O. Box 711
San Marcos, Calif. 92069
(619) 744-3582
By mail only
William Carroll
Automotive

Book Store
132 East Third Avenue
San Mateo, Calif. 94401
(415) 343-2751
9-6 Mon-Sat
Art; Fiction; History; Performing
Arts; New Paperbacks; Paintings

Grapevine Books
P. O. Box 1134
San Mateo, Calif. 94403
(415) 341-7009
By mail only
Sharalyn Spiteri
Children's Books; Western
Americana; Cookbooks; Illustrated
Books; Fiction

David H. Frid
P. O. Box 5266
San Pedro, Calif. 90733
(213) 832-9682
Catalogues issued
David Frid
Americana; Western Americana

Carl Blomgren
P. O. Box 3597
San Rafael, Calif. 94912
(415) 456-7610
By appointment only
Carl Blomgren
Photography; Illustrated Books;
Modern First Editions; Ephemera;
Architecture; Art History &
Reference

R. E. Lewis, Inc.
P. O. Box 1108
San Rafael, Calif. 94915
(415) 461-4161

By appointment only
Catalogues issued
R. E. Lewis
Prints; Sets

Dave Henson
P. O. Box 11402
Santa Ana, Calif. 92711
(714) 542-8839
By appointment only
Catalogues issued
Dave Henson
California; Western Americana

A B I Books
P. O. Box 30564
Santa Barbara, Calif. 93130
(805) 682-9686
By appointment only
Catalogues issued
Jeffrey Akard, Nancy Isakson
*Illustrated Books; Livre d'Artiste;
Decorative Arts; Design; Avant
Garde, Experimental, & Modern
Art*

Again--Books
16-A Helena Avenue
Santa Barbara, Calif. 93101
(805) 966-9312
12-9 Tues-Sat
Catalogues issued
John M. Sloan, Ann Sloan
*Aviation & Aeronautics;
Automotive; Militaria; Children's
Books; Marine & Maritime;
Christian Books*

Book Den
15 East Anapanu Street, Box 733
Santa Barbara, Calif. 93102
(805) 962-3321
10-9 Mon-Fri, 10-6 Sat, 12-5 Sun
Catalogues issued
Eric Kelley
*California; Western Americana;
20th Century Literature; Juveniles*

Drew's Bookshop
31 East Canon Perdido
Santa Barbara, Calif. 93101
(805) 966-3311
11-5 Mon-Sat
Catalogues issued
*Americana; Literary Criticism;
Prints; Maps, Atlases, &
Cartography; Ephemera; General*

Everard Books
P. O. Box 90347
Santa Barbara, Calif. 93190
(805) 569-5647
By appointment only
Catalogues issued
Peter Stalker II
Illustrated Books

Robert Gavora
1232 Laguna Street
Santa Barbara, Calif. 93101
(805) 965-7130
By appointment only
Catalogues issued
Robert Gavora
Science Fiction; Fantasy; Horror

Helen Halbach
116 East de la Guerra, studio 3
Santa Barbara, Calif. 93101
(805) 965-6432
12-5 Mon-Sat
Catalogues issued
Helen Halbach
Sherlock Holmes & A. C. Doyle

Milton Hammer
125 El Paseo
Santa Barbara, Calif. 93101
(805) 965-8901
By appointment only
Catalogues issued
Milton Hammer, Jessica Hammer
*Literature; California; Mexico;
Maps, Atlases, & Cartography; Art
Catalogues, Periodicals, & Books;
General*

Joseph The Provider
10 West Micheltorena
Santa Barbara, Calif. 93101
(805) 962-6862
10-4 Mon-Sat
Catalogues issued
Ralph B. Sipper, Larry Moskowitz,
Lee. G. Campbell
*Modern First Editions; 20th
Century Literature; American
Literature; English Literature;
Manuscripts; Limited & Signed
Editions*

Lance J. Klass
1414 Pacific Avenue
Santa Barbara, Calif. 93109
(805) 966-2941
Lance J. Klass
Science Fiction; Pulps

Lost Horizon Bookstore
703 Anacapa Street
Santa Barbara, Calif. 93101
(805) 962-4606
10-6 Mon-Sun
Catalogues issued
Jerry Jacobs, Angela Perko
*Western Americana; California;
General*

Maurice F. Neville
835 Laguna Street
Santa Barbara, Calif. 93101
(805) 963-1908
9:30-5:30 Mon-Fri, 10-2 Sat
Catalogues issued
Maurice F. Neville, Robert Dagg
*Modern First Editions; Inscribed
Books*

Pepper & Stern
P. O. Box 2711
Santa Barbara, Calif. 93120
(805) 569-0735
By appointment only
Catalogues issued
James Pepper
19th Century Literature; English

*Literature; 20th Century
Literature; Inscribed Books;
Mystery & Detective Fiction;
Cinema & Film*

Randall House
835 Laguna Street
Santa Barbara, Calif. 93101-1509
(805) 963-1909
9-5 Mon-Fri, 10-2 Sat
Catalogues issued
Ronald R. Randall
*Americana; Collection
Development; First Editions; Press
Books & Fine Printing; Rare
Books; Voyages, Travels, &
Exploration*

Michael J. Sherick
P. O. Box 91915
Santa Barbara, Calif. 93190
(805) 966-5819
By appointment only
Catalogues issued
Michael J. Sherick
Literature

Martin A. Silver
643 Willowglen Road
Santa Barbara, Calif. 93105
(805) 687-4198
By appointment only
Catalogues issued
Martin A. Silver
*Music; Musical Scores;
Phonograph Records; Musical
Instruments; Performing Arts;
Opera*

Robert Svoboda
P. O. Box 93110
Santa Barbara, Calif. 93121
(805) 963-8743
Montana

L. S. Kaiser
1820 Graham Hill
Santa Cruz, Calif. 95060
(408) 438-1379

By mail only
Catalogues issued
Lillian Kaiser
*Regional Americana; Religion &
Religious History; Children's
Books*

George Robert Kane
252 Third Avenue
Santa Cruz, Calif. 95062
(408) 426-4133
By appointment only
Catalogues issued
George Robert Kane
*Illustrated Books; Children's
Books; Fashion; Printing &
Printing History; Typography &
Type Specimens*

Tinker & Metaxas
603 California Street
Santa Cruz, Calif. 95060
(408) 426-0359
By appointment only
Don Tinker, Linda Metaxas
*Back Issue Magazines; Children's
Books; Illustrated Books*

Arcana
1256 Santa Monica Mall
Santa Monica, Calif. 90401
(213) 458-4342
10-6 Tues-Sat
Catalogues issued
Lee Kaplan, Gary L. White
*Art Catalogues, Periodicals, &
Books; Art; Photography;
Architecture; Primitive & Pre-
Columbian Art*

A Change Of Hobbit
1853 Lincoln Boulevard
Santa Monica, Calif. 90404
(213) 473-2873
10:30-8 Mon-Fri, 10:30-6 Sat &
Sun
Sherry M. Gottlieb, Bill Glass
*Science Fiction; New Books; New
Paperbacks; Fantasy*

Hennessey & Ingalls, Inc.
1254 Santa Monica Mall
Santa Monica, Calif. 90401
(213) 458-9074
10-6 Mon-Fri, 10-5 Sat
Catalogues issued
*Architecture; Art; Landscape
Architecture; Graphic Arts;
Remainders*

Michael S. Hollander
1433 Santa Monica Boulevard
Santa Monica, Calif. 90404
(213) 828-0773
By appointment only
Catalogues issued
Michael S. Hollander
*Color Plate Books; Voyages,
Travels, & Exploration; Western
Americana; Technology; Illustrated
Books; Children's Books*

Ken Karmiole
1225 Santa Monica Mall
Santa Monica, Calif. 90401
(213) 451-4342
10-5 Mon-Sat
Catalogues issued
Kenneth Karmiole
*Early Printed Books; Press Books
& Fine Printing; Printing &
Printing History; First Editions;
Art; Voyages, Travels, &
Exploration*

Howard Karno
1229 Santa Monica Mall
Santa Monica, Calif. 90401
(213) 458-1619
Catalogues issued
Howard Karno, Beverly Lishner
*Archaeology; Art; Caribbean;
Central America; Latin America;
South America*

Morrison and Kline
309 Arizona Avenue
Santa Monica, Calif. 90401
(213) 395-4747

10-6 Mon-Fri, 11-7 Sat & Sun
Catalogues issued
Eric Chaim Kline, David Morrison
Holocaust; Judaica & Hebrica;
Middle East; Folklore; Myths &
Mythology; Religion & Religious
History

The Phoenix Bookstore
514 Santa Monica Boulevard
Santa Monica, Calif. 90401
(213) 395-9516
10-9 Mon-Sat, 12-8 Sun
Catalogues issued
Michael R. Goth
Metaphysics

Rancho Books
P. O. Box 2040
Santa Monica, Calif. 90406
(213) 396-9567
By appointment only
Catalogues issued
Stan Dahl, John Jones
Western Americana; American
History; Voyages, Travels, &
Exploration; Overland Narratives;
Press Books & Fine Printing;
Printing & Printing History

Twelfth Street Bookseller
P. O. Box 3103
Santa Monica, Calif. 90403
(213) 393-1891
By appointment only
Bernard Axelrod, Lillian Cole
Arctica & Antarctica; Minerology
& Gemology; Children's Books;
Modern First Editions; 19th
Century Literature

Vegetarian Society, Inc.
P. O. Box 5688
Santa Monica, Calif. 90405
By mail only
Blanche Leonardo
Holistic Health & Nutrition;
Vegetarianism

Virginia Burgman
3198 Hidden Valley Drive
Santa Rosa, Calif. 95404
(707) 526-2482
8-noon daily
Catalogues issued
Virginia Burgman
Little Magazines & Literary Small
Presse; Back Issue Periodicals;
Children's Books; Americana,
States; Women; Art History &
Reference

Treehorn Books
522 Wilson Street
Santa Rosa, Calif. 95041
(707) 525-1782
10-5 Mon & Thu-Fri, 10-5:30 Sat
Michael Stephens, Keith Hotaling
Western Americana; California;
Children's Books; Illustrated
Books; Radical Poltics &
Literature

L'Estampe Originale
P. O. Box 3117
Saratoga, Calif. 95071
(408) 867-0833
By appointment only
Sandra Safris
Illustrated Books; Prints; Posters

Edwin V. Glaser
P. O. Box 1765
Sausalito, Calif. 94966
(415) 332-1194
By appointment only
Catalogues issued
Edwin V. Glaser, Peter Glaser
History of Medicine & Science;
Mathematics; Medical &
Medicine; Medicine & Science;
Technology

Chimney Sweep Books
220A Mount Hermon Road
Scotts Valley, Calif. 95066
(408) 438-1379
11-5 Mon-Fri, 10-4 Sat

Catalogues issued
Lillian Kaiser
Children's Books; Religion &
Religious History; Mystery &
Detective Fiction; Gardening &
Horticulture

John Barbier
P. O. Box 1159
Seaside, Calif. 93955
(408) 646-5204
By mail only
John Barbier
Back Issue Magazines; "Harper's
Weekly" Magazine

Betsy Hook
7345 Healdsburg Avenue
Sebastopol, Calif. 95472
(707) 829-0916
By mail only
Betsy Hook
Crafts & Hobbies

Sebastopol Book Shop
133 North Main Street
Sebastopol, Calif. 95472
(707) 823-9788
10-5:30 Mon-Sat
China; Japan; Trade Catalogues;
Technology; Sports; Natural
History

B. Lynch Book Finder
8840 Debra Avenue
Sepulveda, Calif. 91343
(818) 892-8491
By mail only
Bonita Lynch
General

Davis & Schorr
14755 Ventura Boulevard, No. 1-
747
Sherman Oaks, Calif. 91403
(818) 787-1322
By appointment only
Catalogues issued
Cal Davis, Lissa Schorr

Art; Collection Development; Graphic Arts; Fine Arts; 20th Century Literature

Fraser's Books
13760 Valley Vista
Sherman Oaks, Calif. 91423
(818) 788-9878
By mail only
History; Philosophy; Music; Literature; Political Science & Theory; Authors

Arnold Jacobs
5038 Hazeltine Avenue, No. 305
Sherman Oaks, Calif. 91423
(818) 789-6431
9 a.m.-10 p.m. Mon-Sun
Arnold Jacobs
Indians & Eskimos; Military

B. & L. Rootenberg
P. O. Box 5049
Sherman Oaks, Calif. 91403
(818) 788-7765
By appointment only
Catalogues issued
Barbara Rootenberg, Leon Rootenberg, Mollyanne George
Medicine & Science; Manuscripts; Early Printed Books; Philosophy; Continental Books; Rare Books

The Book Loft
1680 Mission Drive
Solvang, Calif. 93463
(805) 688-6010
9:30-6 Mon-Sat, 10-5 Sun
Gary Mullens
European History; Children's Books; Western Americana; General

Parsons Books
519 First Street West
Sonoma, Calif. 95476
(707) 935-0991
11-6 Wed-Sun
Catalogues issued

Gilman Parsons
History; Literature; Art; Rare Books

Alta's
20418 Green Acres Road
Sonora, Calif. 95370
(209) 532-6151
By appointment only
Alta Matthews
General

Heritage Books
52 South Washington Street
Sonora, Calif. 95370
(209) 532-6261
9:30-5:30 Mon-Sat
Catalogues issued
Robert Vance
Religion & Religious History; Americana; Regional Americana

Bay Side Books
P. O. Box 57
Soquel, Calif. 95073
By mail only
Catalogues issued
R. S. Becker
Modern First Editions; Poetry; Fiction; Anthropology

Bunker Books
704 Safford Avenue, Box 1638
Spring Valley, Calif. 92077
(619) 469-3296
By mail only
Melville C. Hill
Used Paperbacks; Back Issue Magazines; Science Fiction; Mystery & Detective Fiction; Science Fiction

Bookland
5648 North Pershing Avenue
Stockton, Calif. 95207
(209) 477-2009
9-9 Mon-Sat, 1-5 Sun
Tom Schuppe

Bonnie Denver
2513 Alexa Way
Stockton, Calif. 93209
(209) 952-8364
By mail only
Bonnie D. Ruttan
General; Aviation & Aeronautics; Illustrated Books

Harvard Book Store
336 East Market Street
Stockton, Calif. 95202
(209) 464-4866
10-6 Tues-Sat
Kelly Rego
Western Americana; Used Paperbacks; Back Issue Magazines; General

Maxwell's Bookmark
2103 Pacific Avenue
Stockton, Calif. 95204
(209) 466-0194
9:30-6 Mon-Sat
Catalogues issued
William Maxwell, Wendi Maxwell
California; Golf; Modern First Editions; Children's Books; Cooking

Fred A. Berk
P. O. Box 1367
Studio City, Calif. 91604
(818) 789-4372
By mail only
Catalogues issued
Fred A. Berk
Americana; California; Travel; Ephemera; Voyages, Travels, & Exploration

Gen Krueger
7840 McGroarty Street
Sunland, Calif. 91040
(818) 353-0525
By appointment only
Catalogues issued
Genevieve Krueger
Children's Books; Christmas

The Antiquarian Archive
160 South Murphy Avenue
Sunnyvale, Calif. 94086
(408) 739-5633
10-6 Tues-Fri, 10-5 Sat
Catalogues issued
David B. Ogle
Elbert Hubbard & Roycrofters;
Western Americana; Railroads;
Aviation & Aeronautics; Naval &
Nautical; Bindings, Decorative
Trade

Norman T. Hopper
1142 Plymouth Drive
Sunnyvale, Calif. 94087
(408) 736-8714
By appointment only
Norman T. Hopper
Juveniles; Pulps; Fiction; General

Lois Gereghty
9521 Orion Avenue
Supulveda, Calif. 91343
(213) 892-1053
By appointment only
Lois Gereghty
General

Pantechnicon
783 East Thousand Oaks
Boulevard
Thousand Oaks, Calif. 91360
(805) 495-9330
Catalogues issued
Myron Cohen-Ross
Science Fiction; Fantasy; Comic
Books; Disneyana; Hollywood

Albatross II Book Shop
100 Main Street
Tiburon, Calif. 94920
(415) 435-1506
11-6 Tues-Sun
Rose Sharp
First Editions; Illustrated Books;
Bindings, Fine & Rare; Postcards

Pendleton Publications
5093 Paradise Drive
Tiburon, Calif. 94920
(415) 435-3325
By mail only
Catalogues issued
Juveniles; Zane Grey; Children's
Books; Aviation & Aeronautics;
Tom Swift; Series Books For Boys
& Girls

Air Age Book Company
P. O. Box 40
Tollhouse, Calif. 93667
(209) 855-8993
By mail only
Catalogues issued
Ron Mahoney
Aviation & Aeronautics; Militaria;
Ephemera; Zeppelins & Dirigibles;
Photography

Boulevard Books
P. O. Box 89
Topanga, Calif. 90290
(213) 455-1036
By mail only
Catalogues issued
Clifford McCarty
Mystery & Detective Fiction; Plays
& Playwrights; Cinema & Film

Books In Transit
2830 Case Way
Turlock, Calif. 95380
(209) 632-6984
By appointment only
Catalogues issued
Mary T. Peterson
Crafts & Hobbies; Graphic Arts;
Illustrated Books; Printing &
Printing History; Typography &
Type Specimens; Woodcut Books

Garcia-Garst
334 North Center Street, No. L-M
Turlock, Calif. 95380
(209) 632-5054
10-5:30 Mon-Sun

Kenneth Garst, Beverly Garst
Illustrated Books; Children's
Books; Western Americana;
General

Chips 'n Books
14181 Newport Avenue
Tustin, Calif. 92680
(714) 838-6008
10-5 Mon-Sat
Chip Hunter
Metaphysics

AlphaBook
P. O. Box 7038
Van Nuys, Calif. 91409
(818) 780-4060
By mail only
Ray Vasin, Betty Vasin
Search Service, Without Stock

Bayshore Books
7409 Amestoy Avenue
Van Nuys, Calif. 91406
(818) 996-5756
By appointment only
Catalogues issued
Roger Jaep, Angeline Jaep
P. G. Wodehouse; Modern First
Editions

Front, Musical Literature
16122 Cohasset Street
Van Nuys, Calif. 91406
(818) 994-1902
12-5 Mon-Sat
Catalogues issued
Music; General

E. H. Mallory
5656 Buffalo Avenue
Van Nuys, Calif. 91401
(818) 988-3975
E. H. Mallory
Cactus & Succulents

E. E. Peters
P. O. Box 8412
Van Nuys, Calif. 91406

(818) 362-8521
Catalogues issued
Steven Peters
Press Books & Fine Printing;
Poetry; Modern First Editions

Lois St. Clair
P. O. Box 247
Van Nuys, Calif. 91408
(818) 781-5376
Catalogues issued
Lois St. Clair
Needlework; Art; Fiction; General

Calico Cat Bookshop
495 East Main Street
Ventura, Calif. 93001
(805) 643-7849
10-5 Mon-Sat, 1-4 Sun
Catalogues issued
Richard Cormack, Bente Margenat
Americana; Cooking; General

Second Time Around Books
391 East Main Street
Ventura, Calif. 93003
(805) 643-3154
10-5 Mon-Sun
James Staley
Metaphysics; Comic Books;
Science Fiction; History; Pulps;
Back Issue Magazines

Connolly & Wade
777 West Vista Way
Vista, Calif. 92083
(619) 758-2488
10-6 Mon-Sun
Catalogues issued
Glory Wade, Daniel Connolly
Science Fiction; History;
Cookbooks; Literature; General

The Book Shop
2687 Cherry Lane
Walnut Creek, Calif. 94596
(415) 937-5040
By appointment only
Catalogues issued

Larry Kimmich
General; Veterinary Medicine

Diablo Books
1317 Canyon Wood Court, Apt. 1
Walnut Creek, Calif. 94595
(415) 987-8644
By appointment only
George Emanuels
John Muir; Western Americana;
Jack London; California; Voyages,
Travels, & Exploration; Railroads

James M. Dourgarian
1595-A Third Avenue
Walnut Creek, Calif. 94596-2604
(415) 935-5033
By appointment only
Catalogues issued
James M. Dourgarian
Modern First Editions; John
Steinbeck; Stephen King; Cinema
& Film

George Hubert
2173-2 Ptarmigan Drive
Walnut Creek, Calif. 94595
(415) 937-6652
By appointment only
Catalogues issued
Occult & Magic; Freemasonry;
Myths & Mythology; Mysticism;
Philosophy; Metaphysics

Blitz Books
P. O. Box 1076
Weaverville, Calif. 96093
(916) 623-5430
By mail only
Catalogues issued
Richard Krieg
Americana

221 Books
760 Carlisle Cyn Road
Westlake Village, Calif. 91361
(213) 889-2640
By mail only
Catalogues issued

Phillip Gold
First Editions; Sherlock Holmes
& A. C. Doyle; Authors

Anderson's Bookshop
7043 Greenleaf
Whittier, Calif. 90601
(213) 693-4408
Mon, Fri 11-7; Tu, W, Sa 11-5:30
Ronald D. Anderson
General

J. E. Reynolds
3801 Ridgewood Road
Willits, Calif. 95490
(707) 459-4321
By mail only
Catalogues issued
J. E. Reynolds
California; Western Americana;
Press Books & Fine Printing;
Outlaws & Rangers; Overland
Narratives; Pacific Region

Book Faire
517 Main Street
Woodland, Calif. 95695
(916) 662-1546
9:30-9 Mon-Fri, 9:30-5 Sat
Bobby Jo Ford
General

Natural History Books
5239 Tendilla Avenue
Woodland Hills, Calif. 91364
(818) 346-7164
By appointment only
Catalogues issued
Rudolph Wm. Sabbot, Irene M.
Sabbot
Natural History; Rare Books

Robert Ross & Company
6101 El Escorpion Road
Woodland Hills, Calif. 91367
(213) 246-6152
By appointment only
Catalogues issued
Robert Ross

Maps, Atlases, & Cartography;
Voyages, Travels, & Exploration;
Color Plate Books; Geography;
19th Century Periodicals; Voyages,
Travels, & Exploration

Geoscience Books
13057-BC California Street
Yucaipa, Calif. 92399
(714) 797-1650

By mail only
Catalogues issued
Russell Filer
Mining & Metallurgy; Minerology
& Gemology; Paleontology;
Geology; Arizona; Western
Americana

J. Arthur Robinson
56149 29 Palms Highway

Yucca Valley, Calif. 92284
(619) 365-1861
9-6 Mon-Sat
Robbie Robinson, Connie
Robinson
Western Americana; Desert;
General

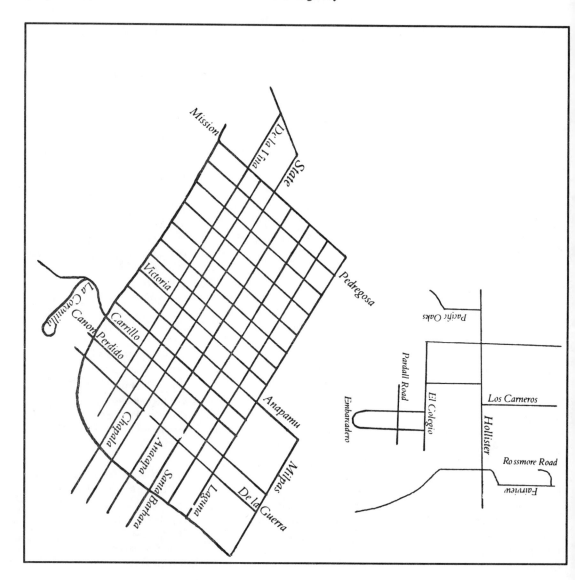

Colorado

The Book Rack
1930 South Havana
Aurora, Colo. 80014
(803) 752-4499
10-5:30 Mon-Sat
Ernest Roy
General

Alon Used Bookshop
1235 Pennsylvania Avenue
Boulder, Colo. 80302
(303) 443-5763
10:30-6 Mon-Sat, 1-5 Sun
Lance Rieker
Mountaineering; Scholarly Books;
General

Books At The Park
P. O. Box 3037
Boulder, Colo. 80307
By appointment only
Carrie Bailey, George Bailey
Colorado; Automobile Racing;
Automobiles, Specific Makes &
Models

The King's Market
P. O. Box 709
Boulder, Colo. 80306
(303) 449-8999
By appointment only
Catalogues issued
Robert Wayne
Science; Mountaineering; Western
Americana; Colorado; Psychiatry,
Psychology, & Psychoanalysis;
Documents

Carol Myers
P. O. Box 7537
Boulder, Colo. 80306
(303) 823-5387
By mail only

Catalogues issued
Carol Myers
First Editions; Western Books;
Children's Books

Rue Morgue Bookshop
942 Pearl Street
Boulder, Colo. 80302
(303) 443-8346
10-5:30 Mon-Sat, 12-5 Sun
Catalogues issued
Tom Schantz, Enid Schantz
Mystery & Detective Fiction;
Sherlock Holmes & A. C. Doyle

Stage House II
1039 Pearl Street
Boulder, Colo. 80302
(303) 447-1433
9-9 Mon-Sun
Richard Schwarz, Nicholas Angelo
General

Trident Booksellers
940 Pearl Street
Boulder, Colo. 80302
(303) 443-3133
10 a.m.-11 p.m. Tues-Sun
Hudson Shotwell, Terry Schultz
General

Barrie D. Watson
18760 Grand, Box 38
Buelah, Colo. 81023-0038
(303) 485-3136
By appointment only
Catalogues issued
Barrie D. Watson
Natural History; Falconry; Law;
American Literature; Western
Americana

Allbooks
1331 Imperial Road
Colorado Springs, Colo. 80918
(303) 548-1273
By appointment only
Catalogues issued
Charles J. Robinove
Geography; Natural History;
Indians & Eskimos; Science Fiction

Book Home, Inc.
P. O. Box 825, 119 East Dale
Colorado Springs, Colo. 80901
(303) 632-0555
9-5 daily
Catalogues issued
Leo Mohl
Botany; Geology; Scholarly Books

Book Sleuth
2423 West Colorado Avenue
Colorado Springs, Colo. 80904
(303) 632-2727
10-5 Mon-Sat
Annette Stith, Diane Stevens
Mystery & Detective Fiction

Chinook Bookshop
210 North Tejon
Colorado Springs, Colo. 80907
(303) 635-1195
9:30-5:30 Mon-Fri, to 4:30 Sat
Richard Noyes, Judith Noyes
General

Academy Books
753 South University Boulevard
Denver, Colo. 80209
(803) 744-8763
10-5 Mon-Sat
A. Jo Poersch
General

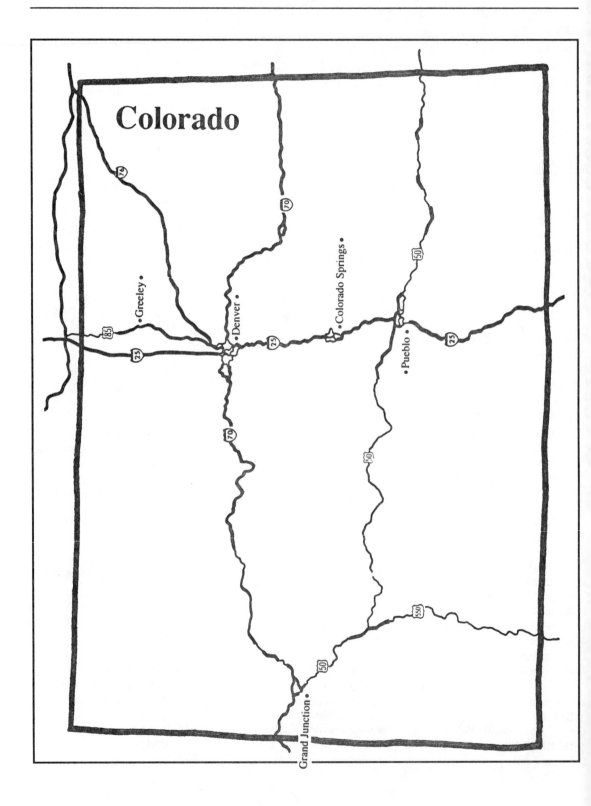

American City Books
5922 East Colfax
Denver, Colo. 80220
(303) 355-1101
10-6 Mon-Sat
Catalogues issued
Steve Wilson, Michael Grano
Modern First Editions; Children's Books; Illustrated Books; Scholarly Books; Rare Books

Black Ace Books
5920 East Colfax Avenue
Denver, Colo. 80220
(803) 355-5389
10-6 Mon-Sun
Jim Pagliasotti
Rare Books; General

Bloomsbury Book Service
2070 South University
Denver, Colo. 80210
(303) 777-6912
By appointment only
Margaret Lake, Joan Lake
Search Service, Without Stock

The Book Exchange
7820 West Jewell Avenue
Denver, Colo. 80226
(303) 989-2338
10-5 Mon-Sat
Wilma Ruscio
Used Paperbacks

Book Forum
709 East 6th Avenue
Denver, Colo. 80203
(303) 837-9069
12-5 Mon-Sat
Edgar Jepson
Scholarly Books

Books & Advice
1435 Estes
Denver, Colo. 80201
(303) 238-6937
9-5 Mon-Sat

Wallace Bauer
Used Paperbacks

Bookseller
2029 East Colfax Avenue
Denver, Colo. 80206
(303) 329-9458
12-6 Mon-Sat
Franklin Carto
Turn-Of-The-Century Novels; Scholarly Books; General

City Spirit
1434 Blake Street
Denver, Colo. 80202
(303) 595-0434
11-7 Mon-Fri, 10-6 Sat
Catalogues issued
Michael Fagin
Art; Architecture; Literature; Modern First Editions; Limited & Signed Editions

The Constant Reader
7031 East Colfax Avenue
Denver, Colo. 80220
(303) 355-2562
11-5 Mon-Wed, Fri, & Sat
Mary Lederer
General

Culpin's Bookshop
3827 West 32nd Avenue
Denver, Colo. 80211-3192
(303) 455-0317
10:30-5:30 Mon-Thurs, 10-4 Fri & Sat
Allan Culpin
Western Americana; Diaries & Narratives; Autographs & Autograph Material; World Wars; Illustrated Books

Denver Book Barter
919 East Colfax Avenue
Denver, Colo. 80218
(202) 894-0416
10-6 Mon-Sat, 12-6 Sun

Doug Robbins
Used Paperbacks

Denver Book Fair
44 South Broadway
Denver, Colo. 80209
(303) 777-9946
10-7 Mon-Fri, 10-6 Sat, 12-5 Sun
Jerry Robinette
Back Issue Magazines; General

The Hermitage
2817 East Third Avenue
Denver, Colo. 80206
(303) 388-6811
7 days a week
Catalogues issued
Americana, States; Western Americana; Modern First Editions; First Editions; Scholarly Books; Literature

Kugelman & Bent
5924 East Colfax Avenue
Denver, Colo. 80220
(803) 333-1269
10-6 Mon-Sat, 10-4 Sun
Mike Harvey
General

Murder By The Book
1574 South Pearl Street
Denver, Colo. 80210
(303) 871-9401
10-5 Tues-Sat
Shirley Beard, Chris McPhee
Mystery & Detective Fiction

Rosenstock Arts
1228 East Colfax
Denver, Colo. 80218
(303) 832-7190
10-5 Mon-Fri, 11-2 Sat
Linda Lebsack, Stephen Good
Western Americana; Art; Railroads

Tattered Cover, Inc.
2955 East 1st Avenue
Denver, Colo. 80206

(303) 322-7727
9:30-9 Mon-Fri, 9:30-6 Sat, 1-4:30
Sun
Joyce Knauer, Matthew Miller,
Linda Millemann
*Judaica & Hebraica; Maps,
Atlases, & Cartography;
Children's Books; Greek & Roman
Classics; Poetry; Psychiatry,
Psychology, & Psychoanalysis*

Together Books
2220 East Colfax Avenue
Denver, Colo. 80206
(303) 388-5171
10-9 Mon-Fri, 9-8 Sat, 10-6:30
Sun
Craig Steele
Metaphysics; Astrology

Southwest Book Trader
1025 Main Avenue
Durango, Colo. 81301
(303) 247-8479
9-6 Mon-Fri, 10-5 Sat
George Hassan
*Western Americana; Railroads;
Mining & Metallurgy;
Photography; Ephemera; General*

Willow Creek Books
P. O. Box 4663
Englewood, Colo. 80155
(303) 773-6941
By appointment only
Don Colberg, Nancy Colberg
*20th Century Literature; Biography
& Autobiography; Western
Americana; General*

Bonaventura Books
P. O. Box 2709
Evergreen, Colo. 80439
(303) 674-4830
By mail only

Catalogues issued
Ann Johnson
Western Americana

Harry & Eleanor Deines
1707 Country Club Road
Fort Collins, Colo. 80524
(303) 493-3682
By mail only
Harry Deines, Eleanor Deines
*Western Americana; Children's
Books*

Stone Lion Books
106 East Mountain
Fort Collins, Colo. 80524
(303) 493-0030
9:30-5 Mon-Fri
Paula Murray, Jacques Ricux
*Western Americana; American
History*

Beryl Claar
13890 Braun Road
Golden, Colo. 80401
(303) 279-8282
By mail only
Beryl Claar
Colorado; General

Mount Falcon Books
926 Ninth Avenue
Greeley, Colo. 80631
(303) 356-9211
9:30-5 Mon-Sat
Ron Stump
*Regional Americana; Military
History; Farming, Ranching, &
Livestock; Civil War &
Confederacy*

E. Fithian
1538 Ingalls Street
Lakewood, Colo. 80214
(303) 238-6283

By mail only
Catalogues issued
E. Fithian, Patricia Crisco
*Mystery & Detective Fiction;
Science Fiction*

Book Prospector
6118 South Hill
Littleton, Colo. 80120-2517
(303) 798-5882
10-5 Tues-Sat
Mel Moore
*Regional Americana; Camping &
Out-Of-Doors; Geology; Marine
& Maritime; Railroads; Natural
History*

The Cache
7157 West U.S. 34
Loveland, Colo. 80537
(303) 667-1081
9-4 daily
Martha Anderson, Ed Anderson
*Colorado; Western Americana;
Zane Grey*

Colorado Bookman
P. O. Box 156
Norwood, Colo. 81423
(303) 327-4616
By appointment only
Gene Beckman
*Colorado; Western Americana;
Photography*

Tumbleweed Books
687 South Union
Pueblo, Colo. 81004
(503) 544-3420
11-5:30 Mon-Fri, 11-5 Sat
Phyllis Fairchild
*Americana; Children's Books; Art;
Rare Books*

Connecticut

The Antiquarium
166 Humiston Drive
Bethany, Conn. 06525
(203) 393-2723
By mail only
Catalogues issued
Lee Ash
Books about Books; Natural History; Medicine & Science; Rare Books; Reference; Scholarly Books

Whitlock Farm Booksellers
20 Sperry Road
Bethany, Conn. 06525
(203) 393-1240
9-5 Tues-Sun
Catalogues issued
Gilbert Whitlock, Everett Whitlock
Gardening & Horticulture; Americana; Sporting; General

Robert B. Williams
57 Lacey Road
Bethany, Conn. 06525
(203) 393-1488
By mail only
Catalogues issued
Robert B. Williams, Diane F. Williams
Dogs

Bethlehem Book Company
P. O. Box 249
Bethlehem, Conn. 06751
(203) 266-7586
By mail only
Gregory Johnson
Folk Art

June 1 Gallery
86 Bellamy Lane
Bethlehem, Conn. 06751
(203) 266-7191

By appointment only
Catalogues issued
June Kraeft, Norman Kraeft
Prints; Art, Books about

Richard Blacher
209 Plymouth Colony, Alps Road
Branford, Conn. 06405
(203) 481-3321
By appointment only
Richard Blacher
Elbert Hubbard & Roycrofters; Press Books & Fine Printing

Branford Rare Books
779 East Main Street
Branford, Conn. 06405
(203) 488-5882
11-5 Tues-Sat, 12-5 Sun
Catalogues issued
John R. Elliott
Voyages, Travels, & Exploration; Americana; Maps, Atlases, & Cartography; Postal History; Folk Art; Fine Arts

Frank R. Joslin III
234 Opening Hill Road
Branford, Conn. 06405-2259
(203) 488-3458
By appointment only
Catalogues issued
Frank Joslin
First Editions; Literary Criticism; Americana; Beat Literature

Chimney Smoke Books
74 Waller Road
Bridgeport, Conn. 06606
(203) 372-8806
By mail only
Al Woebcke
Illustrated Books; Books about

Books; Natural History; Americana; Art; Gardening & Horticulture

Bob Cowell
15 Pearsall Way
Bridgeport, Conn. 06605
(203) 334-3025
By appointment only
Robert P. Cowell
Dogs; General

Murray's Bookfinding Service
292 Jackson Avenue
Bridgeport, Conn. 06606
(203) 335-5598
By mail only
Murray Novick
Search Service, Without Stock

Bert & Phyllis Boyson
23 Cove Road
Brookfield, Conn. 06804
(203) 775-0176
By appointment only
Bert Boyson, Phyllis Boyson
Science; Technology; Children's Books; Illustrated Books; History; Biography & Autobiography

Stone Of Scone Books
19 Water Street
Canterbury, Conn. 06331
(203) 546-9917
12-8 Mon-Fri, 10-8 Sat, 10-5 Sun
Catalogues issued
Jan Stratton, Tom Stratton
Connecticut; New England; General

Chester Book Company
4 Maple Street
Chester, Conn. 06412

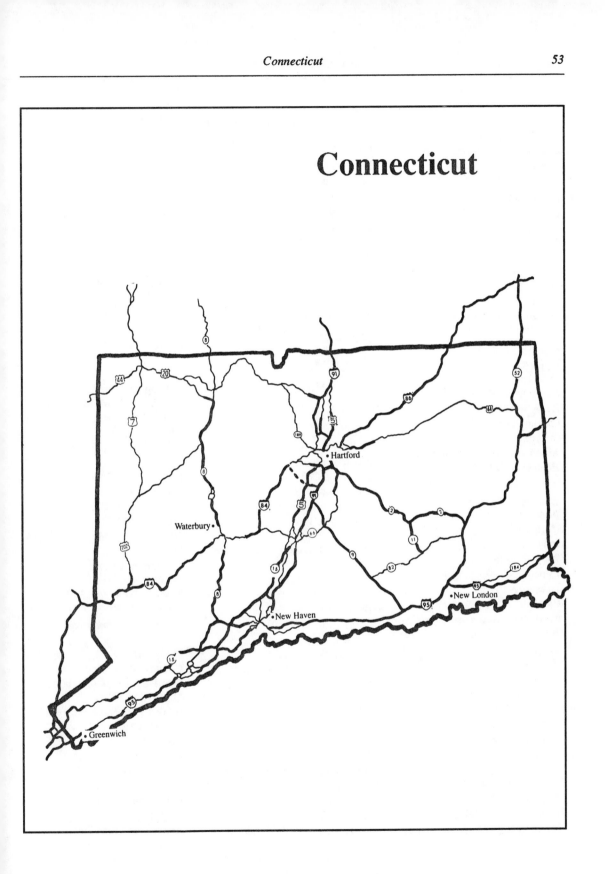

Connecticut

(203) 526-9887
10-5 Mon-Sat, 1-5 Sun
Lois Nadel
New England; General

Colebrook Book Barn
Route 183, Box 108
Colebrook, Conn. 06021
(203) 379-3185
10-5 Sat & Sun (call first)
Catalogues issued
Robert Seymour
Americana; Ephemera; First Editions; Sets; General

Rinhart Galleries
Upper Grey
Colebrook, Conn. 06021
(203) 379-9773
By appointment only
Catalogues issued
George Rinhart
American History; Presidents; Poetry; Graphic Arts

Laurence Golder
P. O. Box 144
Collinsville, Conn. 06022
(203) 693-8110
By mail only
Catalogues issued
Lawrence Golder
American Colonies & the Revolution; Americana; Arctica & Antarctica; Canada & Canadiana; Latin America; Voyages, Travels, & Exploration

The Book Block
8 Loughlin Avenue
Cos Cob, Conn. 06807
(203) 629-2990
By appointment only
Catalogues issued
David M. Block, Shiu-min Block
Illustrated Books; Press Books & Fine Printing; Bindings, Fine & Rare; Autographs & Autograph

Material; Manuscripts; Color Plate Books

Harrington's
333 Cognewaug Road
Cos Cob, Conn. 06807
(203) 869-1070
By appointment only
Catalogues issued
Alton Ketchum
Newspapers; History

Coventry Bookshop
1159 Main Street
Coventry, Conn. 06238
(203) 742-9875
12-5 Tues-Sun
John Gambino
Naval & Nautical; Marine & Maritime; Western Americana; General

Kathleen T. Sullivan
861 Main Street
Coventry, Conn. 06238
(203) 742-7073
By appointment only
Catalogues issued
Kathleen T. Sullivan
Illustrated Books; Children's Books

Barbara Weindling
69 Ball Pon Road
Danbury, Conn. 06811
(203) 746-2514
By mail only
Barbara Weindling
Cooking; Children's Books; Fiction

Gilann Books
P. O. Box 67
Darien, Conn. 06820
(203) 655-4532
By appointment only
Catalogues issued
Gil Rodriguez
Modern First Editions; Americana; Children's Books; Illustrated

Books; Press Books & Fine Printing; General

Mechanical Music Center
P. O. Box 88
Darien, Conn. 06820
(203) 655-9510
9:30-4:30 Tues-Sat
Catalogues issued
Isaac Halsey, Fran Mayer
Music; Mechanical Musical Instruments; Technology

Books By The Falls
253 Roosevelt Drive
Derby, Conn. 06418
(203) 734-6112
9-5 Mon-Sun
Catalogues issued
Ron Knox, Mark Maciag
Greek & Roman Classics; Sets; Philosophy; Religion & Religous History; Art; Poetry

Connecticut River Books
Goodspeed Plaza
East Haddam, Conn. 06423
(203) 873-8881
10-5 Tues-Sat (May-Dec 12-5 Mon-Sun)
Catalogues issued
Frank Crohn
Naval & Nautical; Fishing & Angling; Children's Books; Art; Architecture; Americana

Bibliolatree
Country Store, Route 66
East Hampton, Conn. 06424
(203) 267-8222
From 1 p.m. Sat & Sun only
Paul O. Clark
General

The Bookie
206 Burnside Avenue
East Hartford, Conn. 06108
(203) 289-1208
Afternoons, Tues-Sun

Harold E. Kinney
Comic Books; Science Fiction

Warren Blake
131 Sigwin Drive
Fairfield, Conn. 06430
(203) 259-3278
By appointment only
Catalogues issued
Warren Blake
Astronomy; Physics; General

Connecticut Book Galleries
251 Carroll Road
Fairfield, Conn. 06430
(203) 259-1997
By mail only
Y. J. Skutel
Americana; Aviation &
Aeronautics; Slavery; Maps,
Atlases, & Cartography

A. Lucas
89 Round Hill Road
Fairfield, Conn. 06430
(203) 259-2572
By appointment only
Alexander Lucas, Kathleen P.
Lucas
Modern First Editions; General

Museum Gallery Book Shop
360 Mine Hill Road
Fairfield, Conn. 06430
(203) 259-7114
By appointment only
Catalogues issued
Henry B. Caldwell
Books About Painting; Art, Books
about; Decorative Arts; Graphic
Arts; Architecture

R & D Emerson
The Old Church, Main Street
Falls Village, Conn. 06031
(203) 824-0442
12-5 Mon-Sun (closed Jan & Feb)
Catalogues issued
Robert Emerson, Dorothy Emerson

Art; Literature; Medicine &
Science; Press Books & Fine
Printing; Americana; Voyages,
Travels, & Exploration

Geological Book Center
P. O. Box 235
Falls Village, Conn. 06031
(203) 824-0442
By mail only
Robert Emerson, Dorothy Emerson
Geology; Science; Natural History;
Technology; Petroleum;
Paleontology

Anglers & Shooters Bookshelf
Goshen, Conn. 06756
(203) 491-2500
By mail only
Catalogues issued
Henry A. Siegel
Fishing & Angling; Derrydale
Press; Art

William & Lois Pinkney
240 North Granby Road
Granby, Conn. 06035
(203) 653-7710
9-5 Mon-Fri
Catalogues issued
William Pinkney, Lois Pinkney
Western Americana; First Editions;
Americana; New York State;
Illustrated Books; Limited Editions
Club

Emery Allain
108 Valley Road
Greenwich, Conn. 06807
(203) 661-9459
By mail only
Emery Allain
Biography & Autobiography

American Worlds Books
P. O. Box 6305, Whitneyville Stn.
Hamden, Conn. 06517
(203) 776-3558
By mail only

Catalogues issued
Nolan E. Smith
Literature; Literary Criticism;
Scholarly Books; Humanities;
Regional Americana; American
History

Antique Books
3651 Whitney Avenue
Hamden, Conn. 06518
(203) 281-6606
By appointment only
Catalogues issued
Willis D. Underwood
Children's Books; Civil War &
Confederacy; Education; Farming,
Ranching, & Livestock; History;
Maps, Atlases, & Cartography

Bookcell Books
90 Robinwood Road
Hamden, Conn. 06517
(203) 248-0010
By appointment only
Catalogues issued
Louis Kuslan, Dorothy Kuslan
History of Medicine & Science;
Technology; Children's Books;
Illustrated Books

McBlain Books
48 Thompson Street
Hamden, Conn. 06518
(203) 281-0400
By appointment only
Catalogues issued
Philip McBlain, Sharon McBlain
Africa; Black Literature & Studies;
South America; Middle East; Asia;
Russia & Slavic Countries

Walter E. Hallberg
16 Hawthorn Street
Hartford, Conn. 06105
(203) 524-1618
By appointment only
Walter E. Hallberg
Americana; Connecticut; Maps,
Atlases, & Cartography; Prints

The Jumping Frog
161 South Whitney Street
Hartford, Conn. 06105
(203) 523-1622
10-5:30 Wed-Sat (Thurs to 9), 1-5:30 Sun
Bill McBride
Modern First Editions; First Editions; Fiction; Graphic Arts; Marine & Maritime; Back Issue Periodicals

McBride First Editions
157 Sisson Avenue
Hartford, Conn. 06105
(203) 523-1622
By mail only
Catalogues issued
Bill McBride
Fiction; Poetry; Drama; Humor; Mystery & Detective Fiction; Science Fiction

Julian J. Nadolny
121 Hickory Hill Road
Kensington, Conn. 06037
(203) 225-5353
By mail only
Catalogues issued
Julian J. Nadolny
Natural History; Geology; Botany; Zoology; Paleontology; Gardening & Horticulture

Cobble Court Bookshop
Litchfield, Conn. 06759
(203) 567-0084
9-4:30 Mon-Sat
L. M. Wiggin
New England; Gardening & Horticulture; History; General

The John Steele Book Shop
P. O. Box 1091, South Street
Litchfield, Conn. 06759
(203) 567-0748
11-5:30 Tues-Sat, 1-5 Sun
Catalogues issued
William Keifer

New England; Remainders; General

Ordnance Chest
P. O. Box 905
Madison, Conn. 06443
(203) 245-2387
By appointment only
Catalogues issued
Bleecker Williams, Neil Gutterman
Military; Voyages, Travels, & Exploration; Guns & Weapons; Militaria; Ephemera

R. MacKendrick
P. O. Box 390
Manchester, Conn. 06040
(203) 649-4927
By mail only
Russel MacKendrick
General

Sheila B. Amdur
R.F.D. 3, 630 Sawmill Brook Lane
Mansfield, Conn. 06250
(203) 423-3176
By appointment only
Sheila B. Amdur
Medical & Medicine; Psychiatry, Psychology, & Psychoanalysis; General

Michael C. Dooling
P. O. Box 1047
Middlebury, Conn. 06762
(203) 758-8130
By mail only
Catalogues issued
Michael C. Dooling
Americana; Architecture; Art; Natural History; Bindings, Fine & Rare; Voyages, Travels, & Exploration

P & H Bliss, Inc.
215 East Main Street, Box 1079
Middletown, Conn. 06457
(203) 347-2255
By mail only

Back Issue Periodicals; Renaissance; Reprints; Sets; United States Government Publications

Printer's Devil Bookstore
20 Riverview Center
Middletown, Conn. 06457
(203) 344-0022
9:30-5:30 Mon-Sat
Andreia Flynn
Used Paperbacks; Science Fiction; Fantasy; Metaphysics

Printer's Devil Bookstore
1660 Meriden Waterbery Road
Milldale, Conn. 06467
(203) 628-5429
10-5:30 Mon-Sat (Thurs to 8), 12-5 Sun
Catalogues issued
Andreia Flynn
Used Paperbacks; Science Fiction; Fantasy; Metaphysics

Robert Shuhi
P. O. Box 268
Morris, Conn. 06763
(203) 567-5231
By mail only
Catalogues issued
Bob Shuhi, Pat Shuhi
Americana; Travel; Natural History; Militaria; General

Mystic River Antiques Market
14 Holmes Street (booth 10)
Mystic, Conn. 06355
10-5 Mon-Sat, 11-5 Sun
Bernadine O'Donnell
General

Joseph L. Kapica
60 Hawthorne Street
New Britain, Conn. 06053
(203) 229-7259
By appointment only
Joseph L. Kapica
Americana; Nostalgic Fiction;

Miniature Books; "Harper's Weekly" Magazine; American Illustrative Art; Connecticut

David Howland
99 Marshall Ridge Road
New Canaan, Conn. 06840
(203) 966-2150
By appointment only
David Howland
Juveniles

Alibi Books
252 College Street
New Haven, Conn. 06510
(203) 782-0889
11-6 Mon-Sat
Catalogues issued
Lynden Davis, Lisa Davis
Mystery & Detective Fiction; Children's Books; Greek & Roman Classics

Bryn Mawr Book Shop
56 Whitney Avenue
New Haven, Conn. 06510
(203) 562-4217
12-3 Wed-Fri, 10-1 Sat
General

Communications Consultanting & Services
828 Orange Street
New Haven, Conn. 06511
(203) 777-3786
By mail only
Peter J. O'Connell
General

Old Book & Photo
P. O. Box 1070
New Haven, Conn. 06504
(203) 562-7800
By mail only
Catalogues issued
Russell Norton
Poetry; Stereoviews

Pharos Books
P. O. Box 17, Fair Haven Stn.
New Haven, Conn. 06513
(203) 562-0085
By appointment only
Catalogues issued
Matthew Jennett, Sheila Jennett
19th Century Literature; 20th Century Literature; Poetry; Fiction; Greek & Roman Classics

William Reese Company
409 Temple Street
New Haven, Conn. 06511
(203) 789-8081
10-6 Mon-Fri
Catalogues issued
Terry Halliday, William Reese
Americana; Voyages, Travels, & Exploration; Western Americana; Literature; Modern First Editions; Natural History

C. A. Stonehill, Inc.
282 York Street
New Haven, Conn. 06511
(203) 865-5141
9:30-5:30 Mon-Fri
Robert Barry
English Literature; Manuscripts; Appraisals & Appraisal Services; British History; Autographs & Autograph Material

Whitlock's, Inc.
17 Broadway
New Haven, Conn. 06511
(203) 562-9841
9:30-5:30 Mon-Sat
Reverdy Whitlock
Americana; Bindings, Fine & Rare; Color Plate Books; First Editions

Brown Books
577 Bank Street
New London, Conn. 06320
(203) 443-6608
12-5 Wed-Sat

Paul Brown
Naval & Nautical; Literature

Fourth Estate Plus
P. O. Box 866
New London, Conn. 06320
(203) 447-1361
By appointment only
Jeanne Kontoleon
Almanacs; Back Issue Magazines; Fiction; Naval & Nautical; Newspapers

Mrs. L. M. Brew
105 Squash Hollow Road
New Milford, Conn. 06776
(203) 355-0733
By mail only
Louise M. Brew
General; Cooking; Needlework

Britannia Bookshop
Church Street
New Preston, Conn. 06777
(203) 868-0368
11-5 Wed-Sun
Barbara Tippin
English Literature; Ireland & The Irish

Timothy Mawson
Main Street
New Preston, Conn. 06777
(203) 868-0732
11-5:30 Wed-Sat
Catalogues issued
Timothy Mawson
Gardening & Horticulture; Illustrated Books; Cooking; Decorative Arts

Trebizond Rare Books
P. O. Box 2430, Main Street
New Preston, Conn. 06777
(203) 868-2621
By appointment only
Catalogues issued
Williston R Benedict, Rosalind C. Benedict

Voyages, Travels, & Exploration;
Continental Books; English
Literature; STC & Wing Books;
Poetry; Rare Books

American Political Biography
39 Boggs Hill Road
Newton, Conn. 06470
By mail only
Catalogues issued
J. R. Speirs
Presidents; Biography &
Autobiography; Americana;
Political Science & Theory;
Political, Social, & Cultural
History

Bancroft Book Mews
86 Sugar Lane
Newtown, Conn. 06470
(203) 426-6338
By appointment only
Eleanor Bancroft
Performing Arts; Music; New York
City & Metropolitan Region

The Pages Of Yesteryear
Old Hawleyville Road
Newtown, Conn. 06470
(203) 426-0864
By appointment only
John Renjilian
Imprints; Political, Social, &
Cultural History; Cooking

Samuel N. Bean
26 South Washington
Niantic, Conn. 06357
(203) 739-5381
By appointment only
Samuel Bean
General; New England

Carriage House Books
P. O. Box 344
Northford, Conn. 06472
(203) 484-9724
By mail only
Marilyn Esposito, Charles Esposito

Biography & Autobiography; First
Editions

Elliot's Books
P. O. Box 6
Northford, Conn. 06472
(203) 484-2184
By mail only
Catalogues issued
E. Ephraim, Emma Ephraim
Scholarly Books; General

The Book Admirer
135 East Rocks Road
Norwalk, Conn. 06851
(203) 846-9635
By mail only
Daniel Greifenberger
Africa; Black Literature & Studies;
General

Book Associates
P. O. Box 687
Orange, Conn. 06477
(203) 795-3107
10-4 Mon-Thurs, 10-2 Sat
Catalogues issued
Bob Snell
History; Mathematics; Philosophy;
Science; Languages; Geography

H. Galewitz
612 Grassy Hill Road
Orange, Conn. 06477
(203) 795-6222
By mail only
Herb Galewitz
Humor; Fiction; Children's Books;
Performing Arts; General;
Cartoons & Caricature

The Book Exchange
327 New Britain Avenue
Plainville, Conn. 06062
(203) 747-0770
10-6 Mon-Sat (Thurs & Fri to 8)
Science Fiction; Comic Books;
Remainders; Phonograph Records

Charles Daly Collection
P. O. Box 2697
Ridgefield, Conn. 06877
(203) 438-7341
9-5 Mon-Fri
Catalogues issued
Agnes Grogan
Guns & Weapons; Hunting

Jan Mashman
Nine Saunders Lane
Ridgefield, Conn. 06877
(203) 438-7444
By mail only
Jan Mashman
Neurosciences; Medicine &
Science; Calligraphy; Joyce Carol
Oates

Lion's Head Books
P. O. Box 447
Salisbury, Conn. 06068
(203) 435-9328
10-5 Mon-Sat
Mike McCabe
Books about Books; Gardening &
Horticulture; Natural History; New
Books; Modern First Editions

Chiswick Book Shop, Inc.
98 Walnut Tree Hill Road
Sandy Hook, Conn. 06482
(203) 426-3220
By appointment only
Catalogues issued
Herman Cohen, Aveve Cohen
Press Books & Fine Printing; Rare
Books; Printing & Printing
History; Typography & Type
Specimens; Papermaking &
Marbling; Calligraphy

Scarlet Letter
P. O. Box 117
Sherman, Conn. 06784
By appointment only
Catalogues issued
Kathleen Lazere, Michael Lazere
Original Art For Illustration;

*Woodcut Books; Children's Books;
Color Plate Books; Cooking; Back
Issue Magazines*

The Toxophilite Collector
P. O. Box 363
Simsbury, Conn. 06070
(203) 653-3319
By appointment only
David C. Sterling
Archery; Fishing & Angling; Prints

Phyllis M. Lumb
63 Maple Street, Box 192
Somersville, Conn. 06072
(203) 763-1473
By appointment only
Phyllis M. Lumb
*Natural History; Regional
Americana; General*

Ann Dumler
67 Westway Road
Southport, Conn. 06490
(203) 255-9049
By appointment only
Catalogues issued
Ann Dumler
Children's Books; Illustrated Books

Old Southport Books
65 Station Street
Southport, Conn. 06490
(203) 255-6784
11-5 Tues-Sat
Molly Vogel
*Children's Books; Americana;
Business & Business History;
Sporting; Military; Guns &
Weapons*

Laurence Witten
P. O. Box 490
Southport, Conn. 06490
(203) 255-3474
By appointment only
Catalogues issued
Laurence Witten
Incunabula; Medieval

*Manuscripts; Illustrated Books;
Bindings, Fine & Rare; Autographs
& Autograph Material; Appraisals
& Appraisal Services*

Barry Scott
P. O. Box 207
Stonington, Conn. 06378
By mail only
Catalogues issued
Barry Scott
*Rare Books; Modern First
Editions; Illustrated Books; Press
Books & Fine Printing; Decorative
Arts; Technology*

Seaport Autographs
41 Tipping Rock Road
Stonington, Conn. 06378
(203) 535-1224
By mail only
Catalogues issued
Norman F. Boas
*Autographs & Autograph Material;
American Colonies & the
Revolution; Presidents;
Manuscripts; Documents*

Preston C. Beyer
752A Pontiac Lane
Stratford, Conn. 06497
(203) 375-9073
By appointment only
Catalogues issued
Preston C. Beyer, Helen Beyer
*Books about Books; Modern First
Editions; John Steinbeck; American
Literature; Emily Dickinson*

Attic Books & Records
60 Northside Drive
Torrington, Conn. 06790
(203) 496-9260
By mail only
Catalogues issued
Roger P. Steward
General

Nutmeg Books
354 New Litchfield Street, Route
202
Torrington, Conn. 06790
(203) 482-9696
12-5 daily
Catalogues issued
Bill Goring, Debby Goring
General; Ephemera

Traveler Restaurant Book Cellar
Interstate 84, Exit 74
Union, Conn. 06076
(203) 684-4920
12-8 Sun & Mon & Thurs, 10-2
    Tues & Wed, 10-8 Fri
Juveniles; General

Books & Birds
375 Hartford Turnpike (route 30)
Vernon, Conn. 06066
(203) 875-1876
11-4:30 Tues & Wed, 11-8 Thurs,
11-5 Fri & Sat
Gil Salk
Birds & Ornithology; General

Crofter's Books
P. O. Box 236
Washington, Conn. 06794
By mail only
A. Crofter
*Cinema & Film; Zeppelins &
Dirigibles; Marine & Maritime;
Naval & Nautical; American
History*

A Cabinet Of Books
P. O. Box 195
Watertown, Conn. 06795
(203) 274-4825
By mail only
Catalogues issued
Leland H. Kirk, Suzanne H. Kirk
*Hunting; Natural History; Guns
& Weapons; Figure Skating*

Deborah Benson
River Road

West Cornwall, Conn. 06796
(203) 672-6614
By appointment only
Deborah Benson
19th Century Literature; 20th Century Literature; Books about Books; Children's Books; Fore-Edge Paintings

Barbara Farnsworth
Route 128
West Cornwall, Conn. 06796
(203) 672-6571
By appointment only
Barbara Farnsworth
Illustrated Books; Gardening & Horticulture; Press Books & Fine Printing; Graphic Arts

Poor Farm
P. O. Box 193
West Cornwall, Conn. 06796
(203) 672-6567
By appointment only
Dick Lindsey, Charlotte Lindsey
Automotive; Automobile Racing; Regional Americana

Paula Sterne
R.F.D. 2, Huckleberry Road
West Redding, Conn. 06896
(203) 938-2756
Janice Burgeson, George Burgeson
Dogs; Fishing & Angling; Guns & Weapons

Bankside Books
372 Greens Farms Road
Westport, Conn. 06880
(203) 255-5379
By appointment only
Catalogues issued
Richard A. Lowenstein
Mark Twain; World War II Battlefield Art; First Editions; Ships & The Sea; Prints

Guthman Americana
P. O. Box 392

Westport, Conn. 06881
(203) 259-9763
By appointment only
William Guthman
Americana; Indians & Eskimos; Documents; Militaria; American History; Marine & Maritime

Turkey Hill Books
46 Turkey Hill Road South
Westport, Conn. 06880
(203) 255-0041
By appointment only
Catalogues issued
Jack L. Grogins
Children's Books; First Editions; Fiction; Poetry; Art; Limited & Signed Editions

E. Tatro
60 Goff Road
Wethersfield, Conn. 06109
(203) 563-7884
By mail only
Catalogues issued
E. Tatro
Boxing; Golf; Olympic Games; Sports; Baseball

David Ladner
P. O. Box 6179
Whitneyville, Conn. 06517
(203) 288-6575
By appointment only
Catalogues issued
David Ladner, Annette S. Ladner
Bibliography; Books about Books; Printing & Printing History; Scholarly Books

Auslender
P. O. Box 122
Wilton, Conn. 06897
(203) 762-3455
By mail only
Catalogues issued
Stephen Auslender
Military; Naval & Nautical;

Aviation & Aeronautics; Technology

Wolfgang Schiefer
23 Church Street
Wilton, Conn. 06897
(203) 544-9046
By appoint-ment only
Wolfgang Schiefer
South America; Latin America

Cedric L. Robinson
597 Palisado Avenue
Windsor, Conn. 06095
(203) 688-2582
9-5 Mon-Fri (call first)
Catalogues issued
Cedric L. Robinson
Americana; Architecture; Connecticut; American Literature; Voyages, Travels, & Exploration

Windsor Book Store
284 Broad Street
Windsor, Conn. 06095
(203) 688-2159
11-7 Mon-Fri, 9-5 Sat
Ann Wyllie, Arthur Wyllie
American History; Biography & Autobiography; Science Fiction; Comic Books; General

Verde Antiques & Rare Books
64 Main Street
Winsted, Conn. 06098
(203) 379-3135
By mail only
Roy Dethsy
First Editions; Fore-Edge Paintings; Numismatics

Bernie McManus
494 Main Street South
Woodbury, Conn. 06798
(203) 263-3407
12-5 Thurs-Sun
Bernie McManus
First Editions; Illustrated Books

Woodbury House
494 Main Street South, Route 6
Woodbury, Conn. 06798
(203) 263-3407
12-5 Thurs-Sun
Bernie McManus
First Editions; Illustrated Books

Delaware

Oak Knoll Books
214 Delaware Street
New Castle, Del. 19720
(302) 328-7232
9-5 Mon-Fri
Catalogues issued
Robert D. Fleck
Books about Books; Bibliography;
Printing & Printing History;
Typography & Type Specimens;
Press Books & Fine Printing

Attic Books
1175 Pleasant Hill Road
Newark, Del. 19711
(302) 738-7477

By appointment only
C. W. Mortenson
Delaware; First Editions;
Americana

S. D. Beare
7 East Brookland Avenue
Wilmington, Del. 19805
(302) 998-7651
By mail only
Steven Beare, Karen Beare
Science; Technology

Hollyoak Book Shop
306 West 7th Street

Wilmington, Del. 19801
(302) 798-2708
9-4 Mon-Fri, 9-2 Sat
Mort Rosenblatt
General; Voyages, Travels, &
Exploration

Palma Book Service
P. O. Box 602
Wilmington, Del. 19899
By appointment only
Harry M. Stuart
Biography & Autobiography;
History; Literary Criticism

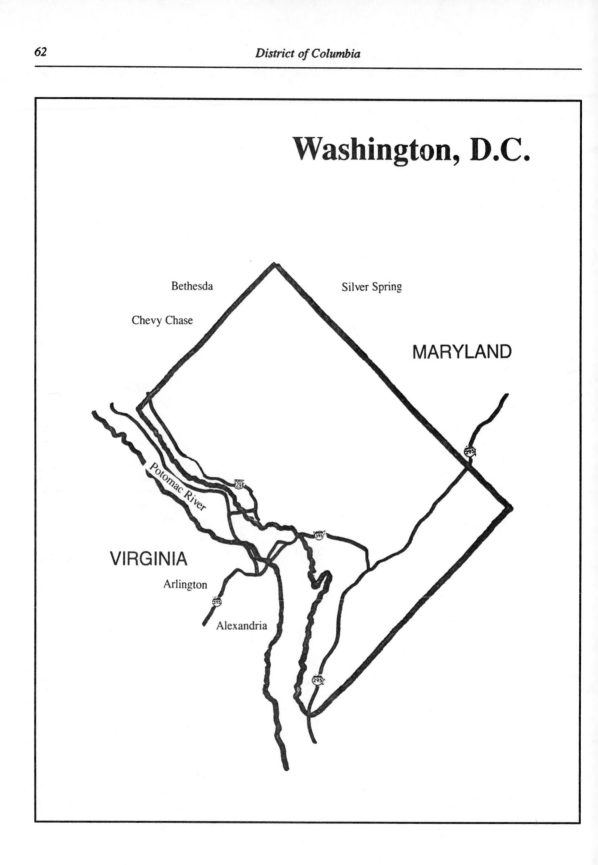

District of Columbia

Booked Up
1209 31st Street, NW
Washington, D.C. 20007
(202) 965-3244
11-3 Mon-Fri, 10-12 Sat
Larry McMurtry
Rare Books; Voyages, Travels, &
Exploration; Literature; Books
about Books; Literary Criticism

Chaos Unlimited
3512 Connecticut Avenue, NW
Washington, D.C. 20008
(202) 244-2710
12-7 Mon-Sat, 12-6 Sun
Catalogues issued
Nelson Freck, Katherine Tuttle
Mystery & Detective Fiction;
Science Fiction

Q. M. Dabney & Co.
P. O. Box 42026
Washington, D.C. 20015
(301) 881-1470
By mail only
Catalogues issued
Michael E. Schnitter
Militaria; Americana; European
History; Law; United States
Government Publications

Earthworks, Inc.
1724 20th Street, NW
Washington, D.C. 20009
(202) 332-4323
10-8 Mon-Fri, 10-7 Sat, 12-5 Sun
Catalogues issued
Bill White, L. Page MacCubbin
Tobacco & Smoking

P. Eisenberg
3729 Massachusetts Avenue, NW
Washington, D.C. 20016

By appointment only
P. Eisenberg
Black Literature & Studies; Africa;
Music

Estate Book Sales
2824 Pennsylvania Avenue, NW
Washington, D.C. 20007
(202) 965-4274
11-9 Mon-Sat, 11-7 Sun
George W. Pollen
American History; Philosophy;
Psychiatry, Psychology, &
Psychoanalysis; Literary Criticism;
Biography & Autobiography

Folger Shakespeare Library
201 East Capitol Street, SE
Washington, D.C. 20003
(202) 544-4600
10-4 Mon-Sat
Janel Frierabend
Shakespeare; Renaissance; Prints;
Press Books & Fine Printing; Art;
Literature

Duff & M. E. Gilfond
1722 19th Street, NW, Apt. 811
Washington, D.C. 20009
(202) 387-1418
By mail only
Duff Gilfond
Search Service, With Stock

William F. Hale
1222 31st Street, NW
Washington, D.C. 20007
(202) 338-8272
11-5 daily
William Hale
Art; Science; Continental Books;
STC & Wing Books

Joshua Heller
P. O. Box 70268
Washington, D.C. 20088
(202) 234-6111
By appointment only
Catalogues issued
Joshua Heller, Phyllis Heller
Press Books & Fine Printing;
Printing & Printing History; Livre
d'Artiste; Bindings, Fine & Rare;
Books about Books

The Holy Land
3041 Normanstone Terrace, NW
Washington, D.C. 20008
(202) 965-4831
By appointment only
Samuel Halperin
Israel; Maps, Atlases, &
Cartography; Judaica & Hebrica;
Voyages, Travels, & Exploration;
Illustrated Books; Rare Books

Jean C. Jones
3701 Massachusetts Avenue, NW
Washington, D.C. 20016
(202) 966-3064
By appointment only
Catalogues issued
Jean C. Jones, Laura Jones
Poetry; History of Medicine &
Science

Lambda Rising, Inc.
1625 Connecticut Avenue, NW
Washington, D.C. 20009
(202) 462-6969
10 a.m.-12 mid. Mon-Sun
Catalogues issued
James M. Bennett, Kent Fordyce
Gay & Lesbian Literature; First
Editions; Ephemera

Shirley B. Lebo
221 "E" Street
Washington, D.C. 20003
(205) 546-9102
By mail only
Shirley Lebo
Appraisals & Appraisal Services

Lloyd Books
145 Dumbarton Street, NW
Washington, D.C. 20007
(202) 333-8989
By appointment only
Catalogues issued
Stacy B. Lloyd
*Americana; Sports; Asia; Pacific
Region; Travel*

Old Print Gallery
1220 31st Street, NW
Washington, D.C. 20007
(202) 965-1818
10-5:45 Mon-Sat
Catalogues issued
Judy Blakely, Jim Blakely
*Prints; Maps, Atlases, &
Cartography; Conservation;
Appraisals & Appraisal Services;
Americana*

The President's Box Bookshop
P. O. Box 1255
Washington, D.C. 20013
(703) 751-5813
By mail only
Catalogues issued
David A. Lovett
*Presidential Assassinations;
Presidents; Famous Trials; True
Crime; Conspiracies & Conspiracy
Theory*

Reprint Bookshop
456 L'Enfant Plaza, SW
Washington, D.C. 20024
(202) 554-5070
9:30-6 Mon-Fri
Michael Osborne
*New Books; Limited & Signed
Editions; First Editions*

Second Story Books
2000 "P" Street, NW
Washington, D.C. 20036
(202) 659-8884
10-10 Mon-Sat
Andrew MacDonald, Chris Cooper
*Greek & Roman Classics;
Scholarly Books; General*

Oscar Shapiro
3726 Connecticut Avenue, NW
Washington, D.C. 20008
(202) 244-4446
By mail only
Catalogues issued
Oscar Shapiro
*Chess; Music; Autographs &
Autograph Material; Violins;
Musical Instruments*

Wehawken Books
4221 45th Street, NW
Washington, D.C. 20016
(202) 362-3185
By mail only
Harris L. Coulter
*Medical & Medicine; History of
Medicine & Science*

Yesterday's Books
4702 Wisconsin Avenue
Washington, D.C. 20016
(202) 363-0581
11-9 Mon-Sat (Fri-Sat to 10), 1-7
Sun
Katina Stockbridge, Don Fleming
Rare Books; General

Florida

Tappin Book Mine
705 Atlantic Boulevard
Atlantic Beach, Fla. 32233
(904) 246-1388
10-6 Mon-Sat (Fri to 7:30)
F. Donald Tappin, Douglas C.
Tappin
*Regional Americana; Civil War
& Confederacy; Comic Books;
Maps, Atlases, & Cartography;
Marine & Maritime*

Books & Things, Inc.
473 NE 20th Street
Boca Raton, Fla. 33431
(305) 395-2229
9:30-5 Mon-Sat
Edward Se Gall
History; Art; General

Herman Herst, Jr., Inc.
P. O. Box 1583
Boca Raton, Fla. 33429-0494
(305) 391-3223

By appointment only
Herman Herst, Jr.
*Philately & Philatelic Literature;
Counterfeit Stamps & Coins*

Jean Cohen
P. O. Box 654
Bonita Springs, Fla. 33923
(813) 992-1262
By mail only
Catalogues issued

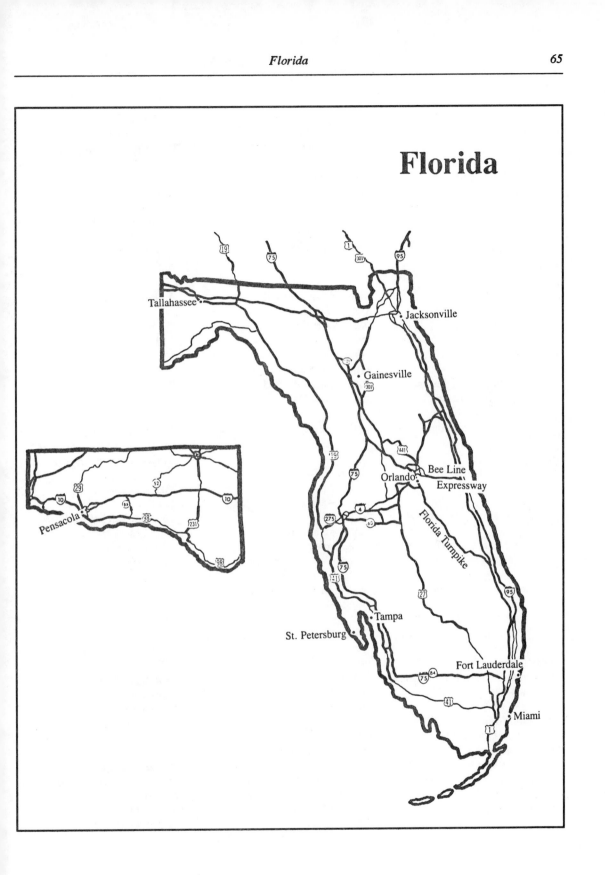

Florida

Jean Cohen
General

One Books
302 Old Main Street
Bradenton, Fla. 33505
(813) 747-1066
10-6 Mon-Sat
Anne Garms
General

Ross Socolof
P. O. Box 1907
Bradenton, Fla. 33506
(813) 758-9378
By mail only
Catalogues issued
Ross Socolof
Fish & Ichthyology; Voyages,
Travels, & Exploration

Harbar Book Exchange
916 East Semoran Boulevard
(Highway 436)
Casselberry, Fla. 32707-5633
(305) 834-0153
10-5 Mon-Sat (to 7 Mon)
Harry J. Oldford, Barbara L.
Oldford
Militaria; Railroads; Cinema &
Film; Cooking; General

Mickler's Antiquarian Books
P. O. Box 38
Chuluota, Fla. 32766
(305) 365-3636
By appointment only
Catalogues issued
Georgine Mickler, Thomas Mickler
Florida

A Blue Moon
1415 Cleveland
Clearwater, Fla. 33515
(813) 443-7444
9-8 Mon-Sat
Lowell Kelly, Jane Jorgensen
Florida; Civil War & Confederacy;
Bindings, Fine & Rare; Art

Book Revue
315 North Fort Harrison Avenue
Clearwater, Fla. 33515
(813) 447-3092
10-4 Mon & Wed-Sat
Louise Robinson
General

The Midnight Bookman
1908 Seagull Drive
Clearwater, Fla. 33546
(813) 536-4029
By appointment only
Lee J. Harrer
Fine Arts; General

Oar House
P. O. Box 3434
Clearwater, Fla. 33515
(813) 441-8288
9-5:30 Mon-Sun
Bill Wheeler
Naval & Nautical

Virgil Wilhite
P. O. Box 10001
Clearwater, Fla. 33517-8001
(813) 447-5722
By appointment only
Catalogues issued
Virgil Wilhite, Colleen Wilhite
Science Fiction; Fantasy; Mystery
& Detective Fiction; Authors;
Western Books

Americana Bookshop & Gallery
1719 Ponce de Leon Boulevard
Coral Gables, Fla. 33134
(305) 442-1776
10-5 Mon-Sat
John Detrick
Maps, Atlases, & Cartography;
Florida; Caribbean; Treasure
Hunting; Napoleon; General

Book Room
3117 Ponce de Leon Boulevard
Coral Gables, Fla. 33134
(305) 445-9716

11-5 Mon-Sat
Duronda Koenig
Art; Maps, Atlases, &
Cartography; General

Books & Books
296 Aragon Avenue
Coral Gables, Fla. 33134
(305) 442-4408
10-8 Mon-Fri, 10-7 Sat, 12-5 Sun
Julius Ser
Literature; Illustrated Books;
Architecture; Design

Barrister, Inc.
4400 SW 95th Avenue
Davie, Fla. 33328
(305) 475-1856
By mail only
Catalogues issued
Sheldon Kurland
Americana; Abraham Lincoln;
Literature; Illustrated Books;
Limited & Signed Editions

Mandala Books
224 South Beach Street
Daytona Beach, Fla. 32074
(904) 255-6728
9:30-6 Mon-Sat, 11-4:30 Sun
Victor Newman
Scholarly Books; St. Louis Area;
Photography; Art; General

Frank Guarino
P. O. Box 89
De Bary, Fla. 32713
(305) 663-5973
Catalogues issued
Frank Guarino
Stock Market & Wall Street;
Antique Stocks & Bonds;
Photography

Helikon Books
112 South Woodland Boulevard
De Land, Fla. 32720
(904) 734-0278
9:30-5:30 Mon-Sat

Catalogues issued
Keith Bollum
Florida; Voyages, Travels, &
Exploration; Natural History;
Naval & Nautical

Pell's Books
2327 South Federal Highway
Delray Beach, Fla. 33444
(305) 272-1210
10-5 Mon-Fri, 10-4 Sat
Robert Kent
Used Paperbacks; Early &
Collectible Paperbacks; Sports;
Sailing & Yachting; Cookbooks;
Fishing & Angling

Raintree Books
432 North Eustis Street
Eustis, Fla. 32726
(904) 357-7145
9:30-5 Mon-Sat
Catalogues issued
Jeff Davis
General

Book Fair
5974 Southwest 40th Avenue
Fort Lauderdale, Fla. 33314
(305) 987-6695
10-5:30 Mon-Fri, 10-1:30 Sat
Marlow Schram
General

Robert A. Hittel
3020 North Federal Highway,
Building 6
Fort Lauderdale, Fla. 33306
(305) 563-1752
10-6 Tues-Sat, Fri to 9
Catalogues issued
Robert A. Hittel
Modern First Editions; Fishing &
Angling; Science Fiction;
Adventure; Cooking; Press Books
& Fine Printing

The Paper Chase
P. O. Box 6632, Stn. 9

Fort Lauderdale, Fla. 33316
(305) 792-9961
By appointment only
Catalogues issued
Elizabeth M Schaffer
Fiction; Modern First Editions;
General

Wake-Brook House
2609 NE 29th Court
Fort Lauderdale, Fla. 33306
(305) 563-9301
9-5 Mon-Fri
Catalogues issued
E. P. Geauque
Florida; Poetry; Cape Cod,
Martha's Vineyard, & Nantucket;
Miniature Books

The Book Den South
2249 First Street
Fort Myers, Fla. 33901
(813) 332-2333
10-5 Mon-Fri (10-5 Sat Winter
only)
Nancy McDougall
Florida; Thomas A. Edison;
General

Cover To Cover Booksellers
9290-1 College Parkway
Fort Myers, Fla. 33907
(813) 481-4647
12-6 Mon, 10-5 Tues-Fri, 10-4
Sun
Rosemary Maurice
General

Book Gallery
1150 North Main Street
Gainesville, Fla. 32601
(904) 378-9117
10-6 Mon-Sat (Fri to 8)
Kaye Henderson, Dan Morgan
Cooking; Metaphysics; Florida;
General

Wildlife Publications Inc
1014 NW 14th Avenue

Gainesville, Fla. 32601
(904) 378-7944
By appointment only
Catalogues issued
Vernon Kisling, Judy Kisling
Natural History

McQuerry Orchid Books
5700 Salerno Road, West
Jacksonville, Fla. 32244
(904) 387-5044
By appointment only
Catalogues issued
Mary N. McQuerry, Jack W.
McQuerry
Natural History; Gardening &
Horticulture; Trades

San Marco Bookstore
1971 San Marco Boulevard
Jacksonville, Fla. 32207
(904) 396-7597
10-5:30 Mon-Fri, 10-4 Sat
John Blauer, Mike Blauer
Florida; General

Key West Island Bookstore
513 Fleming Street
Key West, Fla. 33040
(305) 294-2904
10-6 Mon-Sun
Catalogues issued
John Boisonault
Modern First Editions; Ernest
Hemingway; General

Alla T. Ford
114 South Palmway
Lake Worth, Fla. 33460
(305) 585-1442
By mail only
Catalogues issued
Alla T. Ford
Children's Books; First Editions;
Miniature Books; Rare Books;
Science Fiction; L. Frank Baum
& Oziana

Ray A. Horne
1247 North Wabash Avenue
Lakeland, Fla. 33805
(813) 683-3974
9-9 daily
Ginger C. Horne
First Editions; Indians & Eskimos;
Literature

All Books & Prints Store
4329 SW 8th Street
Miami, Fla. 33134
(305) 444-5001
11-3 Mon-Sat
Al Ledoux
Fiction; New Paperbacks; Poetry;
Religion & Religous History

Book Barn
11047 Bird Road
Miami, Fla. 33165
(305) 223-0531
9:30-5:30 Tues-Sat
Adele Katz
Used Paperbacks

O. Brisky
P. O. Box 585
Micanopy, Fla. 32667
(904) 466-3910
10-5 Fri-Sun
O. Brisky
Naval & Nautical; General

The Book Trader
170 10th Street, North
Naples, Fla. 33940
(813) 262-7562
9:30-5:30 Mon-Sat
Catalogues issued
Ray E. Nugent, Zena A. Nugent
Appraisals & Appraisal Services;
New Books; New Paperbacks; First
Editions

Mycophile Books
1166 Royal Palm
Naples, Fla. 33940
(813) 262-3363

By mail only
Catalogues issued
Robert Demarest
Chemical & Substance
Dependency; Mushrooms

D. E. Whelan--Samadhi
P. O. Box 729
Newberry, Fla. 32669
(904) 472-3451
By mail only
Catalogues issued
Dennis E. Whelan
Astrology; Metaphysics; UFOs;
Herbology & Herbs; Alchemy &
Hermetics

The Scribbling Bookmonger
1613 Silverwood Court
North Fort Myers, Fla. 33903
(813) 995-0222
By mail only
Catalogues issued
Antoinette Gersdorf
Writing Instruction

Aardvarks Booksellers
P. O. Box 15070
Orlando, Fla. 32858
(305) 295-9381
By appointment only
Catalogues issued
Paul Landfried, Claudia Landfried
Mystery & Detective Fiction

Dugas Bookstore
6812 Silver Star Road
Orlando, Fla. 32818
(305) 299-8934
9:30-8 Mon-Fri, 10-6 Sat
Israel Duga
Science Fiction; General

Farley's Old & Rare Books
5855 Tippin Avenue
Pensacola, Fla. 32504
(904) 477-8282
10-5 Tues-Sat
Owen Farley, Moonean Farley

Americana; Children's Books;
Technology; Humanities

King & Queen Books
P. O. Box 15062
Pensacola, Fla. 32514
(904) 477-6811
By mail only
Catalogues issued
Lana Servies
Southern Americana; Florida

Seville Books
660 East Government Street
Pensacola, Fla. 32590
(904) 434-0439
9:30-3:30 Mon-Sat
Gladstone Fluegge
Foreign Languages; Literature;
Voyages, Travels, & Exploration;
Scholarly Books

Quill and Clef Books
7301 55th Street North
Pinellas Park, Fla. 33565
(813) 545-2270
10-5 Fri-Sun only
Catalogues issued
Dick Hazlett
Literature; Jazz; Rock 'n Roll;
Photography; Dance; Art

Ken Kimbel
804 West Russell Drive
Plant City, Fla. 33566
(813) 752-6317
9-12 Mon-Fri
Catalogues issued
Kathleen K. Hicks
Horses & Horse Sports

Carling's Of Florida
P. O. Box 580
Pomona Park, Fla. 32081
(904) 649-9730
By appointment only
Catalogues issued
Carling Gresham

Numismatics; Florida; Latin America

The Bookkeepers Books
190 Shore Drive
Riviera Beach, Fla. 33404
(305) 848-6084
By appointment only
Jim Genovese
Military History

Old City Books
51 King Street
St. Augustine, Fla. 32084
(904) 829-0338
10-9 Mon-Sat, 10-5 Sun
Carolyn T. Olsen, Bill Olsen
Political, Social, & Cultural History; General

Attic Bookshop
5980 66th Street North
St. Petersburg, Fla. 33709
(813) 545-2398
10-6 Mon-Sat
Chris Gomez, Osborne Gomez
Comic Books; Phonograph Records; Encyclopedias; Sheet Music; General

Haslam's Book Store, Inc.
2025 Central Avenue
St. Petersburg, Fla. 33713
(813) 822-8616
9-5:30 Mon-Sat (Fri to 9)
Regional Americana; Religion & Religous History; Children's Books; Americana, States

Lighthouse Books
1735 First Avenue North
St. Petersburg, Fla. 33713
(813) 822-3278
10-5 Mon-Fri, 10-4 Sat
Catalogues issued
Michael Slicker, Catherine Slicker
Florida; Southwestern Americana; Caribbean; Ephemera; Literature

The Oriental Book Shelf
6940 9th Street South
St. Petersburg, Fla. 33705
(813) 894-0766
By appointment only
Catalogues issued
James W. Roberts
The Orient & Orientalia; China; Japan; Pacific Region

Wallace A. Robinson
461 12th Avenue North
St. Petersburg, Fla. 33701
(813) 823-3280
By mail only
Catalogues issued
Wallace Robinson
Early & Collectible Paperbacks; Humor; Children's Books; Maps, Atlases, & Cartography; General

Dorothy Sullivan
P. O. Box 7045
St. Petersburg, Fla. 33734
(813) 821-8254
By appointment only
Catalogues issued
Dorothy Sullivan
Illustrated Books; Southern Americana; Original Art For Illustration; Press Books & Fine Printing; Southern Authors; 20th Century Literature

Aceto Bookmen
5721 Antietam Drive
Sarasota, Fla. 33581
(813) 924-9170
By mail only
Catalogues issued
Charles D. Townsend
Americana, States; Genealogy; American History; Local History

Parmer's Books
1488 Main Street
Sarasota, Fla. 33577
(813) 366-2898
10-5 Mon-Sat

Catalogues issued
Gary Hurst
Americana; Color Plate Books; Press Books & Fine Printing; Illustrated Books

Christine Pegram
1901 Upper Cove Terrace
Sarasota, Fla. 33581
(813) 921-2467
By mail only
Christine Pegram
Search Service, With Stock

Brassers
8701 Seminole Boulevard
Seminole, Fla. 33542
(813) 393-6707
9-5 daily
Thomas Brasser
Sports; Used Paperbacks; Florida; Local History; Regional Americana

Civil War History
P. O. Box 2054
South Miami, Fla. 33143
(305) 665-2613
By mail only
Catalogues issued
Stephen B. Smith
Civil War & Confederacy

Jolie's Books, Inc.
2020 South Federal Highway (U.S. 1)
Stuart, Fla. 33494
(305) 287-7575
9:30-6 Thur-Sat (Fri to 8), 10:30-4 Sun
Jolie Pond, Al Pond
Rare Books; Comic Books; Postcards; New Books

House Of Books
833 West Thorpe
Tallahassee, Fla. 32303
(904) 385-0526
10-5 Mon-Sat

Adene Beal
General

Hyde Park Book Shop
1109 Swann Avenue
Tampa, Fla. 33606
(813) 259-1432
10-6 Mon-Fri, 10-5 Sat
Jim Shelton, Vivian Shelton
General; Children's Books;
Literature; Modern First Editions;
Florida; New Books

McFarland
112 North Gilchrist Avenue
Tampa, Fla. 33606
(813) 251-4858
By appointment only
Catalogues issued
C. S. McFarland
Science Fiction; Fantasy; Mystery
& Detective Fiction

Red Horse At Ybor Square
1901 North 13th Street
Tampa, Fla. 33605
(813) 248-8859
10-6 Mon-Sat, 12-6 Sun
Lucy O'Brien
Literature; Children's Books;
Florida; Postcards; Ephemera;
Back Issue Magazines

Jim Shelton
105-B South Fielding
Tampa, Fla. 33606

(813) 254-4935
By appointment only
Catalogues issued
Jim Shelton
Literature; Modern First Editions;
Florida; Civil War & Confederacy

James Wood
7304 Dixon Avenue
Tampa, Fla. 33604
(813) 232-5221
By appointment only
Catalogues issued
James Wood
Religion & Religious History;
Church History; Florida

Charlotte Krause
P. O. Box 4254
Warrington, Fla. 32507
(904) 455-0931
By appointment only
Catalogues issued
Charlotte Krause
Antiques; Southern Americana;
Local History; Mystery & Detective
Fiction; Science Fiction; General

Book Fair, Farmers Market
1200 South Congress Avenue
West Palm Beach, Fla. 33407
(305) 965-1500
10-9 Thurs-Sat, 10-6 Sun
Marie Smith, Bill Hobson, Lee
Pauline
New Paperbacks; New Books;

Automotive; Bible & Bible Studies;
Crafts & Hobbies

Stanley Roberts
3100 Vincent Road
West Palm Beach, Fla. 33405
(305) 833-8698
By appointment only
Stanley Roberts
Illustrated Books; Documents;
Rare Books

Book Traders Inc.
301 West Central Avenue, Box
9403
Winter Haven, Fla. 33880
(813) 299-4904
9-9 Mon-Sat, 1-6 Sun
Sue Ujlaki
Americana; Comic Books;
Children's Books; Rare Books

Antiquarian Book World
P. O. Box 2682
Winter Park, Fla. 32790
(305) 647-1021
By appointment only
Catalogues issued
D. H. Blanchard
Medical & Medicine; History;
Science; Biography &
Autobiography

Georgia

B. Rogers
P. O. Box 6642
Athens, Ga. 30604
(404) 546-8026
By appointment only
Catalogues issued
Bernard Rogers
Southern Americana; United States Government Publications; Trade Catalogues; Maps, Atlases, & Cartography

Theatricana
P. O. Box 4244
Athens, Ga. 30605
(404) 548-2514
By mail only
Catalogues issued
Gerald Kahan
Theatre; Performing Arts

Harvey Dan Abrams
P. O. Box 13763
Atlanta, Ga. 30324
(404) 982-0460
By appointment only
Harvey Dan Abrams
Georgia; Southern Americana; "Gone With The Wind"; Civil War & Confederacy; Maps, Atlases, & Cartography; First Editions

W. Graham Arader III
2970 Peachtree Road, No. 770
Atlanta, Ga. 30305
(404) 231-5891
9-5 daily
Catalogues issued
Duncan Connelly
Indians & Eskimos; Maps, Atlases, & Cartography; Natural History; Prints; Americana; Color Plate Books

Atlanta Book Exchange
1000 North Highland Avenue
Atlanta, Ga. 30306
(404) 872-2665
10-10 Mon-Fri, 10-6 Sat, 1-6 Sun
Charles Henson
History; Literary Criticism; Biography & Autobiography; Literature; Science Fiction

Ruth Berman
300 Johnson Ferry Road, A-808
Atlanta, Ga. 30328
(404) 256-0723
Ruth Berman
Search Service, Without Stock

Bookfinders
P. O. Box 13692
Atlanta, Ga. 30324-0692
By mail only
Catalogues issued
Thomas Paine
Modern First Editions; Performing Arts; Art; Mystery & Detective Fiction; Science Fiction; Fantasy

The Book Studio
P. O. Box 13335
Atlanta, Ga. 30324
By appointment only
Catalogues issued
John W. White
Civil War & Confederacy; Philately & Philatelic Literature; Art; Occult & Magic; Reference

James W. Burleson
5125 Trimble Road, NE
Atlanta, Ga. 30342
(404) 252-2480
By appointment only
Catalogues issued

James W. Burleson, Cindy Burleson
Medical & Medicine; Medicine & Science; Fore-Edge Paintings

Julian Burnett
P. O. Box 229
Atlanta, Ga. 30301
(404) 252-5812
By appointment only
Catalogues issued
John B. Morris
Naval & Nautical; Arctica & Antarctica; Marine & Maritime; Voyages, Travels, & Exploration; Whaling; America's Cup

C. Dickens
3393 Peachtree Road NE, Lenox Square
Atlanta, Ga. 30326
(404) 231-3825
10-9:30 Mon-Sat, 12:30-5:30 Sun
Tom Hamm, Mike Carnell, Barbara Kleckley
Southern Americana; Juveniles; "Gone With The Wind"; Modern First Editions; 20th Century Literature; Civil War & Confederacy

C. F. Colburn
803 Briarcliff Road, No. D-7
Atlanta, Ga. 30306
(404) 377-1025
By appointment only
Catalogues issued
Chad Colburn
Modern First Editions; Literature

Tom Kuo
P. O. Box 450154
Atlanta, Ga. 30345

(404) 634-7009
By mail only
Catalogues issued
Tom Kuo
Olympic Games; Figure Skating

Robert J. Martin, Jr.
3060 Pharr Court North
Atlanta, Ga. 30305
(404) 659-6700
By appointment only
Robert J. Martin
Maps, Atlases, & Cartography;
Louisiana

Old New York Book Shop
1069 Juniper Street, NE
Atlanta, Ga. 30309
(404) 881-1285
11-6 Mon-Sat
Catalogues issued
Cliff Graubart, Howard McAbee
Modern First Editions; Americana;
Literary Criticism; Religion &
Religious History

Oxford At Williamsburg
2781 Clairemont Road, NE
Atlanta, Ga. 30329
(404) 633-4151
9:30-8 Mon-Fri, 9:30-6 Sat, 11-5
Sun
Rebecca Graham
New Books; Used Paperbacks;
Remainders; General

Oxford Book Store
2345 Peachtree Road, NE
Atlanta, Ga. 30305
(404) 262-3332
9 a.m.-11 p.m. Sun-Thurs, 9-2 Fri-
Sat
Kitty Moran, Rupert LeCraw
New Books; General

Oxford Two Book Store
2395 Peachtree Road, NE
Atlanta, Ga. 30305
(404) 262-3411

9 a.m.-11 p.m. Mon-Sun
Grover DeLuca, Lore Dulson
New Books; Remainders; Used
Paperbacks; Comic Books;
General

Woolf's Den Books
2839 Peachtree Road, NE
Atlanta, Ga. 30305
(404) 233-8053
12-7 Mon-Sat, 1-6 Sun
Catalogues issued
Amelia Woolf, Gene Woolf
Southern Americana; Southern
Authors; Civil War &
Confederacy; Modern First
Editions

Yesteryear Book Shop
3201 Maple Drive, NE
Atlanta, Ga. 30305
(404) 237-0163
10-5:30 Mon-Fri, 11-5 Sat
Catalogues issued
Frank O. Walsh III, Polly G. Fraser
Southern Americana; Civil War
& Confederacy; Militaria; First
Editions; Appraisals & Appraisal
Services; Rare Books

K. Tilden Adamson
1833 Woodrow Street
Augusta, Ga. 30904
(404) 737-8017
By appointment only
K. Tilden Adamson
Medical & Medicine

Book Search Service
36 Kensington Road
Avondale Estates, Ga. 30002
(404) 294-5398
By appointment only
Catalogues issued
Edmond D. Keith, Mrs. Edmond
Keith
Music; Hymns & Hymnals

Tattersalls Book Merchant
902 Center Street, Olde Downtown
Conyers, Ga. 30207
(404) 922-1536
9:30-6 daily
Linda Moulton
General

The Book Dispensary
4588 Memorial Drive
Decatur, Ga. 30032
(404) 296-2186
10-9 Mon-Sat, 12-6 Sun
Chris Cleveland
General

Cooper's Books
2403 Lawrence Highway
Decatur, Ga. 30033
(404) 636-1690
9:30-6 Tues-Sat
Emily Cooper
Children's Books; Greek & Roman
Classics; Early & Collectible
Paperbacks; Prints

Michael D. Brooks
959 Glenridge Drive
Macon, Ga. 31211
(912) 746-0359
By mail only
Michael D. Brooks
Books about Books; English
Literature; Georgia; Vietnam War
& Literature

Downs Books
351 Washington Avenue, NE
Marietta, Ga. 30060
(404) 971-1103
10-4 Wed & Sat only
Katherine Downs
Georgia; Southern Americana;
Americana; Series Books For Boys
& Girls; Civil War & Confederacy

Judith R. Long
2710 Harvest Way
Marietta, Ga. 30062

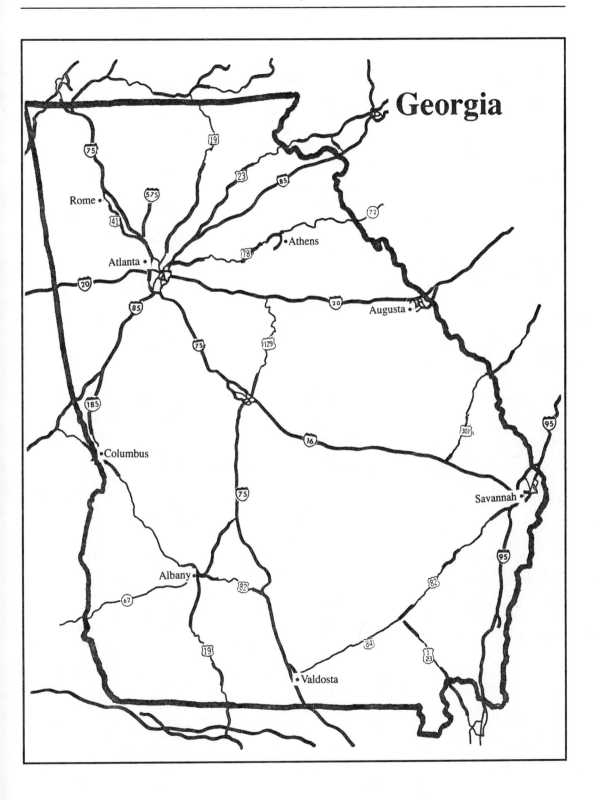

(404) 977-0794
By mail only
Catalogues issued
Judith R. Long
Indiana

Midnight Book Company
3929 Ebeneezer Road
Marietta, Ga. 30066
By mail only
Howard Dricks
*Science Fiction; Fantasy; First
Editions; Sets; Art*

Robert Murphy
3113 Bunker Hill Road
Marietta, Ga. 30062
(404) 973-1523
By appointment only
Catalogues issued
Robert Murphy
Western Americana; Local History

O. G. Lansford
Powersville, Ga. 31008
(912) 956-3484
By mail only
O. G. Lansford, Lucille Lansford
*Phonograph Records; Bible &
Bible Studies; Edgar Rice
Burroughs*

Coosa Valley Book Shop
15 East Third Avenue
Rome, Ga. 30161
(404) 291-7517
8:30-5:30 Mon-Sat
Mrs. John Grigsby
*Americana; Americana, States;
Regional Americana*

G. S. Herron
P. O. Box 1442
Rome, Ga. 30161
(404) 232-1441
G. S. Herron
*Americana; Americana, States;
Regional Americana; Fiction;
Genealogy; General*

Whistles In The Woods
Route 1, Box 265-A
Rossville, Ga. 30741
(404) 375-4326
By appointment only
Catalogues issued
Robert L. Johnson, Mary Ellen
Johnson
*History; Archaeology; Technology;
Trade Catalogues; Forestry; Back
Issue Periodicals*

The Book Lady
17 West York
Savannah, Ga. 31401
(912) 233-3628
9:30-4:30 Mon-Fri
Anita Raskin
*Southern Americana; General;
Literature*

Lonnie E. Evans
804 Drayton Street
Savannah, Ga. 31401
(912) 236-3364
By appointment only
Catalogues issued
Lonnie E. Evans
*Series Books For Boys & Girls;
Georgia; Civil War &
Confederacy; Sherlock Holmes &
A. C. Doyle*

Jacqueline Levine
107 East Oglethorpe Avenue
Savannah, Ga. 31401
(912) 233-8519
By appointment only
Catalogues issued
Jacqueline Levine
*Marine & Maritime; Fore-Edge
Paintings; Americana; Books about
Books; Press Books & Fine
Printing*

Printed Page
211 West Jones
Savannah, Ga. 31401
(912) 234-5612

By appointment only
Rita Trote
*Georgia; Southern Americana;
Civil War & Confederacy;
Americana*

Shaver Booksellers
326 Bull Street
Savannah, Ga. 31401
(912) 234-7257
9-6 Mon-Sat
Esther Shaver
Southwestern Americana

Herb Bridges
P. O. Box 192
Sharpsburg, Ga. 30277
(404) 253-4934
By mail only
Herb Bridges
*"Gone With The Wind"; Southern
Writers*

Forgotten Lore
301 Mendez Avenue
St. Simon Island, Ga. 31522
(912) 638-7897
By appointment only
Ed H. Ginn, Betty Ginn
*Illustrated Books; Press Books &
Fine Printing; Local History;
Cookbooks*

Memorable Books
5380 Manor Drive
Stone Mountain, Ga. 30083
(404) 469-5911
11-5 Tues-Sat
George Hoalk, Ella Hoalk
*Americana; Georgia; Scholarly
Books; Literature; Literary
Criticism; Modern First Editions*

Stone Mountain Relics
968 Main Street
Stone Mountain, Ga. 30083
(404) 469-1425
10-6 Mon-Sat

John Sexton
Civil War & Confederacy

P. R. Rieber
P. O. Box 2202
Thomasville, Ga. 31799
(912) 226-7415
By mail only
Dick Reiber
Juveniles; Modern First Editions;
Southern Americana; Natural
History; Black Literature &
Studies; Jazz

The Bookman Of Arcady
P. O. Box 1259
Tybee Island, Ga. 31328
(912) 786-5842
Daily (Oct-Apr only)
Mary Zeller
Biography & Autobiography;
Fiction; Literature; Poetry;
Broadsides

The Bookstore
Brookwood Plaza
Valdosta, Ga. 31601

(912) 242-5713
9-6:30 daily
Catalogues issued
David Ince
General; Children's Books

Bookshop
Millers Hills Center
Warner Robins, Ga. 31008
(912) 922-7231
10-6 Mon-Sat
Hulda Robuck
General

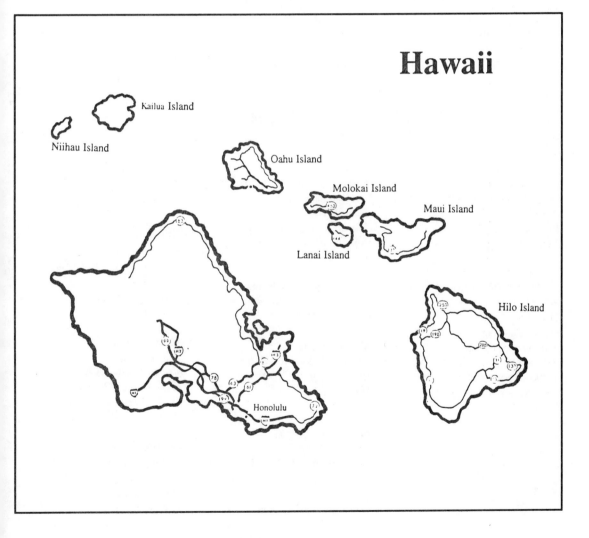

Hawaii

Map of Hawaii on previous page

Academy Shop
900 South Beretania Street
Honolulu, Haw. 96814
(808) 523-1493
10-4 Tues-Sat, 1-5 Sun
Kathee Hoover
*Art; Asia; Pacific Region; The
Orient & Orientalia*

Pacific Book House
1016 Kapahulu, Kilohana Square
Honolulu, Haw. 96816
(808) 737-3475
10-5 Mon-Fri

Catalogues issued
Gay N. Slavsky
*Hawaii; 18th Century Literature;
First Editions; General; Pacific
Region*

Tusitala Bookshop
116 Hekili Street
Kailua, Haw. 96734
(808) 262-6343
10-5:30 Mon-Sat
Lee Reeve, Nancy Abe
*Pacific Region; Hawaii; Voyages,
Travels, & Exploration*

Concord Books
P. O. Box 3380
Kailua-Kona, Haw. 96740
(808) 326-2514
By mail only
Catalogues issued
Charles W. Davis, Evelyn Davis
Conservative Literature & Authors

Idaho

Boise Book Farm
1507 North 13th Street
Boise, Idaho 83702
(208) 344-9205
10-7 Mon-Sat
Catalogues issued
Russell Barnes
*Income Opportunities; Children's
Books; Sheet Music*

Boise Book Mart
612 North Orchard
Boise, Idaho 83706
(208) 342-3161
10-7 Mon-Fri, 10-5:30 Sat
Pat Callahan
General

The Book Shop Inc.
908 Main Street
Boise, Idaho 83702
(208) 342-2659

8:30-5:30 Mon-Fri, 9:30-5:30 Sat
Catalogues issued
Jean Wilson
*Idaho; New Books; Regional
Americana; British Isles*

Hyde Park Book Store
1507 North 13th Street
Boise, Idaho 83702
(208) 383-9035
10-7 Mon-Sat
Russell Barns, Rita Barns
*Idaho; Western Americana;
General*

Parnassus Books
218 North Ninth
Boise, Idaho 83702
(208) 344-7560
11-5:30 Mon-Sat
Judith K. Gaarder, Lorin R.

Gaarder
General

Bonners Books
P. O. Box 1141
Bonners Ferry, Idaho 83505
10-5 Mon-Sat
John O'Connor
General

George Nolan
118 North 2nd
Coeur d'Alene, Idaho 83814
(208) 667-2222
10-5:30 Mon-Sat (Winter open at
10:30)
Catalogues issued
George Nolan
Idaho; Western Americana

Market Place
431 Park

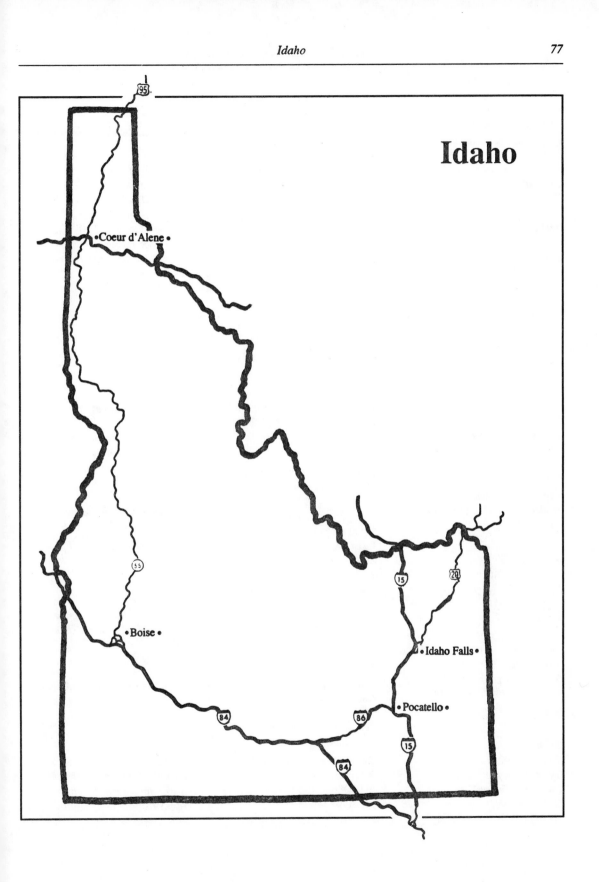

Idaho

Idaho Falls, Idaho 83402
(208) 523-7717
10-6 Mon-Sat
Effie Wildman
Regional Americana; Idaho;
General

Yesteryear Shoppe
1211 First Street, South, Box 797
Nampa, Idaho 83653-0797
(208) 467-3581

11-5:30 Mon-Sat
Dave C. Gonzales
Idaho; Western Americana;
Postcards; Trade Cards; Science
Fiction; Phonograph Records

Ex Libris
P. O. Box 225, Boardwalk Mall
Sun Valley, Idaho 83353
(208) 622-8174
10-5 daily

Rich Bray
Idaho; General

Judi's Bookstore
120 Main Avenue North
Twin Falls, Idaho 83301
(208) 734-4343
9:30-6 Mon-Fri, 9:30-5:30 Sat
Judi Baxter, Bee Stewart
Idaho; Western Americana;
Children's Books

Illinois

Plain Tales Books
P. O. Box 1691
Arlington Heights, Ill. 60006
(312) 253-1472
By mail only
Catalogues issued
Thomas Zimmerman
Modern First Editions; India;
General

Rose Lasley
5827 Burr Oak
Berkeley, Ill. 60163
(312) 547-6239
By mail only
Catalogues issued
Rose Ann Lasley, James L. Lasley
Americana; Children's Books;
General; Rare Books

P. J. Henry
4225 East
Berwyn, Ill. 60402
(312) 484-9047
By mail only
Catalogues issued
H. J. Popinski
Military; Vietnam War &

Literature; World Wars; Civil War
& Confederacy

J. McGovern
1831 South Harvey Avenue
Berwyn, Ill. 60402
(312) 454-8499
By appointment only
Catalogues issued
James McGovern
Science Fiction; Hunting; Fishing
& Angling; Biography &
Autobiography; Sports; Chicago

Provident Bookstore
1500 East Empire Street
Bloomington, Ill. 61701
(309) 662-1432
9:30-6 Mon-Sun (Mon & Fri to 9)
Catalogues issued
Wilbur Bauman
Religion & Religious History

The American Botanist
P. O. Box 143
Brookfield, Ill. 60513
(312) 485-7805
By appointment only

Catalogues issued
Keith Crotz
Agriculture; Herbology & Herbs;
Botany; Gardening & Horticulture;
Landscape Architecture; Botany

Jane Addams Book Shop
208 North Neil Street
Champaign, Ill. 61820
(217) 356-2555
10-5 Tues-Sat
Catalogues issued
Flora Faraci
Women; Children's Books;
Cookbooks; Natural History;
Americana; General

Abraham Lincoln Book Shop
18 East Chestnut Street
Chicago, Ill. 60611
(312) 944-3085
9-5 Mon-Sat
Catalogues issued
Daniel R. Weinberg, John Petersen
Abraham Lincoln; Appraisals &
Appraisal Services; Autographs &
Autograph Material; Civil War &

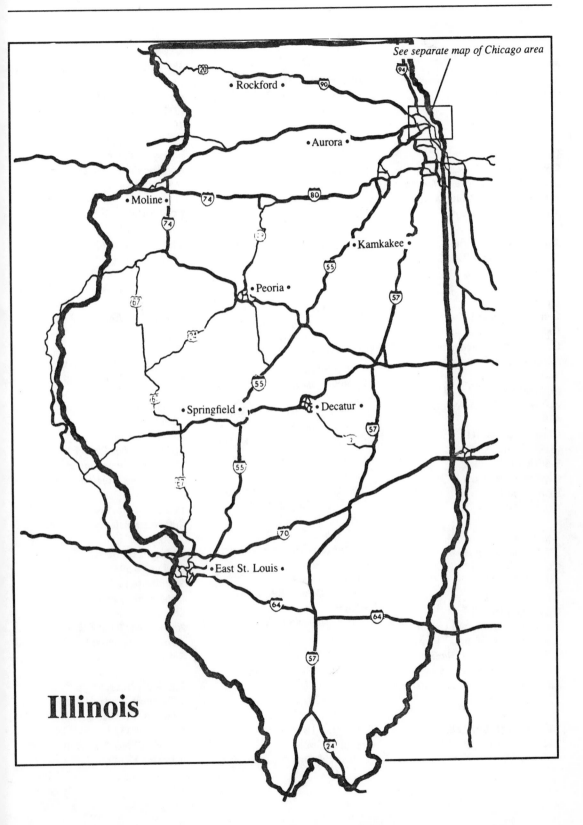

See separate map of Chicago area

Illinois

Confederacy; American History; Presidents

Robert Henry Adams
P. O. Box 11131
Chicago, Ill. 60611
(312) 327-6542
By appointment only
Robert Adams, Robert Bijou
Art; Color Plate Books; Graphic Arts; Paintings; Prints; Maps, Atlases, & Cartography

Appomatox Bookshop
3424 West Irving Park Road
Chicago, Ill. 60618
(312) 539-1863
By mail only
Catalogues issued
Ralph G. Newman
Civil War & Confederacy; Abraham Lincoln

W. Graham Arader III
620 No. Michigan Avenue, suite 470
Chicago, Ill. 60611
(312) 337-6033
9-5 Mon-Fri
Catalogues issued
Esther Sparks
Prints

Beasley Books
1533 West Oakdale
Chicago, Ill. 60657
(312) 472-4528
By appointment only
Catalogues issued
Elizabeth Garon, Paul Garon
Modern First Editions; Mystery & Detective Fiction; Radical Poltics & Literature; Black Literature & Studies; Jazz; Science Fiction

Bookseller's Row Inc.
2445 North Lincoln
Chicago, Ill. 60614

(312) 348-1170
11-10:30 Mon-Sun
Paul Berlanga, Robert Mueller
Fine Arts; Modern First Editions; Rare Books; General

Carol K. Bradshaw
831 Cornelia
Chicago, Ill. 60657
(312) 477-9247
By mail only
Carol Bradshaw
Autographs & Autograph Material; Movie & Fan Magazines; Dance; Postcards; Ephemera; Show Business

Richard Cady
1927 North Hudson Avenue
Chicago, Ill. 60614
(312) 944-0856
By appointment only
Catalogues issued
Richard Cady
Autographs & Autograph Material; Bindings, Fine & Rare; Books about Books; Bibliography; Press Books & Fine Printing; Rare Books

Chicago Law Book Company
4814 South Pulaski Road
Chicago, Ill. 60632
(312) 376-1637
9-5:30 Mon-Fri, 9 a.m.-10 p.m. Sat
Catalogues issued
Joseph J. Gasior, Bernadine Dziedzic
Law; Engineering; Famous Trials

Gerald J. Cielec
2248 North Kedvale Avenue
Chicago, Ill. 60639
(312) 235-2326
By mail only
Catalogues issued
Gerald J. Cielec
General; Americana; Art

N. Fagin
185 North Wabash Avenue, room 1314
Chicago, Ill. 60601
(312) 236-6540
10-5 Mon-Fri, 10-3 Sat
Catalogues issued
Nancy L. Fagin
Anthropology; Archaeology; Botany; Zoology

First Folio
3006 North Sheffield
Chicago, Ill. 60657
(312) 525-0609
12-7 Tues-Thur, 12-9 Fri, 10-6 Sat
Dennis Melhouse, Dennis Hatman
Children's Books; Illustrated Books; First Editions; Freethought; Rare Books; General

Gustafson Books & Antiques
6962 North Clark Street
Chicago, Ill. 60601
(312) 761-0904
12-6 Tues-Sat
Ken Gustafson
Military; Civil War & Confederacy; Technical; Art; Architecture; Regional Americana

Hamill & Barker
400 North Michigan Avenue, suite 2600
Chicago, Ill. 60611
(312) 644-5933
9-4:30 Mon-Fri
Catalogues issued
Terence Tanner
Americana; First Editions; General; Incunabula; Medicine & Science; Rare Books

Hanley's Book Shop
1750 West Jarvis Avenue
Chicago, Ill. 60626
(312) 743-8570
2-8 Mon-Wed & Fri-Sun
Florence Hanley

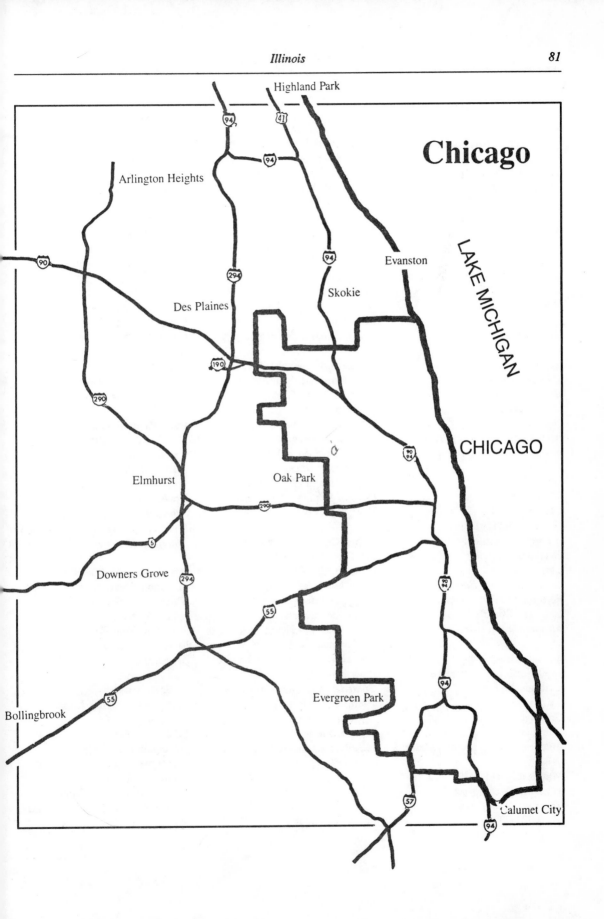

*Fantasy; Horror; Mystery &
Detective Fiction; Myths &
Mythology; Science Fiction*

Thomas J. Joyce & Company
411 South Sangamon, No. 1-D
Chicago, Ill. 60607
(312) 922-0980
By mail only
Catalogues issued
Thomas J. Joyce
*Law; Americana; First Editions;
Ireland & The Irish; Sherlock
Holmes & A. C. Doyle; Rare Books*

N. L. Laird
1240 West Jarvis
Chicago, Ill. 60626
(312) 761-4380
By appointment only
Catalogues issued
Nan Laird
*Art; Illustrated Books; Press Books
& Fine Printing; General*

Larry Laws
831 Cornelia
Chicago, Ill. 60657
(312) 477-9247
By appointment only
Catalogues issued
Larry Laws
*Cinema & Film; Back Issue
Periodicals; Performing Arts;
Chicago; World's Fairs;
Alternative Lifestyles*

London Bookshop
1360 North Lake Shore Drive
Chicago, Ill. 60610
By appointment only
Catalogues issued
Ralph G. Newman
Autographs & Autograph Material

Marshall Field
111 North State Street
Chicago, Ill. 60690
(312) 781-3339

9-5 Mon-Sat
Georgini Paskuly
*First Editions; Bindings, Fine &
Rare; Prints; Maps, Atlases, &
Cartography; Autographs &
Autograph Material*

J. T. Monckton Ltd.
730 North Franklin Street
Chicago, Ill. 60610
(312) 266-1171
9-5 Tues-Sat
Catalogues issued
Bruno H. Schwegmann, John T.
Monckton
Maps, Atlases, & Cartography

Kenneth Nebenzahl, Inc.
333 North Michigan Avenue
Chicago, Ill. 60601
(312) 641-2711
9-5 Mon-Fri
Catalogues issued
Kenneth Nebenzahl, Paul Erling
*Americana; Illustrated Books;
Maps, Atlases, & Cartography;
Natural History; Rare Books;
Voyages, Travels, & Exploration*

Ralph Geoffrey Newman Inc
175 East Delaware Place
Chicago, Ill. 60611
(312) 787-1860
By appointment only
Catalogues issued
Ralph Geoffrey Newman, Patricia
L. Newman
*Appraisals & Appraisal Services;
Americana; Civil War &
Confederacy; American History;
Manuscripts; Presidents*

Joseph Nie
2150 North Lincoln Park West,
suite 509
Chicago, Ill. 60614
(312) 248-7146
By appointment only
Catalogues issued

Joseph Nie, Gertrude Nie
Western Americana

J. E. Pearson
P. O. Box 446
Chicago, Ill. 60690
(312) 776-9566
By mail only
J. E. Pearson, Teresa R. Pearson
*Railroads; Militaria; Aviation &
Aeronautics; Transportation*

Elsie Phalen
2331 West Eastwood
Chicago, Ill. 60625-2031
(312) 583-0513
By appointment only
Elsie Phalen
*First Editions; Children's Books;
Americana; General*

Powell's Bookshop
1501 East 57th Street
Chicago, Ill. 60637
(312) 955-7780
9 a.m.-11 p.m. Mon-Sun
Bradley Jonas
*Scholarly Books; Anthropology;
Philosophy; History; Middle Ages;
American History*

Prairie Avenue Bookshop
711 South Dearborn
Chicago, Ill. 60605
(312) 922-8311
9:30-5:30 Mon-Fri, 10-4 Sat
Marilyn Hasbrouck
Architecture

A. & A. Prosser
3118 North Keating Avenue
Chicago, Ill. 60641
(312) 685-7680
By appointment only
Catalogues issued
Andrew C. Prosser
*Author Collections; Catholica;
Modern First Editions; Literature;
Fiction*

Paul Rohe & Sons
2922 North Clark Street
Chicago, Ill. 60667
(312) 477-1999
7 days a week
Paul Rohe, Christopher Rohe
New Books; Remainders; General

John Rybski
2319 West 47th Place
Chicago, Ill. 60609
(312) 847-5082
By appointment only
Catalogues issued
John Rybski
Indians & Eskimos; Arctica & Antarctica; American History; Civil War & Confederacy; Latin America; Pacific Region

Walter R. Schneemann
5710 South Dorchester Avenue
Chicago, Ill. 60637
By mail only
Catalogues issued
Walter R. Schneemann
General; Scholarly Books; Philosophy; English Literature; Greek & Roman Classics

Harry L. Stern
1 North Wacker Drive, suite 206
Chicago, Ill. 60606
(312) 372-0388
By appointment only
Harry Stern
Voyages, Travels, & Exploration; History of Medicine & Science; Greek & Roman Classics; Maps, Atlases, & Cartography; American Illustrative Art; Rare Books

John Sullivan
3748 North Damen
Chicago, Ill. 60618
(312) 472-2638
By appointment only
John Sullivan

Sporting; Baseball; Boxing; Football

Vintage Volumes
420 Melrose
Chicago, Ill. 60657
(312) 281-9068
12-8 daily
Catalogues issued
Gloria Timmel, Richard Timmel
Children's Books; Illustrated Books; General; Modern First Editions

Dorothy V. Keck
1360 West Riverview
Decatur, Ill. 62522
(217) 428-5100
By mail only
Dorothy V. Keck
Fiction; General; Rare Books

Thomas W. Burrows
P. O. Box 400
Downers Grove, Ill. 60515
By mail only
Catalogues issued
Thomas W. Burrows
Greek & Roman Classics; First Editions; Literature; Rare Books; Scholarly Books

Craig Rohrer
4927 Seeley Avenue
Downers Grove, Ill. 60515
(312) 968-0848
By mail only
Craig Rohrer
Cookbooks

Ye Olde Book Room
161 North York Road
Elmhurst, Ill. 60126
(312) 279-0123
10-5:30 Tues-Fri (Thurs to 8), 10-5 Sat
Ann Brownewell, Dale Brownewell
Science Fiction; General

Adler's Foreign Books Inc
916 Foster Street
Evanston, Ill. 60201-3199
(312) 866-6329
9-6 Mon-Fri, 11-6 Sat
Catalogues issued
Barbara L. Bunce, Peter Connolly
German Books & Literature; Foreign Languages

Alkahest Bookshop
1814 Central Street
Evanston, Ill. 60201
(312) 475-0990
11-5 Wed-Sat
Patricia Martinak-Harmon, David Harmon
Americana; Regional Americana; Illustrated Books; Art

Richard S. Barnes & Co.
821 Foster Street
Evanston, Ill. 60201
(312) 869-2272
10-5 Mon & Thurs-Sat
Richard Barnes, Pat Barnes
Americana; History; Literature; Rare Books; Scholarly Books

Booknook Parnassus
2000 Maple
Evanston, Ill. 60201
(312) 475-3445
12-6 Tues-Sat
I. C. Reaveni
Judaica & Hebrica; Fine Arts; Philosophy; Religion & Religous History; Psychiatry, Psychology, & Psychoanalysis; General

Chicago Historical Bookworks
831 Main Street
Evanston, Ill. 60202
(312) 869-6410
6-9 Thurs, 9-5 Sat
Catalogues issued
Carol Heise
Chicago; WPA & Federal Writers Project; Sets

Midwest European Publications
915 Foster Street
Evanston, Ill. 60201
(312) 866-6262
9-6 Mon-Fri, 11-6 Sat
Catalogues issued
Hubert Mengin, David Chmielnicki
French Books & Literature;
Spanish Books & Literature;
Continental Books

Preservation Book Shop
1911 Central
Evanston, Ill. 60201
(312) 864-4449
11-6 Mon-Sat
Dave Wilhelm
General; History; Literature

George Ritzlin
P. O. Box 6060
Evanston, Ill. 60204
(312) 328-1966
By appointment only
Catalogues issued
George Ritzlin, Mary McMichael
Maps, Atlases, & Cartography

Phyllis Tholin
824 Ridge Terrace
Evanston, Ill. 60201
(312) 475-1174
By appointment only
Catalogues issued
Phyllis Tholin
Women; Chicago

Old Book Barn
Route 51, Box 9
Forsyth, Ill. 62535
(217) 875-0222
11-7 Mon-Sat
Clarke Uhler
Remainders; General

Valley Book Shop
P. O. Box 37
Galena, Ill. 61036
(815) 777-0814

Thomas L. Brisch
Indians & Eskimos; Americana;
Civil War & Confederacy; Outlaws
& Rangers; Overland Narratives;
Railroads

Meyerbooks
235 West Main Street, Box 427
Glenwood, Ill. 60425
(312) 757-4950
By mail only
Catalogues issued
David Meyer
Conjuring & Magic; Circus &
Carnival; Puppetry & Marionettes;
Games & Pastimes; Gambling

Jean Lutz Isador
385 Sumac Road
Highland Park, Ill. 60035
(312) 831-5433
By appointment only
Jean Lutz Isador
Collecting & Collectibles; Rare
Books; General

Titles, Inc.
1931 Sheridan Road
Highland Park, Ill. 60035
(312) 432-3690
10:30-5 Mon-Sat
Florence Shay
Rare Books; Illustrated Books;
Photography; Press Books & Fine
Printing; Children's Books;
Chicago

Little Book Shop, Inc.
11 East First Street
Hinsdale, Ill. 60521
(312) 323-1059
9-5:30 Mon-Sat (Thurs to 8, Sat
to 5)
Caroline C. Wheeler, Phyllis M.
Forward
Children's Books; General

Max Gate Books
641 South Chicago Avenue

Kankakee, Ill. 60901
(815) 939-0422
By appointment only
T. Trafton
Limited & Signed Editions;
Modern First Editions; Series
Books For Boys & Girls; Science
Fiction; Mystery & Detective
Fiction

John Wm. Martin
231 South La Grange Road
La Grange, Ill. 60525
(312) 352-8115
By appointment only
Catalogues issued
John Wm. Martin
18th Century Literature; First
Editions; Literary Criticism; 19th
Century Literature; 20th Century
Literature; Scholarly Books

D. J. Flynn
421 East Westleigh Road
Lake Forest, Ill. 60045
(312) 234-1146
By mail only
Doris Flynn
Fore-Edge Paintings; Illustrated
Books; General

Renaissance Books
10 Trafalgar
Lincolnshire, Ill. 60015
(312) 880-5066
9-5 Mon-Sat
Juanita Shearer
General

Munson Books
3436 Willow Drive
Mattoon, Ill. 61938
(217) 234-8465
8-4:30 Mon-Fri
Anne R. Munson, Donna Nieves
General

About Books
3303 35th Avenue

Moline, Ill. 61265
(309) 797-1583
By appointment only
Catalogues issued
Michael Winne
Books about Books; Bibliography;
Bindings, Fine & Rare; Book Trade
& Catalogues; Collecting &
Collectibles; American Illustrative
Art

Jack's Used Books
718 East Northwest Highway
Mount Prospect, Ill. 60056
(312) 398-7767
9-5 Mon-Sat (Tues & Thurs to 9)
Jack Huggard
Modern First Editions; History;
Science Fiction; Americana

Bank Lane Books
1823 Willow Road
Northfield, Ill. 60093
(312) 441-7570
10-5 Mon-Sat
Jan Hudson, Randy Hudson
General

Booksmith
108 South Marion Street
Oak Park, Ill. 60302
(312) 383-8734
10:30-6 Tues-Sat
Catalogues issued
Thomas O'Brien
Illustrated Books; General

Owen Davies
200 West Harrison Street
Oak Park, Ill. 60304
(312) 848-1186
9-5 Tues-Sat
Catalogues issued
Railroads; Marine & Maritime;
Naval & Nautical

Joyce Klein
818 North Boulevard
Oak Park, Ill. 60302

(312) 383-3033
10-6 Mon-Sat, 11-3 Sun
Joyce Klein
Children's Books; Cooking; Art;
General

Left Bank Bookstall
104 South Oak Park Avenue
Oak Park, Ill. 60302
(312) 383-4700
12-8 Mon-Fri, 10-5 Sat
Catalogues issued
Carole Goodwin, Carol Zientek
Religion & Religious History; Little
Magazines & Literary Small Press

Thomas & Thomas
1138 Erie Street
Oak Park, Ill. 60302
(312) 848-9620
By appointment only
Anne Thomas
Wines; Cookbooks; Cooking

Bern Wheel
834 Wenonah
Oak Park, Ill. 60304
(312) 386-4974
By mail only
Catalogues issued
Bern Wheel
Languages

Old Verities Books
P. O. Box 222
Olympia Fields, Ill. 60461
(312) 747-2211
By mail only
Colleen Dionne, Edward D. Dionne
Criminology; Literature; Sports;
Health; Humor; General

Peter G. Sorrenti
165 North Cady Street
Palatine, Ill. 60067
(312) 358-3055
By mail only
Catalogues issued
Peter G. Sorrenti

Music; Theatre; Cinema & Film;
Military; Sports; Cookbooks

T. A. Swinford
P. O. Box 93
Paris, Ill. 61944
(217) 465-5182
By appointment only
Catalogues issued
Tom A. Swinford, Tonya Y.
Swinford
Civil War & Confederacy;
Montana; Outlaws & Rangers;
Cattle & Range Industry; Indians
& Eskimos; Western Americana

Ken Pierce
P. O. Box 332
Park Forest, Ill. 60466
(312) 672-4457
10-6 Mon-Fri, 11-1 Sat
Catalogues issued
Ken Pierce
Original Art For Illustration

Junction Book Shop, Inc.
Junction City
Peoria, Ill. 61614
(309) 691-4633
10-5 Mon-Sat
Aileen H. Rutherford
Art; Travel

Dick Blomberg
6066 Newburg Road
Rockford, Ill. 61108
By mail only
Dick Blomberg
Indians & Eskimos; Children's
Books; Fishing & Angling; Western
Americana; Overland Narratives;
Civil War & Confederacy

Book Stall Of Rockford
032 Crosby Street
Rockford, Ill. 61107
(815) 963-1671
10-5 Sat only
Karl Moehling, John Peterson

*Americana; Biography &
Autobiography; Farming,
Ranching, & Livestock; Back Issue
Periodicals; Technology*

H. H. Waldo
P. O. Box 350
Rockton, Ill. 61072
(815) 624-2008
By appointment only
Robb Marks, Elizabeth Marks
*Freethought; Humanism; Religion
& Religious History*

Carol Hacker
5 Shagback Road
Rolling Meadows, Ill. 60008
(312) 397-3896
By mail only
Catalogues issued
Carol P. Hacker
Philately & Philatelic Literature

R. J. Hawks Bookstore
215 Main Street
Savanna, Ill. 61074
(815) 273-3070
9-5:30 Mon-Sat (Fri to 8), 11-4
Sun
Ron Deacon, Joanne Deacon
General

Steve Alsberg
9850 Kedvale
Skokie, Ill. 60076
(312) 676-0225
By appointment only
Catalogues issued
Steve Alsberg
*Newspapers; Back Issue
Magazines; Documents; Maps,
Atlases, & Cartography; Outlaws
& Rangers; Chicago*

Articles Of War Ltd.
8806 Bronx Avenue
Skokie, Ill. 60077-1823
(312) 674-7445
11-7 Tues & Wed-Fri (to 9 Thurs),

10-5 Sat
Catalogues issued
Robert Ruman
*Militaria; Marine & Maritime;
History; New Books; Continental
Books*

Historic Newspapers
9850 Kedvale
Skokie, Ill. 60076
(312) 676-9850
By appointment only
Catalogues issued
Steve Alsberg, Linda Alsberg
*Newspapers; Abraham Lincoln;
Manuscripts; Autographs &
Autograph Material; Presidents;
Back Issue Periodicals*

Prairie Archives
641 West Monroe
Springfield, Ill. 62704
(217) 522-9742
11-5 Mon-Sat
Catalogues issued
John R. Paul, Tamar Ehlert
*Americana, States; Civil War &
Confederacy; Ephemera*

J. Dowd
38 West 281, Tom's Trail
St. Charles, Ill. 60174
(312) 584-1930
By appointment only
Catalogues issued
James Dowd, Frances Dowd
*Indians & Eskimos; Western
Americana*

Storeybook Antiques & Books
1325 East State Highway 64
Sycamore, Ill. 60178
(815) 895-5910
11-5 Wed-Sun (Mar-Dec only)
Jean A. Larkin
*Children's Books; Americana;
Christmas; Psychiatry, Psychology,
& Psychoanalysis; Ephemera*

First Impressions
26W580 Butterfield Road
Wheaton, Ill. 60187
(312) 668-9418
By appointment only
Catalogues issued
Jean Jacklin
Children's Books; Illustrated Books

Richard Owen Roberts
P. O. Box 21
Wheaton, Ill. 60189
(312) 584-8069
By mail only
Catalogues issued
Robert Owen Roberts
*Religion & Religous History; Bible
& Bible Studies; Biography &
Autobiography; Christian Books*

Leekley Book Search
P. O. Box 337, 711 Sheridan
Winthrop Harbor, Ill. 60096
(312) 872-2311
Tues-Sat 10-5
Catalogues issued
Brian Leekley, Evelyn Leekley
General; Scholarly Books

Indiana

Cottontail Publications
Route 1, Box 198
Bennington, Ind. 47011
(812) 427-3914
By mail only
Ellyn Kern
Presidents; Chemical & Substance Dependency

Almagre Books
4615 Cranbrook Road
Bloomington, Ind. 47401
(812) 334-0465
By appointment only
Catalogues issued
William Wroth
Western Americana; Mexico; Art, Western; Poetry; New Mexico; Texas

G. J. Rausch
P. O. Box 2346
Bloomington, Ind. 47402
(812) 333-1178
By appointment only
G. J. Rausch
Biography & Autobiography; British Isles; General

Gary Steigerwald
P. O. Box 5236
Bloomington, Ind. 47402
(812) 336-7217
By appointment only
Gary Steigerwald
Books about Books; Illustrated Books; Graphic Arts; Press Books & Fine Printing; Printing & Printing History; Rare Books

Country Bookshelf
933 North State Road, No. 49
Chesterton, Ind. 46304

(219) 926-4694
10-5 Tues-Sat, 12-5 Sun
Virginia McLean
Indiana; Agriculture; Juveniles; Railroads; Local History

Floyd M. Hunt
311 Iowa
Clayton, Ind. 46118
(317) 539-4993
By appointment only
Floyd M. Hunt
Indiana; Series Books For Boys & Girls; Zane Grey

Used Book Place
2027 Hart Street, Box 206
Dyer, Ind. 46311
(219) 322-4247
10-5 Mon-Wed & Fri, Sat
Albert McCasey
Business & Business History; Indiana; Engineering

Bookstack
112 West Lexington Avenue
Elkhart, Ind. 46516
(219) 293-3815
10:30-5:30 Mon-Sat
Catalogues issued
George A. Foster, Jr., Mary Foster, Judy Brothers
Western Americana; Gardening & Horticulture; Fishing & Angling; American History

Book Broker
2127 South Weinbach
Evansville, Ind. 47714-4207
(812) 479-5647
10-9 Mon-Fri, 10-7 Sat, 12-5 Sun
Charles A. Redding
Back Issue Magazines; Comic

Books; Phonograph Records; General

The Bookseller
2922 Braodway
Evansville, Ind. 47712
(812) 424-7472
8:30-4:30 Mon-Fri (Fri to 6), 10-6 Sat
Betty Shultz
General

Campfire Books
6016 Sarabeth Lane
Evansville, Ind. 47712
(812) 425-8549
By appointment only
Catalogues issued
Jerry Madden
Hunting; Fishing & Angling; Alaska

Chanticleer Books
1120 Michigan
Fort Wayne, Ind. 46802
(219) 424-0746
By appointment only
Ralph W. Clark, Mary F. Clark
Indiana; Authors, State & Local

Forest Park Bookshop
1412 Delaware Avenue
Fort Wayne, Ind. 46805
(219) 424-1058
1:30-5:30 Tues-Sat
Lois Morris, J. W. Morris
Regional Americana; Indiana; Illustrated Books; General

Griffith Bookshop
246 South Broad
Griffith, Ind. 46319
(219) 924-8243

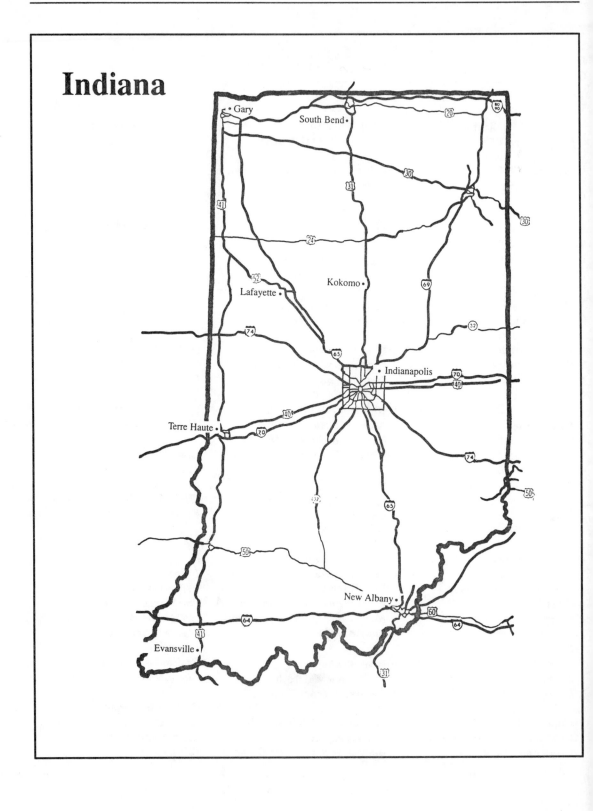

Indiana

10-5 Mon-Sat
Jean McCarty
General

The Abstract
5538 North Pennsylvania Street
Indianapolis, Ind. 46220
(317) 259-1654
By appointment only
Pat Koerber
General

Books & Comics Unlimited #1
922 East Washington
Indianapolis, Ind. 46202
(317) 634-0949
9:30-6 Mon-Sat
James Ware, Mike Stafford
General; Comic Books; Indiana

Books & Comics Unlimited #2
3652 West 16th Street
Indianapolis, Ind. 46222
(317) 635-6447
12-5 Wed, 11-7 Thurs & Fri, 11-5
Sat
Mike Stafford
*Comic Books; Cookbooks; Used
Paperbacks; Science Fiction;
Western Books*

Broad Ripple Bookshop
6407 Ferguson Street
Indianapolis, Ind. 46220
(317) 259-1980
11-6 Tues-Fri, 11-5 Sat
June Sublett
*Indiana; Americana; Modern First
Editions; Children's Books;
Typography & Type Specimens;
General*

Fountain Of Mystery
1119 Prospect Street
Indianapolis, Ind. 46203
(317) 635-1583
12-5 Tues-Fri, 10-6 Sat
Winona Eads

*Mystery & Detective Fiction;
Science Fiction*

Hoosier Bookshop
3820 East 61st Street
Indianapolis, Ind. 46220
(317) 257-0888
Robert R. Russo
*Regional Americana; Civil War
& Confederacy; Appraisals &
Appraisal Services*

Orval J. Imel
424 East Vermont
Indianapolis, Ind. 46202
(317) 638-2618
By appointment only
Orval J. Imel
"National Geographic" Magazine

William S. Johnson
829 East Dr. Woodruff Place
Indianapolis, Ind. 46201
(317) 639-1256
By appointment only
William S. Johnson
*Russia & Slavic Countries; The
Orient & Orientalia; Book Trade
& Catalogues; Humanities*

Lion Enterprises
8608 Old Dominion Court
Indianapolis, Ind. 46231-2539
(317) 243-8048
By mail only
Catalogues issued
Robert Villegas, Irene Kelly
*Political Science & Theory;
Philosophy; Foreign affairs; Art;
Poetry; Humanities*

Odds & Eads
1127 Prospect Avenue
Indianapolis, Ind. 46203
(317) 635-2592
12-5 Tues-Fri, 10-6 Sat
Hereford Eads
General; Indiana

Eleanor Pasotti
5939 Evanston Avenue
Indianapolis, Ind. 46220
(317) 255-2079
By appointment only
Eleanor Fasotti
Children's Books

Coachman Antique Mall
500 Lincolnway
La Porte, Ind. 46350
(219) 326-5933
9-5 Mon-Sat, 12-5 Sun
Jim Rose
General

Readbeard's Books
512 South Baldwin Avenue
Marion, Ind. 46953
(317) 662-0403
9:30-6 Mon-Fri
Anne Haisley, Vivian Stidham
General

Reading Room
P. O. Box 45
Mexico, Ind. 46958
(317) 985-3509
By appointment only
Catalogues issued
Jeanne Sanders, Julie Spears
*Women; Chemical & Substance
Dependency; General*

Robert A. Rhoads
3150 Backmeyer Road
Richmond, Ind. 47374
(317) 962-8056
By mail only
Catalogues issued
Robert A. Rhoads
*Natural History; Color Plate
Books; Illustrated Books*

Good News Books
22 North Plank Street
Rossville, Ind. 46065
(317) 379-3938
10-4 Tues-Sat

Catalogues issued
Ken Jones, Charlie Jones
Religion & Religious History;
Series Books For Boys & Girls;
Turn-Of-Century Novels

Griffon Bookstore
121 West Colfax Street
South Bend, Ind. 46601
(219) 287-5533
10-5:30 Mon-Fri, 10-5 Sat
Sarah Bird, Ken Peczkowski
Philosophy; Religion & Religous
History; Science Fiction;
Literature; Greek & Roman
Classics

Words Of Wisdom
P. O. Box 485
South Bend, Ind. 46624
(219) 233-6922
By appointment only
Catalogues issued
David Eastman
Eastern Religions; Metaphysics;

Holistic Health & Nutrition;
Psychiatry, Psychology, &
Psychoanalysis

Elizabeth H. Bevington
1625 North 8th Street
Terre Haute, Ind. 47804
(812) 234-8989
By appointment only
Elizabeth H. Bevington
General

Willard Goodson
13 North Fifth Street
Vincennes, Ind. 47591
(812) 882-7580
Willard Goodson
Indiana; Local History

Mason's Books
264 South Wabash
Wabash, Ind. 46992
(219) 563-6421
9:30-5 Mon-Sat
Catalogues issued

Jon Mason
Indians & Eskimos; Regional
Americana; Circus & Carnival;
Militaria; General

The Bookworm
P. O. Box 94, 114 South Illinois
Street
Wanatah, Ind. 46390
(219) 733-2403
By appointment only
Laurie Koselke
General

Midnight Bookman
237 Schilling
West Lafayette, Ind. 47906
By appointment only
Catalogues issued
Edwin D. Posey
Books about Books; Press Books
& Fine Printing; Typography &
Type Specimens; Illustrated Books;
Papermaking & Marbling;
Bibliography

Iowa

Broken Kettle Books
Route 1
Akron, Iowa 51001
(712) 568-2114
By appointment only
Catalogues issued
Eldon Bryant
Farming, Ranching, & Livestock;
Automotive; Western Americana;
Trade Catalogues; General

Crawford's Books
339 22nd Avenue, SW
Cedar Rapids, Iowa 52404
(319) 364-0748

By mail only
Joyce Crawford
General

El-Zar Book Bar
P. O. Box 9064
Cedar Rapids, Iowa 52409
(319) 396-3444
By appointment only
Catalogues issued
Karen Laughlin
Horses & Horse Sports

Petersen Book Company
P. O. Box 966

Davenport, Iowa 52805
(319) 355-7051
By mail only
Catalogues issued
Peter C. Petersen, Mary Lou
Petersen
Birds & Ornithology; Natural
History; Botany; Conservation

Different Drummer Books
306 Eighth Street
Des Moines, Iowa 50309
(515) 243-8105
10-4 Mon-Fri
Barbara L. Croft, Norman R. Hane

Ireland & The Irish; Women;
American Literature; Fiction;
Poetry

Checker Book World
3520 Hillcrest, Apt. 9
Dubuque, Iowa 52001
(319) 556-1944
By mail only
Catalogues issued
Don Deweber
Games & Pastimes

Karl Armens
621 Walnut Street
Iowa City, Iowa 52240
(319) 337-7755
By appointment only
Karl Armens
Americana; Modern First Editions;
Mystery & Detective Fiction;
Literature; Science Fiction

William A. Graf
717 Clark Street
Iowa City, Iowa 52240

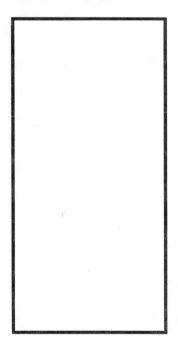

(319) 337-7748
By mail only
Catalogues issued
William A. Graf, Mary K. Graf
Books about Books; American
History; Americana; Militaria;
Press Books & Fine Printing;
Typography & Type Specimens

The Legacy Company
P. O. Box 1303
Iowa City, Iowa 52244
(319) 337-9914
By appointment only
Catalogues issued
John Mullen
Modern First Editions; Americana;
Art; Photography; Medical &
Medicine; Rare Books

The Michauds
1425 Laurel Street
Iowa City, Iowa 52240
(319) 351-5052
By mail only
Catalogues issued
Joe Michaud
Americana; Technology;
Ephemera; General

Murphy-Brookfield Books
219 North Gilbert
Iowa City, Iowa 52240
(319) 338-3077
11-6 Mon-Sat
Jane Murphy
Scholarly Books; Philosophy;
Literary Criticism; History

Vintage Books
507 South Gilbert
Iowa City, Iowa 52240
(319) 354-1822
12-5 Tues-Sat
Catalogues issued
Joe Michaud
Americana; Civil War &
Confederacy; Children's Books;

Technology; Ephemera; Rare
Books

R. Russell Ernest
204 West Maple
Ottumwa, Iowa 52501
(515) 684-5788
By mail only
Rose Russel Ernest
Literature; Scholarly Books

Chris Drumm
P. O. Box 445
Polk City, Iowa 50226
(515) 984-6749
By mail only
Catalogues issued
Chris Drumm
Science Fiction; Fantasy; Horror

Mrs. Velma Johnson
P. O. Box 56
Promise City, Iowa 52583
(515) 874-5980
By mail only
Velma Johnson
General

Gerald Pettinger
Route 2
Russell, Iowa 50238
(515) 535-2239
By mail only
Catalogues issued
Gerald Pettinger
Africa; Fur Trade; Fishing &
Angling; Guns & Weapons;
Western Americana; Voyages,
Travels, & Exploration

D. R. Doerres
P. O. Box 676
Wilton, Iowa 52778
(319) 732-2874
By appointment only
D. R. Doerres
Railroads; Zeppelins & Dirigibles;
Americana, States; Western
Americana; Fur Trade

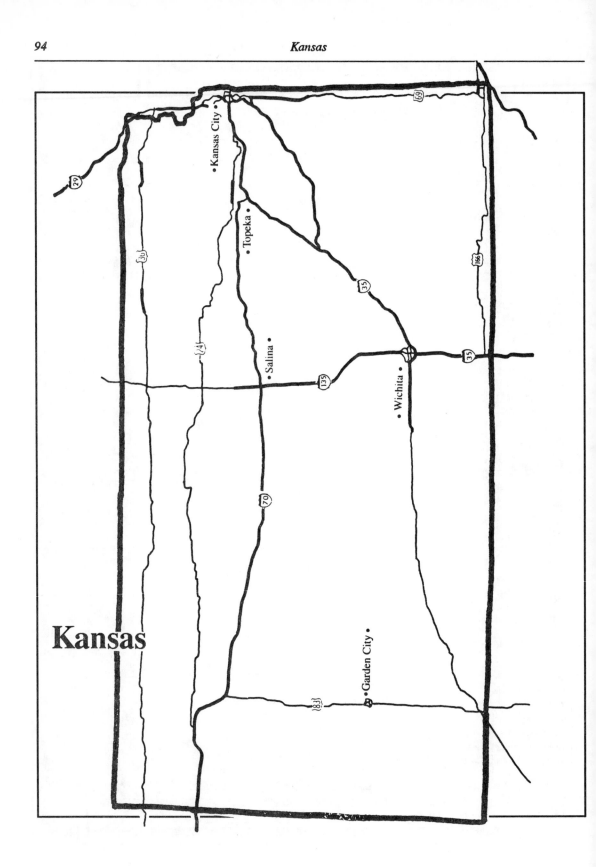

Kansas

Kansas

Bebbah Books
P. O. Box 37
Andover, Kan. 67002
(316) 686-9713
Catalogues issued
Betsy Hobbs, Allen F. Hobbs
Modern First Editions; Americana;
Children's Books; Illustrated
Books; Presidents; Decorative Arts

Charing Cross Road
P. O. Box 2102
Hutchinson, Kan. 67504-2102
(316) 665-7256
9-5 weekdays
Douglas Dible
Search Service, With Stock

David Dary
1101 West 27th Street
Lawrence, Kan. 66044
(913) 843-5268
By appointment only

Catalogues issued
David Dary, Sue Dary
Western Americana; Cattle &
Range Industry; Outlaws &
Rangers; Kansas; Overland
Narratives

J. Hood
1401 Massachusetts
Lawrence, Kan. 66044
(913) 841-4644
11-6 Tues-Sat
John Hood, Chick Hood
Scholarly Books; Psychiatry,
Psychology, & Psychoanalysis;
Literary Criticism; Philosophy

George Keller
8917 West 80th Street
Overland Park, Kan. 66204
(913) 341-3152
By appointment only
George Keller

Western Americana; Illustrated
Books; Kansas; Missouri

Pat's Book Nook
135 South 4th Street
Salina, Kan. 67401
(913) 823-6577
9-5 Mon-Sat
Pat Chalmers
General

Watermark West Rare Books
149 North Broadway
Wichita, Kan. 67202
(316) 263-3007
10-5:30 Mon-Sat
Catalogues issued
Philip C. McComish
Modern First Editions; Limited &
Signed Editions; Western
Americana

Kentucky

Borderland Books
P. O. Box 90
Alvaton, Ky. 42122
(502) 782-3560
By appointment only
Catalogues issued
Philip R. Cloutier
Kentucky; Civil War &
Confederacy; Americana

T. T. Foley
203 East Stephen Foster Avenue

Bardstown, Ky. 40004
(502) 348-6208
By mail only
T. T. Foley
Antiques; Art; Children's Books;
Cooking

Pennyroyal Books
2538 Cox Mill Road
Hopkinsville, Ky. 42240
(502) 885-1532
By appointment only

D. D. Cayce, III
Kentucky; Geography; Herbology
& Herbs; Ephemera

Black Swan Books
505 Maxwell Street
Lexington, Ky. 40507
(606) 252-9255
10-4 Wed-Sat
Catalogues issued
J. Courtney

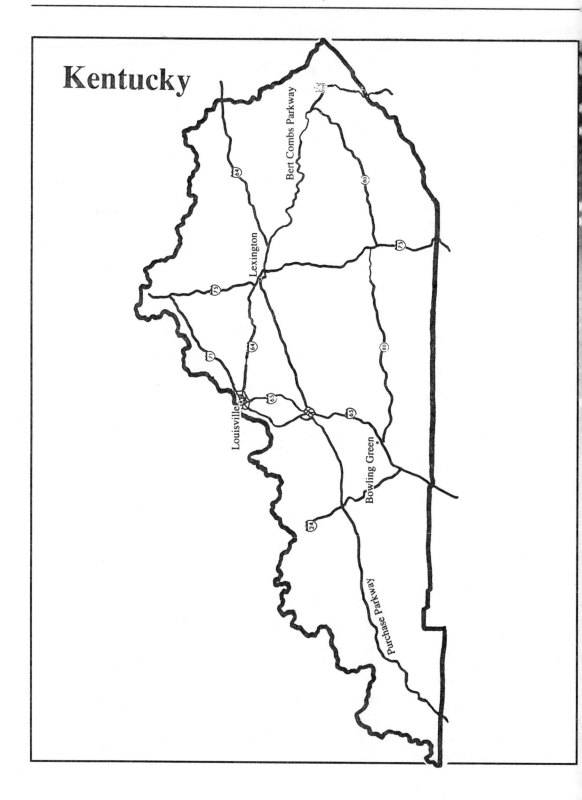

Kentucky; Horses & Horse Sports; General

Glover's Bookery
862 South Broadway
Lexington, Ky. 40504
(606) 253-0614
10-6 Mon-Sat
Catalogues issued
John T. Glover
Americana; Natural History; First Editions; Kentucky; Horses & Horse Sports; Maps, Atlases, & Cartography

The Sail Loft
269 Cassidy Avenue
Lexington, Ky. 40502
(606) 266-6348
By appointment only
Harriet Williams
Children's Books; Illustrated

Books; Color Plate Books; Natural History

Carmichael's Bookstore
1295 Bardstown Road
Louisville, Ky. 40204
(502) 456-6950
10-10 Mon-Sat, 11-6 Sun
Diane Estep
Fiction; New Books; Women

Hawley-Cooke Booksellers
27 Shelbyville Road Plaza
Louisville, Ky. 40207
(502) 893-0133
9:30-5:30 Mon-Sat, 12-6 Sun
Susan Reigler
Sets; Modern First Editions; Authors, State & Local

Philatelic Bibliopole
P. O. Box 36006
Louisville, Ky. 40233

(502) 451-0317
By mail only
Catalogues issued
Leonard H. Hartmann
Philately & Philatelic Literature; Postal History; Local History

Don Smith
3930 Rankin Street
Louisville, Ky. 40214
By mail only
Catalogues issued
Don Smith
"National Geographic" Magazine

The Mt. Sterling Rebel
338 West High Street, Box 481
Mount Sterling, Ky. 40353
(606) 498-5821
9 a.m.-11 p.m. daily
Catalogues issued
Terrence V. Murphy
Civil War & Confederacy

Louisiana

Claitor's Law Books
3165 South Acadian, Box 3333
Baton Rouge, La. 70821
(504) 344-0476
8-4:30 Mon-Fri
Catalogues issued
Rob Claitor
Law

Taylor Clark
2623 Government Street
Baton Rouge, La. 70806
(504) 383-4929
9:30-5:30 Mon-Fri, 9:30-1 Sat
Catalogues issued
Taylor Clark, Mark Stanfield
Color Plate Books; Louisiana

Cottonwood Books
3054 Perkins Road
Baton Rouge, La. 70808
(504) 343-1266
9:30-6 Mon-Fri, 10:30-5:30 Sat
Danny Plaisance
Scholarly Books; Civil War & Confederacy; Fishing & Angling; Hunting

Henry C. Hensel
657-B Rue Perez
Belle Chasse, La. 70037
(504) 393-3323
By appointment only
Catalogues issued
Henry C. Hensel

Americana; Civil War & Confederacy; Maps, Atlases, & Cartography; Philately & Philatelic Literature

G and C Enterprises
612 Alonda Drive
Lafayette, La. 70503
(318) 984-9305
Charles F. Hamsa
Beverages; Wines; Photography; Boy Scouts

Beckham's Bookshop
228 Decatur Street
New Orleans, La. 70130
(504) 522-9875

10-6 Mon-Sun
Alton Cook
*Louisiana; Southern Americana;
General*

Librairie Books
829 Royal Street
New Orleans, La. 70116
(504) 525-4837
10-10 daily
Carey Beckham
Southern Americana; General

Librairie Bookshop
823 Chartres Street
New Orleans, La. 70116
(504) 525-4837
10-8 Mon-Sun
Carey Beckham

*Louisiana; New Orleans; Southern
Americana; General*

Maple Street Rare Bookshop
7529 Maple Street
New Orleans, La. 70118
(504) 866-1163
10-5 Tues-Sat
Louise Coleman
*Illustrated Books; Trade
Catalogues; Modern First
Editions; General*

Frank C. Mrouse
4901 Pauline Drive
New Orleans, La. 70126
(504) 282-2298
By mail only

Frank C. Mrouse
General

Old Books
811 Royal Street
New Orleans, La. 70116
(504) 522-4003
10-6 Mon-Sun
Carey Beckham, Keith Jaggard
*New Orleans; Louisiana; 19th
Century Literature*

J. Raymond Samuel, Ltd.
2727 Pryania Street
New Orleans, La. 70130
(504) 891-9061
10-5 Mon-Sat
Ray Samuel

Maine

Robert Canney
P. O. Box 350
Alfred, Maine 04002
(207) 324-6292
By appointment only
Robert Canney, Connie Canney
*Americana; Association Copies;
Autographs & Autograph Material;
Maine; Rare Books*

Lippincott Books
624 Hammond Street
Bangor, Maine 04401
(207) 942-4398
10-5:30 Tues-Sat
Bill Lippincott
*Science Fiction; Early &
Collectible Paperbacks; Series
Books For Boys & Girls; Mystery
& Detective Fiction; Pulps;
General*

Pro Libris Bookshop
10 Third Street
Bangor, Maine 04401
(207) 942-3019
10-6 Mon-Sat
Eric Furry
General

Steve Powell
The Hideaway
Bar Harbor, Maine 04609
(207) 288-4665
By mail only
Catalogues issued
Steve Powell
*Mystery & Detective Fiction; True
Crime*

Shaw's Bookstore
49 Front Street
Bath, Maine 04530
(207) 443-2283

9-5 Mon-Fri, 9-12:30 Sat
Catalogues issued
John Carter
Maine; Authors, State & Local

Barbara F. Brown
15 Condon Street
Belfast, Maine 04915
(207) 338-2242
By mail only
Barbara F. Brown
*Biography & Autobiography;
History; Maine; Political, Social,
& Cultural History; Voyages,
Travels, & Exploration; Textiles*

Memory Lane Shoppe
P. O. Box 588, 15 Condon Street
Belfast, Maine 04915
(207) 338-2242
By mail only
Barbara F. Brown

Louisiana

*Biography & Autobiography;
Maine; Cinema & Film; Military
History; Travel; Religion &
Religious History*

Marshall E. Bean
P. O. Box 644
Biddeford, Maine 04005
By mail only
Marshall E. Bean
*Mark Twain; Authors; Robert
Frost; Ernest Hemingway;
Autographs & Autograph Material;
Manuscripts*

Maritime Book Shop
P. O. Box 447
Brewer, Maine 04412
(207) 942-3882
By mail only
Catalogues issued
Jon B. Johansen
Marine & Maritime

Bridgton Book House
Depot Street and Route 302
Bridgton, Maine 04009
(207) 647-2546
10-4:30 Mon-Fri (closed Wed), 10-
1 Sat
Sawyer E. Medbury
*Biography & Autobiography;
Children's Books; Turn-Of-The-
Century Novels; Humor; General*

Cross Hill Books
P. O. Box 798
Brunswick, Maine 04011
(207) 729-8531
By appointment only
Catalogues issued
William W. Hill
*Maine; Marine & Maritime;
Voyages, Travels, & Exploration;
Whaling; Naval & Nautical;
Sailing & Yachting*

Leroy Cross
21 Columbia Avenue

Brunswick, Maine 04011
(207) 729-3246
By appointment only
Catalogues issued
Leroy D. Cross
*Mountaineering; Arctica &
Antarctica*

Robert Dysinger, Books
5 Stanwood Street
Brunswick, Maine 04011
(207) 729-1229
By appointment only
Robert Dysinger, Mary Dysinger
*Americana; First Editions;
American Literature*

MacBeans Of Brunswick
134 Maine Street
Brunswick, Maine 04011
(207) 725-8516
9-5:30 Mon-Fri, 9:30-5 Sat
Leilani Dogging, Judy Gardner
Remainders; New Books

Old Books
136 Maine Street (over McBeans)
Brunswick, Maine 04001
(207) 725-4524
10-5 Mon-Sat (Thurs 11-4 Summer
only)
Claire C. Howell
Literature; General

Moll Ockett
Route 26, Box 36
Bryant Pond, Maine 04219
(207) 665-2397
10-5 Thurs-Mon (Apr-Oct only)
Basil Segun
*Maine; Authors, State & Local;
Voyages, Travels, & Exploration;
Agriculture; Gardening &
Horticulture*

Patricia Ledlie
P. O. Box 46, Bean Road
Buckfield, Maine 04220
(207) 336-2969

By appointment only
Catalogues issued
Patricia Ledlie
Natural History

Lillian Berliawsky
23 Bay View Street
Camden, Maine 04843
(207) 236-3903
10:30-5 Mon-Sat (closed Jan-
March)
Lillian Berliawsky
*Americana; European History;
Literature; Music; Art*

Dolphin Bookstore
78 Elm, Box 582
Camden, Maine 04843
(207) 236-3283
10-5 daily (May-Oct, else
weekends)
Leon H. Ballon
*Maine; Americana; Travel;
History; Biography &
Autobiography; Juveniles*

Owl & Turtle
8 Bay View
Camden, Maine 04843
(207) 236-4769
9-5 Mon-Sat
Rebecca G. Cowead
*Juveniles; Art; Antiques; Marine
& Maritime*

Varney's Volumes
P. O. Box 1175, R.F.D. 2
Casco, Maine 04015
(207) 655-4605
10-5 daily, July & August only
Catalogues issued
A. Lois Varney
*Children's Books; Series Books
For Boys & Girls; Maine; Authors,
State & Local; General*

Donna Bishop
48 Cranberry Point Road
Corea, Maine 04624

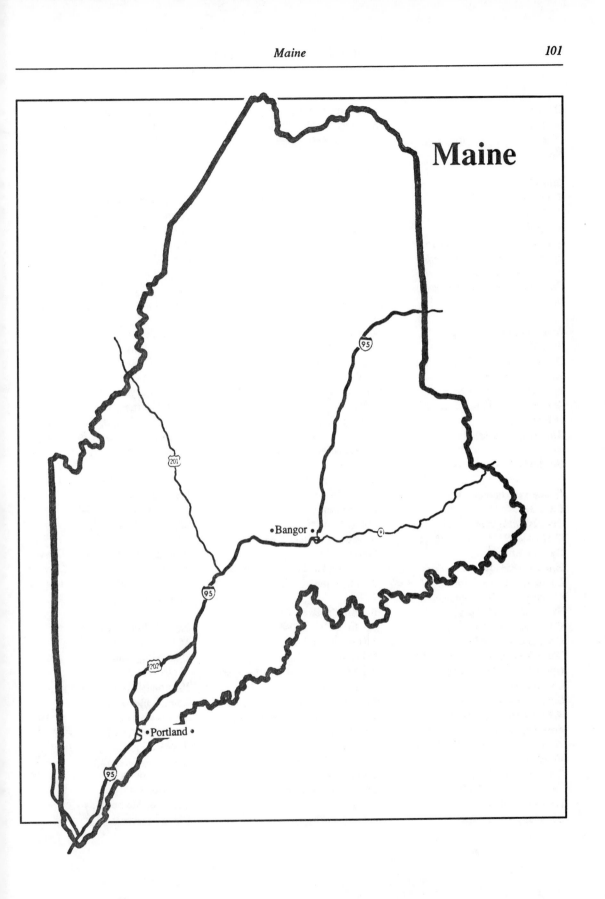

(207) 963-7708
By appointment only
Donna Bishop
Maine; General

Janus Books
Corea, Maine 04624
(207) 963-7100
By mail only
Joan D. Bossi, Sylvia Levin
*Birds & Ornithology; Science
Fiction; Antique Stocks & Bonds;
Cooking; Children's Books;
Illustrated Books*

Book Pedlars
R.D. 2
Cundy's Harbor, Maine 04011
(207) 729-0087
10-5 daily (June 15-Sept 15)
Walter A. O'Brien, Jr., Laura M.
O'Brien
*Children's Books; Illustrated
Books; Americana; Maine;
General*

Grace Perkinson
P. O. Box 7
Deer Isle, Maine 04627
(207) 348-6034
By mail only
Grace Perkinson
Literature; First Editions; General

Skeans & Clifford
P. O. Box 85
Deer Isle, Maine 04627
(207) 348-6864
By mail only
Catalogues issued
Stanley Clifford
*Art; Decorative Arts; Fine Arts;
Rare Books*

Frederica deBeurs
R.F.D. 1, Box 2880
Dexter, Maine 04930
(207) 924-7474
By appointment only

Frederica deBeurs
*Science; Maine; Technology; New
England; Art; General*

Michlestreet Book Company
R.F.D. 1, Box 116
East Lebanon, Maine 04027
(207) 457-1042
By appointment only
Catalogues issued
Hugh S. Morris, Viola Morris
*Medical & Medicine; Architecture;
Americana; Literature; Theatre;
Press Books & Fine Printing*

Alden B. Pratt
Star Route Box 3375
East Livermore, Maine 04228
(207) 897-6979
By appointment only
Alden B. Pratt
Maine; Genealogy; Local History

Books & Autographs
287 Goodwin Road
Eliot, Maine 03903
(207) 439-4739
By appointment only
Catalogues issued
Sherman R. Emery, Harold P.
Merry
*Modern First Editions; Textiles;
Dance; Opera*

Bedford's Used Books
Route 3, Box 150-A
Ellsworth, Maine 04605
(207) 667-7308
9-4 Mon-Sat, 12-4 Sun (Apr-Nov
only)
Annegret Cukierski
*Maine; Marine & Maritime;
General*

MacDonald's Military
Coburn Gore
Eustis, Maine 04936
(207) 297-2751
By appointment only

Catalogues issued
Thomas L. MacDonald
*Civil War & Confederacy;
Ephemera; Photography*

The Falls Book Barn
Main Street, Box 58
Farmington Falls, Maine 04940
(207) 778-3429
9-5 daily
Ethel Emerson
*Biography & Autobiography;
Criminology; Juveniles; Antiques;
New England; New Paperbacks*

Book Cellar
36 Main Street
Freeport, Maine 04032
(207) 865-3157
Mornings, year 'round
Dean Chamberlin
*Nostalgic Fiction; Authors, State
& Local; Juveniles; Biography &
Autobiography*

Bunkhouse Books
Route 5-A, Box 148
Gardiner, Maine 04345
(207) 582-2808
12-9 daily
Isaac Davis, Jr., Beverly Davis
*Authors, State & Local; Local
History; Sporting; Regional
Americana*

Leon Tebbetts Bookstore
164 Water Street
Hallowell, Maine 04347
(207) 623-4670
10-5 daily (June-Oct only)
Leon Tebbetts
*Americana; Color Plate Books;
Remainders; Cinema & Film; Rare
Books*

Island Books
CR Box 33
Isleboro, Maine 04848
(207) 734-6610

9-5 Wed & Fri-Sun (Summers only)
Catalogues issued
Don Roberts, Barbara Roberts
Poetry; Fiction; Literary Criticism; General

River Oaks Books
R.F.D. 2, Box 5505
Jay, Maine 04239
(207) 897-3734
By appointment only
Nicholas J. Bogdon, Barbara J. Bogdon
Americana; Early & Collectible Paperbacks; Maine; Natural History; General

Old Book Shop
61 York Street, Route 1
Kennebunk, Maine 04043
(207) 985-3748
10-5 daily (Summers)
Tom Drysdale, Viola Drysdale
Law; Authors, State & Local; Children's Books; Fiction; Boy Scouts

John F. Rinaldi
P. O. Box 765
Kennebunkport, Maine 04046
(207) 967-3218
By appointment only
Catalogues issued
John F. Rinaldi
Marine & Maritime

Maurice E. Owen
Bowdoin Center Road
Litchfield, Maine 04350
(207) 268-4206
By appointment only
Catalogues issued
Maurice E. Owen
Series Books For Boys & Girls; Fiction; Western Books; Mystery & Detective Fiction; General

Charles Robinson
Pond Road, Box 299
Manchester, Maine 04351
(207) 622-1885
By appointment only
Catalogues issued
Charles Robinson
Appraisals & Appraisal Services; Maps, Atlases, & Cartography; Illustrated Books; Medicine & Science; Voyages, Travels, & Exploration

Wikhegan Rare Books
P. O. Box 370
Mount Desert, Maine 04660
(207) 276-5079
By mail only
Catalogues issued
J. Fuerst
Decorative Arts; Marine & Maritime; Arctica & Antarctica; Indians & Eskimos

The Sail Loft
P. O. Box 248
Newcastle, Maine 04553
(207) 563-3209
By appointment only
Harriet Williams
Children's Books; Illustrated Books; Color Plate Books; Natural History

Snowbound Books
P. O. Box 458
Norridgeweck, Maine 04957
(207) 634-4398
By mail only
Catalogues issued
Nancy Wright, Marla Bottesch
Authors, State & Local; Militaria; General

Joyce B. Keeler
Wilson Pond Road
North Monmouth, Maine 04265
(207) 933-9088
By appointment only

Catalogues issued
Joyce B. Keeler, Donald J. Keeler
Children's Books; Science Fiction; Americana; Nostalgic Fiction; Authors, State & Local

Frank Michelli
P. O. Box 627
Ogunquit, Maine 03907
(207) 646-3886
By mail only
Catalogues issued
Frank Michelli
Children's Books; Fiction

Winter Farm Books
R.F.D. 2, Box 540
Pittsfield, Maine 04967
(207) 938-4141
By appointment only
Catalogues issued
Robert K. Foote
Genealogy; Incunabula

Carlson & Turner Books
241 Congress Street
Portland, Maine 04101
(207) 773-4200
10-5 Tues-Sat
David Turner, Norma Carlson
Birds & Ornithology; Sports; Press Books & Fine Printing; General

Nathan Copeland
72 Groveside Road
Portland, Maine 04102
(207) 773-3647
By appointment only
Catalogues issued
Nathan Copeland
Ships & The Sea; Travel Guides & Baedekers; Wireless Communication

Cunningham Books
P. O. Box 3756
Portland, Maine 04104
(207) 775-2246
11-6 Mon-Sat

Joan Pickard
General

F. M. O'Brien
34 & 36 High Street
Portland, Maine 04101
(207) 774-0931
10-5 daily
F. M. O'Brien
Americana; Maine; Literature

Allen Scott
1-B Dana Street
Portland, Maine 04101
(207) 774-2190
10-6 Mon-Sat
Catalogues issued
Allen Scott
*Books about Books; Literary
Criticism; Marine & Maritime;
Natural History; First Editions*

Kenneth N. Shure
P. O. Box 57
Searsmont, Maine 04973
(207) 342-5441
By appointment only
Catalogues issued
Kenneth N. Shure
Press Books & Fine Printing

Harland H. Eastman
66 Main Street, Box 276
Springvale, Maine 04083
(207) 324-2797
Anytime, but call ahead
Harland H. Eastman
*Maine; Children's Books; Series
Books For Boys & Girls; General*

Lobster Lane Books
Spruce Head, Maine 04859
(207) 594-7520
9-5 Sat & Sun (May-Sept only)
Vivian York

*Maine; Authors, State & Local;
General*

Book Barn
East Main Street
Stockton Springs, Maine 04981
8-7 Mon-Sun
Andrew MacEwen
General

Victorian House
East Main Street
Stockton Springs, Maine 04981
(207) 567-3351
9:30-4:30 Mon-Sat (Apr-Nov only)
Amy MacEwen
General

G. F. Bush
R. D. 1, Box 905
Stonington, Maine 04681
(207) 367-2484
By mail only
G. F. Bush
Fiction; Poetry; General

East Coast Books
P. O. Box 849, Sanford Road
Wells, Maine 04090
(207) 646-3584
10-6 daily (April-Sept.), else 11-5
Merv Slotnick, Kaye Slotnick
*Prints; Autographs & Autograph
Material; Ephemera; Documents;
Rare Books*

Douglas N. Harding
P. O. Box 184, Rte. 1, Webhannet
Farm
Wells, Maine 04090
(207) 646-8785
9-5 daily (July-Oct), else 9-5 Fri-
Sun
Douglas Harding

*Color Plate Books; German Books
& Literature; Arctica & Antarctica*

David Paulhus
Burnt Mill Road
Wells, Maine 04090
(207) 646-7022
10-6 daily (year 'round)
Catalogues issued
A. David Paulhus
Art; General; Prints

Snug Harbor Books
P. O. Box 8, Route 1
Wells, Maine 04090
(207) 646-4124
10-8 Mon-Sun (Winter 10-5 Sat
& Sun)
Gary Austin, Karen Austin
*Western Americana; Bindings, Fine
& Rare; American History*

Wells Bookshop
Burnt Mill Road
Wells, Maine 04090-
(207) 646-7022
By appointment only
Catalogues issued
A. David Paulhus
*Bindings, Fine & Rare; Bindings,
Leather; American Literature;
General*

Sumner & Stillman
P. O. Box 225
Yarmouth, Maine 04096
(207) 846-6070
By appointment only
Catalogues issued
Richard S. Loomis, Jr.
*English Literature; Ireland & The
Irish*

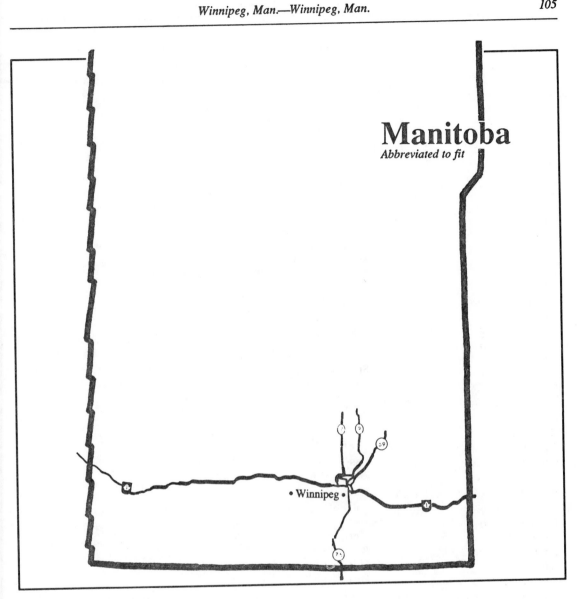

Manitoba

Burton Lysecki
527 Osborne Street
Winnipeg, Man. R3L 2B2
(204) 284-4546
11-6 Mon-Sat

Burton Lysecki
Biography & Autobiography;
Canada & Canadiana; Fiction;
General; Early & Collectible
Paperbacks

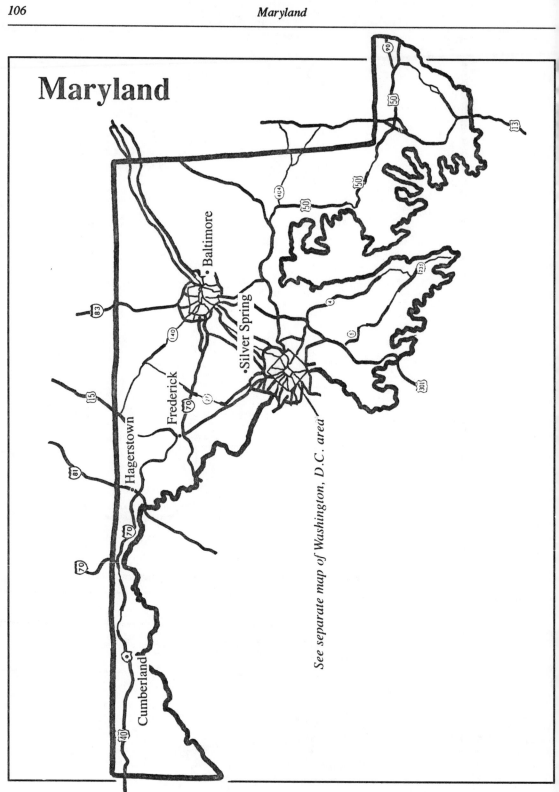

Maryland

Baltimore

Silver Spring

Frederick

Hagerstown

Cumberland

See separate map of Washington, D.C. area

Maryland

Circle West Booksellers
38 West Street
Annapolis, Md. 21401
(301) 267-8761
11-5 Mon-Fri, 10-5 Sat, 12-5 Sun
Catalogues issued
Jeffrey Gordon, Samuel Gordon
*British Isles; Fantasy; Science
Fiction; Sports; Occult & Magic;
Mystery & Detective Fiction*

Dragoman Books
680 Americana Drive, No. 38
Annapolis, Md. 21403
(301) 263-2757
Catalogues issued
Fred Drake
Archaeology; Languages; General

B. R. Artcraft Company
6701 Cherry Hill Road
Baldwin, Md. 21013
(301) 592-2847
By mail only
Catalogues issued
Bernard Rogge, Gloria E. Rogge
*Architecture; Art; Crafts &
Hobbies; Drawings; Graphic Arts;
Paintings*

David Allen
6502 Shelrick Place
Baltimore, Md. 21209
(301) 486-8257
By appointment only
Catalogues issued
David Allen, Ellie Allen
*Performing Arts; Puppetry &
Marionettes; Art; Illustrated
Books; Children's Books; Fashion*

Allen's Bookshop
344 East 33rd Street

Baltimore, Md. 21218
(301) 243-4356
1-6 Mon-Tues, 1-8 Thurs-Fri, 11-5
Sat
David Ray
*Mathematics; Music; Art;
Militaria; Physics; Engineering*

Marilyn Braiterman
20 Whitfield Road
Baltimore, Md. 21210
(301) 235-4848
By appointment only
Catalogues issued
Marilyn Braiterman
*Art; Books about Books;
Architecture; First Editions;
Illustrated Books; Press Books &
Fine Printing*

Camelot Books
2403 Hillhouse Road
Baltimore, Md. 21207
(301) 448-1015
By mail only
Catalogues issued
James A. Kissko
*Americana; Maps, Atlases, &
Cartography; Modern First
Editions; Plays & Playwrights;
Art; Press Books & Fine Printing*

The Chirurgical Bookshop
1211 Cathedral Street
Baltimore, Md. 21201
(301) 539-0872
By appointment only
Catalogues issued
Deborah K. Woolverton, Charlotte
Karin
History of Medicine & Science

Drusilla's Books
859 North Howard Street
Baltimore, Md. 21201
(301) 225-0277
11-4 Wed-Sat
Catalogues issued
Drusilla P. Jones
*Children's Books; Ephemera;
Illustrated Books; Juveniles;
Americana, States*

Key Books
2 West Montgomery Street
Baltimore, Md. 21230
(301) 539-5020
By appointment only
Catalogues issued
Raymond D. Cooper, Carolyn L.
Cooper
*History of Medicine & Science;
Rare Books; Science; Technology*

Richard A. Macksey
107 St. Martin's Road
Baltimore, Md. 21218
(301) 235-6237
By appointment only
Catalogues issued
Dick Macksey
*Americana; Author Collections;
First Editions; Foreign Languages;
Little Magazines & Literary Small
Presses; Scholarly Books*

The 19th Century Shop
1047 Hollins Street
Baltimore, Md. 21223
(301) 539-2586
10-5 Mon-Fri
Catalogues issued
Stephen Loewentheil
19th Century Literature; Evolution;

History of Medicine & Science;
Edgar Allan Poe; Middle East

Cecil Archer Rush
2605 North Charles Street
Baltimore, Md. 21218
(301) 323-7767
By appointment only
Cecil A. Rush, Betty Rush
The Orient & Orientalia; Erotica;
Illustrated Books

Bartleby's Bookshop
7710 Woodmont Avenue
Bethesda, Md. 20814
(301) 654-4373
10-8 Mon-Sat, 12-6 Sun
Catalogues issued
John Thomson, Karen Griffin
Humanities; University Press
Books; Philosophy; Poetry;
Literature; History

The Book Cellar
8227 Woodmont Avenue
Bethesda, Md. 20014
(301) 654-1898
11-6 daily
John Stephens, Martha Hartman
Foreign Languages; Science;
Technology; Music; Art; Literature

Folkways, Scholarly Books
5309 Tuscarawas Road
Bethesda, Md. 20816
(301) 320-5672
By mail only
Catalogues issued
Bradford Gray
Social Sciences; Psychiatry,
Psychology, & Psychoanalysis;
Medicine & Science; Philosophy

Second Story Books
4836 Bethesda Avenue Row
Bethesda, Md. 20814
(301) 656-0170
10-10 Mon-Sun

Allan Stypeck
Phonograph Records; General

Wyngate Manuscripts
5801 Wyngate Drive
Bethesda, Md. 20817
(301) 530-4927
By appointment only
Catalogues issued
Constance R Spande, Thomas F.
Spande
Manuscripts

Old Hickory Bookshop, Ltd
20225 New Hampshire Avenue
Brinklow, Md. 20862
(301) 924-2225
By appointment only
Catalogues issued
Ralph Grimes, Johanna Grimes
History of Medicine & Science

Stewart's Books
6504 Old Branch Avenue
Camp Springs, Md. 20748
(301) 449-6766
11-6 Tues-Sat
Frances M. Stewart, William F.
Stewart
Military History

Wharf House Books
P. O. Box 57
Centreville, Md. 21617
(301) 758-0678
By appointment only
Mary P. Franklin
Cooking; Diaries & Narratives;
Maryland; H. L. Mencken; Marine
& Maritime; Poetry

John Gach
5620 Waterloo Road
Columbia, Md. 21045
(301) 465-9023
By appointment only
Catalogues issued
John Gach, Betty Gach
Psychiatry, Psychology, &

Psychoanalysis; Appraisals &
Appraisal Services; Collection
Development; Rare Books;
Philosophy

Stone House Books
71 Stone House Lane
Elkton, Md. 21921
(301) 398-6835
By appointment only
Catalogues issued
R. M. Eisenberg
Natural History; Mystery &
Detective Fiction; Gardening &
Horticulture; General

Deeds Book Shop
8012 Main Street, Box 85
Ellicott City, Md. 21043
(301) 465-9419
12-5 Tues-Sat, 1-5 Sun
Jean Mattern
Juveniles; Authors; Literature;
Maryland

Wonder Book and Video
1507 West Patrick Street, Route
40 West
Frederick, Md. 21701
(301) 694-5955
10-10 Mon-Sat, 11-6 Sun
Charles Roberts
Remainders; Comic Books;
Maryland; Phonograph Records;
Video Cassette & Compact Disks;
General

Doris Frohnsdorff
P. O. Box 2306
Gaithersburg, Md. 20879
(301) 869-1256
By appointment only
Catalogues issued
Doris Frohnsdorff
Bindings, Fine & Rare; Children's
Books; Drawings; Illustrated
Books; Miniature Books; Rare
Books

**Back Number Magazine
   Company**
7-D Ridge Road
Greenbelt, Md. 20770
(301) 345-7430
By appointment only
Don Bullian, Ronald Bullian
Technical; Back Issue Periodicals

Kensington Used Books
10417 Armory Avenue
Kensington, Md. 20895
(301) 949-9411
11-5 Tues-Sun
Bill Pic
General

Attic Books
357 Main Street
Laurel, Md. 20707
(301) 725-3725
11-7 Mon, Wed-Sat, 1-5 Sun
Richard Cook
*Science Fiction; Mystery &
Detective Fiction; Military History;
General*

Elm
8815 Churchfield Lane
Laurel, Md. 20811
By mail only
*Conspiracies & Conspiracy
Theory; Espionage*

B & B Smith
P. O. Box 158
Mt. Airy, Md. 21771
(301) 549-1227
By mail only
Catalogues issued
William P. Smith
*Ancient History; Archaeology;
Greek & Roman Classics*

Old Quenzel Store
P. O. Box 326
Port Tobacco, Md. 20677
(301) 934-8045
By mail only

Catalogues issued
James L. Barbour
*Maryland; Abraham Lincoln; Civil
War & Confederacy*

Steven C. Bernard
138 New Mark Esplanade
Rockville, Md. 20850
(301) 340-8623
By appointment only
Catalogues issued
Steven C. Bernard
*Modern First Editions; Literature;
First Editions; Mystery & Detective
Fiction; Science Fiction*

Harris Books
12000 Old Georgetown Road, N-
   1209
Rockville, Md. 20852
(301) 770-5183
By appointment only
Catalogues issued
Roberta Harris, Margaret Harris
Horses & Horse Sports; Art

Quill & Brush
P. O. Box 5365
Rockville, Md. 20851
(301) 460-3700
By appointment only
Catalogues issued
Allen Ahearn, Patricia Ahearn
*Modern First Editions; Autographs
& Autograph Material; Fiction;
Rare Books*

Crittenden Schmitt Archives
P. O. Box 4253, Court House Stn.
Rockville, Md. 20850
By appointment only
J. R. Crittenden Schmitt
*Military; Militaria; Submarines;
Hobbies*

Henrietta's Attic
205-B Maryland Avenue
Salisbury, Md. 21801
(301) 546-3700

10-5 Mon-Sat
Catalogues issued
Henrietta J Moore
*Children's Books; Juveniles; Local
History; General*

All Edges Gilt
P. O. Box 7625
Silver Spring, Md. 20907
(301) 593-7465
By mail only
Catalogues issued
Diane Anderson
*Theatre; Cinema & Film; Art;
Natural History; Dogs; Horses &
Horse Sports*

Hirschtritt's "1712"
1712 Republic Road
Silver Spring, Md. 20902
(301) 649-5393
By appointment only
Ralph Hirschtritt
*Americana; Japan; General;
Illustrated Books; 19th Century
Literature; Modern First Editions*

Old Geographics
P. O. Box 649
Sparks, Md. 21152
(301) 343-1569
By mail only
Carolyn R. Mackie
*"National Geographic" Magazine;
General*

Jerome Shochet
6144 Oakland Mills Road
Sykesville, Md. 21784
(301) 795-5879
By mail only
Catalogues issued
Jerome Shochet
Boxing

Unicorn Bookshop
P. O. Box 154
Trappe, Md. 21673
(301) 476-3838

9:30-5 Mon-Sat
James Dawson
Maryland; Civil War &
Confederacy; H. L. Mencken;
Transcendentalism; General

Christian Classics
73 West Main Street
Westminster, Md. 21157

(301) 848-3065
9-4:30 Mon-Fri
Catalogues issued
John J. McHale, Katherine T.
McHale
Religion & Religious History

John A. Desch
2522 University Boulevard West

Wheaton, Md. 20902
(301) 946-9609
12-4 Mon-Sun (Sat to 3)
John A. Desch, Grace Desch
Militaria; Biography &
Autobiography; Americana;
Children's Books; Used
Paperbacks

Massachusetts

Francis G. Walett
369 High Street
Abington, Mass. 02351
(617) 878-1665
By mail only
Catalogues issued
Francis G. Walett
Americana; Regional Americana;
Civil War & Confederacy;
Bibliography; Rare Books

Annie's Book Stop
66-B Great Road
Acton, Mass. 01720
(617) 263-3158
10-6 Mon-Fri (Wed, Fri to 8), 10-5
Sat
Joanne Riddle
New Paperbacks; General

J. Richard Becker
51 Concord Road
Acton Centre, Mass. 01720
(617) 263-3820
By mail only
J. Richard Becker
Canada & Canadiana; Poetry;
Numismatics

Allston Bookshop
169 Brighton Avenue

Allston, Mass. 02134
(617) 254-8228
11-5 Tues-Sat
Robert Franklin
General

Amherst Antiquarian Maps
P. O. Box 12
Amherst, Mass. 01004-0012
(413) 549-4905
By appointment only
Catalogues issued
Jon K. Rosenthal
Maps, Atlases, & Cartography;
Prints; Appraisals & Appraisal
Services

Barbara E. Smith
P. O. Box 563
Amherst, Mass. 01004
(413) 253-3992
By mail only
Barbara Smith
Juveniles; New England; General

Sophia Bookshop
103 North Pleasant
Amherst, Mass. 01002
10-5 Mon-Sat, 12-5 Sun
Catalogues issued
Sandy Lillydahl

Metaphysics; Holistic Health &
Nutrition; Children's Books;
Fiction; Myths & Mythology;
Psychiatry, Psychology, &
Psychoanalysis

Valley Books
5 East Pleasant Street
Amherst, Mass. 01002
(413) 549-6052
10:30-5:30 Mon-Fri, 10-5 Sat, 12-
5 Sun
Catalogues issued
Jerry Pruner, Charmagne Pruner
Literary Criticism; Literature;
Fiction; Art Catalogues,
Periodicals, & Books; Sports

Andover Antique Books &
Gallery
68 Park Street, rear
Andover, Mass. 01810
(617) 475-1645
9:30-5:30 Tues-Sat, 1-4 Sun (Nov-
Feb)
V. David Rodger
New England; Illustrated Books;
Press Books & Fine Printing;
Children's Books; First Editions;
Ephemera

Massachusetts

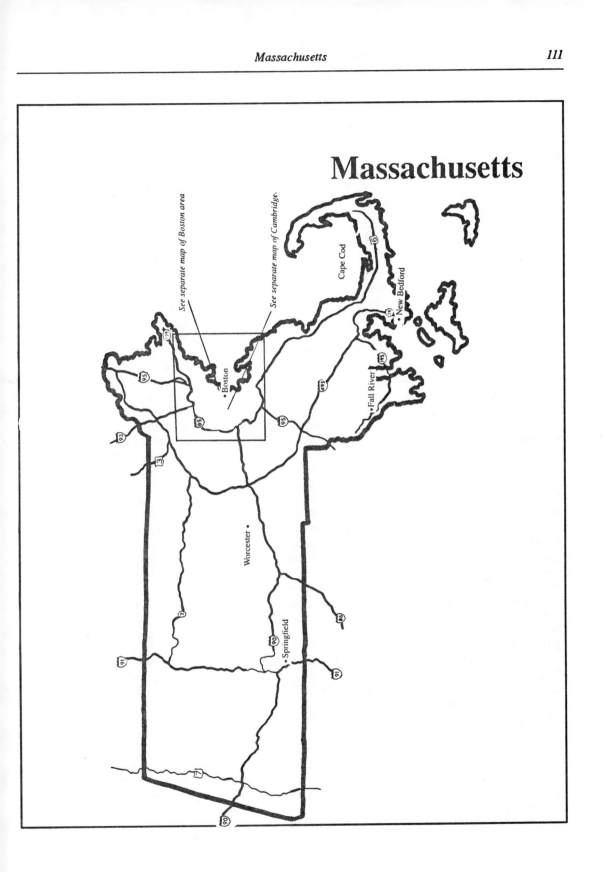

Cape Cod

See separate map of Boston area

See separate map of Cambridge

New Bedford

Fall River

Boston

Worcester

Springfield

John A. Hess
P. O. Box 3062
Andover, Mass. 01810
(617) 470-0327
By mail only
Catalogues issued
John A. Hess
Photography; Civil War &
Confederacy

Hall's Nostalgia
21-25 Mystic Street
Arlington, Mass. 02174
(617) 646-7759
11-6 Tues-Sat
Catalogues issued
Sports; Games & Pastimes; Comic
Books

The Printers' Devil
1 Claremont Court
Arlington, Mass. 02174
(617) 646-6762
By mail only
Catalogues issued
Barry Wiedenkeller, Anne
Wiedenkeller
History of Medicine & Science;
Medical & Medicine; Collection
Development; Psychiatry,
Psychology, & Psychoanalysis;
Neurosciences

Scientia Books
P. O. Box 433
Arlington, Mass. 02174
(617) 643-5725
By appointment only
Catalogues issued
Malcolm Kottler
Medical & Medicine; History of
Medicine & Science; Science;
Evolution

Yesterday's Books
Baptist Corner Road
Ashfield, Mass. 01330
(413) 628-3249
Open shop

Clayton Craft
Greek & Roman Classics;
Literature; Children's Books

History House
P. O. Box 146
Ashley Falls, Mass. 01222
(413) 229-6605
By appointment only
Howard Crockett, Dorothy
Crockett
Americana; Naval & Nautical;
New York City & Metropolitan
Region; Voyages, Travels, &
Exploration

Osee H. Brady
12 Elm Street
Assonet, Mass. 02702
(617) 644-5073
By appointment only
Osee H. Brady, Althea Brady
General; Biography &
Autobiography

Howard T. Glasser
28 Forge Road
Assonet, Mass. 02702
(617) 644-5714
By appointment only
Catalogues issued
Howard Glasser
Calligraphy; Graphic Arts;
Typography & Type Specimens;
Ephemera; Art; British Isles

Charles Conway
P. O. Box 102
Attleboro, Mass. 02703
By mail only
Catalogues issued
Charles Conway
Automotive; Ephemera;
Automobiles, Specific Makes &
Models

Kenneth Anderson
P. O. Box H
Auburn, Mass. 01501

(617) 832-3524
By mail only
Catalogues issued
Kenneth Anderson
Fishing & Angling; Guns &
Weapons; Sporting;
Mountaineering; Natural History;
Golf

Dunham's Book Store
50 Great Road
Bedford, Mass. 01730
(617) 275-9140
11-5 Wed-Sat
Carroll Dunham, Grace Dunham
General

Catholic Book Collector
381 Wrentham Road
Bellingham, Mass. 02019
(617) 883-4344
2-9 daily
Edward J. Fontenarosa
Religion & Religous History;
Bibliography; Reference; Catholica

H. L. Mendelsohn
P. O. Box 317
Belmont, Mass. 02178
(617) 484-7362
10-5 Tues-Sat
Catalogues issued
Harvey L. Mendelsohn
Architecture; City & Urban
Planning; Decorative Arts;
Landscape Architecture

Payson Hall Books
80 Trapelo Road
Belmont, Mass. 02178
(617) 484-2020
10-4 Thurs-Sat
Clare M. Murphy
General

Astronomy Books
P. O. Box 217
Bernardston, Mass. 01337
(413) 648-9500

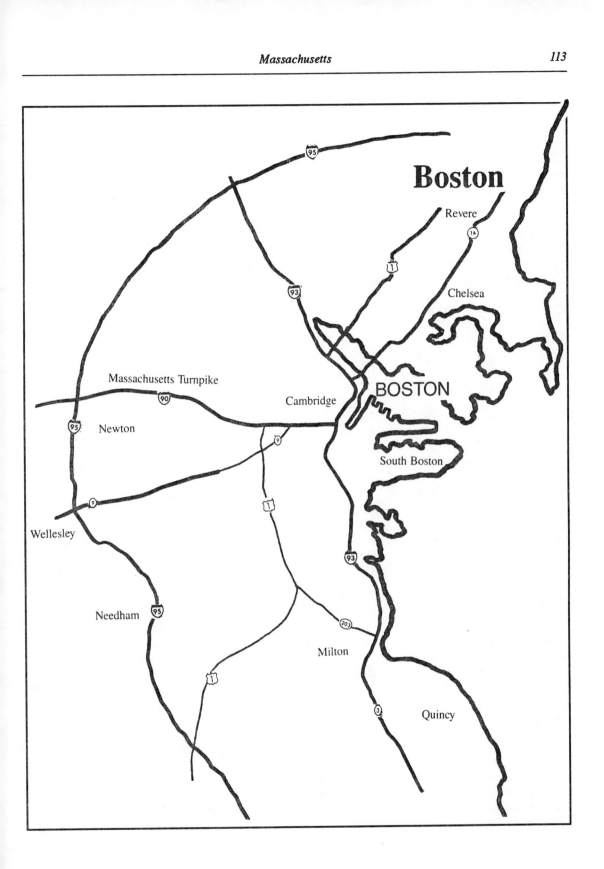

By appointment only
Catalogues issued
Paul W. Luther
Astronomy; Physics; Optics;
History of Medicine & Science;
Appraisals & Appraisal Services

Book Shop
15 Oak Street, Depot Square
Beverly Farms, Mass. 01915
(617) 927-3067
11-5 Tues-Fri, 11-4:30 Sat
Jean S. McKenna
Children's Books; Illustrated
Books; Fiction; General

Robert F. Lucas
P. O. Box 63
Blandford, Mass. 01008
(413) 848-2061
By appointment only
Catalogues issued
Robert F. Lucas
Americana; Voyages, Travels, &
Exploration; Hawaii; Whaling;
Henry David Thoreau; Edgar Allan
Poe

Ars Libri, Ltd.
560 Harrison Avenue
Boston, Mass. 02218
(617) 357-5212
9-6 Mon-Fri, 11-5 Sat
Catalogues issued
Elmar W. Seibel, David Stang,
Gabriele Ouellette
Art; Architecture; Decorative Arts;
Back Issue Periodicals; Illustrated
Books

Artistic Endeavors
24 Emerson Place
Boston, Mass. 02114
(617) 227-1967
By appointment only
Catalogues issued
B. Ratner-Gantsc
Art; Prints; Graphic Arts; Music;

Paintings; Autographs &
Autograph Material

Avenue Victor Hugo Bookshop
339 Newbury Street
Boston, Mass. 02115
(617) 266-7746
9-9 Mon-Fri, 10-8 Sat, 12-8 Sun
Catalogues issued
Vincent McCaffrey, Thomas Owen
Science Fiction; Mystery &
Detective Fiction; Western Books;
Back Issue Magazines; Pulps;
General

Phil Barber
P. O. Box 8694
Boston, Mass. 02114
(617) 492-4653
By mail only
Catalogues issued
Phillip J. Barber
Newspapers; Back Issue
Periodicals; Back Issue Magazines;
Scholarly Books; Early Printed
Books; Incunabula

David Belknap
P. O. Box 1382
Boston, Mass. 02205
(617) 269-5061
By appointment only
Catalogues issued
David Belknap
Mountaineering; Arctica &
Antarctica; Anthropology;
Adventure; Voyages, Travels, &
Exploration

Boston Book Annex
906 Beacon Street
Boston, Mass. 02215
(617) 266-1090
10-10 Mon-Sat, 12-10 Sun
Catalogues issued
Helen Kelly
Literature; Modern First Editions;
General

Brattle Book Shop
9 West Street
Boston, Mass. 02111
(617) 542-0210
9-5:30 Mon-Sat
Kenneth Gloss
General; Rare Books; Prints;
Autographs & Autograph Material;
Maps, Atlases, & Cartography

Bromer Booksellers, Inc.
607 Boylston Street
Boston, Mass. 02116
(617) 247-2818
9:30-5:30 Mon-Fri, 10-4 most Sats
Catalogues issued
Anne C. Bromer, David J. Bromer,
John Wm. Pye
Illustrated Books; Press Books &
Fine Printing; Juveniles; Miniature
Books

Maury A. Bromsen Assoc.
770 Boylston Street
Boston, Mass. 02199
(617) 266-7060
By appointment only
Catalogues issued
Maury A. Bromsen
Latin America; Voyages, Travels,
& Exploration; Bibliography;
Manuscripts; Prints; American
Colonies & the Revolution

Buddenbrooks Books, Inc.
753 Boylston Street
Boston, Mass. 02116
(617) 536-4433
8 a.m.-12 midnight Mon-Sun
Martin Wenkle, Michael Feldman,
Fredi Harris
Children's Books; Illustrated
Books; 19th Century Literature;
Modern First Editions; Bindings,
Fine & Rare; New Books

J. S. Canner Co.
49-65 Lansdowne
Boston, Mass. 02215

(617) 437-1923
Back Issue Periodicals; Reference; Little Magazines & Literary Small Presses; United States Government Publications

Cheng & Tsui Company, Inc
25-31 West Street
Boston, Mass. 02111
(617) 426-6074
9:30-5:30 Mon-Sat
Catalogues issued
Jill Cheng
Asia; Collection Development; Foreign affairs; The Orient & Orientalia; Pacific Region; China

Childs Gallery
169 Newbury Street
Boston, Mass. 02116
(617) 266-1108
9-6 Tues-Fri, 10-5 Sat
Catalogues issued
D. Roger Howlett
Prints; Drawings

ChoreoGraphica
82 Charles Street
Boston, Mass. 02114
(617) 227-4780
9:30-5 daily
Ernest Morrell
Bindings, Decorative Trade; Art; Illustrated Books; Textiles; Literature; General

The Globe Corner Bookstore
3 School Street
Boston, Mass. 02108
(617) 523-6658
9-6 Mon-Fri, 9:30-6 Sat, 12-5 Sun
Catalogues issued
Pat Carrier
New England; Travel; General

Goodspeed's #1
7 Beacon Street
Boston, Mass. 02108
(617) 523-5970

9-5 Mon-Fri, 10-3 Sat
Catalogues issued
Doris Adams, George P. Goodspeed
Americana; Autographs & Autograph Material; Prints; Genealogy; Maps, Atlases, & Cartography; Rare Books

Goodspeed's #2
2 Milk Street
Boston, Mass. 02108
(617) 523-5970
9-5 Mon-Fri, Sat 10-3
Arnold Silverman
Americana; Autographs & Autograph Material; Prints; Genealogy; Maps, Atlases, & Cartography; Rare Books

Harvard Book Store Cafe
190 Newbury Street
Boston, Mass. 02116
(617) 536-0095
9 a.m.-11 p.m. Mon-Sat
Catalogues issued
Michael Bills
General

Priscilla Juvelis, Inc.
150 Huntington Avenue, suite SDL
Boston, Mass. 02115
(617) 424-1895
By appointment only
Catalogues issued
Priscilla Juvelis
Illustrated Books; Color Plate Books; Literature; Bindings, Fine & Rare; First Editions; Livre d'Artiste

Ralph Kristiansen
P. O. Box 524, Kenmore Stn.
Boston, Mass. 02215
(617) 424-1527
By mail only
Catalogues issued
Ralph Kristiansen
Science Fiction; Fantasy; Mystery

& Detective Fiction; Literature; Rare Books; First Editions

Samuel L. Lowe
80 Charles Street
Boston, Mass. 02114
(617) 742-0845
10:3--5 Mon-Fri, 10:30-4 Sat
Samuel L. Lowe, Jr., Fred Campbell
Marine & Maritime; Whaling; Voyages, Travels, & Exploration; American History; Ships & The Sea; Sailing & Yachting

Marlowe's Bookshop
314 Newbury Street
Boston, Mass. 02115
(617) 262-0880
11-10 daily
Martin Langer
Literature; Scholarly Books; Modern First Editions

Charles Martignette
P. O. Box 9295
Boston, Mass. 02114
(617) 739-4500
By appointment only
Charles Martignette
Illustrated Books; Erotica; Original Art For Illustration

David L. O'Neal
131 Newbury Street
Boston, Mass. 02116
(617) 266-5790
10-5 Tues-Sat
Catalogues issued
David L. O'Neal, Mary T. O'Neal
Rare Books; Modern First Editions; Typography & Type Specimens; Pres

Edward T. Pollack
236 Beacon Street
Boston, Mass. 02116
(617) 437-1095
By appointment only

Edward T. Pollack
Art

The Printers' Devil
25 Huntington Avenue
Boston, Mass. 02116
(617) 267-9313
1-6 Tues-Fri, 10-2 Sat
Barry Wiedenkeller, Anne
Wiedenkeller
History of Medicine & Science;
Medicine & Science; Psychiatry,
Psychology, & Psychoanalysis;
Neurosciences; Collection
Development

Spenser's Mystery Bookshop
314 Newbury Street
Boston, Mass. 02115
(617) 262-0880
11-10 Mon-Sat
Andrew Thurnauer
Mystery & Detective Fiction; Early
& Collectible Paperbacks

Starr Book Company, Inc.
186 South Street
Boston, Mass. 02111
(617) 542-2525
9-5 Mon-Fri, 9-4 Sat
Catalogues issued
Ernest Starr, Norman Starr
American Literature; English
Literature; Sets; Fiction; Military;
General

Ivan Stormgart
P. O. Box 1232, GMF
Boston, Mass. 02205
(617) 268-3942
By appointment only
Catalogues issued
Ivan Stormgart
Curiosa; Erotica; Sexology;
Psychiatry, Psychology, &
Psychoanalysis

Charles B. Wood III Inc.
P. O. Box 310

Boston, Mass. 02117
(617) 247-7844
By appointment only
Catalogues issued
Charles Wood
Architecture; Photography;
Decorative Arts; Technology;
Trade Catalogues; Landscape
Architecture

Worldwide Books
37-39 Antwerp Street
Boston, Mass. 02135
(617) 787-9100
By appointment only
Catalogues issued
Brian Gold, Marcia Skalnik
Art Catalogues, Periodicals, &
Books

Kempton J. C. Smith
140 Waite Road
Boxborough, Mass. 01719
(617) 369-9562
By appointment only
Catalogues issued
Kempton J.C Smith
First Editions; General

Organ Literature Foundation
45 Norfolk Road
Braintree, Mass. 02184
(617) 848-1388
By mail only
Catalogues issued
Henry Karl Baker
Music; Phonograph Records;
Video Cassette & Compact Disks

Donald B. Howes
Route 6
Brewster, Mass. 02631
(617) 896-3502
By appointment only
Don Howes
Americana; Autographs &
Autograph Material; Ephemera;
Paintings; Documents; Sporting

Smith's Book Service
Sunsmith House, Route 6-A
Brewster, Mass. 02631
(617) 896-7024
10-5 daily (April-Nov)
Catalogues issued
Wendell Smith
Natural History; Literature; Cape
Cod, Martha's Vineyard, &
Nantucket; General

Book Mart
985 Main Street
Brockton, Mass. 02401
(617) 588-0124
10-6 Mon-Sun
Pam Dernier
Science Fiction; Comic Books;
New Paperbacks; Ephemera;
Pulps; Sports

Stan's Paperback Exchange
7 Montello Street
Brockton, Mass. 02401
(617) 583-6777
10-6 daily (Wed-Fri to 8)
Stan Darcey
New Paperbacks; Western Books;
General; Science Fiction; Comic
Books

Thomas G. Boss
59 Monmouth Street
Brookline, Mass. 02146
(617) 277-1527
By appointment only
Catalogues issued
Tom Boss
Press Books & Fine Printing; Art
Deco & Art Nouveau;
Bibliography; Literature; Bindings,
Fine & Rare; Bookplates & Ex
Libris

Brookline Village Books
23 Harvard Street
Brookline, Mass. 02146
(617) 734-3519
10-6 Mon-Sat

Catalogues issued
James L. Lawton
Rare Books; Naval & Nautical;
Literature; Children's Books;
Appraisals & Appraisal Services;
Americana

David C. Jolly
P. O. Box 931
Brookline, Mass. 02146
(617) 232-6222
By appointment only
David Jolly
Maps, Atlases, & Cartography

Dan Miranda
P. O. Box 145
Brookline, Mass. 02146
(617) 739-1306
By appointment only
Catalogues issued
Dan Miranda
Judaica & Hebrica; Women; Black
Literature & Studies; Postcards

Robert H. Rubin
P. O. Box 267
Brookline, Mass. 02146
(617) 277-7677
By appointment only
Catalogues issued
Robert H. Rubin
Business & Business History; Law;
Social Sciences; Political, Social,
& Cultural History; Political
Science & Theory; Americana

Ann Wilder
299 Tappan Street, No. 9
Brookline, Mass. 02146
(617) 277-4209
By appointment only
Ann Wilder
Children's Books

Hans E. Rohr
P. O. Box 331
Byfield, Mass. 01922
By appointment only

Hans E. Rohr
Illustrated Books; Prints; Rare
Books; Fore-Edge Paintings

Ahab Rare Books
5 John F. Kennedy Street
Cambridge, Mass. 02138
(617) 547-5602
James Randall
English Literature; Manuscripts;
Autographs & Autograph Material;
Americana

Asian Books
12 Arrow Street
Cambridge, Mass. 02138
(617) 354-0005
10-6 Mon-Fri, 11-6 Sat
Catalogues issued
P. Van Zoeren
North Africa; Women; Foreign
Languages; Middle East; The
Orient & Orientalia; Islam

Best Books Ltd.
96 Trowbridge Street
Cambridge, Mass. 02138
(617) 547-1830
By mail only
Catalogues issued
John Best
Asia; Pacific Region; Japan

Blue Rider Books
1640 Massachusetts Avenue (rear)
Cambridge, Mass. 02138
(617) 576-3634
10-5 Tues-Sat
Catalogues issued
Robin Bledsoe
Archaeology; Architecture; Art;
Graphic Design; Landscape
Architecture

The Bookcase
42 Church Street
Cambridge, Mass. 02138
(617) 876-0832
10-5 Mon-Sat

Robert L. Johnson, Wanda M.
Johnson, Colman C. Johnson
Scholarly Books

Grolier Book Shop
6 Plympton Street
Cambridge, Mass. 02138
(617) 547-4648
Tu-Fri 10-6, Sat 10-5:30
Catalogues issued
Louisa Solano
Poetry; Video Cassette & Compact
Disks

In Our Time
P. O. Box 386
Cambridge, Mass. 02139
(617) 523-0549
By mail only
Catalogues issued
Eugene O'Neil
Modern First Editions; American
Literature; British Isles; Press
Books & Fine Printing; Americana

Mandrake Book Store
8 Story Street
Cambridge, Mass. 02138
(617) 864-3088
9-5:30 Mon-Sat
Psychiatry, Psychology, &
Psychoanalysis; Architecture;
Philosophy; Art

Million Year Picnic
99 Mount Auburn Street
Cambridge, Mass. 02138
(617) 492-6763
10-6 Mon-Sat (Fri to 8), 12-6 Sun
Comic Books; Limited & Signed
Editions

Pangloss Bookshop
65 Mount Auburn Street
Cambridge, Mass. 02138
(617) 354-4003
10-7 Mon-Sat, to 10 Thu & Fri
Herbert R. Hillman, Jr.

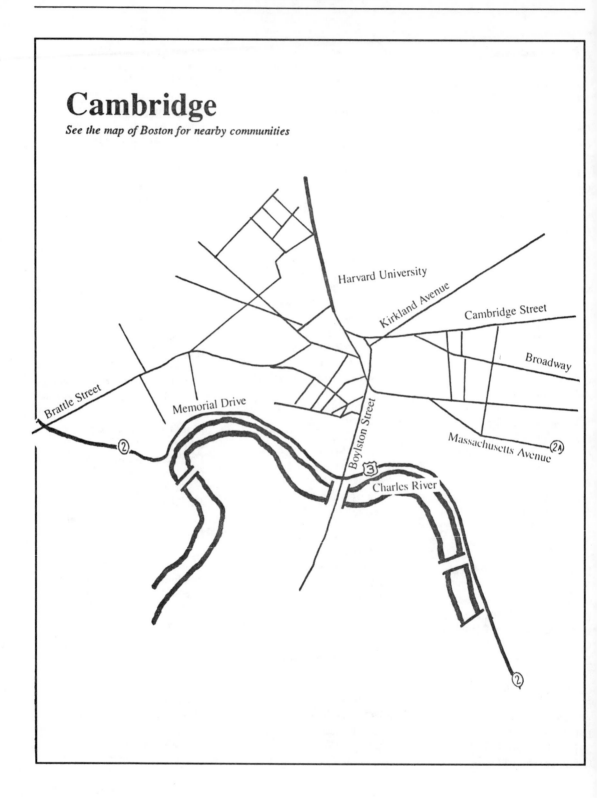

Cambridge

See the map of Boston for nearby communities

Scholarly Books; Literature; History; Social Sciences

Waiting For Godot
P. O. Box 810
Cambridge, Mass. 02139
(617) 661-1824
By appointment only
Catalogues issued
Gary Oleson
Modern First Editions; Vietnam War & Literature; Literature; Literature In English Translation; Black Literature & Studies; Photography

Words Worth
30 Brattle Street
Cambridge, Mass. 02138
(617) 354-5201
8:30 a.m.-11:30 p.m. Mon-Sat
Performing Arts; Science Fiction; Children's Books; Women; Architecture; Cooking

Worldwide Antiquarian
P. O. Box 391
Cambridge, Mass. 02141
(617) 876-6220
Catalogues issued
M. B. Alwan
Middle East; Arab World; Islam; The Orient & Orientalia; North Africa; Color Plate Books

Bohdan Zaremba
3 Livermore Place
Cambridge, Mass. 02141
(617) 491-3246
By appointment only
Catalogues issued
Bohdan Zaremba
Natural History; Birds & Ornithology; Voyages, Travels, & Exploration; Zoology

Ishtar Books
318 Sherman Street
Canton, Mass. 02021

(617) 828-2753
By appointment only
Catalogues issued
Peter R. Sarra
Horses & Horse Sports; Desert

Old Tech, Books & Things
498 Cross Street
Carlisle, Mass. 01741
(617) 369-9770
By mail only
John V. Terrey
Technical; Wireless Communication; Television & Radio; Transportation; Skiing

Royal Oak Bookshop
P. O. Box 23, Jacksonville Stage
Charlemont, Mass. 01339
(413) 337-4809
By mail only
Anne Plunkett
General

Papyrus Books
Shop Ahoy Plaza, Route 28
Chatham, Mass. 02633
(617) 933-7794
Katharine Dalton
General

Cheryl Needle
212 North Road
Chelmsford, Mass. 01824
(617) 256-0455
By appointment only
Cheryl Needle
Travel; Science; Technology; Social Sciences; General

The Book & Tackle Shop
29 Old Colony Road
Chestnut Hill, Mass. 02167
(617) 965-0459
By appointment only
Catalogues issued
B. L. Gordon
Science; Medicine & Science;

Marine & Maritime; Fishing & Angling; Cooking; Art

Sally S. Carver
179 South Street
Chestnut Hill, Mass. 02167
(617) 469-9175
10:30-6 Mon-Sat
Sally S. Carver
Postcards

Magda Tisza
130 Woodcrest Drive
Chestnut Hill, Mass. 02167
(617) 527-5312
By appointment only
Catalogues issued
Magda Tisza
Foreign Languages; Literature; Philosophy; Illustrated Books; Judaica & Hebraica

Barrow Bookstore
79 Main Street
Concord, Mass. 01742
(617) 369-6084
9:30-5 Mon-Sat
Claiborne Dawes
American History; Literature; Children's Books; Transcendentalism; General

Books With A Past
17 Walden Street
Concord, Mass. 01742
(617) 371-0180
10-5 Mon-Sat
Bonnie B. Bracker, Susan C. Tucker
Authors, State & Local; Transcendentalism; Americana; Henry David Thoreau; Americana, States; Music

Joslin Hall Books
P. O. Box 516
Concord, Mass. 01742
(617) 371-3101
By appointment only

Catalogues issued
Forrest Proper, Elizabeth Proper
*Decorative Arts; Fine Arts;
Architecture*

Thoreau Lyceum Bookshop
156 Belknap Street
Concord, Mass. 01742
(617) 369-5912
10-5 Mon-Sat, 2-5 Sun
Catalogues issued
Mrs. Thomas McGrath
*Transcendentalism; Local History;
Natural History*

Robert L. Merriam
Newhall Road
Conway, Mass. 01341
(413) 369-4052
1-5 Sun
Catalogues issued
Robert L. Merriam
*Books about Books; Bibliography;
Americana; Antiques; Miniature
Book*

Back Number Wilkins
P. O. Box 247
Danvers, Mass. 01923
(617) 531-5058
By mail only
James T. Fleming
Back Issue Magazines

The Antiquarian Scientist
P. O. Box 367
Dracut, Mass. 01826
(617) 957-5267
By appointment only
Catalogues issued
Raymond V. Giordano
*Scientific Instruments; Medicine &
Science; Women; Natural History*

W. D. Hall
99 Maple Street
East Longmeadow, Mass. 01028
(413) 525-3064
By mail only

Catalogues issued
W. D. Hall
*Americana; Regional Americana;
Ephemera; Marine & Maritime*

Mildred C. Chamberlin
P. O. Box 794
East Orleans, Mass. 02643
(617) 255-4921
By mail only
Catalogues issued
Mildred C. Chamberlin, Susan C.
Kelley
*Cape Cod, Martha's Vineyard, &
Nantucket; Local History; Joseph
C. Lincoln*

Lyman Books
P. O. Box 853
East Otis, Mass. 01029
(413) 269-6311
By appointment only
Catalogues issued
Peg Freedman, Sam Freedman
Theatre; Performing Arts

Titcomb's Bookshop
P. O. Box 45
East Sandwich, Mass. 02537
(617) 888-2331
10-5 Tues-Sat (1-5 Sun Sept-June
only)
Ralph M. Titcomb, Nancy E.
Titcomb
*Americana; Naval & Nautical;
Marine & Maritime; Local History*

Jim Barilaro
15 Vicki Road
East Weymouth, Mass. 02189
(617) 335-1974
By appointment only
Jim Barilaro
Trade Catalogues; Almanacs

Edward J. Lefkowicz, Inc.
P. O. Box 630
Fairhaven, Mass. 02719
(617) 997-6839

By appointment only
Catalogues issued
Edward J. Lefkowicz
*Hawaii; Ships & The Sea; Marine
& Maritime; Pacific Region;
Voyages, Travels, & Exploration;
Whaling*

Taste Of Honey Bookstore
1755 North Main Street
Fall River, Mass. 02720
(617) 679-8844
10-3 Tues-Fri, 9-5 Sat
James S. McKenna, Mary
McKenna, James F. McKenna
*New England; Naval & Nautical;
Americana; Back Issue Magazines;
Sports; Postcards*

Falmouth Booksellers, Ltd
281 Main Street
Falmouth, Mass. 02540
(617) 540-8639
11-5 Mon-Sat (Summers 9-9 Mon-
Sun)
Jerome Foster
General

The Shire Book Shop
305 Union Street
Franklin, Mass. 02038
(617) 528-5665
9-9 Mon-Fri, 9-5 Sat, 12-5 Sun
Wayne Marshall, Sheila Marshall
General

Book Barn
126 South Main Street
Gardner, Mass. 01440
(617) 632-8501
By appointment only
Paul Drowne, Barbara Drowne
Natural History; Technical

Irene's Book Shop
49 West Broadway
Gardner, Mass. 01440
(617) 632-5574
1-5 daily

Catalogues issued
Irene Walet
Americana; Literature; General

Kenneth & Jane Field
14 North Street
Georgetown, Mass. 01833
(617) 352-6641
By appointment only
Kenneth Field, Jane Field
General; Militaria

Ten Pound Island Book Co.
108 Main Street
Gloucester, Mass. 01930
(617) 283-5299
12-5 Mon-Sat
Catalogues issued
Greg Gibson
Marine & Maritime; New England; Local History; Crafts & Hobbies; Decorative Arts; General

The Bookloft
Barrington Plaza
Great Barrington, Mass. 01230
(413) 528-1521
9:30-9 Mon-Fri, 9:30-5:30 Sat, 12-5 Sun
Eric Wilska
Berkshires; General

Melvins Pharmacy Books
P. O. Box 269
Great Barrington, Mass. 01230
(413) 528-2255
By appointment only
Melvin Katsh
Massachusetts; New England

George Robert Minkoff Inc
P. O. Box 147, R.F.D. 3
Great Barrington, Mass. 01230
(413) 528-4575
By appointment only
Catalogues issued
George Robert Minkoff
English Literature; American Literature; Modern First Editions;

Autographs & Autograph Material; Press Books & Fine Printing; Illustrated Books

Steve Finer
P. O. Box 758
Greenfield, Mass. 01302
(413) 773-5811
By appointment only
Catalogues issued
Steve Finer
Medicine & Science; Gambling; Trade Catalogues; Art; Textiles; Technology

Ken Lopez
51 Huntington Road
Hadley, Mass. 01035
(413) 584-4827
By appointment only
Catalogues issued
Ken Lopez
Modern First Editions; American Indian Literature; Literature; Latin America; Indians & Eskimos; Vietnam War & Literature

Brunsell's Ephemera
55 Spring Street
Hanson, Mass. 02341
(617) 447-5384
By mail only
Rodney C. Brunsell
Ephemera; Medical & Medicine; Automotive; Postcards

Staten Hook Books
705 Main Street
Harwich, Mass. 02645
(617) 432-2155
3-5 Mon-Fri, 11-5 Sat (seasonal)
William D. McCaskie
Cape Cod, Martha's Vineyard, & Nantucket; Fishing & Angling; Natural History; Back Issue Magazines; Joseph C. Lincoln

Knights Book Service
11 Helena Avenue

Harwich Port, Mass. 02646
(617) 432-0557
By mail only
Peter B. Knights
Americana; American History; Political, Social, & Cultural History; Technology

Constance Morelle
1282 Broadway
Haverhill, Mass. 01830
(617) 374-7256
By appointment only
Catalogues issued
Constance Morelle
Biography & Autobiography; Children's Books; Fiction; General

Timothy Wilder
P. O. Box 292
Hubbardston, Mass. 01452
(617) 928-3381
By appointment only
Catalogues issued
Tim Wilder
Philosophy; Political, Social, & Cultural History; Alternative Lifestyles; Science; American Literature; Children's Books

University Book Reserve
75 Main Street & 815 Nantasket Ave.
Hull, Mass. 02045
(617) 925-0570
By mail only
Paul Bassinor
Literature; Social Sciences; Religion & Religious History; Philosophy

Robert & Barbara Paulson
Allen Coit Road
Huntington, Mass. 01050
(413) 667-3208
10-5 Mon-Sun
Robert Paulson, Barbara Paulson
Industry; Literary Criticism; Rockwell Kent; Ephemera; General

Howland & Company
100 Rockwood Street
Jamaica Plain, Mass. 02130
(617) 522-5281
By appointment only
Catalogues issued
Llewellyn Howland III
*Sailing & Yachting; Ships & The
Sea; America's Cup; Modern First
Editions; Whaling*

Savoy Books
Bailey Road, Box 271
Lanesborough, Mass. 01237
(413) 499-9968
By appointment only
Catalogues issued
Robert Fraker
*Farming, Ranching, & Livestock;
Gardening & Horticulture; English
Literature; American Literature;
Rare Books*

Second Life Books, Inc.
Quarry Road, Box 242
Lanesborough, Mass. 01237
(413) 447-8010
By appointment only
Catalogues issued
Russell Freedman, Martha
Freedman
*American Literature; English
Literature; Farming, Ranching, &
Livestock; Gardening &
Horticulture; Women; Radical
Poltics & Literature*

Rita M. Guerrera
P. O. Box 1155
Lawrence, Mass. 01840
By mail only
Samuel Musumeci, Rita
Musumeci, M. L. Marston
*Authors; Stock Market & Wall
Street; Religion & Religious
History; General*

Bookstore
9 Housatonic Street

Lenox, Mass. 01240
(413) 637-3390
10-6 Mon-Sat
Matthew Tannenbaum
*Little Magazines & Literary Small
Presse; Literature; New
Paperbacks; Poetry; Religion &
Religous History; Women*

J. D. Hatch
P. O. Box 1773
Lenox, Mass. 01240
(413) 637-0426
J. D. Hatch
Art History & Reference; Drawings

William T. Gavin
86 Maple Avenue
Leominster, Mass. 01453
(617) 534-4038
By appointment only
William T. Gavin
*Color Plate Books; Graphic Arts;
Maps, Atlases, & Cartography*

Eva Arond
52 Turning Mill Road
Lexington, Mass. 02173
(617) 862-6379
By appointment only
Eva Arond
*Children's Books; Folklore;
Illustrated Books; Literary
Criticism; General*

Patriot Antiquarian Books
28 Woodcliffe Road
Lexington, Mass. 02173
(617) 862-6837
By appointment only
Howard Quinn, Gloria Quinn
*Local History; History; Biography
& Autobiography; Scholarly Books*

Rainy Day Books
44 Bertwell Road
Lexington, Mass. 02173
(617) 861-8656
By appointment only

Catalogues issued
Frank Bequaert, Lucia Bequaert
*Voyages, Travels, & Exploration;
Mountaineering; Natural History;
Children's Books; Technical;
General*

Robin Wilkerson
31 Old Winter Street
Lincoln, Mass. 01773
(617) 969-2678
By appointment only
Catalogues issued
Robin Wilkerson
*Gardening & Horticulture;
Bindings, Decorative Trade*

Peacock Books
P. O. Box 2024
Littleton, Mass. 01460
(617) 456-8404
By appointment only
Catalogues issued
Phyllis J. Parkinson
Birds & Ornithology; Falconry

Anthony G. Ziagos
P. O. Box 28
Lowell, Mass. 01853
(617) 454-7108
By appointment only
Anthony Ziagos
*Freemasonry; Local History;
Appraisals & Appraisal Services;
Rare Books*

Gordon Totty
576 Massachusetts Avenues
Lunenburg, Mass. 01462
(617) 582-7844
By mail only
Catalogues issued
Gordon Totty
*Americana; Civil War &
Confederacy; General; American
History; Newspapers; Voyages,
Travels, & Exploration*

Lewis Street Exchange
171 Lewis Street
Lynn, Mass. 01905
(617) 595-3499
By appointment only
John Donoghue
Numismatics; Local History;
Massachusetts

Irving Galis
357 Atlantic Avenue
Marblehead, Mass. 01945
(617) 631-5351
By appointment only
Irving Galis
Biography & Autobiography;
British History; Military;
Presidential Assassinations;
Presidents; Naval & Nautical

Historical Technology Inc.
6 Mugford Street
Marblehead, Mass. 01945
(617) 631-2275
By mail only
Catalogues issued
Saul Moskowitz
Astronomy; History of Medicine
& Science; Science; Technology;
Naval & Nautical

Much Ado
One Pleasant Street
Marblehead, Mass. 01945
(617) 639-0400
9:30-6 Mon-Sun (call first in
Winter)
Cate Olson, Nash Robbins
Children's Books; New England;
Fiction; Naval & Nautical

Lord Randall Books
22 Main Street
Marshfield, Mass. 02050
(617) 837-1400
11-5 Mon-Sat
Gail Wills
Americana; New England; General

Cape Cod Book Center
Route 28, Box 87
Mashpec, Mass. 02649
(617) 477-9903
10-6 Mon-Sun
Carole Aronson-Plummer
Cape Cod, Martha's Vineyard, &
Nantucket; Marine & Maritime;
Civil War & Confederacy;
Children's Books; Cooking

Busyhaus
P. O. Box 1072
Mattapoisett, Mass. 02739
(617) 763-3307
Robert Hauser
Papermaking & Marbling;
Original Art For Illustration

Robinson Murray III
150 Lynde Street
Melrose, Mass. 02176
(617) 665-3094
By appointment only
Catalogues issued
Robinson Murray III
Americana

Brian E. Cassie
349 Exchange Street
Millis, Mass. 02054
(617) 376-2294
By appointment only
Catalogues issued
Brian E. Cassie
Natural History; Birds &
Ornithology; New England

Peter L. Masi
P. O. Box B
Montague, Mass. 01351
(413) 367-2628
By appointment only
Catalogues issued
Peter L. Masi
Architecture; Business & Business
History; Gardening &
Horticulture; Science; Technology

D. R. Nelson & Company
P. O. Box C-2
New Bedford, Mass. 02741
(617) 992-8897
By appointment only
David R. Nelson, Joyce C. Nelson
Americana; Children's Books;
First Editions; Illustrated Books;
Marine & Maritime; Science
Fiction

Common Reader Bookshop
P. O. Box 32
New Salem, Mass. 01355
(617) 544-3002
10-5 daily (Summer only)
Dorothy A. Johnson, Doris E.
Abramson
Women; First Editions; Ephemera;
Performing Arts; Biography &
Autobiography; General

Bartlett Gould
15 Walnut Street
Newburyport, Mass. 01950
(617) 465-9594
By mail only
Catalogues issued
Bartlett Gould
Aviation & Aeronautics

Grace Munsell
110 High Street
Newburyport, Mass. 01950
(617) 462-3863
By mail only
Catalogues issued
Grace Munsell
Scotland & The Scotish; Wales &
The Welsh; Ireland & The Irish

Newburyport Rare Books
32 Oakland Street
Newburyport, Mass. 01950
(617) 462-7398
By appointment only
Matthew Needee
Illustrated Books; Americana;
Medicine & Science; Architecture;

*Manuscripts; Bindings, Fine &
Rare*

The Book Collector
375 Elliot Street
Newton, Mass. 02164
(617) 964-3599
10-5 Mon-Sat
Theodore Berman
Japan; General

Bethel Charkoudian
18 Maple Avenue
Newton, Mass. 02158
(617) 965-2526
By appointment only
Catalogues issued
Bethel Charkoudian
Cookbooks; Cooking; Pamphlets

**Hard-To-Find Needlework
Books**
96 Roundwood Road
Newton, Mass. 02164
(617) 969-0942
By appointment only
Catalogues issued
Betty S. Feinstein
*Health; Textiles; Needlework;
Fashion*

Kenneth W. Rendell, Inc.
154 Wells Avenue
Newton, Mass. 02159
(800) 447-1007
9-5 daily
Catalogues issued
Kenneth Rendell
*Autographs & Autograph Material;
Manuscripts; Medieval
Manuscripts; Americana;
Appraisals & Appraisal Services*

Suzanne Schlossberg
529 Ward Street
Newton, Mass. 02159
(617) 964-0213
By appointment only
Catalogues issued

Suzanne Schlossberg
*Children's Books; Illustrated
Books; Literature; General*

Edward Morrill & Son
27 Country Club Road
Newton Centre, Mass. 02159
(617) 527-7448
8-5:30 daily
Catalogues issued
Samuel R. Morrill
*Americana; Voyages, Travels, &
Exploration; Militaria; Ephemera;
Marine & Maritime*

Antiques Americana
P. O. Box 19
North Abington, Mass. 02351
(617) 587-6441
By appointment only
Catalogues issued
Ken Owings, Jr.
*American Colonies & the
Revolution; Civil War &
Confederacy*

Imagine That Bookstore
59 Main Street
North Adams, Mass. 01247
(413) 663-5195
10-5 Mon-Sat (Thurs to 9), 12-5
Sun
Elizabeth Wells
*Remainders; Comic Books;
Ephemera; Phonograph Records;
New Books; New Paperbacks*

Magnalia Americana
P. O. Box M
North Amherst, Mass. 01059
(413) 549-6569
By mail only
Catalogues issued
Hugh F. Bell
*Regional Americana; Arctica &
Antarctica; American History;
Law; Marine & Maritime*

Time And Again Books
364 Main Street
North Andover, Mass. 01845
(617) 689-0629
By appointment only
Catalogues issued
Kathy Phillips
Mystery & Detective Fiction

Tom Buckley
645 Old Harbor Road
North Chatham, Mass. 02650
(617) 945-0419
By mail only
Tom Buckley
Search Service, Without Stock

Armchair Bookshop
107 Main Street
North Orange, Mass. 01364
(617) 575-0424
10-4 daily
Ed Rumrill, Pat Rumrill
*New England; Modern First
Editions; Rare Books; General*

British Stamp Exchange
12 Fairlawn
North Weymouth, Mass. 02191
(617) 335-3075
By appointment only
Catalogues issued
Frank E. Mosher
*General; Regional Americana; Art;
Birds & Ornithology*

Gabriel Books
88 Turkey Hill Road
Northampton, Mass. 01060
(413) 586-6272
By appointment only
John Riley
*History of Medicine & Science;
Art History & Reference;
Continental Books; Scholarly
Books*

The Globe Bookshop
38 Pleasant Street

Northampton, Mass. 01060
(413) 584-0374
9-9 Mon-Sat, 10-5 Sun
Mark Brumburg, Wally Swist
Literature; Local History; Poetry;
Philosophy; Fine Arts

Schoen & Son
66 Massasoit Street
Northampton, Mass. 01060
(413) 584-0259
By appointment only
Catalogues issued
Kenneth Schoen, Seth Schoen
Imprints; 20th Century Literature;
Science; Psychiatry, Psychology,
& Psychoanalysis; General

Barbara B. Harris
212 Main Street
Northfield, Mass. 01360
(413) 498-5910
By appointment only
Barbara B. Harris
Americana; Literature; Children's
Books; Natural History; General

The Book Den East
P. O. Box 721, New York Avenue
Oak Bluffs, Mass. 02557
(617) 693-3946
10-5 Mon-Sat & Sun aftns Apr-
Nov
Catalogues issued
Cynthia Meisner
General; Ships & The Sea; Cape
Cod, Martha's Vineyard, &
Nantucket; 20th Century Literature

Joseph A. Dermont
P. O. Box 654
Onset, Mass. 02558
(617) 295-4760
By appointment only
Catalogues issued
Joseph A. Dermont, Joanne M.
Dermont
Author Collections; Modern First
Editions; Children's Books;

Inscribed Books; Little Magazines
& Literary Small Presse; Poetry

The Haunted Bookshop
14 Cove Road
Orleans, Mass. 02653
(617) 255-3780
9-5 Mon-Thurs, 10-5 Fri & Sat
Drucilla Meary
Art; Cape Cod, Martha's Vineyard,
& Nantucket; Mystery & Detective
Fiction; Biography &
Autobiography; History; Fiction

Franc Ladner
P. O. Box 653
Orleans, Mass. 02653
(617) 255-3466
By mail only
Catalogues issued
Franc Ladner
Juveniles; General

Fox Hill Books
436 Main Street, Box 523
Palmer, Mass. 01069
(413) 283-7681
9-5 Mon-Sat
Richard C. Taylor
General; Americana; Children's
Books; Cooking

Cape Ann Antiques
P. O. Box 3502
Peabody, Mass. 01960
(617) 777-3001
By mail only
Catalogues issued
Jed Power
Chemical & Substance
Dependency

Imagine That Bookstore
58 Dalton Avenue
Pittsfield, Mass. 01201
(413) 445-5934
10-5 Mon-Sat (Thurs to 9), 12-5
Sun
Elizabeth Wells

Remainders; Comic Books;
Ephemera; Phonograph Records;
New Books; New Paperbacks

Running Fence Books
148 North Street
Pittsfield, Mass. 01201
(413) 442-6876
10-5:30 Mon-Sat (Thurs to 9)
Robert Juran
Berkshires; Regional Americana

W. L. Avery
31 Spooner Street
Plymouth, Mass. 02360
(617) 747-0288
By appointment only
Winifred Avery, George F. Avery
American History; Civil War &
Confederacy; Modern First
Editions; Autographs & Autograph
Material; Ephemera

The Yankee Book Exchange
10 North Street
Plymouth, Mass. 02360
(617) 747-2691
10-5 Mon-Sat (Fri to 6), 12-4 Sun
Catalogues issued
Charles F. Purro
Local History; Modern First
Editions; Voyages, Travels, &
Exploration; Occult & Magic;
Bindings, Fine & Rare; Art Deco
& Art Nouveau

Bryant's
467 Commercial Street
Provincetown, Mass. 02657
(617) 487-0134
9-6 Mon-Sat
George D. Bryant
Whaling; Cape Cod, Martha's
Vineyard, & Nantucket; Arctica
& Antarctica; Crafts & Hobbies

B & B Autographs
P. O. Box 465
Randolph, Mass. 02368

(617) 986-5695
By appointment only
Barry Bernstein
Autographs & Autograph Material;
Documents; Manuscripts;
Presidents; Whaling; Documents

Grimshaw
15 West Druid Hill Avenue
Randolph, Mass. 02368
Catalogues issued
George Grimshaw
Children's Books; Civil War &
Confederacy; Literature; World
Wars; Indians & Eskimos;
Americana

H. & T. Bond
33 Hartshorn Street
Reading, Mass. 01867
(617) 944-9044
By mail only
Harold Bond, Theresa Bond
Poetry; Fiction; Opera; Music;
Linguistics

Pages Books & Hobbies
25 Harnden Street
Reading, Mass. 01867
(617) 944-9613
10-6 Wed, 10-8 Thur-Fri, 10-5 Sat
Richard W. Eagleston
General; Series Books For Boys
& Girls; Biography &
Autobiography; Comic Books;
History

The Little Farm Bookshop
169 Wheeler Street
Rehoboth, Mass. 02769
(401) 861-5656
12-6 Sat & Sun
Catalogues issued
Ruth E. Conley
Americana; Law; Religion &
Religious History; Rhode Island

Richard Robert Caprio
43 A Vivien Street

Revere, Mass. 02151
(617) 289-4198
By appointment only
Catalogues issued
Richard R. Caprio
Medieval Manuscripts;
Shakespeare; Edgar Allan Poe;
Sets

George Hoyt
P. O. Box 186
Rockport, Mass. 01966
(617) 546-2695
By mail only
Catalogues issued
George Hoyt
Voyages, Travels, & Exploration;
Mountaineering; The Orient &
Orientalia; Middle East

Robert Maier
94 Main Street
Rockport, Mass. 01966
(617) 546-2587
By mail only
Robert Maier
Local History; New England;
Electronics; Massachusetts

G. R. Osgood, Jr.
P. O. Box 195
Rockport, Mass. 01966
(617) 324-1271
By appointment onl
G. R. Osgood
Americana, States; 19th Century
Literature; Greek & Roman
Classics; Reference; General;
Political, Social, & Cultural
History

Southpaw Books
57 Beechglen Street
Roxbury, Mass. 02119
(617) 442-5524
By appointment only
Catalogues issued
Eugene Povirk, Marlene Znoy
Industry; Radical Poltics &

Literature; Women; Photography;
Modern First Editions; 20th
Century Literature

Robert Murphy
14 Derby Square
Salem, Mass. 01970
(617) 745-7170
12-6 Tues-Sat
Catalogues issued
Robert Murphy
Genealogy; Local History

Antiquarian Bookworm
22 Sentry Hill Road
Sharon, Mass. 02067
(617) 784-9411
By appointment only
Catalogues issued
Billie Wetall
Civil War & Confederacy;
Americana; Western Americana;
Architecture; Medical & Medicine

Bland's Book Bin
37 Glendale Road
Sharon, Mass. 02067
(617) 784-8303
By appointment only
Frances E. Memoe
General

Michael Ginsberg
P. O. Box 402
Sharon, Mass. 02067
(617) 784-8181
By appointment only
Catalogues issued
Michael Ginsberg
Americana; Canada & Canadiana;
Latin America; Overland
Narratives; Voyages, Travels, &
Exploration; Western Americana

Pepper & Stern
P. O. Box 160
Sharon, Mass. 02067
(617) 784-7618
By appointment only

Catalogues issued
Peter L. Stern
*19th Century Literature; English
Literature; L. Frank Baum &
Oziana; Inscribed Books; Mystery
& Detective Fiction; Cinema &
Film*

Howard S. Mott, Inc.
South Main Street
Sheffield, Mass. 01257
(413) 229-2019
By appointment only
Catalogues issued
Donald N. Mott, Howard S. Mott,
Phyllis Mott
*Americana; Autographs &
Autograph Material; Children's
Books; Caribbean; Literature;
Ephemera*

Francis Mahard
P. O. Box 326
Sherborn, Mass. 01770
(617) 653-9090
By appointment only
Catalogues issued
Francis Mahard
*Illustrated Books; Architecture;
Decorative Arts*

Webb Dordick
15 Ash Avenue
Somerville, Mass. 02145
(617) 776-1365
By mail only
Catalogues issued
Webb Dordick
*History of Medicine & Science;
Neurosciences; Psychiatry,
Psychology, & Psychoanalysis;
Medical & Medicine*

Bruce and Susan Gventer
P. O. Box 298
South Egremont, Mass. 01258
(413) 528-2327
10:30-5 Wed-Sun
Catalogues issued

Bruce Gventer, Susan Gventer
*Color Plate Books; Prints;
Fashion; Manuscripts; General*

Elmcress Books
161 Bay Road, Route 1-A
South Hamilton, Mass. 01982
(617) 468-3261
12-5 Tues-Sat
Catalogues issued
A. C. Cressy, Jr., Britta K. Cressy
*Books about Books; General;
Horses & Horse Sports; Marine
& Maritime; Press Books & Fine
Printing; Printing & Printing
History*

The Cape Collector
1012 Main Street
South Harwich, Mass. 02661
(617) 432-3701
12-6 daily
H. Jewel Geberth
*Cape Cod, Martha's Vineyard, &
Nantucket; New England; Ships
& The Sea; Antiques; Children's
Books; Fiction*

J. & J. Lubrano
P. O. Box 127, Main Street
South Lee, Mass. 01260
(413) 243-2218
By appointment only
Catalogues issued
John Lubrano, Jude Lubrano
*Music; Dance; Theatre;
Autographs & Autograph Material;
Manuscripts*

Bookstock
P. O. Box 942
South Orleans, Mass. 02662
(617) 255-8566
By appointment only
Cliff Henderson
*Americana; Children's Books; Art;
Rare Books*

Nancy W. Hofmann
P. O. Box 368
South Orleans, Mass. 02662
(617) 255-8318
By mail only
Nancy W. Hofmann
Voyages, Travels, & Exploration

T. Small
P. O. Box 457
South Yarmouth, Mass. 02664
(617) 398-2652
By mail only
Catalogues issued
Ted Small
*Children's Books; Illustrated
Books; Natural History;
Americana; 19th Century
Literature; Press Books & Fine
Printing*

Heritage Books
College Highway, Route 10, Box
48
Southampton, Mass. 01073
(413) 527-6200
11-5 Thurs-Sat (call first)
Rosemarie Coombs
*Children's Books; Fiction;
Ephemera; General*

Ten Eyck Books
P. O. Box 84
Southboro, Mass. 01772
(617) 481-3517
By appointment only
Catalogues issued
Catherine Ten Eyck, Arthur Ten
Eyck
*Literature; Children's Books;
Hunting; Fishing & Angling*

Books 'n Such
789 Page Boulevard
Springfield, Mass. 01104
(413) 732-2213
10-5 Tues-Sat
Marsha Fuller
Children's Books; General

Johnson's Bookstore
1379 Main Street
Springfield, Mass. 01103-1692
(413) 732-6222
9-5:30 Mon-Sat (Thurs to 9)
Mary Lak
New England; Remainders;
"National Geographic" Magazine;
Reprints; General

Trotting Hill Park
P. O. Box 1324
Springfield, Mass. 01101
(413) 567-6466
By appointment only
Catalogues issued
Rocco Verrilli, Barbara Verrilli
Medicine & Science; Natural
History; True Crime; Americana;
Voyages, Travels, & Exploration

Howard John Besnia
Scarab Press
Sterling Junction, Mass. 01564
(617) 422-8869
By mail only
Catalogues issued
Howard John Besnia
Graphic Arts; Illustrated Books;
Press Books & Fine Printing;
Prints; Woodcut Books

John R. Sanderson
West Main Street, Box 844
Stockbridge, Mass. 01262
(413) 274-6093
By appointment only
Catalogues issued
John R. Sanderson
STC & Wing Books; Rare Books;
Modern First Editions; Inscribed
Books; First Editions; Literature

Alan Sample
38 Lynn Falls Parkway
Stoneham, Mass. 02180
(617) 665-7307
By mail only
Alan Sample

Modern First Editions; Islam; Beat
Literature; First Editions

Western Hemisphere
P. O. Box 178
Stoughton, Mass. 02072
(617) 344-8200
By appointment only
Catalogues issued
Eugene L. Schwaab, Jr.
Business & Business History;
Scholarly Books; United States
Government Publications; Back
Issue Periodicals; American
History

Water Row Books, Inc.
P. O. Box 438
Sudbury, Mass. 01776
(617) 443-8910
By mail only
Catalogues issued
Jeffrey H. Weinberg
Beat Literature; Fiction; Modern
First Editions; Literature; Little
Magazines & Literary Small
Presses

Paul C. Richards
High Acres
Templeton, Mass. 01468
(617) 939-8981 or (800) 637-7711
By appointment only
Catalogues issued
Paul C. Richards, Gerard Stodolski
Autographs & Autograph Material;
Documents; Ephemera; Inscribed
Books; Manuscripts; Antique
Stocks & Bonds

American Eagle Sporting
35 North Street, Box 51
Topsfield, Mass. 01983
(617) 887-9734
By mail only
Paul A. Corcoran
Fishing & Angling; Guns &
Weapons; Sporting; New England

Joan Eldredge
P. O. Box 1833
Vineyard Haven, Mass. 02568
(617) 693-4039
By appointment only
Catalogues issued
Joan Eldredge
First Editions; American
Literature; English Literature;
Illustrated Books; Juveniles; Little
Magazines & Literary Small
Presses

Diana J. Rendell, Inc.
177 Collins Road
Waban, Mass. 02168
(617) 969-1774
By appointment only
Catalogues issued
Diana J. Rendell
Autographs & Autograph Material;
Manuscripts; Antiques; Illuminated
Leaves & Pages

Harold M. Burstein & Company
36 Riverside Drive
Waltham, Mass. 02154
(617) 893-7974
By appointment only
Catalogues issued
Americana; Bibliography;
Reference; Literature; Juveniles;
Ephemera

John O. Johnson, Jr.
1106 Trapelo Road
Waltham, Mass. 02154
(617) 893-8861
By mail only
J. O. Johnson, Jr.
Americana; Documents;
Ephemera; Philately & Philatelic
Literature; Voyages, Travels, &
Exploration

Thomas Geagan
Burgess Point, Box 3070
Wareham, Mass. 02571
(617) 295-4506

By mail only
Catalogues issued
Thomas Geagen
Children's Books

Roger F. Casavant
88 Dudley Road
Wayland, Mass. 01778
(617) 653-4104
By mail only
Catalogues issued
Roger F. Casavant
*Americana; American Literature;
Juveniles; Illustrated Books;
Ephemera; Voyages, Travels, &
Exploration*

Barn Owl Books
P. O. Box 323
Wellesley, Mass. 02181
(617) 235-2379
By appointment only
Catalogues issued
Jinnee Macomber
*New Books; Children's Books;
Gardening & Horticulture*

Medallion Books
555 Washington Street
Wellesley, Mass. 02181
(617) 237-5152
10:30-5 daily
Catalogues issued
Elizabeth Morath
*General; Illustrated Books;
Children's Books*

Terramedia Books
19 Homestead Road
Wellesley, Mass. 02181
(617) 237-6485
By appointment only
Catalogues issued
Julianna Saad
*Africa; Asia; Big Game Hunting;
Middle East; The Orient &
Orientalia; Voyages, Travels, &
Exploration*

**Wellfleet Bookstore &
Restaurant**
Mayo Beach, Kendrick Avenue
Wellfleet, Mass. 02667
(617) 349-3154
10-5 daily (June to Sept. only)
Steve Willins
*Comic Books; Back Issue
Magazines; Music; "National
Geographic" Magazine; Pulps;
General*

The Book Bear
Route 9, Box 663
West Brookfield, Mass. 01585
(617) 867-8705
10-6 Wed-Sun
Al Nanitski
*New England; Technical; Occult
& Magic; Social Sciences;
Americana; Psychiatry,
Psychology, & Psychoanalysis*

Marjorie Parrott Adams
P. O. Box 117
West Medway, Mass. 02053
(617) 533-5677
By appointment only
Catalogues issued
Marjorie P. Adams
*Victoriana; Natural History;
Gardening & Horticulture;
Ephemera; Prints; Fine Arts*

Leonard H. Finn
40 Greaton Road
West Roxbury, Mass. 02132
(617) 327-7053
By appointment only
Leonard H. Finn
*Numismatics; Books About
Medals; Counterfeit Stamps &
Coins; Ephemera*

World War I Aero
P. O. Box 142
West Roxbury, Mass. 02132
By mail only
Catalogues issued

Robert D. McGrath Sr., Sean P.
McGrath
*Aviation & Aeronautics; Military
History; World Wars; Miniature
Books; Naval & Nautical; General*

Gustave H. Suhm
81 Llewelyn Drive
Westfield, Mass. 01085
(413) 568-5627
By mail only
Catalogues issued
Gustave H. Suhm
*Americana; Biography &
Autobiography; Fishing &
Angling; Natural History; Guns
& Weapons; General*

Jane Choras
225 Winter Street
Weston, Mass. 02193
(617) 237-9828
By appointment only
Jane Choras
*Fantasy; Science Fiction;
Children's Books; Illustrated
Books; Ephemera; General*

M & S Rare Books, Inc.
P. O. Box 311, 45 Colpitts Road
Weston, Mass. 02193
(617) 891-5650
9-5 Mon-Fri
Catalogues issued
Daniel G. Siegel
*Color Plate Books; First Editions;
Literature; Medicine & Science;
Political, Social, & Cultural
History; Rare Books*

Philip Lozinski
1504 Drift Road, Box C-97
Westport, Mass. 02790
(617) 636-2044
By appointment only
Catalogues issued
Philip Lozinski
Russia & Slavic Countries; The

Orient & Orientalia; Reprints;
Languages

Yesterdays Books
402 Bedford Street
Whitman, Mass. 02382
(617) 447-2730
By mail only
Catalogues issued
Ellie Panos
Cooking; Fiction; Americana;
Series Books For Boys & Girls;
Crafts & Hobbies; Illustrated
Books

Murray Books
473-477 Main Street
Wilbraham, Mass. 01095
(413) 596-3801
By appointment only
Samuel Murray, Paul Murray
Appraisals & Appraisal Services;
Ephemera; General; Rare Books;
Color Plate Books; Marine &
Maritime

Seth Nemeroff, Inc.
35 Spring Street, 2nd Floor
Williamstown, Mass. 01267
(413) 458-9212
By appointment only
Catalogues issued
Seth Nemeroff
Scholarly Books; Art History &
Reference; Illustrated Books; The
Orient & Orientalia; Philosophy;
Myths & Mythology

Williams Bookstore
20 Spring Street
Williamstown, Mass. 01267
(413) 458-5717
9-5 Mon-Sat
Joe Dewey
New Books; Poetry; Poetry; Art

Paula Cronin
460 Mower Street
Worcester, Mass. 01602
(617) 756-8805
By appointment only
Catalogues issued
Paula Cronin
Animals; Prints; Dogs;
Archaeology

House Of Billy Yank
22 Franconia Street
Worcester, Mass. 01602
(617) 754-4814
By appointment only
Catalogues issued
Jack Magune
Civil War & Confederacy; Minor
Wars & Battles

Isaiah Thomas Books & Prints
980 Main Street
Worcester, Mass. 01603
(617) 754-0750
12-5 Tues-Fri (Wed to 8), 9-5 Sat
Jim Visbeck
Appraisals & Appraisal Services;
Art; First Editions; Rare Books;
General

Jeffrey Mancevice
P. O. Box 413, West Side Stn.
Worcester, Mass. 01602
(617) 755-7421
By appointment only
Catalogues issued
Jeffrey Mancevice
Continental Books; Emblem Books;
Illustrated Books; Renaissance;
Early Printed Books

Phenomenologica
P. O. Box 27
Worcester, Mass. 01602
(617) 757-9155
By appointment only
Catalogues issued
Peter Wackell, Mark Roberts
Psychiatry, Psychology, &
Psychoanalysis; Philosophy

Parnassus Book Service
P. O. Box 33
Yarmouthport, Mass. 02675
(617) 362-6420
9-5 daily (June-Aug 9-9 Mon-Sat,
12-5 Sun)
Catalogues issued
Benjamin Muse, Jr.
Cape Cod, Martha's Vineyard, &
Nantucket; Marine & Maritime;
Caribbean; Russia & Slavic
Countries; Central America;
General

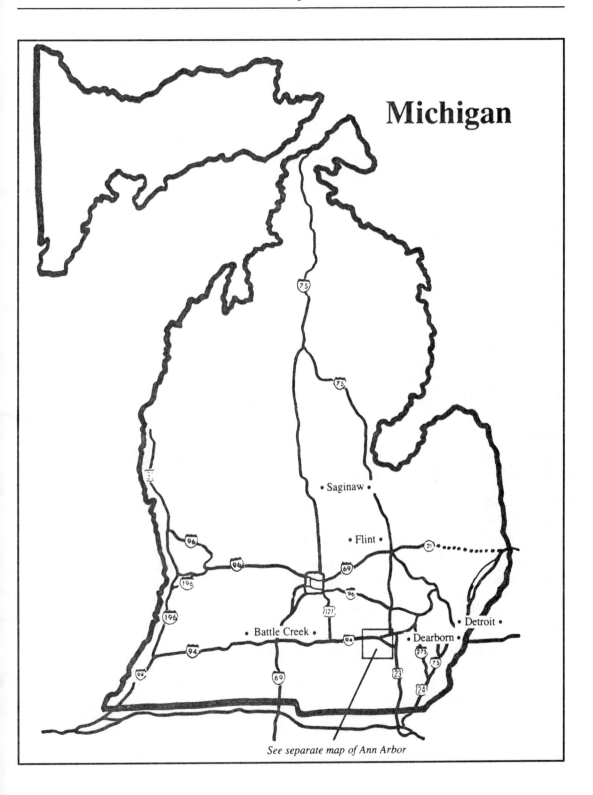

See separate map of Ann Arbor

Michigan

Book OP Shop
64 Swan Lake Drive
Adrian, Mich. 49221
(517) 423-4467
By appointment only
John Nolan, Alice Nolan
Boy Scouts; Illustrated Books;
Americana; General; Children's
Books; Cooking

Pisces & Capricorn
P. O. Box 478, 514 Linden Avenue
Albion, Mich. 49224
(517) 629-3267
By appointment only
Catalogues issued
Joe Wilcox, Claire G. Wilcox
Sporting; Hunting; Fishing &
Angling; Famous Trials

Antiquarian Michiana
P. O. Box 28
Allen, Mich. 49227
(517) 869-2132
By mail only
William Pencelly
Local History; Americana; Horatio
Alger; Civil War & Confederacy;
World Wars; World's Fairs

Faith Hawkins
404 Lincoln
Alpena, Mich. 49707
(517) 354-3846
By mail only
Faith Hawkins
Children's Books

Dawn Treader Books
525 East Liberty
Ann Arbor, Mich. 48104
(313) 995-1008
10-8 Mon-Sat

Catalogues issued
William Gillmore
Western Americana; Autographs
& Autograph Material; Mystery
& Detective Fiction; Science
Fiction; Fantasy

Great Lakes Book Service
208 Montgomery Avenue
Ann Arbor, Mich. 48103
(313) 665-8351
9-5 daily
Catalogues issued
Deborah B. Topliff
Self-Help

Hartfield Fine & Rare Books
117 Dixboro Road
Ann Arbor, Mich. 48105
(313) 662-6035
By appointment only
Catalogues issued
Ruth Iglehart
Rare Books; 18th Century
Literature; Fore-Edge Paintings;
English Literature; Books about
Books; Bindings, Fine & Rare

Keramos
P. O. Box 7500
Ann Arbor, Mich. 48107
(313) 429-7864
By appointment only
Catalogues issued
Marjorie E. Uren
Antiques; Art; Asia; Voyages,
Travels, & Exploration; Rare
Books; The Orient & Orientalia

Leaves Of Grass
2433 Whitmore Lake Road
Ann Arbor, Mich. 48103
(313) 995-2300

By appointment only
Catalogues issued
Tom Nicely
Americana; Appraisals &
Appraisal Services; Books about
Books; First Editions; Press Books
& Fine Printing; Rare Books

The Science Bookshelf
525 Fourth Street
Ann Arbor, Mich. 48103
(313) 665-0537
By appointment only
C. A. Hough
Science; Mathematics; Natural
History; Science Fiction;
Technology; Mystery & Detective
Fiction

Shaman Drum Bookshop
313 South State Street
Ann Arbor, Mich. 48104
(313) 662-7407
10-5:30 Mon-Fri, 10-4:30 Sat
Dick Port, Karl Port
Humanities; Scholarly Books

West Side Book Shop
113 West Liberty
Ann Arbor, Mich. 48103
(313) 995-1891
11-6 daily
Catalogues issued
Jay Platt, Doug Price
Arctica & Antarctica;
Photography; Jack London;
Michigan; Ships & The Sea;
Voyages, Travels, & Exploration

Wine & Food Library
1207 West Madison Street
Ann Arbor, Mich. 48103
(313) 663-4894

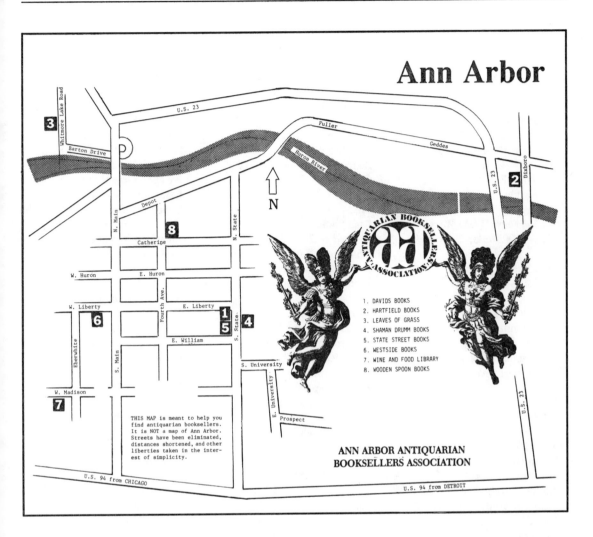

Ann Arbor

1. DAVIDS BOOKS
2. HARTFIELD BOOKS
3. LEAVES OF GRASS
4. SHAMAN DRUMM BOOKS
5. STATE STREET BOOKS
6. WESTSIDE BOOKS
7. WINE AND FOOD LIBRARY
8. WOODEN SPOON BOOKS

THIS MAP is meant to help you find antiquarian booksellers. It is NOT a map of Ann Arbor. Streets have been eliminated, distances shortened, and other liberties taken in the interest of simplicity.

ANN ARBOR ANTIQUARIAN
BOOKSELLERS ASSOCIATION

By appointment only
Catalogues issued
Jan Longons
*Beverages; Cooking; Gardening &
Horticulture; Hotels & Inns; Wines*

Wooden Spoon Books
200 North 4th Avenue
Ann Arbor, Mich. 48104
(313) 769-4775
9:30-4 Mon-Fri (Wed & Fri to 6),
8-5 Sat
David Deye

*Literary Criticism; Regional
Americana; Humanities;
Gardening & Horticulture; World
Wars; Travel*

Gunnerman Books
P. O. Box 4292
Auburn Heights, Mich. 48057
(313) 879-2779
By mail only
Catalogues issued
Larry Barnes, Carol Barnes
Fishing & Angling; Hunting

**Marion The Antiquarian
Librarian**
3660 Shimmons Circle, South
Auburn Hills, Mich. 48057
(313) 373-8414
By appointment only
Marion E. Brodie
First Editions; General

Krickett's Bookshop
69-75 Calhoun
Battle Creek, Mich. 49017
(616) 962-2495

10-5 Mon-Wed, Fri & Sat (Fri to 7)
Paul Ronning
Comic Books; General

Memory Aisle
1162 West Columbia
Battle Creek, Mich. 49015
(616) 964-4293
10-6 Mon-Sat
Joanne Titus
Michigan; Civil War & Confederacy; World Wars; Children's Books; Cookbooks

Julia Sweet Newman
P. O. Box 99
Battle Creek, Mich. 49016
(616) 965-3637
By appointment only
Julia S. Newman
Autographs & Autograph Material; Americana; Ephemera

Nancy Littrup
410 North Grant
Bay City, Mich. 48706
(517) 892-7347
By appointment only
Catalogues issued
Nancy Littrup
Ilustrated Books; Children's Books; First Editions; Turn-Of-The-Century Novels

William J. Delp
615 North State Road, Box 153
Belding, Mich. 48809
(616) 794-3992
By appointment only
William J. Delp
Militaria; Hunting; Crafts & Hobbies; Guns & Weapons; Americana, States; History

Berkley Book Store
3165 West 12 Mile Road
Berkely, Mich. 48072
(313) 547-9644

10-7 Mon-Sat, 12-5 Sun
Edward Jonas
History; Religion & Religous History; Philosophy; Bible & Bible Studies; Archaeology

Birmingham Bookstore
263 Pierce
Birmingham, Mich. 48011
(313) 642-4404
9:30-5:30 Mon-Sat (to 9 Thurs, Fri)
Claudia Seaton
Limited & Signed Editions; Children's Books; Voyages, Travels, & Exploration; Art History & Reference; Architecture

Abbey Books
22103 Michigan Avenue
Dearborn, Mich. 48124
(313) 565-5300
10-6 Mon-Sat
Bill Romero
Used Paperbacks; General

Bygone Book House
12922 Michigan
Dearborn, Mich. 48121
(313) 581-1588
11-7 Mon-Fri, 11-6 Sat
John King
General

Else Fine
P. O. Box 43
Dearborn, Mich. 48121
(313) 834-3255
By appointment only
Catalogues issued
Louise Oberschmidt, Allen Hemlock
Mystery & Detective Fiction; First Editions; Literature

Book Stop
24650 Warren
Dearborn Heights, Mich. 48127
(313) 562-6777

11-7 Mon-Sat
Carol Zimmer
Cookbooks; World Wars; Art; General

Bohling Book Company
P. O. Box 204
Decatur, Mich. 49045
(616) 423-8786
By appointment only
Catalogues issued
Lynette L. Bohling, Curt Bohling
Regional Americana; Middle West, American; Great Lakes; Railroads; Civil War & Confederacy

Big Book Shop #1
3769 Woodward
Detroit, Mich. 48201
(313) 831-8511
9:30-5:30 Mon-Sat
General

Big Book Shop #2
3915 Woodward Avenue
Detroit, Mich. 48201
(313) 831-8511
9:30-5:30 Mon-Sat
Bill Foukes
General

Cellar Book Shop
18090 Wyoming
Detroit, Mich. 48221
(313) 861-1776
By appointment only
Catalogues issued
Petra F. Netzorg
Southeast Asia; Pacific Region; Australia & New Zealand

The Curious Raven Bookstore
10745 Morang Drive (at Cadieux)
Detroit, Mich. 48224
(313) 884-8433
11-7 Mon-Sat, 11-4 Sun
Al Bai, Owen R. Murtagh
Science Fiction; Rare Books; General

Grub Street--A Bookery
17194 East Warren
Detroit, Mich. 48224
(313) 882-7143
12-6 Tues-Sat
Catalogues issued
Mary C. Taylor, James R. Taylor
First Editions; Photography; Art;
Rare Books; Scholarly Books;
Press Books & Fine Printing

John K. King
901 West Lafayette Boulevard,
Box 33363
Detroit, Mich. 48232-5363
(313) 961-0622
9:30-5:30 Mon-Sat
Catalogues issued
John K. King
Illustrated Books; Civil War &
Confederacy; Literature;
Americana; First Editions

Little Read Books
5500 Cass
Detroit, Mich. 48202
(313) 831-2269
9:30-5:30 Mon-Fri, 12-4 Sat, 12-2
Sun
Ernest Franklin
General

The Necessary Press
111 Main Street, Box 313
East Jordan, Mich. 49727
(616) 536-2515
1-4 Mon-Fri
Catalogues issued
Doris Huckle
Ephemera; Poetry; Local History;
General

Curious Book Shop
307 East Grand River
East Lansing, Mich. 48823
(517) 332-0112
10-6 Mon-Sat (Fri to 9)
Catalogues issued
Ray Walsh

Science Fiction; Michigan;
Illustrated Books; Comic Books;
Military; General

Benjamin De Wit
709 Lantern Hill Drive
East Lansing, Mich. 48823
(517) 351-2648
By mail only
Catalogues issued
Benjamin De Wit
Scholarly Books

Fly Creek Bookstall
431 Glenmoor
East Lansing, Mich. 48823
(517) 337-0455
By appointment only
Ruth L. Yule
Poetry; General; Press Books &
Fine Printing

Albert G. Clegg
P. O. Box 306
Eaton Rapids, Mich. 48827
(517) 663-8428
By appointment only
Catalogues issued
Albert G. Clegg
Geology; Paleontology

Jerry's Book Store
23623 Farmington Road
Farmington, Mich. 48024
(313) 477-9545
10:30-6 Mon-Fri (to 8 Fri), 10:30-
5 Sat
Bertha Cunningham
General

Library Book Store
169 West 9 Mile Road
Ferndale, Mich. 48220
(313) 545-4300
10-7 Mon-Sat
M. Sempliner
General

Marion D. Pohrt
1407 West Paterson
Flint, Mich. 48504
(313) 238-2569
By mail only
Marion D. Pohrt
Michigan; Children's Books;
General

R. Wertz
420 East Boulevard, Farmers
Market
Flint, Mich. 48503
(313) 732-6976
10-4:30 Tues, Thurs, Sat
R. Wertz
Michigan; Children's Books;
Authors, State & Local

The Bookman
715 Washington Street
Grand Haven, Mich. 49417
(616) 846-3520
9-9 Mon-Fri, 9-6 Sat, 8-5 Sun
James L. Dana, Mary J. Dana
Great Lakes; Michigan; Children's
Books; Cookbooks

Baker Book House
2768 East Paris
Grand Rapids, Mich. 49506
(616) 957-3110
8:30-5:30 daily
Gary Popma
Religion & Religous History;
Philosophy

Kregel's Bookstore
525 Eastern Avenue, SE, Box 2607
Grand Rapids, Mich. 49501
(616) 459-9444
8:30-5:30 Mon-Fri, 8:30-5 Sat
Catalogues issued
Kenneth L. Kregel, Robert L.
Kregel
Religion & Religious History;
Reprints; Greek & Roman Classics

Memory Aisle II
1509 Lake Drive Southeast
Grand Rapids, Mich. 49506
(616) 456-5908
10-5:30 Mon-Sun
Maxine Hondeman
*Michigan; Western Americana;
Fishing & Angling; Hunting;
Metaphysics; First Editions*

Poor Richard's Books
P. O. Box 68032
Grand Rapids, Mich. 49516
(616) 458-6337
By mail only
Catalogues issued
Terrence S. Todish, Marian Todish
*American Colonies & the
Revolution; History; American
History*

Peter A. Woodruff
P. O. Box 311
Grass Lake, Mich. 49240
(517) 522-8255
By mail only
Peter A. Woodruff
Occult & Magic

J. E. Edger
645 West Green
Hastings, Mich. 49058
(616) 948-2131
By appointment only
Catalogues issued
Julie Ellen Edger
*Civil War & Confederacy;
Michigan; Sherlock Holmes & A.
C. Doyle*

Volume I
104 North Howell
Hillsdale, Mich. 49242
(517) 437-2228
12-6 Mon-Sat
Richard Wunsch, Emily Wunsch
*Labor & Labor History; Radical
Poltics & Literature; Women*

Bargain Book Service
2904 Francis Street
Jackson, Mich. 49203
(517) 782-8195
By appointment only
Catalogues issued
Joseph Fleming
General

George Tramp
709 2nd Street
Jackson, Mich. 49203
(517) 784-1057
By appointment only
George Tramp
*Western Americana; Military
History; Natural History; Ancient
History; Geography; 18th Century
Literature*

Loose Change
1093 U.S. 12
Jerome, Mich. 49249
(517) 688-9673
By appointment only
Robert C. Warner
*Juveniles; Children's Books;
Authors*

Athena Book Shop
300 South Kalamazoo Mall
Kalamazoo, Mich. 49007
(616) 342-4508
10-6 Mon-Sat
Linda Hilton
General

Bicentennial Bookshop
820 South Westnedge
Kalamazoo, Mich. 49008
(616) 345-5987
10-6 Mon-Fri, 10-4 Sat
Vaughn Baber
*Michigan; Fishing & Angling;
Hunting; Militaria; General*

John B. Doukas
3203 Bronson Boulevard
Kalamazoo, Mich. 49008

(616) 342-8155
By appointment only
Catalogues issued
John B. Doukas
*Greece & Turkey; Press Books &
Fine Printing; Greek & Roman
Classics; Rare Books*

Hidden Rooms Book Shoppe
7018 West "H" Avenue
Kalamazoo, Mich. 49009
(616) 375-9398
11-5 Thurs-Sat
Nancy Phillips, Claude Phillips
Women

Yesterday's Books
5580 Gull Road
Kalamazoo, Mich. 49001
(616) 345-1011
11-5 Mon-Sat
Bob Rozandovich, Sue
Rozandovich
General

Leelanau Books
109 Main Street
Leland, Mich. 49654
(616) 256-7111
By appointment only
Prudy Mead, George Ball
*Michigan; Great Lakes; Books
about Books; General*

Snowbound Books
118 North 3rd Street
Marquette, Mich. 49855
(906) 228-4448
10-6 Mon-Fri, 10-5 Sat
Ray Nurmi
General; Local History; Michigan

Bernard A. Margolis
1565 Arbor Avenue
Monroe, Mich. 48161
(313) 243-5213
By mail only
Catalogues issued
Bernard A. Margolis

*Beat Literature; Religion &
Religious History; Indians &
Eskimos*

The Book Trader
1347 Peck Street
Muskegon, Mich. 49441
(616) 728-3181
10-5:30 Mon-Sat
Robert Carr, Mary Carr
General

The First Edition
7 Center Street
Muskegon Heights, Mich. 49444
(616) 733-2176
7:45-6 Mon-Sun
Mary Engen
*Michigan; American Literature;
Back Issue Magazines; General*

Andrews & Rose
749 Maple
Niles, Mich. 49120
(616) 683-4251
By mail only
Jim Rose, Eimi Andrews
General

The Busy Hermit
Antique Mall, 4 Flags Mall
Niles, Mich. 49120
(616) 782-6728
10-5 Mon-Sat, 12-5 Sun
Mary Ann Steimle
General

Casperson Books
1303 Buchanan Road, Box 634
Niles, Mich. 49120
(616) 683-2888
9-7 Wed, Sat, & Sun
Ralph A. Casperson, Doris S.
Casperson
General

Michiana Antique Mall
2809 South 11th Street
Niles, Mich. 49120

(616) 684-7001
10-6 Mon-Sun
Jim Rose
General

Yesterday's Books
25222 Greenfield
Oak Park, Mich. 48237
(313) 968-1510
10-6 Mon-Sat (Thurs to 8), 12-5
Sun
Catalogues issued
Lois Wodika
*Modern First Editions; 20th
Century Literature; General*

Einer Nisula
1931 Osage
Okemos, Mich. 48864
(517) 349-0495
By mail only
Catalogues issued
Einer Nisula
*Philosophy; Science; First
Editions; Limited & Signed
Editions; Bindings, Fine & Rare;
General*

The Book Stop
301 West Mitchell
Petoskey, Mich. 49770
(616) 347-4400
9-5 & 7-9 Mon-Sat
Diane Halford
Used Paperbacks; General

Book Barn Bookstore
125 Main Street
Rochester, Mich. 48063
(313) 651-6787
10-7 Mon-Fri, 10-4 Sat, 10-3 Sun
Alex Novitzsky, Claudia
Novitzsky, Virginia King
*Business & Business History;
Engineering; Technical;
Computers; Medical & Medicine;
Science*

The Fine Books Company
781 East Snell Road
Rochester, Mich. 48064
(313) 651-5735
By appointment only
Catalogues issued
David Aronovitz
*Fiction; Science Fiction; Mystery
& Detective Fiction; Children's
Books; Illustrated Books; Back
Issue Periodicals*

Barbara J. Rule
425 Walnut, Box 215
Rochester, Mich. 48063
(313) 656-0890
10-5 Tues-Sat
Catalogues issued
Barbara J. Rule
*Cooking; Biography &
Autobiography; Fiction; General*

Treasures From The Castle
1720 North Livernois
Rochester, Mich. 48064
(313) 651-7317
By appointment only
Catalogues issued
Connie Castle
Children's Books

Metropolis
1323 North Vermont
Royal Oak, Mich. 48067
(313) 543-2872
By appointment only
Catalogues issued
Laurie M. Ross
*Fine Arts; Art, Books about;
Catalogues Raisonnes;
Architecture; Photography; Art*

Phoenix Bookshop
4126 North Woodward
Royal Oak, Mich. 48072
(313) 549-5559
10-7 Mon-Fri, 10-6 Sat, 12-5 Sun
Mary Joyce
Automotive; Women; General

Call Me Ishmael
P. O. Box 595
Saugatuck, Mich. 49453
(616) 857-2661
By mail only
Catalogues issued
Patricia G. Vinge
Michigan; Great Lakes; Middle
West, American

Roger Koerber
15565 Northland Dr., suite 603
West
Southfield, Mich. 48075
(313) 569-1411
9-5 Mon-Fri, 10-4 Sat
Catalogues issued
Philately & Philatelic Literature;
Postal History

Much Loved Books
P. O. Box 2005
Southfield, Mich. 48037
(313) 355-2040
By mail only
Catalogues issued
Paul M. Branzburg
Americana; Press Books & Fine
Printing; Illustrated Books;
Bibliography; New Jersey; New
York State

Mrs. Charles Rose
12240 Pine Island Drive, Route 2
Sparta, Mich. 49345
(616) 887-7067
By mail only
Dorothy Rose
Book Scouts

The Bookcase
26119 Harper
St. Clair Shores, Mich. 48081
(313) 779-5300
10-7 Mon-Sat
Fred Zaharoff
General

Curiosity Shoppe
3720 Red Arrow Highway
St. Joseph, Mich. 49085
(616) 429-5321
9-5 daily
Arthur Westlake, Roslyn Westlake
Americana; Bindings, Leather;
Illustrated Books; Children's
Books; Photography; General

Ye Olde Curiosity Shop
3720 Red Arrow Way
St. Joseph, Mich. 49085
(616) 429-5321
9-6 daily
A. Westlake
Americana; Bindings, Leather;
Illustrated Books

Middle Earth Book Shop
2791 East 14 Mile
Sterling Heights, Mich. 48310
(313) 979-7340
10-6 Tues-Sat
Catalogues issued
Paul B. Hudson III
Astrology; Metaphysics;
Parapsychology; Occult & Magic;
Parapsychology

The Old Music Shop
P. O. Box 3
Three Oaks, Mich. 49128
(616) 756-9218
By appointment only
Catalogues issued
D. C. Allen, Edith Allen
Performing Arts; Music; Sheet
Music; Dance; Trade Cards

Links To The Past
52631 US 131
Three Rivers, Mich. 49093
(616) 279-7310
By appointment only
Pam Blackburn
Children's Books; Fiction; General

Arnolds Of Michigan
511 South Union Street
Traverse City, Mich. 49684
(616) 946-9212
10:30-5 Mon-Sat (to 3:30 Sat)
Elizabeth Griffin
General

Highwood Books
P. O. Box 1246
Traverse City, Mich. 49685
(616) 271-3898
10-5 daily
Catalogues issued
Lewis L. Razek
Fishing & Angling; Hunting; Guns
& Weapons; Sporting; Derrydale
Press; Back Issue Magazines

Peninsula Books
323 West 11th
Traverse City, Mich. 49684
(616) 941-8745
By appointment only
Catalogues issued
Guy A. Wood
Michigan; Great Lakes

Dale Weber
2899 East Big Beaver, suite 103
Troy, Mich. 48083
By appointment only
Dale A. Weber, Phyllis Weber
Elbert Hubbard & Roycrofters; Sir
Winston Churchill; Edgar Allan
Poe

Exnowski Enterprises
31512 Reed
Warren, Mich. 48092
(313) 264-1686
By mail only
Catalogues issued
Eugene Exnowski
Michigan; Americana; American
History; History; Ethnology

Taylor Search Service
38602 Belliveau

Westland, Mich. 48185
(313) 455-8635
By mail only
Catalogues issued
Tom Taylor
Golf; P. G. Wodehouse

Minnesota

J. & J. O'Donoghue
1926 Second Avenue, South
Anoka, Minn. 55303
(612) 427-4320
10-5:30 Mon-Sat (Thurs to 8)
Catalogues issued
Jean O'Donoghue
*Series Books For Boys & Girls;
Science Fiction; Ireland & The
Irish*

North Woods Books
5400 London Road
Duluth, Minn. 55804
(218) 525-7218
By appointment only
M. Kilen
*Forestry; Hunting; Fishing &
Angling; Great Lakes*

Theodore J. Holsten, Jr.
6400 Smithtown Road
Excelsior, Minn. 55331
(612) 474-5780
By mail only
Catalogues issued
Theodore J. Holsten, Jr.
*Big Game Hunting; Hunting;
Fishing & Angling; Voyages,
Travels, & Exploration; Guns &
Weapons; Natural History*

Melvin McCosh
26500 Edgewood Road

Excelsior, Minn. 55331
(612) 474-8084
By appointment only
*Literature; American History;
Scholarly Books; Literature In
English Translation; First Editions;
Reference*

Once Read
629 South Front
Mankato, Minn. 56001
(507) 388-8144
10-5 Mon-Fri
Mark Hustad
Minnesota

Biermaier's B H Books
809 SE 4th Street
Minneapolis, Minn. 55414
(612) 378-0129
11-5:30 Tues-Sat, Tues to 9
William Biermaier
Art; Literature; General; Fiction

The Book House
429 SE 14th Avenue
Minneapolis, Minn. 55414
(612) 331-1430
11-11 Mon-Sat, 12-6:30 Sun
James Cummings, Kristen
Cummings
Scholarly Books; General

Thomas Dady
2223 Sixth Street NE
Minneapolis, Minn. 55418
(612) 789-5074
By appointment only
Catalogues issued
Thomas Dady
*Television & Radio; Cinema &
Film; Wireless Communication*

Dinkytown Antiquarian Bks
1316 Southeast 4th Street
Minneapolis, Minn. 55414
(612) 378-1286
10:30-5:30 Mon-Sat
Catalogues issued
Larry Dingman, Mary Dingman
*Modern First Editions; 20th
Century Literature; Western
Books; Fiction*

Enrica Fish
814 Washington Avenue SW
Minneapolis, Minn. 55414
(612) 623-0707
8-5 Mon-Wed, 11-3 Sat
Marcia Peterson
Medical & Medicine; Technical

Gregory Gamradt
P. O. Box 22694
Minneapolis, Minn. 55422
(612) 537-0359
By mail only

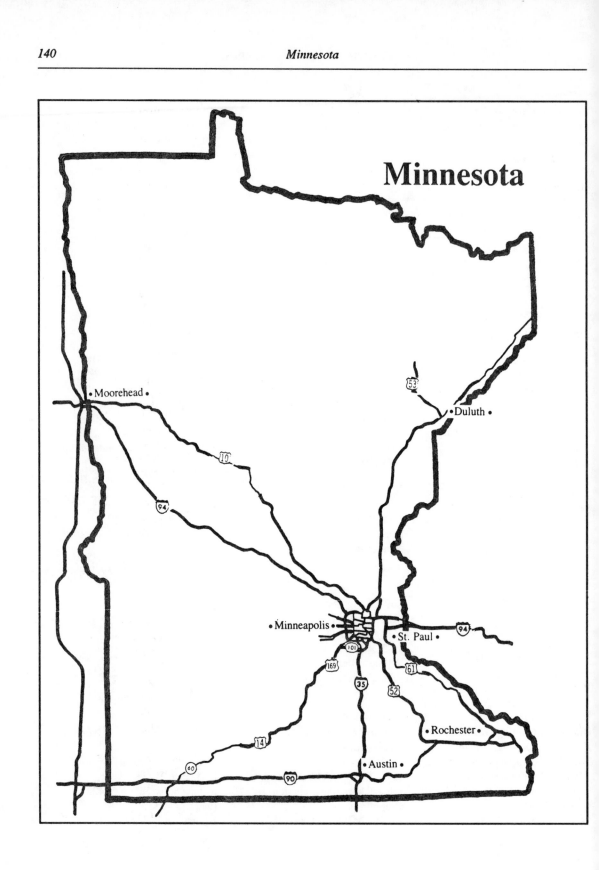

Minnesota

Catalogues issued
Gregory C. Gamradt, Beverly N. Gamradt
Tibet; China; Japan; Asia

Granary Books
212 North 2nd Street
Minneapolis, Minn. 55401
(612) 338-4376
By appointment only
Catalogues issued
Steve Clay, Merce Dostale
Press Books & Fine Printing

Leland N. Lien
413 South 4th Street
Minneapolis, Minn. 55415
(612) 332-7081
10-5 Mon-Sat
Leland N. Lien, Rae T. Lien, Valerie D. Lien
Indians & Eskimos; Civil War & Confederacy; Literature; American History; Rare Books; Voyages, Travels, & Exploration

Minnehaha Bookstore
4901 39th Avenue
Minneapolis, Minn. 55417
(612) 722-3630
By appointment only
Clark B. Hansen
Literature; History; Occult & Magic; Reference; General

Old Theology Book House
P. O. Box 11337
Minneapolis, Minn. 55411
By mail only
Catalogues issued
Matthew G. Alfs
Bible & Bible Studies; Jehovah's Witnesses & Watchtower Books

Rulon-Miller Books
212 North 2nd Street
Minneapolis, Minn. 55401
(612) 339-5779
9-4:30 Mon-Fri

Catalogues issued
Rob Rulon-Miller
Dictionaries; Literature; Americana; Voyages, Travels, & Exploration; Naval & Nautical; Rare Books

Gene Terres
4051 Blaisdell Avenue
Minneapolis, Minn. 55409
(612) 825-4512
By mail only
Gene Terres
First Editions; Fiction; Illustrated Books

Ken Crawford
2735 East 18th Avenue
North St. Paul, Minn. 55109
(612) 777-6877
By appointment only
Catalogues issued
Ken Crawford
Western Americana

Bookdales
46 West 66th Street
Richfield, Minn. 55423
(612) 861-3303
10-6 Mon-Fri, 10-5 Sat
Catalogues issued
David Dale, Joyce Dale
First Editions; Children's Books; Illustrated Books; Cooking; New Books

Ebba Kingstrom
P. O. Box 172
Sacred Heart, Minn. 56285
(612) 765-2534
Ebba Kingstrom
Book Scouts

Five Quail Books
P. O. Box 278
Spring Grove, Minn. 55974
(507) 498-3346
By appointment only
Catalogues issued

C. D. Hellyer
Western Americana; Automotive; Fishing & Angling; California; Documents; General

Julian G. Plante
1603 Cherry Lane
St. Cloud, Minn. 56301-2229
(612) 251-5550
Julian Plante
Religion & Religious History

J. A. Baumhofer
P. O. Box 65943
St. Paul, Minn. 55165
(612) 224-3210
By mail only
Catalogues issued
James A. Baumhofer
Zane Grey; Civil War & Confederacy; Gene Stratton Porter

Booksellers et al.
167 North Snelling
St. Paul, Minn. 55104
(612) 647-1471
9-7 Mon-Fri, 10-5 Sat, 12-5 Sun
Catalogues issued
Harper McKee, Steve Anderson, Ann McKee
Religion & Religous History; Cooking; General; Military; Cinema & Film

G. R. Goodman
1209 Arcade Street
St. Paul, Minn. 55106
(612) 778-1781
By appointment only
Catalogues issued
Gary Goodman
Minnesota; History; First Editions

Harold's Book Shop
186 West 7th Street
St. Paul, Minn. 55102
(612) 222-4524
10:30-5 Mon-Fri, 9:30-5 Sat

Ted Henry, Paul Kisselberg
Minnesota; Military; General

James & Mary Laurie
251 South Snelling Avenue
St. Paul, Minn. 55105
(612) 699-1114
9-6 Mon-Sat
Catalogues issued
James Laurie, Mary Laurie
*English Literature; American
Literature; Books about Books;
Press Books & Fine Printing;
Minnesota; Prints*

S & S Books
80 North Wilder
St. Paul, Minn. 55104
(612) 645-5962
By mail only
Jack Sticha, Pat Sticha
*Mystery & Detective Fiction;
Science Fiction*

James & Kristen Cummings
303 North 4th Street
Stillwater, Minn. 55082

By appointment only
Catalogues issued
James Cummings, Kristen
Cummings
*Folklore; 18th Century Literature;
English Literature; Books about
Books; Bibliography; Diaries &
Narratives*

Thomas & Karen Loome
320 North Fourth Street
Stillwater, Minn. 55082
(612) 430-1092
By appointment only
Catalogues issued
Karen Loome, Thomas Loome
*Religion & Religious History;
Philosophy; Languages;
Renaissance*

Dale Seppa
103 Sixth Avenue
Virginia, Minn. 55792
(218) 749-8108
By appointment only
Catalogues issued
Dale Seppa, Carmen Arroyo

*Hispanica; Holocaust;
Numismatics; Business & Business
History; Latin America*

The Bookpeople
213 South Jefferson
Wadena, Minn. 56482
(218) 631-1739
9-5:30 Mon-Fri (Thurs to 9), 9-5
Sat
Catalogues issued
Linda Stouten, Jack Stouten
General

Mary Twyce
601 East 5th Street
Winona, Minn. 55987
(507) 454-4412
10-5 Mon-Sat (closed Jan-March)
Mary Pendleton, David Pendleton,
John Pendleton
*Americana, States; Regional
Americana; Children's Books;
Americana; Series Books For Boys
& Girls*

Mississippi

Choctaw Books
406 Manship Street
Jackson, Miss. 39202
(601) 352-7281
10:30-5:30 Mon-Sat
Catalogues issued
Fred C. Smith, Kathleen Smith
*Southern Authors; Civil War &
Confederacy; Southern Americana;
History*

Lemuria Bookstore
238 Highland Village,

4500 Interstate 55 North
Jackson, Miss. 39221
(601) 366-7619
10-6 daily
Catalogues issued
John Evans
*20th Century Literature; Modern
First Editions*

Bob Lurate
P. O. Box 13333
Jackson, Miss. 39236
(601) 956-6487

By appointment only
Catalogues issued
Bob Lurate, Carol Lurate
*Civil War & Confederacy;
Virginia; Mississippi*

Nouveau Rare Books
P. O. Box 12471
Jackson, Miss. 39236
(601) 956-9950
By appointment only
Catalogues issued
Stephen Silberman

Drama; Modern First Editions;
20th Century Literature; Inscribed
Books; Poetry; Author Collections

Missouri

David Varner
P. O. Box 306
Belton, Mo. 64012
(816) 331-7911
By appointment only
David Varner
General

The Book House
11475 Burgess Avenue
Bridgeton, Mo. 63044-3010
(314) 968-4491
10-6:30 Mon-Sat (to 9 Mon & Sat)
Michelle Brandt
General

Mostly Books
The Garland Building
Carthage, Mo. 64836
(417) 358-7999
11-5 Mon-Sun
Catalogues issued
Roger O'Connor
Western Americana; First Editions;
Middle West, American; Missouri;
Rare Books; General

DC Book Service
P. O. Box 122
Columbia, Mo. 65205
By mail only
D. M. Christisen
Railroads; Western Americana;
Missouri; Natural History

Becky Thatcher Books
209-211 Hill Street
Hannibal, Mo. 63401
(314) 221-0822
8-6 daily (summer), 9-5 daily
(winter)
Charles Anton, Frank North
Mark Twain; Children's Books

Robert Dobbs
Route 1, Box 192
Higginsville, Mo. 64037
By mail only
Catalogues issued
Robert Dobbs, Cheryl Dobbs
Howard Bell Wright; Authors;
Fiction

Boyce E. McCaslin
P. O. Box 1580, HCR 69
Ironton, Mo. 63650
(314) 546-7923
Catalogues issued
Boyce E. McCaslin
Americana; Regional Americana;
First Editions; Inscribed Books;
Presidents; Press Books & Fine
Printing

William J. Cassidy
P. O. Box 10352
Kansas City, Mo. 64111
By mail only
Terence W. Cassidy
Business & Business History

Cliffside Books
P. O. Box 10352
Kansas City, Mo. 64111-0352
By mail only
Terence W. Cassidy
Railroads; Trolleys; Postcards

Cramer Book Store
P. O. Box 10352
Kansas City, Mo. 64111-0352
By mail only
Philip T. Cassidy, Terence W.
Cassidy, Brian J. Cassidy
Trolleys; Business & Business
History; Railroads; Industry;
Zeppelins & Dirigibles

Glenn Books, Inc.
1227 Baltimore Avenue
Kansas City, Mo. 64105
(816) 842-9777
11-4 Tues-Sat
Catalogues issued
Ardis L. Glenn
Rare Books; Western Americana;
Medieval Manuscripts; Press
Books & Fine Printing; Illustrated
Books; Bindings, Fine & Rare

Klaus Grunewald
807 West 87th Terrace
Kansas City, Mo. 64114
(816) 333-7799
By appointment only
Catalogues issued
Klaus Grunewald
Limited & Signed Editions;
Philosophy; Illustrated Books;
Kansas; Mississippi; General

Red Bridge Books
230 West 75th Street
Kansas City, Mo. 64131
(816) 523-1449
11-5 Wed-Sun
Frank W. Hood
General

Westport Bookstore
14 Westport Road
Kansas City, Mo. 64111
(816) 931-9822
12-6 Mon-Sat
Jane Gilbreath
General

Bonita Summers
P. O. Box 96
Pacific, Mo. 63069

Bonita Summers
Eastern Religions

ABC Theological Index
P. O. Box 2786, Commercial Street Station
Springfield, Mo. 65803
(417) 833-2019
By appointment only
Jerry Flokstra
Religion & Religous History; Americana; Howard Bell Wright

Hooked On Books
2756 South Campbell
Springfield, Mo. 65807
(417) 882-3397
10-8 Mon-Sat (Fri & Sat to 6), 1-5 Sun
Catalogues issued
Lavonne Foster
Science Fiction; Fantasy; Illustrated Books; Children's Books; Mystery & Detective Fiction; Greek & Roman Classics

Shirley's Old Book Shop
1950-V South Glenstone
Springfield, Mo. 65804
(417) 882-3734
11-5 Tues-Fri (Fri to 6), 11-4 Sat
Sherlu R. Walpole
Search Service, With Stock

D. Halloran
7629 Wydown Boulevard
St Louis, Mo. 63105
(314) 863-1690
By appointment only

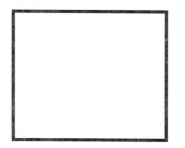

D. Halloran
Appraisals & Appraisal Services; Modern First Editions; Fishing & Angling; Press Books & Fine Printing; Sporting

Amitin Book Shop
711 Washington Avenue
St. Louis, Mo. 63101
(314) 421-9208
11-4:30 Mon-Sat
Catalogues issued
Lawrence Amitin
St. Louis Area; Bindings, Leather; Western Americana; Modern First Editions; Remainders

The Book House
9719 Manchester Road
St. Louis, Mo. 63119
(314) 968-4491
10-9 Mon-Sat (Tues, Th, & Fri to 6:30)
Michelle Y. Brandt
Children's Books; Used Paperbacks; Crafts & Hobbies; History; Technical

M. S. Cohen
727 Craig Road, Box 27479
St. Louis, Mo. 63141
(314) 872-8500
By appointment only
M. S. Cohen
Food & Drink

Elizabeth F. Dunlap
6063 Westminster Place
St. Louis, Mo. 63112
(314) 863-5068
By appointment only
Catalogues issued
Elizabeth F Dunlap
Maps, Atlases, & Cartography; Americana; Regional Americana; American History

Anthony Garnett
P. O. Box 4918

St. Louis, Mo. 63108
(314) 367-8080
By appointment only
Anthony Garnett
Press Books & Fine Printing; First Editions; English Literature; Appraisals & Appraisal Services

Francis T. Guelker
9420 MacKenzie Circle Court
St. Louis, Mo. 63123
(314) 772-6342
By mail only
Francis T. Guelker
Bibliography; Bindings, Fine & Rare; English Literature; Books about Books; Press Books & Fine Printing; Papermaking & Marbling

Eugene M. Hughes
4109 Wilmington
St. Louis, Mo. 63116
(314) 353-1009
Catalogues issued
Eugene M. Hughes
St. Louis Area; Missouri; Americana; Literature; Illustrated Books; Greek & Roman Classics

Readmore Books
3607 Meramec
St. Louis, Mo. 63116
(314) 352-3769
10-4 Mon-Sat
Ed Fix
Fiction

Swiss Village Book Store
711 North First Street
St. Louis, Mo. 63102
(314) 231-2782
Daily
Catalogues issued
Elaine Stratton
History; Children's Books; St. Louis Area; World's Fairs; Women; Civil War & Confederacy

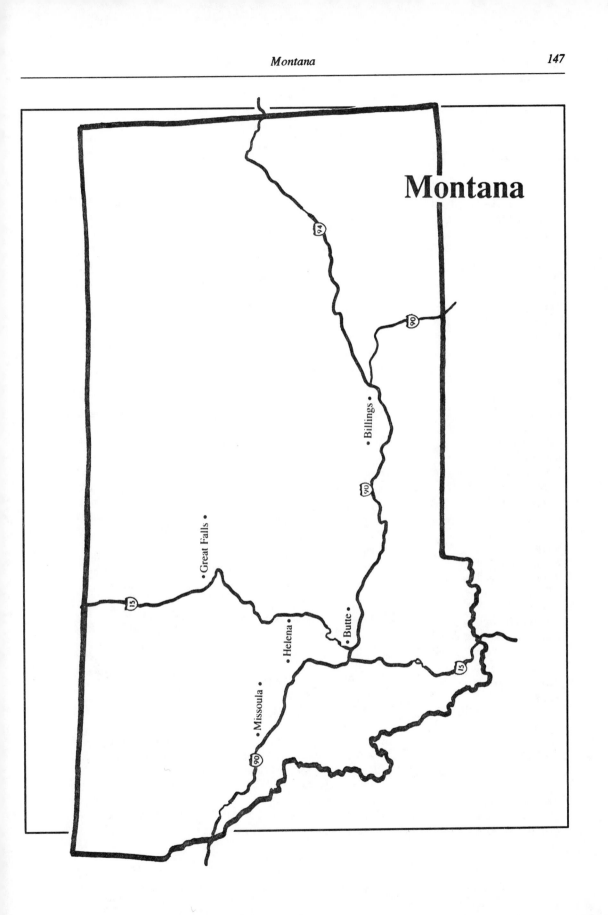

Montana

Gallery Of The Old West
P. O. Box 556
Bigfork, Mont. 59911
(406) 982-3221
By appointment only
Catalogues issued
Bob Borcherdt
Western Americana; Natural History; Hunting; Guns & Weapons; Montana

Log Cabin Books
P. O. Box 108
Bigfork, Mont. 59911
(406) 837-4477
By mail only
Catalogues issued
Joe Eslick
Indians & Eskimos; Farming, Ranching, & Livestock; Fur Trade; Montana; Western Americana; Western Books

Barjon's Books
2718 3rd Avenue North
Billings, Mont. 59101
(406) 252-4398
9:30-5:30 Mon-Sat
Barbara Shenkel
Indians & Eskimos; Northwestern Americana; New Paperbacks

The Bookshelf
113 North 30th
Billings, Mont. 59101
(406) 248-1850
10-6 Mon-Sat, 11-3 Sun
Norma Herndon
General

Thomas Minckler
2907 2nd Avenue North
Billings, Mont. 59101

(406) 245-2969
9-5 daily
Catalogues issued
Thomas Minckler
Montana; Western Books; American Illustrative Art; Autographs & Autograph Material; Photography; Newspapers

Jane Graham
P. O. Box 1624
Bozeman, Mont. 59715-1624
(406) 587-5001
By appointment only
Catalogues issued
Jane Graham
Montana; Western Americana

Vargo's Books
1 East Main
Bozeman, Mont. 59715
(406) 587-5383
10:15-6 Mon-Sat
Cindy Vargo, Fran Vargo
Montana; Local History; Natural History; Remainders; Cookbooks

Books, Begonias & Bargains
P. O. Box 861
Columbia Falls, Mont. 59912
(406) 892-3508
9-5 Mon-Fri, 10-4 Sat
M. Lenora Salandi
General

Jim Combs
417 27th Street Northwest
Great Falls, Mont. 59404
(406) 761-3320
By appointment only
Jim Combs, Fran Combs
Montana; Art, Western; Western

Americana; Hunting; Fishing & Angling; Ephemera

Chapter One
140 North Second Street
Hamilton, Mont. 59840
(406) 363-5220
10-5:30 Mon-Sat
Catalogues issued
Jean Matthews, Russ Lawrence
Montana; Western Americana; Children's Books; General

Books From Yesterday
P. O. Box 6
Helena, Mont. 59624-0006
(406) 442-7950
9:30-9 Mon-Sat (Sat to 7 only)
Dorothy G. Coslet, Walter A. Coslet
Bible & Bible Studies; Christian Books

Golden Hill Books
P. O. Box 5598
Helena, Mont. 59604
(406) 443-0678
By appointment only
Catalogues issued
Margaret Summers
Western Americana; Children's Books; Montana

Iliad Bookstore
112 North Main
Livingston, Mont. 59047
(406) 222-1123
10-5 Tues-Sat
Catalogues issued
Geraldine Callahan
Metaphysics

The Bird's Nest
P. O. Box 8809
Missoula, Mont. 59807
(406) 721-1125
By appointment only
Betty R. Anderson
Western Americana

Book Exchange
Holiday Village Shopping Center
Missoula, Mont. 59801
(406) 728-6342
9-9 Mon-Sat, 10-7 Sun
Rebecca Haddad
*Comic Books; Fiction; New
Paperbacks; Back Issue
Periodicals*

Little Professor Book Center
133 North Higgins Avenue
Missoula, Mont. 59802
(406) 721-3311
9-6 Mon-Sat
John Koelbel
*Children's Books; Local History;
General*

Sidney's Used Books
518 South 4th Street West
Missoula, Mont. 59801
(406) 543-5343
By appointment only
Carol Stern
*Literature; Americana; Sporting;
Natural History; Children's Books*

David A. Lawyer
Route 2, Box 95
Plains, Mont. 59859
(406) 826-3229
By mail only
Catalogues issued
David A. Lawyer
*Gardening & Horticulture;
Conservation; Languages; Greek
& Roman Classics; History*

Nebraska

Research Unlimited
P. O. Box 448
Fremont, Neb. 68025
(402) 727-9833
9-4:30 Mon-Sat
Catalogues issued
Paul Tainter, Joan Tainter
*Adventure; Mining & Metallurgy;
Treasure Hunting; American
History; Civil War & Confederacy;
Western Americana*

Bluestem Books
712 "O" Street
Lincoln, Neb. 68508
(402) 435-7120
11-6 Tues-Sat
Scott Wendt, Pat Wendt
Mystery & Detective Fiction

J. & L. Lee
281 East Park Plaza

Lincoln, Neb. 68505
(402) 467-4416
10-6 daily
Catalogues issued
Jim McKee
*Americana; Nebraska;
Numismatics*

Nebraska Book Store
1300 "Q" Street
Lincoln, Neb. 68508
(402) 476-0111
8-5:30 Mon-Fri (Thurs to 9), 9-
5:30 Sat
Barb Carley
*Scholarly Books; Reference;
Children's Books; General*

D. N. Dupley
9118 Pauline Street
Omaha, Neb. 68124
(402) 393-2906

By appointment only
D. N. Dupley
*Indians & Eskimos; Americana;
Farming, Ranching, & Livestock;
Nebraska; General*

1023 Booksellers
P. O. Box 3668
Omaha, Neb. 68103
(402) 553-8201
By appointment only
Catalogues issued
Richard Flamer
*Press Books & Fine Printing;
Modern First Editions; Illustrated
Books; General*

The Book Barn
R.R. 1, Box 304-H
South Sioux City, Neb. 68776
(402) 494-2936
By mail only

Nebraska

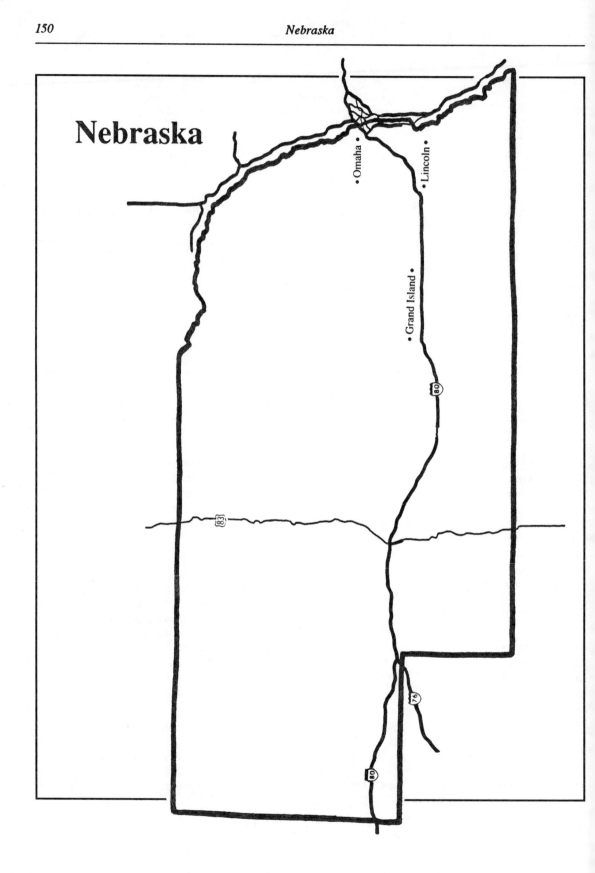

Darleen Volkert
*Art; Travel; Maps, Atlases, &
Cartography; Poetry; Children's
Books*

Wordsmith Books
P. O. Box O
Syracuse, Neb. 68446
(402) 369-2135
By appointment only

Catalogues issued
Francis Moul
*Nebraska; Western Americana;
Political Science & Theory;
Natural History*

Nevada

Nevada map on page 152

Book Stop III
3732 East Flamingo Road
Las Vegas, Nev. 89121
(702) 456-4858
11-7 daily
Gini Segedi
*Children's Books; First Editions;
Psychiatry, Psychology, &
Psychoanalysis; Science Fiction*

Gambler's Book Club
630 South 11th Street
Las Vegas, Nev. 89101
(702) 382-7555
9-5 Mon-Sat
Catalogues issued
Howard Schwartz, Edna Luckman
Gambling

New Brunswick

Harry E. Bagley
P. O. Box 691
Fredericton, N.B. E3B 5B4
(506) 459-3034
9-4 Mon-Fri, 10-2 Sat
Catalogues issued
Harry E. Bagley
Arctica & Antarctica; Canada &

*Canadiana; General; Fishing &
Angling; Maps, Atlases, &
Cartography; Voyages, Travels, &
Exploration*

Pansy Patch
59 Carleton Street
St. Andrews, N.B.

(506) 529-3824
9-6 Mon-Sat, 1-6 Sun (May-Sept
only)
Michael Lazare, Kathleen Lazare
*Biography & Autobiography;
Children's Books; Graphic Arts;
Prints; Maps, Atlases, &
Cartography; Illustrated Books*

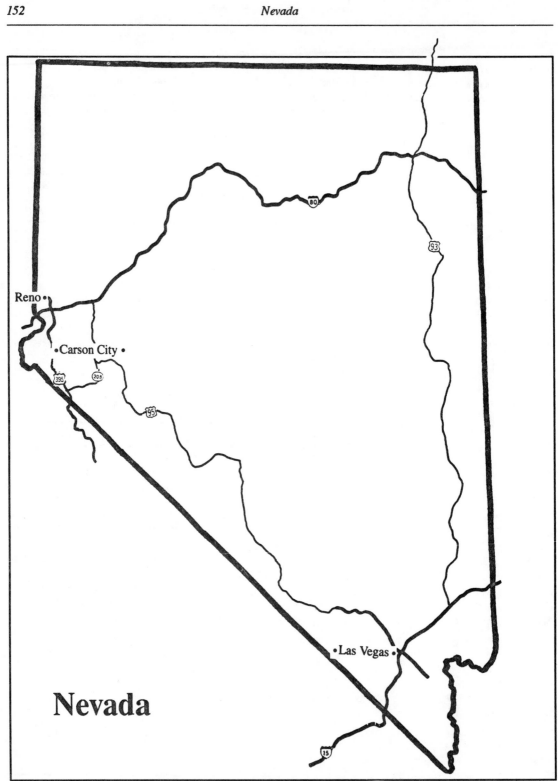

New Hampshire

The Cilleyville Bookstore
P. O. Box 127
Andover, N.H. 03216
(603) 735-5667
10-4 Tues-Sat
E. Leslie Robart, Sands B. Robart
Ireland & The Irish; Cookbooks;
General

Bretton Hall Antiquities
Route 302
Bretton Woods, N.H. 03575
(603) 846-2226
9-5 daily
Richard Force
White Mountains; New Hampshire

Bookshelf Shop
3 Pleasant Street
Concord, N.H. 03301
(603) 224-8496
10:30-5 Tues-Sat
Polly Powers
Cooking; Children's Books;
General

Carr Books
51 North Spring Street
Concord, N.H. 03301
(603) 225-3109
By appointment only
Roberta Carr
Collection Development; Medieval
Manuscripts; General

The Old Almanack Shop
5 South State Street
Concord, N.H. 03301
(603) 225-5411
12-5 Mon-Sat
Craig B. Holmes
Prints; Maps, Atlases, &
Cartography; Ephemera; 19th

Century Literature; 20th Century
Literature; General

Robert M. O'Neill
One Eagle Square
Concord, N.H. 03301
(603) 225-5530
By appointment only
Robert M. O'Neill
Rare Books

The Arnolds
Maple Street
Contoocook, N.H. 03229
(603) 746-3624
By appointment only
Don Arnold, Claire Arnold
Americana; Art; Illustrated Books

Churchill Books
Burrage Road
Contoocook, N.H. 03229
9-5 Mon-Fri
Catalogues issued
Richard M. Langworth
Sir Winston Churchill

Emery's Books
Route 3, Duston Road
Contoocook, N.H. 03229
(603) 746-5787
By mail only
Catalogues issued
Ron Emery
General

La Tienda De Quetzal
P. O. Box 298
Conway, N.H. 03818
(603) 447-5584
By appointment only
Catalogues issued
J. C. Andrews

Central America; Philately &
Philatelic Literature

Bert Babcock
9 East Derry Road, Box 1140
Derry, N.H. 03038
(603) 432-9142
By appointment only
Catalogues issued
Bert Babcock
Association Copies; 20th Century
Literature; Appraisals & Appraisal
Services; Author Collections;
Modern First Editions; Rare Books

The Old Emery Place
21 South Main
Derry, N.H. 03038
(603) 432-9640
By appointment only
Julian Hayes
General

Norman Houle
P. O. Box 1072
Durham, N.H. 03824
(603) 868-2136
By mail only
Norman Houle
Aviation & Aeronautics

Colophon Book Shop
P. O. Box E
Epping, N.H. 03042
(603) 679-8006
By appointment only
Catalogues issued
Robert Liska, Christine Liska
American Literature; English
Literature; Bibliography; Press
Books & Fine Printing; Books
about Books; Printing & Printing
History

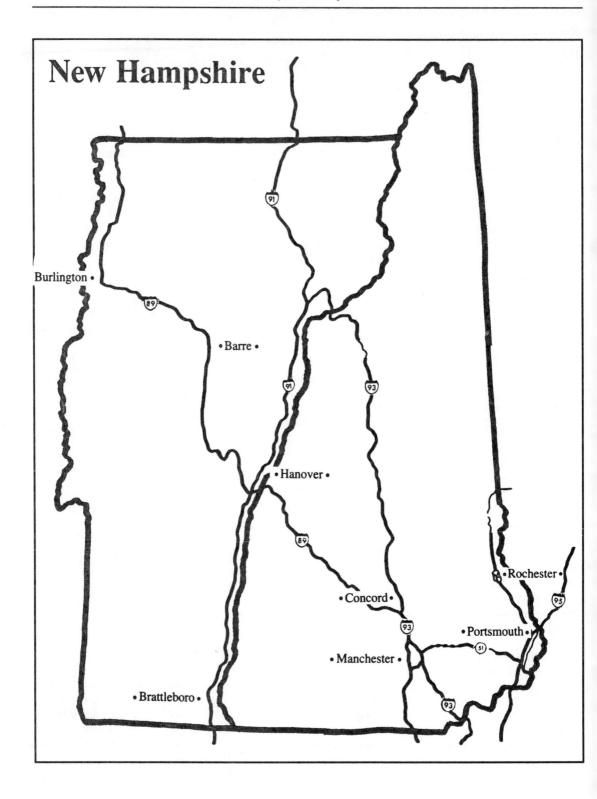

John F. Hendsey
P. O. Box 60
Epping, N.H. 03042
(603) 679-2428
By appointment only
John F. Hendsey
Collection Development; Dance;
Sporting

The Cider House
200 High Street
Exeter, N.H. 03833
(603) 772-8356
10-5 Tues-Sat
Catalogues issued
Anthony M. Tufts
Scotland & The Scotish; Music;
Gardening & Horticulture;
General

Landscape Books
P. O. Box 483
Exeter, N.H. 03833
(603) 964-9333
By mail only
Catalogues issued
Jane W. Robie
Landscape Architecture;
Gardening & Horticulture

A Thousand Words
65 Water Street
Exeter, N.H. 03833
(603) 778-1991
10-6 Mon-Sat
John Segal
Continental Books; Children's
Books; Illustrated Books

Jenny Watson
121 Water Street
Exeter, N.H. 03833
(603) 772-4010
10-5 Mon-Sat
Catalogues issued
Jenny Watson
Asia; The Orient & Orientalia;
General

The Bookery
62 North Main Street
Farmington, N.H. 03835
(603) 755-4471
10-6 Fri
Catalogues issued
Robert M. Colpitt
University Press Books; Latin
America; Central America; Africa;
Arctica & Antarctica; Marine &
Maritime

Rainy Day At Fitzwilliam Center
Route 12
Fitzwilliam, N.H. 03447
(603) 585-9092
10-5 Mon-Sun (Summer), else
close at 4
Marion Legsdin
Antiques; Children's Books;
General

The Typographeum Bookshop
The Stone Cottage, Bennington
Road
Francestown, N.H. 03043
By appointment only
Catalogues issued
R. T. Risk
Literature; First Editions; Rare
Books; Books about Books; Press
Books & Fine Printing

Evelyn Clement
45 Central Street
Franklin, N.H. 03235
(603) 934-5496
By appointment only
Evelyn Clement
Regional Americana; White
Mountains; Technology; Biography
& Autobiography

Louise Frazier
R.D. 8, Box 247, Morrill Street
Gilford, N.H. 03246
(603) 524-2427
By appointment only

Louise Frazier
General

Visually Speaking
Route 11-A, R.F.D. 8, Box 405
Gilford, N.H. 03246
(603) 524-6795
By appointment only
Charles French, Barbara French
General

Sacred and Profane
P. O. Box 321
Goffstown, N.H. 03045
(603) 627-4477
1-4 Sat & Sun
Catalogues issued
H. Donley Wray
Religion & Religous History; Sets;
Archaeology

Nelson Craft & Used Books
Brook Road
Goshen, N.H. 03752
(603) 863-4394
10-5 Mon-Sun (Summer), else 10-
5 Mon-Fri
Audrey Nelson
Children's Books; Crafts &
Hobbies; Art; General

The Bookcase
P. O. Box 33, Forest Road
Greenfield, N.H. 03047
(603) 547-3354
10-6 Mon-Fri
Mrs. William Walsh
General

Alan Lambert
P. O. Box 142
Hancock, N.H. 03449
(603) 525-4035
By appointment only
Alan Lambert, Deece Lambert
Literature; Modern First Editions;
Poetry; Children's Books; L. Frank
Baum & Oziana; General

Old Bennington Books
P. O. Box 142
Hancock, N.H. 03449
(603) 525-4035
By mail only
Alan Lambert, Deece Lambert
*First Editions; Poetry; Children's
Books; L. Frank Baum & Oziana;
Fiction; General*

James C. Tillinghast
P. O. Box 19
Hancock, N.H. 03449-0019
(603) 525-6615
By appointment only
Catalogues issued
James C. Tillinghast
*Guns & Weapons; Postal History;
Antiques*

Dartmouth Bookstore
33 South Main Street
Hanover, N.H. 03755-2098
(603) 643-3616
8:30-5 Mon-Sat (Mon & Wed to 9)
David Cioffi
*Remainders; General; Scholarly
Books; Medical & Medicine;
Technical; Children's Books*

G. B. Manasek, Inc.
35 South Main Street
Hanover, N.H. 03755-0961
(603) 643-2227
10-4 Mon-Sat (call first in Winter)
Catalogues issued
F. J. Manasek
*Astronomy; Physics; Prints; Japan;
Maps, Atlases, & Cartography;
Rare Books*

Carry Back Books
Route 10, Dartmouth College
Highway
Haverhill, N.H. 03765
(603) 989-5943
By mail only
Catalogues issued
Ruth St. John, Donald St. John

*Americana; Vermont; First
Editions; Poetry; Ephemera*

Book Farm
P. O. Box 515, Concord Road
Henniker, N.H. 03242
(603) 428-3429
12-5 Sat & Sun (summer Tues-
Sun)
Catalogues issued
Walter Robinson
*Literature; First Editions; Press
Books & Fine Printing; Inland
Waterways; Poetry; Biography &
Autobiography*

Old Number Six Book Depot
P. O. Box 525, Depot Hill Road
Henniker, N.H. 03242
(603) 428-3334
12:30-5:30 Mon-Sun
Helen Morrison, Ian Morrison
*History; Science; Medicine &
Science; New England; Social
Sciences; Psychiatry, Psychology,
& Psychoanalysis*

The Shadow Shop
Preston Street, Box 1173
Hillsboro, N.H. 03244
(603) 464-5413
By appointment only
Lois Meredith, Barbara Meredith
Ephemera; Juveniles; General

Woman's Words Books
R. R. 4, Box 322, Straw Road
Hopkinton, N.H. 03223
(603) 228-8000
10-5 Tues-Sat, 1-5 Sun
Catalogues issued
Nancy Needham
Women; Metaphysics

Robert B. Stephenson
P. O. Box 67
Jaffrey Center, N.H. 03454
(603) 532-6066
By appointment only

Catalogues issued
Robert B. Stephenson
*Voyages, Travels, & Exploration;
Arctica & Antarctica*

Toadstool Bookshop
222 West Street
Keene, N.H. 03431
(603) 352-8815
10-9 Mon-Sun
Jeff Smull
General

Barn Loft Bookshop
96 Woodland Avenue
Laconia, N.H. 03246
(603) 524-4839
By appointment only
Lee Burt
*Children's Books; New England;
New Hampshire*

Lee Burt
96 Woodland Avenue
Laconia, N.H. 03246
(603) 524-4839
By appointment only
Lee Burt
*Children's Books; New England;
General*

Cotton Hill Books
R.F.D. 6, Box 298
Laconia, N.H. 03246
(603) 524-4967
By appointment only
Elizabeth Emery
*New Hampshire; Maine; New
England; Art; Gardening &
Horticulture; General*

Bretton Hall Antiquities
12 Cottage Street
Lancaster, N.H. 03584
(603) 788-2202
9-5 daily
Richard Force
White Mountains; New Hampshire

Elm Street & Stolcraft Books
20 Elm Street
Lancaster, N.H. 03584
(603) 788-4844
10-5 Mon-Fri, 10-1 Sat
Albert Tetreault
General

Earth Books
37 Main Street
Littleton, N.H. 03561
(603) 444-7740
9-5 Mon-Sat
Catalogues issued
Andrew Gutterman
Geology; Mining & Metallurgy;
General

Village Book Store
102 Main Street
Littleton, N.H. 03561
(603) 444-5263
9-9 Wed-Sat, 9-5:30 Sun-Tues
Ned Densmore
New Hampshire; White Mountains;
General

Anita's Antiquarian Books
1408 Elm Street
Manchester, N.H. 03101
(603) 669-7695
9:30-5 Mon-Sat
Catalogues issued
Anita Danello, Michael Danello
Phonograph Records; Ephemera;
Sheet Music; General

Homestead Bookshop
Route 101, Box 90
Marlborough, N.H. 03455
(603) 876-4213
9-5 Mon-Fri, 9-4:30 Sat & Sun
Harry E. Kenney, Jr., Constance
Kenney, Robert J. Kenney
Children's Books; Regional
Americana; Printing & Printing
History; Cooking; General; Marine
& Maritime

Mary Robertson
P. O. Box 296
Meredith, N.H. 03253
(603) 279-8750
10-5 (Summer), 12-4 (Spring-
Fall), daily
Mary Robertson
Needlework

Paul Henderson
50 Berkeley Street
Nashua, N.H. 03060
(603) 883-8918
By appointment only
Catalogues issued
Paul Henderson
Genealogy; Local History

Burpee Hill Books
Burpee Hill Road, Box 188
New London, N.H. 03257
(603) 526-6654
10-5 daily May to October, else
call
Catalogues issued
Alf E. Jacobson, Sonja Jacobson
Americana; Art; Antiques;
Ephemera; Manuscripts;
Photography

Song Of Sixpence
P. O. Box 166
Newmarket, N.H. 03857
(603) 659-6290
By appointment only
Catalogues issued
Bobbi Cobb
Children's Books; Illustrated Books

Sykes & Flanders
P. O. Box 86, Route 77
North Weare Village, N.H. 03281
(603) 529-7432
By appointment only
Catalogues issued
Mary F. Sykes, Richard L. Sykes
Americana; Fur Trade; First
Editions; Mystery & Detective

Fiction; New Hampshire; White
Mountains

Callahan & Co.
P. O. Box 704
Peterborough, N.H. 03458
(603) 924-3726
By appointment only
Catalogues issued
Kenneth Callahan, Diane Callahan
Fishing & Angling; Natural
History

Antiquarian Book Store
1070 Lafayette Road (U.S. 1)
Portsmouth, N.H. 03801
(603) 436-7250
10-5:30 Mon-Sat
Back Issue Magazines; Erotica;
General

Book Guild Of Portsmouth
85 Daniel Street
Portsmouth, N.H. 03801
(603) 436-1758
10-5 Mon-Sat
Catalogues issued
Martin Held, Phyllis Held
New England; Civil War &
Confederacy; Voyages, Travels, &
Exploration

Cleland's Books
63 Market Street
Portsmouth, N.H. 03801
(603) 431-2369
10-5 Tues-Sat (Mon-Sun in
Summer)
Catalogues issued
William Thompson
Civil War & Confederacy; English
Literature; 18th Century
Literature; Natural History;
General

North Country Bookshop
Route 119, Four Corners
Richmond, N.H. 03470
(603) 239-6547

10-6 Mon-Sun
Catalogues issued
Alan S. Harvey
First Editions; Documents;
Manuscripts; Ephemera

Village Books
Main Street
Rumney Village, N.H. 03266
(603) 786-9300
By appointment only
George N. Kent, Ann S. Kent
Natural History; Americana; New
Hampshire

The Ha'Penny
Star Route
Snowville, N.H. 03849
(603) 447-5314
9-5 Mon-Sat
Catalogues issued
Bette Roden, Tom Roden
Miniature Books; Antiques;
Reference

Abbles Search Service
P. O. Box 36
Temple, N.H. 03084
(603) 878-1758
By mail only

Olga E. Tainter
Search Service, With Stock

Tainters
P. O. Box 36
Temple, N.H. 03084
(603) 878-1758
By mail only
Olga Tainter
General

Spooner's Antiques
P. O. Box 43
Tilton, N.H. 03276
(603) 286-7142
By mail only
Bertrand L. Spooner, Jr., Virginia
I. Spooner
New Hampshire; Local History;
19th Century Literature; Poetry

G. P. Ackerman
P. O. Box 26
Walpole, N.H. 03608
(603) 756-4223
By mail only
G. P. Ackerman
English Literature; Theatre

Colonial Plaza Antiques
Route 12-A
West Lebanon, N.H. 03784
(603) 448-5880
9-5 Mon-Sun
Karl Neary, Kathleen Neary
General

Celtic Cross Books
R.R. 1, Box 160
Westmoreland, N.H. 03467
(603) 399-4342
By appointment only
Catalogues issued
Henry Hurley
Catholica; Religion & Religous
History

Hurley Books
Route 12, R.R. 1, Box 160
Westmoreland, N.H. 03467
(603) 399-4342
By appointment only
Catalogues issued
Henry Hurley
Farming, Ranching, & Livestock;
Gardening & Horticulture;
Miniature Books; Religion &
Religous History; Books about
Books

New Jersey

Antic Hay Books
P. O. Box 2185
Asbury Park, N.J. 07712
By mail only
Catalogues issued
Don Stine
Literature; First Editions; Modern
First Editions; Inscribed Books;
Authors; Autographs & Autograph
Material

White's Galleries
607 Lake Avenue
Asbury Park, N.J. 07712
(201) 774-9300
10-5 Mon-Sat
Evelyn White
Biography & Autobiography; First
Editions; Art; Gardening &
Horticulture; Natural History;
Religion & Religious History

Bauman Rare Books
14 South La Clede Place
Atlantic City, N.J. 08401
(609) 344-0763
By appointment only
Catalogues issued
David L. Bauman, Natalie Bauman
Rare Books; Voyages, Travels, &
Exploration; Humanities; First
Editions; Natural History; Law

New Jersey

Bookbizniz
23 North Florida Avenue
Atlantic City, N.J. 08401
(609) 344-6670
8-7 Mon-Fri, 8-5 Sat
Rhett R. Yap
Search Service, With Stock

Princeton Antiquarian Books
2915-2917 Atlantic Avenue
Atlantic City, N.J. 08401
(609) 344-1943
By appointment only
Robert E. Ruffolo II
*Antiques; Calligraphy; Outlaws &
Rangers; Scholarly Books*

Servant's Knowledge
2915-17 Atlantic Avenue
Atlantic City, N.J. 08401
(609) 344-1943
By appointment only
Robert E. Ruffolo II
*Antiques; Art; Gambling; Scholarly
Books*

Robert C. Auten
Cedar Ridge Road
Bedminster, N.J. 07921
(201) 469-9666
By mail only
Catalogues issued
Robert C. Auten, Rita Wardo
Automotive

Heliochrome Books
74 Webster Drive
Berkeley Heights, N.J. 07922
(201) 464-0805
By appointment only
Catalogues issued
Dr. David Klappholz
Photography; Books about Books

Olde Tyme Music Scene
915 Main Street
Boonton, N.J. 07005
(201) 335-5040
10-5 Tues-Sat, 12-4 Sun

Len Donahue, Nancy Durant
Phonograph Records; Music

Richard W. Spellman
610 Monticello Drive
Brick Town, N.J. 08723
(201) 477-2413
By mail only
Catalogues issued
Richard W. Spellman
*Maps, Atlases, & Cartography;
Newspapers; Prints; Ephemera*

Escargot
503 Route 71, Box 332
Brielle, N.J. 08730
(201) 528-5955
10-5 Mon-Sat
Richard Weiner, Reid Collins
*New Jersey; Rare Books; Comic
Books*

Ruth S. Engle
306 King's Croft
Cherry Hill, N.J. 08034
(609) 482-2377
By mail only
Ruth S. Engle
Search Service, Without Stock

Anthony C. Schmidt
112 East Linden Avenue
Collingswood, N.J. 08108
(609) 858-4719
By appointment only
Catalogues issued
Anthony C. Schmidt
*Art, Books about; Art History &
Reference; Art Catalogues,
Periodicals, & Books; Catalogues
Raisonnes*

Cranbury Book Worm
54 North Main Street
Cranbury, N.J. 08512
(609) 655-1063
9-8 Mon-Fri, 9-5 Sat, 12-5 Sun
Ralph C. Schemp
General

Leo Loewenthal
P. O. Box 938
Dover, N.J. 07801
(201) 328-7196
By mail only
Catalogues issued
Leo Loewenthal
*Architecture; Art; Cinema & Film;
Dance; Photography; Poetry*

Edison Hall Books
5 Ventnor Place
Edison, N.J. 08820
(201) 548-4455
After 6 p.m. and on weekends
George Stang, Florence Stang
*First Editions; Children's Books;
Thomas A. Edison; Tobacco &
Smoking; Edgar Rice Burroughs;
General*

Egg Harbor Books
612 White Horse Pike
Egg Harbor, N.J. 08215
(609) 965-1708
11-6 Mon-Sat
Norman Arrington
General

Book Store at Depot Square
8 Depot Square
Englewood, N.J. 07631
(201) 568-6563
11:30-5:30 Tues-Fri, 10:30-5:30
Sat
Rita Alexander
*Children's Books; Folklore;
Cooking; WPA & Federal Writers
Project; General*

James Tait Goodrich
214 Everett Place
Englewood, N.J. 07631
(201) 567-0199
By appointment only
Catalogues issued
James T. Goodrich
*History of Medicine & Science;
Biography & Autobiography;*

Medical & Medicine;
Neurosciences; Early Printed
Books

Junius Book Distributors
P. O. Box 85
Fairview, N.J. 07022
(201) 868-7725
By appointment only
Catalogues issued
Michael V. Cordasco
Bibliography; Scholarly Books;
Medicine & Science; Reference;
Dictionaries; Encyclopedias

The People's Bookshop
160 Main Street
Flemington, N.J. 08822
(201) 788-4953
9-5 Thurs-Sat
Catalogues issued
Rosemarie Beardsley
Children's Books; Phonograph
Records; Nostalgic Fiction;
General

Peter Scrivener Sloat
R.D. 7, Box 548
Flemington, N.J. 08822
(201) 782-7597
By mail only
Peter S. Sloat
Illustrated Books; Back Issue
Magazines; General

Vathek Books
250 Slocum Way
Fort Lee, N.J. 07024
(201) 585-1760
By appointment only
Daniel Rich
General

Rare Book Company
P. O. Box 957
Freehold, N.J. 07728
(201) 780-1393
9-5 daily
Catalogues issued

Autographs & Autograph Material;
First Editions; Inscribed Books;
Religion & Religious History

Ray Boas
5 Roberts Avenue
Haddonfield, N.J. 08033
(609) 429-9240
Catalogues issued
Ray Boas
Business & Business History

Old Cookbooks
P. O. Box 462
Haddonfield, N.J. 08033
(609) 854-2844
By mail only
Catalogues issued
H. T. Hicks
Cooking; Cookbooks

Nothingham Old Book Store
3720 Nothingham Way
Hamilton Square, N.J. 08690
(609) 587-2991
10-5 and 6:30-8 daily
Howard Tedder
Aviation & Aeronautics; Local
History; Militaria; General

Bernhard J. Kress
7 Cottage Cove, Box 0
Hewitt, N.J. 07421
(201) 728-8683
Bernhard J. Kress
Typography & Type Specimens

Rutgers Book Center
127 Raritan Avenue
Highland Park, N.J. 08904
(201) 545-4344
9-5 Mon-Sat
Catalogues issued
Militaria; World Wars; German
Books & Literature; French Books
& Literature

Elisabeth Woodburn
P. O. Box 398, Booknoll Farm

Hopewell, N.J. 08525
(609) 466-0522
By appointment only
Catalogues issued
Elisabeth Woodburn
Landscape Architecture;
Herbology & Herbs; Gardening
& Horticulture; Farming,
Ranching, & Livestock

Edenite Society
Imlaystown, N.J. 08526
(609) 259-7517
By mail only
Catalogues issued
Frank Muccie, Jr.
Religion & Religous History;
Philosophy; Scholarly Books;
Reprints; Prints

Judy Bieber
14 Dorset Drive
Kenilworth, N.J. 07033
(201) 276-8368
By mail only
Judy Bieber
L. Frank Baum & Oziana;
Children's Books; Illustrated Books

Oz & Ends Book Shoppe
14 Dorset Drive
Kenilworth, N.J. 07033
(201) 276-8368
By mail only
Catalogues issued
Judy A. Bieber
L. Frank Baum & Oziana; Series
Books For Boys & Girls

The Dictionary
P. O. Box 130
Leeds Point, N.J. 08220
(609) 652-1251
By appointment only
R. C. Mills
Computers; Technology; Modern
First Editions; Tobacco &
Smoking; Astronautics & Rocketry

Stephen Viederman
108 High Street
Leonia, N.J. 07605
(201) 947-5292
By appointment only
Catalogues issued
Stephen Viederman
Voyages, Travels, & Exploration;
Asia; Africa

Calderwoods Books
P. O. Box F
Long Valley, N.J. 07853
(201) 876-3001
By mail only
Catalogues issued
Don Frazier, Jo Koch
Derrydale Press

The History House Gallery
152 Zellens Road
Long Valley, N.J. 07853
(201) 852-4442
By appointment only
Marcia Orr, Ronald Orr
Civil War & Confederacy;
American Indian Literature; War;
First Editions; Limited & Signed
Editions; General

The Chatham Bookseller
8 Village Green Road
Madison, N.J. 07940
(201) 822-1361
9-5:30 Mon-Sat
Frank Deodene
General

Jay's Booktique
?????1 Canadian Woods Road (clt
Marlboro, N.J. 07746
(201) 536-7148
By mail only
Catalogues issued
Jay Tominik, Phyllis Tominik,
Barry Tominik
Modern First Editions; Rare
Books; Computers; Technology

Chapter & Verse Books
P. O. Box 954
Maywood, N.J. 07607
(201) 843-3511
By appointment only
C. Sussman
General

Bel Canto Books
P. O. Box 55
Metuchen, N.J. 08840
(201) 548-7371
By mail only
Catalogues issued
Robert Hearn
Opera; Musical Instruments;
Mechanical Musical Instruments;
Violins; Jazz

Keith Egan
522 East Pine Street
Millville, N.J. 08332
(609) 825-8690
By mail only
Keith Egan
Search Service, Without Stock

Montclair Book Center
221 Glen Ridge Avenue
Montclair, N.J. 07042
(201) 783-3630
10-6 Mon-Sat (Thurs to 7, Fri to 8)
General

Abner Schram
36 Park Street
Montclair, N.J. 07042
(201) 744-7755
By appointment only
Catalogues issued
Abner Schram
Art; Architecture; Calligraphy;
Judaica & Hebraica

Patterson Smith
23 Prospect Terrace
Montclair, N.J. 07042
(201) 744-3291
By appointment only

Patterson Smith
Criminology; Gambling;
Technology; Social Sciences; Law

Wangner's Book Shop
9 Midland Avenue
Montclair, N.J. 07042
(201) 744-4211
12-5 Tues-Fri
Victor E. Wangner
First Editions; Sets; General

Whitney McDermut
49 Spring Valley Road
Montvale, N.J. 07645
(201) 391-5905
By mail only
Whitney McDermut
Graphic Arts; Printing & Printing
History; Bookplates & Ex Libris

Old Book Shop
4 John Street
Morristown, N.J. 07960
(201) 538-1210
10-5:30 Mon-Sat
Catalogues issued
Virginia Faulkner, R. Chris Wolff
Americana; New Jersey; General;
Ephemera; Scholarly Books;
Postcards

Trotting Book Shop
Shalebrook Drive
Morristown, N.J. 07960
(201) 766-6111
By mail only
Catalogues issued
S. F. Bergstein
Horses & Horse Sports; Veterinary
Medicine; Prints; Paintings

Angelo Iuspa
474 North 7th Street
Newark, N.J. 07107
(201) 485-0151
By mail only
Angelo Iuspa

Olympic Games; Games & Pastimes

D. Testa
P. O. Box 9064
Newark, N.J. 07104
(201) 484-5291
By appointment only
Catalogues issued
D. Testa
Antiques; Crafts & Hobbies; Photography; Printing & Printing History; United States Government Publications

Northeast Books & Prints
411 East 8th Street
Ocean City, N.J. 08226
(609) 399-9086
9-5 Mon-Sat
Charles Calderone
American History; Naval & Nautical; Art; Antiques; New Jersey; Cookbooks

Morrell's Book Service
50 Broadway
Ocean Grove, N.J. 07756
By mail only
Benjamin C. Morrell, Lillian G. Morrell
Bibliography; Children's Books; Literary Criticism; Books about Books; Back Issue Magazines; Religion & Religious History

Between The Covers
670 B Mapleview
Old Bridge, N.J. 08857
(201) 360-9286
By appointment only
Thomas Congalton, Heidi Congalton
Modern First Editions; Mystery & Detective Fiction; Science Fiction; Photography; Art; Radical Poltics & Literature

Marley & Scrooge
Main Street, Box 358
Oldwick, N.J. 08858
(201) 439-2271
11-5 Tues-Sat
William Michalski
Literature; 18th Century Literature; 19th Century Literature; History; General

Passaic Book Center
594 Main Street
Passaic, N.J. 07055
(201) 778-6646
10-5:45 Mon-Sat (Fri to 8)
General; Science Fiction; Comic Books; Mystery & Detective Fiction

Reliable Books
P. O. Box 2033
Paterson, N.J. 07509
(201) 791-7018
9-6 daily
C. S. Kuzbik
Derrydale Press; Art; Cinema & Film; Military

Joseph Rubinfine
R.F.D. 1
Pleasantville, N.J. 08232
(609) 641-3290
By appointment only
Catalogues issued
Joseph Rubinfine
Autographs & Autograph Material; Manuscripts

James Cummins
P. O. Box 232
Pottersville, N.J. 07979
(201) 439-3803
10-4 Thurs-Sat
Catalogues issued
Anne O'Brien, James Cummins
Bindings, Fine & Rare; Press Books & Fine Printing; Prints; Voyages, Travels, & Exploration; First Editions; Illustrated Books

Joseph J. Felcone Inc.
P. O. Box 366
Princeton, N.J. 08540
(609) 924-0539
By appointment only
Catalogues issued
Joseph J. Felcone
Americana; Books about Books; Literature; Sporting; New Jersey

Roland Roberge
491 Rosedale Road
Princeton, N.J. 08540
(609) 924-6329
By appointment only
Catalogues issued
Roland Roberge
Art Catalogues, Periodicals, & Books; Art History & Reference

Sporting Book Service
P. O. Box 177
Rancocas, N.J. 08073
(609) 267-5506
By appointment only
Catalogues issued
A. A. Williams
Fishing & Angling; Natural History; Guns & Weapons; Sporting

The Keith Library
217 West Front Street
Red Bank, N.J. 07701
(201) 842-7377
11-5 Mon-Sun
Quentin Keith
New Jersey; Bindings, Fine & Rare; Local History

Charles Lloyd
195 West Front St.reet (Red Bank Antiques Center)
Red Bank, N.J. 07701
(201) 842-3393
11-5 Mon-Sun
Charles Lloyd
Prints; Ephemera; General

Kirksco International Bookfinders
70-212 Cedar Road
Ringwood, N.J. 07456
(201) 962-6519
By mail only
William McMasters, J. Berry, Mrs. C. Comer
Book Scouts; Collection Development; General; Americana; Americana

R. & A. Petrilla
P. O. Box 306
Roosevelt, N.J. 08555
(609) 426-4999
By appointment only
Catalogues issued
Robert Petrilla
Appraisals & Appraisal Services; Collection Development; Western Americana; Americana

Gerry & Helen de la Ree
7 Cedarwood Lane
Saddle River, N.J. 07458
(201) 327-6621
By appointment only
Catalogues issued
Gerry de la Ree, Helen de la Ree
Science Fiction; Fantasy; Pulps

Rosemarie Beardsley
1324 Orchard Drive South Br.
Somerville, N.J. 08876
(201) 369-4488
By mail only
Rosemarie Beardsley
Search Service, Without Stock

Heinoldt Books
1325 West Central Avenue
South Egg Harbor, N.J. 08215
(609) 965-2284
By appointment only

Catalogues issued
Theodore Heinoldt, Margaret Heinoldt, Rose Mary Vissage
Americana; Indians & Eskimos; American History; Americana, States; Outlaws & Rangers; Overland Narratives

Little Mermaid Books
411 Park Street
Upper Montclair, N.J. 07043
(201) 744-9157
By appointment only
Nora C. Wertz
Biography & Autobiography; Political Science & Theory; History; Performing Arts; Ireland & The Irish; General

Stephen Koschal
P. O. Box 201
Verona, N.J. 07044
(201) 239-9299
By mail only
Catalogues issued
Stephen Koschal
Association Copies; Autographs & Autograph Material; Inscribed Books; Manuscripts; Presidents; Rare Books

H. Nestler
13 Pennington Avenue
Waldwick, N.J. 07463
(201) 444-7413
By appointment only
Catalogues issued
H. Nestler
New York State; Crafts & Hobbies; Technology; Trade Catalogues; Manuscripts

The Baggage Car
128 Lake Drive East
Wayne, N.J. 07470

(201) 694-6749
By appointment only
Catalogues issued
Thomas A. Bjorkman, Susan Bjorkman
Railroads

Albert Saifer
P. O. Box 51, Town Center
West Orange, N.J. 07052
(201) 731-5701
By mail only
Catalogues issued
Albert Saifer
Trade Catalogues; Technology; Authors; Printing & Printing History; Scholarly Books

Hobbit Rare Books
305 West South Avenue
Westfield, N.J. 07090
(201) 654-4115
10-5 Mon-Sat
General

Richardson Books
209 Stratford Avenue
Westmont, N.J. 08108
(609) 854-3348
By appointment only
Catalogues issued
Herbert Richardson, Christine Richardson
Americana; Architecture; Ephemera; Voyages, Travels, & Exploration

Bookwood Books
P. O. Box 263
Westwood, N.J. 07675
(201) 664-4066
By appointment only
Catalogues issued
Ruth Goodman

New Mexico

Adobe Booksellers
2416 Pennsylvania Street, NE
Albuquerque, N.M. 87110
(505) 299-1670
By appointment only
H. S. Adler
*Americana; Southwestern
Americana*

Books By Mail
1833 Central Avenue, NW
Albuquerque, N.M. 87104
(505) 247-3043
10:30-5:30 Tues-Sat
Katharine Ransom
Regional Americana

Emerson-Lane Booksellers
519 Central Avenue NW
Albuquerque, N.M. 87102
(505) 842-8898
12-5 Wed-Sat
Jerry Lane
*Western Americana; Indians &
Eskimos; Art; Literature; Printing
& Printing History; Geology*

Hummingbird Books
2400 Hannett NE
Albuquerque, N.M. 87106
(505) 268-6277
By appointment only
Catalogues issued
Gail Baker
*Women; Humanities; Literature;
Philosophy*

Ramshorn Booksearch
9513 Villa Del Ray, NE
Albuquerque, N.M. 87111-1650
(505) 299-7244
By mail only
Catalogues issued

Patrick Knupp
*Medicine & Science; Technology;
Western Americana*

Jack D. Rittenhouse
P. O. Box 4422
Albuquerque, N.M. 87196
(505) 255-2479
By appointment only
Catalogues issued
Jack D. Rittenhouse
*Indians & Eskimos; Regional
Americana; Overland Narratives;
Rare Books; Voyages, Travels, &
Exploration*

Robert R. White
P. O. Box 101
Albuquerque, N.M. 87103
(505) 247-3138
By mail only
Catalogues issued
Robert R. White
Art, Western; New Mexico

Jane Zwisohn
524 Solano Drive, NE
Albuquerque, N.M. 87108
(505) 255-4080
By appointment only
Catalogues issued
Jane Zwisohn
*Western Americana; Latin
America; Voyages, Travels, &
Exploration*

La Galeria de Artesanos
P. O. Box 1657
Las Vegas, N.M. 87701
(505) 425-8331
10-5 Mon-Fri, 10-1 Sat
Diana G. Stein, Joseph W. Stein
Indians & Eskimos; Southwestern

*Americana; Outlaws & Rangers;
Folklore; Military; Cattle & Range
Industry*

James Harder
124 Monte Vista Drive
Los Alamos, N.M. 87544
(505) 672-9152
By mail only
James Harder
*Americana; Arctica & Antarctica;
Maps, Atlases, & Cartography;
Militaria; Natural History;
Voyages, Travels, & Exploration*

Abacus Books
P. O. Box 5555
Santa Fe, N.M. 87502-5555
(505) 983-6434
By appointment only
Robert F. Kadlec
*Southwestern Americana; First
Editions*

Ancient City Press
P. O. Box 5401
Santa Fe, N.M. 87502
(505) 982-8195
By appointment only
Catalogues issued
Mary Powell
*Indians & Eskimos; Regional
Americana; First Editions;
Scholarly Books; Travel;
Archaeology*

Richard Fitch
2324 Calle Halcon
Santa Fe, N.M. 87505
(505) 982-2939
By appointment only
Catalogues issued
Richard Fitch

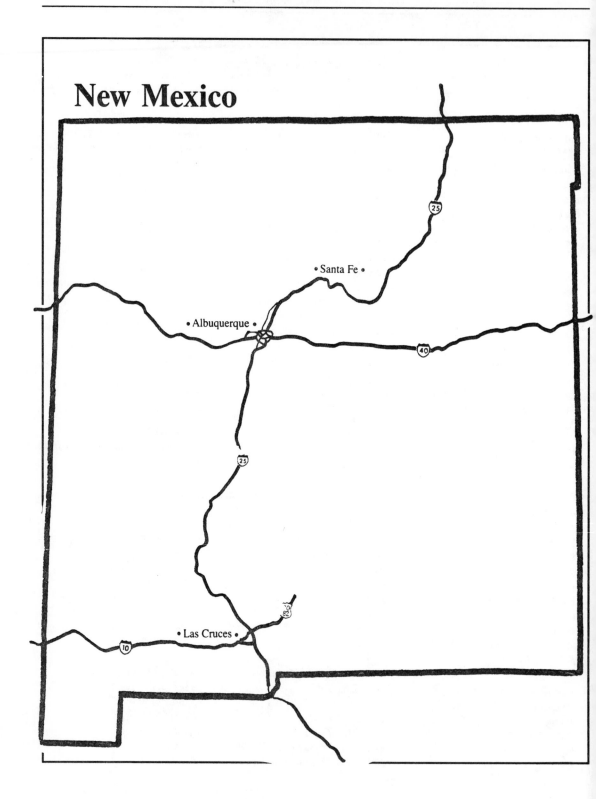

Maps, Atlases, & Cartography;
Prints; Voyages, Travels, &
Exploration; Canada &
Canadiana; Geology; Reference

L. E. Gay
1023 Tierra Drive
Santa Fe, N.M. 87505
(505) 471-2393
By appointment only
Catalogues issued
L. E. Gay, Mary R. Gay
Arizona; New Mexico; Art,
Western; Southwestern Americana

The Great Southwest Books
960 Santander
Santa Fe, N.M. 87501
(505) 983-1680
By appointment only
Clark Kimball
Southwestern Americana; New
Mexico; First Editions; Press
Books & Fine Printing;
Bibliography

Margolis & Moss
129 West San Francisco Street
Santa Fe, N.M. 87504
(505) 982-1028
11-5 Mon-Sat
Catalogues issued
David Margolis, Jean Moss
Western Americana; Ephemera;
Illustrated Books; Photography;
Prints; General

Parker Books Of The West
300 Lomita
Santa Fe, N.M. 87504-8390
(505) 988-1076
10-5 daily
Catalogues issued
Riley Parker, Betty Parker
Western Americana; Southwestern
Americana; New Mexico; Texas

Nicholas Potter
203 East Palace Avenue
Santa Fe, N.M. 87501
(505) 983-5434

10-5 Mon-Sat
Nicholas Potter
General; Southwestern Americana;
Modern First Editions; Poetry;
Music

Talmage N. Luther
P. O. Box 429
Taos, N.M. 87571
(505) 776-8117
By appointment only
Catalogues issued
Talmage N. Luther
Western Americana; Indians &
Eskimos

Taos Book Shop
114 Kit Carson Road, Box 827
Taos, N.M. 87571
(505) 758-3733
9-5:30 Mon-Sat, 10-5 Sun
Catalogues issued
Ron Querry
Western Americana; Authors

New York

Joseph Geraci
R.D. 1, Box 258
Accord, N.Y. 12404
(914) 687-0822
By appointment only
Catalogues issued
Joseph Geraci, Barbara White
Prints; Illuminated Manuscripts;
Autographs & Autograph Material

Bryn Mawr Bookshop
1 Spring Street
Albany, N.Y. 12210
(518) 465-8126
10:30-4 Tues-Sat

Virginia B. Bennett
General

Nelson's Book Stores
26 Central Avenue
Albany, N.Y. 12210
(518) 463-1023
11-5:30 Mon-Sat
John L. Nelson, Sr.
Local History; Literature;
Americana; Cookbooks; General

Thomas W. Shaw
11 Albright Avenue
Albany, N.Y. 12203

(518) 456-5905
By mail only
Catalogues issued
Thomas W. Shaw
Mystery & Detective Fiction;
Fiction; General

Martin B. Raskin
11 Edgemere Drive
Albertson, N.Y. 11507
(516) 621-7418
By mail only
Catalogues issued
Martin B. Raskin
Medical & Medicine

Sandys
P. O. Box 181
Albertson, N.Y. 11507
(516) 484-4299
By mail only
Norman Sandys, Doris Sandys
*Sports; Military; Back Issue
Periodicals; Cookbooks;
Children's Books*

Buffalo Book Store
3131 Sheriden Drive, Century Mall
Amherst, N.Y. 14226
(716) 835-9827
9-9 Mon-Sat
Eugene Musiel
New York State; General

Kevin T. Ransom
P. O. Box 176
Amherst, N.Y. 14226
(716) 839-1510
By appointment only
Catalogues issued
Kevin T. Ransom
*Modern First Editions; Mystery
& Detective Fiction; Children's
Books; Autographs & Autograph
Material; Science Fiction; Press
Books & Fine Printing*

Village Green Bookstore
1089 Niagara Falls Boulevard
Amherst, N.Y. 14226
(716) 836-8960
6 a.m.-11 p.m. Sun-Thurs, 6-noon
Fri & Sat
Jessie Martin
Back Issue Magazines; General

Kenneth Lang
105 Avon Place
Amityville, N.Y. 11701
(516) 598-1964
By appointment only
Kenneth Lang
*General; Publishing History;
Ephemera*

Reston's Booknook
59 Rockton Street
Amsterdam, N.Y. 12010
(518) 843-1601
By appointment only
Catalogues issued
Donna Reston
*Americana; Ephemera; General;
Paintings; Prints; Science Fiction*

Ancramdale Book Barn
Wood's Drive
Ancramdale, N.Y. 12503
(518) 329-0193
By appointment only
John Schultz, Catherine Schultz
General

Talbothay's Books
P. O. Box 118
Aurora, N.Y. 13026
(315) 364-7550
By appointment only
Catalogues issued
Paul Mitchell
*Americana; First Editions; Literary
Criticism; Militaria*

Autobooks East
P. O. Box 1
Babylon, N.Y. 11702
(516) 587-3332
By mail only
David Ficken
*Automobile Racing;
Transportation; Steamboats &
River Travel; World War II
Battlefield Art; Posters*

B. A. Fullam
8 Wigwam Path
Babylon, N.Y. 11702
(516) 587-5974
By mail only
Brandon A. Fullam
*Autographs & Autograph Material;
First Editions; 19th Century
Literature; Juveniles; Stereoviews*

**Thomas J. Wise Memorial
Bookshop**
P. O. Box 259
Baldwin Place, N.Y. 10505
(914) 628-9308
By mail only
John F. Mahony
*Modern First Editions; Modern
Library Publishing Company; Sets;
General*

Pride And Prejudice Books
11 North Hill Road
Ballston Lake, N.Y. 12019
(518) 877-5310
By appointment only
Catalogues issued
Merrill Whitburn, Diane Whitburn
*Writing Instruction; First Editions;
20th Century Literature; 19th
Century Literature; Women;
General*

Bay Shore Books
33 West Main Street
Bay Shore, N.Y. 11706
(516) 665-8385
11-5 daily
Steven Weinkselbaum
General

Maestro
P. O. Box 848
Bayport, N.Y. 11705
(516) 472-1222
By mail only
Maestro Signorelli
*Violins; Dance; Children's Books;
Modern First Editions; Paintings;
Performing Arts*

Thomolsen Books
P. O. Box 180
Bayside, N.Y. 11361
(718) 428-3942
By mail only
Catalogues issued
Joan O. Golder, Walter E. Golder

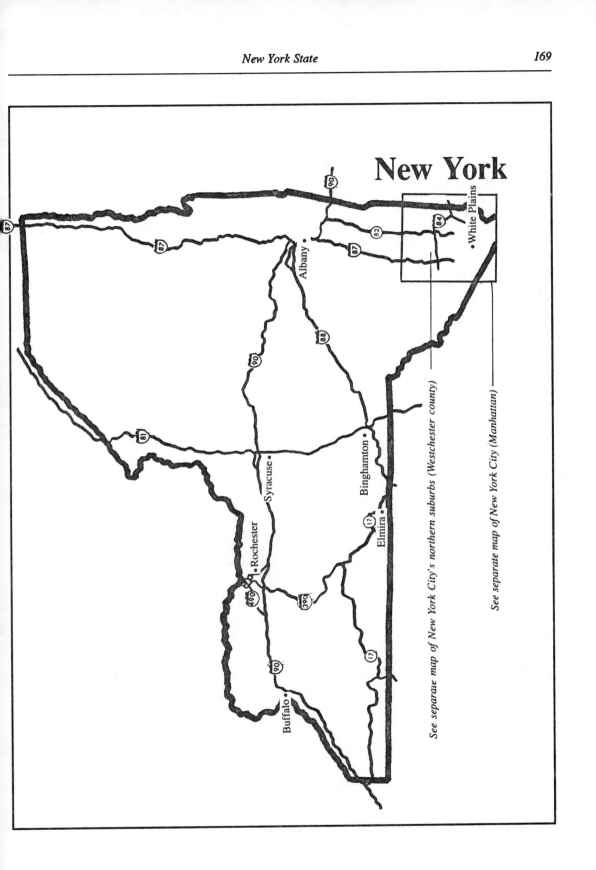

Mystery & Detective Fiction; True Crime

Judith Bowman
Pound Ridge Road
Bedford, N.Y. 10506
(914) 234-7543
By appointment only
Catalogues issued
Judith Bowman
Fishing & Angling

Nancy Doutt
2700 County Line Drive
Big Flats, N.Y. 14814
(607) 562-3781
By mail only
Nancy F. Doutt
General

Editions
Route 28
Boiceville, N.Y. 12412
(914) 657-7000
By mail only
Catalogues issued
Norman Levine, Joan Levine
General

Olana Gallery
P. O. Drawer 9
Brewster, N.Y. 10509
(914) 279-8077
By appointment only
Catalogues issued
Bernard Rosenberg
Books About Painting; Art, Books about; Art Catalogues, Periodicals, & Books

Robert C. Hess
559 Potter Boulevard
Brightwaters, N.Y. 11718
(516) 665-4369
By appointment only
Catalogues issued
Robert C. Hess
Sherlock Holmes & A. C. Doyle

Windsor Books
P. O. Box 280
Brightwaters, N.Y. 11718
By mail only
Catalogues issued
Stephen Schmidt, Jeff Schmidt
Commodities Trading; Stock Market & Wall Street

Lift Bridge Bookshop
71 Main Street
Brockport, N.Y. 14420
(716) 637-8354
9:30-9 Mon-Fri, to 5:30 Sat, 12-5 Sun
A. Kutz
New Books; Western New York State; Regional Americana; Modern First Editions

Abbot Books & Prints
100-26 Benchley Place
The Bronx, N.Y. 10475
(212) 671-9800
By mail only
Catalogues issued
Ira Unschuld
Stock Market & Wall Street; Business & Business History; Antique Stocks & Bonds; Travel Guides & Baedekers; Railroads; The Orient & Orientalia

H. Celnick
2144 Muliner Avenue
The Bronx, N.Y. 10462
(212) 823-5731
By mail only
H. Celnick
Gardening & Horticulture; Judaica & Hebrica; Medicine & Science; Natural History; Natural Healing

J. M. Cohen
P. O. Box 542
The Bronx, N.Y. 10463-0542
(212) 548-7160
By appointment only
Catalogues issued

Judy M. Cohen
Decorative Arts; Antiques; Design; Fashion; Textiles; Jewelry

E. K. Schreiber
3140 Netherland Avenue
The Bronx, N.Y. 10463
(212) 884-9139
By appointment only
Catalogues issued
Fred Schreiber, Ellen Schreiber
Early Printed Books; Incunabula; Renaissance; Greek & Roman Classics

Xanadu
3242 Irwin Avenue
The Bronx, N.Y. 10463
(212) 549-3655
9:30-5:30 Mon-Fri
Don Schlitten
Art; Poetry; Cinema & Film; Theatre; Fantasy; Science Fiction

A C Books
P. O. Box 962, G.P.O.
Brooklyn, N.Y. 11202
(718) 855-0600
By appointment only
Catalogues issued
A. Berube
Religion & Religous History; Philosophy; Law; Sexology

J. Biegeleisen
4409 16th Avenue
Brooklyn, N.Y. 11204
(718) 436-1165
10:30-6:30 Sun-Fri
Sol Biegeleisen, Moses Biegeleisen
Judaica & Hebrica; Manuscripts; Israel

Binkin's Book Center
54 Willoughby Street
Brooklyn, N.Y. 11201
(718) 855-7813
10:30-6 Mon-Sat

Robert Kanatous, Irving Binkin
General

Book Search Service
P. O. Box 168
Brooklyn, N.Y. 11202
Catalogues issued
B. Chaim
Political Science & Theory;
Political, Social, & Cultural
History; Latin America; Back Issue
Periodicals; Social Sciences;
Ballroom Dancing

City Wide Books
P. O. Box 211, WMBS Stn.
Brooklyn, N.Y. 11211
(718) 388-0037
By appointment only
Robert Chalfin
Used Paperbacks; Back Issue
Magazines; General

The Dance Mart
P. O. Box 48, Homecrest Stn.
Brooklyn, N.Y. 11229
(718) 627-0477
By mail only
Catalogues issued
A. J. Pischl
Dance

Enchanted Books
2435 Ocean Avenue, Apt. 6-J
Brooklyn, N.Y. 11229
(718) 891-5241
By appointment only
Susan W. Liebegott
Children's Books; Illustrated
Books; Literature

The Footnote
179 Washington Park
Brooklyn, N.Y. 11205
By mail only
Catalogues issued
David C. Frost, David A. Hovell
Dance; Opera; Music; Cooking;
Americana; Literature

Free Lance Books
163 Joralemon Street, suite 1060
Brooklyn, N.Y. 11201
(718) 522-5455
By appointment only
Catalogues issued
Jason Duberman
H. L. Mencken; Radical Poltics &
Literature; Minor Wars & Battles;
Slavery

Fricelli Associates
P. O. Box 247, Bath Beach Stn.
Brooklyn, N.Y. 11214
(718) 266-0675
By mail only
Catalogues issued
Joseph J. Fricelli
Autographs & Autograph Material

Grand Book, Inc.
659-C Grand Street
Brooklyn, N.Y. 11211
(718) 384-4089
12:30-5:30 daily
Catalogues issued
Comic Books; Fiction; General

Frances Klenett
13 Cranberry Street
Brooklyn, N.Y. 11201
(718) 852-2424
By mail only
Frances Klenett
General

Main Street Booksellers
P. O. Box 103, Vanderveer Stn.
Brooklyn, N.Y. 11210
(718) 275-0331
By mail only
Catalogues issued
Arnold Cohen
Chess; Fiction; Modern First
Editions; Biography &
Autobiography

Jeffrey Meyerson
50 First Place

Brooklyn, N.Y. 11231
(718) 596-7739
By mail only
Catalogues issued
Jeffrey Meyerson
Mystery & Detective Fiction;
General

National Library Publications
P. O. Box 73
Brooklyn, N.Y. 11234
(718) 444-7427
William Summers
Games & Pastimes; Hobbies;
Reference

Opera Box
P. O. Box 48, Homecrest Stn.
Brooklyn, N.Y. 11229
(718) 627-0477
By mail only
Catalogues issued
Tennessee Wilde
Opera; Autographs & Autograph
Material; Sheet Music; Musical
Scores

H. C. Roseman
85 Livingston Street
Brooklyn, N.Y. 11201
(718) 834-8928
By mail only
Catalogues issued
H. G. Roseman
Ballroom Dancing; Cinema &
Film; Criminology; New York City
& Metropolitan Region

C. J. Scheiner
275 Linden Boulevard
Brooklyn, N.Y. 11226
(718) 469-1089
By mail only
Catalogues issued
C. J. Scheiner
Erotica; Curiosa; Sexology

Robert Daunce
P. O. Box 408

Buffalo, N.Y. 14205-0408
(716) 838-2540
By appointment only
Catalogues issued
Robert J. Daunce, Nancy A. Daunce
Science Fiction; Fantasy; Horror; Minor Wars & Battles; Adventure; Erotica

Olga Hoefliger
438 Vermont Street
Buffalo, N.Y. 14213
(716) 886-1898
By mail only
Catalogues issued
Olga Wagensonner
Illustrated Books; Children's Books; Art; Americana; Literature; Latin America

Mahoney & Weekly
513 Virginia Street
Buffalo, N.Y. 14202
(716) 856-6024
11-5 Wed-Sat
Catalogues issued
John W. Weekly
Appraisals & Appraisal Services; Western New York State; Literature; Philosophy; Press Books & Fine Printing; Rare Books

Old Editions Bookshop
3124 Main Street
Buffalo, N.Y. 14214-1306
(716) 836-7354
10-6 Mon-Sat
Ronald L. Cozzi
General; Chess; History; Americana; Religion & Religious History; Prints

Don Fay
4329 Acon-Caledonia Road, Route 5
Caledonia, N.Y. 14423
(716) 226-2288
10-5 daily

Don Fay
Literature; Americana; Hymns & Hymnals; Children's Books; Mystery & Detective Fiction; Religion & Religious History

I. L. Glover
19 Washington Street
Cambridge, N.Y. 12816
(518) 677-3713
2-8 Thurs, 1-5 Fri & Sat
Ida Glover
20th Century Literature; Americana; Fiction; Vietnam War & Literature; Illustrated Books; Regional Americana

C. J. Boardman
R.D. 3, Route 13
Camden, N.Y. 13316
(315) 245-1950
By appointment only
Crager J. Boardman, Sr.
New York State; Americana; Religion & Religous History; Juveniles; General

Sydney R. Smith
Canaan, N.Y. 12029
(518) 794-8998
By appointment only
Catalogues issued
Camila P. Smith
Horses & Horse Sports; Dogs; Fishing & Angling; Guns & Weapons

Jenison's Books
23 Gouverneur Street (Route 11)
Canton, N.Y. 13617
(315) 386-3022
12-5 Thurs-Sat
Catalogues issued
Thomas Jenison
New York State; Trade Catalogues; Americana; Ephemera; Postcards; Prints

Ed Boyce
2 East Drive
Carmel, N.Y. 10512
(914) 225-3577
By appointment only
Ed Boyce
Appraisals & Appraisal Services; Americana; General

McDonald's Book Ends
125 Water Street
Catskill, N.Y. 12414
(518) 943-3520
By appointment only
Francis J. McDonald
New York State; Catskill Mountains; Hudson River Valley

Pan Books & Graphics
401 Main Street
Catskill, N.Y. 12414
(518) 943-4771
10-5 Mon-Sat, 12-4 Sun
Catalogues issued
Ric Zank, Gordon Usticke
Illustrated Books; Art; Children's Books; Sporting; New York State; Prints

Rockland Bookman
P. O. Box 134
Cattaraugus, N.Y. 14719
(716) 257-5121
By appointment only
Catalogues issued
Thomas Cullen, Carol Cullen
Natural History; Americana; Bindings, Fine & Rare; Illustrated Books

Stephen & Carol Resnick
36 Lincklaen Street
Cazenovia, N.Y. 13035
(315) 655-2810
By appointment only
Catalogues issued
Stephen Resnick, Carol Resnick
Ephemera; Autographs &

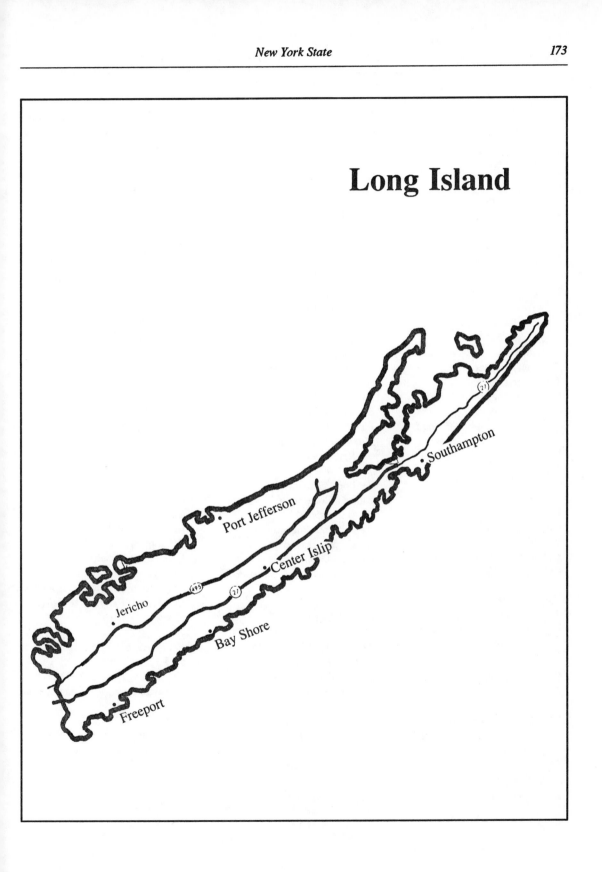

Long Island

*Autograph Material; Manuscripts;
Rare Books*

Evlen Books
P. O. Box 42
Centerport, N.Y. 11721
(516) 421-1632
By appointment only
Catalogues issued
George R. Lenz, Evelyn Lenz
Modern First Editions

Terra Firma Books
P. O. Box 480
Churchville, N.Y. 14428
(716) 494-2264
By mail only
Catalogues issued
T. C. Fabrizio
*Phonograph Records; Trade
Cards; Postcards; Ephemera;
Games & Pastimes; Railroads*

Vi & Si's Antiques Ltd.
8970 Main Street, Route 5
Clarence, N.Y. 14031
(716) 634-4488
10-5 Mon-Sun
Catalogues issued
Vi Altman, Si Altman
*Mechanical Musical Instruments;
Phonograph Records*

Deirdre O'Mahony
8110 Northfield Road
Clarence Center, N.Y. 14032
(716) 741-9236
By appointment only
Deirdre O'Mahony
Juveniles

The Earl Of Clarendon
16286 East Lee Road, Route 31-A,
    Box 176
Clarendon, N.Y. 14429
(716) 638-6982
11-5:30 Sat & Sun (Apr-Oct only)
Catalogues issued
Jason Karp

*Illustrated Books; Children's
Books; L. Frank Baum & Oziana;
Erotica*

Clinton Rare Books
26 Utica Street
Clinton, N.Y. 13323
(315) 853-2137
By appointment only
Richard E. Eckler
General; Bindings, Fine & Rare

Garret Gallery
33 Senaca Turnpike
Clinton, N.Y. 13323
(315) 853-8145
By appointment only
Catalogues issued
Richard Astle
*Arctica & Antarctica; Civil War
& Confederacy; Fur Trade;
Western Americana; Marine &
Maritime; American Colonies &
the Revolution*

Seabook Search
Clinton Corners, N.Y. 12514
(914) 266-5800
By appointment only
Catalogues issued
John G. De Graff
*Naval & Nautical; Ships & The
Sea*

C. G. Fisher
62 East Main Street
Cobleskill, N.Y. 12043
(518) 234-3374
By appointment only
Clifford Fisher
*Americana; New York State; Maps,
Atlases, & Cartography; Natural
History; General*

Antipodean Books
P. O. Box 189
Cold Spring, N.Y. 10516
By appointment only
Catalogues issued

David Lilburne, Cathy Lilburne
*Australia & New Zealand; Pacific
Region*

Nosegay Books
46 Glen Way
Cold Spring Harbor, N.Y. 11724
(516) 692-4315
By mail only
Lorraine Galinsky
*Antiques; Art; Children's Books;
British Isles; Illustrated Books;
Poetry*

Alfred Jaeger, Inc.
66 Austin Boulevard
Commack, N.Y. 11725
(516) 543-1500
By mail only
Catalogues issued
Helen Protasewicz
*Back Issue Magazines; Back Issue
Periodicals; Appraisals &
Appraisal Services*

Willis Monie
R.D. 1, Box 336
Cooperstown, N.Y. 13326
(607) 547-8363
By appointment only
Catalogues issued
Willis Monie
*Americana; Literature; Ephemera;
Presidents; Religion & Religious
History; General*

Willis Monie Book Store
52 Pioneer Street
Cooperstown, N.Y. 13326
Regular hours Mon-Sun (Summers
only)
Willis Monie
*Americana; Literature; Ephemera;
Presidents; Religion & Religious
History; General*

Book Exchange
90 West Market Street
Corning, N.Y. 14830

(607) 936-8536
10:30-5 Mon-Sat
Catalogues issued
Jim Iraggi
Ceramics & Glass; Decorative Arts

Books Of Marvel
37 E. Market Street (@Glass
Menagerie)
Corning, N.Y. 14830
(607) 962-6700
By appointment only
Richard L. Pope
*Tom Swift; Aviation &
Aeronautics; Series Books For
Boys & Girls; Western Books;
Horatio Alger; Edgar Rice
Burroughs*

Hope Farm Bookshop
Strong Road
Cornwallville, N.Y. 12418
(518) 239-4745
Mon-Sun 10-5
Catalogues issued
Charles E. Dornbusch
*New York State; Civil War &
Confederacy; Hudson River Valley*

Cragsmoor Books
P. O. Box 66
Cragsmoor, N.Y. 12420
(914) 647-5588
Catalogues issued
Leni J. Kroul
*Scholarly Books; Women;
Continental Books; Literary
Criticism; Literature; History*

Croton Book Service
P. O. Box 131
Croton-on-Hudson, N.Y. 10520
(914) 271-6575
By mail only
Edith U. Scott, Robert Scott
*Regional Americana; Militaria;
Hudson River Valley; Local
History*

Old Book Room
111 Grand Street
Croton-on-Hudson, N.Y. 10520
(914) 271-6802
10-5 Thurs-Sat
Jane Northshield
*Hudson River Valley; New York
City & Metropolitan Region; New
York State; Westchester County
(New York State); Children's Books*

Berry Hill Bookshop
R.D. Box 118
Deansboro, N.Y. 13328
(315) 821-6188
10-6 Mon-Sat
Catalogues issued
D. L. Swarthout
*New York State; Cinema & Film;
General*

Lincoln Hill Book Shop
Delaware Plaza
Delmar, N.Y. 12054
(518) 439-8241
By mail only
Michael Aikey, Barbara Aikey
Civil War & Confederacy; General

Golden Age
81 Button Drive
Dix Hills, N.Y. 11746
(516) 499-6112
By appointment only
Ron Katzberg, Jane Katzberg
*Children's Books; Illustrated
Books; History; Antiques;
Biography & Autobiography;
Sports*

Frederick Arone
377 Ashforde
Dobbs Ferry, N.Y. 10522
(914) 693-5858
12-5 Sat & Sun
Catalogues issued
Frederick Arone
Railroads

Gordon Beckhorn
23 Ashford Avenue
Dobbs Ferry, N.Y. 10522
(914) 478-5511
By appointment only
Catalogues issued
Gordon Beckhorn
*Modern First Editions; Autographs
& Autograph Material; Americana*

The Brown Bag Bookstore
127A Main Street
Dobbs Ferry, N.Y. 10522
(914) 693-2322
10-5 Tues-Sat
Ruth Rosenblatt
General

N. & N. Pavlov
37 Oakdale Drive
Dobbs Ferry, N.Y. 10522
(914) 693-1776
By appointment only
Nicolai Pavlov, Nina Pavlov
*Prints; Maps, Atlases, &
Cartography; Incunabula; New
York City & Metropolitan Region;
Rare Books; Ephemera*

Roy Young
145 Palisade Street
Dobbs Ferry, N.Y. 10522
(914) 693-6116
By appointment only
Catalogues issued
Roy Young
*Press Books & Fine Printing;
Illustrated Books; Art;
Architecture; Modern First
Editions*

Watkins Natural History
R. D. 1, Box 199
Dolgeville, N.Y. 13329
(518) 568-2280
By appointment only
Catalogues issued
Larry C. Watkins
Natural History; Sporting; Birds

& Ornithology; Mammalogy;
Herpetolo

Librarium
R.F.D. 190, Blackbridge Road
East Chatham, N.Y. 12060
(518) 392-5209
10-6 Fri-Mon (Apr-Dec), else 10-5
Sat-Sun
Sharon S. Lips
General

M. & M. Books
21 Perth Place
East Northport, N.Y. 11731
(516) 368-4858
By mail only
Catalogues issued
M. C. Feinstein, M. S. Feinstein
*Americana; Fiction; First Editions;
Modern First Editions; Literature*

Tintagel Books
County Route 31, Box 125
East Springfield, N.Y. 13333
(607) 264-3669
10-7 Mon-Sun
Catalogues issued
Rabic Shariff, Gail Shariff
*Press Books & Fine Printing; First
Editions; Rare Books*

Jerry Alper, Inc.
P. O. Box 218
Eastchester, N.Y. 10707
(914) 793-2100
By appointment only
Catalogues issued
Jerry Alper, Ken Hoch
*Scholarly Books; Back Issue
Periodicals*

Ingeborg Quitzau
P. O. Box 5160
Edmeston, N.Y. 13335
(607) 965-8605
By appointment only
Catalogues issued
Ingeborg Quitzau

Miniature Books; Children's
Books; Books about Books;
German Books & Literature

L. W. Currey, Inc.
Church Street
Elizabethtown, N.Y. 12932
(518) 873-6477
By appointment only
Catalogues issued
L. W. Currey
*Fantasy; Science Fiction; Modern
First Editions; 19th Century
Literature*

Bud Pearce
55 Hessland
Elma, N.Y. 14059
(716) 655-4134
Bud Pearce
*World Wars; European History;
Guns & Weapons; Military History*

Elysian Fields Booksellers
80-50 Baxter Avenue, suite 339
Elmhurst, N.Y. 11373
(718) 424-2789
By mail only
Catalogues issued
Ed Drucker
*Gay & Lesbian Literature;
Sexology; Erotica*

Anton Gud
41-22 Judge
Elmhurst, N.Y. 11373
(718) 898-2316
By appointment only
Anton Gud
*Americana; First Editions; Press
Books & Fine Printing; Illustrated
Books; Science Fiction;
Autographs & Autograph Material*

Maxwell Scientific International
Fairview Park
Elmsford, N.Y. 10523
(914) 592-7700
By mail only

Catalogues issued
Otto Rapp
*Mathematics; Science; Physics;
Medical & Medicine; Business &
Busine*

Richard E. Donovan
P. O. Box 7070
Endicott, N.Y. 13760
(607) 785-5874
By appointment only
Catalogues issued
Richard E. Donovan, Patrick H.
Donovan
Golf

Purple Mountain Press Ltd
Main Street
Fleischmanns, N.Y. 12430
(914) 254-4062
By appointment only
Catalogues issued
Wray Romingen
Catskill Mountains

**Foreign & International Book
  Co.**
P. O. Box 126
Flushing, N.Y. 11364
(718) 352-2145
9-5 Mon-Fri
Robert N. Schreiner
Latin America

Michael Halpern
67-32 136th Street
Flushing, N.Y. 11367
(718) 544-3885
By appointment only
Michael Halpern
*Illustrated Books; Juveniles;
General; Cinema & Film*

Spiratone, Inc.
135-06 Northern Boulevard
Flushing, N.Y. 11354
(718) 886-2000
9-6 Mon-Fri, 9-5 Sat

Catalogues issued
Photography

Battery Park Book Company
P. O. Box 710
Forest Hills, N.Y. 11375
(718) 261-1216
By appointment only
Catalogues issued
Ruth Lew
*Books about Books; Printing &
Printing History; Typography &
Type Specimens; Papermaking &
Marbling; Press Books & Fine
Printing; Dance*

Biblion, Inc.
P. O. Box 9
Forest Hills, N.Y. 11375
(718) 263-3910
9-5 Mon-Fri
Ludwig Gottschalk
*History of Medicine & Science;
Incunabula; Rare Books*

B. J. S. Autographs
P. O. Box 886
Forest Hills, N.Y. 11375
(718) 897-7275
9-6 Mon-Sat
Catalogues issued
Bill Safka, Arbe Bareis
*Opera; Biography &
Autobiography; Music; Autographs
& Autograph Material*

Henry Feldstein
P. O. Box 398
Forest Hills, N.Y. 11375
(718) 544-3002
By appointment only
Catalogues issued
Henry Feldstein
Photography

Lubrecht & Cramer Ltd.
R.D. 1, Box 244
Forestburgh, N.Y. 12777
(914) 794-8539

By appointment only
Catalogues issued
Anne Lubrecht, Harry Lubrecht
*Science; Botany; Geology;
Mathematics*

Canford Book Corral
P. O. Box 216
Freeville, N.Y. 13068
(607) 844-9784
By appointment only
Catalogues issued
Michael Cancellari
*Science Fiction; Mystery &
Detective Fiction; Western Books;
Comic Books; Early & Collectible
Paperbacks*

The Phoenix
1608 Dryden Road (Route 13),
Bx 230
Freeville, N.Y. 13068
(607) 347-4767
10-6 Tues-Sat, 1-5 Sun
Elizabeth Morrison
Scholarly Books; General

Ann and James Gray
57 Brompton Road
Garden City, N.Y. 11530
(516) 747-2390
By appointment only
General

Bookmart
P. O. Box 101
Gardiner, N.Y. 12525
(914) 255-5141
By appointment only
Mrs. Haig
*United States Government
Publications; Societies &
Associations Publications*

Leslie Poste
P. O. Box 68
Geneseo, N.Y. 14454
(716) 243-3246
By appointment only

Les Poste
*Horses & Horse Sports; New York
State; Indians & Eskimos;
Sporting; Railroads*

The Book Finder
207 Lyons Road (Route 14 North)
Geneva, N.Y. 14456
(315) 789-9388
Tues-Sat 10-5 (to 8:30 Thurs &
Fri), 1-5 Sun
Jeanne S. Busch, Gary Chicoine
*Fiction; Humanities; Early &
Collectible Paperbacks; General*

Calhouns' Books
1510 Routes 5 and 20
Geneva, N.Y. 14456
(315) 789-8599
11-5 Mon-Sun (Apr-Oct only)
Catalogues issued
Douglas Calhoun, Marlene
Calhoun
New York State; General

Roy W. Clare
47 Woodshire South, Box 136
Getzville, N.Y. 14068
(716) 688-8723
By appointment only
Catalogues issued
Roy W. Clare
*Incunabula; Illustrated Books;
Rare Books; Woodcut Books;
Medicine & Science; STC & Wing
Books*

Xerxes Books
P. O. Box 428
Glen Head, N.Y. 11545
(516) 671-6235
By appointment only
Catalogues issued
Dennis Travis, Carol Travis
*Voyages, Travels, & Exploration;
The Orient & Orientalia;
Manuscripts; Photography; Rare
Books; General*

Howard & Gail Rogofsky
P. O. Box 107
Glen Oaks, N.Y. 11004
(718) 723-0954
Catalogues issued
Howard Rogofsky, Gail Rogofsky
Television & Radio; Ephemera;
Back Issue Periodicals

Sea Heritage Foundation
254-26 75th Avenue
Glen Oaks, N.Y. 11004
(718) 343-9575
By mail only
Catalogues issued
Bernie Klay
Marine & Maritime; Naval &
Nautical; Art

Edward J. Kearin
P. O. Box 563
Goldens Bridge, N.Y. 10526
(914) 232-4881
By appointment only
Catalogues issued
Edward J. Kearin
Southwestern Americana; Southern
Americana; North Carolina; South
Carolina

Ernest Kionke
175 Buffalo Street
Gowanda, N.Y. 14070
(716) 532-3714
By appointment only
Ernest J. Kionke, Lee Kionke
Children's Books; Ships & The
Sea; Americana; Fiction

Tona Graphics
P. O. Box 58
Grand Island, N.Y. 14072
(716) 773-1292
By appointment only
Catalogues issued
Paul McKenna
Naval & Nautical

Fred Rosselot
586 Route 9 West
Grand View, N.Y. 10960
(914) 358-0254
By appointment only
Fred Rosselot
Freethought; Geology; Americana;
General

Core Collection
11 Middle Neck Road
Great Neck, N.Y. 11021
(516) 466-3676
By mail only
Janine Hughes
Poetry; Reference; Bibliography

GFS Books
P. O. Box 12
Great River, N.Y. 11739
(516) 581-7076
By mail only
Gertrude F. Schweibish
General

Burton's Bookstore
43 Front Street
Greenport, N.Y. 11944
(516) 477-1161
9:30-5:30 Mon-Sat
Joy Regula, Joyce Burton
General

Owl Pen Books
Route 2, Box 202
Greenwich, N.Y. 12834
(518) 692-7039
12-6 Wed-Sun (May-Oct only)
Hank Howard, Edie Brown
Americana; Children's Books;
Fiction; Gardening &
Horticulture; Natural History;
General

JMD Enterprises
271 Locke Road, Box 155
Groton, N.Y. 13073
(607) 898-5114
By appointment only

Catalogues issued
Jim Doty
Science Fiction; Fantasy; Horror;
Mystery & Detective Fiction;
Adventure; Western Books

East West Books, Inc.
5777 Camp Road
Hamburg, N.Y. 14057
(716) 648-4111
10-5:30 Mon-Fri, 10-5 Sat
Catalogues issued
Salvatore M Latona, Valerie
Latona, Kathleen Vincent
Holistic Health & Nutrition;
Philosophy; Psychiatry,
Psychology, & Psychoanalysis; The
Orient & Orientalia; Religion &
Religous History; Occult & Magic

Alan C. Hunter
Harriman Heights Road
Harriman, N.Y. 10926
(914) 783-1930
10-5 Tues-Sat
Alan C. Hunter
Americana, States; Regional
Americana

Harbor Hill Books, Inc.
P. O. Box 407
Harrison, N.Y. 10528
(914) 698-3495
By appointment only
Catalogues issued
Jens J. Christoffersen
New York State; Genealogy;
Adirondacks; Local History

Herb Levart
566 Secor Road
Hartsdale, N.Y. 10530
(914) 946-2060
By appointment only
Herb Levart
Art

Karl Schick
180 East Hartsdale Avenue

Hartsdale, N.Y. 10530
(914) 725-0408
By appointment only
Catalogues issued
Karl Schick
Medicine & Science; Philosophy;
Psychiatry, Psychology, &
Psychoanalysis; Rare Books;
Neurosciences

Riverrun
7 Washington Avenue
Hastings-on-Hudson, N.Y. 10706
(914) 478-4307
11-6 Sat & Sun
Frank Scioscia
20th Century Literature; Modern
First Editions; General

Christopher P. Stephens
7 Terrace Drive
Hastings-on-Hudson, N.Y. 10706
(914) 478-2522
By appointment only
Catalogues issued
Christopher Stephens
Modern First Editions; American
Literature; Science Fiction;
Literature In English Translation;
Autographs & Autograph Material;
Manuscripts

Tesseract
P. O. Box 151
Hastings-on-Hudson, N.Y. 10706
(914) 478-2594
By appointment only
Catalogues issued
David Coffeen, Yola Coffeen
Scientific Instruments; History of
Medicine & Science; Optics

Clifford K. Travis
5 Harvard Lane, Box 111
Hastings-on-Hudson, N.Y. 10706
(914) 473-0931
By appointment only
Catalogues issued
Poetry; Photographic Manuals

H. & R. Salerno
1 Given Court
Hauppauge, N.Y. 11788
(516) 265-3008
By mail only
Catalogues issued
Hank Salerno, Rose Salerno
Science Fiction; Photography; Art
History & Reference; Local
History; Rare Books

Womrath's Bookshop
229 Fulton Avenue
Hempstead, N.Y. 11550
(516) 483-6338
9-6 daily
 Bernard G. Ames
General; New Paperbacks;
Militaria; Marine & Maritime;
Astrology; New Books

Oceanie-Afrique Noire
Route 22, Box C-12
Hillsdale, N.Y. 12529
(518) 325-5400
10-12 & 2-5 Tues-Thurs
Catalogues issued
Lynda Cunningham, Kevin
Cunningham
Primitive & Pre-Columbian
Culture; Africa; Southeast Asia

Rodgers Book Barn
Rodman Road
Hillsdale, N.Y. 12529
10-6 Sat & Sun, plus seasonal
hours
General

Stephen E. Hughes
P. O. Box 108
Holmes, N.Y. 12531
(914) 855-9228
By appointment only
Stephen Hughes
Comic Books; Science Fiction;
Pulps; Baseball

Daniel Hirsch
P. O. Box 315
Hopewell Junction, N.Y. 12533
(914) 462-7404
By appointment only
Catalogues issued
Daniel Hirsch
Children's Books; Illustrated
Books; Rare Books; Literature;
Original Art For Illustration

Grandview Books
439 Warren Street
Hudson, N.Y. 12534
(518) 943-4704
9-3 Tues-Thurs
Oscar Sorge
General

The Village Booksmith
223 Main Street
Hudson Falls, N.Y. 12839
(518) 747-3261
10-5 Mon-Sat, 1-5 Sun
Clifford E. Bruce, April LaMoy
New York State; Cooking;
Performing Arts; Social Sciences;
General

Walter R. Benjamin
664 Scribner Hollow Road, Box
 255
Hunter, N.Y. 12442
(518) 263-4133
By appointment only
Catalogues issued
Mary A. Benjamin, Christopher
Jaeckel
Autographs & Autograph Material;
Continental Books; Presidents;
Civil War & Confederacy;
Literature; Music

Polyanthos Books, Inc.
8 Green Street
Huntington, N.Y. 11743
(516) 271-5558
11-6:30 Mon-Sun
Catalogues issued

David Nottman, Andrew Nottman
*Modern First Editions; Scholarly
Books; German Books &
Literature; French Books &
Literature; Medical & Medicine;
Rare Books*

Janus Books
36 Wyoming Drive
Huntington Station, N.Y. 11746
(516) 271-6454
By mail only
Joan D. Bossi, Sylvia Levin
*Birds & Ornithology; Science
Fiction; Voyages, Travels, &
Exploration; Cooking; Children's
Books; Illustrated Books*

Merriwell Enterprises
P. O. Box 1
Islip, N.Y. 11751
(516) 581-4545
By mail only
W. Kunz
*Series Books For Boys & Girls;
Automotive; Aviation &
Aeronautics; Back Issue
Periodicals; Television & Radio;
Postcards*

The Bookery
215 North Cayuga Street
Ithaca, N.Y. 14850
(607) 273-5055
10-6 Mon-Sat
Catalogues issued
Jack Goldman, Cory Kerns, Adela
Edwards
*Appraisals & Appraisal Services;
Foreign Languages; Philosophy;
STC & Wing Books; History of
Medicine & Science*

Vladimir Dragan
218 University Avenue
Ithaca, N.Y. 14850
(607) 272-3874
By appointment only
Catalogues issued

Vladimir Dragan
*Architecture; Bookplates & Ex
Libris; Bibliography; Scholarly
Books; Rare Books*

Rick Grunder
669 West King Road
Ithaca, N.Y. 14850
(607) 272-3448
By appointment only
Catalogues issued
Rick Grunder
*Mormons; Local History;
Americana; Religion & Religious
History; Manuscripts; Rare Books*

Lillian Herzig-Cohen
34-41 77th Street
Jackson Heights, N.Y. 11372
(718) 472-2102
By appointment only
Lillian Cohen
Juveniles; Miniature Books

Spector The Collector
34-10 94th Street
Jackson Heights, N.Y. 11372
(718) 458-2553
By appointment only
Gladys Spector, George Spector
*Rockwell Kent; Fore-Edge
Paintings; Illustrated Books;
Bindings, Fine & Rare*

Caravan-Maritime Books
87-06 168th Place
Jamaica, N.Y. 11432
(718) 526-1380
By mail only
Catalogues issued
Anne Klein
*Arctica & Antarctica; Marine &
Maritime; Naval & Nautical;
Voyages, Travels, & Exploration;
Whaling; Ships & The Sea*

Jamaica Book Center
146-16 Jamaica Avenue
Jamaica, N.Y. 11435

9-6 Mon-Sat
Joseph Landau, Jack Saviano, Ken
Guarino
*Ships & The Sea; Philosophy;
Judaica & Hebrica; Religion &
Religious History; Psychiatry,
Psychology, & Psychoanalysis;
Technology*

Old & Rare Love Affair
215 Spring Street
Jamestown, N.Y. 14701
(716) 488-1020
10-5 Mon-Fri, 10-3 Sat
Marjorie L. Coons
*New York State; Women; Natural
History; Children's Books;
Voyages, Travels, & Exploration;
Mystery & Detective Fiction*

Ruth Kravette
9 Lewis Avenue
Jericho, N.Y. 11753
(516) 938-9510
By appointment only
Ruth Kravette
Back Issue Magazines

Mrs. K. R. Dorn Book Service
8 Walnut Avenue
Johnstown, N.Y. 12095
(518) 762-9466
9-9 Mon-Sun (but call first)
Betty Dorn
*Western New York State; Natural
History; Birds & Ornithology;
Fishing & Angling; Hunting;
Americana*

Karl Miller
R.D. 2, Box 20
Johnstown, N.Y. 12095
(518) 762-3551
By mail only
Catalogues issued
Karl Miller
Marine & Maritime; Military

Tryon County Bookshop
R.D. 1, Box 207, Route 29
Johnstown, N.Y. 12095
(518) 762-1060
8-8 Mon-Sun
Roger Montgomery, Alice
Montgomery
Fishing & Angling; Hunting;
General

Dalies Devine
R.D. 2, Box 121-C
Katonah, N.Y. 10536
(914) 962-7750
By appointment only
Dalies Devine
Gene Stratton Porter; Alaska;
Western Americana

Katonah Book Scout
75 Meadow Lane
Katonah, N.Y. 10536
By appointment only
Anne M. Lange
Performing Arts; Fiction;
Children's Books; Early &
Collectible Paperbacks; General

Austin Book Shop
P. O. Box 36
Kew Gardens, N.Y. 11415
(718) 441-1199
12-6 Fri & Sat
Catalogues issued
Bernard Titowsky
Immigration; Judaica & Hebrica;
Law; Holocaust; Baseball; Women

Emil Offenbacher
84-50 Austin Street, Box 96
Kew Gardens, N.Y. 11415
(718) 849-5834
By appointment only
Catalogues issued
Emil Offenbacher
Medicine & Science; Technology;
Rare Books; Continental Books;
Printing & Printing History;
Bibliography

L. E. Gobrecht
Kinderhook Antique Center, Box
531, Route 9-H
Kinderhook, N.Y. 12106
(518) 758-7341
10-4 daily
L. E. Gobrecht
Architecture; Decorative Arts;
Hudson River Valley

Harold J. Shoebridge
Maple Hill, Berry Road
Lafayette, N.Y. 13084
(315) 677-3056
By appointment only
Catalogues issued
Harold J. Shoebridge
Bindings, Fine & Rare; New York
State; Color Plate Books; Fore-
Edge Paintings; Inscribed Books

Many Feathers Books
Route 212, Box 117
Lake Hill, N.Y. 12448
(914) 679-6830
By appointment only
Anthony Sackett
General

With Pipe & Book
91 Main Street
Lake Placid, N.Y. 12946
(518) 523-9096
9-6 Mon-Sat, also Sun in summer
Breck Turner, Julie Turner
Adirondacks; Appraisals &
Appraisal Services

F. A. Bernett Inc.
2001 Palmer Avenue
Larchmont, N.Y. 10538
(914) 834-3026
9-5 daily
Catalogues issued
Peter Bernett
Art; Architecture; Archaeology

Book Clearing House
2089 Boston Post Road

Larchmont, N.Y. 10538
(914) 834-4933
8-5 daily
Nancy Smoller, Arnold Smoller
Technology; Reference; Stock
Market & Wall Street;
Dictionaries; Medicine & Science;
Business & Business History

Dog Ink
46 Cooper Lane
Larchmont, N.Y. 10538
(914) 834-9029
By appointment only
Catalogues issued
Kathy Darling
Dogs

Wild Muse
P. O. Box 509
Larchmont, N.Y. 10538
(212) 320-1394
Catalogues issued
Robert McGuire, Susan Colman
First Editions; Cinema & Film

Yesterday's Books
2130 Boston Post Road
Larchmont, N.Y. 10538
(914) 834-6630
12-5:30 Mon-Sat
Michael Merims
General

Hobby Helpers
7369 East Main Street
Lima, N.Y. 14485
(716) 624-4259
By mail only
William F. Buechel
Children's Books; Dogs;
Ephemera; Authors; World's Fairs

Maxwell's Treasures
Lima, N.Y. 14465
(716) 669-2568
11:30-5:30 Sat, Sun, and holidays
George Kennedy, Ruth Kennedy
Local History; Archaeology;

Literature; Ephemera;
Photography

Herpetological Search Service
117 East Santa Barbara Road
Lindenhurst, N.Y. 11757
(516) 957-3624
By mail only
Catalogues issued
Steven Weinkselbaum
Natural History; Herbology &
Herbs

Howard Frisch
P. O. Box 75, Old Post Road
Livingston, N.Y. 12541
(518) 851-7493
11-4 Sat
Catalogues issued
Howard Frisch, Fred Harris
General; Art

Bill The Booky
P. O. Box 6228
Long Island City, N.Y. 11106
(718) 728-4791
By appointment only
Catalogues issued
Bill Epstein, Irma Epstein
Trades; Cartoons & Caricature;
Original Art For Illustration;
Baseball; Boxing; Autographs &
Autograph Material

Michael Huxley
355 Loudon Road
Loudonville, N.Y. 12211
(518) 449-7280
By mail only
Catalogues issued
Michael Huxley
Natural History; Travel; Birds &
Ornithology; Africa; Mammalogy

Jens J. Christoffersen
221 South Barry Avenue
Mamaroneck, N.Y. 10543
(914) 698-3495
By appointment only

Catalogues issued
Jens J. Christoffersen
Rare Books; Greek & Roman
Classics; Illustrated Books; Press
Books & Fine Printing; Books
about Books

Elaine S. Feiden
P. O. Box 410
Mamaroneck, N.Y. 10543
(914) 698-6504
By appointment only
Catalogues issued
Elaine Feiden
Art; Illustrated Books; Literature

George Lewis
P. O. Box 291
Mamaroneck, N.Y. 10543
(914) 698-4579
By appointment only
Catalogues issued
George Lewis
Golf

Victor Tamerlis
911 Stuart Avenue
Mamaroneck, N.Y. 10543
(914) 698-8950
By appointment only
Victor Tamerlis
Illustrated Books; Prints; Art; First
Editions

JFF Autographs, Inc.
P. O. Box U
Manhasset, N.Y. 11030
(516) 354-5338
By appointment only
Catalogues issued
Joseph F. Fawls, Teresa M. Fawls
Presidents; Civil War &
Confederacy; Militaria; Marine &
Maritime; American History;
Astronautics & Rocketry

Balthasar's Books
P. O. Box 0081
Maryknoll, N.Y. 10545

By mail only
Catalogues issued
Mortimer S. Balthasar
Religion & Religous History; First
Editions; Press Books & Fine
Printing

Craig Ross
P. O. Box 148
Medina, N.Y. 14103
(716) 798-1493
By appointment only
Catalogues issued
Craig W. Ross
Americana; Manuscripts;
Ephemera; Rare Books

Carl Sandler Berkowitz
7 Crane Road
Middletown, N.Y. 10940-1806
(914) 692-5324
By mail only
Catalogues issued
Carl S. Berkowitz
Archaeology; Art; History;
Numismatics; Religion & Religous
History; Middle Ages

Cooper Fox Farm
P. O. Box 763
Millbrook, N.Y. 12545
(914) 677-3013
9-5 Sat & Sun (Winters), else 9-5
Tues-Sun
Catalogues issued
George B. Davis
Appraisals & Appraisal Services;
Gardening & Horticulture;
Antiques; Children's Books

Oblong Books & Records
P. O. Box 495
Millerton, N.Y. 12546
(518) 789-3797
R. Hermans
Conservation; General; Women;
New Paperbacks; Maps, Atlases,
& Cartography; Children's Books

Kraus Antiquarian
Route 100
Millwood, N.Y. 10546
(914) 762-2200
By appointment only
Catalogues issued
Kenneth N. Schoen
Art; Books about Books; First Editions; Rare Books; Scholarly Books; General

William-Roberts Company
P. O. Box 543
Mineola, N.Y. 11501
(516) 741-0781
By mail only
Bob Stenard
Maps, Atlases, & Cartography; Antiques; Horology (Clocks)

Abintra, The Bookseller
P. O. Box 700
Morris, N.Y. 13808
(607) 263-2021
By appointment only
Catalogues issued
David Kherdian
Eastern Religions; Mysticism; Metaphysics; Folklore; Myths & Mythology

Pages Antiquarian Books
16 Dakin Avenue
Mount Kisco, N.Y. 10549
(914) 555-8281
By appointment only
Catalogues issued
Lew Goldmann, Bruce Heckman
Hudson River Valley; Ephemera; Prints; Westchester County (New York State)

Paul P. Appel
216 Washington Street
Mount Vernon, N.Y. 10553
(914) 667-7365
By appointment only
Paul P. Appel
Art; Modern First Editions;

Literary Criticism; Literature; Foreign Languages

The Caren Archive
P. O. Box 303
Nanuet, N.Y. 10954
(914) 624-3693
By appointment only
Catalogues issued
Eric C. Caren
Newspapers; Back Issue Periodicals; Pamphlets; Photography

Hemlock Books
170 Beach 145th Street
Neponsit, N.Y. 11694
(718) 318-0737
By appointment only
Catalogues issued
Sheila Shaftel, Norman Shaftel
Medicine & Science

L. H. McGill
41 Third Street
New City, N.Y. 10956
(914) 634-0729
By appointment only
Lawrence McGill
General

Grover J. Askins
P. O. Box 386, 2 West Street
New Lebanon, N.Y. 12125
(518) 794-8833
10-6 Fri-Mon
Grover J. Askins
Scholarly Books; Americana; General

The Cat Book Center
P. O. Box 112
New Rochelle, N.Y. 10804
(914) 235-2698
By mail only
Catalogues issued
G. Zeehandelaar
Cats

Abraham's Magazine Service
56 East 13th Street
New York, N.Y. 10003
(212) 777-4700
By mail only
Stephen J. Baron
Back Issue Periodicals; Reprints

Academy Book Store
10 West 18th Street
New York, N.Y. 10011
(212) 242-4848
10-9 Mon-Sat, 11-7 Sun
Alan Weiner
First Editions; Literature; Art; Performing Arts; Psychiatry, Psychology, & Psychoanalysis; Philosophy

Acanthus Books
48 West 22nd Street, No. 4
New York, N.Y. 10010
By appointment only
Catalogues issued
Barry Cenower
Decorative Arts; Antiques; Architecture

William Altman
515 Madison Avenue
New York, N.Y. 10022
(212) 838-8987
By mail only
William Altman
Dance; Music; Typography & Type Specimens

Ampersand Books
P. O. Box 674
New York, N.Y. 10276
(212) 674-6795
By mail only
Catalogues issued
George Bixby
Modern First Editions; Ephemera; Little Magazines & Literary Small Presses; 20th Century Literature; Appraisals & Appraisal Services

Antiquarian Booksellers' Center
50 Rockefeller Plaza
New York, N.Y. 10020
(212) 246-2564
10-5 Mon-Fri
Peter Courmont
Rare Books

The Apothecary
P. O. Box 778
New York, N.Y. 10021
By mail only
A. N. Real
History of Medicine & Science;
Ephemera; Cartoons & Caricature

Appelfeld Gallery
1372 York Avenue
New York, N.Y. 10021
(212) 988-7835
10-6 Mon-Fri, 11-3 Sat
Catalogues issued
Louis Appelfeld, Joseph Kaminksy
Appraisals & Appraisal Services;
Bindings, Fine & Rare; Literature;
Color Plate Books; Rare Books;
Sets

W. Graham Arader III
23 East 74th Street
New York, N.Y. 10021
(212) 628-3668
9-5 daily
Catalogues issued
Tom McLaughlin
Indians & Eskimos; Maps, Atlases,
& Cartography; Natural History;
Prints; Americana; Color Plate
Books

Argosy Book Store
116 East 59th Street
New York, N.Y. 10022
(212) 753-4455
9-6 Mon-Fri, 10-5 Sat
Catalogues issued
Louis Cohen, Judith Lowry
Americana; History of Medicine
& Science; Maps, Atlases, &

Cartography; First Editions;
Autographs & Autograph Material

Richard B. Arkway, Inc.
538 Madison Avenue
New York, N.Y. 10022
(212) 751-8135
10-5 Mon-Fri
Catalogues issued
Richard B. Arkway, Robert
Augustine
History of Medicine & Science;
Voyages, Travels, & Exploration;
Maps, Atlases, & Cartography;
Illustrated Books

Arte Primitivo
3 East 65th Street
New York, N.Y. 10021
(212) 355-1433
11-5 Mon-Sat
Mildred F. Kaplan
Primitive & Pre-Columbian
Culture

Asian American Materials
165 West 66th Street
New York, N.Y. 10023
By mail only
Catalogues issued
Yoshio Kishi
Immigration; The Orient &
Orientalia; Japan; Asians in
America

Asian Rare Books
234 Fifth Avenue, 3rd floor
New York, N.Y. 10001
(718) 259-3732
By mail only
Catalogues issued
Stephen Feldman
Asia; Middle East; The Orient &
Orientalia; Voyages, Travels, &
Exploration; Japan

Bart Auerbach, Ltd.
411 West End Avenue
New York, N.Y. 10024

(212) 724-4054
By appointment only
Catalogues issued
Bart Auerbach
English Literature; 19th Century
Literature; 20th Century
Literature; Manuscripts;
Appraisals & Appraisal Services

Fernand Baer Jr.
903 Park Avenue
New York, N.Y. 10021
(212) 861-8357
By appointment only
Fernand Baer Jr.
Art Deco & Art Nouveau

Brian Bailey
496-A Hudson Street, suite D-9
New York, N.Y. 10014
(212) 228-5032
By appointment only
Catalogues issued
Brian Bailey
Art; Modern First Editions;
Autographs & Autograph Material

The Ballet Shop
1887 Broadway
New York, N.Y. 10023
(212) 581-7990
11-8 Mon-Sat, 12-7 Sun
Catalogues issued
Dance; Opera; Show Business

Barnstable Books
799 Broadway
New York, N.Y. 10003
By mail only
Catalogues issued
E. Krastin
Modern First Editions;
Bibliography; Scholarly Books

J. N. Bartfield Galleries
30 West 57th Street
New York, N.Y. 10019
(212) 245-8890
10-5 Mon-Fri, 10-3 Sat

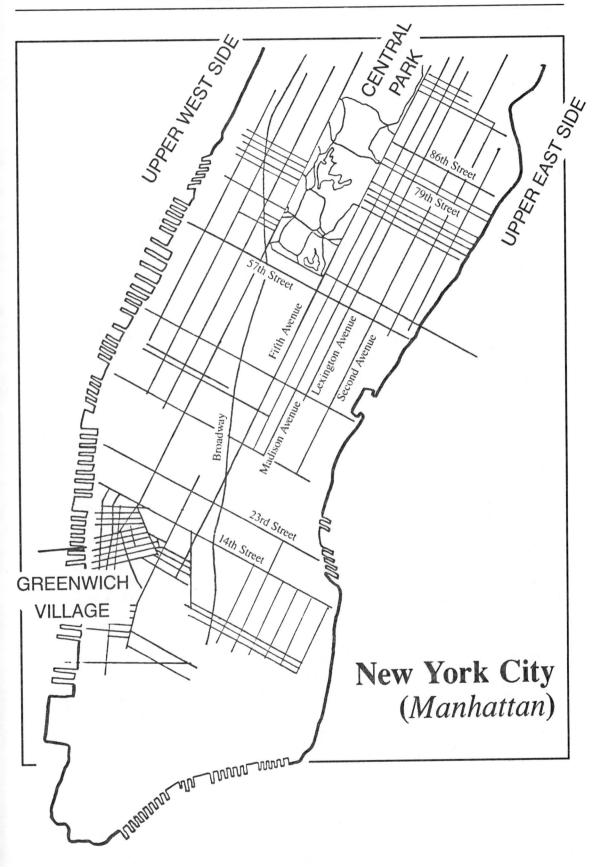

UPPER WEST SIDE

CENTRAL PARK

UPPER EAST SIDE

86th Street

79th Street

57th Street

Fifth Avenue

Lexington Avenue

Second Avenue

Broadway

Madison Avenue

23rd Street

14th Street

GREENWICH
VILLAGE

New York City
(*Manhattan*)

Catalogues issued
Art; Art, Western; Paintings

J. N. Bartfield Books, Inc.
30 West 57th Street
New York, N.Y. 10019
(212) 245-8890
10-5 Mon-Fri, 10-3 Sat
George Murray, Bibi Mohamed
Sets; Color Plate Books; Maps,
Atlases, & Cartography; Voyages,
Travels, & Exploration;
Americana; Natural History

C. Richard Becker
238 West 14th Street
New York, N.Y. 10111
(212) 243-3789
By appointment only
Catalogues issued
C. Richard Becker
Decorative Arts; Art History &
Reference; Collecting &
Collectibles; Books about Books

Bill George International
200 East 66th Street, Suite C-1702
New York, N.Y. 10021
(212) 790-1448
By appointment only
William G. Smith
Bindings, Fine & Rare; Travel;
Geography; Maps, Atlases, &
Cartography

Black Sun Books
220 East 60th Street
New York, N.Y. 10022
(212) 688-6622
9-5 Mon-Fri
Catalogues issued
Linda Tucker, Harvey Tucker
Press Books & Fine Printing; First
Editions; Illustrated Books;
Drawings; Manuscripts; Rare
Books

The Book Chest
300 East 75th Street

New York, N.Y. 10021-3305
(212) 772-3498
By appointment only
Catalogues issued
Estelle Chessid
Humor; Color Plate Books;
Children's Books; Poetry

Booklord's
P. O. Box 177
New York, N.Y. 10009
(212) 677-4547
By mail only
Catalogues issued
Bern Meyer
Television & Radio; Cinema &
Film

Book Quest
301 East 21st Street, suite 13-C
New York, N.Y. 10010
(212) 677-4564
By appointment only
Catalogues issued
Isabel Cymerman
Biography & Autobiography;
General

Book Ranger
105 Charles Street
New York, N.Y. 10014
(212) 924-4957
By appointment only
Americana; Art; Marine &
Maritime; Voyages, Travels, &
Exploration

Books & Company
939 Madison Avenue
New York, N.Y. 10021
(212) 737-1450
10-6 Mon-Sat, 11:30-6 Sun
Peter Philbrook
20th Century Literature; Art;
Philosophy

Books 'n Things
64 East 7th Street
New York, N.Y. 10003

(212) 533-2320
1-6 Mon-Sat
Gertrude Briggs
Performing Arts; Dance; Cinema
& Film; Poetry; Literature;
Postcards

Books Of Wonder
132 Seventh Avenue
New York, N.Y. 10011
(212) 989-3270
11-9 Mon-Sat, 12-6 Sun
Catalogues issued
Peter Glassman, James Carey
Children's Books; Illustrated
Books; L. Frank Baum & Oziana;
Fantasy; Juveniles; Folklore

Brazenhead Book Store
215 East 84th Street
New York, N.Y. 10028
(212) 861-4704
4:30-8:30 Mon-Fri, 2-7 Sat
Michael Seidenberg
Modern First Editions

Martin Breslauer, Inc.
P. O. Box 607
New York, N.Y. 10028
(212) 794-2995
By appointment only
Catalogues issued
Bernard Breslauer, E. W. Grieb
Illustrated Books; Bindings, Fine
& Rare; Incunabula; Manuscripts

Elliott W. Brill
697 West End Avenue
New York, N.Y. 10025
(212) 864-1269
By mail only
Elliott W. Brill
Judaica & Hebraica

Broude Brothers Ltd.
170 Varick Street
New York, N.Y. 10013
(212) 242-7001
By appointment only

Catalogues issued
Art; Music; Performing Arts

Brownstone Books (Phillips)
18 West 9th Street
New York, N.Y. 10011
(212) 982-6495
By appointment only
Martin Hutner
American Literature; Bibliography;
Books about Books; Printing &
Printing History

Bryn Mawr Book Shop
502 East 79th Street
New York, N.Y. 10021
(212) 744-7682
10:30-4:30 Thurs-Sat, 12-4:30 Sun
Jane Rhodes, Lillian Sholin
General; Phonograph Records

Susi Buchanan
325 East 79th Street
New York, N.Y. 10021
(212) 288-4018
By mail only
Susi Buchanan, John Buchanan
Children's Books; Illustrated
Books; Americana; Sporting;
Gardening & Horticulture;
General

Jutta Buck
4 East 95th Street
New York, N.Y. 10128
(212) 289-4577
By appointment only
Jutta Buck
Color Plate Books; Illustrated
Books; Botany; Natural History;
Prints

Camel Book Company
P. O. Box 1936
New York, N.Y. 10025
By mail only
Catalogues issued
Carl Wurtzel, Faith Wurtzel
Middle East; Islam; Israel; Judaica

& Hebrica; Arab World; North
Africa

Carnegie Book Shop
30 East 60th Street
New York, N.Y. 10022
(212) 755-4861
9-4 Mon-Fri
David Kirschenbaum
Rare Books; Autographs &
Autograph Material; Manuscripts;
Americana

James F. Carr
220 East 81st Street
New York, N.Y. 10028
(212) 535-8110
12-5 Tues-Fri, 10-5 Sat
James F. Carr, Leonard E. Piasecki
Art; Inscribed Books; Rare Books;
General

JoAnn & Richard Casten Ltd
101 West 81st Street
New York, N.Y. 10024
(212) 496-5483
By appointment only
Catalogues issued
JoAnn Casten, Richard Casten
Maps, Atlases, & Cartography;
Rare Books

Richard Chalfin
118 West 72nd Street
New York, N.Y. 10023
By appointment only
Richard Chalfin
Book Scouts; Jack London

Chartwell Booksellers
55 East 52nd Street
New York, N.Y. 10055
9:30-6:30 Mon-Fri (11-5 Sat in
Fall)
Catalogues issued
Barry Singer, Suzanne Vuillet
Sir Winston Churchill; Modern
First Editions

Michael Chessler
90 Hudson Street
New York, N.Y. 10013
(212) 219-1696
By appointment only
Catalogues issued
Michael Chessler
Mountaineering; Voyages, Travels,
& Exploration; Tibet; Asia; Skiing

Chip's Booksearch
P. O. Box 123
New York, N.Y. 10024
(212) 580-9434
By appointment only
Catalogues issued
Chip Greenberg
Modern First Editions; Literature;
Literary Criticism

Chip's Bookshop, Inc.
P. O. Box 639
New York, N.Y. 10003
(212) 362-9336
Catalogues issued
Emily Pearlman
English Literature; First Editions;
Literary Criticism; Scholarly
Books; Collection Development

Cinemabilia, Inc.
611 Broadway, suite 203
New York, N.Y. 10012
(212) 533-6686
11-7 Mon-Sat (to 6 Mon and Sat)
Catalogues issued
Ernest Burns
Cinema & Film

Collectors' Editions
P. O. Box 20422, Cherokee Station
New York, N.Y. 10028-9991
(212) 288-3649
By appointment only
Catalogues issued
Carol Fruchter
Photography; Decorative Arts;
Books about Books; Trade

Catalogues; Illustrated Books;
Posters

Comic Art Shop
231 East 53rd Street
New York, N.Y. 10022
(212) 759-6255
11-7 Mon-Sat (Thur & Fri to 8)
Comic Books

The Compulsive Collector
1082 Madison Avenue
New York, N.Y. 10028
(212) 879-7443
1-6 Wed-Sat
Ami Megiddo, Cindy Megiddo
Art; Illustrated Books; Scholarly
Books; Judaica & Hebrica

Continental Book Search
P. O. Box 1183
New York, N.Y. 10009
(212) 254-8719
By mail only
Catalogues issued
Alvin M. Katz
Search Service, With Stock

James Cummins, Inc.
859 Lexington Avenue, 2nd floor
New York, N.Y. 10017
(212) 249-6901
10-6 Mon-Fri
Catalogues issued
James Cummins, Timothy Johns,
Melvin Krapola
Sporting; Press Books & Fine
Printing; Color Plate Books;
Voyages, Travels, & Exploration;
First Editions; Illustrated Books

Mitchell R. Cutler
61 West 37th Street
New York, N.Y. 10018
(212) 921-9234
By appointment only
Mitchell R. Cutler
American Illustrative Art; Design

Howard C. Daitz
P. O. Box 530
New York, N.Y. 10113-0530
(212) 929-8987
9-9 daily
Howard C. Daitz
Photography; Photographically
Illustrated Books

Keith de Lellis
520 East 72nd Street
New York, N.Y. 10021
(212) 288-1827
By appointment only
Catalogues issued
Keith de Lellis
Photography; Photographically
Illustrated Books

Donan Books, Inc.
235 East 53rd Street
New York, N.Y. 10022
(212) 421-6210
9-4 Mon-Fri
Mr. Dreyfuss
Search Service, With Stock

Philip C. Duschnes, Inc.
201 East 66th Street, Apt. 17-L
New York, N.Y. 10021
(212) 861-7832
By appointment only
Catalogues issued
Mrs. P. C. Duschnes
Books about Books; Modern First
Editions; Illuminated Manuscripts;
Illustrated Books; Press Books &
Fine Printing; Limited Editions
Club

Eeyore's Books for Children #1
1066 Madison Avenue
New York, N.Y. 10028
(212) 988-3404
10-6 Mon-Sat, 12-5 Sun
Catalogues issued
Children's Books; Parenting &
Child Care; Games & Pastimes;

Education; Video Cassette &
Compact Disks

Eeyore's Books For Children #2
2212 Broadway
New York, N.Y. 10024
(212) 362-0634
10-6 Mon-Sat, 10:30-5 Sun
Catalogues issued
Children's Books; Parenting &
Child Care; Games & Pastimes;
Education; Video Cassette &
Compact Disks

M. M. Einhorn Maxwell
80 East 11th Street
New York, N.Y. 10003
(212) 228-6767
By mail only
Catalogues issued
Marilyn M. Einhorn, Lawrence R.
Maxwell
Beverages; Dance; Cooking;
Shakespeare; Puppetry &
Marionettes

El Cascajero
506 West Broadway (LaGuardia
Place)
New York, N.Y. 10012
(212) 254-0905
By appointment only
Catalogues issued
Anthony Gran, Sally Gran
Latin America; Archaeology;
Architecture; Art

Fay Elliott
149 East 73rd Street
New York, N.Y. 10021
(212) 772-1271
By appointment only
Catalogues issued
Fay Elliott
Modern First Editions; 19th
Century Literature; 20th Century
Literature; Literature;
Manuscripts; Association Copies

Allan Elsner Book Shop
900 First Avenue
New York, N.Y. 10022
(212) 688-4577
11:30-5:30 daily
Allan Elsner
General

L'Estampe Originale
120 E. 36th Street (Dolmatch
Group)
New York, N.Y. 10016
By appointment only
Catalogues issued
Sandra Safris
Illustrated Books; Prints; Posters

Ex Libris
160A East 70th Street
New York, N.Y. 10021
(212) 249-2618
10-5 daily
Catalogues issued
W. Michael Sheehe, Elaine L.
Cohen
*Avant Garde, Experimental, &
Modern Art; Architecture; Graphic
Arts; Little Magazines & Literary
Small Presse; Posters;
Photography*

Facsimile Book Shop
16 West 55th Street
New York, N.Y. 10019
(212) 581-2672
10-6:30 daily
Catalogues issued
Kevin T. McEneaney
*Ireland & The Irish; Folklore;
Poetry*

Fantasy Archives
71 Eighth Avenue
New York, N.Y. 10014
(212) 929-5391
By appointment only
Catalogues issued
Eric Kramer
Science Fiction; Fantasy; Horror;

*Edgar Rice Burroughs; Original
Art For Illustration; Stephen King*

Bob Fein
150 Fifth Avenue
New York, N.Y. 10011
(212) 807-0489
12-6 Mon-Sat
Catalogues issued
Bob Fein
*Indians & Eskimos; Archaeology;
Primitive & Pre-Columbian
Culture; Latin America; South
America*

William Fern
180 East 79th Street
New York, N.Y. 10021
(212) 988-1312
By appointment only
William Fern
*English Literature; Judaica &
Hebrica*

Firsts & Company
1066 Madison Avenue
New York, N.Y. 10028
(212) 249-4122
By appointment only
Catalogues issued
Arnold A. Rogow
*Modern First Editions; Autographs
& Autograph Material; Rare Books*

Peter Thomas Fisher
41 Union Square West
New York, N.Y. 10003
(212) 255-6789
By mail only
Peter Thomas Fisher
*New Books; German Books &
Literature*

John F. Fleming, Inc.
322 East 57th Street
New York, N.Y. 10022
(212) 755-3242
By appointment only
John F. Fleming

*First Editions; Rare Books;
Manuscripts*

Linda Campbell Franklin
P. O. Box 383
New York, N.Y. 10156
(212) 679-6038
By mail only
Catalogues issued
Linda C. Franklin
Cooking

Ralph Gardner
135 Central Park West
New York, N.Y. 10023
(212) 877-6820
By mail only
Ralph Gardner
*Authors; Autographs & Autograph
Material; Bibliography; Books
about Books; Children's Books;
First Editions*

John Taylor Gatto
235 West 76th Street
New York, N.Y. 10023
(212) 874-3631
By appointment only
Catalogues issued
*Mushrooms; Fantasy; Arctica &
Antarctica; Erotica; Chemical &
Substance Abuse*

Gem Antiques
1088 Madison Avenue
New York, N.Y. 10028
(212) 535-7399
10:30-5:30 Mon-Sat
Jack Feingold
Ceramics & Glass; Decorative Arts

Stanley Gilman
P. O. Box 131, Cooper Stn.
New York, N.Y. 10276
Stanley Gilman
General

Nancy Sheiry Glaister
P. O. Box 6477

New York, N.Y. 10128
(212) 348-5284
By appointment only
Catalogues issued
Nancy S. Glaister
*Architecture; City & Urban
Planning; Landscape Architecture;
Gardening & Horticulture*

Eileen Campbell Gordon
109 St. Marks Place
New York, N.Y. 10009
(212) 254-6544
12-8 daily
Catalogues issued
E. C. Gordon
*Ireland & The Irish; Languages;
Myths & Mythology; Folklore;
Fantasy; Arthurian Legend*

Elliot Gordon
250 West 94th Street
New York, N.Y. 10025
(212) 861-2892
By appointment only
Elliot Gordon
Art; Books about Books

Martin Gordon, Inc.
25 East 83rd Street
New York, N.Y. 10028
(212) 249-7350
By appointment only
Martin Gordon
*Art; Reference; Prints; Catalogues
Raisonnes*

Gotham Book Mart
41 West 47th Street
New York, N.Y. 10036
(212) 719-4448
9:30-6:30 Mon-Sat
Catalogues issued
Andreas Brown, Matthew
Monahan, Philip Lyman
*Modern First Editions; Cinema &
Film; Literature; Little Magazines
& Literary Small Presses;
Performing Arts; Poetry*

K. Gregory
222 East 71st Street
New York, N.Y. 10021
(212) 288-2119
By appointment only
Catalogues issued
K. Gregory
*Botany; Color Plate Books;
Miniature Books; Prints*

Gryphon Bookshop #2
220 West 80th Street
New York, N.Y. 10024
(212) 496-7911
1 p.m.-9 p.m. Mon.-Sun
Musical Scores; Scholarly Books

Gryphon Bookshop #1
2246 Broadway
New York, N.Y. 10024
(212) 362-0706
10 a.m.-midnight Mon-Sun
Henry Holman
*Children's Books; Modern First
Editions; Art; Performing Arts;
Phonograph Records; General*

Gryphon Record Shop
606 Amsterdam Avenue
New York, N.Y. 10024
(212) 874-1588
10:30-6:30 Mon-Sat
Phonograph Records

Hacker Art Books, Inc.
54 West 57th Street
New York, N.Y. 10019
(212) 757-1450
9-6 Mon-Sat
Catalogues issued
Seymour Hacker
*Art; Archaeology; Architecture;
Antiques; Illustrated Books; Africa*

Lathrop C. Harper Inc.
175 Fifth Avenue
New York, N.Y. 10010
(212) 529-1960
By appointment only

Catalogues issued
Felix Oyens
*Incunabula; Illustrated Books;
Bindings, Fine & Rare;
Manuscripts*

W. S. Heinman
P. O. Box 926
New York, N.Y. 10023
(212) 787-3154
By appointment only
W. S. Heinman
Dictionaries

J.-N. Herlin, Inc.
68 Thompson Street
New York, N.Y. 10012
(212) 431-8732
11-6:30 Mon-Fri, 2-6:30 Sat
Jean-Noel Herlin
*Art; Avant Garde, Experimental,
& Modern Art; Ephemera; Posters;
Art Catalogues, Periodicals, &
Books; Livre d'Artiste*

Jonathan A. Hill
470 West End Avenue
New York, N.Y. 10024
(212) 496-7856
By appointment only
Catalogues issued
Jonathan A. Hill, Jane R. Folger
*Medicine & Science; Bibliography;
Printing & Printing History;
Voyages, Travels, & Exploration*

Hillman Books
53 East 75th Street, suite 3-A
New York, N.Y. 10021
(212) 737-2287
10-5 Mon-Fri
Catalogues issued
Giampiero Zazzera, Liz Marcucci
*Cooking; Wines; Medicine &
Science; Natural History; Rare
Books*

Glenn Horowitz
141 East 44th Street

New York, N.Y. 10017
(212) 557-1381
10-5:30 daily
Catalogues issued
Glenn Horowitz, Aaron Horowitz
Modern First Editions;
Manuscripts; Autographs &
Autograph Material

Edward Howe
280 Rector Place
New York, N.Y. 10280
By mail only
Ed Howe
Architecture; Printing & Printing
History; Press Books & Fine
Printing; Graphic Arts;
Calligraphy; Ephemera

Ideal Book Store
1125 Amsterdam Avenue
New York, N.Y. 10025
(212) 662-1909
10-6 Mon-Sat
Catalogues issued
A. Lutwak
Russia & Slavic Countries; Judaica
& Hebrica; Middle East;
Philosophy

Inner Circle Books
6 West 18th Street
New York, N.Y. 10011
(212) 691-2596
By appointment only
Anatole Kondratieff
Imprints; Foreign Languages;
Travel; Science

International University Books
30 Irving Place
New York, N.Y. 10003
(212) 254-4100
9-5 daily
Catalogues issued
Africa; Collection Development;
Business & Business History;
Medicine & Science; Back Issue
Periodicals; Social Sciences

Harmer Johnson Books Ltd.
38 East 64th Street
New York, N.Y. 10021
(212) 752-1189
11-5 Mon-Fri
Catalogues issued
Harmer Johnson, Peter Sharrer
Art, African; Indians & Eskimos;
Primitive & Pre-Columbian
Culture; Archaeology

Maxine Kaplan
60 East 12th Street
New York, N.Y. 10003
(212) 260-5173
By mail only
Maxine Kaplan, Howard Kopelson
Art; Architecture; Photography;
General

Kim Kaufman
1370 Lexington Avenue
New York, N.Y. 10128
(212) 369-3384
By appointment only
Catalogues issued
Kim Kaufman, Sean Devlin
Fiction; Children's Books;
Illustrated Books; Original Art For
Illustration; Reference

The Keshcarrigan Bookshop
90 West Broadway
New York, N.Y. 10007
(212) 962-4237
11-5 Mon-Fri, 12-5 Sat
Angela Carter
Ireland & The Irish

Yoshio Kishi
165 West 66th Street
New York, N.Y. 10023
(212) 787-7954
By mail only
Catalogues issued
Yoshio Kishi
Authors; Modern First Editions;
Asians in America

J. & P. Klemperer
400 Second Avenue
New York, N.Y. 10010
(212) 684-5970
By appointment only
Catalogues issued
Peter Klemperer, Judith Klemperer
New York City & Metropolitan
Region; Ephemera; Postcards;
General

H. P. Kraus
16 East 46th Street
New York, N.Y. 10017
(212) 687-4808
9:30-5 Mon-Fri
Catalogues issued
Hans P. Kraus, Kit Currie, Roland
Folter
Incunabula; Maps, Atlases, &
Cartography; Americana;
Medieval Manuscripts; Science

Madeline Kripke
317 West 11th Street
New York, N.Y. 10014
(212) 989-6832
By appointment only
Catalogues issued
Madeline Kripke
Dictionaries; Linguistics; Rare
Books

Lambeth Books
143 East 37th Street
New York, N.Y. 10016
(212) 679-0163
By mail only
Catalogues issued
Richard Newman
Black Literature & Studies; Africa

Landmark Book Company
260 Fifth Avenue
New York, N.Y. 10001
(212) 696-5430
By mail only
Catalogues issued
Henry Shelley, Dee Shelley

Art; Architecture; Poetry;
Bibliography; Decorative Arts

La Valois Books
P. O. Box 386
New York, N.Y. 10028
(212) 722-1877
By mail only
Henry K. Fried, David L. Caraway
French Books & Literature;
Documents; Ephemera; Rare
Books

Larry Lawrence
P. O. Box 265
New York, N.Y. 10013
(212) 362-8593
By mail only
Catalogues issued
Larry Lawrence
Americana; Autographs &
Autograph Material; Books about
Books; Television & Radio; Golf;
Bindings, Fine & Rare

Janet Lehr
P. O. Box 617
New York, N.Y. 10028
(212) 288-6234
By appointment only
Catalogues issued
Janet Lehr
Photography; Illustrated Books;
Reference; Manuscripts

Barbara Leibowits
80 Central Park West
New York, N.Y. 10023
(212) 769-0105
By appointment only
Catalogues issued
Barbara Leibowits
Drawings; Illustrated Books;
Posters; Prints

Lion Heart Autographs
12 West 37th Street
New York, N.Y. 10018
(212) 695-1310

8:30-5 daily
Catalogues issued
David H. Lowenherz
Autographs & Autograph Material;
Documents; Manuscripts;
Photography

James Lowe
30 East 60th Street
New York, N.Y. 10022
(212) 759-0795
9-5 Mon-Fri
Catalogues issued
James Lowe, Sal Alberti
Appraisals & Appraisal Services;
Autographs & Autograph Material;
Documents; Manuscripts;
Photography

Magazine Center
1133 Broadway
New York, N.Y. 10010
(212) 929-5255
11-8 Mon-Fri
Catalogues issued
H. B. Quoyoon
Art; Little Magazines & Literary
Small Presses; Back Issue
Periodicals; Back Issue Magazines;
P. G. Wodehouse

Manor Gems
305 West 24th Street, suite 18-C
New York, N.Y. 10010
(212) 889-0498
By appointment only
Catalogues issued
Norma Ponard
Middle East; Asia; The Orient &
Orientalia; Africa; Rare Books

Martayan/Lan
36 West 9th Street
New York, N.Y. 10011
(212) 529-6688
By appointment only
Catalogues issued
Seyla Martayan, Richard Lan
Science; Americana; Architecture;

Maps, Atlases, & Cartography;
Prints

Memory Shop
109 East 12th Street
New York, N.Y. 10003
(212) 473-2404
10-6 Mon-Sat
Mark Ricci
Cinema & Film; Photography;
Posters

Isaac Mendoza Book Company
15 Ann Street
New York, N.Y. 10038
(212) 227-8777
10-6 Mon-Fri, 11-5 Sat
Walter Caron, Gilbert Farley
Science Fiction; Modern First
Editions; Mystery & Detective
Fiction

Marjorie Miele
145 East 35th Street, No. 3-FW
New York, N.Y. 10016
(212) 725-1429
By appointment only
Marjorie Miele
First Editions

Milestone Books Inc.
303 Fifth Avenue, suite 1503
New York, N.Y. 10016
(212) 679-6332
10-5 daily
Irving Zucker, Zucker Mrs.
Illustrated Books; Natural History;
Rare Books

The Military Bookman Ltd.
29 East 93rd Street
New York, N.Y. 10128
(212) 348-1280
10:30-5:30 Tues-Sat
Catalogues issued
Margaret Colt, Harris Colt, Jason
Duberman
Militaria; Marine & Maritime;
Aviation & Aeronautics; Civil War

& *Confederacy; World Wars;*
American History

Arthur H. Minters
39 West 14th Street, No. 401
New York, N.Y. 10011
(212) 989-0593
10-6 Mon-Fri
Catalogues issued
Arthur H. Minters
Architecture; Art; Ephemera;
Literature; Back Issue Periodicals;
Photography

P. Matthew Monahan
214 Riverside Drive, No. 410
New York, N.Y. 10025
(212) 663-8232
By appointment only
Matthew Monahan
Modern First Editions; 20th
Century Literature; Poetry; Fiction

Moriah Antique Judaica
699 Madison Avenue
New York, N.Y. 10021
(212) 751-7090
9-5 Mon-Thurs, 9-4 Fri
Peter Ehrenthal, Michael Ehrenthal
Illuminated Manuscripts; Judaica
& Hebrica

Bradford Morrow
33 West 9th Street
New York, N.Y. 10011
(212) 477-1136
By appointment only
Bradford Morrow
Modern First Editions;
Manuscripts; Bibliography; Books
about Books; Press Books & Fine
Printing; Autographs & Autograph
Material

Museum Books, Inc.
6 West 37th Street
New York, N.Y. 10018
(212) 563-2770
10-5 Mon-Fri

Catalogues issued
Nicole Kostean
Graphic Arts; Printing & Printing
History; Art, Books about

New York Bound Bookshop
43 West 54th Street
New York, N.Y. 10019
(212) 245-8503
10-5:30 Tues-Fri, 12-5 Sat (Sat in
Winter only)
Catalogues issued
Barbara Cohen
New York City & Metropolitan
Region; New York State;
Americana; World's Fairs;
Ephemera

999 Bookshop
999 Madison Avenue
New York, N.Y. 10021
(212) 288-9439
9:30-6 Mon-Fri, 10-5 Sat, 12-5
Sun
Catalogues issued
Joan Gers, Betty Ellsworth, Morris
Bender
Art; Reference; Decorative Arts;
Fiction; Gardening & Horticulture

NRS Books
1181 Amsterdam Avenue
New York, N.Y. 10027
10-7 daily
Paul Solano
Sets; Modern Library Publishing
Company; Poetry; Drama; Fiction;
Biography & Autobiography

Harry Nudel
135 Spring Street
New York, N.Y. 10012
(212) 966-5624
By appointment only
Catalogues issued
Harry Nudel
Modern First Editions; Illustrated
Books; Photography; Black
Literature & Studies

Oceanic Primitive Arts
88 East 10th Street, 2nd floor
New York, N.Y. 10003
(212) 982-8060
By appointment only
Catalogues issued
Lynda Cunningham, Kevin
Cunningham
Art, African; Southeast Asia;
Australia & New Zealand; Jewelry;
Textiles

The Old Print Shop, Inc.
150 Lexington Avenue
New York, N.Y. 10016
(212) 683-3950
9-5 daily
Catalogues issued
Maps, Atlases, & Cartography;
Prints; Paintings

Pageant Book & Print Shop
109 East 9th Street
New York, N.Y. 10003
(212) 674-5296
10-6:30 Mon-Sat
Shirley Solomon
First Editions; Prints; Maps,
Atlases, & Cartography;
Literature; Americana; Rare Books

Paperback Exchange
355 East 86th Street
New York, N.Y. 10028
(212) 369-5023
11-10 Mon-Thurs, 10-11 Fri-Sat,
12-9 Sun
Gennaro Pugliese
Mystery & Detective Fiction; New
Paperbacks; Greek & Roman
Classics

Paragon Book Gallery
2130 Broadway
New York, N.Y. 10023
(212) 496-2378
10-5:45 Mon-Fri, 11-5 Sat
Catalogues issued
Linda Kramer, Roberta Huber

The Orient & Orientalia; China;
Japan; Asia; Middle East

Paths Untrodden
P. O. Box 459
New York, N.Y. 10014-0459
(212) 924-5421
Walter J. Phillips
Gay & Lesbian Literature

Performing Arts Books
18 East 16th Street, room 202
New York, N.Y. 10003
(212) 645-9576
11-6 Mon-Tues & Thurs-Sat
Catalogues issued
Richard Stoddard
Appraisals & Appraisal Services;
Cinema & Film; Ephemera;
Performing Arts; Fashion

Elizabeth Phillips
108 East 38th Street
New York, N.Y. 10016
(212) 684-2369
By appointment only
Catalogues issued
Elizabeth Phillips
Illustrated Books;
Photographically Illustrated
Books; Livre d'Artiste

Philosophical Library
200 West 57th Street
New York, N.Y. 10019
(212) 265-6050
9:30-5 daily
Catalogues issued
Rose Runes
Philosophy; Religion & Religous
History; Psychiatry, Psychology,
& Psychoanalysis; Literature;
History; Social Sciences

Phoenix Book Shop
22 Jones Street
New York, N.Y. 10014
(212) 675-2795
12-6 Mon-Fri, 12-5 Sun

Catalogues issued
Robert A. Wilson, Richard
Schaubeck
Modern First Editions; Poetry;
Little Magazines & Literary Small
Presses

A Photographers Place
133 Mercer Street
New York, N.Y. 10012
(212) 431-9358
11-6 Mon-Sat, 12-5 Sun
Catalogues issued
Harvey Zucker, Gene Bourne
Photography; Stereoviews

Photographica Ltd.
224 East 68th Street
New York, N.Y. 10021
(212) 288-7741
1-6 Wed-Sat
Marjorie Neikrug
Civil War & Confederacy;
Photography; Photographically
Illustrated Books

Pomander Book Shop
252 West 95th Street
New York, N.Y. 10025
(212) 866-1777
12-8 every day
Suzanne Zavrian, C. R. Goez
Art; Philosophy; Religion &
Religious History; History;
Biography & Autobiography;
Literature

Poster America
138 West 18th Street
New York, N.Y. 10011
(212) 206-0499
11-6 Tues-Sat, 1-5 Sun
Jack Banning, Sandra Elm
Posters

Printed Matter
7 Lispenard Street
New York, N.Y. 10013
(212) 925-0325

10-6 Tues-Sat
Catalogues issued
Susan Wheeler
Livre d'Artiste; Press Books &
Fine Printing

Professional Photography
Collector
1199 Park Avenue
New York, N.Y. 10028
(212) 289-8411
By appointment only
Catalogues issued
Victor F. Germack
Photography

Radio City Books Store
324 West 47th Street
New York, N.Y. 10036
(212) 245-5754
10-3 daily
Catalogues issued
Seymour Gaynor
Cooking; Hotels & Inns

Bruce J Ramer/Experimenta
401 East 80th Street
New York, N.Y. 10021
(212) 772-6211
By appointment only
Catalogues issued
Bruce J. Ramer
Medicine & Science; Science;
Technology; Mathematics; Natural
History; Rare Books

Richard C. Ramer
225 East 70th Street
New York, N.Y. 10021
(212) 737-0222
By appointment only
Catalogues issued
Richard C. Ramer, Diane Durante
Central America; Latin America;
South America; Voyages, Travels,
& Exploration; Spanish Books &
Literature

The Rare Book Room
125 Greenwich Street
New York, N.Y. 10014
(212) 206-6766
12-7 Mon-Sat
Catalogues issued
Roger Richards, Irvine Richards
*Modern First Editions; Autographs
& Autograph Material; Beat
Literature; Bindings, Fine & Rare;
19th Century Literature*

Reference Book Center
175 Fifth Avenue
New York, N.Y. 10010
(212) 677-2160
10-4 Mon-Fri
Catalogues issued
Saul Shine, Margery Shine
Dictionaries; Reference; Sets

A. Rinen
105 East 2nd Street
New York, N.Y. 10009
(212) 777-1468
By appointment only
Catalogues issued
Sonny Rinen
Asia

Rizzoli International Books
31 West 57th Street
New York, N.Y. 10019
(212) 759-2424
10-10 Mon-Sun
Catalogues issued
Robert Sheeby
*Art; Architecture; Poetry; Back
Issue Periodicals*

Michael F. Robinson, Inc.
505 East 79th Street
New York, N.Y. 10021
(212) 517-3819
By appointment only
Michael F. Robinson
*Autographs & Autograph Material;
Western Americana; Illustrated*

*Books; Association Copies;
Appraisals & Appraisal Services*

Paulette Rose Ltd.
360 East 72nd Street
New York, N.Y. 10021
(212) 861-5607
By appointment only
Catalogues issued
Paulette Rose
*Women; English Literature;
French Books & Literature; 18th
Century Literature; 19th Century
Literature*

Rostenberg & Stern
40 East 88th Street
New York, N.Y. 10128
(212) 831-6628
By appointment only
Catalogues issued
Leona Rostenberg, Madeleine B
Stern
*Books about Books; Ephemera;
History; Political Science &
Theory; Rare Books; Renaissance*

Ruby's Book Sale
119 Chambers Street
New York, N.Y. 10007
(212) 732-8676
10-6 Mon-Fri, 10-5 Sat
Roberta Sadofsky, Martin Sadofsky
General; Remainders

Joel Rudikoff
300 Mercer Street
New York, N.Y. 10003
(212) 674-0219
By appointment only
Catalogues issued
Joel Rudikoff
Art

Russica Book & Art Shop
799 Broadway
New York, N.Y. 10003
(212) 473-7480
9-6 Mon-Fri, 11-4 Sat

Catalogues issued
Irena Kuharets
*Russia & Slavic Countries; Rare
Books; Art; Reference; Literature*

Charlotte F. Safir
1349 Lexington Avenue, Apt. 9-B
New York, N.Y. 10128
(212) 534-7933
By mail only
Charlotte F Safir
*Children's Books; Cooking;
Judaica & Hebraica*

William H. Schab Gallery
11 East 57th Street
New York, N.Y. 10022
(212) 758-0327
9:30-5:30 Mon-Sat
Catalogues issued
Frederick G Schab
*Woodcut Books; Science; Medical
& Medicine; Prints; Drawings*

Justin G. Schiller, Ltd.
1 East 61st Street
New York, N.Y. 10021
(212) 832-8231
10-6 Mon-Fri
Catalogues issued
Justin G. Schiller, Raymond M.
Wapner
*Children's Books; Illustrated
Books; Original Art For
Illustration; Autographs &
Autograph Material; Illuminated
Manuscripts*

Schiller-Wapner Galleries
1 East 61st Street
New York, N.Y. 10021
(212) 758-0329
10-5:30 Tues-Sat
Raymond M. Wapner
*Original Art For Illustration; Fine
Arts*

Oscar Schreyer
230 East 79th Street

Oscar Schreyer
230 East 79th Street
New York, N.Y. 10021
(212) 628-6227
By appointment only
Dr. Oscar Schreyer
North Africa; Islam; Posters; Rare Books

David Schulson
11 East 68th Street
New York, N.Y. 10021
(212) 517-8300
By appointment only
Catalogues issued
David Schulson
Autographs & Autograph Material

Science Fiction Shop
56 Eighth Avenue
New York, N.Y. 10014
(212) 741-0270
11:30-7 Mon-Fri, 11-6 Sat, 12-5 Sun
Catalogues issued
Martin Last
Science Fiction; Fantasy; Rare Books

S. R. Shapiro
29 East 10th Street
New York, N.Y. 10003
(212) 673-0610
11-7 daily
Catalogues issued
S. R. Shapiro
Art; Bibliography; Press Books & Fine Printing; Folklore; Rare Books; Typography & Type Specimens

Sky Books International
48 East 50th Street
New York, N.Y. 10022
(212) 688-5086
10-7 Mon-Sat
Catalogues issued
Bill Dean

Aviation & Aeronautics; Militaria; Marine & Maritime

Rosejeanne Slifer
30 Park Avenue
New York, N.Y. 10016
(212) 685-2040
By appointment only
Rosejeanne Slifer
Autographs & Autograph Material; Documents; Maps, Atlases, & Cartography

Soldier Shop
1222 Madison Avenue
New York, N.Y. 10128
(212) 535-6788
10-6 Mon-Fri, 10-5 Sat
Catalogues issued
Peter J. Blum
Civil War & Confederacy; History; Militaria; Marine & Maritime; Guns & Weapons

Spiratone, Inc.
130 West 31st Street
New York, N.Y. 10001
(212) 594-5269
9-6 Mon-Fri, 9-5 Sat
Catalogues issued
Photography

Strand Book Store
828 Broadway
New York, N.Y. 10003
(212) 473-1452
9:30-9:30 Mon-Fri, 9-6 Sat, 11-5 Sun
Catalogues issued
Fred Bass
Art; Remainders; Fiction; New Books; General

Strand Book Store (Rare Book Dept.)
828 Broadway, upstairs
New York, N.Y. 10003
(212) 473-1452
10-6 Mon-Sat

Catalogues issued
Marvin Mondlin, Craig Anderson
Art; Books about Books; Modern First Editions; Appraisals & Appraisal Services; Rare Books; General

John H. Stubbs
28 East 18th Street
New York, N.Y. 10003
(212) 982-8368
10-6 Tues-Sat
Catalogues issued
John H. Stubbs, Jane Stubbs
Architecture; Archaeology; Landscape Architecture; Architectural Design; Prints

Thomas Suarez
215 West 75th Street, No. 2-D
New York, N.Y. 10023
(212) 877-7468
By appointment only
Catalogues issued
Thomas Suarez, Ahngsana Suarez
Maps, Atlases, & Cartography; Voyages, Travels, & Exploration; Prints

George Sullivan
330 East 33rd Street
New York, N.Y. 10016
(212) 689-9745
By mail only
Sporting; Children's Books; Occult & Magic; Tobacco & Smoking; Military

Melvin Tanditash
P. O. Box 27, Peck Slip Stn.
New York, N.Y. 10272
By mail only
Catalogues issued
Melvin Tanditash
Business & Business History; Engineering

Theatrebooks, Inc.
1576 Broadway, suite 312

New York, N.Y. 10036
(212) 757-2834
10:30-6 Mon-Fri, 12-5 Sat
Catalogues issued
Bob Emerson
*Performing Arts; Theatre;
Inscribed Books*

Tollett & Harman
175 West 76th Street
New York, N.Y. 10023
(212) 573-1566
By appointment only
Catalogues issued
Robert Tollett, Donn Harman
*Autographs & Autograph Material;
Inscribed Books; Photography*

Francis H. Touchet
365 West End Avenue, Apt. 5-C
New York, N.Y. 10024
(212) 937-6942
Catalogues issued
Dr. Francis Touchet
*Religion & Religious History;
Eastern Orthodoxy; History; Art;
Bindings, Fine & Rare; Travel*

Peter Tumarkin
310 East 70th Street
New York, N.Y. 10021
(212) 757-8783
By appointment only
Catalogues issued
Peter Tumarkin
*German Books & Literature; Rare
Books; First Editions*

David Tunick, Inc.
12 East 81st Street
New York, N.Y. 10028
(212) 570-0090
By mail only
Catalogues issued
David Tunick, Linda Colarusso
Prints; Drawings

University Place Bookshop
821 Broadway

New York, N.Y. 10003
(212) 254-5998
10-5 Mon-Fri
Catalogues issued
William P. French
*Africa; Black Literature & Studies;
Caribbean; Chess; Early Printed
Books*

Untitled II #1
159 Prince Street
New York, N.Y. 10012
(212) 982-2088
10-9 Mon-Sat, 12-8 Sun
Catalogues issued
Bevan Davies, Michele Davies
Art; Architecture; Photography

Untitled II #2
680 Broadway
New York, N.Y. 10012
(212) 982-1145
10-9 Mon-Sat, 12-8 Sun
Catalogues issued
Bevan Davies, Michele Davies
Art; Architecture; Photography

Urban Center Books
457 Madison Avenue
New York, N.Y. 10022
(212) 935-3592
10-6 Mon-Sat
Catalogues issued
John Frazier
Architecture

Ursus Books Ltd.
39 East 78th Street
New York, N.Y. 10021
(212) 772-8787
10-6 Mon-Fri, 11-5 Sat
Catalogues issued
T. Peter Kraus, William Wyer
*Art; Art, Books about; Color Plate
Books; Illustrated Books*

Ursus Prints
39 East 78th Street
New York, N.Y. 10021

(212) 772-8787
10-6 Mon-Fri, 11-5 Sat
Evelyn Kraus
Automotive

U.S. Games Systems
38 East 32nd Street
New York, N.Y. 10016
(212) 685-4300
9:30-4 Mon-Fri
Catalogues issued
Stuart R. Kaplan
*Tarot; Games & Pastimes; Occult
& Magic*

Vasta Images/Books
95 Van Dam Street
New York, N.Y. 10013
(212) 243-3475
By appointment only
Catalogues issued
Joseph Vasta
Poetry; Erotica

Victoria Book Shop
303 Fifth Avenue
New York, N.Y. 10016
(212) 683-7849
10-4 Mon-Fri
Catalogues issued
Milton Reissman
*Children's Books; Illustrated
Books; Miniature Books; Rare
Books; Original Art For
Illustration*

Viewpoint Gallery
41 Union Square West, suite 307
New York, N.Y. 10003
(212) 242-5478
By mail only
Robert H. Pettit, James Vanderberg
Art

Village Comic Shop
227 Sullivan Street
New York, N.Y. 10014
(212) 777-2770
11-8 Mon-Wed, 10-9:30 Thurs-

Sat, 12-6 Su
Andrew Melhato
Comic Books

Andrew Washton
411 East 83rd Street
New York, N.Y. 10028
(212) 861-0513
By appointment only
Catalogues issued
Andrew Washton
*Art History & Reference; Art,
Books about*

Michael Weintraub #1
306 West 100th Street
New York, N.Y. 10025
(212) 678-0174
By appointment only
Michael Weintraub
*Illustrated Books; Architecture;
Poetry; Performing Arts*

Michael Weintraub #2
263 West 90th Street
New York, N.Y. 10024
(212) 769-1178
By appointment only
Michael Weintraub
*Illustrated Books; Architecture;
Poetry; Performing Arts*

Samuel Weiser, Inc.
132 East 24th Street
New York, N.Y. 10010-3622
(212) 777-6363
9-5:30 Mon-Wed & Fri, 10-6:50
Thurs
Henry Suzuki
*Astrology; Occult & Magic; The
Orient & Orientalia; Religion &
Religious History; Philosophy;
Archaeology*

L. & H. Weitz
1377 Lexington Avenue
New York, N.Y. 10028
(212) 831-2213
9-5 Mon-Fri, 12-5 Sat

Catalogues issued
Herbert Weitz, Elspeth Coleman
*Appraisals & Appraisal Services;
Bindings, Fine & Rare; Fore-Edge
Paintings; Illustrated Books; Sets*

Weyhe Art Books
794 Lexington Avenue
New York, N.Y. 10021
(212) 838-5466
9:30-5:15 Mon-Sat
Catalogues issued
Gertrude Dennis
Art; Architecture

Jonathan White
98 Riverside Drive, Apt. 10-G
New York, N.Y. 10024
(212) 496-8854
By appointment only
Catalogues issued
Jonathan White
Science Fiction; Fantasy; Science

James Wilson Gallery
1015 Madison Avenue
New York, N.Y. 10028
(212) 772-6338
11-5 Tues-Sat
James Wilson, Anthony Fair
Prints; Decorative Arts

Witkin Gallery
415 West Broadway
New York, N.Y. 10012
(212) 925-5510
11-6 Tues-Fri, 12-6 Sat
Catalogues issued
Edmund Yankov, Evelyne Daitz
Poetry

Wittenborn Art Books
1018 Madison Avenue
New York, N.Y. 10021
(212) 288-1558
10-5 Mon-Sat
Catalogues issued
Gabriel Austin
Art; Architecture; Graphic Arts

Daniel Wolf, Inc.
30 West 57th Street
New York, N.Y. 10019
(212) 586-8432
10-6 Mon-Sat
Daniel Wolf, Bonnie Benrubi
Photography

Womanbooks
656 Amsterdam Avenue
New York, N.Y. 10025
(212) 873-4121
12-7 Tues-Fri, 10-7 Sat, 12-6 Sun
Martita Midence
Women; New Books

Jeffrey Wortman Fine Arts
401 West End Avenue
New York, N.Y. 10023
(212) 595-7006
By appointment only
Catalogues issued
Jeffrey Wortman, Elizabeth
Hamilton
Prints

Wurlitzer-Bruck Music
60 Riverside Drive
New York, N.Y. 10024
(212) 787-6431
By appointment only
Gene Bruck, Mareanne Wurlitzer
*Music; Performing Arts;
Photography; Prints; Autographs
& Autograph Material; Rare Books*

Ximenes Rare Books
19 East 69th Street
New York, N.Y. 10021
(212) 744-0226
9-5 daily
Catalogues issued
Stephen Weisman
*First Editions; Literature;
Americana; STC & Wing Books;
Business & Business History;
Medicine & Science*

Morris N. Young
150 Broadway, suite 1110
New York, N.Y. 10038
(212) 227-4714
By appointment only
Morris N. Young
Games & Pastimes

Alfred F. Zambelli
156 Fifth Avenue
New York, N.Y. 10010
(212) 734-2141
By mail only
Catalogues issued
Alfred F. Zambelli, Maria D.
Zambelli
Middle Ages; Renaissance;
Philosophy; Bibliography;
Paleontology

Zita Books
760 West End Avenue
New York, N.Y. 10025
(212) 866-4715
By appointment only
Catalogues issued
Carol Cavat
Original Art For Illustration;
Photographically Illustrated
Books; Art; Comic Books; Sheet
Music; Illustrated Books

Irving Zucker
303 Fifth Avenue, suite 1503
New York, N.Y. 10016
(212) 679-6332
10-5:30 daily
Irving Zucker
Illustrated Books; Natural History;
French Books & Literature; Color
Plate Books

Tony Zwicker
15 Gramercy Park South
New York, N.Y. 10003
(212) 982-7441
By appointment only
Catalogues issued
Tony Zwicker

Livre d'Artiste; Press Books &
Fine Printing

Marvin Sommer
P. O. Box 442
Niagara Falls, N.Y. 14305
(416) 354-9761
10-5:30 daily
Catalogues issued
Marv Sommer, Sheila Bolton
Mystery & Detective Fiction; Early
& Collectible Paperbacks; Food
& Drink; Militaria; General

Antheil Booksellers
2177 Isabelle Court
North Bellmore, N.Y. 11710
(516) 826-2094
By appointment only
Catalogues issued
Sheila Rind, Nate Rind
Marine & Maritime; Ships & The
Sea; Aviation & Aeronautics;
Militaria; World Wars

Bayview Books & Bindery
P. O. Box 710
Northport, N.Y. 11768
(516) 757-3563
By appointment only
Catalogues issued
Hilda Robbins, Norman V.
Robbins
Africa; Arctica & Antarctica;
Marine & Maritime; Voyages,
Travels, & Exploration; Whaling

Dee Cee Books
P. O. Box 506
Nyack, N.Y. 10960
(914) 358-3989
By mail only
David Carpenter
Africa; Asia; First Editions;
Political Science & Theory; Russia
& Slavic Countries; Social
Sciences

Herbert A. Luft
69-11 229th Street
Oakland Gardens, N.Y. 11364
(718) 428-2770
By mail only
Catalogues issued
Herbert A. Luft
Astronomy; Optics; Science

Oceanside Books Unlimited
2856 St. John Road
Oceanside, N.Y. 11572
(516) 764-3378
9:30-f:30 Mon-Fri
Catalogues issued
Adrienne Williams
Sherlock Holmes & A. C. Doyle;
Mystery & Detective Fiction;
Bibliography

Stan's Book Bin
234 Merrick Road
Oceanside, N.Y. 11572
(516) 766-4949
12-6 Mon-Sat
Stanley Simon
General

G. Montlack
12 Harrow Lane
Old Bethpage, N.Y. 11804
(516) 249-5632
By appointment only
Gloria Montlack
Decorative Arts; Antiques;
Collecting & Collectibles;
Children's Books

Wildwood Books & Prints
P. O. Box 560, Route 28
Old Forge, N.Y. 13420
(315) 369-3397
9:30-5 Mon-Sat (Nov-May only)
Ted Comstock, Sarah Comstock
Regional Americana; Fishing &
Angling; Natural History; Art;
Prints; Adirondacks

Wilsey Rare Books
HC1, Box 23, Mill Road
Olivebridge, N.Y. 12461
(914) 657-7057
By appointment only
Catalogues issued
Edward Ripley-Duggan, Carol
Maltby
Bindings, Fine & Rare;
Bibliography; Press Books & Fine
Printing; Calligraphy; Illustrated
Books; Color Plate Books

Carney Books
44 Elm Street
Oneonta, N.Y. 13820
(607) 432-5360
By appointment only
Margaret Carney, John J. Carney,
Jr.
Ephemera; General

Serpent & Eagle Books
1 Dietz Street
Oneonta, N.Y. 13820
(607) 432-5604
10-5 Mon-Sat (Thurs to 9)
Catalogues issued
Jo Mish
Folklore; New York State; General

Poster City
3 Henry Street, Box 94
Orangeburg, N.Y. 10962
(914) 359-0177
By mail only
Catalogues issued
Todd Feiertag
Posters

Bev Chaney, Jr.
73 Croton Avenue
Ossining, N.Y. 10562
(914) 941-1002
By appointment only
Catalogues issued
Bev Chaney, Jr.
Modern First Editions; Literature;
Books about Books

Josephine Lazarus, Inc.
56 Grace Lane
Ossining, N.Y. 10562
(914) 941-6066
By appointment only
Herb Lazarus
Presidents; Autographs &
Autograph Material; Americana;
Inscribed Books

William Salloch
Pines Bridge Road
Ossining, N.Y. 10562
(914) 941-8363
By appointment only
Catalogues issued
William Salloch
Rare Books; Renaissance;
Incunabula; Emblem Books;
Middle Ages; Greek & Roman
Classics

Mary B. Schaefer
56 Sherwood Avenue
Ossining, N.Y. 10562
By mail only
Mary B. Schaefer
Horses & Horse Sports;
Computers; Illustrated Books

Indian Head Books
P. O. Box 383
Owego, N.Y. 13827
(607) 798-0844
By mail only
Catalogues issued
Webb T. Comfort
American History; American
Colonies & the Revolution; Indians
& Eskimos

Riverow Bookshop
187 Front Street
Owego, N.Y. 13827
(607) 687-4094
9:30-5:30 Mon-Sat, Thu to 8
Catalogues issued
John D. Spencer
Technology; Architecture;

Antiques; Crafts & Hobbies;
Ephemera; Scholarly Books

K. George Arthurton
1783 Maple Avenue
Palmyra, N.Y. 14522
(315) 597-5275
By mail only
K. George Arthurton
Indians & Eskimos; Americana;
Criminology; Law; Outlaws &
Rangers; American History

Peter Stockman
1191 Johnson Road
Palmyra, N.Y. 14522
(315) 597-9696
By mail only
Peter Stockman
Little Magazines & Literary Small
Presses; General

Peter Hennessey
P. O. Box 393
Peconic, N.Y. 11958
(516) 734-5650
By mail only
Catalogues issued
Peter Hennessey, Marianne
Hennessey
Fiction

Chang Tang Books
35 Di Rubbo Drive
Peekskill, N.Y. 10566
(914) 739-8167
By appointment only
Catalogues issued
Donald E. Roy
Dogs; Asia; Tibet

Timothy Trace
144 Red Mill Road
Peekskill, N.Y. 10566
(914) 528-4074
By appointment only
Elizabeth Trace
Architecture; Decorative Arts;
Antiques; Crafts & Hobbies

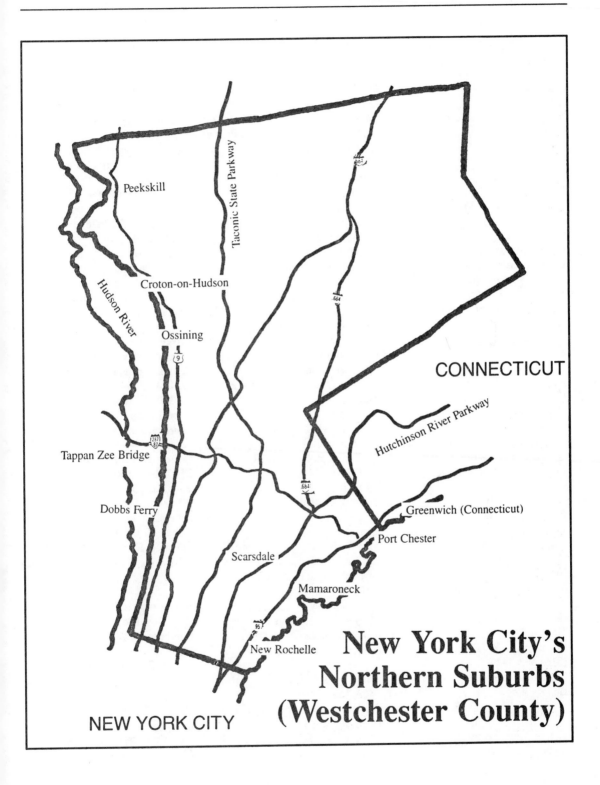

New York City's Northern Suburbs (Westchester County)

Vincent Prestianni
175 Lazy Trail
Penfield, N.Y. 14526
(716) 377-7369
By mail only
Vincent Prestianni, Susanne S.
Prestianni
Sets; Modern First Editions

Pier Books, Inc.
P. O. Box 5
Piermont, N.Y. 10968
(914) 353-0232
By mail only
Catalogues issued
David C. Roach
*Marine & Maritime; Ships & The
Sea; Naval & Nautical; Sailing &
Yachting; America's Cup; Ships
& Ship Building*

Bonmark Books
998 Old Country Road
Plainview, N.Y. 11803
(516) 938-9000
10:30-7 Mon-Fri, 10:30-5 Sat, 11-
4 Sun
Mark Blinderman, Rita Blinderman
*Bindings, Fine & Rare; First
Editions; Illustrated Books;
Cookbooks; Art; Science Fiction*

Phoenix Bookfinders
17 Sheridan Court
Plainview, N.Y. 11803
(516) 938-8192
Jean Louis, Arthur Louis
Search Service, Without Stock

Bengta Woo
1 Sorgi Court
Plainview, N.Y. 11803
(516) 692-4426
By appointment only
Bengta Woo
Mystery & Detective Fiction

Lee & Mike Temares
50 Heights Road

Plandome, N.Y. 11030
(516) 627-7822
By appointment only
Lee Temares, Mike Temares
*Limited Editions Club; Series
Books For Boys & Girls;
Children's Books; Heritage Press;
Modern First Editions*

Corner-Stone Bookshop
110 Margaret Street
Plattsburgh, N.Y. 12901
(518) 561-0520
9-9 Mon-Sat
Nancy Duniho
General; Comic Books

Colonial O.P. Book Service
P. O. Box 451
Pleasantville, N.Y. 10570
(914) 769-1704
By mail only
Al Scheinbaum
*Literary Criticism; Literature;
Biography & Autobiography*

Andrew Wittenborn
152 Mountain Road
Pleasantville, N.Y. 10570
(914) 941-2744
By mail only
Andrew Wittenborn
Automotive

The Good Times Bookshop
150 East Main Street
Port Jefferson, N.Y. 11777
(516) 928-2664
11-6 Tues-Sat
Mary J. Mart, Michael A. Mart
*Humanities; Labor & Labor
History; Scholarly Books*

Collector's Antiques
286A Main Street
Port Washington, N.Y. 11050
(516) 883-2098
10-3:30 Tues-Fri, 10-5:30 Sat &
Sun

Jean Feigenbaum
General

Signed Limited Editions
P. O. Box 631
Port Washington, N.Y. 11050
R. E. Gauvey
*Inscribed Books; Modern First
Editions; Woodcut Books*

Cabin In The Pines
Route 2
Potsdam, N.Y. 13676
(315) 265-9036
9-5 Mon-Sat
Charles Penrose
*Adirondacks; Fiction; Biography
& Autobiography; American
History; Science Fiction*

Three Arts
3 Collegeview Avenue
Poughkeepsie, N.Y. 12603
(914) 471-3640
9:30-5:30 Mon-Sat
Jesse Effron
Regional Americana; Prints

Robert E. Underhill
85 Underhill Road
Poughkeepsie, N.Y. 12603
(914) 452-5986
By mail only
Robert E. Underhill
*Farming, Ranching, & Livestock;
Gardening & Horticulture; Natural
History; New Books*

Art Book Finders
P. O. Box 156
Purchase, N.Y. 10577
By mail only
Joel R. Ruduloff
Art

Book-O-Rama
89-85 Springfield Boulevard
Queens Village, N.Y. 11432
(718) 963-9365

8-4 daily
Bruce Kopet
Chess

B. & J. Books
91-16 63rd Drive
Rego Park, N.Y. 11374
(718) 896-1272
11-6 Mon-Sat, 12-5 Sun
Catalogues issued
Barry Skolnick
Military History; General

E. K. Book Service
P. O. Box 83
Rego Park, N.Y. 11374
(718) 263-8980
By mail only
Catalogues issued
N. J. Effress
*Physics; Mathematics; Technical;
Psychiatry, Psychology, &
Psychoanalysis; Scholarly Books*

Austin Book Shop
104-29 Jamaica Avenue
Richmond Hill, N.Y. 11418
(718) 441-1199
12-6 Fri & Sat
Catalogues issued
Bernard Titowsky
*Immigration; Judaica & Hebrica;
Law; Baseball; American History;
Women*

Abra Cadavar
110 Dunrovin Lane
Rochester, N.Y. 14618
(716) 244-7665
By appointment only
Catalogues issued
Dick Moskowitz
*Mystery & Detective Fiction; True
Crime; Fiction; First Editions;
American History; Tobacco &
Smoking*

Brownbag Bookshop
678 Monroe Avenue

Rochester, N.Y. 14607
(716) 271-3494
11-6 Mon-Sat (to 8 Thurs), 12-5
Sun
Catalogues issued
James Gould
*Art; Biography & Autobiography;
Science Fiction; Philosophy;
History; General*

Bryn Mawr Book Shop
147 State Street
Rochester, N.Y. 14614
(716) 454-2910
10-3 Mon-Fri, 9:30-12:30 Sat
Marian Greswold, Mary Schwertz
General

Ray Diamond
80 Southview Terrace
Rochester, N.Y. 14620
(716) 244-9349
Ray Diamond
*Americana; Modern First Editions;
Illustrated Books; Press Books &
Fine Printing; Art; Voyages,
Travels, & Exploration*

Gutenberg's
675 Monroe Avenue
Rochester, N.Y. 14607
(716) 442-4620
12-6 daily
Martha Kelly
*Art; Political, Social, & Cultural
History; General*

C. F. Heindl
P. O. Box 8345
Rochester, N.Y. 14618
(716) 271-1423
By mail only
Charles Heindl
Charles Dickens

Jeffrey H. Marks
36 Main Street West
Rochester, N.Y. 14614
(716) 232-3464

By appointment only
Jeffrey H. Marks
Modern First Editions

Village Green Bookstore
766 Monroe Avenue
Rochester, N.Y. 14607
(716) 442-1151
6 a.m.-11 p.m. Sun-Thurs, 6-noon
Fri & Sat
Jessie Marvin
Back Issue Magazines; General

Yankee Peddler Bookshop
274 North Goodman Street, Village
Gate Square
Rochester, N.Y. 14607
(716) 271-5080
10-5 Mon-Fri (to 9 Thurs), 11-5
Sat, 12-5 Sun
John Westerberg, Janet Westerberg,
Douglas Westerberg
*New York State; First Editions;
Civil War & Confederacy;
Americana; Aviation &
Aeronautics; Illustrated Books*

Elgen Books
336 DeMott Avenue
Rockville Centre, N.Y. 11570
(516) 536-6276
By appointment only
Catalogues issued
Leonard Geller, Esther Geller
*Medicine & Science; Technology;
Mathematics; Voyages, Travels, &
Exploration*

Paulette Greene
140 Princeton Road
Rockville Centre, N.Y. 11570
(516) 766-8602
By appointment only
Catalogues issued
Paulette Greene, Robert J. Greene
*Mystery & Detective Fiction;
Sherlock Holmes & A. C. Doyle;
Modern First Editions; 19th
Century Literature; Autographs &*

Autograph Material; Press Books & Fine Printing

Rolls-Royce Archives
5 Brouwer Lane
Rockville Centre, N.Y. 11570
(516) 764-9086
By mail only
David M. King
Automobiles, Specific Makes & Models; Automotive; Travel; Transportation

Ed Moran
P. O. Box 1231
Rocky Point, N.Y. 11778
By mail only
Ed Moran
Trolleys; Railroads; Fires & Firefighting

Bridgman Books
906 Roosevelt Avenue
Rome, N.Y. 13440
(315) 337-7252
By mail only
Catalogues issued
Patrick H. Bridgman
Ephemera; Used Paperbacks; General

Tom Delle Donne
816 Johnson Avenue
Ronkonkoma, N.Y. 11779
(516) 981-6766
By appointment only
Catalogues issued
Tom Delle Donne
American Illustrative Art; Rockwell Kent; Prints; WPA & Federal Writers Project

Bookmarx
28 Lincoln Avenue
Roslyn Heights, N.Y. 11577
(516) 621-8382
11-6 Mon-Sat
Stan Marx, Evan Marx

Children's Books; First Editions; Art; Neurosciences; Baseball; Golf

Blossom Resnik
58 Midland Road
Roslyn Heights, N.Y. 11577
(516) 621-4898
By appointment only
Blossom Resnik
Illustrated Books; Back Issue Periodicals; Juveniles; Ephemera; Prints

High Ridge Books, Inc.
P. O. Box 286
Rye, N.Y. 10580
(914) 967-3332
By appointment only
Catalogues issued
Howard Baron, Frederick Baron
Maps, Atlases, & Cartography; Americana; Color Plate Books; Ephemera

Lighthouse Bookstore
20 Purchase Street
Rye, N.Y. 10580
(914) 967-0966
9-6 Mon-Sat
Patrick Corcoran
New Paperbacks; Fiction

Denning House
P. O. Box 42
Salisbury Mills, N.Y. 12577
(914) 496-6771
By appointment only
Catalogues issued
Patricia McTague
General

Anglican Bibliopole
Church Street, R.D. 3, Box 116
Saratoga Springs, N.Y. 12866
(518) 587-7470
By appointment only
Catalogues issued
Paul Evans, Robert Kearney
Religion & Religous History;

Church History; Catholica; Eastern Orthodoxy

The Hennesseys
Fourth & Woodlawn
Saratoga Springs, N.Y. 12866
(518) 584-4921
By appointment only
Catalogues issued
Ellen Hennessey
Sporting; General

Lyrical Ballad Books
7 Phila Street
Saratoga Springs, N.Y. 12866
(518) 584-8779
10-5:30 Tues-Sat (Sun in July & Aug only)
John J. DeMarco
General; Children's Books; Dance; Horses & Horse Sports; Illustrated Books; Sporting

Nancy Scheck
164 Boulevard
Scarsdale, N.Y. 10583
(914) 723-6974
By appointment only
Catalogues issued
Nancy Scheck
American Illustrative Art; Prints; Fine Arts

Annemarie Schnase
120 Brown Road, Box 119
Scarsdale, N.Y. 10583
(914) 725-1284
By appointment only
Catalogues issued
Annemarie Schnase
Back Issue Periodicals; Music; Reprints; Societies & Associations Publications; Scholarly Books

Beatific Books & Prints
P. O. Box 943
Schenectady, N.Y. 12301
(518) 895-2444
By appointment only

Catalogues issued
Michael Greene, Denise Greene
Beat Literature; Modern First Editions; Limited & Signed Editions; Broadsides; Prints

Bibliomania
129 Jay Street
Schenectady, N.Y. 12305
(518) 393-8069
10-5:30 Mon-Sat (Thurs to 9)
Catalogues issued
Bill Healy
Literature; Americana; Mountaineering; Fishing & Angling; Art; Photography

Hammer Mountain Book Halls
841 Union Street
Schenectady, N.Y. 12308
(518) 393-5266
1-5 Mon-Fri, 10-5 Sat
Catalogues issued
Wayne Somers
Scholarly Books; Social Sciences; Business & Business History; Foreign Languages; European History

Nelson's Book Store
173 Jay Street
Schenectady, N.Y. 12305
11-5:30 Mon-Sat
General

Parkway Classics
P. O. Box 452
Schenectady, N.Y. 12305
Walter C. Brzoza
Golf

William Frost Mobley
P. O. Box 10
Schoharie, N.Y. 12157
(518) 295-7978
By appointment only
William F. Mobley
Ephemera; Prints; Appraisals &

Appraisal Services; Trade Cards; Posters; Broadsides

Speleobooks
P. O. Box 10
Schoharie, N.Y. 12157
(518) 295-7978
By appointment only
Catalogues issued
Emily Mobley
Natural History

Paul Olinkiewicz Associates
17 Grand Avenue
Shelter Island, N.Y. 11965
(516) 749-8925
12-8 daily (Winter), 10-8 daily (Summer)
Paul Olinkiewicz, Janet Olinkiewicz
Americana; Regional Americana; Ephemera; General

Norman Levine's Bookshop
Route 28
Shokan, N.Y. 12481
(914) 657-7000
10-5 Wed-Sun
Norman Levine, Joan Levine
General

S. Lombardo
P. O. Box 133
Shoreham, N.Y. 11786
(516) 744-3656
By appointment only
Catalogues issued
Sal Lombardo
Imprints; Newspapers; Ephemera

Havemeyer Booksellers
Eibert Road
Skaneafeles, N.Y. 13152
(315) 685-7573
By appointment only
Catalogues issued
John Havemeyer, Nancy Havemeyer

Rare Books; Modern First Editions; Children's Books; Christmas; Books about Books; Civil War & Confederacy

Liberty Rock Books
P. O. Box 143
Sloatsburg, N.Y. 10974
(914) 753-2071
By mail only
Virginia M. Mahoney, James J. Mahoney
Regional Americana; Architecture; Antiques; Catholica

Cadenza Booksellers
8 Brilner Drive
Smithtown, N.Y. 11787
(516) 265-0122
By appointment only
Catalogues issued
Mimi Taube
Music; Performing Arts

GBI Antiques
94 Craft Lane
Smithtown, N.Y. 11787
(516) 724-7781
By appointment only
Gabor Inke
Paintings; Prints

Robert Keene
21 South Main Street
Southampton, N.Y. 11968
(516) 283-1612
10-4 Mon-Sat
Robert Keene
Whaling; Steamboats & River Travel; New York City & Metropolitan Region

Edna Bennett
495 Northfield Lane
Southold, N.Y. 11971
(516) 765-5816
Catalogues issued
Edna Bennett
Photography; Gardening &

Horticulture; Natural History; Dogs; Horses & Horse Sports

Europe Unie Books
60 Reynolds Street
Staten Island, N.Y. 10305
(718) 273-0475
By appointment only
Michael Speer
German Books & Literature

Great Expectations
20 Barton Avenue
Staten Island, N.Y. 10306
(718) 447-8377
By appointment only
Catalogues issued
Modern First Editions; Literature; Illustrated Books; Americana; Children's Books

Harlow McMillen
131 Manor Road
Staten Island, N.Y. 10310
(718) 981-7781
By appointment only
Harlow McMillen
Local History; General

Book-In-Hand
R. D. 2, Condon Road
Stillwater, N.Y. 12170
(518) 587-0040
By appointment only
Helen Crawshaw, Bill Crawshaw
American Colonies & the Revolution; Children's Books; New York State; General

Ridge Books
P. O. Box 58
Stone Ridge, N.Y. 12484
(914) 687-9774
By appointment only
Catalogues issued
Peter E. Scott
Modern First Editions; American Literature; Hudson River Valley;

Plays & Playwrights; 20th Century Literature

Columbia Trading Company
2 Rocklyn Drive
Suffern, N.Y. 10901
(914) 368-3078
By appointment only
Catalogues issued
Bob Glick
Naval & Nautical; Marine & Maritime; Ships & The Sea; Ships & Ship Building; Sailing & Yachting

Cornucopia
R. D. Box 2108
Syosset, N.Y. 11791
(516) 921-4813
By appointment only
Carol A. Greenberg
True Crime; Mystery & Detective Fiction; Cooking; Crafts & Hobbies; Children's Books

The Books End
2443 James Street
Syracuse, N.Y. 13206
(315) 437-2312
10-6 Mon-Fri, 10-5 Sat
Lois M. Favier
General

Bruce Calman
1508 Park Street
Syracuse, N.Y. 13208
(315) 471-6300
By mail only
Catalogues issued
Bruce Calman
Evolution; Natural History; History of Medicine & Science

Jim Hodgson
3600 East Genesee Street
Syracuse, N.Y. 13214
(315) 446-1930
By mail only
Catalogues issued

Jim Hodgson
Civil War & Confederacy

Johnson & O'Donnell
1015 State Tower Building
Syracuse, N.Y. 13202
(315) 476-5312
By appointment only
Catalogues issued
Bruce Johnson, Ed O'Donnell
First Editions; Modern First Editions; Author Collections; Autographs & Autograph Material; Rare Books; Bindings, Fine & Rare

Walter Miller
6710 Brooklawn Parkway
Syracuse, N.Y. 13211
(315) 432-8282
9-5 daily
Walter Miller
Automobiles, Specific Makes & Models

Edward J. Monarski
1050 Wadsworth Street
Syracuse, N.Y. 13208
(315) 455-1716
9-5 Mon-Fri
Catalogues issued
Ed Monarski
New York State; World Wars; Ephemera; Military; Militaria; Rare Books

William Loewy
P. O. Box 186
Tallman, N.Y. 10982-0186
(914) 425-2924
By appointment only
William Loewy
Judaica & Hebrica

Milton Slater
P. O. Box 501
Tarrytown, N.Y. 10591
(914) 631-1888
By mail only
Catalogues issued

Milton Slater
Autographs & Autograph Material;
Inscribed Books; Americana; First
Editions; Ephemera; Mormons

Chris Fessler
R.D. 1
Theresa, N.Y. 13691
(315) 628-5560
By mail only
Catalogues issued
Chris Fessler
Anthropology; Archaeology;
History; Primitive & Pre-
Columbian Culture

Grace Block
90 Eton Road
Thornwood, N.Y. 10594
(914) 769-3387
By mail only
Grace Block
General

Barn East Books
29 Montgomery Street
Tivoli, N.Y. 12583
(914) 757-4294
By appointment only
Richard Wiles
Local History; American History;
Literature

Nelson's Book Store
22 4th Street
Troy, N.Y. 12180
(518) 273-6588
11-5:30, Mon-Sat
John Nelson, Jr.
Technical; Literature; General

Paul J. Drabeck
32 Oak Avenue
Tuckahoe, N.Y. 10707
By appointment only
Catalogues issued
Paul J. Drabeck
Archery; Falconry; Big Game

Hunting; Guns & Weapons; Art,
Western; Derrydale Press

Ben Franklin Book Shop
318 North Broadway
Upper Nyack, N.Y. 10960
(914) 358-0440
12-5 Mon-Fri (ex Wed), 11-6 Sat
& Sun
Michael Houghton
Scholarly Books; General

Educo Services International
   Limited
P. O. Box 226, 75 North Kensico
Avenue
Valhalla, N.Y. 10595
(914) 997-7044
Open shop
Catalogues issued
Charles N. Cecere
Back Issue Periodicals; Collection
Development; General

Aleph-Bet Books
670 Waters Edge
Valley Cottage, N.Y. 10989
(914) 268-7410
By appointment only
Catalogues issued
Helen Younger
Children's Books; Illustrated
Books; Juveniles

Charles Apfelbaum
39 Flower Road
Valley Stream, N.Y. 11581
(516) 791-2801
By mail only
Catalogues issued
Charles Apfelbaum
Author Collections; Autographs &
Autograph Material; Collection
Development; Manuscripts; First
Editions; Documents

Collectabilia
475 West Merrick Road
Valley Stream, N.Y. 11580

(516) 825-8000
10-5 Mon-Sat
Catalogues issued
Philip R. Weiss
Literature; First Editions; General

Edward L. Kreinheder
197 Main Street
Warrensburg, N.Y. 12885
(518) 623-2149
9-5 Mon-Sat (closed Jan & Feb)
Edward L. Kreinheder, Pearl
Kreinheder
Western New York State;
Adirondacks; Fishing & Angling;
Military; Hudson River Valley;
Natural History

Book Look
51 Maple Avenue
Warwick, N.Y. 10990
(914) 986-1981
By mail only
Catalogues issued
Jerry Dodd
Hudson River Valley; Business &
Business History

New & Used
15-17 River Street
Warwick, N.Y. 10990
(914) 986-2665
10-5 Mon-Sat
Catalogues issued
Jerry Dodd
General

Backroom Bookstore
P. O. Box 223
Webster, N.Y. 14580-0223
(716) 671-0437
By appointment only
Catalogues issued
Ron Hein
Elbert Hubbard & Roycrofters;
Poetry; Photography

Collectrix
366 Woodfield Road

West Hempstead, N.Y. 11552
(516) 538-3388
10-6 Mon-Sat
Alida Roochvarg
Antiques; Collecting & Collectibles

Once Upon A Time Books
366 Woodfield Road
West Hempstead, N.Y. 11552
(516) 486-9427
11-6 Mon-Sat
James Dore
Art, Books about; Military;
General

Helmut & Horn Antiques
602 Higbie Lane
West Islip, N.Y. 11795
(516) 661-1828
By mail only
Catalogues issued
Arnold Merkitch
Fires & Firefighting; Criminology;
Hobbies

C. Moebius
484 Winthrop Street
Westbury, N.Y. 11590
(516) 333-3797
By mail only
C. Moebius
Automotive; Automobiles, Specific
Makes & Models

Avonlea Books
P. O. Box 74, Main Stn.
White Plains, N.Y. 10602
(914) 946-5923
By mail only
Leone E. Bushkin
Search Service, Without Stock

Michael E. Bennett
38 Ridgeway Circle
White Plains, N.Y. 10605
By mail only

Michael E. Bennett
New York City & Metropolitan
Region; Cooking; Ephemera;
Americana, States

Bryn Mawr Book Shop
170 Grand Street
White Plains, N.Y. 10601
(914) 946-5356
10-4 Mon-Sat
Eleanor Forman, Leon Bushkin
General

Albert J. Phiebig, Inc.
P. O. Box 352
White Plains, N.Y. 10602
(914) 948-0138
By mail only
Albert J. Phiebig
Collection Development;
Continental Books; Back Issue
Periodicals; Societies &
Associations Publications

Yankee Peddler
3895 Route 104
Williamson, N.Y. 14589
(315) 589-2063
10-5 Mon-Wed, 1-5 Thurs-Sun
Catalogues issued
John Westerberg, Douglas
Westerberg
New York State; Photography;
Civil War & Confederacy;
Americana; Aviation &
Aeronautics; Illustrated Books

Jerry Granat
P. O. Box 92
Woodmere, N.Y. 11598
(516) 374-7809
By appointment only
Catalogues issued
Ellen Granat, Jerry Granat
Autographs & Autograph Material;
Manuscripts; Documents; Limited

& Signed Editions; Association
Copies

Three Geese In Flight
12 Tinker Street
Woodstock, N.Y. 12498
(914) 679-8787
11-5 Mon & Wed-Sun
Catalogues issued
Sam Wenger, Moira Joyce
Ireland & The Irish; Myths &
Mythology; Arthurian Legend;
New York State; Indians & Eskimos

aGatherin'
P. O. Box 175
Wynantskill, N.Y. 12198
(518) 674-2979
By appointment only
Catalogues issued
Robert D. Harris, Diane DeBlois
Postal History; Aviation &
Aeronautics; Railroads; Trade
Catalogues; Ephemera;
Manuscripts

All Photography Books
P. O. Box 429
Yonkers, N.Y. 10702
(914) 423-6473
By mail only
Catalogues issued
Arnold Sadow
Photography

Cohasco, Inc.
P. O. Box 821
Yonkers, N.Y. 10702
(914) 476-8500
9-5 daily
Catalogues issued
Robert H. Snider
Documents; Manuscripts;
Autographs & Autograph Material;
Newspapers; Maps, Atlases, &
Cartography

Solve Bookselling
Problems 5 Ways By Taking
American Book Collector Regularly

1. **Read Every Issue.** *American Book Collector* is America's most interesting and most widely read book collector's magazine. Read regularly, it will help you keep up with what's being talked about in book collecting circles.

2. **Advertise Regularly.** There's no substitute for keeping your name in front of the book collecting public. Your competitors are out there working hard for name recognition—so should you! Write for our free rate card for display and classified advertisements.

3. **Promote Your Catalogues—Free!** Our "Catalogues Received" section lists hundreds of catalogues in every issue—free! Get your share of this free publicity by adding *ABC* to your mailing list (see address below).

4. **Give Us Away.** *American Book Collector* makes a great gift (any time of the year) for that favored client or budding collector you want to keep in touch with. Discounted subscriptions available (when purchased in quantity): write for information.

5. **Write To Our Readers.** The mailing list of *American Book Collector* is available for rent. Write for free flyer with all details.

... And then there is this Directory. Mailing labels for dealers listed in this Directory (we add new dealers every week), grouped by any one or a combination of the specialties shown in this book, are also available. Write for further information to *American Book Collector*

North Carolina

Book Mart
7 Biltmore Plaza, Box 5094
Asheville, N.C. 28803
(704) 274-2241
10-5 Tues-Sat
Nancy Brown
Authors; North Carolina; Regional Americana; Southern Writers; General

Richard A. Pandich
12 Ridgefield Place
Asheville, N.C. 28803
(704) 274-9537
By appointment only
Richard A. Pandich
Southern Americana; Civil War & Confederacy; North Carolina; Military

Captain's Bookshelf
26 Battery Park Avenue
Asheville, N.C. 28801
(704) 253-6631
11-5:30 Tues-Sat
Catalogues issued
Chandler Gordon
First Editions; Literature; North Carolina; Southern Americana; Art

The Bookshop
400 West Franklin Street
Chapel Hill, N.C. 27514
(919) 942-5178
11-9 Mon-Fri, 11-6 Sat, 1-5 Sun
Catalogues issued
Bill Loeser, Linda Saaremaa
Southern Americana; New Paperbacks; Civil War & Confederacy

L. & T. Respess
P. O. Box 1284

Chapel Hill, N.C. 27514
(919) 489-8135
By appointment only
Catalogues issued
Lin Respess
Americana; American Literature; English Literature; Modern First Editions; Sporting

Carolina Bookshop
1601 East Independence Boulevard
Charlotte, N.C. 28205
(704) 375-7305
11-6 Tues-Sat
Catalogues issued
Gordon Briscoe
Regional Americana; Black Literature & Studies; Civil War & Confederacy; American History; North Carolina

B. L. Means
5935 Creola Road
Charlotte, N.C. 28226
(704) 364-3117
By mail only
Catalogues issued
Betty Means
General

L. & T. Respess
Brightleaf Sq., 905 West Main
Durham, N.C. 27707
(919) 668-5311
11-6 Mon-Sat
Catalogues issued
Lin Respess
Americana; American Literature; English Literature; Modern First Editions; Sporting

Autos & Autos
P. O. Box 280

Elizabeth City, N.C. 27909
(919) 335-1117
By appointment only
Catalogues issued
B. C. West, Jr.
Autographs & Autograph Material; Medicine & Science; Voyages, Travels, & Exploration; Aviation & Aeronautics

Book Trader
P. O. Box 603
Fairmont, N.C. 28340
(919) 628-0945
By appointment only
Catalogues issued
Billy Whitted
North Carolina; South Carolina

Cyrano's Bookshop
Main Street
Highlands, N.C. 28741
(704) 526-5488
10-5 Mon-Sat
Randolph P. Shaffner
Juveniles; Natural History; North Carolina; Art

Pacificana
P. O. Box 398
Jamestown, N.C. 27282
(919) 454-4938
By appointment only
Catalogues issued
Mary A. Browning
Pacific Region; Voyages, Travels, & Exploration

Chris Hartmann
Route 10, Box 120
Morganton, N.C. 28655
(704) 433-5478
By appointment only

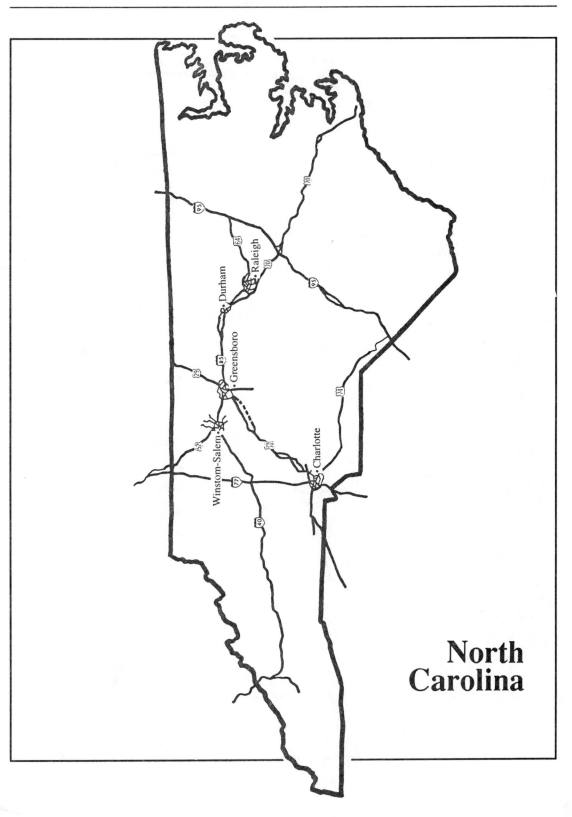

North Carolina

Catalogues issued
Chris Hartmann
General; Social Sciences;
Humanities; Americana

Bolingbroke Books
P. O. Box 153
Pinnacle, N.C. 27043
(919) 325-2210
By mail only
Catalogues issued
Lee Cheek, Ann Cheek
Conservative Literature & Authors;
Political Science & Theory;
Religion & Religious History

H. E. Turlington
P. O. Box 146
Pittsboro, N.C. 27312
(919) 542-3403
By appointment only
Catalogues issued
Henry Turlington
Modern First Editions; 20th
Century Literature; Southern
Americana; English Literature;
Inscribed Books

October Farm
Route 2, Box 183-C
Raleigh, N.C. 27610
(919) 772-0482
By appointment only
Catalogues issued
Barbara Cole
Horses & Horse Sports

The Reader's Corner
3201 Hillsborough Street
Raleigh, N.C. 27607
(919) 828-7024
10-9 Mon-Fri, 10-6 Sat, 1-6 Sun
Irv Coats, Christine Buakus
Art; Fiction; Phonograph Records;
Technology; Science Fiction

Avocet Books
827 South Harner
Sanford, N.C. 27330
(919) 775-7928
By mail only
Catalogues issued
John D. Cheesborough
Natural History; Sports;
Americana; Voyages, Travels, &
Exploration; Medical & Medicine;
North Carolina

Grandpa's Books
Route 3, Box 292, Highway 24-27
West
Troy, N.C. 27371
(919) 572-3484
By appointment only
Mary R. Parks, Albert L. Parks
North Carolina; Ephemera; Back
Issue Periodicals; Rare Books;
General

Stevens Book Shop
245 East Roosevelt Avenue
Wake Forest, N.C. 27587
(919) 556-3830
9-5:30 Mon-Sat
Catalogues issued
Richard L. Stevens
Religion & Religious History; Bible
& Bible Studies; Biography &
Autobiography; North Carolina;
American History

Sloan's Book Shop
289 North Main Street
Waynesville, N.C. 28786
(704) 456-8062
9:30-5:30 Mon-Sat
Charles Sloan
Used Paperbacks

V. O. Smith
202 South Haywood Street

Waynesville, N.C. 28786
By mail only
V. O. Smith
General

Broadfoot's Wendell
6624 Robertson Pond Road
Wendell, N.C. 27591
8:30-5:30 daily
Catalogues issued
Joyce Barrow
Civil War & Confederacy; General

Broadfoot's Bookmark
Route 4, Box 508-C
Wilmington, N.C. 28405
(919) 686-4379
8:30-5:30 daily
Catalogues issued
Tom Broadfoot
Civil War & Confederacy; Maps,
Atlases, & Cartography; Prints;
Naval & Nautical

Larry D. Laster
2416 Maplewood Avenue
Winston-Salem, N.C. 27103
(919) 724-7544
By appointment only
Larry D. Laster, Susan G. Laster
Bindings, Fine & Rare; German
Books & Literature; Americana;
Law; Appraisals & Appraisal
Services

Lovett & Lovett
110 North Hawthorne Road
Winston-Salem, N.C. 27104
(919) 722-5499
10-6 Tues-Fri, 10-5 Sat
Catalogues issued
Charles Lovett, Stephanie Lovett
Children's Books; First Editions;
General

North Dakota

Howard O. Berg
317 7th Street
Devils Lake, N.D. 58301
(701) 662-2343
By mail only
Howard O. Berg
Local History

Rollie Bullock
313 North "P" Avenue
Fargo, N.D. 58107
(701) 234-0954
11-7 Mon-Sat
Catalogues issued
Rollie Bulock
Travel

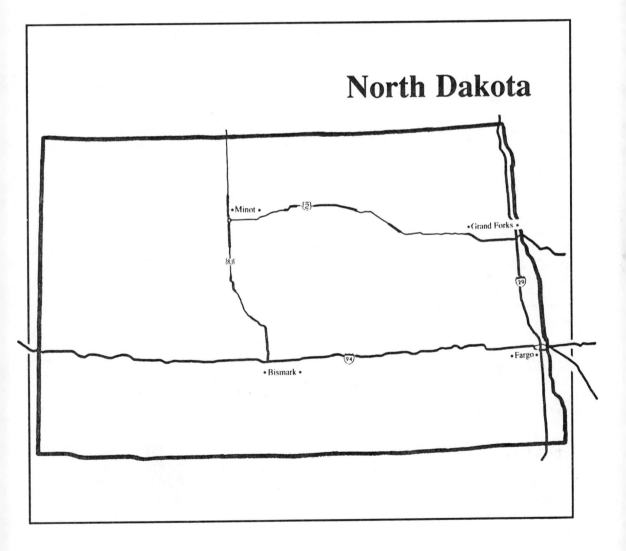

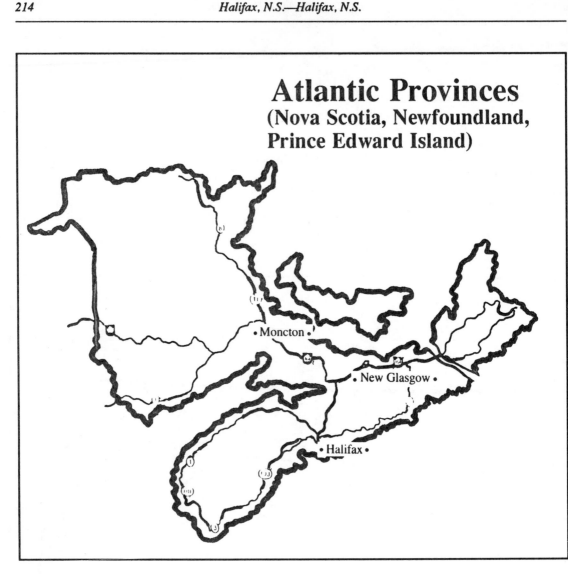

Atlantic Provinces
(Nova Scotia, Newfoundland, Prince Edward Island)

Moncton •

• New Glasgow •

• Halifax •

Nova Scotia

Back Pages
1520 Queen Street
Halifax, N.S. B3J 2H8
(902) 423-4750
10-5:30 Mon-Sat

Marcia Orr, Ronald Orr
Canada & Canadiana; Local
History; Horses & Horse Sports

Nautica Booksellers
1579 Dresden Row
Halifax, N.S. B3J 2K4
(902) 429-2741
10-5 daily (call first)

Catalogues issued
John Holland
*Naval & Nautical; Arctica &
Antarctica; Voyages, Travels, &
Exploration; Whaling; Sailing &
Yachting; Marine Biology*

Rainy Day Books
5802 South Street
Halifax, N.S. B3H 1S5
(902) 422-2433
10-5:30 Mon-Sat
Paul Conrad
General

Schooner Books Ltd.
5378 Inglis Street
Halifax, N.S. B3H 1J5
(902) 423-8419
9:30-6 Mon-Sun (to 9 Thurs & Fri)
Catalogues issued
Canada & Canadiana; General

Ohio

The Bookseller, Inc.
521 West Exchange Street
Akron, Ohio 44302
(216) 762-3101
10-6 Mon-Fri, 10-5 Sat
Catalogues issued
Frank S. Klein
*Military; Aviation & Aeronautics;
Ohio; General*

Bruce P. Ferrini
933 West Exchange Street
Akron, Ohio 44302
(216) 867-2665
By appointment only
Catalogues issued
Bruce Ferrini
Illuminated Leaves & Pages

**Bruce Ferrini & Michael
Greenberg**
933 West Exchange Street
Akron, Ohio 44302
(800) 321-3753
By appointment only
Bruce Ferrini
Illuminated Manuscripts

Fickes Crime Fiction
1471 Burkhardt Avenue
Akron, Ohio 44301
(216) 773-4223
By appointment only
Catalogues issued

Patricia A. Fickes
*Mystery & Detective Fiction;
Adventure*

Croissant & Company
P. O. Box 282
Athens, Ohio 45701
(614) 593-3008
By mail only
Catalogues issued
Duane Schneider
Thomas Wolfe; Joyce Carol Oates

Carpenter Books
P. O. Box 96
Barlow, Ohio 45712
(614) 678-2602
By mail only
Glen Carpenter
General

D. Gratz
8990 Augsburger Road, Route 2
Bluffton, Ohio 45817
(419) 358-7431
By mail only
Catalogues issued
D. Gratz
Genealogy

Ryan D. Tweney
413 Sand Ridge
Bowling Green, Ohio 43402
(419) 352-6771

By appointment only
Catalogues issued
Ryan D. Tweney, Karin G. Hubert
*Neurosciences; Psychiatry,
Psychology, & Psychoanalysis;
History of Medicine & Science;
Philosophy*

Robert G. Hayman
P. O. Box 188
Carey, Ohio 43316
(419) 396-6933
By appointment only
Catalogues issued
Bob Hayman, Arne Hayman
*Americana; Americana, States;
Regional Americana; American
History; Political, Social, &
Cultural History; Rare Books*

Barbara Agranoff
P. O. Box 6501
Cincinnati, Ohio 45206
(513) 281-5095
By appointment only
Catalogues issued
Barbara Agranoff, Joseph Agranoff
*Americana; Crafts & Hobbies;
Ephemera; General; Illustrated
Books*

Crawford' Books
4527 Reading Road
Cincinnati, Ohio 45229

(513) 561-7355
12-5 daily
Charles C. Ellsworth
Railroads; Transportation

The Dust Jacket
3200 Linwood Avenue
Cincinnati, Ohio 45226
(513) 871-4224
6-9 Wed-Thurs, 12-5 Sat
Catalogues issued
S. H. Jenike, P. V. Metz
*Local History; Americana; Books
about Books; Natural History;
History; Biography &
Autobiography*

R. McCarty
613 Ellen Drive
Cincinnati, Ohio 45230
(513) 752-2689
By mail only
Romilda McCarty
General

Ohio Book Store, Inc.
726 Main Street
Cincinnati, Ohio 45202
(513) 621-5142
9-5 Mon-Sat
Catalogues issued
James Fallon
*Americana; Local History; First
Editions*

Robert Richshafer
1800 Vine Street
Cincinnati, Ohio 45210
(513) 421-2665
By appointment only
Catalogues issued
Robert Richshafer, Stacy
Richshafer
*Americana; Documents;
Newspapers; Photography; Rare
Books; Voyages, Travels, &
Exploration*

Significant Books
2053 Madison Road
Cincinnati, Ohio 45209
(513) 321-7567
12-6 Mon-Sat (Tues-Thurs to 9)
Catalogues issued
Carolyn Downing, Bill Downing
*History of Medicine & Science;
Natural History; Technology;
General*

John Wade
P. O. Box 991041
Cincinnati, Ohio 45201
(513) 661-2890
By appointment only
Catalogues issued
John Wade
*Middle West, American;
Americana; Science; History;
Documents; Manuscripts*

A. L. Feldman
488 The Arcade
Cleveland, Ohio 44114
(216) 861-3580
10-5:30 daily
Arthur L. Feldman
*Art; Illustrated Books; Miniature
Books; Press Books & Fine
Printing; Printing & Printing
History*

Susan Heller
22611 Halburton Road
Cleveland, Ohio 44122
(216) 283-2665
By appointment only
Catalogues issued
Susan Heller
*Scholarly Books; Modern First
Editions; Voyages, Travels, &
Exploration; Illustrated Books;
Americana*

Old Erie Street Bookstore
2128 East 9th Street
Cleveland, Ohio 44115
(216) 575-0743

10:30-5:30 Mon-Sat
Catalogues issued
Mark Stueve
*Ohio; Great Lakes; Military;
Indians & Eskimos; Civil War &
Confederacy; Literature*

Publix Book Mart
2037 East 14th Street
Cleveland, Ohio 44115
(216) 621-6624
9:30-5:30 Mon-Fri, 10-4 Sat
Wesley C. Williams
*General; Rare Books; Literature;
Local History*

John T. Zubel, Inc.
2969 West 25th Street
Cleveland, Ohio 44113
(216) 241-7640
8-4 Mon-Fri
Catalogues issued
John Zubel, Michael Zubel
*Back Issue Periodicals; Literary
Criticism; Literature; Russia &
Slavic Countries; First Editions;
Collection Development*

Books & Buttons
P. O. Box 3228
Columbus, Ohio 43210
Emanuel D. Rudolph
*Natural History; Fashion; History
of Medicine & Science; Arctica &
Antarctica*

Heritage Books
4280 Cody Road
Columbus, Ohio 43224
(614) 267-0752
By appointment only
Larry Cosner
*Civil War & Confederacy; Military
History*

Photo Place Bookshop & Gallery
211 East Arcadia Avenue
Columbus, Ohio 43202
(614) 267-0203

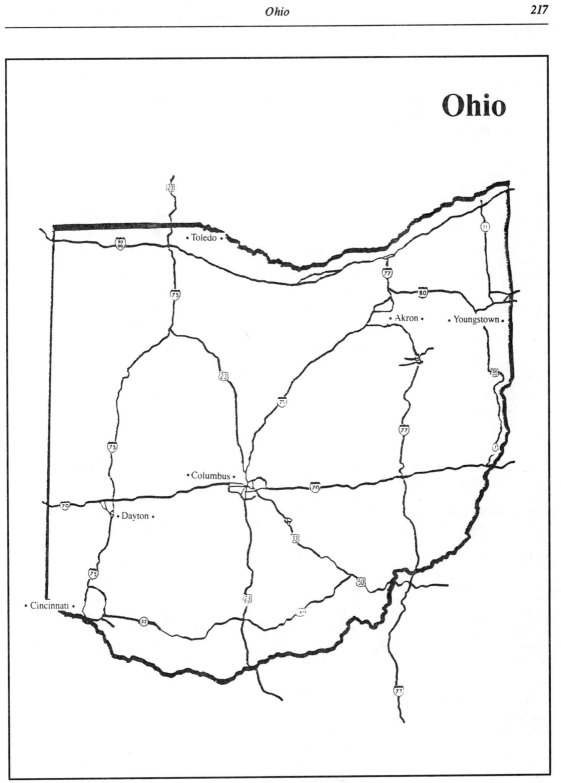

11-5 Tues-Sat
Catalogues issued
Ed Hoffman, Tina Hoffman
*Photography; Photographic
Manuals; Ohio; Humor; Modern
First Editions; Cooking*

L. J. Ryan
P. O. Box 243
Columbus, Ohio 43216
(614) 258-6558
By appointment only
Catalogues issued
Louis J. Ryan
*Americana; Foreign Affairs;
Political, Social, & Cultural
History; Religion & Religous
History; Scholarly Books; Social
Sciences*

Roy Willis
195 Thurman
Columbus, Ohio 43206
(614) 443-0004
11-5 Tues-Sun
Roy Willis
*Children's Books; Illustrated
Books; Science Fiction; Mystery
& Detective Fiction; General*

The Dragon's Lair, Inc.
110 West Fifth Street
Dayton, Ohio 45402
(513) 222-1479
10-6:45 Mon-Sat
Richard A. Vorpe, Glenn Marcus,
Richard E. Clear
*Science Fiction; Back Issue
Periodicals; Comic Books;
General; Illustrated Books; New
Paperbacks*

Owen D. Kubik
3474 Clar-Von Drive
Dayton, Ohio 45430
(513) 426-8460
By appointment only
Catalogues issued
Owen D. Kubik

*British History; Presidents;
Scholarly Books*

Morningside Bookshop
260 Oak Street, Box 1087
Dayton, Ohio 45410
(513) 461-6736
9-5 Mon-Fri
Bob Younger, Mary Younger
Civil War & Confederacy

Bibliomania
13 North Sandusky Street
Delaware, Ohio 43015
(614) 369-7904
9:30-6 Mon-Sat
Fran Chennells
Ohio; General

Saturdays' Gallery
565 East 185th Street
Euclid, Ohio 44119
(216) 486-9199
2-6 Tues-Fri, 10-5 Sat, 2-5 Sun
Catalogues issued
Jarmila Sobota, Jan Sobota
*Livre d'Artiste; Bindings, Fine &
Rare*

Bookery Fantasy & Comics
11 South Wright Avenue
Fairborn, Ohio 45324
(513) 879-1408
11-6 Mon-Fri (closed Wed), 10-6
Sat
Timothy A. Cottrill
*Science Fiction; Comic Books;
Back Issue Magazines; Trade
Cards; Games & Pastimes; Posters*

Ron Dot Bookfinders
4700 Masillon Road
Greensburg, Ohio 44232
(216) 896-3482
10-6 Mon-Sat
Ron Clewell
*Jehovah's Witnesses &
Watchtower Books; Americana;
First Editions; Ohio*

Archer's Used & Rare Bks.
164 East Main Street
Kent, Ohio 44240
(216) 673-0945
11-9 Mon-Fri, 11-6 Sat
Paul Bauer
*Natural History; Mystery &
Detective Fiction; 20th Century
Literature; General*

The Bookman Of Kent
608 Fairchild Avenue
Kent, Ohio 44240
(216) 673-1894
By appointment only
Jim Best, Linda Best
*Illustrated Books; Children's
Books; Americana; Literature*

Elaine Consolo
503 South Lexington-Springmill
Road
Mansfield, Ohio 44906
(419) 529-5755
By appointment only
Elaine Consolo
*Western Americana; Children's
Books; Natural History; General*

Ohio Bookhunter
564 East Townview Circle
Mansfield, Ohio 44907
(419) 756-0655
By appointment only
Catalogues issued
John Stark
*Americana; Indians & Eskimos;
First Editions; Western Americana;
Press Books & Fine Printing;
Limited & Signed Editions*

Mad Anthony Books
702 West Wayne Street
Maumee, Ohio 43537
(419) 893-5404
By appointment only
Catalogues issued
Don Stonestreet, Sandra Stonestreet
Antiques

Cotswold Corner Books
538 Granger Road
Medina, Ohio 44256
(216) 239-2222
10-5 Sat & Sun
Catalogues issued
Paul Duke
Cookbooks; Ancient History;
Literature; Thomas Wolfe;
Authors; Children's Books

Jack Roderick
361 Forest Meadows Drive
Medina, Ohio 44256
(216) 722-5354
By appointment only
Catalogues issued
Jack Roderick, Nancy Roderick
Aviation & Aeronautics; Railroads;
Transportation

Glenn Armitage
108 Fifth Avenue
Miamisburg, Ohio 45342
(513) 423-9569
By appointment only
Catalogues issued
Glenn Armitage
Americana; Art; First Editions;
Humanities; Literature;
Performing Arts

Owl Creek Books
309 West Vine Street
Mount Vernon, Ohio 43050
(614) 397-9337
5-9 Mon
B. K. Clinker
Americana; Authors; Biography &
Autobiography; Children's Books;
First Editions; Religion &
Religious History

Irving M. Roth
89 Whittlesey Avenue
Norwalk, Ohio 44857
(419) 668-2893
Catalogues issued
Irving M. Roth

Freemasonry; Ohio; Trade Cards;
Americana; Trade Catalogues

Backlot Books
26 South Main Street, Box 306
Oberlin, Ohio 44074
(216) 775-1296
12-6 Mon-Sat
Milton Jordan
General

Elmer G. Harris
10941 Quarry Road
Oberlin, Ohio 44074
(216) 774-4113
By appointment only
Elmer G. Harris
Children's Books

Lois Ward
P. O. Box 368
Prospect, Ohio 43342
(614) 494–2117
By appointment only
Catalogues issued
Lois H. Ward
Religion & Religious History;
Cooking; Mystery & Detective
Fiction

Under Cover Books
20201 Van Aken Boulevard
Shaker Heights, Ohio 44122
(216) 991-3600
10-6 Mon-Sat (Tues & Thurs to
9), 12-4 Sun
Catalogues issued
Joel Turner
Archaeology; Architecture;
Judaica & Hebraica; Press Books
& Fine Printing; Typography &
Type Specimens

Paper Peddlers
4425 Mayfield Road
South Euclid, Ohio 44121
(216) 382-6383
10-6 Sun
Janet Blakeley, Carole Lazarus

Ephemera; Americana; Ohio;
Fiction; Children's Books

Springbook Haus
851 East High Street
Springfield, Ohio 45505
(513) 322-1123
By appointment only
Catalogues issued
Dorothy J. Snyder, Philip D.
Snyder
Art; Architecture; Children's
Books; Military

Bishop Of Books Ltd.
328 Market
Steubenville, Ohio 43952
(614) 283-2665
9-5 Mon-Fri
Catalogues issued
Roger Bertoia, Charles Bishop, Jr.
West Virginia; Western
Pennsylvania; Western Americana;
Autographs & Autograph Material;
Modern First Editions; Chemical
& Substance Dependency

Steve Kirch
12162 Route 188
Thornville, Ohio 43076
(614) 246-4660
By appointment only
Catalogues issued
Steve Kirch
Children's Books; Back Issue
Magazines; Trade Catalogues;
Fiction

Antiquarian Book House
718 Heidelberg Road
Toledo, Ohio 43615
(419) 531-6995
12-5 Mon-Sat
Pete Baughman, Cheryl Baughman
Illustrated Books; Modern First
Editions; General

G. D. Brown
7001 Bancroft Street

Toledo, Ohio 43617
(419) 841-4979
1-5 Tues-Sat
Alberta Brown, George D. Brown
General; Great Lakes; Americana;
Archaeology; Architecture; Bible
& Bible Studies

Burley & Books, Inc.
348 Franklin Park Mall
Toledo, Ohio 43623
(419) 472-0775
10-9 Mon-Sat, 12-5 Sun
Michael W. Lora
Modern First Editions; Tobacco
& Smoking; Books about Books;
Bibliography; Appraisals &
Appraisal Services; Book Trade
& Catalogues

Lawrence A. Leo
2246 Midlawn Drive
Toledo, Ohio 43614
(419) 385-4793
By appointment only
Lawrence A. Leo
General

Bob & Doris Lutz
523 East Temple Street
Washington C. H., Ohio 43160
(614) 335-0317
By appointment only
Catalogues issued
Bob Lutz, Doris Lutz
"National Geographic" Magazine;
General

The World Of Books
37231 Euclid Avenue
Willoughby, Ohio 44094
(216) 951-1252
10-6 Sat
Lynn Robinson
Poetry; Children's Books; Art;
Illustrated Books; Drama; History

Robert E. Morgan
P. O. Box 5483
Willowick, Ohio 44094
(216) 943-6374
By mail only
Catalogues issued
Robert E. Morgan, Michele
Morgan
Television & Radio; Electronics

Historical Realia
1059 Douglas Drive
Wooster, Ohio 44691
(216) 262-3103
By appointment only
Catalogues issued
Garry E. Gibbons
Indians & Eskimos; Americana;
Autographs & Autograph Material;
Civil War & Confederacy; Rare
Books; Voyages, Travels, &
Exploration

A. & J. Lynn Book Service
1973 West Grandville Road
Worthington, Ohio 43085
(614) 436-0646
By appointment only
Austin Lynn, Jean Lynn
Civil War & Confederacy

Jerry Merkel
2281 Spahr Road
Xenia, Ohio 45385
(513) 848-2359
By mail only
Catalogues issued
Jerry Merkel
Biography & Autobiography;
Literary Criticism; Humor;
Americana

Gary Houseman
327 Dayton Street
Yellow Springs, Ohio 45387
(513) 767-5531
By mail only
Gary Houseman

Science Fiction; Americana; Occult
& Magic

Mysteries From The Yard
101 Cemetary
Yellow Springs, Ohio 45387
(513) 767-2111
12-6 Fri-Sun
M. Frost-Pierson
Mystery & Detective Fiction; Early
& Collectible Paperbacks;
Television & Radio; Sherlock
Holmes & A. C. Doyle

Bolotin Books
P. O. Box 1325
Youngstown, Ohio 44501
By appointment only
J. Warren Bolotin
Business & Business History;
Engineering; Architecture

Carol Butcher
3955 New Road
Youngstown, Ohio 44515
(216) 793-6832
Catalogues issued
Carol Butcher
Dogs; Fishing & Angling;
Hunting; Horses & Horse Sports;
Christian Books

Albert Cohen
457 Arbor Circle
Youngstown, Ohio 44504
(216) 759-8131
By appointment only
Albert Cohen
First Editions; Illustrated Books;
Rare Books

Twice-Loved Books
19 East Middlethian Boulevard
Youngstown, Ohio 44507
(216) 783-2016
10-8 Mon-Fri, 10-5 Sat
Peggy McKissick, Jack Peterson
General

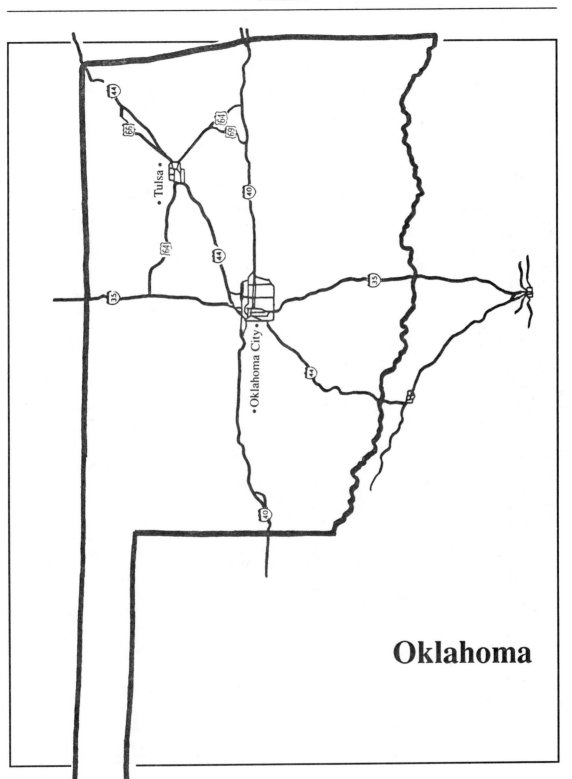

Oklahoma

Oklahoma

Ron Bever
Route 3, Box 243-B
Edmond, Okla. 73013
(405) 478-0125
By mail only
Catalogues issued
Ron Bever
Stock Market & Wall Street;
Commodities Trading; Western
Books; Oklahoma (& Indian
Territory); Religion & Religous
History

A Points Northe
3630 NW 32nd
Oklahoma City, Okla. 73107-2893
(405) 949-0675
9-12 daily
James Neil Northe
Oklahoma (& Indian Territory);
Western Americana

Arcane Books
3120 Harvey Parkway
Oklahoma City, Okla. 73118
(405) 525-6260
By appointment only
Catalogues issued
Oliver Delaney
Ireland & The Irish; Bibliography;
Appraisals & Appraisal Services

E. B. Dean
P. O. Drawer 60450

Oklahoma City, Okla. 73146
(405) 528-5857
By appointment only
E. B. Dean
Western Americana; Oklahoma (&
Indian Territory); Regional
Americana

Lutes Book Store
404 West Main
Oklahoma City, Okla. 73102
(405) 232-2621
9-5 Mon-Sat
Dick Berger
General

Melvin Marcher
6204 North Vermont
Oklahoma City, Okla. 73112
(405) 946-6270
By mail only
Catalogues issued
Melvin Marcher
Guns & Weapons; Archery;
Fishing & Angling; Hunting;
Natural History; Militaria

Michael's Old Books
3636 North Western
Oklahoma City, Okla. 73118
(405) 525-0123
10-6 Mon-Sat
Nguy Lee
Western Americana; Oklahoma (&

Indian Territory); Authors;
General

Caravan Books
221 South Knoblock, Box 861
Stillwater, Okla. 74074
(405) 372-6227
12-6 Mon-Fri (closed Wed), 12-5
Sat
Catalogues issued
Della Thomas, John E. Thomas
Southwestern Americana; Black
Literature & Studies; Children's
Books; Oklahoma (& Indian
Territory); Science Fiction

The First Edition Book Shop
1502 East 15th Street
Tulsa, Okla. 74120
(918) 582-1967
11-6 Mon-Sat
Della Kay McCulloch
Art; Americana

Oklahoma Bookman
1107 Foreman Road, NE
Yukon, Okla. 73099
By mail only
Catalogues issued
Ted Goulden
Natural History; Botany; Zoology

Ontario

Lewis Sherman
865 Danforth Place
Burlington, Ont. L7T 1S1
(416) 522-9082
By appointment only
Ruth Sherman, Lewis Sherman
Voyages, Travels, & Exploration;
Cooking; Victoriana

Madonna House Bookshop
Combermere, Ont. K0J 1L0
(613) 756-3149
2-5 daily (Summers only)
Catalogues issued
Karen Van De Loop
Americana; Canada & Canadiana;
Religion & Religious History;
General; Catholica

William Matthews
16 Jarvis Street
Fort Erie, Ont. L2A 2S1
(416) 871-7859
9-5:30 Mon-Sat
Catalogues issued
William Matthews, Ann Hall
Modern First Editions; Science
Fiction; English Literature; Rare
Books

Lyndsay Dobson
P. O. Box 285
Grimsby, Ont. L3M 4G5
(416) 945-3268
By mail only
Catalogues issued
Lyndsay Dobson, William Poole
Canada & Canadiana; Press
Books & Fine Printing; Printing
& Printing History

John Rush
396 Herkimer Street

Hamilton, Ont.
(416) 522-7096
By mail only
Catalogues issued
John Rush
Canada & Canadiana

Berry and Peterson
112 Montreal Street
Kingston, Ont. K7K 3E8
(613) 548-4871
By appointment only
John Berry, Richard Peterson
Maps, Atlases, & Cartography;
Voyages, Travels, & Exploration;
Illustrated Books; Modern First
Editions; Books about Books

Book Bin
225 Princess Street
Kingston, Ont. K7L 1B3
(613) 548-4871
10-5:30 Mon-Sun
Catalogues issued
Richard Peterson, John C. Berry
Art; First Editions; Canada &
Canadiana; Mountaineering;
Science Fiction; Voyages, Travels,
& Exploration

Gail Wilson
P. O. Box 2833, Stn. B
Kitchener, Ont. H2H 6N3
10-6 Mon-Sat
Gail Wilson
Books about Books; Cooking;
Farming, Ranching, & Livestock;
Folklore; Political, Social, &
Cultural History; Technology

Attic Books
388 Clarence Street
London, Ont. N6A 3M7

(519) 432-6636
10-6 Mon-Sat (Fri to 9)
Catalogues issued
Marvin Post, Nancy Buckingham
Voyages, Travels, & Exploration;
True Crime; Technical; New
Paperbacks; New Paperbacks;
General

Sportsman's Cabinet
P. O. Box 15
Manotick, Ont. K0A 2N0
(613) 692-3618
By mail only
Catalogues issued
W. A. McClure, K. H. McClure
Sporting; Guns & Weapons;
Fishing & Angling; Dogs;
Mountaineering; Natural History

Allison The Bookman
342 Main Street, East
North Bay, Ont. P1B 1B4
(705) 476-1450
10-9 Mon-Sun
Patricia Castle-Doucet, G. S.
Allison
Canada & Canadiana; Literature;
Cooking; General

Treasure Island
250 Kerr Street
Oakville, Ont. L6K 3B1
(416) 845-8009
10-6 Mon-Sat
J. Bruce Ferrier
Canada & Canadiana; Children's
Books; Illustrated Books; Comic
Books; Phonograph Records

Iroqrafts Ltd.
R.R. 2
Ohsweken, Ont. N0A 1M0

Ontario

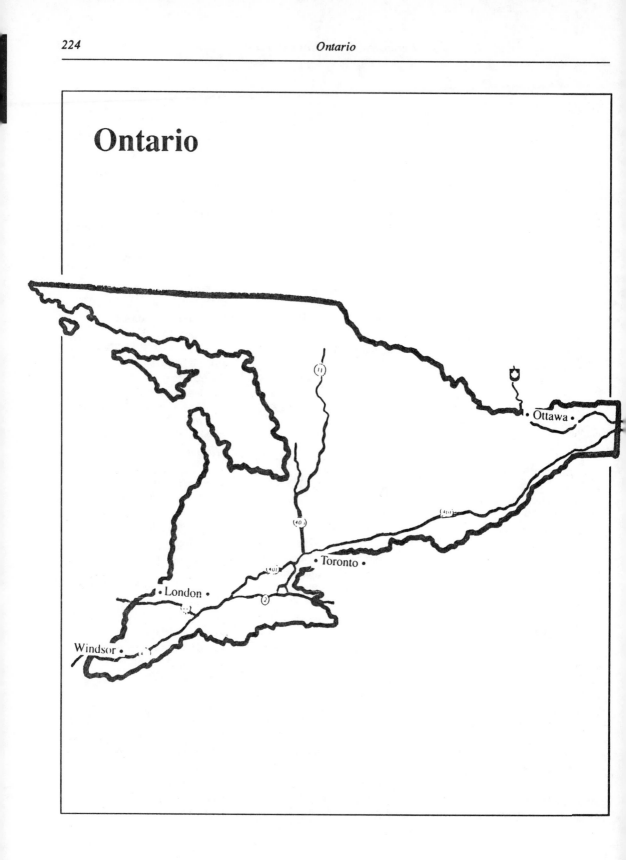

(416) 765-4206
8:30-6 daily
Catalogues issued
W. G. Spittal, N. Hill
Indians & Eskimos

Mrs. A. L. Ashton
49 Birch Avenue
Ottawa, Ont. K1K 3G5
(613) 749-1741
By appointment only
Catalogues issued
Mrs. A. L. Ashton
*Canada & Canadiana; Children's
Books; History; Militaria; Poetry;
Rare Books*

Ken Benson
58 Armstrong Avenue
Ottawa, Ont. K1Y 2V7
(613) 238-7509
11:30-4 Tue-Sat
Ken Benson
Canada & Canadiana; Militaria

The Book Bazaar
755 Bank Street
Ottawa, Ont. K1S 3V3
(613) 233-4380
10-5:30 Tues-Sat
Beryl McLeod
*Canada & Canadiana; Music; Art;
Literature*

Dyment Books
319 Wilbrod Street
Ottawa, Ont. K1N 6M4
(613) 235-0565
10-6 daily
Catalogues issued
Margaret Dyment, Paul Dyment
*Philosophy; Political Science &
Theory; Literature; Political,
Social, & Cultural History;
Psychiatry, Psychology, &
Psychoanalysis*

J. Patrick McGahern
783 Bank Street

Ottawa, Ont. K1S 3V5
(613) 233-2215
10-6 Mon-Sat
Catalogues issued
Patrick McGahern
*Arctica & Antarctica; Canada &
Canadiana; First Editions;
Voyages, Travels, & Exploration;
Ireland & The Irish; Rare Books*

Nelson Ball
31 Willow Street
Paris, Ont. N3L 2K7
(519) 442-6113
By appointment only
Catalogues issued
Nelson Ball
*Canadian Literature; History;
Literary Criticism; Little
Magazines & Literary Small
Presses; Poetry*

Glooscap Study
R.R. 1
Pefferlaw, Ont. L0E 1N0
(705) 437-2346
10-10 daily
Catalogues issued
R. T. Seaman, Alison Seaman
*Sailing & Yachting; Biography &
Autobiography; Fiction; First
Editions*

Pomona Book Exchange
953 Highway 52
Rockton, Ont. L0R 1X0
(519) 621-8897
By appointment only
Catalogues issued
H. Fred Janson, Walda Janson
*Agriculture; Botany; Gardening &
Horticulture; Landscape
Architecture; Herbology & Herbs;
Forestry*

Hannelore Headley
71 Queen Street
St. Catherines, Ont. L2R 5G9
(416) 684-6145

10-5 Mon-Sat
Hannelore Headley
*Canada & Canadiana; Literature;
General*

The House Of Antique Books
150 York Hill Boulevard
Thornhill, Ont. L4J 2P6
(416) 630-8457
By mail only
Harold Medjuck
Canada & Canadiana; Caribbean

Abelard Bookshop
519 Queen Street West
Toronto, Ont. M5V 2B4
(416) 366-0021
10-6 Mon-Sun
Paul Lockwood, Joyce Blair
*Religion & Religous History;
Philosophy; Literature; History;
Greek & Roman Classics;
Archaeology*

About Books
280 Queen Street West
Toronto, Ont. M5V 2A1
(416) 593-0792
10-9 Mon-Fri, 10-6 Sat, 11-6 Sun
Catalogues issued
L. A. Wallrich, A. Greenwood
*Modern First Editions; Literature;
Scholarly Books; Mountaineering;
Dogs; General*

Alphabet Bookshop
656 Spadina Avenue
Toronto, Ont. M5S 2H9
(416) 924-4926
10-6 Mon-Sat
Catalogues issued
Richard Shuh, Linda Woolley
*Canadian Literature; First
Editions; Modern First Editions;
Poetry; Literature; Appraisals &
Appraisal Services*

Annex Books
1083 Bathurst Street

Toronto, Ont. M5R 3G8
(416) 537-1852
11-6 Mon-Fri, 10-6 Sat
Catalogues issued
Janet Fetherling
Literature; Canada & Canadiana

Hugh Anson-Cartwright
229 College Street
Toronto, Ont. M5T 1R4
(416) 979-2441
9:30-5:30 Mon-Fri, 10-5 Sat
Catalogues issued
Hugh Anson-Cartwright
Canada & Canadiana; Literature;
Arctica & Antarctica; Bindings,
Leather

Atticus Books
84 Harbord Street
Toronto, Ont. M5S 1G5
(416) 922-6045
11:30-6 Mon-Sat (Sat to 5:30),
12-5 Sun
Catalogues issued
Michael Freedman, Shirley
Josephs, Donald Smith
Philosophy; Greek & Roman
Classics; Linguistics; History of
Medicine & Science; Psychiatry,
Psychology, & Psychoanalysis;
Literary Criticism

Bakka
282 Queen Street West
Toronto, Ont. M5V 2A1
(416) 596-8161
10-6 Mon-Sat (Fri to 9)
John Rose
Science Fiction

Batta Book Store
710 The Queensway
Toronto, Ont. M8Y 1L3
(416) 259-2618
2-7 Mon-Sat
Bela Batta
20th Century Literature; General

Glad Day Bookshop
598-A Yonge Street
Toronto, Ont. M4Y 1Z3
(416) 961-4161
10-9 Mon-Fri, 10-6 Sat, 12-6 Sun
Jearld Moldenhauer
Gay & Lesbian Literature

J. L. Heath
66 Isabella Street, suite 105
Toronto, Ont. M4Y 1N3
(416) 926-0643
9-5 Mon-Sat
Catalogues issued
Jack Heath, Krista Cliu
Law; True Crime; Criminology

Heritage Books
866 Palmerston Avenue
Toronto, Ont. M6G 2S2
(416) 533-6816
By appointment only
Catalogues issued
Robert M. Stamp
Canada & Canadiana

House Of Sarah
P. O. Box 670, Stn. P
Toronto, Ont. M5S 2Y4
(416) 977-5152
By appointment only
Catalogues issued
Mary Tardiff
Women; Religion & Religious
History

D. & E. Lake, Ltd.
106 Berkeley Street
Toronto, Ont. M5A 2W7
(416) 863-9930
9-6 Mon-Sat
Catalogues issued
Donald Lake, Elaine Lake, Sandra
Lake
Philosophy; Business & Business
History; Canada & Canadiana;
Maps, Atlases, & Cartography;
Voyages, Travels, & Exploration;
Rare Books

David Mason
342 Queen Street, West
Toronto, Ont. M5V 2A2
(416) 598-1015
11-6 Mon-Sat, Sun 12-6
Catalogues issued
David Mason
Canada & Canadiana; 19th
Century Literature; Modern First
Editions; Literature; Rare Books;
History

Murder By Request
261 Broadway Avenue
Toronto, Ont. M4P 1W1
(416) 486-6557
By appointment only
Catalogues issued
Mary L. Pitblado
Mystery & Detective Fiction;
Sherlock Holmes & A. C. Doyle

Old Favorites Bookshop
250 Adelaide, West
Toronto, Ont. M5H 1X8
(416) 977-2944
10-9 Tues, Thu, Sat
Catalogues issued
K. E. Saunders
Canada & Canadiana; Fiction;
Horses & Horse Sports; General

Joseph Patrick Books
1600 Bloor Street West
Toronto, Ont. M6P 1A7
(416) 531-1891
9-5 Mon-Fri, 10-5 Sat
Catalogues issued
J. G. Sherlock, W. Wiles
Canada & Canadiana; Arctica &
Antarctica; Catholica; Scholarly
Books; Autographs & Autograph
Material; Maps, Atlases, &
Cartography

St. Nicholas Books
P. O. Box 863, Stn. F
Toronto, Ont. M4Y 2N7
(416) 922-9640

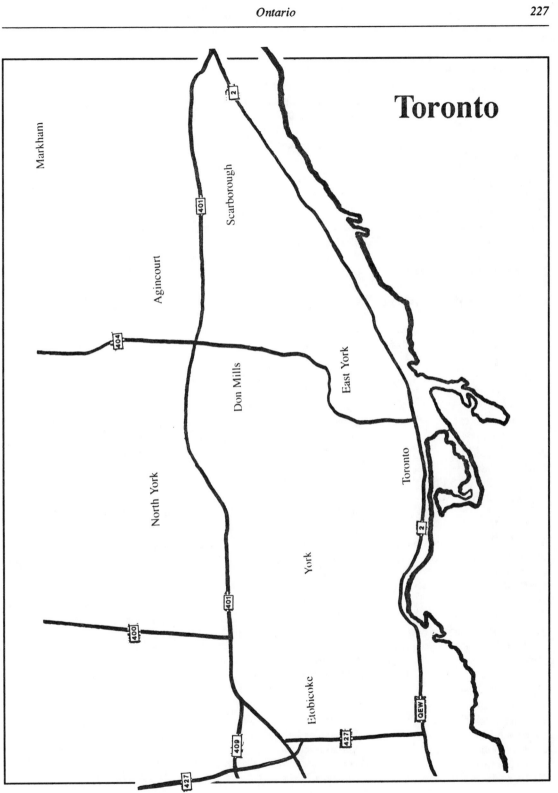

Toronto

Markham

Scarborough

Agincourt

Don Mills

East York

North York

Toronto

York

Etobicoke

By appointment only
Catalogues issued
Yvonne Knight
Children's Books

Steven Temple
483 Queen Street West
Toronto, Ont. M5V 2A9
(416) 865-9908
11-7 Mon-Fri, 11-6 Sat
Catalogues issued
Steve Temple
*Canadian Literature; Modern First
Editions; Mystery & Detective
Fiction; Literature; Poetry;
Literature In English Translation*

Arthur Wharton
652 Queen Street West
Toronto, Ont. M6J 1E5
(416) 865-9907
11-7 Mon-Fri, 11-6 Sat
Catalogues issued
Arthur Wharton
*History of Medicine & Science;
General*

Peter L. Jackson
23 Castle Green Crescent
Weston, Ont. M9R 1N5
(416) 249-4796
By appointment only
Catalogues issued

Peter L. Jackson, Rosemarie M.
Jackson
*Militaria; Napoleon; Books About
Medals; Military History; British
History*

The Past & Present Shop
3277 Sandwich Street
Windsor, Ont. N9C 1A9
(519) 255-7810
10-5 Mon-Sat
W. R. Ransome, E. J. Ransome
*Canada & Canadiana; Children's
Books; History; General*

Oregon

Book Bin
121 West First Avenue
Albany, Ore. 97321
(503) 926-6869
10-6 Mon-Sat (to 8 Fri)
Bob McMaster
General

The Blue Dragon Book Shop
283 East Main Street
Ashland, Ore. 97520
(503) 482-2142
10-6 daily
Bob Peterson
*Arctica & Antarctica; Metaphysics;
Western Americana; Theatre; Rare
Books*

Hermeticus Books
P. O. Box 1166
Ashland, Ore. 97520
(503) 488-0142
By appointment only
Catalogues issued
Richard Miller

*Myths & Mythology; Alchemy &
Hermetics; Religion & Religous
History; Occult & Magic; Asia;
Eastern Religions*

R. Plapinger
144 4th Street
Ashland, Ore. 97520
(503) 488-1220
By mail only
Catalogues issued
R. Plapinger
Baseball

Soundpeace
199 East Main Street
Ashland, Ore. 97520
(503) 482-3633
10-5 Mon-Sat, 11-4 Sun
Catalogues issued
Mariam Schwab
*Metaphysics; Video Cassette &
Compact Disks; Art*

Automobile Books & Literature
P. O. Box 922
Beaverton, Ore. 97075
(503) 292-4227
By mail only
Logan Gray
Automotive; Automobile Racing

Book Vault
3125 SW Cedar Hills Boulevard
Beaverton, Ore. 97005
(503) 646-8119
10-9 Mon-Fri, 10-6 Sat, 12-5 Sun
Doreen Kelley
General

Ernest & Margaret Ediger
12680 SW Farmington Road
Beaverton, Ore. 97005
(503) 643-7222
10-6 Tues-Sat
Ernest Ediger, Margaret Ediger
*Fiction; Biography &
Autobiography*

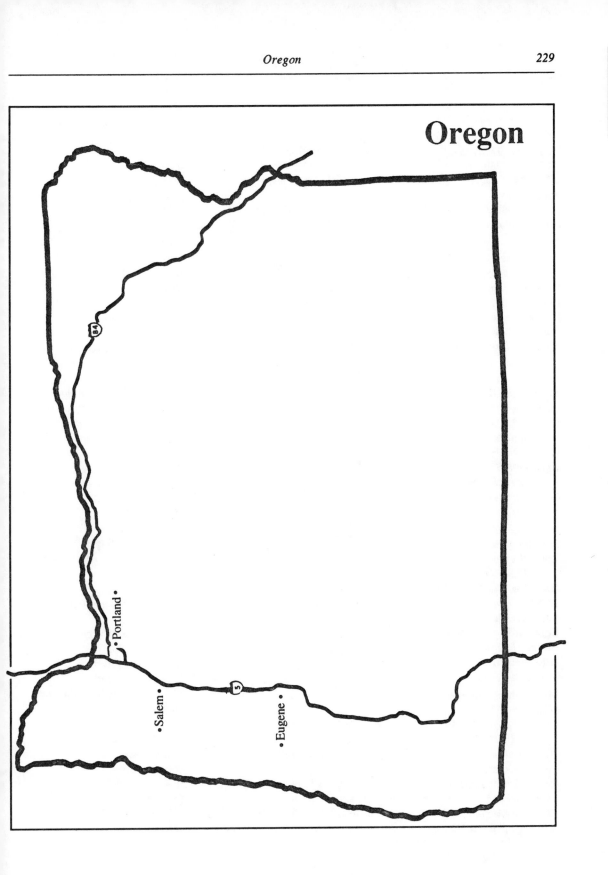

Oregon

The Book Barn
124 Northwest Minnesota
Bend, Ore. 97701
(503) 389-4589
9-5:30 Mon-Sat
Sally Irving
*Northwestern Americana; New
Books; General*

Diva Books
P. O. Box 1439
Coos Bay, Ore. 97420
(503) 269-5220
By appointment only
James R. Soladay
Fiction; Illustrated Books

Avocet Used Books
614 SW 3rd Street
Corvallis, Ore. 97333
(503) 753-4119
10-6 Mon-Sat
Howard Mills, Saundra A. Mills
*Children's Books; Cooking;
Literature; Natural History;
Science Fiction*

Book Bin
351 NW Jackson
Corvallis, Ore. 97330
(503) 752-0040
10-6 Mon-Thu & Sat, 10-8 Fri,
12-5 Sun
Catalogues issued
Bob Baird
*Hawaii; Pacific Region; Religion
& Religous History; General*

McLaughlin's Books
P. O. Box 753
Cottage Grove, Ore. 97424
(503) 942-0745
By appointment only
Catalogues issued
Robert F. McLaughlin
*Idaho; Arctica & Antarctica;
Fishing & Angling; Guns &
Weapons; Natural History*

Allen A. Dunn
1255 Oak Villa Road
Dallas, Ore. 97338
(503) 623-5136
By appointment only
Allen A. Dunn
*Dogs; Hunting; Big Game
Hunting; Natural History; Western
Americana*

Authors Of The West
191 Dogwood Drive
Dundee, Ore. 97115
(503) 538-8132
By appointment only
Catalogues issued
Lee Nash, Grayce Nash
*Western Americana; Western
Books; Modern First Editions;
Indians & Eskimos; Literature;
Poetry*

Joy A. Wheeler
Route 1, Box 49-K
Elgin, Ore. 97827
(503) 437-8641
By appointment only
Catalogues issued
Joy A. Wheeler
*Regional Americana; Children's
Books*

The Bookloft
107 East Main Street
Enterprise, Ore. 97828
(503) 426-3351
9:30-5:30 Fri, 10-4 Sat
Rich Wandschneider
*Local History; Western Americana;
New Books*

Backstage Books
P. O. Box 3676
Eugene, Ore. 97403
By mail only
Catalogues issued
Howard L. Ramey
*Drama; Performing Arts; Circus
& Carnival; Fashion;*

*Shakespeare; Puppetry &
Marionettes*

Book Fair
1409 Oak Street
Eugene, Ore. 97401
(503) 343-3033
10-5:30 Mon-Fri (Fri to 8), 9:30-5
Sat
Jerry Leedy
*Series Books For Boys & Girls;
General*

Cellar Of Books
P. O. Box 10863
Eugene, Ore. 97440
(503) 343-0262
C. J. Houser
*Children's Books; Juveniles;
Regional Americana; Religion &
Religious History; Cooking;
General*

Dakota Antiques & Crafts
201 Spring Creek Drive
Eugene, Ore. 97404
(503) 689-5640
9-5 Mon-Sat
Josephine Zollinger
*Fiction; Western Americana;
General*

Lonesome Water Books
2051 Monroe
Eugene, Ore. 97405
(503) 343-1502
By appointment only
Catalogues issued
Thomas R. Hughes, Margaret
Hughes
Western Americana

J. Michaels
160 East Broadway
Eugene, Ore. 97401-3128
(503) 342-2002
9:30-5:30 Mon-Fri, 10-5 Sat
Jeremy Nissel

Art; Modern First Editions;
Photography; Illustrated Books

Old Eugene Bookstore
207 East 5th Street, suite 101
Eugene, Ore. 97401
(503) 683-2133
10-5:30 Mon-Sat, 12-5 Sun
Nancy Burgraff
Western Americana; General

T. W. Palmer
259 West 23rd Avenue
Eugene, Ore. 97405
(503) 343-6536
By appointment only
Theodore W. Palmer
Western Americana; Maps, Atlases,
& Cartography; Voyages, Travels,
& Exploration; Natural History;
Railroads

The Bay Window
P. O. Box 930
Florence, Ore. 97439
(503) 997-2002
10-5 Mon-Sat, 12-3 Sun
General

Western Book Company
P. O. Box 271
Gaston, Ore. 97119
(503) 662-3618
By appointment only
Catalogues issued
Pam Konschu
Railroads; Sporting

John G. Stein
P. O. Box 1329
Gold Beach, Ore. 97444
(503) 247-2474
Catalogues issued
John G. Stein
Naval & Nautical; Curiosa

B. L. Bibby
1225 Sardine Creek Road
Gold Hill, Ore. 97525

(503) 855-1621
By mail only
Catalogues issued
George Bibby
Gardening & Horticulture; Natural
History

Golden Gull Bookstore
1885 NE 7th Street
Grants Pass, Ore. 97526
(503) 476-7323
9-9 Mon-Fri, 9-6 Sat, 11-6 Sun
Susan Elzea
New Books; Search Service,
Without Stock

Ernest L. Sackett
100 Waverly Drive
Grants Pass, Ore. 97526
(503) 476-6404
By appointment only
Catalogues issued
Ernest L. Sackett
Western Americana; Christian
Books; Fishing & Angling;
Juveniles

Jacksonville Books
120 East California Street
Jacksonville, Ore. 97530
(503) 899-8520
11-5 Tues-Sat, 12-5 Sun
James Goodreau
Remainders; General

Phillip J. Pirages
P. O. Box 504
McMinnville, Ore. 97128
(503) 472-5555
By appointment only
Catalogues issued
Phillip J. Pirages, Phyllis Turner
Rare Books; Press Books & Fine
Printing; Manuscripts; Literature;
Appraisals & Appraisal Services;
Incunabula

Bartlett Street Book Store
16 South Bartlett Street

Medford, Ore. 97501
(503) 772-8049
10-5 Mon-Sat
Ken Corliss
General

Eldora's Books
814 East Hancock
Newberg, Ore. 97132
(503) 538-1279
9-6 Wed-Sat
Eldora Acott
Children's Books; Fiction; General

Ken-L-Questor
32255 North Highway 99 East
Newberg, Ore. 97132
(503) 538-2051
By appointment only
Catalogues issued
Kenneth M. Lewis
Dogs; Mushrooms; Cactus &
Succulents; Natural History;
Sporting

Scott Arden
20457 Highway 126
Noti, Ore. 97461
(503) 935-1619
By appointment only
Catalogues issued
Scott Arden
Railroads; Transportation

Academic Book Center
5600 NE Hassalo Street
Portland, Ore. 97213-3640
(503) 287-6657
By mail only
Catalogues issued
Bob Schatz
Technical; Reference; University
Press Books

Annie Bloom's Books #1
7834 SW Capitol Highway
Portland, Ore. 97219
(503) 246-0053
9:30-7 Mon-Fri, 9:30-5 Sat, 12-4

Sun
Roberta Tichenor
Judaica & Hebrica; Children's
Books; Women; Cooking;
Literature; Poetry

Annie Bloom's Books #2
406 NW 23rd Avenue
Portland, Ore. 97210
(503) 221-4224
9:30-7 Mon-Fri, 9:30-5 Sat, 12-4
Sun
Roberta Tichenor
Judaica & Hebrica; Children's
Books; Women; Cooking;
Literature; Poetry

Beaver Book Store
3747 Southeast Hawthorne
Boulevard
Portland, Ore. 97214
(503) 238-1668
10-6 Tues-Sat
Ken Isbell
General

The Book Manifest Ltd.
2585 SW 87th Avenue
Portland, Ore. 97225
(503) 292-1050
By appointment only
Christoper Skagen
Metaphysics; Tibet; Eastern
Religions

Cameron's Books
336 SW Third Avenue
Portland, Ore. 97204
(503) 228-2391
10-6 daily
Fred Goetz
General; 19th Century Periodicals;
Postcards; Sheet Music

The Catbird Seed Bookstore
913 SW Broadway
Portland, Ore. 97205
(503) 222-5817
9:30 a.m.-9:30 p.m. Mon-Fri (to

11 p.m. Fri), 10 a.m.-11 p.m. Sat
Catalogues issued
Debra Robboy, Mary Swanson
Chemical & Substance
Dependency; Psychiatry,
Psychology, & Psychoanalysis;
Women; Health; Metaphysics;
Gardening & Horticulture

Green Dolphin Bookshop
1300 SW Washington
Portland, Ore. 97205
(503) 224-3060
11-9 Mon-Sat, 11-5 Sun
Wright Lewis
Northwestern Americana; Modern
First Editions; Marine & Maritime

Raymond Kimeldorf
1925 Southeast 59th Avenue
Portland, Ore. 97215
(503) 236-1848
By mail only
Raymond Kimeldorf
Judaica & Hebrica

McDuffie's Old Books
P. O. Box 42282
Portland, Ore. 97242-0282
By appointment only
Catalogues issued
McDuffie Owen
Medicine & Science; Technology;
Mining & Metallurgy; Geology;
Western Americana; Trade
Catalogues

Midvale Books
155 SW Midvale Road
Portland, Ore. 97219
(503) 636-7952
By mail only
Catalogues issued
Cheryl Clevenger, Ron Clevenger
New Books; Rare Books

Old Oregon Book Store
1128 SW Alder
Portland, Ore. 97205

(503) 227-2742
11-5 daily
Catalogues issued
Preston McMann
Regional Americana; General;
Rare Books; Scholarly Books

Paper Moon Bookstore
3538 SE Hawthorne
Portland, Ore. 97214
(503) 236-5195
12-5 Mon-Sun
Andrea Drenard
Children's Books; Illustrated
Books; Photography; Art

Robert Ellis Rudolph
Corporation
1119 SW Park Avenue
Portland, Ore. 97205
(503) 223-7518
10-3 Mon-Fri
Robert E. Rudolph
Autographs & Autograph Material;
Prints; Maps, Atlases, &
Cartography; Western Books;
Illuminated Leaves & Pages; Early
Printed Books

Charles Seluzicki
3733 NE 24th Avenue
Portland, Ore. 97212
(503) 284-4749
By appointment only
Catalogues issued
Charles Seluzicki
Modern First Editions; Autographs
& Autograph Material; Press
Books & Fine Printing; Illustrated
Books; Literature In English
Translation

Tom Stewart
P. O. Box 5998
Portland, Ore. 97228
(503) 281-4401
By mail only
Catalogues issued
Tom Stewart

*Black Literature & Studies; Fishing
& Angling; Hunting; Guns &
Weapons; Derrydale Press;
Presidents*

The Webfoot Bookman
334 SE 62nd Avenue
Portland, Ore. 97215
(503) 236-3040
By appointment only
Catalogues issued
Charles Gould
*Western Americana; Fishing &
Angling; Hunting*

Hole In The Wall Bookstore
439 Fir Avenue

Reedsport, Ore. 97467
9:30-5:30 Mon-Sat
Cindy Haines
Regional Americana; General

Doug Bearce
P. O. Box 7081
Salem, Ore. 97303
(503) 393-1767
By appointment only
Catalogues issued
Doug Bearce, Robyn DeVilliers
Boy Scouts

Dale C. Schmidt
610 Howell Prairie Road, SE
Salem, Ore. 97301

(503) 364-0499
By appointment only
Dale C. Schmidt
*Regional Americana; Postcards;
Ephemera; Trade Catalogues*

Gerry Aboud
836 East Kathy Street
Stayton, Ore. 97383
(503) 769-7505
By mail only
Gerry Aboud
*Back Issue Magazines;
Newspapers; Ephemera; Back
Issue Periodicals*

Pennsylvania

Otzinachson Book Shop
R. R. 1, Box 30
Allenwood, Pa. 17810
(717) 538-1800
10-5 Mon-Sun
Catalogues issued
Marjorie O. Steininger
*General; Modern First Editions;
Pennsylvania*

Robert Batchelder
1 West Butler Avenue
Ambler, Pa. 19002
(215) 643-1430
9:30-4 Mon-Fri
Catalogues issued
Robert Batchelder, Eileen Keiter
*Autographs & Autograph Material;
Documents; Manuscripts*

Mark E. Battersby
P. O. Box 527
Ardmore, Pa. 19003

(215) 649-0311
Catalogues issued
Mark E. Battersby
*Bindings, Fine & Rare; Farming,
Ranching, & Livestock; Mystery
& Detective Fiction; Business &
Business History; Economics;
Stock Market & Wall Street*

The Saurus
109 East Third Street
Bethlehem, Pa. 18015
(215) 691-2005
11-5 Tues-Sat
Adrienne Redd
*Literature; Philosophy; Psychiatry,
Psychology, & Psychoanalysis;
Science Fiction; History; Political,
Social, & Cultural History*

The Epistemologist
P. O. Box 63
Bryn Mawr, Pa. 19010

(215) 527-1065
By appointment only
Catalogues issued
Lynn Wozniak, Rob Wozniak
*Psychiatry, Psychology, &
Psychoanalysis; Philosophy; Social
Sciences*

The Owl Bookshop
Morris Avenue & Yarrow Street
Bryn Mawr, Pa. 19010
(215) 525-6117
1-5 Tues, Thurs-Fri, 10-2 Sat
General

Chadds Ford Antique Mall
Route 1
Chadds Ford, Pa. 19317
(215) 388-6480
11-5 Sat & Sun
Judith S. Helms
General

George Hall, Jr.
1441 Lincoln Way, East
Chambersburg, Pa. 17201
(717) 263-4388
Catalogues issued
George Hall, Jr.
Americana; Fishing & Angling;
Militaria; Technology; Hunting

Cesi Kellinger
735 Philadelphia Avenue
Chambersburg, Pa. 17201
(717) 263-4474
By appointment only
Catalogues issued
Cesi Kellinger
Americana; Art; Books about
Books; Dance

Lincoln Way Books
136 Lincoln Way West
Chambersburg, Pa. 17201
(717) 264-7120
11-5 Mon-Sat
William B. Earley
Pennsylvania; Press Books & Fine
Printing; Modern First Editions;
Phonograph Records; Civil War
& Confederacy; General

Doe Run Valley Books
P. O. Box 255
Cochranville, Pa. 19330
(215) 593-6997
By appointment only
Judith S. Helms
Illustrated Books; Regional
Americana; General

Darby Books
842 Main Street
Darby, Pa. 19023
(215) 583-4550
9-5 Mon-Fri
Jerry Weiman, Hassie Weiman
Literary Criticism; Literature;
Humanities; Folklore; Reprints

Stanley Gorski
2667 Furlong Road
Doylestown, Pa. 18901
(215) 794-5377
By appointment only
Stanley Gorski
Science; Technology; Science
Fiction; Psychiatry, Psychology, &
Psychoanalysis

The East-West Room
3139 Alpin Drive
Dresher, Pa. 19025
(215) 657-0178
By appointment only
Catalogues issued
Myrna Bloom
Textiles

Hive Of Industry
P. O. Box 602
Easton, Pa. 18042
(215) 258-6663
By mail only
Catalogues issued
I. Y. Mayer, Oliver Mayer, Ms.
Dudley Katt
Political Science & Theory;
Technology; Business & Business
History; Engineering; Social
Sciences; Psychiatry, Psychology,
& Psychoanalysis

Quadrant Book Mart
20 North 3rd Street
Easton, Pa. 18042
(215) 252-1188
9:30-5:30 Mon-Sat (Tues, Fri to 9)
Richard Epstein, Barbara Epstein
Biography & Autobiography;
Fiction; Scholarly Books

Zellner's Book Service
2839 Norton Avenue
Easton, Pa. 18042
(215) 258-3882
By appointment only
Catalogues issued
Maurice A. Zellner, Geraldine C

Zellner
Series Books For Boys & Girls;
Western Books; Civil War &
Confederacy; Pennsylvania;
Nostalgic Fiction

Beverly Green
7946 Park Avenue
Elkins Park, Pa. 19117
(215) 635-4589
By appointment only
Beverly Green
Original Art For Illustration;
Children's Books; Illustrated Books

The Erie Book Store
717 French Street
Erie, Pa. 16501
(814) 452-3354
9-6 Mon-Sat
Kathleen Cantrell
General; Great Lakes; Petroleum;
Western Pennsylvania

The Gateway
Ferndale, Pa. 18921
(215) 847-5644
By mail only
Catalogues issued
Jeanne Gorham
Occult & Magic; Mysticism;
Astrology; Religion & Religious
History

W. C. Darrah
2235 Baltimore Pike
Gettysburg, Pa. 17325
(717) 334-2272
By mail only
Catalogues issued
W. C. Darrah
Photography; Technology

Obsolescence
24 Chambersburg Street
Gettysburg, Pa. 17325
(717) 334-8634
9-5 Mon-Sat
Catalogues issued

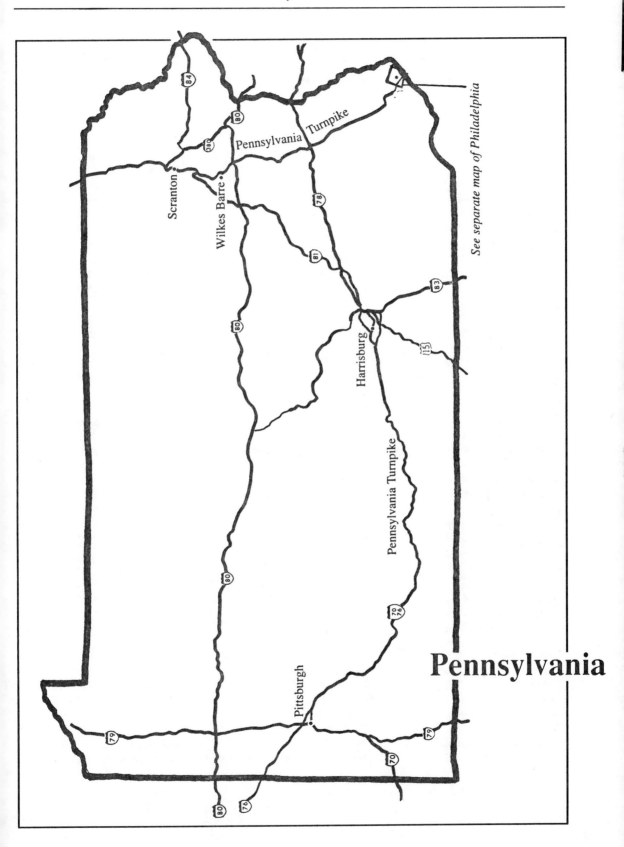

Pennsylvania

German Books & Literature;
Pennsylvania; Children's Books

The Family Album
R.D. 1, Box 42
Glen Rock, Pa. 17327
(717) 235-2134
By appointment only
Catalogues issued
Ronald Lieberman
*Imprints; Incunabula; Fore-Edge
Paintings; Pennsylvania;
Illustrated Books; Appraisals &
Appraisal Services*

Legacy Books
P. O. Box 494
Hatboro, Pa. 19040
(215) 675-6762
By mail only
Catalogues issued
Lillian Krelove, Richard K. Burns
*Folklore; Americana; Folk Art;
Music*

James S. Jaffe
P. O. Box 496
Haverford, Pa. 19041
(215) 649-4221
By appointment only
Catalogues issued
James Jaffe
*Modern First Editions; First
Editions; Illustrated Books; Press
Books & Fine Printing; Appraisals
& Appraisal Services*

Tamerlane Books
P. O. Box C
Havertown, Pa. 19083
(215) 449-4400
John Freas
*Illustrated Books; Sporting;
Voyages, Travels, & Exploration;
Natural History; Art Catalogues,
Periodicals, & Books*

Modern Manor Books
P. O. Box 312

Huntingdon Valley, Pa. 19006
(215) 637-9255
By mail only
Pat McGarvey
*Modern First Editions; First
Editions; Literature; English
Literature; Fiction*

Mystery Manor Books
P. O. Box 135
Huntingdon Valley, Pa. 19006
(215) 637-9255
By mail only
Catalogues issued
Pat McGarvey
*First Editions; Mystery & Detective
Fiction*

Manor House Books
P. O. Box 6
Huntington Valley, Pa. 19006
(215) 637-9255
By mail only
Catalogues issued
Pat McGarvey
*Modern First Editions; Literature;
English Literature; 18th Century
Literature; 19th Century Literature*

Hobson's Choice
511 Runnymede Avenue
Jenkintown, Pa. 19046
(215) 884-4853
By appointment only
Catalogues issued
Jane Hobson Walker
*Biography & Autobiography;
Books about Books; First Editions;
Poetry; Press Books & Fine
Printing*

Medical Manor Books
P. O. Box 647
Jenkintown, Pa. 19046
(215) 637-9255
By mail only
Catalogues issued
Pat McGarvey
Medical & Medicine; History of

Medicine & Science; Medicine &
Science

Robert L. Sadoff
326 Benjamin Fox Pavillion
Jenkintown, Pa. 19046
(215) 887-6144
By appointment only
Robert L. Sadoff
*Criminology; Law; Medicine &
Science; Psychiatry, Psychology,
& Psychoanalysis; Social Sciences;
Medical & Medicine*

Thomas Macaluso
111 South Union Street
Kennett Square, Pa. 19348
(215) 444-1063
1-5 Wed-Fri, 11-5 Sat
Catalogues issued
Thomas P. Macaluso
*Americana; Science; Art; First
Editions; Illustrated Books;
General*

W. Graham Arader III
1000 Boxwood Court
King Of Prussia, Pa. 19406
(215) 825-6570
9-5 Mon-Fri
Catalogues issued
W. Graham Arader III
*Maps, Atlases, & Cartography;
Natural History; Color Plate Books*

Book Haven
146 North Prince Street
Lancaster, Pa. 17603
(717) 393-0920
10-5 Mon-Thurs, 10-9 Fri, 10-4
Sat
Catalogues issued
Kinsey Baker, Kelly Constable
*Pennsylvania; Illustrated Books;
Children's Books; First Editions;
General*

Antonio Raimo
144 Amsterdam Road

Lancaster, Pa. 17608
(717) 285-3861
By appointment only
Catalogues issued
Anthonio Raimo
*Fore-Edge Paintings; Color Plate
Books; Continental Books; Judaica
& Hebrica; Bible & Bible Studies;
Bindings, Fine & Rare*

R. Robertson
278 Birch Drive
Levittown, Pa. 19054
(215) 946-0643
By appointment only
Roger Roberton
*General; Americana; Geology;
Natural History; Voyages, Travels,
& Exploration*

Geoffrey Steele, Inc.
Lumberville, Pa. 18933
(215) 297-5187
By appointment only
Catalogues issued
Geoffrey Steele
Architecture; Art

William Thomas
210 West Marble Street
Mechanicsburg, Pa. 17055
(717) 766-7778
By appointment only
Catalogues issued
Americana; Pennsylvania

Cramer Book Store
P. O. Box 165
Media, Pa. 19063
By mail only
Terence W. Cassidy
Trolleys; Railroads; Postcards

Andrew Cahan
31 North Narberth Avenue
Narberth, Pa. 19072
(215) 668-1716
10-7 Wed & Fri, 10-5 Sat
Catalogues issued

Andrew Cahan
*Americana; Southern Americana;
Art; Poetry; Literature*

Miscellaneous Man
P. O. Box 1776
New Freedom, Pa. 17349
(717) 235-4766
By mail only
Catalogues issued
George Theofiles
*Typography & Type Specimens;
Ephemera; Printing & Printing
History; Posters*

W. L. Zeigler
10 Lincolnway West
New Oxford, Pa. 17350
(717) 624-2347
Catalogues issued
W. L. Zeigler
Poultry

S. & C. Najarian
852 Milmar Road
Newtown Square, Pa. 19073
By appointment only
Chris Najarian, Steve Najarian
*Americana; Ephemera;
Newspapers; Sheet Music*

Cantrells' Books
15 South Pearl Street
North East, Pa. 16429
By appointment only
Glenn W. Cantrell, Sabra Cantrell
*Inland Waterways; Steamboats &
River Travel*

Debra Books
321 Elm Avenue
North Hills, Pa. 19038
By mail only
*Modern First Editions; English
Literature; Science Fiction;
Natural History; Children's Books;
Mystery & Detective Fiction*

The Sporting Scene
181 Delaware Avenue
Palmerton, Pa. 18071
(215) 826-5500
By appointment only
Catalogues issued
Richard D. George
*Camping & Out-Of-Doors; Fishing
& Angling; Hunting; Natural
History*

John E. Norris
P. O. Box 442
Paoli, Pa. 19301
(215) 644-5957
By mail only
Catalogues issued
John E. Norris
Poultry; Birds & Ornithology

James W. Beattie
R.D. 1, Box 242
Parkesburg, Pa. 19385
(215) 857-5686
By appointment only
Catalogues issued
James W. Beattie, Terry Beattie
*Art; Architecture; Trades;
Veterinary Medicine; Medical &
Medicine; Travel*

William H. Allen
2031 Walnut Street
Philadelphia, Pa. 19103
(215) 563-3398
8:30-5 Mon-Fri, 8:30-1 Sat
Catalogues issued
George Allen
*Scholarly Books; Literature; Latin
America; Americana; Greek &
Roman Classics*

**Arader Gallery At Charles
Sessler, Inc.**
1308 Walnut Street
Philadelphia, Pa. 19107
(215) 735-8811
10-6 Mon-Fri
Catalogues issued

Karen Nathan
Americana; Natural History;
Voyages, Travels, & Exploration;
Prints; Bindings, Fine & Rare;
Autographs & Autograph Material

G. H. Arrow Company
1133-39 North 4th Street
Philadelphia, Pa. 19123
(215) 922-3211
By mail only
Catalogues issued
Louis Kohn
Back Issue Periodicals

Catherine Barnes
2031 Walnut Street, 3rd floor
Philadelphia, Pa. 19103
(215) 854-0175
10-5 Mon-Fri (call first)
Catalogues issued
Catherine Barnes
Autographs & Autograph Material;
Documents; Inscribed Books;
Manuscripts; History; Presidents

Bauman Rare Books
1807 Chestnut Street
Philadelphia, Pa. 19103
(215) 564-4274
10-5 daily
David L. Bauman, Natalie Bauman
Rare Books; Voyages, Travels, &
Exploration; Law; Humanities;
First Editions; Natural History

John Benjamins, Books
1 Buttonwood Square
Philadelphia, Pa. 19130
(215) 564-6379
By appointment only
Catalogues issued
John Benjamins, Paul Peranteau
Back Issue Periodicals; Art;
Architecture; Little Magazines &
Literary Small Presses; Judaica
& Hebrica

Book Mark
2049 West Rittenhouse Square
Philadelphia, Pa. 19103
(215) 735-5546
10-6 Mon-Sat
Catalogues issued
Valerie J. Polin, Robert C.
Langmuir, Jr.
Architecture; Literature; General;
Natural History; Landscape
Architecture; Illustrated Books

Art Carduner
6228 Greene Street
Philadelphia, Pa. 19144
(215) 843-6071
By appointment only
Catalogues issued
Art Carduner
Americana; Fiction; Poetry;
Literature; Military History;
Performing Arts

Bernard Conwell Carlitz
1901 Chestnut Street
Philadelphia, Pa. 19103
(215) 563-6608
12-5 daily
Catalogues issued
Bernard C. Carlitz, Bob Carlitz
Photography; First Editions;
Illustrated Books; Manuscripts;
Maps, Atlases, & Cartography;
Medicine & Science

Fran's Bookhouse
6617 Lincoln Drive
Philadelphia, Pa. 19119
(215) 438-2729
4-8 Mon-Fri
Catalogues issued
Francenva Emery, Charles H.
Emery, Jr.
Children's Books; General

Frisk & Borodin
2043 Walnut Street
Philadelphia, Pa. 19103
(215) 963-0572

By appointment only
John Frisk
Appraisals & Appraisal Services

C. Green
P. O. Box 21111
Philadelphia, Pa. 19114-0311
(215) 824-1452
By mail only
Catalogues issued
C. Green
Methodism; English Literature;
Religion & Religious History;
Christian Books; Bible & Bible
Studies; Philosophy

David J. Holmes
230 South Broad Street, 3rd floor
Philadelphia, Pa. 19102
(215) 735-1083
By appointment only
Catalogues issued
David J. Holmes, Ellis H. Neel, Jr.
Autographs & Autograph Material;
Manuscripts; First Editions;
Association Copies; Drawings

Mr, & Mrs. Eric Lee Jordan
1600 Pine Street, No. 2-A
Philadelphia, Pa. 19103
(215) 732-1548
By appointment only
Catalogues issued
Florence Jordan
Regional Americana; Art;
Bindings, Fine & Rare; Literature;
Texas; History

Maxine & Michael Kam
514 Fitzwater Street
Philadelphia, Pa. 19147
(215) 925-1991
By mail only
Maxine Kam, Michael Kam
Art Deco & Art Nouveau; Judaica
& Hebrica; Art

George S. MacManus
1317 Irving Street

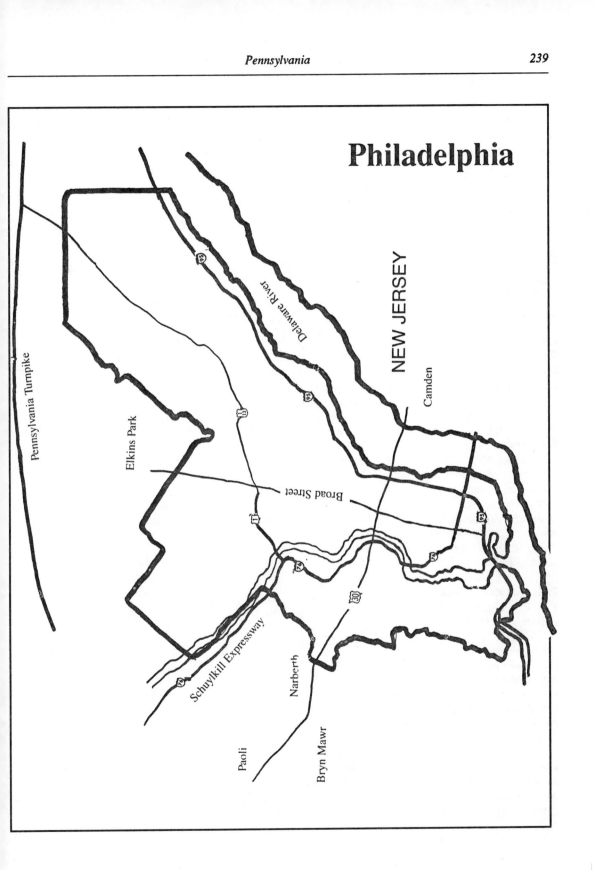

Philadelphia

Philadelphia, Pa. 19107
(215) 735-4456
9-5:30 Mon-Fri
Catalogues issued
Clarence Wolf
Americana; Regional Americana;
First Editions; Literature;
Association Copies

Bruce McKittrick
2240 Fairmount Avenue
Philadelphia, Pa. 19130
(215) 235-3209
By appointment only
Catalogues issued
Bruce McKittrick
Renaissance; Incunabula;
Medicine & Science; Continental
Books; History; Rare Books

Wilbur L. Norman
P. O. Box 516
Philadelphia, Pa. 19105
(215) 735-5356
By appointment only
Catalogues issued
Wilbur Norman
Science; Medicine & Science;
Anthropology; Mountaineering;
Political, Social, & Cultural
History; Prints

Palinurus Rare Books
P. O. Box 15923
Philadelphia, Pa. 19103
(215) 735-2970
By appointment only
Catalogues issued
John Hellebrand
Medicine & Science; Engineering;
Technology; Mathematics;
Economics; Political Science &
Theory

The Petersons
6324 Langdon Street
Philadelphia, Pa. 19111
(215) 744-5671
By mail only

Selma Peterson, Murray Peterson
Children's Books; Illustrated
Books; Ephemera

Philadelphia Print Shop
8441 Germantown Avenue
Philadelphia, Pa. 19118
(215) 242-4750
10-5 Mon-Sat (Wed to 9)
Catalogues issued
Christopher Lane, Donald H.
Cresswell
Maps, Atlases, & Cartography;
Travel; Voyages, Travels, &
Exploration; Natural History;
Color Plate Books

Philadelphia Rare Book &
Mmanuscript Company
P. O. Box 9536
Philadelphia, Pa. 19124
(215) 744-6734
By appointment only
Catalogues issued
Cynthia Davis-Buffington, David
Szewczyk
Law; Music; Latin America; Early
Printed Books; Hispanica;
Manuscripts

Quixote Books
105 South 11th Street, Box 1991
Philadelphia, Pa. 19107
By mail only
Catalogues issued
William Askins
Children's Books

Reedmor Magazine Company
1229 Walnut Street
Philadelphia, Pa. 19107
(215) 922-6643
10:30-5:30 Mon-Fri
David Bagelman
Comic Books; Search Service, With
Stock; Science Fiction; Back Issue
Magazines; Pulps

Lisa M. Reisman
2015 Delancey Place
Philadelphia, Pa. 19103
(215) 985-4695
By appointment only
Lisa Halterman
Art; Livre d'Artiste; Posters; Art
Deco & Art Nouveau; Catalogues
Raisonnes

Ray Riling Arms Book Co.
6844 Gorsten Street
Philadelphia, Pa. 19119
(215) 438-2456
By mail only
Catalogues issued
Joseph Riling
Guns & Weapons; Hunting;
Fishing & Angling

Rittenhouse Book Store
1706 Rittenhouse Square
Philadelphia, Pa. 19103
(215) 545-6072
9-5 Mon-Fri, 10-5 Sat
Catalogues issued
Richard W. Foster
Medical & Medicine; Health

Robin's Bookstore
1837 Chestnut Street
Philadelphia, Pa. 19103
(215) 567-2615
Paul Hogan
General

Mr. Carmen D. Valentino
2956 Richmond Street
Philadelphia, Pa. 19134
(215) 739-6056
By appointment only
Catalogues issued
Carmen D. Valentino
Manuscripts; Ephemera;
Newspapers; Art; Americana;
Numismatics

John F. Warren
124 South 19th Street

Philadelphia, Pa. 19103
(215) 561-6422
10-5 Mon-Fri
Catalogues issued
John F. Warren
*Color Plate Books; Illustrated
Books; Art; Drawings; Art
Catalogues, Periodicals, & Books*

Bryn Mawr-Vassar Bookstore
4612 Winthrop Street
Pittsburgh, Pa. 15213
(412) 687-3433
10-4 Tues-Sat
General

Calliope Children's Crnr.
9600 Perry Highway
Pittsburgh, Pa. 15237
(412) 367-2110
10-6 Mon-Fri, 10-5 Sat
Heidi Savage
Children's Books

The Literary Cat
1505 Asbury Place
Pittsburgh, Pa. 15217
(412) 422-0280
12-6 Mon-Tues & Thurs-Fri, 10-4
Sat
E. J. Polonsky, Sarah Polonsky
General

Pinocchio Bookstore
26 South Aiken Avenue
Pittsburgh, Pa. 15232
(412) 621-1323
10-5:30 Mon-Sat (Wed to 9)
Catalogues issued
Marilyn Hollinshead
Children's Books

Arthur Scharf
5040 Carolyn Drive
Pittsburgh, Pa. 15236
(412) 653-4402
By appointment only
Catalogues issued
Arthur Scharf

*Africa; Americana, States; Asia;
Latin America; The Orient &
Orientalia; Voyages, Travels, &
Exploration*

Betty Schmid
485 Sleepy Hollow
Pittsburgh, Pa. 15228
(412) 341-4597
By mail only
Catalogues issued
Betty Schmid, Earl Schmid
Circus & Carnival

Schoyer's Books
1404 South Negley
Pittsburgh, Pa. 15217
(412) 521-8464
11-6 Tues-Sat
Catalogues issued
Donnis de Camp, Marc Selvaggio
*Americana; Art; Ephemera;
Literature; Books about Books;
General*

Olga Snyder
1107 Federal Street
Pittsburgh, Pa. 15212
(412) 231-6564
10-4 daily
Olga Snyder
*"National Geographic" Magazine;
Back Issue Magazines; Used
Paperbacks; General*

The Tuckers
2236 Murray Avenue
Pittsburgh, Pa. 15217
(412) 521-0249
1-5 Mon-Fri, 10-5 Sat
Catalogues issued
Esther J. Tucker
*Middle Ages; Appraisals &
Appraisal Services; Humanities;
Western Pennsylvania; General*

The Antiquarians
P. O. Box 112
Plainfield, Pa. 17081

(717) 243-8053
By appointment only
Edward L. Rosenberry, Linda K.
Rosenberry
Imprints; Broadsides

The Americanist
1525 Shenkel Road
Pottstown, Pa. 19464
(215) 323-5289
9:30-5:30 Mon-Sat, 10-5 Sun
Catalogues issued
*Americana; Poetry; Women;
Manuscripts; Rare Books; General*

S. F. Collins' Bookcellar
266 Concord Drive
Pottstown, Pa. 19464
(215) 323-2495
By appointment only
Catalogues issued
Sue Collins
*Children's Books; Illustrated
Books; Steamboats & River Travel;
Press Books & Fine Printing*

Stephanie F. Chapin
R. D. 7, Box 303
Reading, Pa. 19606
(215) 779-1512
By appointment only
Stephanie Chapin
Children's Books; Illustrated Books

J. Howard Woolmer
Marienstein Road
Revere, Pa. 18953
(215) 847-5074
By appointment only
Catalogues issued
J. Howard Woolmer
*Appraisals & Appraisal Services;
Author Collections; Modern First
Editions; Inscribed Books;
Literature; Manuscripts*

Hoffman Research Services
P. O. Box 342
Rillton, Pa. 15678

(412) 446-3374
By appointment only
Catalogues issued
Ralph Hoffman
Science; Medical & Medicine;
Medicine & Science; Technical;
Psychiatry, Psychology, &
Psychoanalysis; Sports

Robert M. Grabowski
Route 2, Box 426, Hartman Bridge
Road
Ronks, Pa. 17572
(717) 687-0924
By appointment only
Catalogues issued
Robert M. Grabowski
First Editions; Association Copies;
Autographs & Autograph Material;
Bookplates & Ex Libris;
Astronomy; Voyages, Travels, &
Exploration

D. J. Ernst
R. D. 3, Box 258-P
Selinsgrove, Pa. 17870
(717) 374-9461
9-4 Mon-Tues & Sat, 9-12 Wed,
9-5:30 Fri
Donald J. Ernst, Donald H. Ernst
Pennsylvania; Americana; General

On The Road Books
P. O. Box 334
Shippensburg, Pa. 17257
(717) 532-4426
By mail only
Catalogues issued
Michael M. Kohler
Fishing & Angling; Modern First
Editions; Cooking; Jazz

Dale W. Starry, Sr.
115 North Washington Street
Shippensburg, Pa. 17257
(717) 532-2690
By appointment only
Dale W. Starry, Sr.

Pennsylvania; Illustrated Books;
Authors; Western Books

Manuscript Manor
P. O. Box 562
Southampton, Pa. 18966
(215) 637-9255
By mail only
Catalogues issued
Pat McGarvey
Manuscripts; Autographs &
Autograph Material; Documents;
Maps, Atlases, & Cartography

Harvey Abrams
P. O. Box 732
State College, Pa. 16801
By mail only
Catalogues issued
Harvey Abrams
Sports; Olympic Games

Michael Gibbs
666 Devonshire Drive
State College, Pa. 16803
(814) 234-1745
By mail only
Catalogues issued
Michael Gibbs, Peggy Gibbs
Western Americana; Appraisals &
Appraisal Services; Farming,
Ranching, & Livestock; Petroleum;
Texas; Outlaws & Rangers

Keane-Egan Books
P. O. Box 529
State College, Pa. 16804
(814) 237-2288
By appointment only
Catalogues issued
John Egan
Modern First Editions; Fiction;
Poetry; Ireland & The Irish;
Limited & Signed Editions

Jesse H. Brubacher
R.D. 2, Box 218
Stevens, Pa. 17578-9529
(215) 267-5982

By appointment only
Jesse H. Brubacher
General

F. Thomas Heller
P. O. Box 356
Swarthmore, Pa. 19081
(215) 543-3582
By appointment only
Catalogues issued
James A. Hinz, Christopher Wolfe
Medicine & Science; Science;
Technology; Psychiatry,
Psychology, & Psychoanalysis;
History of Medicine & Science

Robert J. Kalanja
247 East Fairmont Avenue
Trafford, Pa. 15085
(412) 372-8096
By mail only
Catalogues issued
Robert J. Kalanja
Africa; Birds & Ornithology;
Natural History; Fishing &
Angling; Russia & Slavic
Countries; Presidential
Assassinations

Talvin Enterprises
P. O. Box F
Trafford, Pa. 15085
By mail only
Catalogues issued
Robert J. Kalanja, Mary Lou
Kalanja, Robert A. Kalanja
Presidential Assassinations; Africa;
Russia & Slavic Countries; Birds
& Ornithology; Railroads;
Ephemera

Ernest C. Miller
P. O. Box 1
Warren, Pa. 16365
(814) 723-8335
By appointment only
Ernest C. Miller
Petroleum; Pennsylvania

Washington Crossing Books
1112 Taylorsville Road
Washington Crossing, Pa. 18977
(215) 321-9191
11-5 Wed-Sat
Charlie Lloyd
Voyages, Travels, & Exploration;
Geography; Maps, Atlases, &
Cartography; General

Konigsmark Books
309 Midland Avenue
Wayne, Pa. 19087
(215) 687-5965
By appointment only
Catalogues issued
Jocelyn Konigsmark
Literature; Art; Bindings, Fine &
Rare; Illustrated Books; First
Editions; Children's Books

Emerson Company
36 East Avenue
Wellsboro, Pa. 16901
(717) 724-3139
By appointment only
Catalogues issued
Jay Gertzman
English Literature

Baldwin's Book Barn
865 Lenape Road
West Chester, Pa. 19380
(215) 696-0816
9-5 Mon-Sat, 12-5 Sun
Catalogues issued
Thomas M. Baldwin, Paul Jung
Pennsylvania; Delaware; Sporting;

Local History

Maiden Voyage
120 East Virginia
West Chester, Pa. 19350
(215) 430-0529
By mail only
Catalogues issued
Literature; Modern First Editions;
Rare Books; Black Literature &
Studies

Do Fisher
1631 Sheridan Street
Williamsport, Pa. 17701
(717) 323-3573
By mail only
Catalogues issued
Dolores Fisher, Robert Fisher
Pennsylvania; Autographs &
Autograph Material; Limited &
Signed Editions; First Editions;
Illustrated Books; Derrydale Press

Tim Hughes
2410 North Hills Drive
Williamsport, Pa. 17701
(717) 326-1045
By appointment only
Catalogues issued
Tim Hughes
Newspapers; Civil War &
Confederacy; Documents; Back
Issue Periodicals; Americana

The Last Hurrah Bookshop
937 Memorial Avenue
Williamsport, Pa. 17701

(717) 327-9338
9-6 Wed-Fri
Catalogues issued
Andrew Winiarczyk, Linda
Winiarczyk
Presidential Assassinations;
Political, Social, & Cultural
History

Earl Moore Associates Inc
P. O. Box 243
Wynnewood, Pa. 19096
(215) 649-1549
By mail only
Catalogues issued
Earl E. Moore
Americana; Appraisals &
Appraisal Services; Autographs &
Autograph Material; Marine &
Maritime; Railroads; Whaling

The Hermit's Book House
34 Mt. Zion Road
Wyoming, Pa. 18644
(717) 696-1474
12-5 Fri-Sun
Catalogues issued
Stephen Casterlin
Local History; Fiction; Nostalgic
Fiction; Children's Books; General

George C. Bullock
940 Queens Drive
Yardley, Pa. 19067
(215) 493-2047
By mail only
George C. Bullock
Americana; History; Military

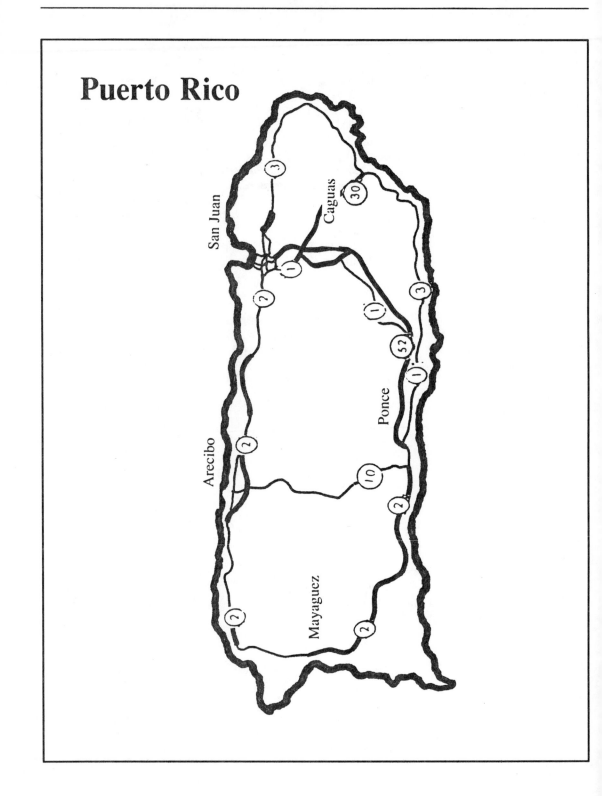

Puerto Rico

Puerto Rico

Poe Book Shop
Bzn 6348, Barrio Mani, Route 18
Mayaguez, P.R. 00708

(809) 833-6906
8-6 daily
Al Luckton, Maria Luckton

Caribbean; Geography; Geology; Jewelry; Latin America; Mining & Metallurgy

Quebec

J. A. Benoit
3465 Sherbrooke East, No. 1
Montreal, Que. H1W 1C9
(514) 527-1137
By appointment only
Catalogues issued
J. A. Benoit
Canada & Canadiana; French Books & Literature

Wilfrid DeFreitas
P. O. Box 883, Stock Exch. Tower
Montreal, Que. H4Z 1K2
(514) 935-9581
By appointment only
Wilfrid DeFreitas
Modern First Editions; Authors; Sherlock Holmes & A. C. Doyle; Golf

Guerin Editeur Ltee.
4501 rue Drolet
Montreal, Que. H2T 2G2
(514) 843-6241
9-5 Mon-Fri
Catalogues issued
Education; Children's Books; Geography; History; General; Literature

Mme. Lucie Javitch
1589 Dr. Penfield Avenue
Montreal, Que. H3G 1C6
(514) 932-4366
By appointment only
Lucie Javitch
Canada & Canadiana; Indians & Eskimos; Americana

Helen R. Kahn
P. O. Box 323, Victoria Stn.
Montreal, Que. H3Z 2V8
(514) 844-5344
By appointment only
Catalogues issued
Helen R. Kahn
Voyages, Travels, & Exploration; Americana; Arctica & Antarctica; Canada & Canadiana; Rare Books

La Librairie Quebecoise
1417 rue Amherst
Montreal, Que. H2L 2L2
(514) 523-3305
12-5:30 Mon-Wed, 12-9 Thur-Fri
General

Russell Books
275 St. Antoine Street West
Montreal, Que. H2Z 1N5
(514) 866-0564

9-6 Mon-Fri, 9-5 Sat, 11-5 Sun
Niall Russell, Reg Russell
Limited & Signed Editions; Modern First Editions; General

Stryker's Books Regained
5947 Park Avenue
Montreal, Que. H2V 4H4
(514) 487-0793
By mail only
Catalogues issued
T. G. Stryker
Health; Natural Healing

Grant Woolmer
4823 Sherbrooke Street West
Montreal, Que. H3Z 1G7
(514) 933-3968
9-4:30 Mon-Fri, 10-3 Sat
Catalogues issued
Grant Woolmer
Canada & Canadiana

Word Bookstore
469 Milton Street
Montreal, Que. H2X 1W3
(514) 845-5540
10-6 Mon-Fri (Fri to 9), 12-6 Sat
Adrian King-Edwards
Humanities; Literature; Poetry; Drama; Scholarly Books

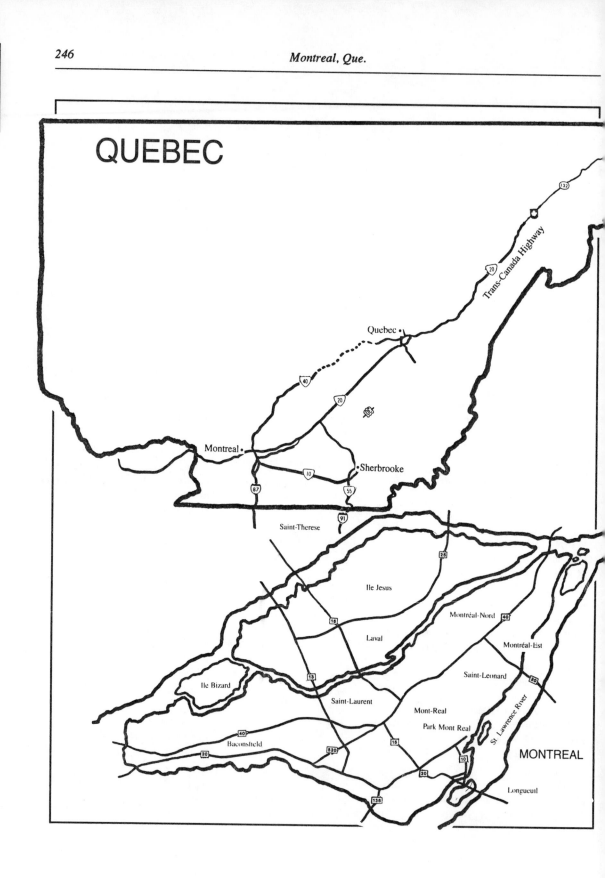

Galerie Tayaut
C.P. 43, 985 rue Massawippi
North Hatley, Que. J0B 2C0
(819) 842-2695
10-5 Mon-Sun
Catalogues issued
Serge Dupre
Natural History; Sporting; Fishing & Angling; Hunting

William P. Wolfe, Inc.
P. O. Box 1190
Pt. Claire, Que. H9S 5K7
(514) 697-1630
By appointment only
Catalogues issued
Patricia Brown
Judaica & Hebraica; Canada & Canadiana; Americana; Voyages, Travels, & Exploration; Rare Books

Jean Gagnon
402-764 St. Joseph St., Bp 653
H-V
Quebec, Que. G1R 4S2
(418) 523-6760
By mail only
Catalogues issued
Jean Gagnon
Canada & Canadiana; French Books & Literature

Rhode Island

Lincoln O.P. Book Search Ltd.
Mount Hygeia Road, Box 100
Foster, R.I. 02825
(401) 647-2825
By mail only
Harold S. Ephraim, Linda F. Ephraim
Literary Criticism; Social Sciences; Business & Business History; Political Science & Theory; History

William T. O'Malley
55 Linden Drive
Kingston, R.I. 02881
(401) 789-0355
By appointment only
William T. O'Malley
Modern First Editions; Books about Books; Press Books & Fine Printing; Ireland & The Irish; Bibliography; Little Magazines & Literary Small Presses

Theophrastus
P. O. Box 458
Little Compton, R.I. 02837
Augustus M. Kelley

Cooking; Rhode Island; Gardening & Horticulture

Anchor & Dolphin Books
30 Franklin Street
Newport, R.I. 02840
(401) 846-6890
Afternoons daily
Catalogues issued
Ann Marie Wall, James Hinck
Landscape Architecture; Decorative Arts; Architecture; Gardening & Horticulture; City & Urban Planning; Design

Armchair Sailor Bookstore
Lee's Wharf
Newport, R.I. 02840
(401) 847-4252
9-5 Mon-Sat
Catalogues issued
Ron Barr, Sandy Parks
America's Cup; Sailing & Yachting

Edward J. Craig
11 Clarke Street
Newport, R.I. 02840
(401) 847-6498

By appointment only
Catalogues issued
Edward J. Craig
Americana; Manuscripts; Autographs & Autograph Material; Postal History; Slavery; American Colonies & the Revolution

Scribe's Perch Bookstore
62 Thames Street
Newport, R.I. 02840
(800) 242-5461
9-6 Mon-Sat, 1-6 Sun
Donna Gibson, Jim Weyant
General

John Kashmanian
38 Forest View Drive
North Providence, R.I. 02904
(401) 353-4503
By appointment only
Catalogues issued
John Kashmanian
Baseball; Boxing; Football

Michael Borden
2774 East Main Road
Portsmouth, R.I. 02871

(401) 683-4872
By appointment only
Catalogues issued
Michael Borden
Fantasy; Horror; Mystery &
Detective Fiction; Books about
Books; Autographs & Autograph
Material; Manuscripts

Cellar Stories
190 Matthewson Street
Providence, R.I. 02903
(401) 521-2665
11-6 Mon-Sat
Michael Chandley
Modern First Editions; Science
Fiction; Fantasy; Rhode Island

Cornerstone Books
P. O. Box 2591
Providence, R.I. 02906
(401) 331-1340
9-7 Mon-Sat
Catalogues issued
Ray Rickman, Robb Dimmick
Black Literature & Studies;
Slavery; New England; Rhode
Island

Merlin's Closet
166 Valley Street
Providence, R.I. 02909
(401) 351-9272
12-6 Mon-Thur, 10-8 Fri-Sat, 12-6
Sun
Catalogues issued
Elliot Kay Shorter
First Editions; Illustrated Books;
Science Fiction; Children's Books;
Literature

Metacomet Books
P. O. Box 2479
Providence, R.I. 02906
(401) 861-7182

By appointment only
Catalogues issued
James Sanford
History of Medicine & Science;
American Literature; English
Literature; Women; Industry;
General

Sewards' Folly Books
139 Brook Street
Providence, R.I. 02906
(401) 272-4454
12-8 Wed-Fri, 9-8 Sat, 12-6 Sun
Schuyler Seward, J. Peterkin
Seward
Modern First Editions; Rhode
Island; Scholarly Books; Rare
Books; General

Tyson Books
334 Westminster Mall
Providence, R.I. 02903
(401) 421-3939
11-5 Mon-Fri, 11-4 Sat
Catalogues issued
Marriet Bedard
Americana; Rhode Island; First
Editions; American History;
General

Barbara Walzer
P. O. Box 2536
Providence, R.I. 02906
(401) 351-6330
By appointment only
Catalogues issued
Barbara Walzer
Women; General

Fortunate Finds Bookstore
16 West Natick Road
Warwick, R.I. 02886
(401) 737-8160
9-5 Fri-Sat
Catalogues issued

Mildred E. Santille
Ephemera; Trade Cards;
Postcards; Trade Catalogues;
Documents; Maps, Atlases, &
Cartography

J. W. Morritt
3 Colgate Street
Warwick, R.I. 02888
(401) 467-3364
By mail only
J. W. Morritt, B. O. Morritt
Joseph C. Lincoln

The Book & Tackle Shop
7 Bay Street
Watch Hill, R.I. 02891
(401) 596-0700
10-8 Mon-Sun (June-Sept only)
Catalogues issued
B. L. Gordon
Medical & Medicine; Naval &
Nautical; New England;
Cookbooks; Children's Books;
Fishing & Angling

New Age Metaphysical
Bookshop
30 Canal
Westerly, R.I. 02891
(401) 596-2879
11-2:30 Mon-Fri, 10-5 Sat, 1-4
Sun
James Faiella, Helen Faiella
Metaphysics; Rare Books

The Wayside Bookshop
Langworthy Road, Box 501, R.
R. 3
Westerly, R.I. 02891
(401) 322-1698
By appointment only
Catalogues issued
Bernadine O'Donnell
General

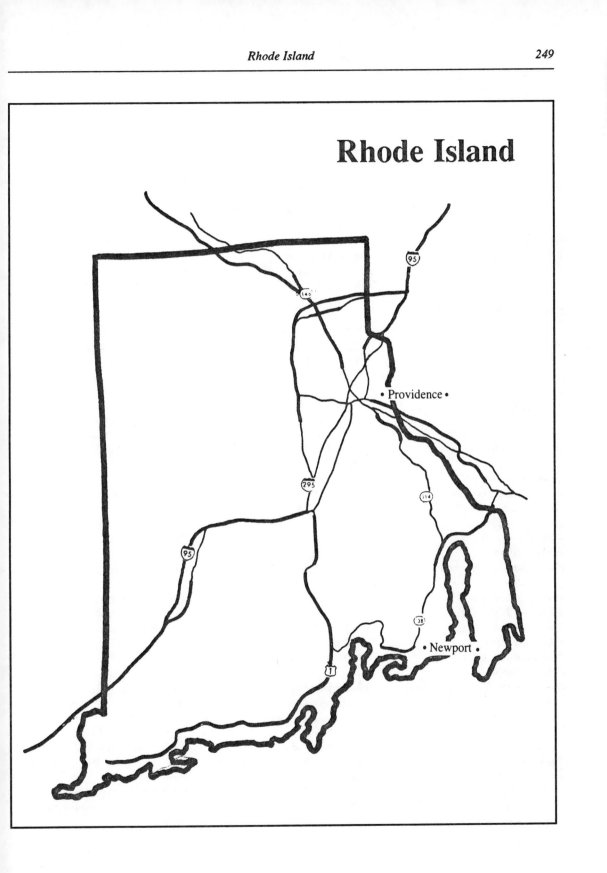

Rhode Island

South Carolina

Joel Patrick
P. O. Box 992
Beaufort, S.C. 29902
(803) 324-4258
By appointment only
Catalogues issued
Joel Patrick
*Southern Americana; South
Carolina; North Carolina*

Book Dispensary #1
1600 Broad River Road
Columbia, S.C. 29210
(803) 798-4739
10-9 Mon-Sat, 1-6 Sun
Becky Pearson
*South Carolina; Authors, State &
Local; Juveniles; Fiction*

Book Dispensary #2
6800 Garners Ferry Road
Columbia, S.C. 29209
(803) 783-4608
10-9 Mon-Sat, 1-6 Sun
Alyce Ballard
South Carolina; General

Book Dispensary #3
7359 Two Notch Road
Columbia, S.C. 29204
(803) 736-4033
10-9 Mon-Sat, 1-6 Sun
Becky Pearson
*Modern First Editions; Fiction;
Authors, State & Local; Juveniles*

The Book Place
3129 Millwood Avenue
Columbia, S.C. 29205
(803) 799-6561
10-5 Mon-Sat
F. Hampton Alvey
South Carolina; Civil War &

*Confederacy; Southern Americana;
Rare Books; General; Fishing &
Angling*

Maggie DuPriest
1230 Pendleton Street
Columbia, S.C. 29201
(803) 252-0690
10-5 Tues-Sat
Catalogues issued
Maggie DuPriest
*Southern Americana; South
Carolina; Rare Books*

St. Andrews Books
P. O. Box 210756
Columbia, S.C. 29221
(803) 772-4551
By appointment only
Catalogues issued
Jill Bettendorf, Tom Bettendorf
*Ships & The Sea; South Carolina;
Wildflowers*

Robbins' Rarities
28 2038-C Laurens Road
Greenville, S.C. 29606
(803) 297-7948
11-5 Mon-Fri (closed Wed)
LeRoy Robbins
*Civil War & Confederacy;
Illustrated Books; General*

Volume I Books
407 Augusta Street
Greenville, S.C. 29601
(803) 235-6419
10-6 Mon-Sat
Mike Bailey, Deane Bailey
Southern Authors; General

Noah's Ark Book Attic
Stony Point, Route 2

Greenwood, S.C. 29646
(803) 374-3013
9-5 Sat
Catalogues issued
Donald Hawthorne
*Religion & Religious History;
Collection Development*

Branimir M. Rieger
936 Sunset Drive
Greenwood, S.C. 29646
(803) 223-7977
By appointment only
Catalogues issued
Branimir M. Rieger
*Americana; History; Literature;
Voyages, Travels, & Exploration;
Travel Guides & Baedekers;
Authors*

The Attic, Inc.
P. O. Box 128
Hodges, S.C. 29653
(803) 374-3013
9-5 Sat
Catalogues issued
Donald Hawthorne
*Americana; Collection
Development; South Carolina; 18th
Century Literature; English
Literature*

The Book Shoppe
9900 C Kings Highway North
Myrtle Beach, S.C. 29577
(803) 449-8302
10-9 Mon-Sat, 12-9 Sun
Catalogues issued
Nate Shulimson, Bob Caldwell,
Kevin Ferguson
*Civil War & Confederacy; South
Carolina; Comic Books; Military
History; Southern Authors*

Hampton Books
Route 1, Box 202
Newberry, S.C. 29108
(803) 276-6870
10-5:30 Mon-Sun
Catalogues issued
Muriel P. Hamilton, Ben Hamilton
Cinema & Film; Television &
Radio; Sporting; Photography;

Southern Writers; Children's
Books

LeRoy C. Brown, Jr.
339 Blanchard Road
North Augusta, S.C. 29841
(803) 279-4967
By mail only
Catalogues issued
LeRoy C. Brown, Jr., Jeanette

Brown
Aviation & Aeronautics; World
Wars; Western Books; Authors;
Pulps

James S. Pipkin
2324-A Rosewood Drive
Rock Hill, S.C. 29730
(803) 366-3839
By appointment only

James S. Pipkin
South Carolina; Ephemera; Series
Books For Boys & Girls;
Postcards; Comic Books; Civil
War & Confederacy

Norm Burleson
104 First Avenue
Spartanburg, S.C. 29302
(803) 583-8845
By mail only
Catalogues issued
Norm Burleson
Christian Books; Religion &
Religous History

Kitemaug Books
229 Mohawk Drive
Spartanburg, S.C. 29301
(803) 576-3338
By appointment only
Catalogues issued
Frank J. Anderson
Submarines; Ships & The Sea;
Miniature Books; General

South Dakota

The Bookshelf
P. O. Box 67
Miller, S.D. 57362
(605) 853-2197
By appointment only
John Pugh, Ellebeth Pugh
Western Americana; Americana,
States; Fiction; General

Buteo Books
P. O. Box 481
Vermillion, S.D. 57069
(605) 624-4343
By mail only
Catalogues issued
Joyce Harrell
Natural History; Birds &

Ornithology; Zoology; Science;
Falconry; Voyages, Travels, &
Exploration

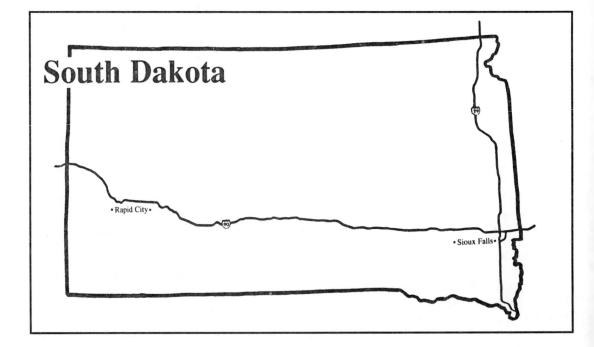

Tennessee

John L. Heflin, Jr.
5708 Brentwood Trace
Brentwood, Tenn. 37027
(615) 373-2917
By mail only
Catalogues issued
John L. Heflin, Jr.
Civil War & Confederacy

Book Shelf
3765 Hillsdale Drive, NE
Cleveland, Tenn. 37312
(615) 472-8408
By appointment only
Catalogues issued
William R. Snell
*Alabama; Tennessee; Southern
Americana; Presidents*

Robert L. George
3705 Northwood Drive, NW
Cleveland, Tenn. 37311
(615) 472-7750
By appointment only
Catalogues issued
R. L. George
*Religion & Religious History;
Judaica & Hebrica; Science
Fiction; Children's Books; Boy
Scouts; Series Books For Boys &
Girls*

Gary F. Smalley
205-B Creek Trail
Columbia, Tenn. 38401
(615) 388-1654
Gary F. Smalley
Religion & Religious History

Murray Hudson
Route 1, Box 362
Dyersburg, Tenn. 38024
(901) 285-0666

By appointment only
Catalogues issued
Murray Hudson
*Maps, Atlases, & Cartography;
Regional Americana; Voyages,
Travels, & Exploration;
Southwestern Americana;
Southwestern Americana; Geology*

Antiquaria
P. O. Box 1226
Franklin, Tenn. 37064
(615) 790-0391
By appointment only
Catalogues issued
Linda Tune, Bob Tune
*Americana; Civil War &
Confederacy; Travel; Sports;
Maps, Atlases, & Cartography;
Ephemera*

Magic Lantern Books
219 East Main Street
Johnson City, Tenn. 37601
9-9 Mon-Sat
Catalogues issued
Gil Moody, Linda Moody
*Limited & Signed Editions;
Manuscripts; Art; Musical Scores;
Rare Books*

Moody Bookstore
107 Broyles Drive, Holiday Plaza
Johnson City, Tenn. 37601
(615) 282-6004
9-9 Mon-Sat
Gil Moody
General

F. M. Hill
P. O. Box 1037
Kingsport, Tenn. 37662
(615) 247-8704

By appointment only
Catalogues issued
F. Maynard Hill, Ann Hill, Lori
Hackler
*Tennessee; Southern Americana;
Bibliography; Books about Books;
Civil War & Confederacy*

Andover Square Books
805 Norgate Road
Knoxville, Tenn. 37919
(615) 693-8984
By mail only
Catalogues issued
G. A. Yeomans
Americana; History; First Editions

Donaldson's Books
600 Inskip Road, Apt. A102
Knoxville, Tenn. 37912
(615) 687-8872
Catalogues issued
Irene Donaldson
*Illustrated Books; Children's
Books; General; Literature;
Americana*

Fox Books
1420 Neely Bend Road
Madison, Tenn. 37115
(615) 868-2078
By appointment only
Vivian P. Fox, Richard B. Fox
*Americana; Regional Americana;
Tennessee; Civil War &
Confederacy; Authors; Children's
Books*

Burke's Book Store, Inc.
634 Poplar Avenue
Memphis, Tenn. 38105
(901) 527-7484
9-5 Mon-Fri (Thurs to 5:30), 10-4

Tennessee

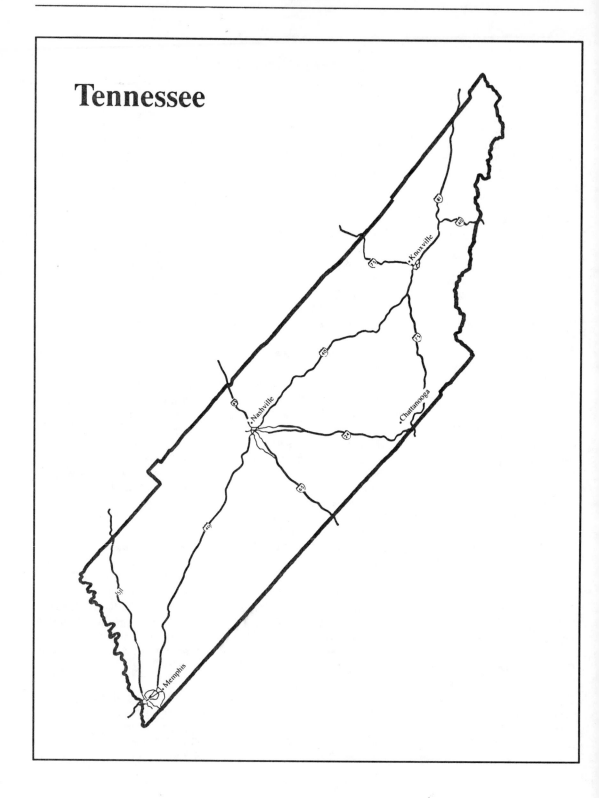

Sat
Harriette M Beeson, David Clark,
Lauren Johnson
*Regional Americana; First
Editions; Civil War &
Confederacy; Rare Books*

Ollie's Books
3218 Boxdale Street
Memphis, Tenn. 38118
(901) 363-1996
By appointment only
Ollie McGarrh
*Astrology; Religion & Religious
History*

The Battery Book Shop
P. O. Box 3107, Uptown Stn.
Nashville, Tenn. 37219
(615) 298-1401

9-4 daily
Catalogues issued
Richard Gardner
Military

Book Treasury
3404 West End Avenue
Nashville, Tenn. 37203
(615) 269-3358
10-5 Tues-Sat
Lori Bender
*First Editions; Fiction; Children's
Books; General*

Fugitive Books
P. O. Box 50293
Nashville, Tenn. 37205
(615) 297-6055
By appointment only
Catalogues issued

Pamela S. Chenery
*Southern Authors; 20th Century
Literature; First Editions*

Crabtree Booksellers
P. O. Box 366
Signal Mountain, Tenn. 37377
(615) 886-5944
10-5 Tues-Sat
R. Harry Crabtree
*Rare Books; Civil War &
Confederacy; Southern Americana;
Tennessee*

Hillcrest Books
Route 2, Box 162
Spring City, Tenn. 37381
By mail only
Catalogues issued
Trade Catalogues

Texas

American Southwest Books
P. O. Box 148
Amarillo, Texas 79105
(806) 372-3444
By mail only
Catalogues issued
R. D. Hollingsworth, R. R.
Hollingsworth, J. R. Hollingsworth
*Texas; Farming, Ranching, &
Livestock; Voyages, Travels, &
Exploration; Law*

Mrs. R. H. Arthur
5402 George Terrace
Amarillo, Texas 79106
(806) 355-0901
By mail only
Mrs. R. H. Arthur
Texas; Western Americana

R. J. Sayers
P. O. Box 246
Andrews, Texas 79714
(915) 523-2902
By appointment only
Catalogues issued
R. J. Sayers, R. J. Sayers, Jr.
*Boy Scouts; Civil War &
Confederacy; Camping & Out-Of-
Doors; Texas*

Michael D. Heaston Co.
5614 Wagon Train Road
Austin, Texas 78749
(512) 892-3730
By appointment only
Catalogues issued
Michael Heaston
Western Americana; Maps, Atlases,

*& Cartography; Manuscripts;
Americana; Photography*

The Jenkins Company
P. O. Box 2085
Austin, Texas 78768
(512) 280-2940
By appointment only
Catalogues issued
John Jenkins, Michael Parrish
*Western Americana; Texas; Latin
America; Civil War &
Confederacy; Literature;
Americana*

Mac Donnell Rare Books
9307 Glenlake Drive
Austin, Texas 78738
(512) 345-4139
By appointment only

Kevin Mac Donnell
American Literature; English
Literature; 19th Century
Literature; 20th Century
Literature; Association Copies;
Autographs & Autograph Material

Photo-Eye
P. O. Box 2686
Austin, Texas 78768
(512) 480-8409
By appointment only
Catalogues issued
Rixon Reed
Photography

Dorothy Sloan
P. O. Box 49670
Austin, Texas 78765-9670
(512) 477-8442
By appointment only
Catalogues issued
Dorothy Sloan, Julie Sloan
Americana; Southwestern
Americana; Texas; Latin America;
Women; Indians & Eskimos

W. Thomas Taylor
1906 Miriam Street
Austin, Texas 78722
(512) 478-7628
By appointment only
Catalogues issued
Tom Taylor, Elaine Smyth
Early Printed Books; English
Literature; Press Books & Fine
Printing; Bindings, Fine & Rare

Terrapin Station
613 Wilmes Drive
Austin, Texas 78752
(512) 454-0643
By appointment only
Catalogues issued
A. Gula
Fiction; Texas; Southwestern
Americana

Maggie Lambeth
Star Route 4, Box 361
Blanco, Texas 78606
By appointment only
Catalogues issued
Maggie Lambeth
Texas; American Literature;
English Literature; Western
Americana; General

Frontier American Corporation
P. O. Box 3698
Bryan, Texas 77805
(409) 846-4462
By appointment only
Catalogues issued
Fred White, Jr.
Western Americana; Americana;
Regional Americana; Voyages,
Travels, & Exploration;
Photography; Civil War &
Confederacy

Hi Books
P. O. Box 1409
Canutillo, Texas 79835
(915) 581-8188
By mail only
Harriet G. Brown, Irving R. Brown
Western Americana; Texas;
Illustrated Books; Children's
Books; Modern First Editions;
Mystery & Detective Fiction

CGT Company
1115 Langford Street
College Station, Texas 77840
By appointment only
Catalogues issued
Garret M. Ihler
Archaeology; Americana; Voyages,
Travels, & Exploration; History;
Medicine & Science

Federation Book Search
P. O. Box 9654
College Station, Texas 77840
(409) 696-2168
By appointment only

Cassandra McDonough
Science Fiction; New Books;
Archaeology; Ireland & The Irish

Gierspeck & Roper
1132 West Dallas
Conroe, Texas 77301
(409) 756-6188
9-6 Mon-Sat
Vicki Roper
Aviation & Aeronautics

Conway Barker
4126 Meadowdale Lane, Box
670625
Dallas, Texas 75367-0625
(214) 358-3786
Conway Barker
Autographs & Autograph Material

Finders Keepers
P. O. Box 820247
Dallas, Texas 75382-0247
(214) 341-3961
Judi Fouts
General

David Grossblatt
P. O. Box 25042
Dallas, Texas 75225
(214) 373-0218
By appointment only
Catalogues issued
David Grossblatt
Texas; Southwestern Americana;
Civil War & Confederacy;
Appraisals & Appraisal Services;
Cattle & Range Industry; Western
Americana

Library Books
P. O. Box 7240
Dallas, Texas 75209
(214) 690-5882
By mail only
Catalogues issued
Bibliography; Author Collections;
Modern First Editions; Literary
Criticism; Poetry; Reference

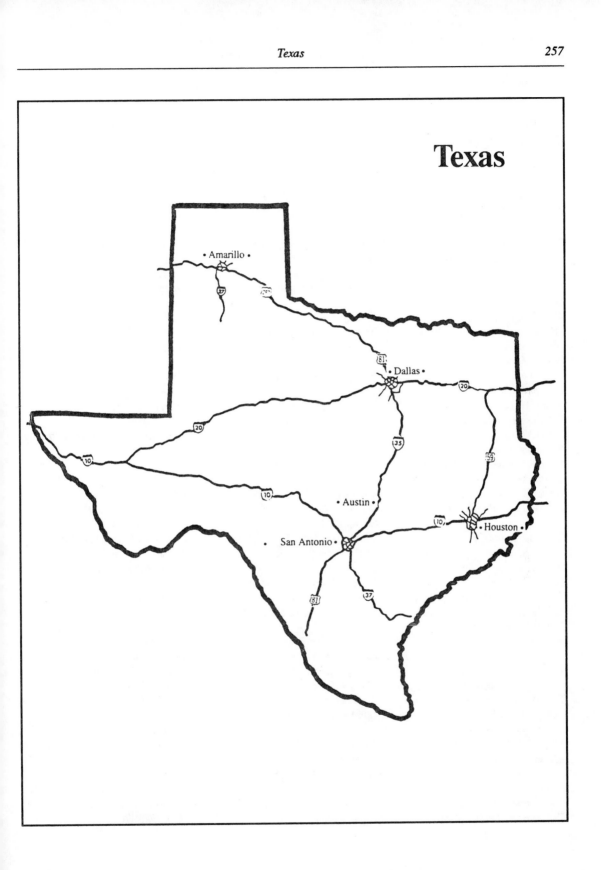

Texas

The Tracery
P. O. Box 670236
Dallas, Texas 75367-0236
(214) 361-5269
10-4 daily
Catalogues issued
Julie Clem, Onnie Clem
Christmas; World Wars

The Bookshop
1808 North Main Street
Del Rio, Texas 78840
(512) 775-5935
By appointment only
Jim Croom, Sue Croom
Texas; Southwestern Americana;
Western Americana; Western
Books; Mexico; Art, Western

Schroeder's Bookhaven
Route 1, Box 2820
Dickinson, Texas 77539
(713) 337-1002
By appointment only
Bert Schroeder, Faye Schroeder
Texas; Art; Cooking; Crafts &
Hobbies; American History;
Scholarly Books

The Stevensons
316 Sage Lane
Euless, Texas 76039-7906
(817) 354-8903
By appointment only
Catalogues issued
James G. Stevenson
Boy Scouts

Barber's Book Store
215 West 8th Street
Fort Worth, Texas 76102
(817) 335-5469
9-7:30 Mon-Fri, 9-5:30 Sat
Brian Perkins, Larue Perkins
Militaria; Texas

Evergreen Books
1500 West Magnolia
Fort Worth, Texas 76104

(817) 335-1911
10-5:30 Mon-Sat
Bobbie Simms
General; Texas; Literary Criticism

Murder In Print
2880 Hulen Street, suite 625
Fort Worth, Texas 76107
(817) 731-8877
By appointment only
Catalogues issued
Steven W. Strange
Mystery & Detective Fiction

The Quest
3524 Race Street
Fort Worth, Texas 76111
(817) 838-8865
By appointment only
Pauline Nunley, James B. Nunley
Dictionaries; Christian Books;
Travel; Children's Books; Medical
& Medicine; Phonograph Records

Limestone Hills Book Shop
P. O. Box 1125
Glen Rose, Texas 76043
(817) 897-4991
By appointment only
Catalogues issued
Lyle Harris Kendall, Jr., Aubyn
Kendall
English Literature; American
Literature; Mystery & Detective
Fiction; Books about Books

White Cross Press
Route 1, Box 592
Granger, Texas 76530
(512) 859-2814
C. W. Horton, Sr.
Linguistics; Physics; Geology

Noble Enterprises
5319 Vale
Greenville, Texas 75401
(214) 455-1231
By appointment only
Catalogues issued

Donnell Noble
Inscribed Books; Autographs &
Autograph Material; Documents

W. Graham Arader III
2800 Virginia Street
Houston, Texas 77098
(713) 527-8055
9-5 Mon-Fri
Catalogues issued
Gary Fishman
Prints; Maps, Atlases, &
Cartography; Western Americana;
Natural History

A Book Buyers Shop
711 Studewood
Houston, Texas 77007
(713) 868-3910
11-6 Mon-Sun
Catalogues issued
Chester Doby
Books about Books; Texas; Indians
& Eskimos; General

Book Case
2419 South Shepherd
Houston, Texas 77019
(713) 527-9293
11-8 Mon-Thurs, 11-6 Fri & Sat
Richard A. Goodrum, Dorothy D.
Goodrum
Americana; Fiction; Science
Fiction; American History;
General

The Chickadee, Inc.
440 Wilchester
Houston, Texas 77079
(713) 932-1408
10-4:30 Tues-Fri, 9-6 Sat, 1-5 Sun
Martha Henschen
Natural History; New Books; Birds
& Ornithology; Children's Books

Colleen's Books
6880 Telephone Road
Houston, Texas 77061
(713) 641-1753

10-4 daily
Colleen Urbanek
Regional Americana; Militaria

Detering Book Gallery
2311 Bissonnet
Houston, Texas 77005
(713) 526-6974
10-6 Mon-Sat, 10-5 Sun
Catalogues issued
Herman E. Detering III, Oscar D.
Graham II, Jeffery A. Scoggins
*Bindings, Fine & Rare; First
Editions; Press Books & Fine
Printing; Humanities; Illustrated
Books; Rare Books*

Norumbega Books
P. O. Box 25246
Houston, Texas 77265
(713) 523-6660
By appointment only
Elizabeth Labandwski
*Rare Books; First Editions;
Literature; Inscribed Books;
Africa; Law*

Trackside Books
P. O. Box 770264
Houston, Texas 77215-0264
(713) 772-8107
By mail only
Catalogues issued
Lawrence E. Madole
*Railroads; Texas; Americana;
Outlaws & Rangers*

Aileen T. Taylor
1701 Ranchero Drive
Kerrville, Texas 78028
(512) 257-6017
Aileen T. Taylor
Book Scouts

Traveller Books
P. O. Box 2323
Laredo, Texas 78040
(512) 727-8505
By mail only

Catalogues issued
John H. Keck
*Civil War & Confederacy;
Virginia; Texas; Americana*

G. N. Gabbard
P. O. Box 781
New Boston, Texas 75570
By mail only
Catalogues issued
G. N. Gabbard
*Science Fiction; Comic Books;
Humanities; Middle Ages; Mystery
& Detective Fiction*

Fletcher's Books
Main Street & Mill Creek Drive
Salado, Texas 76571
(817) 947-5414
10-5 Mon-Fri
Thelma R. Fletcher
*Appraisals & Appraisal Services;
Texas; Southwestern Americana;
Bindings, Fine & Rare; General*

Info Books
P. O. Box 5200
San Angelo, Texas 76902
(915) 653-1795
Jerry Mack
*Southwestern Americana; Authors;
Farming, Ranching, & Livestock;
Folklore; Australia & New
Zealand; Commodities Trading*

Ye Olde Fantastique Books
1218 West Beauregard
San Angelo, Texas 76901
(915) 653-1031
10-12 & 1-6 Mon-Sat
Charles N. Hall
*American History; Texas; Religion
& Religious History; Metaphysics;
Occult & Magic; General*

Booketeria
3323 Fredericksburg Road
San Antonio, Texas 78201
(512) 734-8760

9:30-5 Tues-Sat
Paul Harwell, Carol Harwell
*Sets; Texas; Military History;
Bindings, Fine & Rare*

Book Mart
3127 Broadway
San Antonio, Texas 78209
(512) 828-4885
10-6 Mon-Sat
Frank Kellel, Jr., Lois M. Kellel,
Robert F. Kellel
*Americana; Regional Americana;
First Editions; American History;
Militaria; Outlaws & Rangers*

Book Mart Annex
3132 Avenue "B"
San Antonio, Texas 78209
(512) 828-7433
11-5 Thurs-Sat
Dr. Frank Kellel
*Americana; Americana, States;
Railroads; Outlaws & Rangers;
Press Books & Fine Printing; Guns
& Weapons*

The Clipper Ship Book Store
150 West Olmos
San Antonio, Texas 78212
(512) 826-1237
10:30-5:30 daily
Catalogues issued
Philip Krumm
*20th Century Literature; Poetry;
Art; Music; Metaphysics; Political
Science & Theory*

Rick Bandas
P. O. Box 1115
Temple, Texas 76501
(817) 773-4384
By appointment only
Rick Bandas
*Texas; Press Books & Fine
Printing*

Book Cellar
2 South Main

Temple, Texas 76501
(817) 773-7545
9:30-5 daily
Bob Jones
*General; Regional Americana;
New Paperbacks; Texas*

Carousel
2920 Fry Avenue
Tyler, Texas 75701
(214) 597-9202
By mail only
Catalogues issued

Ann Hatchell, Mike Hatchell
*Avant Garde, Experimental, &
Modern Art; German Books &
Literature; Graphic Arts;
Illustrated Books; Egypt &
Egyptology; Prints*

Von Blon's Books
1111 Colcord Avenue
Waco, Texas 76707
9-5:15 Mon-Sat
A. F. Von Blon, Jr.
Railroads; Civil War &

*Confederacy; Texas; Postcards;
Authors, State & Local*

Clark Wright
409 Royal Street
Waxahachie, Texas 75165
(214) 937-6502
By appointment only
Catalogues issued
Hugh M. Wright, Bessie L. Wright
*Regional Americana; Farming,
Ranching, & Livestock; Latin
America; Outlaws & Rangers*

Utah

Distinctive Documents
P. O. Box 100
Cedar City, Utah 84720
(801) 586-9497
Catalogues issued
Warren Anderson
*Western Americana; Ephemera;
Autographs & Autograph Material*

The Bookshelf
2456 Washington
Ogden, Utah 84401
(801) 621-4752
10-6 Mon-Sat
Paricio Ortega, Tim Chase
*American Literature; History;
Biography & Autobiography;
Science Fiction*

Walt West Books
1355 Riverside
Provo, Utah 84604
(801) 377-1298
11-5:30 Tues-Fri, 1-5 Sat
Walt West

*Mormons; Utah; Idaho; Western
Americana; Scholarly Books*

Basil's
515 East 3rd South
Salt Lake City, Utah 84102
(801) 355-1012
10-6 Mon-Sat
Brent Evans
General

Brennan Books
P. O. Box 9002
Salt Lake City, Utah 84109-0002
(801) 278-7946
By appointment only
Ed Brennan, Anna Brennan
*Appraisals & Appraisal Services;
Western Americana; Mormons;
Middle East*

Cosmic Aeroplane Books
258 East First Street, South
Salt Lake City, Utah 84111
(801) 533-9409
10-9 Mon-Sat, 12-7 Sun

Catalogues issued
Steve Barnett
*Mormons; Western Americana;
Science Fiction; Utah; Autographs
& Autograph Material*

Deseret Fine & Rare Books
44 East South Temple, Box 30178
Salt Lake City, Utah 84130
(801) 328-8191
10-6 Mon-Sat
Catalogues issued
Curt Bench, Wade Lillywhite
*Mormons; Utah; Western
Americana*

Scallawagiana Books
P. O. Box 2441
Salt Lake City, Utah 84110
(801) 467-3011
By appointment only
Catalogues issued
Kent Walgren
*Mormons; Freemasonry; Occult &
Magic; First Editions; Myths &
Mythology*

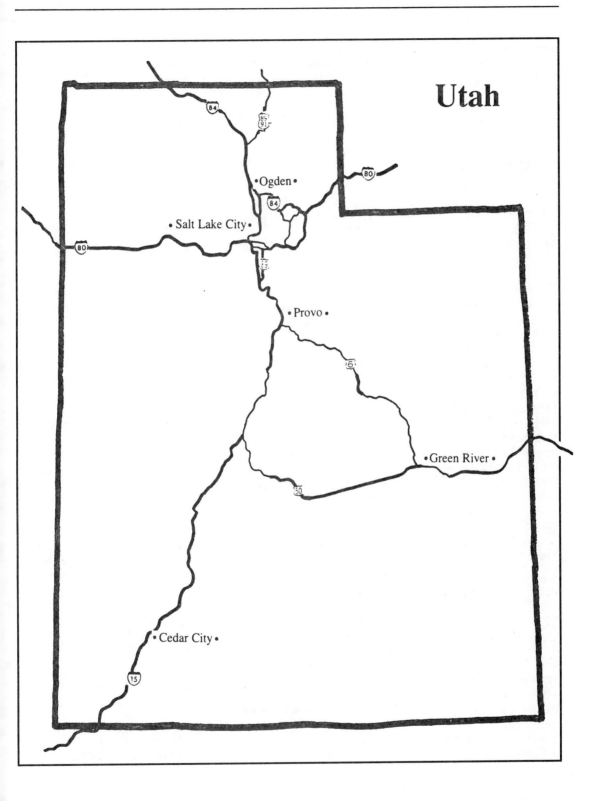

Ute-Or-Ida Books
P. O. Box 279
West Jordan, Utah 84084

(801) 566-1145
By mail only
Paul Meilin

Idaho; Utah; Mormons; Western
Americana; Rare Books

Vermont

State map of Vermont on
page 154 (New Hampshire)

Hill Haven Books
P. O. Box 292
Barton Village, Vt. 05822
(802) 525-4716
By appointment only
Catalogues issued
William M. Moroney, Judith A.
Henault
Mystery & Detective Fiction; True
Crime; Civil War & Confederacy;
Arctica & Antarctica

Arch Bridge Bookshop
142 Westminster Street, 2nd floor
Bellows Falls, Vt. 05101
(802) 463-9395
By appointment only
Duane Whitehead, Barbara
Whitehead
Indians & Eskimos; Aviation &
Aeronautics; Western Americana;
Civil War & Confederacy;
Biography & Autobiography;
World Wars

Bennington Bookshop
439 Main Street
Bennington, Vt. 05201
(802) 442-5059
9-5:30 Mon-Sat (Fri to 9)
Ellen Havlak, Richard Havlak
Vermont; New England; Fiction

Bradford Books
West Road
Bennington, Vt. 05201
(802) 447-0387

11-5 Wed-Sat, 1-5 Sun (May-Oct.
only)
Margaret L. Craig, W. Bradford
Craig
General

New Englandiana
121 Benmount Street, Box 589
Bennington, Vt. 05201
(802) 447-1695
By mail only
Catalogues issued
Roger D. Harris
Americana; Biography &
Autobiography; Genealogy;
History; Religion & Religious
History; Social Sciences

Old Book & Ephemera
Route 107
Bethel, Vt. 05032
(802) 234-9505
1-5 Mon-Sun
Patricia S. Smith
Ephemera; General

Book Cellar
120 Main Street
Brattleboro, Vt. 05301
(8-2) 254-6026
9-5:30 Mon-Sat (Fri to 9)
Betsy Bonin
Children's Books; Cooking; Crafts
& Hobbies; Literature; Poetry

Kenneth Leach
P. O. Box 78

Brattleboro, Vt. 05301
(802) 257-7918
By appointment only
Catalogues issued
Kenneth Leach
Americana; Ephemera; Literature;
American History; Rare Books

Terry Harper
P. O. Box 37
Bristol, Vt. 05443-0037
(802) 453-5088
By appointment only
Terry Harper
Americana; Natural History; Rare
Books; Voyages, Travels, &
Exploration

Ashley Book Company
P. O. Box 534
Burlington, Vt. 05402
(802) 863-3854
By appointment only
George C. Singer, Gloria B. Singer
Press Books & Fine Printing;
Illustrated Books; Skiing

Bygone Books
91 College Street
Burlington, Vt. 05401
(802) 862-4397
9:30-5:30 Mon-Sat
Vermont

Everyday Bookshop
106 Church Street
Burlington, Vt. 05401

(802) 862-5191
9-9 Mon-Sat, 10-7 Sun
Elizabeth M. Borr
Juveniles; Children's Books;
General

Fraser Publishing
309 South Willard
Burlington, Vt. 05401
(802) 658-0322
By mail only
Catalogues issued
Karla Ferrelli
Business & Business History; Stock
Market & Wall Street; Industry;
Biography & Autobiography

Mill Village Books
Mill Village
Craftsbury Common, Vt. 05827
(802) 586-9677
By appointment only
Ralph Lewis, Nancy Lewis
Marine & Maritime; Americana;
Illustrated Books; Literature;
General

Haunted Mansion Bookshop
Route 103
Cuttingsville, Vt. 05738
(802) 492-3462
10-5 Mon-Sat (May-Oct. only)
Clint Fiske, Lucille Fiske
Vermont; General

Breadloaf Bookshop
East Middlebury, Vt. 05740
(802) 388-3502
10-5 Mon-Fri
Lawrence Washington
German Books & Literature;
French Books & Literature;
General

Virginia R. Powers
P. O. Box 474
Essex Junction, Vt. 05452
Virginia Powers
Search Service, Without Stock

The Old Book Store
P. O. Box 3
Fairlee, Vt. 05045
(802) 333-4784
9-6 Mon-Sat, 9-2 Sun
John Larson, Odie Chapman
General

Recovery Books
P. O. Box 232
Greensboro, Vt. 05841
(802) 586-2846
9-9 daily
Catalogues issued
John M. Jeffrey, Mary Anne Jeffrey
Robert Frost

Ray's Used Books
3 Depot Street
Hartford, Vt. 05047
(802) 295-2267
By appointment only
Leslie Ray
Gothics & Romantic Novels;
Western Books; Cats; Rare Books;
General

Green Mountain Books & Prints
100 Broad Street
Lyndonville, Vt. 05851
(802) 626-5051
10-4 Mon-Thurs, 10-6 Fri, 10-1
Sat
Catalogues issued
Americana; History; Art

Johnny Appleseed Bookshop
Main Street
Manchester, Vt. 05254
(802) 362-2458
9:30-5 Mon-Sat, 10-5 Sun
Frederic Taylor, Mrs. Fritz
Dillmann
Regional Americana; Bindings,
Fine & Rare; First Editions;
American History; Fishing &
Angling; Rare Books

Wyman W. Parker
13 South Street
Middlebury, Vt. 05753
(802) 388-7840
Wyman Parker
Appraisals & Appraisal Services

Vermont Book Shop
38 Main Street
Middlebury, Vt. 05753
(802) 388-2061
8:30-5:30 Mon-Sat
Robert Blair
Vermont; Robert Frost

Brick House Book Shop
Morristown Corners, Box 3020
Morrisville, Vt. 05661
(802) 888-4300
10-5 daily (closed some Mon)
Alexandra Heller
General

Michael Dunn
P. O. Box 436
Newport, Vt. 05855
(802) 334-2768
By appointment only
Catalogues issued
Michael Dunn
Americana; Canada & Canadiana;
Vermont; Fishing & Angling;
Mountaineering; Bibliography

John Johnson
R.D. 1, Box 513
North Bennington, Vt. 05257
(802) 442-6738
By mail only
Catalogues issued
Betty Johnson
Botany; Fish & Ichthyology;
Mammalogy; Voyages, Travels, &
Exploration; Birds & Ornithology;
Entomology

Anne Blackmer
P. O. Box 46
North Ferrisburg, Vt. 05473

(802) 425-3148
By appointment only
Catalogues issued
Anne Blackmer
*Women; First Editions; Mystery
& Detective Fiction*

Richard H. Adelson
Cloudland Road
North Pomfret, Vt. 05053
(802) 457-2608
By appointment only
Catalogues issued
Richard H. Adelson, Jane K.
Adelson
*Voyages, Travels, & Exploration;
Americana; Pacific Region; Africa;
Children's Books; Appraisals &
Appraisal Services*

Lilac Hedge Bookshop
Main Street
Norwich, Vt. 05055
(802) 649-2921
10-5 Thurs-Sun
Katharine M Ericson, Robert P.
Ericson
Art, Books about; General

G. B. Manasek, Inc.
P. O. Box 705
Norwich, Vt. 05055
(802) 649-3962
By mail only
Catalogues issued
F. J. Manasek
*Astronomy; Physics; Prints; Japan;
Maps, Atlases, & Cartography;
Rare Books*

The Country Bookshop
R.F.D. 2
Plainfield, Vt. 05667
(802) 454-8439
By appointment only
Catalogues issued
Benjamin Koenig, Alexandra
Koenig

*Anthropology; Folklore; Vermont;
Bells; Music*

Sean Moye
Kimball Hill, Box 434
Putney, Vt. 05346
(802) 387-4159
By appointment only
Sean Moye
*Art; Architecture; Printing &
Printing History; Illustrated Books;
Rare Books*

The Unique Antique
P. O. Box 485
Putney, Vt. 05346
(802) 387-4488
By appointment only
Johnathan Flaccus
*Americana; Art; Drawings;
Paintings; Prints; Photography*

Quechee Books
P. O. Box 597
Quechee, Vt. 05059
(802) 295-1681
9:30-5:30 Mon-Sun
Catalogues issued
Duane Whitehead, Barbara
Whitehead, Ian Morrison
*British History; Western
Americana; Science; Civil War &
Confederacy; Psychiatry,
Psychology, & Psychoanalysis;
World Wars*

F. P. Elwert
19 Crescent Street
Rutland, Vt. 05701
(802) 773-3417
By mail only
Catalogues issued
Frederic Elwert
Architecture; Technology

Tuttle Antiquarian Books
28 South Main Street
Rutland, Vt. 05701
(802) 773-8930

8-5 Mon-Sat
Catalogues issued
Charles E. Tuttle, Jon H. Mayo
*General; Genealogy; Local
History; Americana, States;
Regional Americana*

William L. Parkinson
R.R. 1, Box 1330
Shelburne, Vt. 05482-9106
(802) 482-3113
By mail only
Catalogues issued
William L. Parkinson
Vermont

Sheila Scanlon-Towers
12 Hillside Terrace
Shelburne, Vt. 05462
(802) 985-8552
By mail only
Sheila Scanlon-Towers
Search Service, With Stock

Green Mountain Book Company
Broad Brook Road
South Royalton, Vt. 05068
(802) 763-7224
By appointment only
Catalogues issued
Bryant Urstadt, Thomas Powers
Science Fiction; Fantasy

Abatis Books
P. O. Box 451
Springfield, Vt. 05156
(802) 885-3151
By mail only
Irving Bell
*Almanacs; Bells; Alaska; Scotland
& The Scotish*

Una Galleries
P. O. Box 183
St. Johnsbury Center, Vt. 05863
(802) 748-5034
By appointment only
Catalogues issued
Jeanne Douglas

Children's Books; Education;
History; Rare Books

Tempest Book Shop
Route 100, Village Square
Waitsfield, Vt. 05673
(802) 496-2022
10-6 Mon-Sat, 12-5 Sun
Rick Rayfield, Roberta Tracy
Fiction; Cookbooks; Gardening &
Horticulture; Vermont; New
England; Children's Books

Green Acre Books
P. O.Box 787
Wells, Vt. 05774
(802) 645-1997
By appointment only
Henry A. Robidoux, Sheila A.
Robidoux
Americana; Illustrated Books;

Autographs & Autograph Material;
Mystery & Detective Fiction; Used
Paperbacks; General

Bear Book Shop
R.F.D. 4, Box 219
West Brattleboro, Vt. 05301
(802) 464-2260
10-5 Mon-Sun (May-Aug), else
call
Catalogues issued
John Greenberg
Music; Art; Illustrated Books;
Bibliography; Vermont; Scholarly
Books

Weston Books
R.D. 1, Box 90, Landgrove Road
Weston, Vt. 05161
(802) 824-3033
By mail only

Catalogues issued
Michael F. Speers
Espionage; History; Military

Stanley Books
P. O. Box 434
Wilder, Vt. 05088
(802) 295-9058
By appointment only
Kathleen Stnaley, Thomas Stanley
Literary Criticism; Art; General

Pleasant Street Books
48 Pleasant Street
Woodstock, Vt. 05091
(802) 457-4050
11-5 daily (Winter 11-5 Tues-Sun)
Catalogues issued
Harry Soul, Jr.
Ephemera; General

Virginia

Bookstop
109 South Alfred Street
Alexandria, Va. 22314
(703) 548-6566
11-5 Mon-Sat (closed Thurs), 1-5
Sun
Toby Cedar
Architecture; Local History;
Postcards; Sheet Music

Barbara & Mike Keck
6440 Richmond Highway
Alexandria, Va. 22306
(703) 768-7827
11-6 Tues-Sat
Barbara Keck, Mike Keck
Back Issue Periodicals

Old Mill Books
P. O. Box 21561
Alexandria, Va. 22320-2561
(703) 683-1831
By appointment only
Catalogues issued
Sam Tomlin, George Loukides
Southeast Asia; Arctica &
Antarctica

Ben Robinson
8705 Sudbury Place
Alexandria, Va. 22309
(703) 780-4469
By appointment only
Ben Robinson
Americana; Voyages, Travels, &
Exploration

Seminary Book Service
3737 Seminary Road
Alexandria, Va. 22304
(703) 370-6161
10-5 Mon-Sat
Catalogues issued
Tom Bass
Religion & Religious History

Alfabooks
2615 Columbia Pike
Arlington, Va. 22204
(703) 920-6644
10-6 Mon-Sat
Dick Gibson
Foreign Languages

Book House
805 North Emerson
Arlington, Va. 22205
(703) 527-7797
11-5 Tues-Sat (to 7 Tues & Thurs),
1-5 Sun
Catalogues issued
Natalie Hughes, Edward Hughes
Americana; Art; Civil War &
Confederacy; Illustrated Books;
Militaria; Natural History

David Jaffe
P. O. Box 4173
Arlington, Va. 22204
(703) 920-4943
David Jaffe
Humanities; Literary Criticism;
Literature; Pacific Region;
Scholarly Books; Mystery &
Detective Fiction

Virginia Book Company
114 South Church Street, Box 431
Berryville, Va. 22611
(703) 955-1428
9-4 Mon-Fri
Catalogues issued
Mrs. Myers
Virginia; Local History;
Genealogy; Manuscripts

B. Tauscher
102 Norwood Drive
Bristol, Va. 24201
(703) 669-2994
By mail only
Catalogues issued
Bill Tauscher
Civil War & Confederacy; Science
Fiction

Especially Books
8707 Wooden Spoke Road
Burke, Va. 22015
By mail only
Alan Meyrowitz, Barbara
Meyrowitz

Modern First Editions; Autographs
& Autograph Material

Essential Press
5512 Buggy Whip Drive
Centreville, Va. 22020-1663
(804) 272-5558
By mail only
C. L. Batson
Civil War & Confederacy;
Militaria; Military; Treasure
Hunting

The Book Broker
114 Bollingwood Road
Charlottesville, Va. 22903
(804) 295-5586
By appointment only
Catalogues issued
Vesta Lee Gordon
Press Books & Fine Printing;
Children's Books; Bindings,
Decorative Trade

Clover Hill Books
P. O. Box 6278
Charlottesville, Va. 22906
(804) 973-1506
By appointment only
Catalogues issued
Candace C. Crosby
English Literature; Chicago; 20th
Century Literature

Barbara H. Clower
2671 Cardinal Ridge Road
Charlottesville, Va. 22901
(804) 295-2548
By mail only
Catalogues issued
Barbara H. Clower
Needlework; Crafts & Hobbies

Daedalus
121 Fourth Street, NE
Charlottesville, Va. 22901
(804) 293-7595
10-6 Mon-Thurs, 10-5 Fri-Sat, 12-
4 Sun

Sandy McAdams
Fiction; Little Magazines &
Literary Small Presses; General

Franklin Gilliam
112 Fourth Street Northeast
Charlottesville, Va. 22901
(804) 979-2512
By appointment only
Franklin Gilliam
English Literature; American
Literature; Southern Writers;
Southern Americana

Heartwood Books
5 & 9 Elliewood Avenue
Charlottesville, Va. 22903
(804) 295-7083
11-6 daily
Catalogues issued
Paul Collinge, Mike Evans, Sher
Joseph
Southwestern Americana; Virginia;
Literature; 19th Century
Literature; Local History; General

Magnum Opus
201 West Main, Box 1301
Charlottesville, Va. 22902
(804) 293-7273
11:30-5:30 Mon-Fri, 11-3:30 Sat
Catalogues issued
Jon Guillot
English Literature; American
Literature; Western Americana;
Southern Americana; Art;
Bindings, Fine & Rare

Dalley Books
90 Kimball Lane
Christiansburg, Va. 24073
(703) 382-8949
By appointment only
Catalogues issued
George W. Dalley
Vietnam War & Literature

Antiquarian Tobacciana
5101 Willowmeade Drive

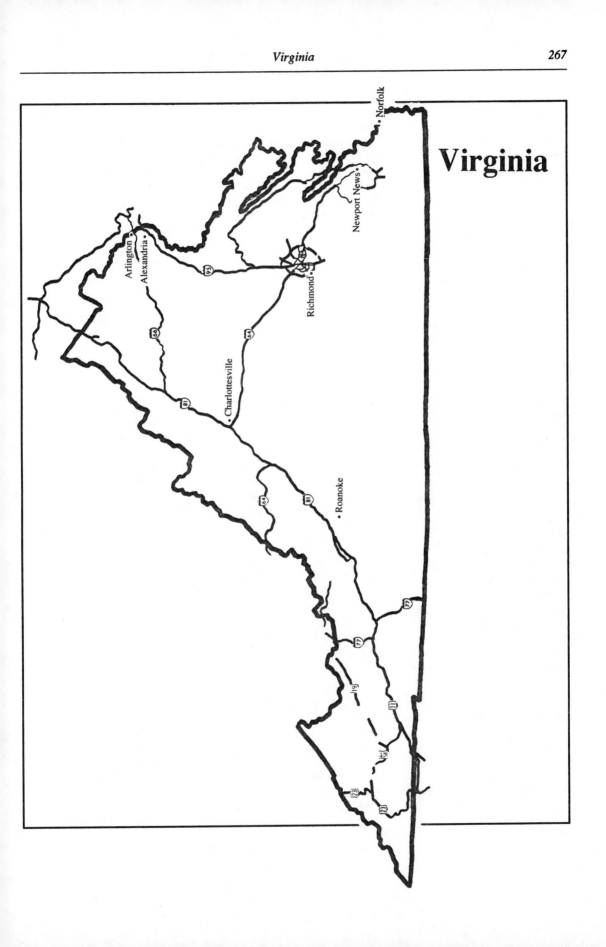

Fairfax, Va. 22030
(703) 830-8584
By mail only
Catalogues issued
Benjamin Rapaport
Tobacco & Smoking

Novel Ideas
3940 Old Lee Highway
Fairfax, Va. 22030
(703) 385-5951
10-5 Mon-Sat
Irma Ryan
General

The Associates
P. O. Box 4214
Falls Church, Va. 22044
(703) 578-3810
By appointment only
Catalogues issued
R. William Selander, Nanci
Langley
*Modern First Editions; 20th
Century Literature; Vietnam War
& Literature*

Hooper's Books
6 Loudoun Street, SW
Leesburg, Va. 22075
(703) 777-8301
10:30-5 Tues-Sat
Catalogues issued
Richard Hooper
*Horses & Horse Sports;
Agriculture; Civil War &
Confederacy; Virginia; Press
Books & Fine Printing; General*

Doctor Nostalgia
3237 Downing Drive
Lynchburg, Va. 24503
(804) 384-8303
By mail only
Catalogues issued
Bob Gardner, Mrs. Bob Gardner
*Series Books For Boys & Girls;
Postcards; Ephemera*

Jack R. Levien
Route 1, Box 18
McDowell, Va. 24458
(703) 396-3345
By mail only
Jack R. Levien
*Miniature Books; Mathematics;
Horses & Horse Sports*

Buckingham Books
R.F.D. 1, Box 186
New Canton, Va. 23123-9742
(804) 627-2267
11:30-5:30 Tues-Fri, 10-5:30 Sat
Bill Hudnall
General

Cheap Street
Route 2, Box 293
New Castle, Va. 24127
(703) 864-6288
By mail only
Catalogues issued
Jan O'Nale, George O'Nale
*Science Fiction; Press Books &
Fine Printing; Juveniles; Fantasy*

Hilton Village Book Shop
10375 Warwick Boulevard
Newport News, Va. 23601
(804) 595-5866
10-5 Mon-Sat
Jack Hamilton
*Rare Books; Civil War &
Confederacy; Art; Virginia; Naval
& Nautical; Travel*

Bargain Books—Ward's Corner
7524 Granby Street
Norfolk, Va. 23505
(804) 587-3303
10-9 Mon-Fri, 10-6 Sat
Harvey D. Eluto, Irene Snyder,
Renee Porter
*General; Rare Books; Science
Fiction; New Paperbacks; Civil
War & Confederacy*

E. Wharton & Company
3232 History Court
Oakton, Va. 22124
(703) 264-0129
By appointment only
Catalogues issued
Sarah Baldwin
*19th Century Literature; 20th
Century Literature; First Editions;
Women; Autographs & Autograph
Material; Manuscripts*

Book Search
1741 Fairfax Street
Petersburg, Va. 23803
(804) 862-2288
7-7 Mon-Sun
Joan Black, Reading Black
Search Service, Without Stock

Louis Ginsberg
P. O. Box 1502
Petersburg, Va. 23805
(804) 732-8188
By appointment only
Catalogues issued
L. Ginsberg
*Ephemera; Food & Drink; Civil
War & Confederacy; Mormons;
Colorado; Photography*

W. B. O'Neill
11609 Hunters Green Court
Reston, Va. 22091
(703) 860-0782
By appointment only
Catalogues issued
*Greece & Turkey; Voyages,
Travels, & Exploration; Travel
Guides & Baedekers; Middle East;
Rare Books; History*

Collectors' Old Bookshop
15 South Fifth Street
Richmond, Va. 23219
(804) 644-2097
11-5 Mon-Fri, 11-3 Sat
Mary Clark Roone
Americana, States; Civil War &

Confederacy; Regional Americana; Americana; Appraisals & Appraisal Services; Genealogy

First Editions Bookshop
4040 MacArthur Avenue
Richmond, Va. 23227
(804) 264-7276
12-5 Mon-Sat
Catalogues issued
Damon Persiani
Books about Books; Mystery & Detective Fiction; Modern First Editions; Graphic Arts; Literature; Jazz

Old Favorites Bookshop
610 North Sheppard Street
Richmond, Va. 23221
(804) 355-2437
11-5 Mon-Fri, 10-6 Sat
Catalogues issued
Gary O'Neal
Science Fiction; Fantasy; Civil War & Confederacy

Owens Civil War Books
P. O. Box 13622
Richmond, Va. 23225
(804) 272-8888
By appointment only
Catalogues issued
Michael Owens, Linda Owens
Civil War & Confederacy; Virginia

Nelson Bond
4724 Easthill Drive
Roanoke, Va. 24018
(703) 774-2674
By mail only
Catalogues issued
Nelson Bond
First Editions; Southern Writers

Terry Alford
P. O. Box 1151
Springfield, Va. 22151
(703) 256-6748
By appointment only

Terry Alford
Manuscripts; Appraisals & Appraisal Services; Autographs & Autograph Material; Documents; General

Audubon Prints & Books
9720 Spring Ridge Lane
Vienna, Va. 22180
(202) 484-3334
By mail only
Catalogues issued
Ed Kenney
Prints; Rare Books; Birds & Ornithology; Animals

Jo Ann Reisler
360 Glyndon Street, NE
Vienna, Va. 22180
(703) 938-2967
By appointment only
Catalogues issued
JoAnn Reisler, Donald Reisler
Children's Books; Illustrated Books; Original Art For Illustration; Hobbies; L. Frank Baum & Oziana; Miniature Books

Irene Rouse
Route 195 at Route 169
Wattsville, Va. 23483
(804) 824-4090
11-5 Mon-Fri, 11-6 Sat, 1-5 Sun
Catalogues issued
Irene Rouse
Folklore; Music; Americana; Poetry

Karl Altau
800 Warwick Circle
Waynesboro, Va. 22980
(703) 949-8867
By appointment only
Karl Altau
Americana; Virginia; Western Americana; Southern Americana; Civil War & Confederacy; Sporting

The Book House
421-A Prince George Street
Williamsburg, Va. 23185
(804) 229-3603
10-5 Mon-Fri, 10-4 Sat
M. L. Chapman
General

The Bookpress Ltd.
411 West Duke of Gloucester Street, Box KP
Williamsburg, Va. 23187
(804) 229-1260
10-5 Mon-Sat
Catalogues issued
John R. Curtis, Jr., John Ballinger, Emily Ballinger
Americana; Architecture; Voyages, Travels, & Exploration; Books about Books

George H. Garrison, Jr.
Drawer JH
Williamsburg, Va. 23187
(804) 220-3838
By appointment only
Catalogues issued
George H. Garrison, Jr.
Ephemera; Stock Market & Wall Street

Hamilton's Book Store
1784 Jamestown Road
Williamsburg, Va. 23185
(804) 693-2005
10-5 Mon-Sat
Catalogues issued
Jack D. Hamilton
Virginia; Religion & Religious History; World Wars; Juveniles; Naval & Nautical; Literature

Henry Stevens Son & Stiles
P. O. Box 1299
Williamsburg, Va. 23187
(804) 220-0925
By mail only
Catalogues issued
Thomas P. MacDonnell

Rare Books; Americana; American
History; Maps, Atlases, &
Cartography; Voyages, Travels, &
Exploration

Appleland Books
446 North Braddock Street
Winchester, Va. 22601
(703) 662-1980
By appointment only
Catalogues issued
Gene Miller
Virginia; Civil War &

Confederacy; Regional Americana;
Americana, States; Americana

Olin O. Evans
371 West Spring Street
Woodstock, Va. 22664
(703) 459-2914
By mail only
Catalogues issued
Olin O. Evans
Farming, Ranching, & Livestock;
"National Geographic" Magazine;

Civil War & Confederacy;
Regional Americana

Bookworm & Silverfish
P. O. Box 639
Wytheville, Va. 24382
(703) 686-5813
8:30-4:30 Mon-Fri
Catalogues issued
James S. Presgraves, Betty W.
Presgraves
Technology; Trade Catalogues;

Virgin Islands

Jeltrups'
51 ABC Company St.,
Christiansted
St. Croix, V.I. 00820
(809) 773-1018
9-5 Mon-Sat
Janice M. James
Caribbean; New Books; New
Paperbacks

Rulon-Miller Books
Red Hook Box 41
St. Thomas, V.I. 00802
(800) 524-2053
By appointment only
Catalogues issued
Robert Rulon-Miller Sr.
Caribbean; Central America;
South America

Washington

Comstock's Bindery & Books
257 East Main Street
Auburn, Wash. 98002
(206) 939-8770
10-6 Mon-Sat, 12-5 Sun
David Comstock, Anita Comstock
Aviation & Aeronautics; Militaria;
Mountaineering; Marine &
Maritime

High Latitude
P. O. Box 11254
Bainbridge Island, Wash. 98110
(206) 842-0202
By appointment only
Catalogues issued
Robert J. Finch
Arctica & Antarctica; Alaska;
Voyages, Travels, & Exploration

P. T. Mallahan
307 130th, SE
Bellevue, Wash. 98005
(206) 454-1663
By mail only
Patrick Mallahan
World Wars; Russia & Slavic
Countries

Steven Pirtle
P. O. Box 3422
Bellevue, Wash. 98009
Steven L. Pirtle, Jeanine Reddaway
Back Issue Magazines;
Phonograph Records

Village Books
1210 11th Street
Bellingham, Wash. 98225
(206) 671-2626
10-10 Mon-Sat, 10-6 Sun
Dee Robinson, Chuck Robinson
Chemical & Substance

Dependency; Women; Children's
Books; Self-Help; General

Nancy Filler
615 4th Street
Bremerton, Wash. 98310
(206) 377-4343
11-5 Mon-Sat
Nancy Filler
Naval & Nautical; Military;
Western Americana; Northwestern
Americana; British Isles

Huckleberry Books
105 South Tower Avenue
Centralia, Wash. 98531
(206) 736-0325
10:30-5 daily
Bill Moeller
Northwestern Americana; Sheet
Music; General

Jane Sutley
1105 West Cherry Street
Centralia, Wash. 98351
(206) 736-5251
By mail only
Catalogues issued
Jane Sutley
Gardening & Horticulture;
Farming, Ranching, & Livestock;
Forestry; Cats; Wildflowers

Peggatty Books
609 Maple Street
Clarkston, Wash. 99403
(509) 758-9517
11-5:30 Mon-Sat
Margaret H. Behrens, Philip T.
Soucy
New Books; New Paperbacks; Rare
Books

Richard T. Kennedy
1017 South 251st Street
Des Moines, Wash. 98198-8548
(206) 824-2635
By mail only
Richard T. Kennedy
"National Geographic" Magazine;
Back Issue Periodicals; Maps,
Atlases, & Cartography; Technical

Darvill's Book Store
1 Main Street, Box 166
Eastsound, Wash. 98245
(206) 376-2135
10-5:30 Mon-Sat
Kieffer Denning
Naval & Nautical; Marine &
Maritime; Northwest Americana;
Children's Books; General

Darvill's Rare Print Shop
P. O. Box 47
Eastsound, Wash. 98245
(206) 376-2351
10-5:30 Mon-Sat
Dale Pederson, Catherine Pederson
Prints

Derek Lowe
Route 1, Box 84
Eastsound, Wash. 98245
(206) 376-4344
By appointment only
Derek Lowe
Bindings, Fine & Rare;
Bibliography; Literature; English
Literature

J. D. Holmes
P. O. Box 623
Edmonds, Wash. 98020
(206) 771-2701
By appointment only

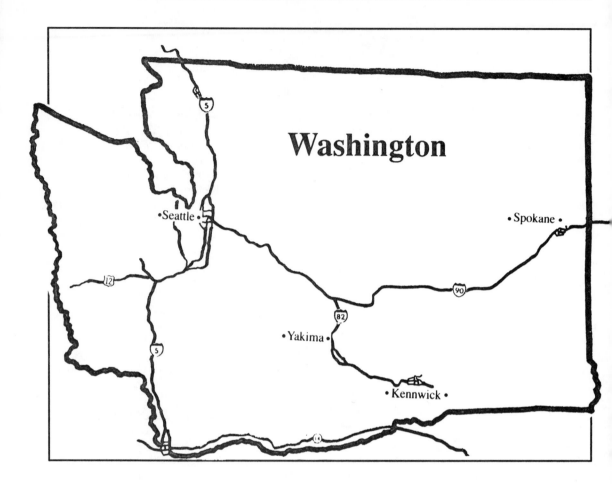

Catalogues issued
J. D. Holmes
Asia; Religion & Religous History;
Occult & Magic; Alchemy &
Hermetics; Scholarly Books

Boardwalk Books
P. O. Box 283
Friday Harbor, Wash. 98250
(206) 378-2787
9-5:30 Mon-Sun
Dorthea Augusztiny
Marine & Maritime

Fortuna Books
113 Lake Street

Kirkland, Wash. 98033
(206) 827-7294
10-6 Mon-Sat, 12-6 Sun
Ruth Williams
Foreign Languages; Art; General

R. L. Shep
P. O. Box C-20
Lopez Island, Wash. 98261
(206) 468-2023
By mail only
Catalogues issued
R. L. Shep
Textiles; Fashion; Needlework

Stephen M. James
1175 Van Dyk Road
Lynden, Wash. 98264-9447
(206) 354-1931
By appointment only
Stephen M. James
Metaphysics; Occult & Magic;
Astrology

Island Books
3014 78th, SE
Mercer Island, Wash. 98040
(206) 232-6970
10-6 Mon-Sat (Thurs to 8)
Children's Books; Fiction

R. M. Weatherford
10902 Woods Creek Road
Monroe, Wash. 98272
(206) 794-4318
By mail only
Catalogues issued
R. M. Weatherford
Indians & Eskimos; Americana;
Appraisals & Appraisal Services;
Outlaws & Rangers; Overland
Narratives; Voyages, Travels, &
Exploration

C. L. Easton
223 South First
Mount Vernon, Wash. 98273
(206) 336-2066
10:30-5 Mon-Sat
Dianna Cornelius
Fiction

Browsers' Book Shop
107 North Capitol Way
Olympia, Wash. 98501
(206) 357-7462
10-5:30 Mon-Sat, 12-4 Sun
Jennifer Stewart
General

Dohm's Ex Libris
625 South Foote Street
Olympia, Wash. 98502
By mail only
Janice H. Dohm
Children's Books; Illustrated
Books; Folklore

Ookkees Bookshop
929 South Bay Road
Olympia, Wash. 98506
(206) 352-8622
By mail only
David H. Schlottmann
Jack London; General

Book Stop
18954-A Front Street NE
Poulsbo, Wash. 98370
(206) 779-9773

10-5:30 Mon-Sat, 12:30-4 Sun
Megan Holmberg
General

The Bookmark
611 6th Street
Prosser, Wash. 99350
(509) 786-2626
8-5 Mon-Sat
Dixie Koenig, Glenn Koenig
General

Brused Books
North 105 Grand
Pullman, Wash. 99163
(509) 334-7898
11-6 Tues-Sat
Bruce Calkins
Northwest Americana; General

Book Place
1330 Jadwin
Richland, Wash. 99352
(509) 946-6046
10-6 Mon-Wed, 10-8 Thurs-Fri,
10-5 Sat
Phyllis Bowersock, Shirley Miller
General

Antiques & Art Associates
2113 Third Avenue
Seattle, Wash. 98121
(206) 624-4378
10-5 Mon-Sat
George Harder
Northwestern Americana;
Americana; Modern First Editions;
Illustrated Books; Children's Books

Bibelots & Books, Inc.
112 East Lynn
Seattle, Wash. 98102
(206) 329-6676
12-5:30 Tues-Sat
Shirley Schneider, Reba Schneider
Children's Books; Illustrated
Books; Modern First Editions;
Literary Criticism

M. Taylor Bowie
2613 Fifth Avenue
Seattle, Wash. 98121
(206) 682-5363
11-5 Tues-Sat
Catalogues issued
M. Taylor Bowie
Modern First Editions; Illustrated
Books; Performing Arts;
Literature; Books about Books;
Voyages, Travels, & Exploration

Collins Rare Books
1211 East Denny Way
Seattle, Wash. 98122
(306) 323-3999
By appointment only
Catalogues issued
Louis B. Collins, Jr.
Ethnology; Modern First Editions;
Scholarly Books

Dennis Books
P. O. Box 99142
Seattle, Wash. 98199
(206) 283-0532
12-5 Sat & Sun
Catalogues issued
Dennis E. Jellam
Children's Books; Comic Books;
Disneyana; Games & Pastimes;
Original Art For Illustration; L.
Frank Baum & Oziana

Donnally New & Used Books
1915 First Avenue
Seattle, Wash. 98101
(206) 448-9673
10:30-5:30 Mon-Sat
Elizabeth Donnally
Art; Photography; Literature,
Architecture

Elliott Bay Book Company
101 South Main Street
Seattle, Wash. 98104
(206) 624-6600
10:30 a.m.-11 p.m. Mon-Sat, 12-6
Sun

Catalogues issued
Kristin Kennell, Rick Simonson
*Northwest Americana; Local
History; General*

Flora & Fauna Books
2231 2nd Avenue
Seattle, Wash. 98121
(206) 328-5175
10-5 Mon-Sat
Catalogues issued
D. Hutchinson
*Natural History; Science; Western
Americana*

Golden Age Collectibles
1501 Pike Place Market
Seattle, Wash. 98101
(206) 622-9799
10:30-5:30 Mon-Sat
*Comic Books; Cinema & Film;
Science Fiction; Stephen King;
Disneyana*

Helen Harte
6253 54th Avenue, NE
Seattle, Wash. 98115
(206) 526-5284
By appointment only
Catalogues issued
Helen Harte
Ireland & The Irish

Horizon Books
425 15th Avenue, East
Seattle, Wash. 98112
(206) 329-3586
10-10 Mon-Fri, 10-8 Sat, 10-6 Sun
Don Glover
*Science Fiction; Literature;
Literary Criticism; Folklore*

David Ishii
212 First Avenue, South
Seattle, Wash. 98104
(206) 622-4719
10-6 Mon-Sat, 10-5 Sun
David Ishii

*Asians in America; Fishing &
Angling; Hunting; General*

Elaine Katz
1319 NE 56th Street
Seattle, Wash. 98105
(206) 525-3777
By appointment only
Catalogues issued
Elaine Katz
Women

J. James Lewis
1439 NW 65th Street, No. 4
Seattle, Wash. 98117
(206) 789-0783
By mail only
Catalogues issued
Don Moreland, Harold Mick
*China; Asia; Vietnam War &
Literature; Asians in America;
India*

Magus Bookstore
1408 NE 42nd Street
Seattle, Wash. 98105
(206) 633-1800
10-8 Mon-Fri (to 10 Thurs & Fri),
11-6 Sat
David L. Bell, Kristi Austin
Scholarly Books

Robert W. Mattila
P. O. Box 4038, Pioneer Square
Stn.
Seattle, Wash. 98104
(206) 622-9455
By appointment only
Catalogues issued
Robert W. Mattila
*Arctica & Antarctica;
Northwestern Americana; Voyages,
Travels, & Exploration*

Peter Miller
1909 First Avenue
Seattle, Wash. 98101
(206) 623-5563
10-6 Mon-Fri, 10-5 Sat

Catalogues issued
Peter Miller
Architecture; Design

Moving Books Inc.
P. O. Box 20037
Seattle, Wash. 98102
(206) 325-9077
8-5 daily
Catalogues issued
Doug Benecke
*Chemical & Substance
Dependency; Self-Help; Health;
Psychiatry, Psychology, &
Psychoanalysis*

W. O. Moye
7717 Aurora Avenue North
Seattle, Wash. 98103
(206) 783-8701
By appointment only
Catalogues issued
Wayne Moye
*Voyages, Travels, & Exploration;
Natural History; General*

Edward D. Nudelman
P. O. Box 20704, Broadway Stn.
Seattle, Wash. 98102
(206) 367-4644
By appointment only
Catalogues issued
Edward D. Nudelman
*Press Books & Fine Printing;
English Literature; American
Literature; Bindings, Fine & Rare;
Autographs & Autograph Material;
Children's Books*

Simon Ottenberg
P. O. Box 15509
Seattle, Wash. 98115
(206) 322-5398
By appointment only
Catalogues issued
Simon Ottenberg
Africa; Art

Pioneer-West Bookshop
4519 California Avenue SW
Seattle, Wash. 98116
(206) 935-8440
10-6 Mon-Sat (Fri to 7)
Russell W. Miller
Chess; General

Seattle Book Center
2031 Second Avenue
Seattle, Wash. 98121
(206) 625-1533
10-5 Mon-Sat
Catalogues issued
John L. Polley
General

Shorey Book Store
110 Union Street
Seattle, Wash. 98111
(206) 624-0221
9-6 Mon-Sat (Fri to 8), 12-5 Sun
Catalogues issued
J. W. Todd, Jr., James Todd
Western Americana; Alaska;
Arctica & Antarctica; American
History; Religion & Religious
History; Indians & Eskimos

Spade & Archer
1502 East Olive Way
Seattle, Wash. 98122
(206) 328-6321
4-6 Mon, 12-4:30 Tues & Thurs,
12-6 Fri & Sat
Catalogues issued
D. W. Nyback, Beth Rozier
Mystery & Detective Fiction; True
Crime; Criminology

George H. Tweney
16660 Marine View Drive, SW
Seattle, Wash. 98166
(206) 243-8243
By appointment only
Catalogues issued
George H. Tweney, Maxine R.
Tweney
Americana; Appraisals &

Appraisal Services; Books about
Books; Overland Narratives;
Voyages, Travels, & Exploration

Way's Magazines Unlimited
P. O. Box AB-193
Seattle, Wash. 98111
(206) 633-2262
By mail only
Jack Way
Back Issue Magazines

L. T. Myers
119 Clallam Bay Street
Sequim, Wash. 98382
(206) 683-8641
By mail only
Lawrence Myers
20th Century Literature; History;
Biography & Autobiography;
Books about Books; Bibliography;
General

Robert H. Redding
1301 South 3rd, Apt. 18-D
Sequim, Wash. 98382
(206) 683-8202
By mail only
Catalogues issued
Robert Redding
Alaska; Northwestern Americana;
Literature

Clark's Old Bookstore
318 West Sprague Avenue
Spokane, Wash. 99204
(509) 624-1846
10-5 Tues-Sat
James R. Simon, Irene Simon
Regional Americana; Children's
Books; Gardening & Horticulture;
History; Literature; Poetry

Fox Book Company
737 St. Helens
Tacoma, Wash. 98402
(206) 627-2223
10-5:30 Mon-Sat
Catalogues issued

Barbara Fox
Rare Books; Local History; First
Editions

George E. Linthicum
P. O. Box 98762
Tacoma, Wash. 98499
(206) 584-7123
By appointment only
Catalogues issued
George Linthicum
Modern First Editions

O'Leary's Books
4021 100th Street, SW
Tacoma, Wash. 98499
(206) 588-2503
10-9 Mon-Fri, 10-6 Sat, 12-5 Sun
Catalogues issued
Ron Trimble
Children's Books; Northwestern
Americana; Comic Books; Science
Fiction

World Mountain Books
P. O. Box 11174
Tacoma, Wash. 98411-0174
By mail only
Catalogues issued
Charles G. Hubbell
General

Spencer's Bookstore
10415 NE Fourth Plain Road
Vancouver, Wash. 98662
(206) 892-9862
10-8 Mon-Fri, 10-4 Sat
Darwin Spencer
Used Paperbacks; General

Homesteader
26 North Wenatchee Avenue
Wenatchee, Wash. 98801
(509) 662-7988
9:30-6 Mon-Fri, 10-4:30 Sat
Judy Soule, Fran Taber
Regional Americana; New Books;
Children's Books

Book Nook
722 Summitview
Yakima, Wash. 98902
(509) 453-3762
10-6 Mon-Fri, 10-4 Sat
Dorothy C. Emmert
Indians & Eskimos; Children's Books; Metaphysics; Philosophy; Chemical & Substance Dependency; General

Cheshire Books
310 Yakima Avenue
Yakima, Wash. 98901
(509) 457-0930
9-5 Mon-Sat
Walter Toop
Northwest Americana; Children's Books; General

Jay Woods
1 Bohoskey Drive
Yakima, Wash. 98901
(509) 452-9133
By appointment only
Jay Woods, Betty Schulte
Geology; Medieval Manuscripts; Middle Ages; Natural History; Scholarly Books; Science Fiction

West Virginia

West Virginia

Appalachia Book Shop
1316 Pen Mar Avenue
Bluefield, W.Va. 24701
(304) 327-5493
12-5 Mon-Sat
Arnold Porterfield
*Civil War & Confederacy;
Genealogy; Geography; Comic
Books*

Unicorn Ltd.
P. O. Box 397
Bruceton Mills, W.Va. 26525
(304) 379-8803
By mail only
Catalogues issued
W. R. McLeod, Vicki McLeod
Scotland & The Scotish

Book Store
104 South Jefferson Street
Lewisburg, W.Va. 24901
(304) 645-6910
10-5 Tues-Sat
Catalogues issued
Robert Head, Darlene Fife
*General; Poetry; History;
Philosophy; Evolution*

Wooden Porch Books
Route 1, Box 262
Middlebourne, W.Va. 26149
(304) 386-4434
By mail only
Catalogues issued
Lois Mueller, Bill Mueller
*Fashion; Textiles; Cooking;
Steamboats & River Travel*

Pinocchio's
180 Willey Street
Morgantown, W.Va. 26505
(304) 296-2332

10-5 Mon-Sat (Mon to 8)
Jeanne Goodman
Children's Books

Ruth E. Robinson
Route 7, Box 162-A
Morgantown, W.Va. 26505
(304) 594-3140
By appointment only
Ruth E. Robinson
*Regional Americana; Americana,
States; Books about Books;
Bibliography*

Stilwell Bookshop
150 Pleasant Street
Morgantown, W.Va. 26505
(304) 296-6378
10-5:30 Mon-Sat
Margaret Stilwell
General

Wolf's Head Books
198 Foundary Street
Morgantown, W.Va. 26507
(304) 296-0706
11-5 Mon-Sat
Catalogues issued
Barbara E. Nailler, Harvey J. Wolf
*Americana; Military; Illustrated
Books; West Virginia*

Sebert Books
Route 3, Box 325
Mount Nebo, W.Va. 26679
(304) 438-8180
By mail only
Elvin Sebert, Marcia Bragg
*Western Books; Science Fiction;
Mystery & Detective Fiction;
Cookbooks; Children's Books*

Mt. Zion Books
P. O. Box 25
Mount Zion, W.Va. 26151
(304) 354-6141
By mail only
Michael Lebowitz
*Religion & Religious History;
Health; Vegetarianism*

Trans Allegheny Books Inc
725 Green Street
Parkersburg, W.Va. 26101
(304) 422-4499
10-7 Tues-Fri, 10-5 Sat, 12-5 Sun
Catalogues issued
Rebecca Farnsworth
*West Virginia; Regional
Americana; Ohio; Western
Pennsylvania; Authors*

Richard A. Hand
81 Lynwood Avenue
Wheeling, W.Va. 26003
(304) 242-8853
By appointment only
Catalogues issued
Richard Hand, Jeannette Hand
*Western Americana; Indians &
Eskimos; Archaeology; Voyages,
Travels, & Exploration; Arctica
& Antarctica*

Stroud Booksellers
Star Route, Box 94
Williamsburg, W.Va. 24991
(304) 645-7169
By mail only
Catalogues issued
John Nathan Stroud, Elizabeth
Daigle
*Religion & Religious History; Bible
& Bible Studies; Methodism;
Agriculture*

Wisconsin

Badger Trading Company
2620 North Mason Street, No. 7
Appleton, Wisc. 54914
(414) 739-1339
By appointment only
Tod Loberg
Graphic Design; General

Dan's Books
111 South Appleton Street
Appleton, Wisc. 54911
(414) 739-6118
11-5 Mon-Fri
Catalogues issued
Daniel K. Shenan
Science Fiction

Shenandoah Books
133 East Wisconsin Avenue
Appleton, Wisc. 54911
10-7 Mon-Sat (Thurs to 8, Fri to 9)
Catalogues issued
Paul A. Skenadors
*Indians & Eskimos; History;
Wisconsin; Religion & Religious
History; Psychiatry, Psychology,
& Psychoanalysis; Political,
Social, & Cultural History*

Decline & Fall
P. O. Box 368
Clinton, Wisc. 53525
(608) 676-5102
By mail only
Catalogues issued
Mr. Clair A Schulz
Modern First Editions

Sadlon's Ltd.
109 North Broadway
De Pere, Wisc. 54115
(414) 336-6665
Catalogues issued

Ramona J. Sadlon
Rare Books

West's Booking Agency
P. O. Box 406
Elm Grove, Wisc. 53122
(414) 786-7084
By mail only
Catalogues issued
Richard West
*Mystery & Detective Fiction;
Americana; First Editions; Science
Fiction; Illustrated Books;
Children's Books*

Pages/Booktraders #1
801 South Irwin Avenue
Green Bay, Wisc. 54301
(414) 437-9566
10-6 Mon-Fri, 10-5 Sat
Catalogues issued
*Wisconsin; Fore-Edge Paintings;
General*

Pages/Booktraders #2
426 South Military
Green Bay, Wisc. 54303
(414) 498-3370
10-9 Mon-Sat, 10-6 Sun
Catalogues issued
Jeanne Kartz
*Modern First Editions; Fore-Edge
Paintings; Great Lakes; General*

Wise Owl Books
P. O. Box 377
Lake Dalton, Wisc. 53941
(608) 254-2092
9-8 Mon-Sat, 1-8 Sun
Percy H. Seamans
*Children's Books; Americana,
States; Series Books For Boys &
Girls; Wisconsin; Horatio Alger*

Avol's Books
405 West Gilman Street
Madison, Wisc. 53703
(608) 255-4730
10-6:30 Mon-Sat
Richard Avol, Carol Avol
Scholarly Books; General

James C. Dast
1910 Keyes Avenue
Madison, Wisc. 53711
(608) 257-5172
By appointment only
Catalogues issued
James C. Dast
Medicine & Science

G. F. Glaeve
6654 Odana Road
Madison, Wisc. 53719
(608) 833-3113
10-8 Mon-Fri, 10-5 Sat
G. F. Glaeve
*Prints; Ephemera; Antiques; Maps,
Atlases, & Cartography*

Paul's Book Store
670 State Street
Madison, Wisc. 53703
(608) 257-2968
Daily
General

J. Tuttle
1806 Laurel Crest
Madison, Wisc. 53705
(608) 238-3668
By mail only
Catalogues issued
Judith A. Tuttle, Robert P. Tuttle
*Marine & Maritime; Ships & The
Sea*

20th Century Books
108 King Street
Madison, Wisc. 53703
(608) 251-6226
10:30-5:30 Mon-Sat, 2-5 Sun
Catalogues issued
Hank Luttrell
Science Fiction; Mystery &
Detective Fiction; Military History;
Comic Books

Waite Collection
402 Clemons Avenue
Madison, Wisc. 53704
By mail only
Paul Waite
English Literature; Woodcut
Books; Prints; Drawings; True
Crime; Illustrated Books

The Book Nook
2516 Wollmer Street
Manitowoc, Wisc. 54220
(414) 682-2665
9-5 daily
Fred Eppler, Judy Eppler
General

W. Bruce Fye
1607 North Wood Avenue
Marshfield, Wisc. 54449
(715) 384-8128
By mail only
Catalogues issued
W. Bruce Fye, Lois B. Fye
Medicine & Science; History of
Medicine & Science; Bibliography;
Neurosciences; Back Issue
Periodicals; Autographs &
Autograph Material

T. S. Vandoros
5827 Highland Terrace
Middleton, Wisc. 53562
(608) 836-8254
By appointment only
Catalogues issued
Takis Vandoros
English Literature; Charles

Dickens; Association Copies;
Limited & Signed Editions; Press
Books & Fine Printing

Constant Reader Bookshop
1625-27E Irving Place
Milwaukee, Wisc. 53202
(414) 291-0452
11-8 daily
Catalogues issued
John M. Esser, David Hurlbutt
Americana; Cinema & Film;
Fiction; Fishing & Angling;
Literary Criticism; Religion &
Religious History

Just Books
845 North Marshall Street
Milwaukee, Wisc. 53202
(414) 278-8478
12-6 daily
Hartwin W. Just
Appraisals & Appraisal Services

Spectrum Books
2110 West Wells Street
Milwaukee, Wisc. 53233
(414) 344-5522
1-7 Mon-Sat
Robert Stein
Science Fiction

Webster's Books
2559 North Downer Avenue
Milwaukee, Wisc. 53211
(414) 332-4610
9:30-midnight Mon-Sat, 12-5 Sun
Catalogues issued
Francis J. Reich, Lynn Gilliam,
Pegi Taylor
Foreign Languages; Mystery &
Detective Fiction; Gay & Lesbian
Literature; Fiction; Women;
History

New Miner Trading Post
P. O. Box 188
Necedah, Wisc. 54646
(608) 565-2822

By appointment only
Catalogues issued
Charles Mayer
Catholica; Church History; Series
Books For Boys & Girls

Winstead Shop
140 South Winsted Street
Spring Green, Wisc. 53588
(608) 588-2042
8-5 daily
Virgil Steele, Helen Steele
Americana; Wisconsin;
Architectural Design; Architecture

Bill's Books
3323 Lindbergh Avenue
Stevens Point, Wisc. 54481
(715) 341-2035
By mail only
Catalogues issued
William L. Ohm
Baseball

The Gamebag
P. O. Box 838
Twin Lakes, Wisc. 53181
(414) 279-5478
By appointment only
Catalogues issued
Carol McNally
Hunting; Big Game Hunting;
Natural History

The Untamed Shrew
N7609 Airport Road
Waterloo, Wisc. 53594
(414) 478-3644
Catalogues issued
Joan Hyer
Women

Baptist Book Bourse
745 West Main Street
Watertown, Wisc. 53094
(414) 261-9300
By mail only
Dr. Richard Weeks
Religion & Religous History;

Biography & Autobiography; Bible & Bible Studies; Church History

Littlewoods Book House
200 East Park Avenue
Waukesha, Wisc. 53186

(414) 549-1125
11-5 Fri-Sat
Catalogues issued
William Littlewood, Marion Littlewood
General; Americana; Biography &

Autobiography; History of Medicine & Science; Series Books For Boys & Girls; Wireless Communication

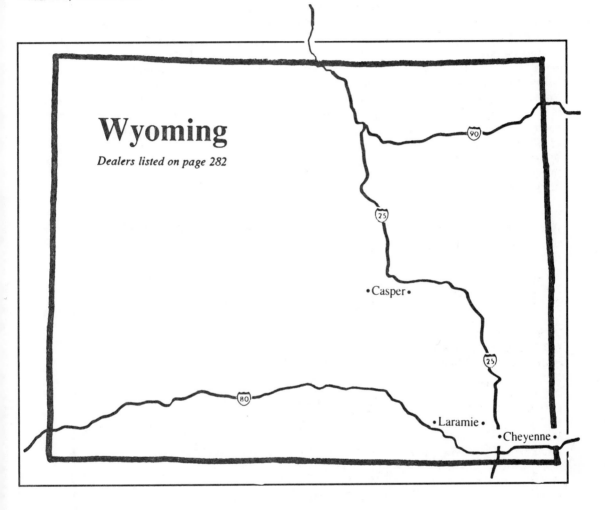

Wyoming

Dealers listed on page 282

Wyoming

Summerhouse Books
P. O. Box 66
Dayton, Wyo. 82836
(307) 655-9714
9-5 Mon-Sat (May-Oct)
Bonnie Switzer, Janet Wolney
Western Americana; Wyoming;
General

High Country Books
111 Grand Avenue
Laramie, Wyo. 82070
(307) 742-5640
10-6 Mon-Sat, 12-4 Sun

Ken Crawford
Wyoming; Geology; Western
Americana; Western Books;
Railroads

Lee Douglas
46 Wakeley
Sheridan, Wyo. 82801
(307) 737-2222
By appointment only
Catalogues issued
Lee Douglas
Authors, State & Local

Backpocket Ranch Bookshop
Star Route 4, Box 27
Sundance, Wyo. 82729
(307) 283-2665
By appointment only
Catalogues issued
Gaydell Collier
Wyoming; Western Americana;
Farming, Ranching, & Livestock;
Horses & Horse Sports

Specialties

Adirondacks

Cabin In (Potsdam, N.Y.)
Harbor Hill (Harrison, N.Y.)

Kreinheder (Warrensburg, N.Y.)
Wildwood (Old Forge, N.Y.)

With (Lake Placid, N.Y.)

Adventure

Belknap (Boston, Mass.)
Book Carnival (Orange, Calif.)
Daunce (Buffalo, N.Y.)

Discher (Castro Valley, Calif.)
Fickes (Akron, Ohio)
Hittel (Ft. Lauderdale, Fla.)

JMD (Groton, N.Y.)
Research (Fremont, Neb.)
Silver (Redondo Bch., Calif.)

Africa

Adelson (No. Pomfret, Vt.)
Bayview (Northport, N.Y.)
Berkelouw (Los Angeles, Calif.)
Book Admirer (Norwalk, Conn.)
Bookery (Farmington, N.H.)
Dee Cee (Nyack, N.Y.)
Eisenberg (Washington, D.C.)
Hacker (New York, N.Y.)
Huxley (Loudonville, N.Y.)

Int'l. Univ. (New York, N.Y.)
Kalanja (Trafford, Pa.)
Lambeth (New York, N.Y.)
Manor (New York, N.Y.)
McBlain (Hamden, Conn.)
Norumbega (Houston, Texas)
Oceanie (Hlllsdale, N.Y.)
Ottenberg (Seattle, Wash.)
Parmer (San Diego, Calif.)

Pettinger (Russell, Iowa)
Scharf (Pittsburgh, Pa.)
Talvin (Trafford, Pa.)
Terramedia (Wellesley, Mass.)
Trophy (Agoura, Calif.)
University (New York, N.Y.)
Vanderstoel (El Cerrito, Calif.)
Viederman (Leonia, N.J.)

North Africa

Asian Books (Cambridge, Mass.)
Camel (New York, N.Y.)

Feltus (Berkeley, Calif.)
Schreyer (New York, N.Y.)

Worldwide (Cambridge, Mass.)

Agriculture

Amer. Botanist (Brookfield, Ill.)
Black Swan (Sacramento, Calif.)
Country (Chesterton, Ind.)

Hooper's (Leesburg, Va.)
Ockett (Bryant Pond, Maine)
Pomona (Rockton, Ont.)

Stroud (Williamsburg, W.Va.)

Alabama

Book Shelf (Cleveland, Tenn.)

Cather/Brown (Birmingham, Ala.)

R E (Fairhope, Ala.)

Alaska

Abatis (Springfield, Vt.)
Campfire (Evansville, Ind.)
Devine (Katonah, N.Y.)
High Lat. (Bainbridge, Wash.)

Hilscher (Anchorage, Alk.)
Jack London (Glen Ellen, Calif.)
Martin's (Fairbanks, Alk.)
Observatory (Sitka, Alk.)

Old Harbor (Sitka, Alk.)
Redding (Sequim, Wash.)
Shorey (Seattle, Wash.)
Wilson (Bull Shoals, Ark.)

Alchemy & Hermetics

Fields (San Francisco, Calif.)
Hermeticus (Ashland, Ore.)

Holmes (Edmonds, Wash.)

Whelan (Newberry, Fla.)

Horatio Alger

Antiq. Michiana (Allen, Mich.)

Books Of (Corning, N.Y.)

Wise (Lake Delton, Wisc.)

Almanacs

Abatis (Springfield, Vt.)

Barilaro (E. Weymouth, Mass.)

4th Estate (New London, Conn.)

Alternative Lifestyles

Laws (Chicago, Ill.)

Wilder (Hubbardston, Mass.)

Americana

ABC Theo. (Springfield, Mo.)
Academic (No. Vancouver, B.C.)
Adelson (No. Pomfret, Vt.)
Adobe (Albuquerque, N.M.)
Agranoff (Cincinnati, Ohio)
Ahab (Cambridge, Mass.)
Alkahest (Evanston, Ill.)
Allen (Philadelphia, Pa.)
Altau (Waynesboro, Va.)
Amer. Book (Fresno, Calif.)
Americanist (Pottstown, Pa.)
Amer. Pol. (Newtown, Conn.)
Andover Sq. (Knoxville, Tenn.)
Antiquaria (Franklin, Tenn.)
Antiq. Bookworm (Sharon, Mass.)
Antiq. Michiana (Allen, Mich.)
Antiques/Art (Seattle, Wash.)
Antiquus (San Francisco, Calif.)
Appleland (Winchester, Va.)
Arader/Sessler (Philadelphia, Pa.)
Arader (Atlanta, Ga.)
Arader (New York, N.Y.)
Argosy (New York, N.Y.)
Armens (Iowa City, Iowa)
Armitage (Miamisburg, Ohio)
Arnolds (Contoocook, N.H.)
Arthurton (Palmyra, N.Y.)
Askins (New Lebanon, N.Y.)

Attic (Hodges, S.C.)
Attic (Newark, Del.)
Avocet (Sanford, N.C.)
Bargain (Long Beach, Calif.)
Barnes (Evanston, Ill.)
Barrister (Davie, Fla.)
Bartfield (New York, N.Y.)
Bebbah (Andover, Kan.)
Beckhorn (Dobbs Ferry, N.Y.)
Berk (Studio City, Calif.)
Berliawsky (Camden, Maine)
Bibliomania (Schenectady, N.Y.)
Blitz (Weaverville, Calif.)
Boardman (Camden, N.Y.)
Book Bear (W. Brookfield, Mass.)
Book-Bind (Anaheim, Calif.)
Book Case (Houston, Texas)
Book Cellar (Fullerton, Calif.)
Book House (Arlington, Va.)
Bookman (Kent, Ohio)
Book Mart (San Antonio, Texas)
Book Mart Annex (San Antonio, Tex.)
Bookmine (Old Scaramento, Calif.)
Book OP (Adrian, Mich.)
Book Pedlars (Cundy's Harbor, Maine)
Bookpress (Williamsburg, Va.)

Book Ranger (New York, N.Y.)
Book Stall (Rockford, Ill.)
Bookstock (So. Orleans, Mass.)
Books With (Concord, Mass.)
Book Traders (Winter Haven, Fla.)
Bookworm (Wytheville, Va.)
Borderland (Alvaton, Ky.)
Bowling (Rancho Palos Verdes, Calif.)
Boyce (Carmel, N.Y.)
Branford (Branford, Conn.)
Brick Row (San Francisco, Calif.)
Broad Ripple (Indianapolis, Ind.)
Brookline (Brookline, Mass.)
Brown (Toledo, Ohio)
Buchanan (New York, N.Y.)
Bullock (Yardley, Pa.)
Burpee Hill (New London, N.H.)
Burstein (Waltham, Mass.)
Cahan (Narberth, Pa.)
Calico Cat (Ventura, Calif.)
Camelot (Baltimore, Md.)
Canney (Alfred, Maine)
Carduner (Philadelphia, Pa.)
Carnegie (New York, N.Y.)
Carry Back (Haverhill, N.H.)
Casavant (Wayland, Mass.)
Cather/Brown (Birmingham, Ala.)

Cavallo (Altadena, Calif.)
CGT (College Stn., Texas)
Chimney (Bridgeport, Conn.)
Cielec (Chicago, Ill.)
Colebrook (Colebrook, Conn.)
Collectors' (Richmond, Va.)
Conn. Book (Fairfield, Conn.)
Connecticut (E. Haddam, Conn.)
Constant (Milwaukee, Wisc.)
Coosa Valley (Rome, Ga.)
Craig (Newport, R. I.)
Curiosity (St. Joseph, Mich.)
Dabny (Washington, D.C.)
Desch (Wheaton, Md.)
Diamond (Rochester, N.Y.)
Dolphin (Camden, Maine)
Donaldson's (Knoxville, Tenn.)
Dooling (Middlebury, Conn.)
Dorn (Johntown, N.Y.)
Downs (Marietta, Ga.)
Drew's (Santa Barbara, Calif.)
Dunlap (St. Louis, Mo.)
Dunn (Newport, Vt.)
Dupley (Omaha, Neb.)
Dust (Cincinnati, Ohio)
Dysinger (Brunswick, Maine)
Emerson (Falls Village, Conn.)
Ernst (Selinsgrove, Pa.)
Exnowski (Warren, Mich.)
Farley's (Pensacola, Fla.)
Fay (Caledonia, N.Y.)
Felcone (Princeton, N.J.)
1st Edtn. (Tulsa, Okla.)
Fisher (Cobleskill, N.Y.)
Footnote (Brooklyn, N.Y.)
Fox (Madison, Tenn.)
Fox Hill (Palmer, Mass.)
Frid (San Pedro, Calif.)
Frontier (Bryan, Texas)
Gilann (Darien, Conn.)
Gilbo (Carpinteria, Calif.)
Ginsberg (Sharon, Mass.)
Glover (Cambridge, N.Y.)
Glover's (Lexington, Ky.)
Golder (Collinsville, Conn.)
Goodspeed's #1 (Boston, Mass.)
Goodspeed's #2 (Boston, Mass.)
Graf (Iowa City, Iowa)
Grt. Expect. (Staten Isl., N.Y.)

Green Acre (Wells, Vt.)
Green Mtn. (Lyndonville, Vt.)
Grimshaw (Randolph, Mass.)
Grunder (Ithaca, N.Y.)
Gud (Elmhurst, N.Y.)
Guthman (Westport, Conn.)
Hallberg (Hartford, Conn.)
Hall (Chambersburg, Pa.)
Hall (E. Longmeadow, Mass.)
Hamill (Chicago, Ill.)
Harder (Los Alamos, N.M.)
Harper (Bristol, Vt.)
Harris (Northfield, Mass.)
Hartmann (Morganton, N.C.)
Hayman (Carey, Ohio)
Heaston (Austin, Texas)
Heinoldt (So. Egg, N.J.)
Heller (Cleveland, Ohio)
Hensel (Belle Chasse, La.)
Heritage (Sonora, Calif.)
Herron (Rome, Ga.)
High Ridge (Rye, N.Y.)
Hirschtritt's (Silver Spg., Md.)
Hist. Realia (Wooster, Ohio)
History (Ashley Falls, Mass.)
Hoefliger (Buffalo, N.Y.)
Holmes (San Francisco, Calif.)
Houseman (Yellow Spgs., Ohio)
Howes (Brewster, Mass.)
Hughes (St. Louis, Mo.)
Hughes (Williamsport, Pa.)
In Our (Cambridge, Mass.)
Irene's (So. Gardner, Mass.)
Ivey (Brewton, Ala.)
Jack's (Mt. Prospect, Ill.)
Jane Addams (Champaign, Ill.)
Javitch (Montreal, Que.)
Jenison's (Canton, N.Y.)
Jenkins (Austin, Texas)
Johnson (Waltham, Mass.)
Joslin (Springfield, Mass.)
Joyce (Chicago, Ill.)
Kahn (Montreal, Que.)
Kapica (New Britain, Conn.)
Keeler (No. Monmouth, Maine)
Kellinger (Chambersburg, Pa.)
King (Detroit, Mich.)
Kionke (Gowanda, N.Y.)
Kirksco (Ringwood, N.J.)

Klemm (Apple Valley, Calif.)
Knights (Harwich Port, Mass.)
Kraus (New York, N.Y.)
Lasley (Berkeley, Ill.)
Laster (Winston-Salem, N.C.)
Lawrence (New York, N.Y.)
Lazarus (Ossining, N.Y.)
Leach (Brattleboro, Vt.)
Leaves (Ann Arbor, Mich.)
Leech (Ormand Bch., Fla.)
Lee (Lincoln, Neb.)
Legacy (Hatboro, Pa.)
Legacy (Iowa City, Iowa)
Lemon (Lemon Grove, Calif.)
Levine (Savannah, Ga.)
Liberty (Concord, Calif.)
Little (Rehobeth, Mass.)
Littlewoods (Waukesha, Wisc.)
Lloyd (Washington, D.C.)
Lord (Marshfield, Mass.)
Lorson's (Fullerton, Calif.)
Lucas (Blandford, Mass.)
Lunsford (No. Vancouver, B.C.)
Macauluso (Kennett Sq., Pa.)
Macksey (Baltimore, Md.)
MacManus (Philadelphia, Pa.)
Madonna (Combermere, Ont.)
Martayan (New York, N.Y.)
McCaslin (Ironton, Mo.)
Memorable (Stone Mtn., Ga.)
Merkel (Xenia, Ohio)
Merriam (Conway, Mass.)
Michauds (Iowa City, Iowa)
Michlestreet (E. Lebanon, Maine)
Mill (Craftsbury Common, Vt.)
M. & M. (E. Northport, N.Y.)
Monie (Cooperstown, N.Y.)
Monie Shop (Cooperstown, N.Y.)
Moore (Wynnewood, Pa.)
Morrill (Newton Centre, Mass.)
Mott (Sheffield, Mass.)
Much (Southfield, Mich.)
Marray (Melrose, Mass.)
Najarian (Newtown Sq., Pa.)
Natural (Scottsdale, Ariz.)
Nebenzahl (Chicago, Ill.)
Nelson (New Bedford, Mass.)
Nelson's (Albany, N.Y.)
Newburyport (Newburyport,

Mass.)
New Engl. (Bennington, Vt.)
Newman (Battle Creek, Mich.)
Newman (Chicago, Ill.)
N.Y. Bound (New York, N.Y.)
O'Brien (Portland, Maine)
Ohio (Mansfield, Ohio)
Ohio (Cincinnati, Ohio)
Old Book (Morristown, N.J.)
Old Edtns. (Buffalo, N.Y.)
Old N.Y. (Atlanta, Ga.)
Old Print (Washington, D.C.)
Old Southport (Southport, Conn.)
Olinkiewicz (Shelter Isl., N.Y.)
Owl Creek (Mt. Vernon, Ohio)
Owl (Greenwich, N.Y.)
Pageant (New York, N.Y.)
Paper (So. Euclid, Ohio)
Parmer's (Sarasota, Fla.)
Perry's (San Jose, Calif.)
Petrilla (Roosevelt, N.J.)
Phalen (Chicago, Ill.)
Pinkney (Granby, Conn.)
Printed (Savannah, Ga.)
Randall (Santa Barbara, Calif.)
Ravenstree (Yuma, Ariz.)
Ray (Baldwin Park, Calif.)
Reese (New Haven, Conn.)
Rendell (Newton, Mass.)
Respess (Durham, N.C.)
Respess (Chapel Hill, N.C.)
Reston's (Amsterdam, N.Y.)

Richardson (Westmont, N.J.)
Richshafer (Cincinnati, Ohio)
Rieger (Greenwood, S.C.)
River Oaks (Jay, Maine)
Robertson (Levittown, Pa.)
Robinson (Alexandria, Va.)
Robinson (Windsor, Conn.)
Rockland (Cattaraugus, N.Y.)
Ron Dot (Greensburg, Ohio)
Ross (Redwood City, Calif.)
Ross (Medina, N.Y.)
Rosselot (Grand View, N.Y.)
Roth (Norwalk, Ohio)
Rouse (Wattsville, Va.)
Rubin (Brookline, Mass.)
Rulon-Miller (Minneapolis, Minn.)
Ryan (Columbus, Ohio)
Schoyer's (Pittsburgh, Pa.)
Shuhi (Morris, Conn.)
Sidney's (Missoula, Mont.)
Slater (Tarrytown, N.Y.)
Sloan (Austin, Texas)
Small (So. Yarmouth, Mass.)
Stevens (Williamsburg, Va.)
Storeybook (Sycamore, Ill.)
Suhm (Westfield, Mass.)
Sykes (No. Weare, N.H.)
Talbothay's (Aurora, N.Y.)
Taste (Fall River, Mass.)
Tebbetts (Hallowell, Maine)
Thomas (Mechanicsburg, Pa.)
Thomas (San Francisco, Calif.)

Titcomb's (E. Sandwich, Mass.)
Totty (Lunenburg, Mass.)
Trackside (Houston, Texas)
Traveller (Laredo, Texas)
Trotting (Springfield, Mass.)
Tumbleweed (Pueblo, Colo.)
Tweney (Seattle, Wash.)
Twyce (Winona, Minn.)
Tyson (Providence, R.I.)
Unique (Putney, Vt.)
Valentino (Philadelphia, Pa.)
Valley (Galena, Ill.)
Village (Rumney Village, N.H.)
Vinik (Tucson, Ariz.)
Vintage (Iowa City, Iowa)
Wade (Cincinnati, Ohio)
Walett (Abington, Mass.)
Weatherford (Monroe, Wash.)
West's (Elm Grove, Wisc.)
Whitlock (Bethany, Conn.)
Whitlock's (New Haven, Conn.)
Wilson (Bull Shoals, Ark.)
Winsted (Spg. Green, Wisc.)
Wolfe (Pt. Claire, Que.)
Wolf's (Morgantown, W.Va.)
Ximenes (New York, N.Y.)
Yankee (Williamson, N.Y.)
Yankee (Rochester, N.Y.)
Ye Olde (St. Joseph, Mich.)
Yesterday's (San Diego, Calif.)
Yesterday's (Hot Springs, Ark.)
Yesterdays (Whitman, Mass.)

See also individual states # Northwestern Americana

Antiques/Art (Seattle, Wash.)
Barjon's (Billings, Mont.)
Book Barn (Bend, Ore.)
Brused (Pullman, Wash.)
Cheshire (Yakima, Wash.)

Darvill's Book (Eastsound, Wash.)
Elliot Bay (Seattle, Wash.)
Filler (Bremerton, Wash.)
Green Dolphin (Portland, Ore.)
Huckleberry (Centralia, Wash.)

Mattila (Seattle, Wash.)
O'Leary's (Tacoma, Wash.)
Redding (Sequim, Wash.)

Regional Americana

Alkahest (Evanston, Ill.)
Amer. Worlds (Hamden, Conn.)
Ancient (Santa Fe, N.M.)
Appleland (Winchester, Va.)
Avalon (Hayward, Calif.)
Bohling (Decatur, Mich.)
Book Cellar (Temple, Texas)
Book Mart (San Antonio, Texas)
Book Mart (Asheville, N.C.)
Bookmonger (Montgomery, Ala.)
Book Prospector (Littleton, Colo.)
Books By (Albuquerque, N.M.)
Book Shop (Boise, Idaho)
Book Stop (Tucson, Ariz.)
Brassers (Seminole, Fla.)
British (No. Weymouth, Mass.)
Bunkhouse (Gardiner, Maine)
Burke's (Memphis, Tenn.)
Carolina (Charlotte, N.C.)
Cellar (Eugene, Ore.)
Clark's (Spokane, Wash.)
Clement (Franklin, N.H.)
Collectors' (Richmond, Va.)
Colleen's (Houston, Texas)
Coosa Valley (Rome, Ga.)
Croton (Croton, N.Y.)

Dean (Oklahoma City, Okla.)
Doe Run (Cochranville, Pa.)
Dunlap (St. Louis, Mo.)
Evans (Woodstock, Va.)
Forest Park (Ft. Wayne, Ind.)
Fox (Madison, Tenn.)
Frontier (Bryan, Texas)
Glover (Cambridge, N.Y.)
Gustafson (Chicago, Ill.)
Hall (E. Longmeadow, Mass.)
Haslam's (St. Pete., Fla.)
Hayman (Carey, Ohio)
Heritage (Sonora, Calif.)
Herron (Rome, Ga.)
Hole (Reedsport, Ore.)
Homestead (Marlborough, N.H.)
Homesteader (Wenatchee, Wash.)
Hoosier (Indianapolis, Ind.)
Hudson (Dyersburg, Tenn.)
Hunter (Harriman, N.Y.)
Johnny (Manchester, Vt.)
Jordan (Philadelphia, Pa.)
Kaiser (Santa Cruz, Calif.)
Liberty (Sloatsburg, N.Y.)
Lift (Brockport, N.Y.)
Lumb (Somersville, Conn.)

MacManus (Philadelphia, Pa.)
Magnalia (No. Amherst, Mass.)
Market (Idaho Falls, Idaho)
Mason's (Wabash, Ind.)
McCaslin (Ironton, Mo.)
Mt. Falcon (Greeley, Colo.)
Old Oregon (Portland, Ore.)
Olinkiewicz (Shelter Isl., N.Y.)
Poor Farm (W. Cornwall, Conn.)
Porter (Phoenix, Ariz.)
Rittenhouse (Albuquerque, N.M.)
Robinson (Morgantown, W.Va.)
Rosetree (Tombstone, Ariz.)
Running (Pittsfield, Mass.)
Schmidt (Salem, Ore.)
Tappin (Atlantic Bch., Fla.)
3 Arts (Poughkeepsie, N.Y.)
Trans (Parkersburg, W.Va.)
Tuttle (Ruthland, Vt.)
Twyce (Winona, Minn.)
Walett (Abington, Mass.)
Wheeler (Elgin, Ore.)
Wildwood (Old Forge, N.Y.)
Wooden (Ann Arbor, Mich.)
Wright (Waxahachie, Texas)

Southern Americana

See also Southern Authors

Abrams (Atlanta, Ga.)
Altau (Waynesboro, Va.)
Beckham's (New Orleans, La.)
Book Lady (Savannah, Ga.)
Book Place (Columbia, S.C.)
Book Shelf (Cleveland, Tenn.)
Bookshop (Chapel Hill, N.C.)
Cahan (Narberth, Pa.)
Captain's (Ashville, N.C.)
Cather/Brown (Birmingham, Ala.)
C. Dickens (Atlanta, Ga.)
Choctaw (Jackson, Miss.)
Crabtree (Signal Mtn., Tenn.)

Downs (Marietta, Ga.)
DuPriest (Columbia, S.C.)
Gilliam (Charlottesville, Va.)
Hill (Kingsport, Tenn.)
Ivey (Brewton, Ala.)
Kearin (Goldens Bridge, N.Y.)
King (Pensacola, Fla.)
Krause (Warrington, Fla.)
Librairie (Royal) (New Orleans, La.)
Librairie (Chartres) (New Orleans, La.)
Magnum (Charlottesville, Va.)

Natural (Scottsdale, Ariz.)
Pandich (Asheville, N.C.)
Patrick (Beaufort, S.C.)
Printed (Savannah, Ga.)
Rieber (Thomasville, Ga.)
Rogers (Athens, Ga.)
Smith (Pleasant Hill, Calif.)
Sullivan (St. Pete., Fla.)
Turlington (Pittsboro, N.C.)
Woolf's (Atlanta, Ga.)
Yesteryear (Atlanta, Ga.)

Southwestern Americana

Abacus (Santa Fe, N.M.)
Adobe (Albuquerque, N.M.)
Associated (Long Beach, Calif.)
Bargain (San Diego, Calif.)
Booklover's (Tucson, Ariz.)
Bookmans (Tucson, Ariz.)
Bookshop (Del Rio, Texas)
Caldwell (Arkadelphia, Ark.)
Caravan (Stillwater, Okla.)
Davidson (San Diego, Calif.)
Eshner (Bisbee, Ariz.)

Fletcher's (Salado, Texas)
Gay (Santa Fe, N.M.)
Grand (Redwood City, Calif.)
Grt. Southwest (Santa Fe, N.M.)
Grossblatt (Dallas, Texas)
Heartwood (Charlottesville, Va.)
Hudson (Dyersburg, Tenn.)
Info (San Angelo, Texas)
Kearin (Goldens Bridge, N.Y.)
La Galeria (Las Vegas, N.M.)
Lighthouse (St. Pete., Fla.)

Parker (Santa Fe, N.M.)
Potter (Santa Fe, N.M.)
Robles (Tucson, Ariz.)
Shaver (Savannah, Ga.)
Sloan (Austin, Texas)
Terrapin (Austin, Texas)
Todd (Cave Creek, Ariz.)
Trail (Tucson, Ariz.)

Americana, States

See also individual states

Aceto (Sarasota, Fla.)
Appleland (Winchester, Va.)
Bennett (White Plains, N.Y.)
Book Mart Annex (San Antonio, Tex.)
Bookshelf (Miller, S.D.)

Books With (Concord, Mass.)
Burgman (Santa Rosa, Calif.)
Collectors' (Richmond, Va.)
Coosa Valley (Rome, Ga.)
Delp (Belding, Mich.)
Doerres (Wilton, Iowa)

Drusilla's (Baltimore, Md.)
Haslam's (St. Pete., Fla.)
Hayman (Carey, Ohio)
Heinoldt (So. Egg, N.J.)
Hermitage (Denver, Colo.)
Herron (Rome, Ga.)

Hills (San Francisco, Calif.)
Hunter (Harriman, N.Y.)
Mitch's (Menlo Park, Calif.)
Osgood (Rockport, Mass.)

Prairie (Springfield, Ill.)
Robinson (Morgantown, W.Va.)
Scharf (Pittsburgh, Pa.)
Tuttle (Ruthland, Vt.)

Twyce (Winona, Minn.)
Vogt (Meadow Vista, Calif.)
Wise (Lake Delton, Wisc.)

See also
Outlaws & Rangers

Western Americana

Abbey (Los Angeles, Calif.)
Acorn (San Francisco, Calif.)
Albatross (San Francisco, Calif.)
Almagre (Bloomington, Ind.)
Altau (Waynesboro, Va.)
Amitin (St. Louis, Mo.)
Annegan (San Marcos, Calif.)
Antiq. Archive (Sunnyvale, Calif.)
Antiq. Bookworm (Sharon, Mass.)
A Points (Okla. City, Okla.)
Arader (Houston, Texas)
Arch (Bellows Falls, Vt.)
Argonaut (San Francisco, Calif.)
Argus (Sacramento, Calif.)
Arthur (Amarillo, Texas)
Authors (Dundee, Ore.)
Backpocket (Sundance, Wyo.)
Bird's Nest (Missoula, Mont.)
Bishop (Steubenville, Ohio)
Blomberg (Rockford, Ill.)
Blue Dragon (Ashland, Ore.)
Bonaventura (Evergreen, Colo.)
Book Attic (San Bernardino, Calif.)
Book-Bind (Anaheim, Calif.)
Book Den (Santa Barbara, Calif.)
Bookloft (Enterprise, Ore.)
Book Loft (Solvang, Calif.)
Bookshelf (Miller, S.D.)
Bookshop (Del Rio, Texas)
Bookstack (Elkhart, Ind.)
Brauns (Sacramento, Calif.)
Brennan (Salt Lake City, Utah)
Broken Kettle (Akron, Iowa)
Burger (Pine Grove, Calif.)
Cache (Loveland, Colo.)
Caddo (Cartaro, Ariz.)
Carpenter (Balboa Isl., Calif.)
Cassidy (Sacramento, Calif.)

Cavallo (Altadena, Calif.)
Chapter 1 (Hamilton, Mont.)
Clark (Glendale, Calif.)
Coffman (Cambria, Calif.)
Colorado (Norwood, Colo.)
Combs (Great Falls, Mont.)
Consolo (Mansfield, Ohio)
Cook (Los Angeles, Calif.)
Cosmic (Salt Lake City, Utah)
Coventry (Coventry, Conn.)
Cow Country (Prescott, Ariz.)
Crawford (No. St. Paul, Minn.)
Culpin's (Denver, Colo.)
Dakota (Eugene, Ore.)
Dary (Lawrence, Kan.)
Dawn (Ann Arbor, Mich.)
Dawson's (Los Angeles, Calif.)
Day's (Quincy, Calif.)
DC Service (Columbia, Mo.)
Dean (Oklahoma City, Okla.)
Deines (Ft. Collins, Colo.)
Deseret (Salt Lake City, Utah)
Devine (Katonah, N.Y.)
Diablo (Walnut Creek, Calif.)
Distinctive (Cedar City, Utah)
Doerres (Wilton, Iowa)
Dowd (St. Charles, Ill.)
Duck's (Flagstaff, Ariz.)
Dunn (Dallas, Ore.)
Emerson (Albuquerque, N.M.)
Filler (Bremerton, Wash.)
Fischler (San Jose, Calif.)
5 Quail (Spg. Grove, Minn.)
Flora (Seattle, Wash.)
Frid (San Pedro, Calif.)
Frontier (Bryan, Texas)
Gallery Of (Bigfork, Mont.)
Carcia (Turlock, Calif.)

Garret (Clinton, N.Y.)
Geoscience (Yucaipa, Calif.)
Gibbs (State College, Pa.)
Ginsberg (Sharon, Mass.)
Glenn (Kansas City, Mo.)
Golden Hill (Helena, Mont.)
Graham (Bozeman, Mont.)
Grapevine (San Mateo, Calif.)
Grossblatt (Dallas, Texas)
Guidon (Scottsdale, Ariz.)
Hall (San Francisco, Calif.)
Hand (Wheeling, W.Va.)
Harvard (Stockton, Calif.)
Heaston (Austin, Texas)
Henson (Santa Ana, Calif.)
Hermitage (Denver, Colo.)
Hi (Canutillo, Texas)
High Country (Laramie, Wyo.)
Hollander (Santa Monica, Calif.)
Holmes (San Francisco, Calif.)
Holmes (Oakland, Calif.)
Houle (Los Angeles, Calif.)
Howard (Burlingame, Calif.)
Hyde Park (Boise, Idaho)
Jack London (Glen Ellen, Calif.)
Jenkins (Austin, Texas)
Judi's (Twin Falls, Idaho)
Keller (Overland Park, Kan.)
King's (Boulder, Colo.)
Kuehn (Bisbee, Ariz.)
Lambeth (San Antonio, Texas)
Log Cabin (Bigfork, Mont.)
Lonesome (Eugene, Ore.)
Lost (Santa Barbara, Calif.)
Luther (Taos, N.M.)
Magnum (Charlottesville, Va.)
Margolis (Santa Fe, N.M.)
McDuffie's (Portland, Ore.)

Memory (Grand Rapids, Mich.)
Michael's (Okla. City, Okla.)
Monroe (Fresno, Calif.)
Mostly (Carthage, Mo.)
Murphy (Marietta, Ga.)
Nie (Chicago, Ill.)
Nolan (Coeur d'Alene, Idaho)
Ohio (Mansfield, Ohio)
Old Eugene (Eugene, Ore.)
Old Town (Tempe, Ariz.)
Palmer (Eugene, Ore.)
Parker (Santa Fe, N.M.)
Parmer (San Diego, Calif.)
Perata (Oakland, Calif.)
Persoff (Alameda, Calif.)
Petrilla (Roosevelt, N.J.)
Pettinger (Russell, Iowa)
Pinkney (Granby, Conn.)
Prufrock (Pasadena, Calif.)
Quechee (Quechee, Vt.)

Ramshorn (Albuquerque, N.M.)
Rancho (Santa Monica, Calif.)
Reese (New Haven, Conn.)
Research (Fremont, Neb.)
Reynolds (Willits, Calif.)
Robinson (Yucca Valley, Calif.)
Robinson (New York, N.Y.)
Robles (Tucson, Ariz.)
Rosenstock (Denver, Colo.)
Ross (Redwood City, Calif.)
Ross (Albany, Calif.)
Sackett (Grants Pass, Ore.)
Sagebrush (Morongo Valley, Calif.)
Scottsdale (Scottsdale, Ariz.)
Shorey (Seattle, Wash.)
Sleepy (Moraga, Calif.)
Snug Harbor (Wells, Maine)
Southwest (Durango, Colo.)
Stickel (Colma, Calif.)

Stone Lion (Ft. Collins, Colo.)
Summerhouse (Dayton, Wyo.)
Swinford (Paris, Ill.)
Talisman (Georgetown, Calif.)
Taos (Taos, N.M.)
Todd (Cave Creek, Ariz.)
Trail (Tucson, Ariz.)
Tramp (Jackson, Mich.)
Treehorn (Santa Rosa, Calif.)
Ute-Or (W. Jordan, Utah)
Watermark W. (Wichita, Kan.)
Watson (Buelah, Colo.)
Webfoot (Portland, Ore.)
West (Provo, Utah)
Willow (Englewood, Colo.)
Wordsmith (Syracuse, Neb.)
Wreden (Palo Alto, Calif.)
Yesteryear (Nampa, Idaho)
Zwisohn (Albuquerque, N.M.)

American Colonies & The Revolution

Annegan (San Marcos, Calif.)
Antiques (No. Abington, Mass.)
Book-In (Stillwater, N.Y.)
Bromsen (Boston, Mass.)

Craig (Newport, R. I.)
Garret (Clinton, N.Y.)
Golder (Collinsville, Conn.)
Indian Head (Owego, N.Y.)

Merlin's (Isla Vista, Calif.)
Poor Richard's (Grand Rapids, Mich.)
Seaport (Stonington, Conn.)

American Indian Literature

History (Long Valley, N.J.)

Lopez (Hadley, Mass.)

American Middle West

Bohling (Decatur, Mich.)
Call Me (Saugatuck, Mich.)

Mostly (Carthage, Mo.)
Wade (Cincinnati, Ohio)

America's Cup

Armchair (Newport, R.I.)
Burnett (Atlanta, Ga.)

Howland (Jamaica Plain, Mass.)
Pier (Piermont, N.Y.)

Animals

Audubon (Vienna, Va.)

Cronin (Worcester, Mass.)

Anthropology

Bay Side (Soquel, Calif.)
Belknap (Boston, Mass.)
Collins (San Francisco, Calif.)
Country (Plainfield, Vt.)

Engard (Tucson, Ariz.)
Fagin (Chicago, Ill.)
Fessler (Theresa, N.Y.)
Maynard's (Pasadena, Calif.)

Norman (Philadelphia, Pa.)
Powell's (Chicago, Ill.)

Antiques

Acanthus (New York, N.Y.)
Avalon (Hayward, Calif.)
Bargain (Long Beach, Calif.)
Burpee Hill (New London, N.H.)

Cape Collector (So. Harwich, Mass.)
Cohen (Bronx, N.Y.)
Collectrix (W. Hempstead, N.Y.)

Cooper Fox (Millbrook, N.Y.)
Falls (Farmington Falls, Maine)
Foley (Bardstown, Ky.)
Glaeve (Madison, Wisc.)

Golden Age (Dix Hills, N.Y.)
Hacker (New York, N.Y.)
Ha'Penny (Snowville, N.H.)
Houle (Los Angeles, Calif.)
Keramos (Ann Arbor, Mich.)
Krause (Warrington, Fla.)
Liberty (Sloatsburg, N.Y.)
Mad (Maumee, Ohio)
Merriam (Conway, Mass.)
Montlack (Old Bethpage, N.Y.)

Northeast (Ocean City, N.J.)
Nosegay (Cold Spg. Harbor, N.Y.)
Owl (Camden, Maine)
Princeton (Atlantic City, N.J.)
Qualman (San Diego, Calif.)
Rainy (Fitzwilliam, N.H.)
Rendell (Waban, Mass.)
Riverow (Owego, N.Y.)
San Fernando (San Fernando,
   Calif.)

Servant's (Atlantic City, N.J.)
Starosciak (San Francisco, Calif.)
Testa (No. Newark, N.J.)
Those Were (Tempe, Ariz.)
Tillinghast (Hancock, N.H.)
Trace (Peekskill, N.Y.)
William (Mineola, N.Y.)
Wilson (Bull Shoals, Ark.)

Antique Stocks & Bonds

Abbot (Bronx, N.Y.)
Guarino (De Bary, Fla.)

Janus (Corea, Maine)
Rails (Rosemead, Calif.)

Richards (Templeton, Mass.)

Appraisals & Appraisal Services

Abe. Lincoln (Chicago, Ill.)
Acoma (Ramona, Calif.)
Adelson (No. Pomfret, Vt.)
Alford (Springfield, Va.)
Alphabet (Toronto, Ont.)
Amherst (Amherst, Mass.)
Ampersand (New York, N.Y.)
Appelfeld (New York, N.Y.)
Arcane (Okla. City, Okla.)
Astronomy (Bernardston, Mass.)
Auerbach (New York, N.Y.)
Babcock (Derry, N.H.)
Bookery (Ithaca, N.Y.)
Book Trader (Naples, Fla.)
Boyce (Carmel, N.Y.)
Brennan (Salt Lake City, Utah)
Brookline (Brookline, Mass.)
Buckabest (Palo Alto, Calif.)
Burley/Books (Toledo, Ohio)
Collectors' (Richmond, Va.)

Cooper Fox (Millbrook, N.Y.)
Family Album (Glen Rock, Pa.)
Fletcher's (Salado, Texas)
Frisk (Philadelphia, Pa.)
Gach (Columbia, Md.)
Garnett (St. Louis, Mo.)
Gibbs (State College, Pa.)
Grossblatt (Dallas, Texas)
Halloran (St. Louis, Mo.)
Hoosier (Indianapolis, Ind.)
Isaiah (Worcester, Mass.)
Jaeger (Commack, N.Y.)
Jaffe (Haverford, Pa.)
Just (Milwaukee, Wisc.)
Lake (San Francisco, Calif.)
Laster (Winston-Salem, N.C.)
Laub (Berkeley, Calif.)
Leaves (Ann Arbor, Mich.)
Lebo (Washington, D.C.)
Leishman (Menlo Park, Calif.)

Lowe (New York, N.Y.)
Mahoney (Buffalo, N.Y.)
McGilvery (La Jolla, Calif.)
Mobley (Schoharie, N.Y.)
Moore (Wynnewood, Pa.)
Murray (Wilbraham, Mass.)
Newman (Chicago, Ill.)
Old Print (Washington, D.C.)
Otento (San Diego, Calif.)
Parker (Middlebury, Vt.)
Performing (New York, N.Y.)
Petrilla (Roosevelt, N.J.)
Pirages (McMinnville, Ore.)
Rendell (Newton, Mass.)
Robinson (Manchester, Maine)
Robinson (New York, N.Y.)
Sand (Berkeley, Calif.)
Scriptorium (Beverly Hills, Calif.)
Serendipity (Berkeley, Calif.)
Stonehill (New Haven, Conn.)

Strand Rare (New York, N.Y.)
Tuckers (Pittsburgh, Pa.)
Tweney (Seattle, Wash.)
Venkatesa (Tofino, B.C.)

Weatherford (Monroe, Wash.)
Weitz (New York, N.Y.)
With (Lake Placid, N.Y.)
Witten (Southport, Conn.)

Woolmer (Revere, Pa.)
Yesteryear (Atlanta, Ga.)
Ziagos (Lowell, Mass.)

Arab World

Abelard (Toronto, Ont.)
Acoma (Ramona, Calif.)

Ancient (Santa Fe, N.M.)
Camel (New York, N.Y.)

Feltus (Berkeley, Calif.)
Worldwide (Cambridge, Mass.)

Archaeology

Archaeologia (Oakland, Calif.)
Berkley (Berkley, Minn.)
Berkowitz (Chester, N.Y.)
Bernett (Larchmont, N.Y.)
Blue Rider (Cambridge, Mass.)
Brown (Toledo, Ohio)
CGT (College Stn., Texas)
Cronin (Worcester, Mass.)
Dragoman (Annapolis, Md.)
El Cascajero (New York, N.Y.)

Fagin (Chicago, Ill.)
Federation (College St., Texas)
Fein (New York, N.Y.)
Ferndale (Ferndale, Calif.)
Fessler (Theresa, N.Y.)
Hacker (New York, N.Y.)
Hand (Wheeling, W.Va.)
Hyman (Los Angeles, Calif.)
Johnson (New York, N.Y.)
Karno (Santa Monica, Calif.)

Libros (Redlands, Calif.)
Maxwell's (Lima, N.Y.)
Maynard's (Pasadena, Calif.)
Sacred (Goffstown, N.H.)
2nd Front (San Francisco, Calif.)
Smith (Mt. Airy, Md.)
Stubbs (New York, N.Y.)
Under (Shaker Hgts., Ohio)
Weiser (New York, N.Y.)
Whistles (Rossville, Ga.)

Archery

Berman (Los Angeles, Calif.)
Drabeck (Tuckahoe, N.Y.)

Marcher (Okla. City, Okla.)
Toxophilite (Simsbury, Conn.)

Architecture

Acanthus (New York, N.Y.)
Anchor (Newport, R.I.)
Antiq. Bookworm (Sharon, Mass.)
Arcana (Santa Monica, Calif.)
Ars Libri (Boston, Mass.)
Art Cats. (Los Angeles, Calif.)
Artcraft (Baldwin, Md.)
Bamberger (San Francisco, Calif.)
Bargain (San Diego, Calif.)
Beattie (Parkesburg, Pa.)
Benjamins (Philadelphia, Pa.)
Bernett (Larchmont, N.Y.)
Bibliofile (San Francisco, Calif.)
Birmingham (Birmingham, Mich.)
Blomgren (San Rafael, Calif.)
Blue Rider (Cambridge, Mass.)
Bolotin (Youngstown, Ohio)
Book Cellar (Fullerton, Calif.)
Book Mark (Philadelphia, Pa.)
Bookpress (Williamsburg, Va.)
Books/Books (Coral Gables, Fla.)
Bookstop (Alexandria, Va.)
Braiterman (Baltimore, Md.)
Brown (Toledo, Ohio)
Buck (San Francisco, Calif.)
City Spirit (Denver, Colo.)
Connecticut (E. Haddam, Conn.)
Donnally (Seattle, Wash.)
Dooling (Middlebury, Conn.)
Dragan (Ithaca, N.Y.)

El Cascajero (New York, N.Y.)
Elwert (Rutland, Vt.)
Ex Libris (New York, N.Y.)
Glaister (New York, N.Y.)
Gobrecht (Kinderhook, N.Y.)
Gustafson (Chicago, Ill.)
Hacker (New York, N.Y.)
Hennessey (Santa Monica, Calif.)
Howe (New York, N.Y.)
Jense (Los Angeles, Calif.)
Joslin (Concord, Mass.)
Kaplan (New York, N.Y.)
Landmark (New York, N.Y.)
Liberty (Sloatsburg, N.Y.)
Loewenthal (Dover, N.J.)
Mahard (Sherborn, Mass.)
Mandrake (Cambridge, Mass.)
Martayan (New York, N.Y.)
Masi (Montague, Mass.)
Mendelsohn (Cambridge, Mass.)
Metropolis (Royal Oak, Mich.)
Michlestreet (E. Lebanon, Maine)
Miller (Seattle, Wash.)
Minters (New York, N.Y.)
Moye (Putney, Vt.)
Muns (Berkeley, Calif.)
Museum (Fairfield, Conn.)
Newburyport (Newburyport, Mass.)
Pacific (No. Vancouver, B.C.)

Prairie (Chicago, Ill.)
Prufrock (Pasadena, Calif.)
Richardson (Westmont, N.J.)
Riverow (Owego, N.Y.)
Rizzoli (New York, N.Y.)
Robinson (Windsor, Conn.)
Schram (Montclair, N.J.)
Springbook (Springfield, Ohio)
Starosciak (San Francisco, Calif.)
Steele (Lumberville, Pa.)
Stubbs (New York, N.Y.)
Trace (Peekskill, N.Y.)
Transition (San Francisco, Calif.)
Under (Shaker Hgts., Ohio)
Untitled II #2 (New York, N.Y.)
Untitled II #1 (New York, N.Y.)
Urban (New York, N.Y.)
Weintraub #2 (New York, N.Y.)
Weintraub #1 (New York, N.Y.)
Weyhe (New York, N.Y.)
Winsted (Spg. Green, Wisc.)
Wittenborn (New York, N.Y.)
Wofsy (San Francisco, Calif.)
Wood (Boston, Mass.)
Words (San Deigo, Calif.)
Words (Cambridge, Mass.)
Young (Dobbs Ferry, N.Y.)

Landscape Architecture

Amer. Botanist (Brookfield, Ill.)
Anchor (Newport, R.I.)
Blue Rider (Cambridge, Mass.)
Book Mark (Philadelphia, Pa.)

Glaister (New York, N.Y.)
Hennessey (Santa Monica, Calif.)
Landscape (Exeter, N.H.)
Mendelsohn (Cambridge, Mass.)

Pomona (Rockton, Ont.)
Stubbs (New York, N.Y.)
Wood (Boston, Mass.)
Woodburn (Hopewell, N.J.)

Arctica & Antarctica

Academic (No. Vancouver, B.C.)
Anson-Cartwright (Toronto, Ont.)
Bagley (Fredericton, N.B.)
Bayview (Northport, N.Y.)
Belknap (Boston, Mass.)
Blue Dragon (Ashland, Ore.)
Bookery (Farmington, N.H.)
Books/Buttons (Columbus, Ohio)
Bowes (Vancouver, B.C.)
Bryant's (Provincetown, Mass.)
Burnett (Atlanta, Ga.)
Caravan-Maritime (Jamaica, N.Y.)
Cross (Brunswick, Maine)
Frontier (Los Angeles, Calif.)
Garret (Clinton, N.Y.)

Gatto (New York, N.Y.)
Golder (Collinsville, Conn.)
Hand (Wheeling, W.Va.)
Harder (Los Alamos, N.M.)
Harding (Wells, Maine)
High Lat. (Bainbridge, Wash.)
Hill Haven (Barton, Vt.)
Kahn (Montreal, Que.)
Lunsford (No. Vancouver, B.C.)
Magnalia (No. Amherst, Mass.)
Martin's (Fairbanks, Alk.)
Mattila (Seattle, Wash.)
McGahern (Ottawa, Ont.)
McLaughlin's (Cottage Grove, Ore.)

Nautica (Halifax, N.S.)
Observatory (Sitka, Alk.)
Old Harbor (Sitka, Alk.)
Old Mill (Alexandria, Va.)
Parmer (San Diego, Calif.)
Patrick (Toronto, Ont.)
Rybski (Chicago, Ill.)
Shorey (Seattle, Wash.)
Stephenson (Jaffrey, N.H.)
Thunderbird (Aldergrove, B.C.)
12th St. (Santa Monica, Calif.)
West Side (Ann Arbor, Mich.)
Wikehgan (Mt. Desert, Maine)
Williams (Calgary, Alt.)

Arizona

Bookmans (Tucson, Ariz.)
Cow Country (Prescott, Ariz.)
Gay (Santa Fe, N.M.)

Geoscience (Yucaipa, Calif.)
Kuehn (Bisbee, Ariz.)
Robles (Tucson, Ariz.)

Trail (Tucson, Ariz.)

Arkansas

Dickson St. (Fayetteville, Ark.)

Yesterday's (Hot Springs, Ark.)

Yesterday's (Hot Springs, Ark.)

Art

Aardvark (San Francisco, Calif.)
Academy (New York, N.Y.)
Academy (Honolulu, Haw.)
Acorn (San Francisco, Calif.)
Adams (Chicago, Ill.)
Alkahest (Evanston, Ill.)
All Edges (Silver Spg., Md.)
Allen (Baltimore, Md.)
Allen's (Baltimore, Md.)
Anglers (Goshen, Conn.)
Appel (Mt. Vernon, N.Y.)
Arcana (Santa Monica, Calif.)
Armitage (Miamisburg, Ohio)
Arnolds (Contoocook, N.H.)
Ars Libri (Boston, Mass.)
Art (Purchase, N.Y.)
Art Cats. (Los Angeles, Calif.)
Artcraft (Baldwin, Md.)
Artistic (Boston, Mass.)
Bailey (New York, N.Y.)
Bamberger (San Francisco, Calif.)
Bargain (San Diego, Calif.)
Bartfield Gall. (New York, N.Y.)
Bear (W. Brattleboro, Vt.)
Beattie (Parkesburg, Pa.)
Benjamins (Philadelphia, Pa.)
Berkowitz (Chester, N.Y.)
Berliawsky (Camden, Maine)
Bernett (Larchmont, N.Y.)
Between (Old Bridge, N.J.)
Bibliofile (San Francisco, Calif.)
Bibliomania (Schenectady, N.Y.)
Biermaier's (Minneapolis, Minn.)
Black Oak (Berkeley, Calif.)
Black Swan (Sacramento, Calif.)
Blue Moon (Clearwater, Fla.)
Blue Rider (Cambridge, Mass.)
Bonmark (Plainview, N.Y.)
Book Barn (So. Sioux City, Neb.)
Book Bazaar (Ottawa, Ont.)
Book Bin (Kingston, Ont.)
Book Cellar (Fullerton, Calif.)
Book Cellar (Bethesda, Md.)

Bookfinders (Atlanta, Ga.)
Book House (Arlington, Va.)
Bookmarx (Roslyn, N.Y.)
Book Ranger (New York, N.Y.)
Book Room (Coral Gables, Fla.)
Books By (Derby, Conn.)
Books/Coll. (Encino, Calif.)
Books & Co. (New York, N.Y.)
Books/Things (Boca Raton, Fla.)
Bookstock (So. Orleans, Mass.)
Book Stop (Dearborn Hgts., Mich.)
Book Store (San Mateo, Calif.)
Book Studio (Atlanta, Ga.)
Book/Tackle (Chestnut Hill, Mass.)
Braiterman (Baltimore, Md.)
Brannan (Garberville, Calif.)
British (No. Weymouth, Mass.)
Broude (New York, N.Y.)
Brownbag (Rochester, N.Y.)
Burpee Hill (New London, N.H.)
Caddo (Cartaro, Ariz.)
Cahan (Narberth, Pa.)
Califia (San Francisco, Calif.)
Camelot (Baltimore, Md.)
Captain's (Ashville, N.C.)
Carr (New York, N.Y.)
Chimney (Bridgeport, Conn.)
ChoreoGraphica (Boston, Mass.)
Cielec (Chicago, Ill.)
City Spirit (Denver, Colo.)
Clipper Ship (San Antonio, Texas)
Cole's (La Jolla, Calif.)
Compulsive (New York, N.Y.)
Connecticut (E. Haddam, Conn.)
Cotton Hill (Laconia, N.H.)
Cyrano's (Highlands, N.C.)
Dailey (Los Angeles, Calif.)
Davis (Sherman Oaks, Calif.)
deBeurs (Dexter, Maine)
Diamond (Burbank, Calif.)
Diamond (Rochester, N.Y.)
Donnally (Seattle, Wash.)
Dooling (Middlebury, Conn.)

El Cascajero (New York, N.Y.)
Emerson (Falls Village, Conn.)
Emerson (Albuquerque, N.M.)
Engard (Tucson, Ariz.)
Ethnographic (Mill Valley, Calif.)
Feiden (Mamaroneck, N.Y.)
Feldman (Cleveland, Ohio)
50,000 (El Cajon, Calif.)
Finer (Greenfield, Mass.)
1st Edtn. (Tulsa, Okla.)
Foley (Bardstown, Ky.)
Folger (Washington, D.C.)
Fortuna (Kirkland, Wash.)
Frisch (Livingston, N.Y.)
Glasser (Assonet, Mass.)
E. Gordon (New York, N.Y.)
M. Gordon (New York, N.Y.)
Green Mtn. (Lyndonville, Vt.)
Grub Street (Detroit, Mich.)
Gryphon #1 (New York, N.Y.)
Gull Gall. (Oakland, Calif.)
Gustafson (Chicago, Ill.)
Gutenberg's (Rochester, N.Y.)
Hacker (New York, N.Y.)
Hale (Washington, D.C.)
Harris (Rockville, Md.)
Haunted (Orleans, Mass.)
Hennessey (Santa Monica, Calif.)
Herlin (New York, N.Y.)
Hilton Village (Newport News, Va.)
Hoefliger (Buffalo, N.Y.)
Hollywood City (Hollywood, Calif.)
Houle (Los Angeles, Calif.)
In #1 (San Francisco, Calif.)
In #2 (San Francisco, Calif.)
Isaiah (Worcester, Mass.)
Jense (Los Angeles, Calif.)
Jordan (Philadelphia, Pa.)
Junction (Peoria, Ill.)
Kam (Philadelphia, Pa.)
Kaplan (New York, N.Y.)

Karmiole (Santa Monica, Calif.)
Karno (Santa Monica, Calif.)
Kaufman (Tempe, Ariz.)
Kellinger (Chambersburg, Pa.)
Keramos (Ann Arbor, Mich.)
Klein (Oak Park, Ill.)
Konigsmark (Wayne, Pa.)
Kraft (Palm Desert, Calif.)
Kraus (Millwood, N.Y.)
Laird (Chicago, Ill.)
Landmark (New York, N.Y.)
Legacy (Iowa City, Iowa)
Lemon (Lemon Grove, Calif.)
Levart (Hartsdale, N.Y.)
Libros (Redlands, Calif.)
Lion (Indianapolis, Ind.)
Loewenthal (Dover, N.J.)
Macauluso (Kennett Sq., Pa.)
Maelstrom (San Francisco, Calif.)
Magazine (New York, N.Y.)
Magic (Johnson City, Tenn.)
Magnum (Charlottesville, Va.)
Mandala (Daytona Bch., Fla.)
Mandrake (Cambridge, Mass.)
Maynard's (Pasadena, Calif.)
McGilvery (La Jolla, Calif.)
Metropolis (Royal Oak, Mich.)
Michaels (Eugene, Ore.)
Midnight (Marietta, Ga.)
Minters (New York, N.Y.)
Moye (Putney, Vt.)
Muns (Berkeley, Calif.)
Nelson (Goshen, N.H.)
999 (New York, N.Y.)

Northeast (Ocean City, N.J.)
Nosegay (Cold Spg. Harbor, N.Y.)
Ottenberg (Seattle, Wash.)
Owl (Camden, Maine)
Pacific (No. Vancouver, B.C.)
Pan (Catskill, N.Y.)
Paper (Portland, Ore.)
Parsons (Sonoma, Calif.)
Paulhus (Wells, Maine)
Phoenix (San Luis Obispo, Calif.)
Pollack (Boston, Mass.)
Pollock (Palo Alto, Calif.)
Pomander (New York, N.Y.)
Prufrock (Pasadena, Calif.)
Quill (Pinellas Park, Fla.)
Rare Oriental (Aptos, Calif.)
Reader's (Raleigh, N.C.)
Reisman (Philadelphia, Pa.)
Reliable (Paterson, N.J.)
Rizzoli (New York, N.Y.)
Rosenstock (Denver, Colo.)
Rudikoff (New York, N.Y.)
Russica (New York, N.Y.)
Sackheim (Tucson, Ariz.)
St. Clair (Van Nuys, Calif.)
Schoyer's (Pittsburgh, Pa.)
Schram (Montclair, N.J.)
Schroeder's (Dickinson, Texas)
Scopazzi (San Francisco, Calif.)
Sea (Glen Oaks, N.Y.)
Servant's (Atlantic City, N.J.)
Shapiro (New York, N.Y.)
Skeans (Deer Isle, Maine)
Soundpeace (Ashland, Ore.)

Springbook (Springfield, Ohio)
Stanley (Wilder, Vt.)
Starosciak (San Francisco, Calif.)
Steele (Lumberville, Pa.)
Strand (New York, N.Y.)
Strand Rare (New York, N.Y.)
Sunset (San Francisco, Calif.)
Tamerlis (Mamaroneck, N.Y.)
Touchet (New York, N.Y.)
Tumbleweed (Pueblo, Colo.)
Tupper (Vancouver, B.C.)
Turkey (Westport, Conn.)
Unique (Putney, Vt.)
Untitled II #2 (New York, N.Y.)
Untitled II #1 (New York, N.Y.)
Ursus (New York, N.Y.)
Valentino (Philadelphia, Pa.)
Valley (No. Hollywood, Calif.)
Vanderstoel (El Cerrito, Calif.)
Viewpoint (New York, N.Y.)
Warren (Philadelphia, Pa.)
West L.A. (Los Angeles, Calif.)
Weyhe (New York, N.Y.)
White's (Asbury Park, N.J.)
Wildwood (Old Forge, N.Y.)
Williams (Williamstown, Mass.)
Wittenborn (New York, N.Y.)
Wofsy (San Francisco, Calif.)
Words (San Deigo, Calif.)
World Of (Willoughby, Ohio)
Xanadu (Bronx, N.Y.)
Young (Dobbs Ferry, N.Y.)
Zeitlin (Los Angeles, Calif.)
Zita (New York, N.Y.)

African Art

Ethnographic (Mill Valley, Calif.)   Johnson (New York, N.Y.)   Oceanic (New York, N.Y.)

American Illustrative Art

Art About (Moline, Ill.)
Cutler (New York, N.Y.)
Delle Donne (Ronkonkoma, N.Y.)

Kapica (New Britain, Conn.)
Minckler (Billings, Mont.)
Scheck (Scarsdale, N.Y.)

Stern (Chicago, Ill.)

Avant Garde, Experimental, & Modern Art

A B I (Santa Barbara, Calif.)
Carousel (Tyler, Texas)
Ex Libris (New York, N.Y.)

Gull Gall. (Oakland, Calif.)
Herlin (New York, N.Y.)
McGilvery (La Jolla, Calif.)

Transition (San Francisco, Calif.)

Books About Art

Books & Co. (San Francisco, Calif.)
June 1 (Bethlehem, Conn.)
Lilac Hedge (Norwich, Vt.)

Metropolis (Royal Oak, Mich.)
Museum (Fairfield, Conn.)
Museum (New York, N.Y.)
Olana (Brewster, N.Y.)

Once Upon (W. Hempstead, N.Y.)
Schmidt (Collingswood, N.J.)
Scottsdale (Scottsdale, Ariz.)
Ursus (New York, N.Y.)

Art Catalogues, Periodicals, & Books

Arcana (Santa Monica, Calif.)
Art Cats. (Los Angeles, Calif.)
Hammer (Santa Barbara, Calif.)
Herlin (New York, N.Y.)

McGilvery (La Jolla, Calif.)
Olana (Brewster, N.Y.)
Roberge (Princeton, N.J.)
Schmidt (Collingswood, N.J.)

Tamerlane (Havertown, Pa.)
Valley (Amherst, Mass.)
Warren (Philadelphia, Pa.)
Worldwide (Boston, Mass.)

Art Deco & Art Nouveau

Baer (New York, N.Y.)
Boss (Brookline, Mass.)

Kam (Philadelphia, Pa.)
Reisman (Philadelphia, Pa.)

Yankee (Plymouth, Mass.)

Folk Art

Bethlehem (Bethlehem, Conn.)
Branford (Branford, Conn.)

Folk (Long Beach, Calif.)
Legacy (Hatboro, Pa.)

Art History & Reference

Becker (New York, N.Y.)
Birmingham (Birmingham, Mich.)
Blomgren (San Rafael, Calif.)
Burgman (Santa Rosa, Calif.)

Carlton (Camino, Calif.)
Gabriel (Northampton, Mass.)
Hatch (Lenox, Mass.)
Nemeroff (Williamstown, Mass.)

Roberge (Princeton, N.J.)
Salerno (Hauppauge, N.Y.)
Schmidt (Collingswood, N.J.)
Washton (New York, N.Y.)

Arthurian Legend

E. C. Gordon (New York, N.Y.)

3 Geese (Woodstock, N.Y.)

Wyatt (San Diego, Calif.)

Original Art For Illustration

Bill (Long I. City, N.Y.)
Books/Coll. (Encino, Calif.)
Busyhaus (Mattapoisett, Mass.)

Dennis (Seattle, Wash.)
Docheff (Berkeley, Calif.)
Fantasy (New York, N.Y.)

Green (Elkins Park, Pa.)
Hirsch (Hopewell Jctn., N.Y.)
Kaufman (New York, N.Y.)

Klemm (Apple Valley, Calif.)
Martignette (Boston, Mass.)
Pierce (Park Forest, Ill.)
Reisler (Vienna, Va.)

Scarlet (New Milford, Conn.)
Schiller (New York, N.Y.)
Schiller-Wapner (New York, N.Y.)
Starratt (Palo Alto, Calif.)

Sullivan (St. Pete., Fla.)
Transition (San Francisco, Calif.)
Victoria (New York, N.Y.)
Zita (New York, N.Y.)

Decorative Arts

A B I (Santa Barbara, Calif.)
Acanthus (New York, N.Y.)
Anchor (Newport, R.I.)
Ars Libri (Boston, Mass.)
Bamberger (San Francisco, Calif.)
Bebbah (Andover, Kan.)
Becker (New York, N.Y.)
Book Exch. (Corning, N.Y.)
Coffman (Cambria, Calif.)
Cohen (Bronx, N.Y.)

Collectors' (New York, N.Y.)
Gem (New York, N.Y.)
Gobrecht (Kinderhook, N.Y.)
Joslin (Concord, Mass.)
Landmark (New York, N.Y.)
Mahard (Sherborn, Mass.)
Mawson (New Preston, Conn.)
Mendelsohn (Cambridge, Mass.)
Montlack (Old Bethpage, N.Y.)
Museum (Fairfield, Conn.)

999 (New York, N.Y.)
Scott (Stonington, Conn.)
Skeans (Deer Isle, Maine)
10 Pound (Gloucester, Mass.)
Trace (Peekskill, N.Y.)
Wikehgan (Mt. Desert, Maine)
Wilson (New York, N.Y.)
Wood (Boston, Mass.)

Western Art

Almagre (Bloomington, Ind.)
Bartfield Gall. (New York, N.Y.)
Books/Coll. (Encino, Calif.)
Bookshop (Del Rio, Texas)

Combs (Great Falls, Mont.)
Drabeck (Tuckahoe, N.Y.)
Gay (Santa Fe, N.M.)
Guidon (Scottsdale, Ariz.)

Porter (Phoenix, Ariz.)
Scottsdale (Scottsdale, Ariz.)
White (Albuquerque, N.M.)

World War II Battlefield Art

Autobooks (Babylon, N.Y.)

Bankside (Westport, Conn.)

Asia

Academy (Honolulu, Haw.)	Gamradt (Minneapolis, Minn.)	Paragon (New York, N.Y.)
Asian Rare (New York, N.Y.)	Hermeticus (Ashland, Ore.)	Rinen (New York, N.Y.)
Berkelouw (Los Angeles, Calif.)	Holmes (Edmonds, Wash.)	Scharf (Pittsburgh, Pa.)
Best (Cambridge, Mass.)	Keramos (Ann Arbor, Mich.)	Terramedia (Wellesley, Mass.)
Chang Tang (Peekskill, N.Y.)	Lewis (Seattle, Wash.)	Trophy (Agoura, Calif.)
Cheng (Boston, Mass.)	Lloyd (Washington, D.C.)	Vanderstoel (El Cerrito, Calif.)
Chessler (New York, N.Y.)	Manor (New York, N.Y.)	Viederman (Leonia, N.J.)
Dee Cee (Nyack, N.Y.)	McBlain (Hamden, Conn.)	Watson (Exeter, N.H.)

Asians In America

Asian Amer. (New York, N.Y.)	Ishii (Seattle, Wash.)	Lewis (Seattle, Wash.)
Doi (San Jose, Calif.)	Kishi (New York, N.Y.)	Oriental (Pasadena, Calif.)

Southeast Asia

Cellar (Detroit, Mich.)	Oceanie (Hlllsdale, N.Y.)	Oriental (Pasadena, Calif.)
Oceanic (New York, N.Y.)	Old Mill (Alexandria, Va.)	

Association Copies

Babcock (Derry, N.H.)	Granat (Woodmere, N.Y.)	MacManus (Philadelphia, Pa.)
Canney (Alfred, Maine)	Harris (Los Angeles, Calif.)	Robinson (New York, N.Y.)
Cassidy (Sacramento, Calif.)	Holmes (Philadelphia, Pa.)	Vandoros (Middleton, Wisc.)
Elliott (New York, N.Y.)	Koschal (Verona, N.J.)	
Grabowski (Ronks, Pa.)	Mac Donnell (Austin, Texas)	

Astrology

Gateway (Ferndale, Pa.)
James (Lynden, Wash.)
Middle (Sterling Hgts., Mich.)

Ollie's (Memphis, Tenn.)
Together (Denver, Colo.)
Weiser (New York, N.Y.)

Whelan (Newberry, Fla.)
Womrath's (Hempstead, N.Y.)

Astronautics & Rocketry

Dictionary (Leeds Point, N.J.)

JFF (Manhasset, N.Y.)

Astronomy

Alcala (San Diego, Calif.)
Astronomy (Bernardston, Mass.)
Blake (Fairfield, Conn.)

Grabowski (Ronks, Pa.)
Hist. Tech (Marblehead, Mass.)
Luft (Oakland Gdns., N.Y.)

Manasek (Hanover, N.H.)
Manasek (Norwich, Vt.)
Univelt (San Diego, Calif.)

Australia & New Zealand

Antipodean (Cold Spg., N.Y.)
Cellar (Detroit, Mich.)
Chapman (Los Angeles, Calif.)

Info (San Angelo, Texas)
Oceanic (New York, N.Y.)
Tin Can (Arcata, Calif.)

Vanderstoel (El Cerrito, Calif.)

Author Collections

Apfelbaum (Valley Stream, N.Y.)
Babcock (Derry, N.H.)

Butterworth (Claremont, Calif.)
Dermont (Onset, Mass.)

Hansen (Carlsbad, Calif.)
Johnson (Syracuse, N.Y.)

Library (Dallas, Texas)
Macksey (Baltimore, Md.)
Nouveau (Jackson, Miss.)

Prosser (Chicago, Ill.)
Serendipity (Berkeley, Calif.)
Smith (Pleasant Hill, Calif.)

Thelema (King Bch., Calif.)
Venkatesa (Tofino, B.C.)
Woolmer (Revere, Pa.)

Authors

Antic Hay (W. Caldwell, N.J.)
Bean (Biddeford, Maine)
Book Mart (Asheville, N.C.)
Brown (No. Augusta, S.C.)
Cotswold (Medina, Ohio)
Dabbs (Higginsville, Mo.)
Deeds (Ellicott City, Md.)
DeFreitas (Montreal, Que.)
Fox (Madison, Tenn.)
Fraser's (Sherman Oaks, Calif.)

Gardner (New York, N.Y.)
Good News (Rossville, Ind.)
Guerrera (Lawrence, Mass.)
Hobby Helpers (Lima, N.Y.)
Info (San Angelo, Texas)
Kishi (New York, N.Y.)
Loose (Jerome, Mich.)
Michael's (Okla. City, Okla.)
Mullins (Encinitas, Calif.)
Owl Creek (Mt. Vernon, Ohio)

Richert (Fresno, Calif.)
Rieger (Greenwood, S.C.)
Saifer (W. Orange, N.J.)
Starry (Shippensburg, Pa.)
Taos (Taos, N.M.)
Trans (Parkersburg, W.Va.)
221 (Westlake Village, Calif.)
Venkatesa (Tofino, B.C.)
Wilhite (Clearwater, Fla.)

Southern Authors

Book Shoppe (Myrtle Bch., S.C.)
Choctaw (Jackson, Miss.)

Fugitive (Nashville, Tenn.)
Sullivan (St. Pete., Fla.)

Vol. I (Greenville, S.C.)
Woolf's (Atlanta, Ga.)

State & Local Authors

Book Cellar (Freeport, Maine)
Book Disp. #1 (Columbia, S.C.)
Book Disp. #3 (Columbia, S.C.)
Books With (Concord, Mass.)
Bunkhouse (Gardiner, Maine)
Chanticleer (Ft. Wayne, Ind.)

Douglas (Sheridan, Wyo.)
Hawley (Louisville, Ky.)
Keeler (No. Monmouth, Maine)
Lobster (Spruce Head, Maine)
Ockett (Bryant Pond, Maine)
Old Book (Kennebunk, Maine)

Shaw's (Bath, Maine)
Snowbound (Norridgeweck, Maine)
Varney's (Casco, Maine)
Von Blon's (Waco, Texas)
Wertz (Flint, Mich.)

Autographs & Autograph Material

Abe. Lincoln (Chicago, Ill.)
Ahab (Cambridge, Mass.)
Aldrich (Groveland, Calif.)
Alford (Springfield, Va.)
Antic Hay (W. Caldwell, N.J.)
Apfelbaum (Valley Stream, N.Y.)
Arader/Sessler (Philadelphia, Pa.)
Argosy (New York, N.Y.)
Artistic (Boston, Mass.)
Autos (Eliz. City, N.C.)
Avery (Plymouth, Mass.)
Bailey (New York, N.Y.)
Barker (Dallas, Texas)
Barnes (Philadelphia, Pa.)
Batchelder (Ambler, Pa.)
B & B (Randolph, Mass.)
Bean (Biddeford, Maine)
Beckhorn (Dobbs Ferry, N.Y.)
Benjamin (Hunter, N.Y.)
Bill (Long I. City, N.Y.)
Bishop (Steubenville, Ohio)
B.J.S. (Forest Hills, N.Y.)
Book Block (Cos Cob, Conn.)
Book City (Hollywood, Calif.)
Borden (Portsmouth, R. I.)
Bradshaw (Chicago, Ill.)
Brattle Book (Boston, Mass.)
Burger (Pine Grove, Calif.)
Cady (Chicago, Ill.)
Canney (Alfred, Maine)
Carnegie (New York, N.Y.)
Cohasco (Yonkers, N.Y.)
Cosmic (Salt Lake City, Utah)
Craig (Newport, R. I.)
Culpin's (Denver, Colo.)
Dawn (Ann Arbor, Mich.)
Desmarais (Palo Alto, Calif.)
Distinctive (Cedar City, Utah)
E. Coast (Wells, Maine)

Especially (Burke, Va.)
E. Wharton (Oakton, Va.)
Firsts (New York, N.Y.)
Fisher (Williamsport, Pa.)
Fricelli (Brooklyn, N.Y.)
Fullam (Babylon, N.Y.)
Fye (Marshfield, Wisc.)
Gardner (New York, N.Y.)
Geraci (Accord, N.Y.)
Goodspeed's #1 (Boston, Mass.)
Goodspeed's #2 (Boston, Mass.)
Grabowski (Ronks, Pa.)
Granat (Woodmere, N.Y.)
Green Acre (Wells, Vt.)
Greene (Rockville Centre, N.Y.)
Gud (Elmhurst, N.Y.)
Harris (Los Angeles, Calif.)
Hist. Realia (Wooster, Ohio)
Hist. News (Skokie, Ill.)
Holmes (Philadelphia, Pa.)
Horowitz (New York, N.Y.)
Houle (Los Angeles, Calif.)
Howes (Brewster, Mass.)
Johnson (Syracuse, N.Y.)
Koschal (Verona, N.J.)
Lawrence (New York, N.Y.)
Lazarus (Ossining, N.Y.)
Lion (New York, N.Y.)
London (Chicago, Ill.)
Lowe (New York, N.Y.)
Lubrano (So. Lee, Mass.)
Mac Donnell (Austin, Texas)
Manuscript (Southampton, Pa.)
Marshall Field (Chicago, Ill.)
Mil-Air (Compton, Calif.)
Minckler (Billings, Mont.)
Minkoff (Grt. Barrington, Mass.)
Mitch's (Menlo Park, Calif.)
Moore (Wynnewood, Pa.)

Morrow (New York, N.Y.)
Mott (Sheffield, Mass.)
Muns (Berkeley, Calif.)
Newman (Battle Creek, Mich.)
Noble (Greenville, Texas)
Nudelman (Seattle, Wash.)
Opera Box (Brooklyn, N.Y.)
Patrick (Toronto, Ont.)
Quill (Rockville, Md.)
Ransom (Amherst, N.Y.)
Rare Book (Freehold, N.J.)
Rare Book (New York, N.Y.)
Rendell (Newton, Mass.)
Rendell (Waban, Mass.)
Resnick (Cazenovia, N.Y.)
Richards (Templeton, Mass.)
Robinson (New York, N.Y.)
Rubinfine (Pleasantville, N.J.)
Rudolph (Portland, Ore.)
Sackheim (Tucson, Ariz.)
Sand (Berkeley, Calif.)
Schiller (New York, N.Y.)
Schulson (New York, N.Y.)
Scriptorium (Beverly Hills, Calif.)
Seaport (Stonington, Conn.)
Seluzicki (Portland, Ore.)
Shapiro (Washington, D.C.)
Singer (Buena Park, Calif.)
Slater (Tarrytown, N.Y.)
Slifer (New York, N.Y.)
Stephens (Hastings, N.Y.)
Stickel (Colma, Calif.)
Stonehill (New Haven, Conn.)
Tollett (New York, N.Y.)
Wahrenbrock's (San Diego, Calif.)
Witten (Southport, Conn.)
Wofsy (San Francisco, Calif.)
Wurlitzer (New York, N.Y.)

Automobile Racing

Autobooks (Babylon, N.Y.)   Books At (Boulder, Colo.)
Automobile (Beaverton, Ore.)   Poor Farm (W. Cornwall, Conn.)

Specific Makes & Models
Of Automobiles

Books At (Boulder, Colo.)   Miller (Syracuse, N.Y.)   Moebius (Westbury, N.Y.)
Conway (Attleboro, Mass.)   Rolls (Rockville Centre, N.Y.)

Automotive

Again (Santa Barbara, Calif.)   Carlton (Camino, Calif.)   Phoenix (Royal Oak, Mich.)
Auten (Bedminster, N.J.)   Carroll (San Marcos, Calif.)   Poor Farm (W. Cornwall, Conn.)
Automobile (Beaverton, Ore.)   Conway (Attleboro, Mass.)   Ray (Baldwin Park, Calif.)
Book Fair (W. Palm Beach, Fla.)   5 Quail (Spg. Grove, Minn.)   Rolls (Rockville Centre, N.Y.)
Broken Kettle (Akron, Iowa)   Merriwell (Islip, N.Y.)   Ursus Prints (New York, N.Y.)
Brunsell's (Hanson, Mass.)   Moebius (Westbury, N.Y.)   Wittenborn (Pleasantville, N.Y.)

Aviation & Aeronautics

Again (Santa Barbara, Calif.)   Auslender (Wilton, Conn.)   Comstock's (Auburn, Wash.)
aGatherin' (Wynantskill, N.Y.)   Autos (Eliz. City, N.C.)   Conn. Book (Fairfield, Conn.)
Air Age (Tollhouse, Calif.)   Aviation (Glendale, Calif.)   Denver (Stockton, Calif.)
Aldrich (Groveland, Calif.)   Barnstormer (Sacramento, Calif.)   Gierspeck (Conroe, Texas)
Antheil (No. Bellmore, N.Y.)   Bookseller (Akron, Ohio)   Gould (Newburyport, Mass.)
Antiq. Archive (Sunnyvale, Calif.)   Books Of (Corning, N.Y.)   Houle (Durham, N.H.)
Arch (Bellows Falls, Vt.)   Brown (No. Augusta, S.C.)   Merriwell (Islip, N.Y.)
Argus (Sacramento, Calif.)   Caravan (Los Angeles, Calif.)   Mil-Air (Compton, Calif.)

Military (New York, N.Y.)
Northingham (Hamilton Sq., N.J.)
Pearson (Chicago, Ill.)
Pendleton (Tiburon, Calif.)
Roby (San Diego, Calif.)

Roderick (Medina, Ohio)
Sky (New York, N.Y.)
Thunderbird (Aldergrove, B.C.)
Univelt (San Diego, Calif.)
World War (W. Roxbury, Mass.)

Yankee (Williamson, N.Y.)
Yankee (Rochester, N.Y.)
Yesterday's (San Diego, Calif.)

Baseball

Austin (Richmond Hill, N.Y.)
Austin (Kew Gardens, N.Y.)
Bill (Long I. City, N.Y.)
Bill's (Stevens Pt., Wisc.)

Bookmarx (Roslyn, N.Y.)
Hughes (Holmes, N.Y.)
Kashmanian (No. Providence, R.I.)
Plapinger (Ashland, Ore.)

Sullivan (Chicago, Ill.)
Tatro (Wethersfield, Conn.)

L. Frank Baum & Oziana

Bieber (Kenilworth, N.J.)
Books Of (New York, N.Y.)
Bookstall (San Francisco, Calif.)
Dennis (Seattle, Wash.)

Earl (Clarendon, N.Y.)
Ford (Lake Worth, Fla.)
Lambert (Hancock, N.H.)
Old Benn. (Hancock, N.H.)

Oz (Kenilworth, N.J.)
Pepper/Stern (Sharon, Mass.)
Reisler (Vienna, Va.)
Toy (San Francisco, Calif.)

Bells

Abatis (Springfield, Vt.)

Country (Plainfield, Vt.)

Berkshires

Bookloft (Grt. Barrington, Mass.)

Running (Pittsfield, Mass.)

Beverages

Einhorn (New York, N.Y.)
G & C (Lafayette, La.)

Gore (San Gabriel, Calif.)
Household (Berkeley, Calif.)

Wine (Ann Arbor, Mich.)

Bible & Bible Studies

Allenson (Geneva, Ala.)
Baptist (Watertown, Wisc.)
Berkley (Berkley, Minn.)
Bible (El Cajon, Calif.)
Book Fair (W. Palm Beach, Fla.)

Books From (Helena, Mont.)
Brown (Toledo, Ohio)
Green (Philadelphia, Pa.)
Lansford (Powersville, Ga.)
Old Theo. (Minneapolis, Minn.)

Raimo (Lancaster, Pa.)
Roberts (Wheaton, Ill.)
Stevens (Wake Forest, N.C.)
Stroud (Williamsburg, W.Va.)
Yesterday's (Modesto, Calif.)

Bibliography

About (Moline, Ill.)
Allenson (Geneva, Ala.)
Arcane (Okla. City, Okla.)
Barnstable (New York, N.Y.)
Bear (W. Brattleboro, Vt.)
Boss (Brookline, Mass.)
Brick Row (San Francisco, Calif.)
Bromsen (Boston, Mass.)
Brownstone (New York, N.Y.)
Burley/Books (Toledo, Ohio)
Burstein (Waltham, Mass.)
Cady (Chicago, Ill.)
Catholic (Bellingham, Mass.)
Colophon (Epping, N.H.)
Core Coll. (Great Neck, N.Y.)
Cummings (Stillwater, Minn.)
Dragan (Ithaca, N.Y.)

Dunn (Newport, Vt.)
Fye (Marshfield, Wisc.)
Gardner (New York, N.Y.)
Grt. Southwest (Santa Fe, N.M.)
Guelker (St. Louis, Mo.)
Hill (Kingsport, Tenn.)
Hill (New York, N.Y.)
Household (Berkeley, Calif.)
Junius (Fairview, N.J.)
Ladner (Whitneyville, Conn.)
Landmark (New York, N.Y.)
Levinson (Beverly Hills, Calif.)
Library (Dallas, Texas)
Lorson's (Fullerton, Calif.)
Lowe (Eastsound, Wash.)
Merriam (Conway, Mass.)
Midnight (W. Lafayette, Ind.)

Morrell's (Ocean Grove, N.J.)
Morrow (New York, N.Y.)
Much (Southfield, Mich.)
Myers (Sequim, Wash.)
Oak Knoll (New Castle, Del.)
Oceanside (Oceanside, N.Y.)
Offenbacher (Kew Gardens, N.Y.)
O'Malley (Kingston, R.I.)
Ravenstree (Yuma, Ariz.)
Robinson (Morgantown, W.Va.)
Rosenthal (San Francisco, Calif.)
Shapiro (New York, N.Y.)
Walett (Abington, Mass.)
Wilsey (Olivebridge, N.Y.)
Wofsy (San Francisco, Calif.)
Zambelli (New York, N.Y.)

Decorative Trade Bindings

Antiq. Archive (Sunnyvale, Calif.)
Book Broker (Charlottesville, Va.)
ChoreoGraphica (Boston, Mass.)
Wilkerson (Lincoln, Mass.)

Fine & Rare Bindings

About (Moline, Ill.)
Albatross II (Tiburon, Calif.)
Appelfeld (New York, N.Y.)
Arader/Sessler (Philadelphia, Pa.)
Battersby (Ardmore, Pa.)
Bill (New York, N.Y.)
Blue Moon (Clearwater, Fla.)
Bonmark (Plainview, N.Y.)
Book Block (Cos Cob, Conn.)
Booketeria (San Antonio, Texas)
Book Sail (Orange, Calif.)
Boss (Brookline, Mass.)
Breslauer (New York, N.Y.)
Buddenbrooks (Boston, Mass.)
Cady (Chicago, Ill.)
Caravan (Los Angeles, Calif.)
Cherokee (Hollywood, Calif.)
Clinton (Clinton, N.Y.)
Cummins (Pottersville, N.J.)
Detering (Houston, Texas)
Dooling (Middlebury, Conn.)
Fletcher's (Salado, Texas)

Frohnsdorff (Gaithersburg, Md.)
Glenn (Kansas City, Mo.)
Guelker (St. Louis, Mo.)
Harper (New York, N.Y.)
Harris (Little Rock, Ark.)
Hartfield (Ann Arbor, Mich.)
Heller (Washington, D.C.)
Heritage (Los Angeles, Calif.)
Johnny (Manchester, Vt.)
Johnson (Syracuse, N.Y.)
Jordan (Philadelphia, Pa.)
Juvelis (Boston, Mass.)
Keith (Red Bank, N.J.)
Konigsmark (Wayne, Pa.)
Laster (Winston-Salem, N.C.)
Lawrence (New York, N.Y.)
Lowe (Eastsound, Wash.)
Magnum (Charlottesville, Va.)
Marshall Field (Chicago, Ill.)
Newburyport (Newburyport, Mass.)
Nisula (Okemos, Mich.)

Nudelman (Seattle, Wash.)
Otento (San Diego, Calif.)
Perata (Oakland, Calif.)
Raimo (Lancaster, Pa.)
Rare Book (New York, N.Y.)
Rockland (Cattaraugus, N.Y.)
Saturdays' (Euclid, Ohio)
Scopazzi (San Francisco, Calif.)
Shoebridge (Lafayette, N.Y.)
Snug Harbor (Wells, Maine)
Spector (Jackson Hgts., N.Y.)
Taylor (Austin, Texas)
Touchet (New York, N.Y.)
Weitz (New York, N.Y.)
Wells (Wells, Maine)
Whitlock's (New Haven, Conn.)
Wilsey (Olivebridge, N.Y.)
Witten (Southport, Conn.)
Yankee (Plymouth, Mass.)

Leather Bindings

Amitin (St. Louis, Mo.)
Anson-Cartwright (Toronto, Ont.)
Curiosity (St. Joseph, Mich.)
Morgan (Tucson, Ariz.)
Wells (Wells, Maine)
Ye Olde (St. Joseph, Mich.)

Biography & Autobiography

Allain (Greenwich, Conn,)
Amer. Pol. (Newtown, Conn.)
Antiq. Book (Winter Park, Fla.)
Appletree (Williford, Ark.)
Arch (Bellows Falls, Vt.)
Atlanta (Atlanta, Ga.)
Baptist (Watertown, Wisc.)
B.J.S. (Forest Hills, N.Y.)
Book Cellar (Freeport, Maine)
Book End (Monterey, Calif.)
Book Farm (Henniker, N.H.)
Bookman (Tybee Isl., Ga.)
Book Quest (New York, N.Y.)
Bookshelf (Ogden, Utah)
Book Stall (Rockford, Ill.)
Bookwood (Westwood, N.J.)
Boyson (Brookfield, Conn.)
Brady (Assonet, Mass.)
Bridgton (Bridgton, Maine)
Brownbag (Rochester, N.Y.)
Brown (Belfast, Maine)
Cabin/Pines (Potsdam, N.Y.)
Carriage (Northford, Conn.)
Clement (Franklin, N.H.)
Colonial (Pleasantville, N.Y.)

Common (New Salem, Mass.)
Desch (Wheaton, Md.)
Dolphin (Camden, Maine)
Dust (Cincinnati, Ohio)
Ediger (Beaverton, Ore.)
Estate (Washington, D.C.)
Falls (Farmington Falls, Maine)
Fraser (Burlington, Vt.)
Gallis (Marblehead, Mass.)
George Sand (Los Angeles, Calif.)
Glassman (Corte Madera, Calif.)
Glooscap (Pefferlaw, Ont.)
Golden Age (Dix Hills, N.Y.)
Goodrich (Englewood, N.J.)
Gordon (Pasadena, Calif.)
Haunted (Orleans, Mass.)
Hobson's (Jenkintown, Pa.)
Little (U. Montclair, N.J.)
Littlewoods (Waukesha, Wisc.)
Lysecki (Winnipeg, Man.)
Main St. (Brooklyn, N.Y.)
McGovern (Berwyn, Ill.)
Memory (Belfast, Maine)
Merkel (Xenia, Ohio)
Merlin's (Isla Vista, Calif.)

Morelle (Haverhill, Mass.)
Myers (Sequim, Wash.)
New Engl. (Bennington, Vt.)
NRS (New York, N.Y.)
Owl Creek (Mt. Vernon, Ohio)
Pages (Reading, Mass.)
Palma (Wilmington, Del.)
Pansy (St. Andrews, N.B.)
Patriot (Lexington, Mass.)
Perry's (San Jose, Calif.)
Pomander (New York, N.Y.)
Quadrant (Easton, Pa.)
Rausch (Bloomington, Ind.)
Roberts (Wheaton, Ill.)
Rule (Rochester, Mich.)
Stevens (Wake Forest, N.C.)
Suhm (Westfield, Mass.)
Valley (No. Hollywood, Calif.)
Vinik (Tucson, Ariz.)
Vogt (Meadow Vista, Calif.)
White's (Asbury Park, N.J.)
Willow (Englewood, Colo.)
Windsor (Windsor, Conn.)
Words (San Deigo, Calif.)

Birds & Ornithology

Audubon (Vienna, Va.)
Avalon (Hayward, Calif.)
Books/Birds (Vernon, Conn.)
British (No. Weymouth, Mass.)
Buteo (Vermillion, S.D.)
Carlson (Portland, Maine)
Cassie (Millis, Mass.)
Chickadee (Houston, Texas)

Dorn (Johntown, N.Y.)
Huxley (Loudonville, N.Y.)
Janus (Corea, Maine)
Janus (Hungtinton Stn., N.Y.)
Johnson (No. Bennington, Vt.)
Kalanja (Trafford, Pa.)
Martin's (Fairbanks, Alk.)
Norris (Paoli, Pa.)

Peacock (Littleton, Mass.)
Petersen (Davenport, Iowa)
Talvin (Trafford, Pa.)
Tolliver's (Los Angeles, Calif.)
Watkins (Dolgeville, N.Y.)
Zaremba (Cambridge, Mass.)

Black Literature & Studies

Beasley (Chicago, Ill.)
Book Admirer (Norwalk, Conn.)
Caravan (Stillwater, Okla.)
Carolina (Charlotte, N.C.)
Cornerstone (Providence, R.I.)
Docheff (Berkeley, Calif.)
Eisenberg (Washington, D.C.)
Gilbo (Carpinteria, Calif.)

Gull Gall. (Oakland, Calif.)
Invisible (Berkeley, Calif.)
Lambeth (New York, N.Y.)
Maiden (W. Chester, Pa.)
McBlain (Hamden, Conn.)
Miranda (Brookline, Mass.)
Mullins (Encinitas, Calif.)
Nudel (New York, N.Y.)

Prufrock (Pasadena, Calif.)
Rieber (Thomasville, Ga.)
Serendipity (Berkeley, Calif.)
Stewart (Portland, Ore.)
University (New York, N.Y.)
Waiting (Cambridge, Mass.)

Book Plates & Ex Libris

Boss (Brookline, Mass.)
Dragan (Ithaca, N.Y.)

Grabowski (Ronks, Pa.)
McDermut (Montvale, N.J.)

Books About Books

About (Moline, Ill.)
Antiquarium (Bethany, Conn.)
Associated (Long Beach, Calif.)
Bargain (Long Beach, Calif.)
Battery (Forest Hills, N.Y.)
Becker (New York, N.Y.)
Benson (W. Cornwall, Conn.)
Berry (Kingston, Ont.)
Beyer (Stratford, Conn.)
Book Buyers (Houston, Texas)
Booked Up (Washington, D.C.)
Bookpress (Williamsburg, Va.)
Books/Coll. (Encino, Calif.)
Borden (Portsmouth, R. I.)
Bowie (Seattle, Wash.)
Braiterman (Baltimore, Md.)
Brick Row (San Francisco, Calif.)
Brooks (Macon, Ga.)

Brownstone (New York, N.Y.)
Burley/Books (Toledo, Ohio)
Cady (Chicago, Ill.)
Cassidy (Sacramento, Calif.)
Chaney (Ossining, N.Y.)
Chimney (Bridgeport, Conn.)
Christoffersen (Mamaroneck, N.Y.)
Collectors' (New York, N.Y.)
Colophon (Epping, N.H.)
Cummings (Stillwater, Minn.)
Dawson's (Los Angeles, Calif.)
Duschnes (New York, N.Y.)
Dust (Cincinnati, Ohio)
Elmcress (So. Hamilton, Mass.)
Felcone (Princeton, N.J.)
First Edtns. (Richmond, Va.)
Gardner (New York, N.Y.)
E. Gordon (New York, N.Y.)

Graf (Iowa City, Iowa)
Guelker (St. Louis, Mo.)
Hartfield (Ann Arbor, Mich.)
Havemeyer (Skaneafeles, N.Y.)
Heliochrome (Berkeley Hgts., N.J.)
Heller (Washington, D.C.)
Hill (Kingsport, Tenn.)
Hobson's (Jenkintown, Pa.)
Hurley (Westmoreland, N.H.)
Kellinger (Chambersburg, Pa.)
Kraus (Millwood, N.Y.)
Ladner (Whitneyville, Conn.)
Laurie (St. Paul, Minn.)
Lawrence (New York, N.Y.)
Leaves (Ann Arbor, Mich.)
Leech (Ormand Bch., Fla.)
Leelanau (Leland, Mich.)
Levine (Savannah, Ga.)

Limestone (Glen Rose, Texas)
Lion's (Salisbury, Conn.)
Merriam (Conway, Mass.)
Midnight (W. Lafayette, Ind.)
Morrell's (Ocean Grove, N.J.)
Morrow (New York, N.Y.)
Myers (Sequim, Wash.)
Oak Knoll (New Castle, Del.)
O'Malley (Kingston, R.I.)

Printers' (Palo Alto, Calif.)
Quitzau (Edmeston, N.Y.)
Robinson (Morgantown, W.Va.)
Rostenberg (New York, N.Y.)
Schoyer's (Pittsburgh, Pa.)
Scott (Portland, Maine)
Sleepy (Moraga, Calif.)
Starosciak (San Francisco, Calif.)
Steigerwald (Bloomington, Ind.)

Stickel (Colma, Calif.)
Strand Rare (New York, N.Y.)
Tweney (Seattle, Wash.)
Typographeum (Francestown, N.H.)
Wilson (Kitchener, Ont.)
Yerba (San Francisco, Calif.)

Book Scouts

Baseball (Tucson, Ariz.)
Chalfin (New York, N.Y.)

Kingstrom (Sacred Heart, Minn.)
Kirksco (Ringwood, N.J.)

Rose (Sparta, Mich.)
Taylor (Kerrville, Texas)

Book Trade & Catalogues

About (Moline, Ill.)
Bargain (Long Beach, Calif.)

Burley/Books (Toledo, Ohio)
Hall (San Francisco, Calif.)

Johnson (Indianapolis, Ind.)

Botany

Amer. Botanist (Brookfield, Ill.)
Book Home (Colo. Spgs., Colo.)
Buck (New York, N.Y.)
Carpenter (Balboa Isl., Calif.)
Engard (Tucson, Ariz.)
Fagin (Chicago, Ill.)

Gregory (New York, N.Y.)
Jackson (Berkeley, Calif.)
Johnson (No. Bennington, Vt.)
Lubrecht (Forestburgh, N.Y.)
Nadolny (Kensington, Conn.)
Oklahoma (Yukon, Okla.)

Orange (Garberville, Calif.)
Petersen (Davenport, Iowa)
Pomona (Rockton, Ont.)
Wayner (Ft. Payne, Ala.)

Boxing

Bill (Long I. City, N.Y.)
Kashmanian (No. Providence, R.I.)

Pollock (Palo Alto, Calif.)
Shochet (Sykesville, Md.)

Sullivan (Chicago, Ill.)
Tatro (Wethersfield, Conn.)

Boy Scouts

Bearce (Salem, Ore.)
Book OP (Adrian, Mich.)
G & C (Lafayette, La.)

George (Cleveland, Tenn.)
Old Book (Kennebunk, Maine)
Sayers (Andrews, Texas)

Stevensons (Euless, Texas)

British Isles

Book Shop (Boise, Idaho)
Circle West (Annapolis, Md.)
Filler (Bremerton, Wash.)

Glasser (Assonet, Mass.)
In Our (Cambridge, Mass.)
Nosegay (Cold Spg. Harbor, N.Y.)

Rausch (Bloomington, Ind.)

Broadsides

Antiquarians (Plainfield, Pa.)
Beatific (Schenectady, N.Y.)

Bookman (Tybee Isl., Ga.)
Mobley (Schoharie, N.Y.)

Edgar Rice Burroughs

Books Of (Corning, N.Y.)
Edison Hall (Edison, N.J.)

Fantasy (New York, N.Y.)
Lansford (Powersville, Ga.)

Perry's (San Jose, Calif.)
Toy (San Francisco, Calif.)

Business & Business History

Abbot (Bronx, N.Y.)
Annegan (San Marcos, Calif.)
Battersby (Ardmore, Pa.)
Boas (Haddonfield, N.J.)
Bolotin (Youngstown, Ohio)
Book Barn (Rochester, Mich.)
Book Clearing (Larchmont, N.Y.)
Book Look (Warwick, N.Y.)
Cassidy (Kansas City, Mo.)
Cramer (Kansas City, Mo.)

Fraser (Burlington, Vt.)
Hammer Mtn. (Schenectady, N.Y.)
Hive (Easton, Pa.)
Int'l. Univ. (New York, N.Y.)
Lake (Toronto, Ont.)
Lincoln (Foster, R.I.)
Masi (Montague, Mass.)
Mason (Phoenix, Ariz.)
Maxwell (Elmsford, N.Y.)
Norman (San Francisco, Calif.)

Old Southport (Southport, Conn.)
Perry's (San Jose, Calif.)
Qualman (San Diego, Calif.)
Rubin (Brookline, Mass.)
Seppa (Virginia, Minn.)
Tanditash (New York, N.Y.)
Used (Dyer, Ind.)
Western (Stoughton, Mass.)
Ximenes (New York, N.Y.)

Cactus & Succulents

Engard (Tucson, Ariz.)

Ken-L (Newberg, Ore.)

Mallory (Van Nuys, Calif.)

California

Allen (Altadena, Calif.)
Argonaut (San Francisco, Calif.)
Associated (Long Beach, Calif.)
Berk (Studio City, Calif.)
Book Attic (San Bernardino, Calif.)
Book Den (Santa Barbara, Calif.)
Burger (Pine Grove, Calif.)
Campbell (Campbell, Calif.)
Caravan (Los Angeles, Calif.)
Carpenter (Balboa Isl., Calif.)
Cassidy (Sacramento, Calif.)
Coffman (Cambria, Calif.)
Davidson (San Diego, Calif.)

Diablo (Walnut Creek, Calif.)
Ferndale (Ferndale, Calif.)
Fischler (San Jose, Calif.)
5 Quail (Spg. Grove, Minn.)
Hammer (Santa Barbara, Calif.)
Hansen (Carlsbad, Calif.)
Henson (Santa Ana, Calif.)
Holmes (Oakland, Calif.)
Holmes (San Francisco, Calif.)
Lost (Santa Barbara, Calif.)
Manning's (San Francisco, Calif.)
Marchioness (Laguna Bch., Calif.)
Maxwell's (Stockton, Calif.)

Monroe (Fresno, Calif.)
Noto (Cupertino, Calif.)
Old Book (San Francisco, Calif.)
Reynolds (Willits, Calif.)
Talisman (Georgetown, Calif.)
Thomas (San Francisco, Calif.)
Time (Sacramento, Calif.)
Treehorn (Santa Rosa, Calif.)
Wahrenbrock's (San Diego, Calif.)
Yerba (San Francisco, Calif.)
Zeitlin (Los Angeles, Calif.)

Calligraphy

Chiswick (Sandy Hook, Conn.)
Glasser (Assonet, Mass.)
Howe (New York, N.Y.)

Mashman (Ridgefield, Conn.)
Memory (Corona Del Mar, Calif.)
Princeton (Atlantic City, N.J.)

Schram (Montclair, N.J.)
Wilsey (Olivebridge, N.Y.)

Camping & Out-Of-Doors

Book Prospector (Littleton, Colo.)   Sayers (Andrews, Texas)   Sporting (Palmerton, Pa.)

Canada & Canadiana

Academic (No. Vancouver, B.C.)
Allison (No. Bay, Ont.)
Annex (Toronto, Ont.)
Anson-Cartwright (Toronto, Ont.)
Ashton (Ottawa, Ont.)
Back Pages (Halifax, N.S.)
Bagley (Fredericton, N.B.)
Becker (Acton Centre, Mass.)
Benoit (Montreal, Que.)
Benson (Ottawa, Ont.)
Book Bazaar (Ottawa, Ont.)
Book Bin (Kingston, Ont.)
Bowes (Vancouver, B.C.)
Dobson (Grimsby, Ont.)
Dunn (Newport, Vt.)

Fitch (Santa Fe, N.M.)
Frontier (Los Angeles, Calif.)
Gagnon (Quebec, Que.)
Ginsberg (Sharon, Mass.)
Golder (Collinsville, Conn.)
Haunted (Victoria, B.C.)
Headley (St. Catherines, Ont.)
Heritage (Toronto, Ont.)
House (Thornhill, Ont.)
Javitch (Montreal, Que.)
Kahn (Montreal, Que.)
Lake (Toronto, Ont.)
Lunsford (No. Vancouver, B.C.)
Lysecki (Winnipeg, Man.)
MacLeod's (Vancouver, B.C.)

Madonna (Combermere, Ont.)
Mason (Toronto, Ont.)
McGahern (Ottawa, Ont.)
Old Favs. (Toronto, Ont.)
Past (Windsor, Ont.)
Patrick (Toronto, Ont.)
Rush (Hamilton, Ont.)
Scace (Calgary, Alt.)
Schooner (Halifax, N.S.)
Thunderbird (Aldergrove, B.C.)
Treasure (Oakville, Ont.)
Williams (Calgary, Alt.)
Wolfe (Pt. Claire, Que.)
Woolmer (Montreal, Que.)

Cape Cod, Martha's Vineyard, & Nantucket

Book Den E. (Oak Bluffs, Mass.)
Bryant's (Provincetown, Mass.)
Cape (Mashpec, Mass.)
Cape Collector (So. Harwich,

Mass.)
Chamberlin (E. Orleans, Mass.)
Haunted (Orleans, Mass.)
Parnassus (Yarmouthport, Mass.)

Smith's (Brewster, Mass.)
Staten (Harwich, Mass.)
Wake (Ft. Lauderdale, Fla.)

Caribbean

Americana (Coral Gables, Fla.)
House (Thornhill, Ont.)
Jeltrups' St. Croix, V.I.)
Karno (Santa Monica, Calif.)

Libros (Redlands, Calif.)
Lighthouse (St. Pete., Fla.)
Mott (Sheffield, Mass.)
Parnassus (Yarmouthport, Mass.)

Poe (Mayaguez, P.R.)
Rulon-Miller (St. Thomas, V.I.)
University (New York, N.Y.)

Cartoons & Caricatures

Apothecary (New York, N.Y.)
Bill (Long I. City, N.Y.)

Galewitz (Orange, Conn.)
Graham (Forestville, Calif.)

Words (San Deigo, Calif.)

Catalogues Raisonnes

M. Gordon (New York, N.Y.)
Metropolis (Royal Oak, Mich.)

Reisman (Philadelphia, Pa.)
Schmidt (Collingswood, N.J.)

Catholica

Anglican (Saratoga Spgs., N.Y.)
Booklover's (Tucson, Ariz.)
Catholic (Bellingham, Mass.)

Celtic (Westmoreland, N.H.)
Liberty (Sloatsburg, N.Y.)
Madonna (Combermere, Ont.)

New Miner (Necedah, Wisc.)
Patrick (Toronto, Ont.)
Prosser (Chicago, Ill.)

Cats

Cat (New Rochelle, N.Y.)

Ray's (Hartford, Vt.)

Sutley (Centralia, Wash.)

Catskill Mountains

McDonald's (Catskill, N.Y.)

Purple (Fleischmanns, N.Y.)

Cattle & Range Industry

Cow Country (Prescott, Ariz.)
Dary (Lawrence, Kan.)

Grossblatt (Dallas, Texas)
La Galeria (Las Vegas, N.M.)

Swinford (Paris, Ill.)
Trail (Tucson, Ariz.)

Central America

Acoma (Ramona, Calif.)
Bookery (Farmington, N.H.)
Eshner (Bisbee, Ariz.)

Karno (Santa Monica, Calif.)
La Tienda (Conway, N.H.)
Libros (Redlands, Calif.)

Parnassus (Yarmouthport, Mass.)
R. Ramer (New York, N.Y.)
Rulon-Miller (St. Thomas, V.I.)

Ceramics & Glass

Book Exch. (Corning, N.Y.)   Gem (New York, N.Y.)

Chemical & Substance Dependency

Bishop (Steubenville, Ohio)   Cottontail (Bennington, Ind.)   Reading (Mexico, Ind.)
Book Nook (Yakima, Wash.)   Gatto (New York, N.Y.)   Village (Bellingham, Wash.)
Cape Ann (Peabody, Mass.)   Moving (Seattle, Wash.)
Catbird (Portland, Ore.)   Mycophile (Naples, Fla.)

Chess

Book-O (Queens Vill., N.Y.)   Old Edtns. (Buffalo, N.Y.)   Shapiro (Washington, D.C.)
Main St. (Brooklyn, N.Y.)   Pioneer (Seattle, Wash.)   University (New York, N.Y.)

Chicago

Alsberg (Skokie, Ill.)   Laws (Chicago, Ill.)   Tholin (Evanston, Ill.)
Chicago (Evanston, Ill.)   Left Bank (Oak Park, Ill.)   Titles (Highland Park, Ill.)
Clover (Charlottesville, Va.)   McGovern (Berwyn, Ill.)

Children's Books

Adelson (No. Pomfret, Vt.)   Aleph-Bet (Valley Cottage, N.Y.)   Allen (Baltimore, Md.)
Again (Santa Barbara, Calif.)   Alibi (New Haven, Conn.)   Allen (Altadena, Calif.)

Amer. City (Denver, Colo.)
Amer. Frag. (Escondido, Calif.)
Andover (Andover, Mass.)
Annie's #1 (Portland, Ore.)
Annie's #2 (Portland, Ore.)
Antique Books (Hamden, Conn.)
Antiques/Art (Seattle, Wash.)
Antiquus (San Francisco, Calif.)
Arond (Lexington, Mass.)
Asendorf (Los Altos Hills, Calif.)
Ashton (Ottawa, Ont.)
Avocet (Corvallis, Ore.)
Bargain (Long Beach, Calif.)
Barn Loft (Laconia, N.H.)
Barn Owl (Wellesley, Mass.)
Barrow (Concord, Mass.)
Bebbah (Andover, Kan.)
Becky (Hannibal, Mo.)
Benson (W. Cornwall, Conn.)
Bibelots (Seattle, Wash.)
Bieber (Kenilworth, N.J.)
Birmingham (Birmingham, Mich.)
Blomberg (Rockford, Ill.)
Blue Lantern (San Diego, Calif.)
Boise Farm (Boise, Idaho)
Book/Art (Dothan, Ala.)
Book Barn (So. Sioux City, Neb.)
Book Broker (Charlottesville, Va.)
Book Cellar (Brattleboro, Vt.)
Bookcell (Hamden, Conn.)
Book Chest (New York, N.Y.)
Bookdales (Richfield, Minn.)
Book End (Monterey, Calif.)
Book Haven (Lancaster, Pa.)
Book House (St. Louis, Mo.)
Book-In (Stillwater, N.Y.)
Book Loft (Solvang, Calif.)
Bookman (Kent, Ohio)
Bookman (Grand Haven, Mich.)
Bookmarx (Roslyn, N.Y.)
Bookmine (Old Scaramento, Calif.)
Book Nook (Yakima, Wash.)
Book OP (Adrian, Mich.)
Book Pedlars (Cundy's Harbor,
  Maine)
Bookshelf (Concord, N.H.)
Book Shop (Beverly Farms, Mass.)
Books 'n (El Dorado, Ark.)
Books 'n (Springfield, Mass.)

Books Of (New York, N.Y.)
Bookstall (San Francisco, Calif.)
Bookstock (So. Orleans, Mass.)
Book Stop (Las Vegas, Nev.)
Bookstore (Valdosta, Ga.)
Book Store (Englewood, N.J.)
Books Unltd. (Nat'l City, Calif.)
Book/Tackle (Watch Hill, R.I.)
Book Traders (Winter Haven, Fla.)
Book Treasury (Nashville, Tenn.)
Boyson (Brookfield, Conn.)
Bridgton (Bridgton, Maine)
Broad Ripple (Indianapolis, Ind.)
Brookline (Brookline, Mass.)
Buchanan (New York, N.Y.)
Buddenbrooks (Boston, Mass.)
Burgman (Santa Rosa, Calif.)
Burt (Laconia, N.H.)
Caldwell (Arkadelphia, Ark.)
Califia (San Francisco, Calif.)
Calliope (Pittsburgh, Pa.)
Campbell (Campbell, Calif.)
Cape (Mashpec, Mass.)
Cape Collector (So. Harwich,
  Mass.)
Caravan (Stillwater, Okla.)
Cellar (Eugene, Ore.)
Chapin (Reading, Pa.)
Chapter 1 (Hamilton, Mont.)
Cherokee (Hollywood, Calif.)
Cheshire (Yakima, Wash.)
Chickadee (Houston, Texas)
Chimney (Scotts Valley, Calif.)
Choras (Weston, Mass.)
Clark's (Spokane, Wash.)
Cole's (La Jolla, Calif.)
Collins' (Pottstown, Pa.)
Connecticut (E. Haddam, Conn.)
Consolo (Mansfield, Ohio)
Cooper Fox (Millbrook, N.Y.)
Cooper's (Decatur, Ga.)
Cornucopia (Syosset, N.Y.)
Cotswold (Medina, Ohio)
Curiosity (St. Joseph, Mich.)
Dartmouth (Hanover, N.H.)
Darvill's Book (Eastsound, Wash.)
Debra (No. Hills, Pa.)
Deines (Ft. Collins, Colo.)
Dennis (Seattle, Wash.)

Dermont (Onset, Mass.)
Desch (Wheaton, Md.)
Docheff (Berkeley, Calif.)
Dohm's (Olympia, Wash.)
Donaldson's (Knoxville, Tenn.)
Drusilla's (Baltimore, Md.)
Dumler (Southport, Conn.)
Earl (Clarendon, N.Y.)
Eastman (Springvale, Maine)
Edison Hall (Edison, N.J.)
Eeyore's #1 (New York, N.Y.)
Eeyore's #2 (New York, N.Y.)
Eldora's (Newberg, Ore.)
Ellam (Los Angeles, Calif.)
Enchanted (Brooklyn, N.Y.)
Everyday (Burlington, Vt.)
Farley's (Pensacola, Fla.)
Fay (Caledonia, N.Y.)
Fine (Rochester, Mich.)
First (Chicago, Ill.)
First Impressions (Wheaton, Ill.)
Foley (Bardstown, Ky.)
Ford (Lake Worth, Fla.)
Fox (Madison, Tenn.)
Fox Hill (Palmer, Mass.)
Fran's (Philadelphia, Pa.)
Frohnsdorff (Gaithersburg, Md.)
Frontier (Los Angeles, Calif.)
Galewitz (Orange, Conn.)
Carcia (Turlock, Calif.)
Gardner (New York, N.Y.)
Geagan (Wareham, Mass.)
George (Cleveland, Tenn.)
Gilann (Darien, Conn.)
Glassman (Corte Madera, Calif.)
Golden Age (Dix Hills, N.Y.)
Golden Hill (Helena, Mont.)
Grapevine (San Mateo, Calif.)
Grt. Expect. (Staten Isl., N.Y.)
Green (Elkins Park, Pa.)
Grimshaw (Randolph, Mass.)
Gryphon #1 (New York, N.Y.)
Guerin (Montreal, Que.)
Hampton (Newberry, S.C.)
Harris (Northfield, Mass.)
Harris (Oberlin, Ohio)
Haslam's (St. Pete., Fla.)
Haunted (Victoria, B.C.)
Havemeyer (Skaneafeles, N.Y.)

Hawkins (Alpena, Mich.)
Henrietta's (Salisbury, Md.)
Heritage (Southampton, Mass.)
Hermit's (Wyoming, Pa.)
Hi (Canutillo, Texas)
Hirsch (Hopewell Jctn., N.Y.)
Hobby Helpers (Lima, N.Y.)
Hoefliger (Buffalo, N.Y.)
Hollander (Santa Monica, Calif.)
Homestead (Marlborough, N.H.)
Homesteader (Wenatchee, Wash.)
Hooked (Springfield, Mo.)
Hyde Park (Tampa, Fla.)
In #1 (San Francisco, Calif.)
In #2 (San Francisco, Calif.)
Island (Mercer, Wash.)
Jane Addams (Champaign, Ill.)
Janus (Corea, Maine)
Janus (Hungtinton Stn., N.Y.)
Judi's (Twin Falls, Idaho)
Kaiser (Santa Cruz, Calif.)
Kane (Santa Cruz, Calif.)
Katonah (Katonah, N.Y.)
Kaufman (New York, N.Y.)
Kaufman (Tempe, Ariz.)
Keeler (No. Monmouth, Maine)
Kern (Glendale, Ariz.)
Kionke (Gowanda, N.Y.)
Kirch (Thornville, Ohio)
Klein (Oak Park, Ill.)
Klemm (Apple Valley, Calif.)
Konigsmark (Wayne, Pa.)
Kraft (Palm Desert, Calif.)
Krueger (Sunland, Calif.)
Lambert (Hancock, N.H.)
Lasley (Berkeley, Ill.)
Links (3 Rivers, Mich.)
Little (Hinsdale, Ill.)
Little (Missoula, Mont.)
Littrup (Bay City, Mich.)
Loose (Jerome, Mich.)
Lovett (Winston-Salem, N.C.)
Lyrical (Saratoga Spgs., N.Y.)
Maestro (Bayport, N.Y.)
Mannatt (San Diego, Calif.)
Maxwell's (Stockton, Calif.)
Medallion (Wellesley, Mass.)
Memory (Battle Creek, Mich.)
Memory (Corona Del Mar, Calif.)

Merlin's (Providence, R.I.)
Michelli (Ogunquit, Maine)
Montlack (Old Bethpage, N.Y.)
Morelle (Haverhill, Mass.)
Morgan (Tucson, Ariz.)
Morrell's (Ocean Grove, N.J.)
Mott (Sheffield, Mass.)
Much (Marblehead, Mass.)
Myers (Boulder, Colo.)
Nebraska (Lincoln, Neb.)
Nelson (Goshen, N.H.)
Nelson (New Bedford, Mass.)
Nosegay (Cold Spg. Harbor, N.Y.)
Nudelman (Seattle, Wash.)
Oblong (Millerton, N.Y.)
Obsolescence (Gettysburg, Pa.)
Old Benn. (Hancock, N.H.)
Old Book (Croton, N.Y.)
Old Book (Kennebunk, Maine)
Old Rare (Jamestown, N.Y.)
Old Southport (Southport, Conn.)
O'Leary's (Tacoma, Wash.)
Orange (Garberville, Calif.)
Owl Creek (Mt. Vernon, Ohio)
Owl (Greenwich, N.Y.)
Pan (Catskill, N.Y.)
Pansy (St. Andrews, N.B.)
Paper (Portland, Ore.)
Paper (So. Euclid, Ohio)
Pasotti (Indianapolis, Ind.)
Past (Windsor, Ont.)
Pendleton (Tiburon, Calif.)
People's (Flemington, N.J.)
Petersons (Philadelphia, Pa.)
Phalen (Chicago, Ill.)
Pierce (Oroville, Calif.)
Pinocchio (Pittsburgh, Pa.)
Pinocchio's (Morgantown, W.Va.)
Pohrt (Flint, Mich.)
Quest (Ft. Worth, Texas)
Quitzau (Edmeston, N.Y.)
Quixote (Philadelphia, Pa.)
Rainy (Fitzwilliam, N.H.)
Rainy (Lexington, Mass.)
Ralston (Fullerton, Calif.)
Ransom (Amherst, N.Y.)
Red Horse (Tampa, Fla.)
Reisler (Vienna, Va.)
Robinson (St. Pete., Fla.)

Robles (Tucson, Ariz.)
Safir (New York, N.Y.)
Sail (Newcastle, Maine)
Sail (Lexington, Ky.)
St. Nicholas (Toronto, Ont.)
Sandys (Albertson, N.Y.)
Scarlet (New Milford, Conn.)
Schiller (New York, N.Y.)
Schlossberg (Newton, Mass.)
Sebert (Mt. Nebo, W.Va.)
Sidney's (Missoula, Mont.)
Small (So. Yarmouth, Mass.)
Song Of (Newmarket, N.H.)
Sophia (Amherst, Mass.)
Springbook (Springfield, Ohio)
Storeybook (Sycamore, Ill.)
Sullivan (New York, N.Y.)
Sullivan (Coventry, Conn.)
Swiss (St. Louis, Mo.)
Tattered (Denver, Colo.)
Temares (Plandome, N.Y.)
Tempest (Waitsville, Vt.)
Ten Eyck (Southboro, Mass.)
1000 Words (Exeter, N.H.)
Time (Sacramento, Calif.)
Tinker (Santa Cruz, Calif.)
Titles (Highland Park, Ill.)
Toad (Berkeley, Calif.)
Toy (San Francisco, Calif.)
Treasure (Oakville, Ont.)
Treasures (Rochester, Mich.)
Treehorn (Santa Rosa, Calif.)
Tumbleweed (Pueblo, Colo.)
Turkey (Westport, Conn.)
12th St. (Santa Monica, Calif.)
Twyce (Winona, Minn.)
Una (St. Johnsbury, Vt.)
Varney's (Casco, Maine)
Venkatesa (Tofino, B.C.)
Victoria (New York, N.Y.)
Village (Bellingham, Wash.)
Vintage (Iowa City, Iowa)
Vintage (Wheaton, Ill.)
Weindling (Danbury, Conn.)
Wertz (Flint, Mich.)
West's (Elm Grove, Wisc.)
Wheeler (Elgin, Ore.)
White (La Jolla, Calif.)
Wilder (Brookline, Mass.)

Wilder (Hubbardston, Mass.)
Willis (Columbus, Ohio)
Wilson (Bull Shoals, Ark.)

Wise (Lake Delton, Wisc.)
Words (Cambridge, Mass.)
World Of (Willoughby, Ohio)

Yesterday's (Ashfield, Mass.)

China

Cheng (Boston, Mass.)
Gamradt (Minneapolis, Minn.)
Lewis (Seattle, Wash.)

Oriental (St. Pete., Fla.)
Paragon (New York, N.Y.)
Rare Oriental (Aptos, Calif.)

Sebastopol (Sebastopol, Calif.)

Christian Books

Again (Santa Barbara, Calif.)
Books From (Helena, Mont.)
Burleson (Spartanburg, S.C.)

Butcher (Youngstown, Ohio)
Green (Philadelphia, Pa.)
Quest (Ft. Worth, Texas)

Roberts (Wheaton, Ill.)
Sackett (Grants Pass, Ore.)

Christmas

Havemeyer (Skaneafeles, N.Y.)
Krueger (Sunland, Calif.)

Storeybook (Sycamore, Ill.)
Tracery (Dallas, Texas)

Church History

Anglican (Saratoga Spgs., N.Y.)
Baptist (Watertown, Wisc.)

Bible (El Cajon, Calif.)
Kern (Glendale, Ariz.)

New Miner (Necedah, Wisc.)
Wood (Tampa, Fla.)

Sir Winston Churchill

Chartwell (New York, N.Y.)
Churchill (Contoocook, N.H.)
Churchilliana (Sacramento, Calif.)
Weber (Troy, Minn.)

Cinema & Film

Aladdin (Fullerton, Calif.)
All Edges (Silver Spg., Md.)
Berry Hill (Deansboro, N.Y.)
Blue Lantern (San Diego, Calif.)
Book City (Hollywood, Calif.)
Booklord's (New York, N.Y.)
Booksellers (St. Paul, Minn.)
Books 'n (New York, N.Y.)
Boulevard (Topanga, Calif.)
Cinemabilia (New York, N.Y.)
Cinema (Hollywood, Calif.)
City Lights (San Francisco, Calif.)
Constant (Milwaukee, Wisc.)
Cook (Los Angeles, Calif.)
Crofter's (Washington, Conn.)
Dady (Minneapolis, Minn.)

Dourgarian (Walnut Creek, Calif.)
Edmunds (Hollywood, Calif.)
George Sand (Los Angeles, Calif.)
Golden Age (Seattle, Wash.)
Gotham (New York, N.Y.)
Halpern (Flushing, N.Y.)
Hampton (Newberry, S.C.)
Harbar (Casselberry, Fla.)
Hollywood City (Hollywood, Calif.)
Hollywood Service (Hollywood, Calif.)
Laws (Chicago, Ill.)
Limelight (San Francisco, Calif.)
Loewenthal (Dover, N.J.)
Memory (Belfast, Maine)

Memory (New York, N.Y.)
Pepper/Stern (Sharon, Mass.)
Pepper/Stern (Santa Barbara, Calif.)
Performing (New York, N.Y.)
Plant (Grass Valley, Calif.)
Ray (Baldwin Park, Calif.)
Reliable (Paterson, N.J.)
Roseman (Brooklyn, N.Y.)
Sorrenti (Palatine, Ill.)
Tebbetts (Hallowell, Maine)
Valley (No. Hollywood, Calif.)
Wild (Larchmont, N.Y.)
Xanadu (Bronx, N.Y.)

Circus & Carnival

Backstage (Eugene, Ore.)
Katt (Los Angeles, Calif.)
Mason's (Wabash, Ind.)
Meyerbooks (Glenwood, Ill.)
Schmid (Pittsburgh, Pa.)
Theater (Palo Alto, Calif.)

Civil War & Confederacy

Abbey (Los Angeles, Calif.)
Abe. Lincoln (Chicago, Ill.)
Abrams (Atlanta, Ga.)
Altau (Waynesboro, Va.)
Annegan (San Marcos, Calif.)
Antiquaria (Franklin, Tenn.)
Antiq. Bookworm (Sharon, Mass.)
Antiq. Michiana (Allen, Mich.)
Antique Books (Hamden, Conn.)
Antiques (No. Abington, Mass.)
Appalachia (Bluefield, W.Va.)
Appleland (Winchester, Va.)
Appomatox (Chicago, Ill.)
Arch (Bellows Falls, Vt.)
Avery (Plymouth, Mass.)
Bargain (Norfolk, Va.)
Baumhofer (St. Paul, Minn.)
Benjamin (Hunter, N.Y.)
Blomberg (Rockford, Ill.)
Blue Moon (Clearwater, Fla.)
Bohling (Decatur, Mich.)
Book Guild (Portsmouth, N.H.)
Book House (Arlington, Va.)
Book Place (Columbia, S.C.)
Bookshop (Chapel Hill, N.C.)
Book Shoppe (Myrtle Bch., S.C.)
Book Studio (Atlanta, Ga.)
Bookworm (Wytheville, Va.)
Borderland (Alvaton, Ky.)
Broadfoot's (Wilmington, N.C.)
Broadfoot's (Wendell, N.C.)
Burke's (Memphis, Tenn.)
Cape (Mashpec, Mass.)
Carolina (Charlotte, N.C.)
Cather/Brown (Birmingham, Ala.)
C. Dickens (Atlanta, Ga.)
Choctaw (Jackson, Miss.)
Civil War (So. Miami, Fla.)
Cleland's (Portsmouth, N.H.)
Collectors' (Richmond, Va.)
Cottonwood (Baton Rouge, La.)
Crabtree (Signal Mtn., Tenn.)

Downs (Marietta, Ga.)
Edger (Hastings, Mich.)
R E (Fairhope, Ala.)
Essential (Centreville, Va.)
Evans (Savannah, Ga.)
Evans (Woodstock, Va.)
Fox (Madison, Tenn.)
Frontier (Bryan, Texas)
Garret (Clinton, N.Y.)
Ginsberg (Petersburg, Va.)
Grimshaw (Randolph, Mass.)
Grossblatt (Dallas, Texas)
Guidon (Scottsdale, Ariz.)
Gustafson (Chicago, Ill.)
Havemeyer (Skaneafeles, N.Y.)
Heflin (Brentwood, Tenn.)
Henry (Berwyn, Ill.)
Hensel (Belle Chasse, La.)
Heritage (Columbus, Ohio)
Hess (Andover, Mass.)
Hill (Kingsport, Tenn.)
Hill Haven (Barton, Vt.)
Hilton Village (Newport News, Va.)
Hist. Realia (Wooster, Ohio)
History (Long Valley, N.J.)
Hodgson (Syracuse, N.Y.)
Hooper's (Leesburg, Va.)
Hoosier (Indianapolis, Ind.)
Hope Farm (Cornwallville, N.Y.)
House (Worcester, Mass.)
Hughes (Williamsport, Pa.)
Jenkins (Austin, Texas)
JFF (Manhasset, N.Y.)
Katt (Los Angeles, Calif.)
King (Detroit, Mich.)
Lien (Minneapolis, Minn.)
Lincoln (Delmar, N.Y.)
Lincoln (Chambersburg, Pa.)
Lurate (Jackson, Miss.)
Lynn (Worthington, Ohio)
MacDonald's (Eustis, Maine)

Memory (Battle Creek, Mich.)
Mil-Air (Compton, Calif.)
Military (New York, N.Y.)
Morningside (Dayton, Ohio)
Mt. Falcon (Greeley, Colo.)
Mt. Sterling (Mt. Sterling, Ky.)
Newman (Chicago, Ill.)
Old Erie (Cleveland, Ohio)
Old Favs. (Richmond, Va.)
Old Quenzel (Pt. Tobacco, Md.)
Owens (Richmond, Va.)
Pandich (Asheville, N.C.)
Photographica (New York, N.Y.)
Pipkin (Rock Hill, S.C.)
Prairie (Springfield, Ill.)
Printed (Savannah, Ga.)
Quechee (Quechee, Vt.)
Research (Fremont, Neb.)
Robbins (Greenville, S.C.)
Rybski (Chicago, Ill.)
Sayers (Andrews, Texas)
Shelton (Tampa, Fla.)
Soldier (New York, N.Y.)
Stone Mtn. (Stone Mountain, Ga.)
Swinford (Paris, Ill.)
Swiss (St. Louis, Mo.)
Tappin (Atlantic Bch., Fla.)
Tauscher (Bristol, Va.)
Totty (Lunenburg, Mass.)
Traveller (Laredo, Texas)
Unicorn (Trappe, Md.)
Valley (Galena, Ill.)
Vintage (Iowa City, Iowa)
Von Blon's (Waco, Texas)
Walett (Abington, Mass.)
Woolf's (Atlanta, Ga.)
Yankee (Williamson, N.Y.)
Yankee (Rochester, N.Y.)
Yesteryear (Atlanta, Ga.)
Zellner's (Easton, Pa.)

Greek & Roman Classics

Abelard (Toronto, Ont.)
Alibi (New Haven, Conn.)
Allen (Philadelphia, Pa.)
Atticus (Toronto, Ont.)
Black Oak (Berkeley, Calif.)
Bolerium (San Francisco, Calif.)
Books By (Derby, Conn.)
Burrows (Downers Grove, Ill.)
Chimera (Palo Alto, Calif.)
Christoffersen (Mamaroneck, N.Y.)
Cooper's (Decatur, Ga.)

Doukas (Kalamazoo, Mich.)
Griffon (So. Bend, Ind.)
Hooked (Springfield, Mo.)
Hughes (St. Louis, Mo.)
Huntley (Claremont, Calif.)
Kregel's (Grand Rapids, Mich.)
Lawyer (Plains, Mont.)
Osgood (Rockport, Mass.)
Paperback (New York, N.Y.)
Pharos (New Haven, Conn.)
Ravenstree (Yuma, Ariz.)

Salloch (Ossining, N.Y.)
Schneeman (Chicago, Ill.)
Schreiber (Bronx, N.Y.)
2nd Story (Washington, D.C.)
Smith (Mt. Airy, Md.)
Stern (Chicago, Ill.)
Stuart (Yuma, Ariz.)
Tattered (Denver, Colo.)
Yesterday's (Ashfield, Mass.)

Collecting & Collectibles

About (Moline, Ill.)
Becker (New York, N.Y.)

Book Nook (Escondido, Calif.)
Collectrix (W. Hempstead, N.Y.)

Isador (Highland Park, Ill.)
Montlack (Old Bethpage, N.Y.)

Collection Development

Apfelbaum (Valley Stream, N.Y.)
Attic (Hodges, S.C.)
Baseball (Tucson, Ariz.)
Carr (Concord, N.H.)
Cheng (Boston, Mass.)
Chip's Shop (New York, N.Y.)
Davis (Sherman Oaks, Calif.)
Educo (Valhalla, N.Y.)

Gach (Columbia, Md.)
Hendsey (Epping, N.H.)
Int'l. Univ. (New York, N.Y.)
Kirksco (Ringwood, N.J.)
Klemm (Apple Valley, Calif.)
Noah's (Greenwood, S.C.)
Petrilla (Roosevelt, N.J.)
Phiebig (White Plains, N.Y.)

Printers' (Arlington, Mass.)
Printers' (Boston, Mass.)
Randall (Santa Barbara, Calif.)
Sylvester (Los Angeles, Calif.)
Thelema (King Bch., Calif.)
Todd (Cave Creek, Ariz.)
Zubel (Cleveland, Ohio)

Colorado

Books At (Boulder, Colo.)
Cache (Loveland, Colo.)
Claar (Golden, Colo.)
Colorado (Norwood, Colo.)
Ginsberg (Petersburg, Va.)
Grand (Redwood City, Calif.)
King's (Boulder, Colo.)

Color Plate Books

Adams (Chicago, Ill.)
Amer. Frag. (Escondido, Calif.)
Appelfeld (New York, N.Y.)
Arader (New York, N.Y.)
Arader (Atlanta, Ga.)
Arader (King of Prussia, Pa.)
Bargain (Long Beach, Calif.)
Bartfield (New York, N.Y.)
Book Block (Cos Cob, Conn.)
Book Chest (New York, N.Y.)
Buck (New York, N.Y.)
Clark (Baton Rouge, La.)
Cummins (New York, N.Y.)
Gavin (Leominster, Mass.)
Gregory (New York, N.Y.)
Gventer (So. Egremont, Mass.)
Harding (Wells, Maine)
Harris (Little Rock, Ark.)
High Ridge (Rye, N.Y.)
Hollander (Santa Monica, Calif.)
House (San Diego, Calif.)
Juvelis (Boston, Mass.)
M & S (Weston, Mass.)
Murray (Wilbraham, Mass.)
Parmer's (Sarasota, Fla.)
Phila. Print (Philadelphia, Pa.)
Raimo (Lancaster, Pa.)
Rhoads (Richmond, Ind.)
Ross (Woodland Hills, Calif.)
Sail (Newcastle, Maine)
Sail (Lexington, Ky.)
Scarlet (New Milford, Conn.)
Scopazzi (San Francisco, Calif.)
Shoebridge (Lafayette, N.Y.)
Tebbetts (Hallowell, Maine)
Ursus (New York, N.Y.)
Venkatesa (Tofino, B.C.)
Warren (Philadelphia, Pa.)
Whitlock's (New Haven, Conn.)
Wilsey (Olivebridge, N.Y.)
Worldwide (Cambridge, Mass.)
Zucker (New York, N.Y.)

Comic Books

Appalachia (Bluefield, W.Va.)
Attic (St. Pete., Fla.)
Book Broker (Evansville, Ind.)
Bookery (Fairborn, Ohio)
Book Exch. (Missoula, Mont.)
Book Exch. (Plainville, Conn.)
Bookie (E. Hartford, Conn.)
Book Mart (Brockton, Mass.)
Books/Comics #1 (Indianapolis, Ind.)
Books/Comics #2 (Indianapolis, Ind.)
Book Shoppe (Myrtle Bch., S.C.)
Book Traders (Winter Haven, Fla.)
Canford (Freeville, N.Y.)
Comic (New York, N.Y.)
Corner-Stone (Plattsburgh, N.Y.)
Curious Book (E. Lansing, Mich.)
Dennis (Seattle, Wash.)
Dragon's Lair (Dayton, Ohio)
Escargot (Brielle, N.J.)
Fantasy (Garden Grove, Calif.)
Gabbard (New Boston, Texas)
Golden Age (Seattle, Wash.)
Grand (Brooklyn, N.Y.)
Hall's (Arlington, Mass.)
Hughes (Holmes, N.Y.)
Imagine That (Pittsfield, Mass.)
Imagine That (No. Adams, Mass.)
Jolie's (Stuart, Fla.)

Krickett's (Battle Creek, Mich.)
Million (Cambridge, Mass.)
O'Leary's (Tacoma, Wash.)
Oxford Two (Atlanta, Ga.)
Pages (Reading, Mass.)
Pantechnicon (1000 Oaks, Calif.)
Passaic (Passaic, N.J.)

Pipkin (Rock Hill, S.C.)
Plant (Grass Valley, Calif.)
Reedmor (Philadelphia, Pa.)
Rodden's (Long Bch., Calif.)
2nd Time (Ventura, Calif.)
Stan's (Brockton, Mass.)
Tappin (Atlantic Bch., Fla.)

Treasure (Oakville, Ont.)
20th Century (Madison, Wisc.)
Village (New York, N.Y.)
Wellfleet (Wellfleet, Mass.)
Windsor (Windsor, Conn.)
Wonder (Frederick, Md.)
Zita (New York, N.Y.)

Commodities Trading

Trading Bever (Edmond, Okla.) Info (San Angelo, Texas) Windsor (Brightwaters, N.Y.)

Computers

Assoc. Stu. (Chico, Calif.)
Book Barn (Rochester, Mich.)
Bookmans (Tucson, Ariz.)

Dictionary (Leeds Point, N.J.)
Jay's (Marlboro, N.J.)
Oasis (San Deigo, Calif.)

Schaefer (Ossining, N.Y.)

Conjuring & Magic

Aladdin (Fullerton, Calif.) Meyerbooks (Glenwood, Ill.)

Connecticut

Hallberg (Hartford, Conn.)
Kapica (New Britain, Conn.)

Robinson (Windsor, Conn.)
Stone Of (Canterbury, Conn.)

Conservation

Buckabest (Palo Alto, Calif.)
Lawyer (Plains, Mont.)

Oblong (Millerton, N.Y.)
Old Print (Washington, D.C.)

Petersen (Davenport, Iowa)
Scace (Calgary, Alt.)

Conspiracies & Conspiracy Theory

Elm (Laurel, Md.)

President's (Washington, D.C.)

Sessions (Birmingham, Ala.)

Continental Books

Articles (Skokie, Ill.)
Benjamin (Hunter, N.Y.)
Cragsmoor (Cragsmoor, N.Y.)
Gabriel (Northampton, Mass.)
Hale (Washington, D.C.)

Mancevice (Worcester, Mass.)
McKittrick (Philadelphia, Pa.)
Midwest (Evanston, Ill.)
Offenbacher (Kew Gardens, N.Y.)
Phiebig (White Plains, N.Y.)

Raimo (Lancaster, Pa.)
Rootenberg (Sherman Oaks, Calif.)
Stuart (Yuma, Ariz.)
1000 Words (Exeter, N.H.)
Trebizond (New Preston, Conn.)

Cookbooks

Assoc. Stu. (Chico, Calif.)
Bonmark (Plainview, N.Y.)
Bookman (Grand Haven, Mich.)
Books/Comics #2 (Indianapolis, Ind.)
Books & Co. (San Francisco, Calif.)
Book Stop (Dearborn Hgts., Mich.)
Book/Tackle (Watch Hill, R.I.)
Charkoudian (Newton, Mass.)
Cilleyville (Andover, N.H.)

Connolly (Vista, Calif.)
Cookbooks (Yuma, Ariz.)
Cotswold (Medina, Ohio)
Forgotten (St. Simon Isl., Ga.)
Gore (San Gabriel, Calif.)
Grapevine (San Mateo, Calif.)
Jane Addams (Champaign, Ill.)
Memory (Battle Creek, Mich.)
Nelson's (Albany, N.Y.)
Northeast (Ocean City, N.J.)
Old Cook. (Haddonfield, N.J.)

Pell's (Delray Bch., Fla.)
Rohrer (Downers Grove, Ill.)
Sandys (Albertson, N.Y.)
Sebert (Mt. Nebo, W.Va.)
Sorrenti (Palatine, Ill.)
Tempest (Waitsville, Vt.)
Thomas (Oak Park, Ill.)
Vargo's (Bozeman, Mont.)
Wilson (Bull Shoals, Ark.)
Words (San Deigo, Calif.)
Yesterday's (Hot Springs, Ark.)

Cooking

Allison (No. Bay, Ont.)
Annie's #1 (Portland, Ore.)
Annie's #2 (Portland, Ore.)
Antiquus (San Francisco, Calif.)
Appletree (Williford, Ark.)
Avocet (Corvallis, Ore.)
Bennett (White Plains, N.Y.)
Black Oak (Berkeley, Calif.)
Book Cellar (Brattleboro, Vt.)
Bookdales (Richfield, Minn.)
Book Gall. (Gainesville, Fla.)
Book Harbor (Fullerton, Calif.)
Bookmans (Tucson, Ariz.)
Book Nook (Escondido, Calif.)
Book OP (Adrian, Mich.)
Booksellers (St. Paul, Minn.)
Bookshelf (Concord, N.H.)
Book Store (Englewood, N.J.)
Books Unltd. (Nat'l City, Calif.)
Book/Tackle (Chestnut Hill, Mass.)
Bowling (Rancho Palos Verdes, Calif.)
Brew (New Milford, Conn.)
Calico Cat (Ventura, Calif.)
Cape (Mashpec, Mass.)

Caravan (Los Angeles, Calif.)
Cellar (Eugene, Ore.)
Charkoudian (Newton, Mass.)
Chimera (Palo Alto, Calif.)
Cookbooks (Yuma, Ariz.)
Cornucopia (Syosset, N.Y.)
Einhorn (New York, N.Y.)
Foley (Bardstown, Ky.)
Footnote (Brooklyn, N.Y.)
Fox Hill (Palmer, Mass.)
Franklin (New York, N.Y.)
Frontier (Los Angeles, Calif.)
Gore (San Gabriel, Calif.)
Harbar (Casselberry, Fla.)
Hillman (New York, N.Y.)
Hittel (Ft. Lauderdale, Fla.)
Homestead (Marlborough, N.H.)
Household (Berkeley, Calif.)
Janus (Corea, Maine)
Janus (Hungtinton Stn., N.Y.)
Klein (Oak Park, Ill.)
Mawson (New Preston, Conn.)
Maxwell's (Stockton, Calif.)
Old Cook. (Haddonfield, N.J.)
On The (Chambersburg, Pa.)

Orange (Garberville, Calif.)
Pages (Newton, Conn.)
Photo (Columbus, Ohio)
Radio (New York, N.Y.)
Rule (Rochester, Mich.)
Safir (New York, N.Y.)
Scarlet (New Milford, Conn.)
Schroeder's (Dickinson, Texas)
Sherman (Burlington, Ont.)
Sunset (San Francisco, Calif.)
Theophrastus (Little Compton, R.I.)
This Old (Montclair, Calif.)
Thomas (Oak Park, Ill.)
Village (Hudson Falls, N.Y.)
Ward (Prospect, Ohio)
Weindling (Danbury, Conn.)
Wharf (Centreville, Md.)
Wilson (Kitchener, Ont.)
Wine (Ann Arbor, Mich.)
Wooden (Middlebourne, W.Va.)
Words (Cambridge, Mass.)
Yesterdays (Whitman, Mass.)

Counterfeit Stamps & Coins

Finn (W. Roxbury, Mass.)

Herst (Boca Raton, Fla.)

Crafts & Hobbies

Agranoff (Cincinnati, Ohio)
Appletree (Williford, Ark.)
Artcraft (Baldwin, Md.)
Book Cellar (Brattleboro, Vt.)

Book Fair (W. Palm Beach, Fla.)
Book House (St. Louis, Mo.)
Books In (Turlock, Calif.)
Bryant's (Provincetown, Mass.)

Clower (Charlottesville, Va.)
Cornucopia (Syosset, N.Y.)
Delp (Belding, Mich.)
Hook (Sebastopol, Calif.)

Nelson (Goshen, N.H.)
Nestler (Waldwick, N.J.)
Prufrock (Pasadena, Calif.)
Riverow (Owego, N.Y.)

Schroeder's (Dickinson, Texas)
Singer (Buena Park, Calif.)
10 Pound (Gloucester, Mass.)
Testa (No. Newark, N.J.)

This Old (Montclair, Calif.)
Trace (Peekskill, N.Y.)
Yesterdays (Whitman, Mass.)

Criminology

Alcala (San Diego, Calif.)
Arthurton (Palmyra, N.Y.)
Falls (Farmington Falls, Maine)
Heath (Toronto, Ont.)

Helmet (W. Islip, N.Y.)
Old Ver. (Olympia Falls, Ill.)
Roseman (Brooklyn, N.Y.)
Sadoff (Jenkintown, Pa.)

Silver (Redondo Bch., Calif.)
Smith (Montclair, N.J.)
Spade (Seattle, Wash.)

Curiosa

Scheiner (Brooklyn, N.Y.)

Stein (Gold Beach, Ore.)

Stormgart (Boston, Mass.)

Dance

Altman (New York, N.Y.)
Ballet (New York, N.Y.)
Battery (Forest Hills, N.Y.)
Books/Autographs (Eliot, Maine)
Books 'n (New York, N.Y.)
Bradshaw (Chicago, Ill.)
Dance Mart (Brooklyn, N.Y.)

Einhorn (New York, N.Y.)
Footnote (Brooklyn, N.Y.)
Golden Legend (Los Angeles, Calif.)
Hendsey (Epping, N.H.)
Katt (Los Angeles, Calif.)
Kellinger (Chambersburg, Pa.)

Loewenthal (Dover, N.J.)
Lubrano (So. Lee, Mass.)
Lyrical (Saratoga Spgs., N.Y.)
Maestro (Bayport, N.Y.)
Old Music (3 Oaks, Mich.)
Quill (Pinellas Park, Fla.)
Sand (Berkeley, Calif.)

Ballroom Dancing

Book Search (Brooklyn, N.Y.)

Roseman (Brooklyn, N.Y.)

Delaware

Attic (Newark, Del.)　　　　　Baldwin's (W. Chester, Pa.)

Derrydale Press

Anglers (Goshen, Conn.)　　　　Fisher (Williamsport, Pa.)　　　　Stewart (Portland, Ore.)
Calderwoods (Long Valley, N.J.)　　Highwood (Traverse City, Mich.)
Drabeck (Tuckahoe, N.Y.)　　　　Reliable (Paterson, N.J.)

Desert

Associated (Long Beach, Calif.)　　Ishtar (Canton, Mass.)　　　　Robinson (Yucca Valley, Calif.)
Carpenter (Balboa Isl., Calif.)　　Persoff (Alameda, Calif.)

Design

A B I (Santa Barbara, Calif.)　　Books/Books (Coral Gables, Fla.)　　Miller (Seattle, Wash.)
Anchor (Newport, R.I.)　　　　Cohen (Bronx, N.Y.)
Bamberger (San Francisco, Calif.)　Cutler (New York, N.Y.)

Architectural Design

Stubbs (New York, N.Y.)　　　　Winsted (Spg. Green, Wisc.)

Graphic Design

Badger (Appleton, Wisc.)   Blue Rider (Cambridge, Mass.)

Diaries & Narratives

Culpin's (Denver, Colo.)   Cummings (Stillwater, Minn.)   Wharf (Centreville, Md.)

Charles Dickens

Heindl (Rochester, N.Y.)   Vandoros (Middleton, Wisc.)

Emily Dickenson

Beyer (Stratford, Conn.)   Lowenberg (Lafayette, Calif.)

Dictionaries

Book Clearing (Larchmont, N.Y.)   Junius (Fairview, N.J.)   Reference (New York, N.Y.)
Books Unltd. (Nat'l City, Calif.)   Kripke (New York, N.Y.)   Rulon-Miller (Minneapolis, Minn.)
Heinman (New York, N.Y.)   Quest (Ft. Worth, Texas)

Disneyana

Dennis (Seattle, Wash.)   Golden Age (Seattle, Wash.)   Toy (San Francisco, Calif.)
Fantasy (Garden Grove, Calif.)   Pantechnicon (1000 Oaks, Calif.)

Documents

Aldrich (Groveland, Calif.)
Alford (Springfield, Va.)
Alsberg (Skokie, Ill.)
Apfelbaum (Valley Stream, N.Y.)
Barnes (Philadelphia, Pa.)
Batchelder (Ambler, Pa.)
B & B (Randolph, Mass.)
Bowling (Rancho Palos Verdes, Calif.)
Cohasco (Yonkers, N.Y.)
E. Coast (Wells, Maine)
5 Quail (Spg. Grove, Minn.)

Fortunate Finds (Warwick, R.I.)
Granat (Woodmere, N.Y.)
Guthman (Westport, Conn.)
Harris (Los Angeles, Calif.)
Howes (Brewster, Mass.)
Hughes (Williamsport, Pa.)
Johnson (Waltham, Mass.)
King's (Boulder, Colo.)
La Valois (New York, N.Y.)
Lion (New York, N.Y.)
Lowe (New York, N.Y.)
Manuscript (Southampton, Pa.)

Mitch's (Menlo Park, Calif.)
Noble (Greenville, Texas)
No. Country (Richmond, N.H.)
Prag (San Francisco, Calif.)
Richards (Templeton, Mass.)
Richshafer (Cincinnati, Ohio)
Roberts (W. Palm Bch., Fla.)
Scriptorium (Beverly Hills, Calif.)
Seaport (Stonington, Conn.)
Slifer (New York, N.Y.)
Wade (Cincinnati, Ohio)

Dogs

About (Toronto, Ont.)
All Edges (Silver Spg., Md.)
Bennett (Southold, N.Y.)
Butcher (Youngstown, Ohio)
Chang Tang (Peekskill, N.Y.)

Cowell (Bridgeport, Conn.)
Cronin (Worcester, Mass.)
Dog (Larchmont, N.Y.)
Dunn (Dallas, Ore.)
Hobby Helpers (Lima, N.Y.)

Ken-L (Newberg, Ore.)
Smith (Canaan, N.Y.)
Sportsman's (Manotick, Ont.)
Sterne (W. Redding, Conn.)
Williams (Bethany, Conn.)

Drama

Backstage (Eugene, Ore.)
McBride (Hartford, Conn.)

Nouveau (Jackson, Miss.)
NRS (New York, N.Y.)

Word (Montreal, Que.)
World Of (Willoughby, Ohio)

Drawings

Artcraft (Baldwin, Md.)
Black Sun (New York, N.Y.)
Childs (Boston, Mass.)
Frohnsdorff (Gaithersburg, Md.)

Hatch (Lenox, Mass.)
Holmes (Philadelphia, Pa.)
Leibowits (New York, N.Y.)
Schab (New York, N.Y.)

Tunick (New York, N.Y.)
Unique (Putney, Vt.)
Waite (Madison, Wisc.)
Warren (Philadelphia, Pa.)

Early Printed Books

Barber (Boston, Mass.)
Gilbert (Los Angeles, Calif.)
Goodrich (Englewood, N.J.)
Karmiole (Santa Monica, Calif.)

Mancevice (Worcester, Mass.)
Phila. Rare (Philadelphia, Pa.)
Rootenberg (Sherman Oaks, Calif.)
Rudolph (Portland, Ore.)

Schreiber (Bronx, N.Y.)
Stuart (Yuma, Ariz.)
Taylor (Austin, Texas)
University (New York, N.Y.)

Eastern Orthodoxy

Anglican (Saratoga Spgs., N.Y.)

Touchet (New York, N.Y.)

Economics

Battersby (Ardmore, Pa.)

Palinurus (Philadelphia, Pa.)

Thomas A. Edison

Book Den (Ft. Myers, Fla.)

Edison Hall (Edison, N.J.)

Education

Antique Books (Hamden, Conn.)
Assoc. Stu. (Chico, Calif.)
Eeyore's #1 (New York, N.Y.)

Eeyore's #2 (New York, N.Y.)
Guerin (Montreal, Que.)
Lowenberg (Lafayette, Calif.)

Una (St. Johnsbury, Vt.)

Egypt & Egyptology

Carousel (Tyler, Texas)　　　　　Hyman (Los Angeles, Calif.)

Electronics

Maier (Rockport, Mass.)　　　　　Morgan (Willowick, Ohio)

Emblem Books

Mancevice (Worcester, Mass.)　　　Salloch (Ossining, N.Y.)

Encyclopedias

Attic (St. Petersburg, Fla.)　　　　Junius (Fairview, N.J.)

Engineering

Allen's (Baltimore, Md.)　　　Chicago Law (Chicago, Ill.)　　　Palinurus (Philadelphia, Pa.)
Bolotin (Youngstown, Ohio)　　Hive (Easton, Pa.)　　　　　Tanditash (New York, N.Y.)
Book Barn (Rochester, Mich.)　Merlin's (Isla Vista, Calif.)　　Used (Dyer, Ind.)

Entomology

Hahn (Cottonwood, Ariz.)　　　Johnson (No. Bennington, Vt.)

Ephemera

Aboud (Stayton, Ore.)
Adams (W. Medway, Mass.)
aGatherin' (Wynantskill, N.Y.)
Agranoff (Cincinnati, Ohio)
Air Age (Tollhouse, Calif.)
Aldrich (Groveland, Calif.)
Ampersand (New York, N.Y.)
Anacapa (Berkeley, Calif.)
Andover (Andover, Mass.)
Anita's (Manchester, N.H.)
Annegan (San Marcos, Calif.)
Antiquaria (Franklin, Tenn.)
Apothecary (New York, N.Y.)
Argus (Sacramento, Calif.)
Avery (Plymouth, Mass.)
Bennett (White Plains, N.Y.)
Berk (Studio City, Calif.)
Blomgren (San Rafael, Calif.)
Book City (Hollywood, Calif.)
Book Mart (Brockton, Mass.)
Bowling (Rancho Palos Verdes, Calif.)
Bradshaw (Chicago, Ill.)
Brauns (Sacramento, Calif.)
Bridgman (Rome, N.Y.)
Brunsell's (Hanson, Mass.)
Burpee Hill (New London, N.H.)
Burstein (Waltham, Mass.)
Carney (Oneonta, N.Y.)
Carry Back (Haverhill, N.H.)
Casavant (Wayland, Mass.)
Chapman (Los Angeles, Calif.)
Choras (Weston, Mass.)
Cinema (Hollywood, Calif.)
Colebrook (Colebrook, Conn.)
Combs (Great Falls, Mont.)
Common (New Salem, Mass.)
Conway (Attleboro, Mass.)
Distinctive (Cedar City, Utah)
Dr. Nostalgia (Lynchburg, Va.)
Drew's (Santa Barbara, Calif.)
Drusilla's (Baltimore, Md.)
E. Coast (Wells, Maine)
Finn (W. Roxbury, Mass.)

Fortunate Finds (Warwick, R.I.)
Garrison (Williamsburg, Va.)
Ginsberg (Petersburg, Va.)
Glaeve (Madison, Wisc.)
Glasser (Assonet, Mass.)
Grandpa's (Troy, N.C.)
Hall (E. Longmeadow, Mass.)
Heritage (Southampton, Mass.)
Herlin (New York, N.Y.)
High Ridge (Rye, N.Y.)
Hobby Helpers (Lima, N.Y.)
Household (Berkeley, Calif.)
Howe (New York, N.Y.)
Howes (Brewster, Mass.)
Imagine That (Pittsfield, Mass.)
Imagine That (No. Adams, Mass.)
Jenison's (Canton, N.Y.)
Johnson (Waltham, Mass.)
Klemperer (New York, N.Y.)
Lambda (Washington, D.C.)
Lang (Amityville, N.Y.)
La Valois (New York, N.Y.)
Leach (Brattleboro, Vt.)
Lighthouse (St. Pete., Fla.)
Lloyd (Red Bank, N.J.)
Lombardo (Shoreham, N.Y.)
MacDonald's (Eustis, Maine)
Magazine (San Francisco, Calif.)
Margolis (Santa Fe, N.M.)
Maxwell's (Lima, N.Y.)
Memory (Corona Del Mar, Calif.)
Michauds (Iowa City, Iowa)
Minters (New York, N.Y.)
Miscellaneous (New Freedom, Pa.)
Mitch's (Menlo Park, Calif.)
Mobley (Schoharie, N.Y.)
Monarski (Syracuse, N.Y.)
Monie (Cooperstown, N.Y.)
Monie Shop (Cooperstown, N.Y.)
Morrill (Newton Centre, Mass.)
Mott (Sheffield, Mass.)
Murray (Wilbraham, Mass.)
Najarian (Newtown Sq., Pa.)
Necessary (E. Jordan, Mich.)

Newman (Battle Creek, Mich.)
New Steamship (El Cajon, Calif.)
N.Y. Bound (New York, N.Y.)
No. Country (Richmond, N.H.)
Nutmeg (Torrington, Conn.)
Old Almanack (Concord, N.H.)
Old Book (Bethel, Vt.)
Old Book (Morristown, N.J.)
Olinkiewicz (Shelter Isl., N.Y.)
Ordnance (Madison, Conn.)
Pages (Mt. Kisco, N.Y.)
Paper (So. Euclid, Ohio)
Paulson (Huntington, Mass.)
Pavlov (Dobbs Ferry, N.Y.)
Pennyroyal (Hopkinsville, Ky.)
Perata (Oakland, Calif.)
Performing (New York, N.Y.)
Petersons (Philadelphia, Pa.)
Pipkin (Rock Hill, S.C.)
Pleasant St. (Woodstock, Vt.)
Prag (San Francisco, Calif.)
Prairie (Springfield, Ill.)
Red Horse (Tampa, Fla.)
Resnick (Cazenovia, N.Y.)
Resnik (Roslyn Hgts., N.Y.)
Reston's (Amsterdam, N.Y.)
Richards (Templeton, Mass.)
Richardson (Westmont, N.J.)
Riverow (Owego, N.Y.)
Rogofsky (Glen Oaks, N.Y.)
Ross (Medina, N.Y.)
Rostenberg (New York, N.Y.)
Schmidt (Salem, Ore.)
Schoyer's (Pittsburgh, Pa.)
Shadow (Hillsboro, N.H.)
Slater (Tarrytown, N.Y.)
Southwest (Durango, Colo.)
Spellman (Brick Town, N.J.)
Storeybook (Sycamore, Ill.)
Talvin (Trafford, Pa.)
Terra (Churchville, N.Y.)
Valentino (Philadelphia, Pa.)
Vintage (Iowa City, Iowa)

Erotica

Antiq. Book (Portsmouth, N.H.)
Daunce (Buffalo, N.Y.)
Earl (Clarendon, N.Y.)
Elysian (Elmhurst, N.Y.)

Gatto (New York, N.Y.)
Martignette (Boston, Mass.)
Pollock (Palo Alto, Calif.)
Rush (Baltimore, Md.)

Scheiner (Brooklyn, N.Y.)
Stormgart (Boston, Mass.)
Vasta (New York, N.Y.)

Espionage

Elm (Laurel, Md.)
Sessions (Birmingham, Ala.)

Silver (Redondo Bch., Calif.)
Weston (Weston, Vt.)

Ethnology

Collins (Seattle, Wash.)

Exnowski (Warren, Mich.)

Evolution

Book Store (Lewisburg, W.Va.)
Calman (Syracuse, N.Y.)

19th Cent. (Baltimore, Md.)
Scientia (Arlington, Mass.)

Falconry

Buteo (Vermillion, S.D.)
Drabeck (Tuckahoe, N.Y.)

Natural (Scottsdale, Ariz.)
Peacock (Littleton, Mass.)

Watson (Buelah, Colo.)

Fantasy

See also
Science Fiction

Avalon (Hayward, Calif.)

Book Carnival (Orange, Calif.)

Bookfinders (Atlanta, Ga.)

Books Of (New York, N.Y.)
Borden (Portsmouth, R. I.)
Cellar (Providence, R.I.)
Change. (Santa Monica, Calif.)
Cheap St. (New Castle, Va.)
Choras (Weston, Mass.)
Circle West (Annapolis, Md.)
Currey (Elizabethtown, N.Y.)
Daunce (Buffalo, N.Y.)
Dawn (Ann Arbor, Mich.)
de la Ree (Saddle River, N.J.)
Drumm (Polk City, Iowa)
Fantasy (New York, N.Y.)

Fantasy (Carmichael, Calif.)
Gatto (New York, N.Y.)
Gavora (Santa Barbara, Calif.)
E. C. Gordon (New York, N.Y.)
Green Mtn. (So. Royalton, Vt.)
Hanley's (Chicago, Ill.)
Hooked (Springfield, Mo.)
JMD (Groton, N.Y.)
Kristiansen (Boston, Mass.)
Levin (Los Angeles, Calif.)
McFarland (Tampa, Fla.)
Midnight (Marietta, Ga.)
Old Favs. (Richmond, Va.)

Pantechnicon (1000 Oaks, Calif.)
Plant (Grass Valley, Calif.)
Printer's (Milldale, Conn.)
Printer's (Middletown, Conn.)
Sci Fict. (New York, N.Y.)
Slater (Bakersfield, Calif.)
Squires (Glendale, Calif.)
Sun Dance (Hollywood, Calif.)
White (New York, N.Y.)
Wilhite (Clearwater, Fla.)
Wyatt (San Diego, Calif.)
Xanadu (Bronx, N.Y.)

Farming, Ranching, & Livestock

Amer. SW (Amarillo, Texas)
Antique Books (Hamden, Conn.)
Backpocket (Sundance, Wyo.)
Battersby (Ardmore, Pa.)
Book Stall (Rockford, Ill.)
Broken Kettle (Akron, Iowa)
Dupley (Omaha, Neb.)

Evans (Woodstock, Va.)
Gibbs (State College, Pa.)
Hurley (Westmoreland, N.H.)
Info (San Angelo, Texas)
Jan-Er (Eureka Spgs., Ark.)
Log Cabin (Bigfork, Mont.)
Mt. Falcon (Greeley, Colo.)

Savoy (Lanesborough, Mass.)
2nd Life (Lanesborough, Mass.)
Sutley (Centralia, Wash.)
Underhill (Poughkeepsie, N.Y.)
Wilson (Kitchener, Ont.)
Woodburn (Hopewell, N.J.)
Wright (Waxahachie, Texas)

Fashion

Allen (Baltimore, Md.)
Annegan (San Marcos, Calif.)
Backstage (Eugene, Ore.)
Books/Buttons (Columbus, Ohio)

Cohen (Bronx, N.Y.)
Gventer (So. Egremont, Mass.)
Hard-To (Newton, Mass.)
Kane (Santa Cruz, Calif.)

Lincoln (San Jose, Calif.)
Performing (New York, N.Y.)
Shep (Lopez Isl., Wash.)
Wooden (Middlebourne, W.Va.)

Fiction

*See also
Literature*

Abra (Rochester, N.Y.)
All Books (Miami, Fla.)

Anacapa (Berkeley, Calif.)
Bay Side (Soquel, Calif.)

Bennington (Bennington, Vt.)
Biblioctopus (Idyllwild, Calif.)

Bibliofile (San Francisco, Calif.)
Biermaier's (Minneapolis, Minn.)
Bond (Reading, Mass.)
Book Case (Houston, Texas)
Book Disp. #1 (Columbia, S.C.)
Book Disp. #3 (Columbia, S.C.)
Book Exch. (Missoula, Mont.)
Book Finder (Geneva, N.Y.)
Bookman (Tybee Isl., Ga.)
Bookshelf (Miller, S.D.)
Book Shop (Beverly Farms, Mass.)
Book Store (San Mateo, Calif.)
Book Treasury (Nashville, Tenn.)
Bookwood (Westwood, N.J.)
Bush (Stonington, Maine)
Cabin/Pines (Potsdam, N.Y.)
Cape Collector (So. Harwich, Mass.)
Carduner (Philadelphia, Pa.)
Carmichael's (Louisville, Ky.)
Constant (Milwaukee, Wisc.)
Dabbs (Higginsville, Mo.)
Daedalus (Charlottesville, Va.)
Dakota (Eugene, Ore.)
Different (Des Moines, Iowa)
Dinkytown (Minneapolis, Minn.)
Diva (Coos Bay, Ore.)
Easton (Mt. Vernon, Wash.)
Ediger (Beaverton, Ore.)
Eldora's (Newberg, Ore.)
Fine (Rochester, Mich.)
4th Estate (New London, Conn.)
Galewitz (Orange, Conn.)
Glooscap (Pefferlaw, Ont.)
Glover (Cambridge, N.Y.)

Gordon (Pasadena, Calif.)
Grand (Brooklyn, N.Y.)
Grapevine (San Mateo, Calif.)
Gull Shop (Oakland, Calif.)
Haunted (Orleans, Mass.)
Hennessey (Peconic, N.Y.)
Heritage (Southampton, Mass.)
Hermit's (Wyoming, Pa.)
Herron (Rome, Ga.)
Hopper (Sunnyvale, Calif.)
Island (Isleboro, Maine)
Island (Mercer, Wash.)
Joyce (Martinez, Calif.)
Jumping (Hartford, Conn.)
Katonah (Katonah, N.Y.)
Kaufman (New York, N.Y.)
Keane (State College, Pa.)
Keck (Decatur, Ill.)
Kionke (Gowanda, N.Y.)
Kirch (Thornville, Ohio)
Knaus (Ft. Bragg, Calif.)
Lighthouse (Rye, N.Y.)
Links (3 Rivers, Mich.)
Lysecki (Winnipeg, Man.)
Main St. (Brooklyn, N.Y.)
McBride (Hartford, Conn.)
Michelli (Ogunquit, Maine)
M. & M. (E. Northport, N.Y.)
Modern (Huntingdon Valley, Pa.)
Monahan (New York, N.Y.)
Monroe (Fresno, Calif.)
Morelle (Haverhill, Mass.)
Much (Marblehead, Mass.)
999 (New York, N.Y.)
NRS (New York, N.Y.)

Old Benn. (Hancock, N.H.)
Old Book (Kennebunk, Maine)
Old Favs. (Toronto, Ont.)
Owen (Litchfield, Maine)
Owl (Greenwich, N.Y.)
Paper (Ft. Lauderdale, Fla.)
Paper (So. Euclid, Ohio)
Pharos (New Haven, Conn.)
Pierce (Oroville, Calif.)
Prosser (Chicago, Ill.)
Quadrant (Easton, Pa.)
Quill (Rockville, Md.)
Ralston (Fullerton, Calif.)
Ray (Baldwin Park, Calif.)
Reader's (Raleigh, N.C.)
Readmore (St. Louis, Mo.)
Rule (Rochester, Mich.)
St. Clair (Van Nuys, Calif.)
Shaw (Albany, N.Y.)
Sophia (Amherst, Mass.)
Starr (Boston, Mass.)
Strand (New York, N.Y.)
Tempest (Waitsville, Vt.)
Terrapin (Austin, Texas)
Terres (Minneapolis, Minn.)
Turkey (Westport, Conn.)
Valley (Amherst, Mass.)
Vinik (Tucson, Ariz.)
Vogt (Meadow Vista, Calif.)
Water Row (Sudbury, Mass.)
Webster's (Milwaukee, Wisc.)
Weindling (Danbury, Conn.)
Wessex (Menlo Park, Calif.)
Yesterdays (Whitman, Mass.)

Figure Skating

Cabinet Of (Watertown, Conn.)

Kuo (Atlanta, Ga.)

Fine Arts

Adams (W. Medway, Mass.)
Bamberger (San Francisco, Calif.)
Booknook (Evanston, Ill.)
Bookseller's (Chicago, Ill.)
Branford (Branford, Conn.)
Davis (Sherman Oaks, Calif.)

Globe (Northampton, Mass.)
Green Apple (San Francisco, Calif.)
Joslin (Concord, Mass.)
McGilvery (La Jolla, Calif.)
Metropolis (Royal Oak, Mich.)

Midnight (Clearwater, Fla.)
Phoenix (San Luis Obispo, Calif.)
Scheck (Scarsdale, N.Y.)
Schiller-Wapner (New York, N.Y.)
Skeans (Deer Isle, Maine)

Fires & Firefighting

Helmet (W. Islip, N.Y.)

Kern (Glendale, Ariz.)

Moran (Rocky Point, N.Y.)

First Editions

Abacus (Santa Fe, N.M.)
Abra (Rochester, N.Y.)
Abrams (Atlanta, Ga.)
Academy (New York, N.Y.)
Albatross (San Francisco, Calif.)
Albatross II (Tiburon, Calif.)
Alphabet (Toronto, Ont.)
Ancient (Santa Fe, N.M.)
Andover (Andover, Mass.)
Andover Sq. (Knoxville, Tenn.)
Antic Hay (W. Caldwell, N.J.)
Apfelbaum (Valley Stream, N.Y.)
Argosy (New York, N.Y.)
Armitage (Miamisburg, Ohio)
Attic (Newark, Del.)
Balthasar's (Maryknoll, N.Y.)
Bankside (Westport, Conn.)
Bauman (Atlantic City, N.J.)
Bauman (Philadelphia, Pa.)
Bernard (Rockville, Md.)
Biblioctopus (Idyllwild, Calif.)
Blackmer (North Ferrisburg, Vt.)
Black Sun (New York, N.Y.)
Bond (Roanoke, Va.)

Bonmark (Plainview, N.Y.)
Book Baron (Anaheim, Calif.)
Book Bin (Kingston, Ont.)
Bookdales (Richfield, Minn.)
Book Farm (Henniker, N.H.)
Book Harbor (Fullerton, Calif.)
Book Haven (Lancaster, Pa.)
Book Mart (San Antonio, Texas)
Bookmarx (Roslyn, N.Y.)
Book Stop (Las Vegas, Nev.)
Book Trader (Naples, Fla.)
Book Treasury (Nashville, Tenn.)
Braiterman (Baltimore, Md.)
Burke's (Memphis, Tenn.)
Burrows (Downers Grove, Ill.)
Captain's (Ashville, N.C.)
Carlitz (Philadelphia, Pa.)
Carriage (Northford, Conn.)
Carry Back (Haverhill, N.H.)
Cherokee (Hollywood, Calif.)
Chip's Shop (New York, N.Y.)
Chloe's (Sacramento, Calif.)
Cohen (Youngstown, Ohio)
Colebrook (Colebrook, Conn.)

Collectabilia (Valley Stream, N.Y.)
Common (New Salem, Mass.)
Cummins (New York, N.Y.)
Cummins (Pottersville, N.J.)
Dee Cee (Nyack, N.Y.)
Desmarais (Palo Alto, Calif.)
Detering (Houston, Texas)
Dysinger (Brunswick, Maine)
Edison Hall (Edison, N.J.)
Eldredge (Vineyard Haven, Mass.)
Else Fine (Dearborn, Mich.)
E. Wharton (Oakton, Va.)
Fantasy (San Francisco, Calif.)
First (Chicago, Ill.)
Fischler (San Jose, Calif.)
Fisher (Williamsport, Pa.)
Fleming (New York, N.Y.)
Ford (Lake Worth, Fla.)
Fox (Tacoma, Wash.)
Fugitive (Nashville, Tenn.)
Fullam (Babylon, N.Y.)
Gardner (New York, N.Y.)
Garnett (St. Louis, Mo.)
Glooscap (Pefferlaw, Ont.)

Glover's (Lexington, Ky.)
Goodman (St. Paul, Minn.)
Grabowski (Ronks, Pa.)
Grt. Southwest (Santa Fe, N.M.)
Grub Street (Detroit, Mich.)
Gud (Elmhurst, N.Y.)
Hamill (Chicago, Ill.)
Heritage (Los Angeles, Calif.)
Hermitage (Denver, Colo.)
History (Long Valley, N.J.)
Hobson's (Jenkintown, Pa.)
Holmes (Oakland, Calif.)
Holmes (Philadelphia, Pa.)
Horne (Lakeland, Fla.)
Houle (Los Angeles, Calif.)
Isaiah (Worcester, Mass.)
Jack London (Glen Ellen, Calif.)
Jaffe (Haverford, Pa.)
Johnny (Manchester, Vt.)
Johnson (Syracuse, N.Y.)
Joslin (Springfield, Mass.)
Joyce (Chicago, Ill.)
Jumping (Hartford, Conn.)
Juvelis (Boston, Mass.)
Karmiole (Santa Monica, Calif.)
King (Detroit, Mich.)
Konigsmark (Wayne, Pa.)
Kraft (Palm Desert, Calif.)
Kraus (Millwood, N.Y.)
Kristiansen (Boston, Mass.)
Lambda (Washington, D.C.)
Leaves (Ann Arbor, Mich.)
Littrup (Bay City, Mich.)
Lorson's (Fullerton, Calif.)
Lovett (Winston-Salem, N.C.)
Macauluso (Kennett Sq., Pa.)
Macksey (Baltimore, Md.)
MacManus (Philadelphia, Pa.)

Marion (Auburn Hills, Mich.)
Marshall Field (Chicago, Ill.)
Martin (La Grange, Ill.)
McCaslin (Ironton, Mo.)
McCosh (Excelsior, Minn.)
McGahern (Ottawa, Ont.)
McManus (Woodbury, Conn.)
Memory (Grand Rapids, Mich.)
Merlin's (Providence, R.I.)
Midnight (Marietta, Ga.)
Miele (New York, N.Y.)
M. & M. (E. Northport, N.Y.)
Modern (Huntingdon Valley, Pa.)
Monroe (Fresno, Calif.)
Mostly (Carthage, Mo.)
M & S (Weston, Mass.)
Mullins (Encinitas, Calif.)
Myers (Boulder, Colo.)
Mystery (Huntingdon Valley, Pa.)
Nelson (New Bedford, Mass.)
Nisula (Okemos, Mich.)
No. Country (Richmond, N.H.)
Norumbega (Houston, Texas)
Ohio (Mansfield, Ohio)
Ohio (Cincinnati, Ohio)
Old Benn. (Hancock, N.H.)
Old Mont. (Monterey, Calif.)
Owl Creek (Mt. Vernon, Ohio)
Pacific (Honolulu, Haw.)
Pageant (New York, N.Y.)
Perkinson (Deer Isle, Maine)
Phalen (Chicago, Ill.)
Pinkney (Granby, Conn.)
Porter (Phoenix, Ariz.)
Pride (Ballston Lake, N.Y.)
Randall (Santa Barbara, Calif.)
Rare Book (Freehold, N.J.)
Reprint (Washington, D.C.)

Ron Dot (Greensburg, Ohio)
Sample (Stoneham, Mass.)
Sanderson (Stockbridge, Mass.)
Scallawagiana (Salt Lake City, Utah)
Scott (Portland, Maine)
Slater (Tarrytown, N.Y.)
Smith (Boxborough, Mass.)
Starosciak (San Francisco, Calif.)
Sykes (No. Weare, N.H.)
Talbothay's (Aurora, N.Y.)
Tamerlis (Mamaroneck, N.Y.)
Terres (Minneapolis, Minn.)
Thelema (King Bch., Calif.)
Tintagel (E. Springfield, N.Y.)
Truepenny (Tucson, Ariz.)
Tumarkin (New York, N.Y.)
Turkey (Westport, Conn.)
221 (Westlake Village, Calif.)
Typographeum (Francestown, N.H.)
Tyson (Providence, R.I.)
Venkatesa (Tofino, B.C.)
Verde (Winsted, Conn.)
Wangner's (Montclair, N.J.)
West L.A. (Los Angeles, Calif.)
West's (Elm Grove, Wisc.)
White's (Asbury Park, N.J.)
Whitlock's (New Haven, Conn.)
Wild (Larchmont, N.Y.)
Woodbury (Woodbury, Conn.)
Ximenes (New York, N.Y.)
Yankee (Rochester, N.Y.)
Yellin (Northridge, Calif.)
Yesteryear (Atlanta, Ga.)
Zubel (Cleveland, Ohio)

Modern First Editions

Aardvark (San Francisco, Calif.)
About (Toronto, Ont.)
Aladdin (Fullerton, Calif.)
Alphabet (Toronto, Ont.)

Amer. City (Denver, Colo.)
Amitin (St. Louis, Mo.)
Ampersand (New York, N.Y.)
Anacapa (Berkeley, Calif.)

Antic Hay (W. Caldwell, N.J.)
Antiq. Book (Toledo, Ohio)
Antiques/Art (Seattle, Wash.)
Antiquus (San Francisco, Calif.)

Appel (Mt. Vernon, N.Y.)
Armchair (No. Orange, Mass.)
Armens (Iowa City, Iowa)
Asendorf (Los Altos Hills, Calif.)
Associates (Falls Church, Va.)
Authors (Dundee, Ore.)
Avery (Plymouth, Mass.)
Babcock (Derry, N.H.)
Bailey (New York, N.Y.)
Bargain (San Diego, Calif.)
Barnstable (New York, N.Y.)
Baroque (Hollywood, Calif.)
Bayshore (Van Nuys, Calif.)
Bay Side (Soquel, Calif.)
Beasley (Chicago, Ill.)
Beatific (Schenectady, N.Y.)
Bebbah (Andover, Kan.)
Beckhorn (Dobbs Ferry, N.Y.)
Bernard (Rockville, Md.)
Berry (Kingston, Ont.)
Between (Old Bridge, N.J.)
Beyer (Stratford, Conn.)
Bibelots (Seattle, Wash.)
Bishop (Steubenville, Ohio)
Blomgren (San Rafael, Calif.)
Book-Bind (Anaheim, Calif.)
Book Disp. #3 (Columbia, S.C.)
Bookfinders (Atlanta, Ga.)
Book Sail (Orange, Calif.)
Books/Autographs (Eliot, Maine)
Bookseller's (Chicago, Ill.)
Boston Annex (Boston, Mass.)
Bowie (Seattle, Wash.)
Brazenhead (New York, N.Y.)
Broad Ripple (Indianapolis, Ind.)
Buddenbrooks (Boston, Mass.)
Burley/Books (Toledo, Ohio)
Butterworth (Claremont, Calif.)
Camelot (Baltimore, Md.)
C. Dickens (Atlanta, Ga.)
Cellar (Providence, R.I.)
Chaney (Ossining, N.Y.)
Chartwell (New York, N.Y.)
Chip's Search (New York, N.Y.)
Chloe's (Sacramento, Calif.)
City Spirit (Denver, Colo.)
Colburn (Atlanta, Ga.)
Collins (San Francisco, Calif.)
Collins (Seattle, Wash.)

Cook (Los Angeles, Calif.)
Currey (Elizabethtown, N.Y.)
Debra (No. Hills, Pa.)
Decline (Clinton, Wisc.)
DeFreitas (Montreal, Que.)
Dermont (Onset, Mass.)
Diamond (Rochester, N.Y.)
Dictionary (Leeds Point, N.J.)
Dinkytown (Minneapolis, Minn.)
Dourgarian (Walnut Creek, Calif.)
Duschnes (New York, N.Y.)
Elliott (New York, N.Y.)
Especially (Burke, Va.)
Evlen (Centerport, N.Y.)
First Edtns. (Richmond, Va.)
Firsts (New York, N.Y.)
Gilann (Darien, Conn.)
Gotham (New York, N.Y.)
Grt. Expect. (Staten Isl., N.Y.)
Green Dolphin (Portland, Ore.)
Greene (Rockville Centre, N.Y.)
Gryphon #1 (New York, N.Y.)
Hall (San Francisco, Calif.)
Halloran (St. Louis, Mo.)
Hansen (Carlsbad, Calif.)
Havemeyer (Skaneafeles, N.Y.)
Hawley (Louisville, Ky.)
Heller (Cleveland, Ohio)
Hermitage (Denver, Colo.)
Hi (Canutillo, Texas)
Hirschtritt's (Silver Spg., Md.)
Hittel (Ft. Lauderdale, Fla.)
Horowitz (New York, N.Y.)
Howland (Jamaica Plain, Mass.)
Hyde Park (Tampa, Fla.)
In Our (Cambridge, Mass.)
Invisible (Berkeley, Calif.)
Jack's (Mt. Prospect, Ill.)
Jaffe (Haverford, Pa.)
Jay's (Marlboro, N.J.)
Joe the Pro (Santa Barbara, Calif.)
Johnson (Syracuse, N.Y.)
Jumping (Hartford, Conn.)
Keane (State College, Pa.)
Key (Key West, Fla.)
Kishi (New York, N.Y.)
Lambert (Hancock, N.H.)
Legacy (Iowa City, Iowa)
Lemuria (Jackson, Miss.)

Library (Dallas, Texas)
Lift (Brockport, N.Y.)
Lincoln (Chambersburg, Pa.)
Link (Redding, Calif.)
Linthicum (Tacoma, Wash.)
Lion's (Salisbury, Conn.)
Lopez (Hadley, Mass.)
Lucas (Fairfield, Conn.)
Maestro (Bayport, N.Y.)
Maiden (W. Chester, Pa.)
Main St. (Brooklyn, N.Y.)
Mannatt (San Diego, Calif.)
Manor (Huntington Valley, Pa.)
Maple St. (New Orleans, La.)
Marks (Rochester, N.Y.)
Marlowe's (Boston, Mass.)
Mason (Toronto, Ont.)
Matthews (Ft. Erie, Ont.)
Max Gate (Kankakee, Ill.)
Maxwell's (Stockton, Calif.)
Memorable (Stone Mtn., Ga.)
Mendoza (New York, N.Y.)
Mermaid (Oakland, Calif.)
Michaels (Eugene, Ore.)
Minkoff (Grt. Barrington, Mass.)
Mitchell (Pasadena, Calif.)
M. & M. (E. Northport, N.Y.)
Modern (Huntingdon Valley, Pa.)
Monahan (New York, N.Y.)
Morrow (New York, N.Y.)
Neville (Santa Barbara, Calif.)
Nouveau (Jackson, Miss.)
Nudel (New York, N.Y.)
Old N.Y. (Atlanta, Ga.)
O'Malley (Kingston, R.I.)
O'Neal (Boston, Mass.)
On The (Chambersburg, Pa.)
Otzinachson (Allenwood, Pa.)
Pages #2 (Green Bay, Wisc.)
Paper (Ft. Lauderdale, Fla.)
Peters (Van Nuys, Calif.)
Pettler (Los Angeles, Calif.)
Phoenix (New York, N.Y.)
Photo (Columbus, Ohio)
Plain (Arlington Hgts., Ill.)
Polyanthos (Huntington, N.Y.)
Potter (Santa Fe, N.M.)
Prestianni (Penfield, N.Y.)
Prosser (Chicago, Ill.)

Quill (Rockville, Md.)
Ralston (Fullerton, Calif.)
Ransom (Amherst, N.Y.)
Rare Book (New York, N.Y.)
Reese (New Haven, Conn.)
Respess (Durham, N.C.)
Respess (Chapel Hill, N.C.)
Ridge (Stone Ridge, N.Y.)
Rieber (Thomasville, Ga.)
Riverrun (Hastings, N.Y.)
Ross (Redwood City, Calif.)
Russell (Montreal, Que.)
Sackheim (Tucson, Ariz.)
Sample (Stoneham, Mass.)
Sand (Berkeley, Calif.)
Sanderson (Stockbridge, Mass.)

Scott (Stonington, Conn.)
Seluzicki (Portland, Ore.)
Serendipity (Berkeley, Calif.)
Sewards' (Providence, R.I.)
Shelton (Tampa, Fla.)
Signed (Pt. Washington, N.Y.)
Smith (Pleasant Hill, Calif.)
Southpaw (Roxbury, Mass.)
Stahr (Los Angeles, Calif.)
Stephens (Hastings, N.Y.)
Strand Rare (New York, N.Y.)
Sylvester (Los Angeles, Calif.)
Temares (Plandome, N.Y.)
Temple (Toronto, Ont.)
1023 (Omaha, Neb.)
This Old (Montclair, Calif.)

Todd (Cave Creek, Ariz.)
Transition (San Francisco, Calif.)
Turlington (Pittsboro, N.C.)
12th St. (Santa Monica, Calif.)
Vintage (Wheaton, Ill.)
Waiting (Cambridge, Mass.)
Watermark W. (Wichita, Kan.)
Water Row (Sudbury, Mass.)
Wessex (Menlo Park, Calif.)
Wise (Baldwin Pl., N.Y.)
Woolf's (Atlanta, Ga.)
Woolmer (Revere, Pa.)
Yankee (Plymouth, Mass.)
Yellin (Northridge, Calif.)
Yesterday's (Oak Park, Mich.)
Young (Dobbs Ferry, N.Y.)

Fish & Ichthyology

Hahn (Cottonwood, Ariz.)
Johnson (No. Bennington, Vt.)

Socolof (Bradenton, Fla.)
Tolliver's (Los Angeles, Calif.)

Fishing & Angling

Amer. Eagle (Topsfield, Mass.)
Anderson (Auburn, Mass.)
Anglers (Goshen, Conn.)
Bagley (Fredericton, N.B.)
Bibliomania (Schenectady, N.Y.)
Bicentennial (Kalamazoo, Mich.)
Blomberg (Rockford, Ill.)
Book Place (Columbia, S.C.)
Bookstack (Elkhart, Ind.)
Book/Tackle (Chestnut Hill, Mass.)
Book/Tackle (Watch Hill, R.I.)
Bowman (Bedford, N.Y.)
Butcher (Youngstown, Ohio)
Callahan (Peterborough, N.H.)
Campfire (Evansville, Ind.)
Collector's (Phoenix, Ariz.)
Combs (Great Falls, Mont.)
Connecticut (E. Haddam, Conn.)

Constant (Milwaukee, Wisc.)
Cottonwood (Baton Rouge, La.)
Dorn (Johntown, N.Y.)
Dunn (Newport, Vt.)
5 Quail (Spg. Grove, Minn.)
Good News (Rossville, Ind.)
Gunnerman (Auburn Hgts., Mich.)
Hall (Chambersburg, Pa.)
Halloran (St. Louis, Mo.)
Highwood (Traverse City, Mich.)
Hittel (Ft. Lauderdale, Fla.)
Holsten (Excelsior, Minn.)
Ishii (Seattle, Wash.)
Johnny (Manchester, Vt.)
Kalanja (Trafford, Pa.)
Kreinheder (Warrensburg, N.Y.)
Marcher (Okla. City, Okla.)
Martin's (Fairbanks, Alk.)

McGovern (Berwyn, Ill.)
McLaughlin's (Cottage Grove, Ore.)
Memory (Grand Rapids, Mich.)
No. Woods (Duluth, Minn.)
Old Town (Tempe, Ariz.)
On The (Chambersburg, Pa.)
Pell's (Delray Bch., Fla.)
Pettinger (Russell, Iowa)
Pisces (Albion, Mich.)
Riling (Philadelphia, Pa.)
Sackett (Grants Pass, Ore.)
Smith (Canaan, N.Y.)
Sporting (Rancocas, N.J.)
Sporting (Palmerton, Pa.)
Sportsman's (Manotick, Ont.)
Staten (Harwich, Mass.)
Sterne (W. Redding, Conn.)

Stewart (Portland, Ore.)
Suhm (Westfield, Mass.)
Tayaut (No. Hatley, Que.)

Ten Eyck (Southboro, Mass.)
Thunderbird (Aldergrove, B.C.)
Toxophilite (Simsbury, Conn.)

Tryon (Johnstown, N.Y.)
Webfoot (Portland, Ore.)
Wildwood (Old Forge, N.Y.)

Florida

Americana (Coral Gables, Fla.)
Blue Moon (Clearwater, Fla.)
Book Den (Ft. Myers, Fla.)
Book Gall. (Gainesville, Fla.)
Brassers (Seminole, Fla.)
Carling's (Pomona Park, Fla.)

Helikon (De Land, Fla.)
Hyde Park (Tampa, Fla.)
King (Pensacola, Fla.)
Lighthouse (St. Pete., Fla.)
Mickler's (Chuluota, Fla.)
Red Horse (Tampa, Fla.)

San Marco (Jacksonville, Fla.)
Shelton (Tampa, Fla.)
Wake (Ft. Lauderdale, Fla.)
Wood (Tampa, Fla.)

Folklore

Abintra (Morris, N.Y.)
Arond (Lexington, Mass.)
Books Of (New York, N.Y.)
Book Store (Englewood, N.J.)
Country (Plainfield, Vt.)
Cummings (Stillwater, Minn.)
Darby (Darby, Pa.)

Dohm's (Olympia, Wash.)
Facsimile (New York, N.Y.)
E. C. Gordon (New York, N.Y.)
Horizon (Seattle, Wash.)
Info (San Angelo, Texas)
La Galeria (Las Vegas, N.M.)
Legacy (Hatboro, Pa.)

Morrison (Santa Monica, Calif.)
Rouse (Wattsville, Va.)
Serpent (Oneonta, N.Y.)
Shapiro (New York, N.Y.)
Wilson (Kitchener, Ont.)

Food & Drink

Book Cellar (Fullerton, Calif.)
Cohen (St. Louis, Mo.)

Ginsberg (Petersburg, Va.)
Sommer (Niagara Falls, N.Y.)

Football

Kashmanian (No. Providence, R.I.)　　Sullivan (Chicago, Ill.)

Fore-Edge Paintings

Benson (W. Cornwall, Conn.)　　Levine (Savannah, Ga.)　　Shoebridge (Lafayette, N.Y.)
Burleson (Atlanta, Ga.)　　Pages #1 (Green Bay, Wisc.)　　Spector (Jackson Hgts., N.Y.)
Family Album (Glen Rock, Pa.)　　Pages #2 (Green Bay, Wisc.)　　Verde (Winsted, Conn.)
Flynn (Lake Forest, Ill.)　　Raimo (Lancaster, Pa.)　　Weitz (New York, N.Y.)
Hartfield (Ann Arbor, Mich.)　　Rohr (Byfield, Mass.)　　Zeitlin (Los Angeles, Calif.)

Foreign Affairs

Cheng (Boston, Mass.)　　McCullough (Los Angeles, Calif.)
Lion (Indianapolis, Ind.)　　Ryan (Columbus, Ohio)

Foreign Languages

Adler's (Evanston, Ill.)　　Bookery (Ithaca, N.Y.)　　Macksey (Baltimore, Md.)
Alfabooks (Arlington, Va.)　　Fortuna (Kirkland, Wash.)　　Seville (Pensacola, Fla.)
Appel (Mt. Vernon, N.Y.)　　Gull Shop (Oakland, Calif.)　　Tisza (Chestnut Hill, Mass.)
Asian Books (Cambridge, Mass.)　　Hammer Mtn. (Schenectady, N.Y.)　　Webster's (Milwaukee, Wisc.)
Book Cellar (Bethesda, Md.)　　Inner Circle (New York, N.Y.)　　Wessex (Menlo Park, Calif.)
Book End (Monterey, Calif.)　　Joyce (Martinez, Calif.)

Forestry

No. Woods (Duluth, Minn.)　　Sorsky (Fresno, Calif.)　　Whistles (Rossville, Ga.)
Pomona (Rockton, Ont.)　　Sutley (Centralia, Wash.)

Freemasonry

Hubert (Walnut Creek, Calif.)
Roth (Norwalk, Ohio)

Scallawagiana (Salt Lake City, Utah)

Ziagos (Lowell, Mass.)

Freethought

First (Chicago, Ill.)

Rosselot (Grand View, N.Y.)

Waldo (Rockton, Ill.)

French Books

Benoit (Montreal, Que.)
Breadloaf (E. Middlebury, Vt.)
Gagnon (Quebec, Que.)

La Valois (New York, N.Y.)
Midwest (Evanston, Ill.)
Polyanthos (Huntington, N.Y.)

Rose (New York, N.Y.)
Rutgers (Highland Park, N.J.)
Zucker (New York, N.Y.)

Robert Frost

Bean (Biddeford, Maine)

Recovery (Greensboro, Vt.)

Vermont (Middlebury, Vt.)

Fur Trade

Beaver (Daly City, Calif.)
Doerres (Wilton, Iowa)

Garret (Clinton, N.Y.)
Log Cabin (Bigfork, Mont.)

Pettinger (Russell, Iowa)
Sykes (No. Weare, N.H.)

Gambling

Finer (Greenfield, Mass.)
Gambler's (Las Vegas, Nev.)
Meyerbooks (Glenwood, Ill.)

Servant's (Atlantic City, N.J.)
Smith (Montclair, N.J.)
Sun Dance (Hollywood, Calif.)

Walker (San Leandro, Calif.)
Wilshire (No. Hollywood, Calif.)

Games & Pastimes

Bookery (Fairborn, Ohio)
Checker (Dubuque, Iowa)
Dennis (Seattle, Wash.)
Eeyore's #1 (New York, N.Y.)
Eeyore's #2 (New York, N.Y.)

Hall's (Arlington, Mass.)
Iuspa (Newark, N.J.)
Meyerbooks (Glenwood, Ill.)
National (Brooklyn, N.Y.)
Terra (Churchville, N.Y.)

U.S. Games (New York, N.Y.)
Wilshire (No. Hollywood, Calif.)
Young (New York, N.Y.)

Gardening & Horticulture

Adams (W. Medway, Mass.)
Amer. Botanist (Brookfield, Ill.)
Anchor (Newport, R.I.)
Appletree (Williford, Ark.)
Barn Owl (Wellesley, Mass.)
Bennett (Southold, N.Y.)
Bibby (Gold Hill, Ore.)
Black Swan (Sacramento, Calif.)
Bookstack (Elkhart, Ind.)
Buchanan (New York, N.Y.)
Catbird (Portland, Ore.)
Celnick (Bronx, N.Y.)
Chimney (Bridgeport, Conn.)
Chimney (Scotts Valley, Calif.)
Cider (Exeter, N.H.)
Clark's (Spokane, Wash.)
Cobble Crt. (Litchfield, Conn.)
Cooper Fox (Millbrook, N.Y.)

Cotton Hill (Laconia, N.H.)
Farnsworth (W. Cornwall, Conn.)
Glaister (New York, N.Y.)
Hurley (Westmoreland, N.H.)
Jackson (Berkeley, Calif.)
Jan-Er (Eureka Spgs., Ark.)
Knaus (Ft. Bragg, Calif.)
Landscape (Exeter, N.H.)
Lawyer (Plains, Mont.)
Lion's (Salisbury, Conn.)
Masi (Montague, Mass.)
Mawson (New Preston, Conn.)
McQuerry (Jacksonville, Fla.)
Nadolny (Kensington, Conn.)
999 (New York, N.Y.)
Ockett (Bryant Pond, Maine)
Orange (Garberville, Calif.)
Owl (Greenwich, N.Y.)

Pomona (Rockton, Ont.)
Savoy (Lanesborough, Mass.)
2nd Life (Lanesborough, Mass.)
Stone House (Elkton, Md.)
Stroud (Williamsburg, W.Va.)
Sutley (Centralia, Wash.)
Tempest (Waitsville, Vt.)
Theophrastus (Little Compton,
   R.I.)
Toad (Berkeley, Calif.)
Underhill (Poughkeepsie, N.Y.)
Wayner (Ft. Payne, Ala.)
White's (Asbury Park, N.J.)
Whitlock (Bethany, Conn.)
Wilkerson (Lincoln, Mass.)
Wine (Ann Arbor, Mich.)
Woodburn (Hopewell, N.J.)
Wooden (Ann Arbor, Mich.)

Geneology

Aceto (Sarasota, Fla.)
Appalachia (Bluefield, W.Va.)
Collectors' (Richmond, Va.)
Goodspeed's #1 (Boston, Mass.)
Goodspeed's #2 (Boston, Mass.)
Gratz (Bluffton, Ohio)

Harbor Hill (Harrison, N.Y.)
Henderson (Nashua, N.H.)
Herron (Rome, Ga.)
Murphy (Salem, Mass.)
New Engl. (Bennington, Vt.)
Pratt (E. Livermore, Maine)

Sharp's (No. Hollywood, Calif.)
Tuttle (Ruthland, Vt.)
Virginia (Berryville, Va.)
Winter (Pittsfield, Maine)

General

Abbey (Dearborn, Mich.)
Abbey (Los Angeles, Calif.)
About (Toronto, Ont.)
Abstract (Indianapolis, Ind.)
Academy (Denver, Colo.)
Agranoff (Cincinnati, Ohio)
Aion (Boulder, Colo.)
Albatross (San Francisco, Calif.)
Alford (Springfield, Va.)
Allison (No. Bay, Ont.)
Allston (Allston, Mass.)
Alta's (Sonora, Calif.)
Amdur (Mansfield, Conn.)
Americana (Coral Gables, Fla.)
Americanist (Pottstown, Pa.)
Ancramdale (Ancramdale, N.Y.)
Anderson's (Whittier, Calif.)
Andrews (Niles, Minn.)
Anita's (Manchester, N.H.)
Annie's (Acton, Mass.)
Antiq. Book (Portsmouth, N.H.)
Antiq. Book (Toledo, Ohio)
Archer's (Kent, Ohio)
Armchair (No. Orange, Mass.)
Arnolds (Traverse City, Mich.)
Arond (Lexington, Mass.)
Asendorf (Los Altos Hills, Calif.)
Askins (New Lebanon, N.Y.)
Athena (Kalamazoo, Mich.)
Attic (Laurel, Md.)

Attic (London, Ont.)
Attic (Torrington, Conn.)
Attic (St. Pete., Fla.)
Avenue (Boston, Mass.)
Avol's (Madison, Wisc.)
Backlot (Oberlin, Ohio)
Badger (Appleton, Wisc.)
Bagley (Fredericton, N.B.)
Bank (Northfield, Ill.)
Bargain (Jackson, Mich.)
Bargain (Norfolk, Va.)
Barrow (Concord, Mass.)
Bartlett St. (Medford, Ore.)
Basil's (Salt Lake City, Utah)
Batta (Toronto, Ont.)
Bay Shore (Bay Shore, N.Y.)
Bay Window (Florence, Ore.)
Bean (Niantic, Conn.)
Beaver (Portland, Ore.)
Beckham's (New Orleans, La.)
Bedford's (Ellsworth, Maine)
Ben Franklin (U. Nyack, N.Y.)
Berkelouw (Los Angeles, Calif.)
Berry Hill (Deansboro, N.Y.)
Bevington (Terre Haute, Ind.)
Bibliolatree (E. Hampton, Conn.)
Bibliomania (Delaware, Ohio)
Bibliomania (Berkeley, Calif.)
Bibliomania (Oakland, Calif.)
Bicentennial (Kalamazoo, Mich.)

Biermaier's (Minneapolis, Minn.)
Big #1 (Detroit, Mich.)
Big #2 (Detroit, Mich.)
Binkin's (Brooklyn, N.Y.)
Bishop (Corea, Maine)
B. & J. (Rego Park, N.Y.)
Black Ace (Denver, Colo.)
Black Swan (Lexington, Ky.)
Blake (Fairfield, Conn.)
Bland's (Sharon, Mass.)
Block (Thornwood, N.Y.)
Blue Lantern (San Diego, Calif.)
Boardman (Camden, N.Y.)
Boise Mart (Boise, Idaho)
Bonners (Bonners Ferry, Ind.)
Book Admirer (Norwalk, Conn.)
Book/Art (Dothan, Ala.)
Book Barn (Stockton Spgs., Maine)
Book Barn (Bend, Ore.)
Book Baron (Anaheim, Calif.)
Book Barrel (Los Angeles, Calif.)
Book Bin (Albany, Ore.)
Book Bin (Corvallis, Ore.)
Book Broker (Evansville, Ind.)
Book Buyers (Houston, Texas)
Bookcase (Greenfield, N.H.)
Bookcase (St. Clair Shores, Mich.)
Book Case (Houston, Texas)
Book Cellar (Temple, Texas)
Book Collector (Newton, Mass.)

Book Co. (Pasadena, Calif.)
Book Connect. (Mariposa, Calif.)
Book Den E. (Oak Bluffs, Mass.)
Book Den (Ft. Myers, Fla.)
Book Disp. (Decatur, Ga.)
Book Disp. #2 (Columbia, S.C.)
Book Fair (Ft. Lauderdale, Fla.)
Book Fair (Eugene, Ore.)
Book Faire (Woodland, Calif.)
Bookfinder (Eureka, Calif.)
Book Finder (Geneva, N.Y.)
Book Gall. (Gainesville, Fla.)
Book Haven (Lancaster, Pa.)
Book House (Williamsburg, Va.)
Book House (Bridgeton, Mo.)
Book House (Minneapolis, Minn.)
Book-In (Stillwater, N.Y.)
Book Lady (Savannah, Ga.)
Bookloft (Grt. Barrington, Mass.)
Book Loft (Solvang, Calif.)
Bookmark (Prosser, Wash.)
Book Mark (Philadelphia, Pa.)
Book Mart (Asheville, N.C.)
Book Nook (Manitowoc, Wisc.)
Book Nook (Ft. Smith, Ark.)
Book Nook (Escondido, Calif.)
Book Nook (Yakima, Wash.)
Booknook (Evanston, Ill.)
Book OP (Adrian, Mich.)
Book Pedlars (Cundy's Harbor,
  Maine)
Bookpeople (Wadena, Minn.)
Book Place (Richland, Wash.)
Book Place (Columbia, S.C.)
Book Quest (New York, N.Y.)
Book Rack (Aurora, Colo.)
Book Revue (Clearwater, Fla.)
Book Room (Coral Gables, Fla.)
Books/Begonias (Columbia,
  Mont.)
Books/Birds (Vernon, Conn.)
Books/Comics #1 (Indianapolis,
  Ind.)
Books & Co. (San Francisco,
  Calif.)
Bookseller (Evansville, Ind.)
Bookseller (Denver, Colo.)
Bookseller (Akron, Ohio)
Booksellers (St. Paul, Minn.)

Bookseller's (Chicago, Ill.)
Books End (Syracuse, N.Y.)
Bookshelf (Billings, Mont.)
Bookshelf (Miller, S.D.)
Bookshelf (Concord, N.H.)
Bookshop (Warner Robins, Ga.)
Book Shop (Walnut Creek, Calif.)
Book Shop (Beverly Farms, Mass.)
Booksmith (Oak Park, Ill.)
Books 'n (Springfield, Mass.)
Books/Things (Boca Raton, Fla.)
Book Stop (Lafayette, Calif.)
Book Stop (Poulsbo, Wash.)
Book Stop (Petoskey, Mich.)
Book Stop (Dearborn Hgts., Mich.)
Bookstore (Valdosta, Ga.)
Book Store (Lewisburg, W.Va.)
Book Store (Englewood, N.J.)
Booksville (Montrose, Calif.)
Book Trader (Muskegon, Mich.)
Book Treasury (Nashville, Tenn.)
Book Vault (Beaverton, Ore.)
Bookwood (Westwood, N.J.)
Bookworm (Wanatah, Ind.)
Boston Annex (Boston, Mass.)
Boyce (Carmel, N.Y.)
Bradford (Bennington, Vt.)
Brady (Assonet, Mass.)
Brattle Book (Boston, Mass.)
Breadloaf (E. Middlebury, Vt.)
Brew (New Milford, Conn.)
Brick House (Morristown Crnrs.,
  Vt.)
Bridgman (Rome, N.Y.)
Bridgton (Bridgton, Maine)
Brisky (Micanopy, Fla.)
British (No. Weymouth, Mass.)
Broadfoot's (Wendell, N.C.)
Broad Ripple (Indianapolis, Ind.)
Broken Kettle (Akron, Iowa)
Brown (Toledo, Ohio)
Brown Bag (Dobbs Ferry, N.Y.)
Brownbag (Rochester, N.Y.)
Browsers' (Olympia, Wash.)
Brubacher (Stevens, Pa.)
Brused (Pullman, Wash.)
Bryn Mawr (New Haven, Conn.)
Bryn Mawr (Rochester, N.Y.)
Bryn Mawr (White Plains, N.Y.)

Bryn Mawr (New York, N.Y.)
Bryn Mawr (Albany, N.Y.)
Bryn Mawr (Pittsburgh, Pa.)
Buchanan (New York, N.Y.)
Buckabest (Palo Alto, Calif.)
Buckingham (New Canton, Va.)
Buffalo (Amherst, N.Y.)
Burt (Laconia, N.H.)
Burton's (Greenport, N.Y.)
Bush (Stonington, Maine)
Busy Hermit (Niles, Mich.)
Bygone (Dearborn, Mich.)
Caldwell (Arkadelphia, Ark.)
Calhouns' (Geneva, N.Y.)
Calico Cat (Ventura, Calif.)
Cameron's (Portland, Ore.)
Carlson (Portland, Maine)
Carney (Oneonta, N.Y.)
Carpenter (Barlow, Ohio)
Carr (Concord, N.H.)
Carr (New York, N.Y.)
Casperson (Niles, Mich.)
Cellar (Eugene, Ore.)
Chadds (Chadds Ford, Pa.)
Chapter 1 (Hamilton, Mont.)
Chapter/Verse (Maywood, N.J.)
Chatham (Madison, N.J.)
Cheshire (Yakima, Wash.)
Chester (Chester, Conn.)
Chinook (Colo. Spgs., Colo.)
Choras (Weston, Mass.)
ChoreoGraphica (Boston, Mass.)
Cider (Exeter, N.H.)
Cielec (Chicago, Ill.)
Cilleyville (Andover, N.H.)
City Wide (Brooklyn, N.Y.)
Claar (Golden, Colo.)
Cleland's (Portsmouth, N.H.)
Clinton (Clinton, N.Y.)
Coachman (La Porte, Ind.)
Cobble Crt. (Litchfield, Conn.)
Cohen (Bonita Spgs., Fla.)
Colebrook (Colebrook, Conn.)
Collectabilia (Valley Stream, N.Y.)
Collector's (Pt. Washington, N.Y.)
Colonial (W. Lebanon, N.H.)
Columbus (San Francisco, Calif.)
Common (New Salem, Mass.)
Communications (New Haven,

Conn.)
Connolly (Vista, Calif.)
Consolo (Mansfield, Ohio)
Constant (Denver, Colo.)
Corner-Stone (Plattsburgh, N.Y.)
Cotton Hill (Laconia, N.H.)
Coventry (Coventry, Conn.)
Cover (Ft. Myers, Fla.)
Cowell (Bridgeport, Conn.)
Cranbury (Cranbury, N.J.)
Crawford's (Cedar Rapids, Iowa)
Cunningham (Portland, Maine)
Curiosity (St. Joseph, Mich.)
Curious Book (E. Lansing, Mich.)
Curious Raven (Detroit, Mich.)
Daedalus (Charlottesville, Va.)
Dakota (Eugene, Ore.)
Dartmouth (Hanover, N.H.)
Darvill's Book (Eastsound, Wash.)
deBeurs (Dexter, Maine)
De Chene (Los Angeles, Calif.)
Denning (Salisbury Mills, N.Y.)
Denver (Stockton, Calif.)
Denver Fair (Denver, Colo.)
Doe Run (Cochranville, Pa.)
Donaldson's (Knoxville, Tenn.)
Doutt (Big Flats, N.Y.)
Dragoman (Annapolis, Md.)
Dragon's Lair (Dayton, Ohio)
Drew's (Santa Barbara, Calif.)
Dugas (Orlando, Fla.)
Dunham's (Bedford, Mass.)
Dupley (Omaha, Neb.)
Earth (Littleton, N.H.)
Eastman (Springvale, Maine)
Edison Hall (Edison, N.J.)
Editions (Boiceville, N.Y.)
Educo (Valhalla, N.Y.)
Eeyore (Cotati, Calif.)
Egg Harbor (Egg Harbor, N.J.)
Eldora's (Newberg, Ore.)
Elliot's (Northford, Conn.)
Elliot Bay (Seattle, Wash.)
Elmcress (So. Hamilton, Mass.)
Elm St. (Lancaster, N.H.)
Elsner (New York, N.Y.)
Emery's (Contoocook, N.H.)
Erie (Erie, Pa.)
Ernst (Selinsgrove, Pa.)

Evergreen (Ft. Worth, Texas)
Everyday (Burlington, Vt.)
Ex Libris (Sun Valley, Idaho)
Falmouth (Falmouth, Mass.)
Far Corners (Mobile, Ala.)
Field (Georgetown, Mass.)
Finders (Dallas, Texas)
1st Edtn. (Muskegon Hgts., Mich.)
First (Chicago, Ill.)
Fisher (Cobleskill, N.Y.)
5 Quail (Spg. Grove, Minn.)
Fletcher's (Salado, Texas)
Fly Creek (E. Lansing, Mich.)
Flynn (Lake Forest, Ill.)
Forest Park (Ft. Wayne, Ind.)
Fortuna (Kirkland, Wash.)
Fox Hill (Palmer, Mass.)
Fran's (Philadelphia, Pa.)
Frazier (Gilford, N.H.)
Frisch (Livingston, N.Y.)
Frontier (Los Angeles, Calif.)
Front (Van Nuys, Calif.)
Galewitz (Orange, Conn.)
Carcia (Turlock, Calif.)
Gereghty (Sepulveda, Calif.)
GFS (Great River, N.Y.)
Gilann (Darien, Conn.)
Gilman (New York, N.Y.)
Globe Crnr. (Boston, Mass.)
Grand (Brooklyn, N.Y.)
Grandpa's (Troy, N.C.)
Grandview (Hudson, N.Y.)
Gray (Garden City, N.Y.)
Green Acre (Wells, Vt.)
Green Apple (San Francisco, Calif.)
Griffith (Griffith, Ind.)
Grunewald (Kansas City, Mo.)
Gryphon #1 (New York, N.Y.)
Guerin (Montreal, Que.)
Guerrera (Lawrence, Mass.)
Gull Shop (Oakland, Calif.)
Gull Gall. (Oakland, Calif.)
Gutenberg's (Rochester, N.Y.)
Gventer (So. Egremont, Mass.)
Halpern (Flushing, N.Y.)
Hamill (Chicago, Ill.)
Hammer (Santa Barbara, Calif.)
Harbar (Casselberry, Fla.)

Harold's (St. Paul, Minn.)
Harris (Northfield, Mass.)
Hartmann (Morganton, N.C.)
Harvard (Stockton, Calif.)
Harvard (Boston, Mass.)
Haunted (Victoria, B.C.)
Haunted (Cuttingsville, Vt.)
Hawks (Savanna, Ill.)
Headley (St. Catherines, Ont.)
Heartwood (Charlottesville, Va.)
Hennesseys (Saratoga Spgs., N.Y.)
Henrietta's (Salisbury, Md.)
Heritage (Southampton, Mass.)
Hermit's (Wyoming, Pa.)
Herron (Rome, Ga.)
Hirschtritt's (Silver Spg., Md.)
History (Long Valley, N.J.)
Hobbit (Westfield, N.J.)
Hole (Reedsport, Ore.)
Hollyoak (Wilmington, Del.)
Hollywood City (Hollywood, Calif.)
Holmes (San Francisco, Calif.)
Homestead (Marlborough, N.H.)
Hooper's (Leesburg, Va.)
Hopper (Sunnyvale, Calif.)
House (Tallahassee, Fla.)
Howard (Burlingame, Calif.)
Huckleberry (Centralia, Wash.)
Hyde Park (Tampa, Fla.)
Hyde Park (Boise, Idaho)
Irene's (So. Gardner, Mass.)
Isador (Highland Park, Ill.)
Isaiah (Worcester, Mass.)
Ishii (Seattle, Wash.)
Island (Isleboro, Maine)
Jacksonville (Jacksonville, Ore.)
Jane Addams (Champaign, Ill.)
Jerry's (Farmington, Mich.)
J. & L. (Mesa, Ariz.)
Johnson's (Springfield, Mass.)
Johnson's (Los Angeles, Calif.)
Johnson (Promise City, Iowa)
John Steele (Litchfield, Conn.)
Joyce (Martinez, Calif.)
Kaplan (New York, N.Y.)
Katonah (Katonah, N.Y.)
Keck (Decatur, Ill.)
Kensington (Kensington, Md.)

Key (Key West, Fla.)
Kieffer (Los Angeles, Calif.)
Kirksco (Ringwood, N.J.)
Kitemaug (Spartanburg, S.C.)
Klein (Oak Park, Ill.)
Klemperer (New York, N.Y.)
Klenett (Brooklyn, N.Y.)
Kraus (Millwood, N.Y.)
Krause (Warrington, Fla.)
Krickett's (Battle Creek, Mich.)
Kugelman (Denver, Colo.)
Ladner (Orleans, Mass.)
Lady (Lower Lake, Calif.)
Laird (Chicago, Ill.)
Lambert (Hancock, N.H.)
Lambert (Mission Hills, Calif.)
Lambeth (San Antonio, Texas)
Lang (Amityville, N.Y.)
Lasley (Berkeley, Ill.)
Leekley (Winthrop Harbor, Ill.)
Leelanau (Leland, Mich.)
Leo (Toledo, Ohio)
Levine's (Shokan, N.Y.)
Librairie (Royal) (New Orleans, La.)
Librairie (Chartres) (New Orleans, La.)
Librarium (E. Chatham, N.Y.)
Library (Ferndale, Mich.)
Lilac Hedge (Norwich, Vt.)
Lincoln (Delmar, N.Y.)
Lincoln (Chambersburg, Pa.)
Links (3 Rivers, Mich.)
Lippincott (Bangor, Maine)
Literary (Pittsburgh, Pa.)
Little (Hinsdale, Ill.)
Little (U. Montclair, N.J.)
Little (Missoula, Mont.)
Little (Detroit, Mich.)
Littlewoods (Waukesha, Wisc.)
Lloyd (Red Bank, N.J.)
Lobster (Spruce Head, Maine)
Lord (Marshfield, Mass.)
Lorson's (Fullerton, Calif.)
Lost (Santa Barbara, Calif.)
Lovett (Winston-Salem, N.C.)
Lucas (Fairfield, Conn.)
Lumb (Somersville, Conn.)
Lutes (Okla. City, Okla.)

Lutz (Washington C. H., Ohio)
Lynch (Sepulveda, Calif.)
Lyrical (Saratoga Spgs., N.Y.)
Lysecki (Winnipeg, Man.)
Macauluso (Kennett Sq., Pa.)
MacKendrick (Manchester, Conn.)
Mackensen (Lake San Marcos, Calif.)
MacLeod's (Vancouver, B.C.)
Madonna (Combermere, Ont.)
Maelstrom (San Francisco, Calif.)
Mandala (Daytona Bch., Fla.)
Many (Lake Hill, N.Y.)
Maple St. (New Orleans, La.)
Margolis (Santa Fe, N.M.)
Marion (Auburn Hills, Mich.)
Market (Idaho Falls, Idaho)
Marley (Oldwick, N.J.)
Mason's (Wabash, Ind.)
McCarty (Cincinnati, Ohio)
McDonald's (San Francisco, Calif.)
McGill (New City, N.Y.)
McMillen (Staten Isl., N.Y.)
Means (Charlotte, N.C.)
Medallion (Wellesley, Mass.)
Metacomet (Providence, R.I.)
Meyerfeld (San Carlos, Calif.)
Meyerson (Brooklyn, N.Y.)
Michael's (Okla. City, Okla.)
Michauds (Iowa City, Iowa)
Michiana (Niles, Mich.)
Midnight (Clearwater, Fla.)
Mill (Craftsbury Common, Vt.)
Minnehaha (Minneapolis, Minn.)
Monie Shop (Cooperstown, N.Y.)
Monie (Cooperstown, N.Y.)
Montclair (Montclair, N.J.)
Moody (Johnson City, Tenn.)
Morelle (Haverhill, Mass.)
Mostly (Carthage, Mo.)
Moye (Seattle, Wash.)
Mrouse (New Orleans, La.)
Mullins (Encinitas, Calif.)
Munson (Mattoon, Ill.)
Murray (Wilbraham, Mass.)
Myers (Sequim, Wash.)
Mystic (Mystic, Conn.)
Nebraska (Lincoln, Neb.)
Necessary (E. Jordan, Mich.)

Needle (Chelmsford, Mass.)
Nelson (Goshen, N.H.)
Nelson's (Schenectady, N.Y.)
Nelson's (Troy, N.Y.)
Nelson's (Albany, N.Y.)
New/Used (Warwick, N.Y.)
Nisula (Okemos, Mich.)
Northingham (Hamilton Sq., N.J.)
Novel (Fairfax, Va.)
Nutmeg (Torrington, Conn.)
Oblong (Millerton, N.Y.)
Odds (Indianapolis, Ind.)
Old Almanack (Concord, N.H.)
Old Benn. (Hancock, N.H.)
Old Barn (Forsyth, Ill.)
Old Book (Bethel, Vt.)
Old Books (Brunswick, Maine)
Old Book (San Francisco, Calif.)
Old Book (Morristown, N.J.)
Old Book (Fairlee, Vt.)
Old City (St. Augustine, Fla.)
Old Edtns. (Buffalo, N.Y.)
Old Emery (Derry, N.H.)
Old Eugene (Eugene, Ore.)
Old Favs. (Toronto, Ont.)
Old Geog. (Sparks, Md.)
Old Oregon (Portland, Ore.)
Old Town (Tempe, Ariz.)
Old Ver. (Olympia Falls, Ill.)
Olinkiewicz (Shelter Isl., N.Y.)
Once Upon (W. Hempstead, N.Y.)
One (Bradenton, Fla.)
Ookkees (Olympia, Wash.)
Oriole (Fremont, Calif.)
Osgood (Rockport, Mass.)
Otento (San Diego, Calif.)
Otzinachson (Allenwood, Pa.)
Out-Of (San Clemente, Calif.)
Owen (Litchfield, Maine)
Owl (Bryn Mawr, Pa.)
Owl (Greenwich, N.Y.)
Oxford At (Atlanta, Ga.)
Oxford (Atlanta, Ga.)
Oxford Two (Atlanta, Ga.)
Pacific (Honolulu, Haw.)
Pages (Reading, Mass.)
Pages #1 (Green Bay, Wisc.)
Pages #2 (Green Bay, Wisc.)
Paper (Ft. Lauderdale, Fla.)

Papyrus (Chatham, Mass.)
Parnassus (Yarmouthport, Mass.)
Parnassus (Boise, Idaho)
Passaic (Passaic, N.J.)
Past (Windsor, Ont.)
Pat's (Salina, Kan.)
Paulhus (Wells, Maine)
Paul's (Madison, Wisc.)
Paulson (Huntington, Mass.)
Payson (Belmont, Mass.)
People's (Flemington, N.J.)
Perkinson (Deer Isle, Maine)
Phalen (Chicago, Ill.)
Phoenix (Freeville, N.Y.)
Phoenix (Royal Oak, Mich.)
Pioneer (Seattle, Wash.)
Plain (Arlington Hgts., Ill.)
Pleasant St. (Woodstock, Vt.)
Pohrt (Flint, Mich.)
Potter (Santa Fe, N.M.)
Preservation (Evanston, Ill.)
Pride (Ballston Lake, N.Y.)
Pro Libris (Bangor, Maine)
Publix (Cleveland, Ohio)
Quebecoise (Montral, Que.)
Raintree (Eustis, Fla.)
Rainy (Halifax, N.S.)
Rainy (Fitzwilliam, N.H.)
Rainy (Lexington, Mass.)
Rausch (Bloomington, Ind.)
Ray's (Hartford, Vt.)
Readbeard's (Marion, Ind.)
Reading (Mexico, Ind.)
Red Bridge (Kansas City, Mo.)
Red House (Montgomery, Ala.)
Renaisscance (Lincolnshire, Ill.)
Reston's (Amsterdam, N.Y.)
River Oaks (Jay, Maine)
Riverrun (Hastings, N.Y.)
Robbins (Greenville, S.C.)
Robertson (Levittown, Pa.)
Robin's (Philadelphia, Pa.)
Robinson (Yucca Valley, Calif.)
Robinson (St. Pete., Fla.)
Rodden's (Long Bch., Calif.)
Rodgers (Hillsdale, N.Y.)
Rohe (Chicago, Ill.)
Rosselot (Grand View, N.Y.)
Royal (Charlemont, Mass.)

Ruby's (New York, N.Y.)
Rule (Rochester, Mich.)
Russell (Montreal, Que.)
St. Clair (Van Nuys, Calif.)
San Marco (Jacksonville, Fla.)
Schlossberg (Newton, Mass.)
Schneeman (Chicago, Ill.)
Schoen (Northampton, Mass.)
Schooner (Halifax, N.S.)
Schoyer's (Pittsburgh, Pa.)
Scribe's (Newport, R.I.)
Seattle (Seattle, Wash.)
2nd Story (Bethesda, Md.)
2nd Story (Washington, D.C.)
Serpent (Oneonta, N.Y.)
Sewards' (Providence, R.I.)
Shadow (Hillsboro, N.H.)
Shaw (Albany, N.Y.)
Shire (Franklin, Mass.)
Shuey (Elk Grove, Calif.)
Shuhi (Morris, Conn.)
Significant (Cincinnati, Ohio)
Sloat (Flemington, N.J.)
Smith (Amherst, Mass.)
Smith (Boxborough, Mass.)
Smith's (Brewster, Mass.)
Smith (Waynesville, N.C.)
Snowbound (Marquette, Mich.)
Snowbound (Norridgeweck,
  Maine)
Snyder (Pittsburgh, Pa.)
Sommer (Niagara Falls, N.Y.)
Southwest (Durango, Colo.)
Spencer's (Vancouver, Wash.)
Stage (Boulder, Colo.)
Stanley (Wilder, Vt.)
Stan's (Oceanside, N.Y.)
Stan's (Brockton, Mass.)
Starr (Boston, Mass.)
Stilwell (Morgantown, W.Va.)
Stockman (Palmyra, N.Y.)
Stone (Huntsville, Ala.)
Stone House (Elkton, Md.)
Stone Of (Canterbury, Conn.)
Strand (New York, N.Y.)
Strand Rare (New York, N.Y.)
Suhm (Westfield, Mass.)
Summerhouse (Dayton, Wyo.)
Tainters (Temple, N.H.)

Tattersalls (Conyers, Ga.)
10 Pound (Gloucester, Mass.)
1023 (Omaha, Neb.)
Toadstool (Keene, N.H.)
Totty (Lunenburg, Mass.)
Traveler (Union, Conn.)
Trident (Boulder, Colo.)
Truepenny (Tucson, Ariz.)
Tryon (Johnstown, N.Y.)
Tuckers (Pittsburgh, Pa.)
Tupper (Vancouver, B.C.)
Tuttle (Ruthland, Vt.)
Twice-Loved (Youngstown, Ohio)
Tyson (Providence, R.I.)
Unicorn (Trappe, Md.)
Varner (Belton, Mo.)
Varney's (Casco, Maine)
Vathek (Ft. Lee, N.J.)
Victorian (Stockton Spgs., Maine)
Village (Bellingham, Wash.)
Village (Hudson Falls, N.Y.)
Village (Littleton, N.H.)
Village (Rochester, N.Y.)
Village (Amherst, N.Y.)
Vintage (Wheaton, Ill.)
Visually (Gilford, N.H.)
Vol. I (Greenville, S.C.)
Walzer (Providence, R.I.)
Wangner's (Montclair, N.J.)
Washington (Washington Cr., Pa.)
Watson (Exeter, N.H.)
Wayside (Westerly, R.I.)
Wellfleet (Wellfleet, Mass.)
Wells (Wells, Maine)
West L.A. (Los Angeles, Calif.)
Westport (Kansas City, Mo.)
Wharton (Toronto, Ont.)
Whitlock (Bethany, Conn.)
Willis (Columbus, Ohio)
Willow (Englewood, Colo.)
Windsor (Windsor, Conn.)
Wise (Baldwin Pl., N.Y.)
Wolf (Orcutt, Calif.)
Womrath's (Hempstead, N.Y.)
Wonder (Frederick, Md.)
World Mtn. (Tacoma, Wash.)
World War (W. Roxbury, Mass.)
Xerxes (Glen Head, N.Y.)
Ye Olde (Elmhurst, Ill.)

Ye Olde (San Angelo, Texas)
Yesterday's (Kalamazoo, Mich.)

Yesterday's (Larchmont, N.Y.)
Yesterday's (Washington, D.C.)

Yesterday's (Oak Park, Mich.)
Yesterday's (Hot Springs, Ark.)

Geography

Allbooks (Colo. Spgs., Colo.)
Appalachia (Bluefield, W.Va.)
Bill (New York, N.Y.)
Book Assoc. (Orange, Conn.)
Ferndale (Ferndale, Calif.)

Guerin (Montreal, Que.)
Mt. Eden (Mt. Eden, Calif.)
Pennyroyal (Hopkinsville, Ky.)
Poe (Mayaguez, P.R.)
Rodden's (Long Bch., Calif.)

Ross (Woodland Hills, Calif.)
Tramp (Jackson, Mich.)
Washington (Washington Cr., Pa.)

Geology

Book Home (Colo. Spgs., Colo.)
Bookmine (Old Scaramento, Calif.)
Book Prospector (Littleton, Colo.)
Clegg (Eaton Rapids, Mich.)
Earth (Littleton, N.H.)
Emerson (Albuquerque, N.M.)
Ferndale (Ferndale, Calif.)
Fitch (Santa Fe, N.M.)

Geological (Falls Village, Conn.)
Geoscience (Yucaipa, Calif.)
High Country (Laramie, Wyo.)
Hudson (Dyersburg, Tenn.)
Leishman (Menlo Park, Calif.)
Lubrecht (Forestburgh, N.Y.)
McDuffie's (Portland, Ore.)
Mt. Eden (Mt. Eden, Calif.)

Nadolny (Kensington, Conn.)
Peri (San Diego, Calif.)
Poe (Mayaguez, P.R.)
Robertson (Levittown, Pa.)
Rosselot (Grand View, N.Y.)
White (Granger, Texas)
Woods (Yakima, Wash.)

Georgia

Abrams (Atlanta, Ga.)
Brooks (Macon, Ga.)

Downs (Marietta, Ga.)
Evans (Savannah, Ga.)

Memorable (Stone Mtn., Ga.)
Printed (Savannah, Ga.)

German Books & Literature

Adler's (Evanston, Ill.)
Breadloaf (E. Middlebury, Vt.)
Carousel (Tyler, Texas)
Europe (Staten Isl., N.Y.)
Fisher (New York, N.Y.)

Harding (Wells, Maine)
Kostman (Glendora, Calif.)
Laster (Winston-Salem, N.C.)
Obsolescence (Gettysburg, Pa.)
Polyanthos (Huntington, N.Y.)

Quitzau (Edmeston, N.Y.)
Rutgers (Highland Park, N.J.)
Tumarkin (New York, N.Y.)

Golf

Anderson (Auburn, Mass.)
Berman (Los Angeles, Calif.)
Bookmarx (Roslyn, N.Y.)
DeFreitas (Montreal, Que.)

Donovan (Endicott, N.Y.)
Lawrence (New York, N.Y.)
Lewis (Mamaroneck, N.Y.)
Maxwell's (Stockton, Calif.)

Parkway (Schenectady, N.Y.)
Tatro (Wethersfield, Conn.)
Taylor (Westland, Mich.)

"Gone With The Wind"

Abrams (Atlanta, Ga.)

Bridges (Sharpsburg, Ga.)

C. Dickens (Atlanta, Ga.)

Gothic & Romance Novels

Ray's (Hartford, Vt.)

Singer (Beuna Park, Calif.)

Graphic Arts

Adams (Chicago, Ill.)
Artcraft (Baldwin, Md.)

Artistic (Boston, Mass.)
Besnia (Sterling Jctn., Mass.)

Books In (Turlock, Calif.)
Carousel (Tyler, Texas)

Davis (Sherman Oaks, Calif.)
Ex Libris (New York, N.Y.)
Farnsworth (W. Cornwall, Conn.)
First Edtns. (Richmond, Va.)
Gavin (Leominster, Mass.)
Glasser (Assonet, Mass.)
Hennessey (Santa Monica, Calif.)

Howe (New York, N.Y.)
Jumping (Hartford, Conn.)
McDermut (Montvale, N.J.)
Memory (Corona Del Mar, Calif.)
Museum (Fairfield, Conn.)
Museum (New York, N.Y.)
Pansy (St. Andrews, N.B.)

Printers' (Palo Alto, Calif.)
Rinhart (Colebrook, Conn.)
Steigerwald (Bloomington, Ind.)
Wittenborn (New York, N.Y.)
Wofsy (San Francisco, Calif.)

Great Lakes

Bohling (Decatur, Mich.)
Bookman (Grand Haven, Mich.)
Brown (Toledo, Ohio)
Call Me (Saugatuck, Mich.)

Erie (Erie, Pa.)
Leelanau (Leland, Mich.)
No. Woods (Duluth, Minn.)
Old Erie (Cleveland, Ohio)

Pages #2 (Green Bay, Wisc.)
Peninsula (Traverse City, Mich.)

Greece, Turkey, & Cyprus

Doukas (Kalamazoo, Mich.)

Hyman (Los Angeles, Calif.)

O'Neill (Reston, Va.)

Zane Grey

Baumhofer (St. Paul, Minn.)
Cache (Loveland, Colo.)

Hunt (Clayton, Ind.)
Pendleton (Tiburon, Calif.)

Guns & Weapons

Amer. Eagle (Topsfield, Mass.)
Anderson (Auburn, Mass.)
Book Mart Annex (San Antonio,
   Tex.)
Cabinet/Books (Watertown, Conn.)
Collector's (Phoenix, Ariz.)

Daly (Ridgefield, Conn.)
Delp (Belding, Mich.)
Drabeck (Tuckahoe, N.Y.)
Gallery Of (Bigfork, Mont.)
Highwood (Traverse City, Mich.)
Holsten (Excelsior, Minn.)

Marcher (Okla. City, Okla.)
McLaughlin's (Cottage Grove,
   Ore.)
Old Southport (Southport, Conn.)
Ordnance (Madison, Conn.)
Pearce (Elma, N.Y.)

Pettinger (Russell, Iowa)
Riling (Philadelphia, Pa.)
Smith (Canaan, N.Y.)
Soldier (New York, N.Y.)

Sporting (Rancocas, N.J.)
Sportsman's (Manotick, Ont.)
Sterne (W. Redding, Conn.)
Stewart (Portland, Ore.)

Suhm (Westfield, Mass.)
Tillinghast (Hancock, N.H.)

"Harper's Weekly" Magazine

Barbier (Seaside, Calif.)

Kapica (New Britain, Conn.)

Hawaii

Book Bin (Corvallis, Ore.)
Chapman (Los Angeles, Calif.)
Jack London (Glen Ellen, Calif.)

Lefkowicz (Fairhaven, Mass.)
Lucas (Blandford, Mass.)
Pacific (Honolulu, Haw.)

Tusitala (Kailua, Haw.)

Natural Healing

Celnick (Bronx, N.Y.)

Stryker's (Montreal, Que.)

Health

Catbird (Portland, Ore.)
Hard-To (Newton, Mass.)
Jan-Er (Eureka Spgs., Ark.)

Mt. Zion (Mt. Zion, W.Va.)
Moving (Seattle, Wash.)
Old Ver. (Olympia Falls, Ill.)

Rittenhouse (Philadelphia, Pa.)
Stryker's (Montreal, Que.)

Lafcadio Hearn

R E (Fairhope, Ala.)   Rare Oriental (Aptos, Calif.)

Ernest Hemingway

Bean (Biddeford, Maine)   Key (Key West, Fla.)

Herbology & Herbs

Amer. Botanist (Brookfield, Ill.)   Pennyroyal (Hopkinsville, Ky.)   Woodburn (Hopewell, N.J.)
Herpetological (Lindenhurst, N.Y.)   Pomona (Rockton, Ont.)
Jan-Er (Eureka Spgs., Ark.)   Whelan (Newberry, Fla.)

Heritage Press

Book Harbor (Fullerton, Calif.)   Temares (Plandome, N.Y.)

Herpetology

Hahn (Cottonwood, Ariz.)   Tolliver's (Los Angeles, Calif.)
Pollock (Palo Alto, Calif.)   Watkins (Dolgeville, N.Y.)

Hispanica

Phila. Rare (Philadelphia, Pa.)   Seppa (Virginia, Minn.)

History

Abelard (Toronto, Ont.)
Amer. Book (Fresno, Calif.)
Andover Sq. (Knoxville, Tenn.)
Antiq. Book (Winter Park, Fla.)
Antique Books (Hamden, Conn.)
Appletree (Williford, Ark.)
Articles (Skokie, Ill.)
Ashton (Ottawa, Ont.)
Atlanta (Atlanta, Ga.)
Ball (Paris, Ont.)
Barnes (Philadelphia, Pa.)
Barnes (Evanston, Ill.)
Bartleby's (Bethesda, Md.)
Berkley (Berkley, Minn.)
Berkowitz (Chester, N.Y.)
Berman (Los Angeles, Calif.)
Book Assoc. (Orange, Conn.)
Book House (St. Louis, Mo.)
Bookshelf (Ogden, Utah)
Books/Things (Boca Raton, Fla.)
Book Store (San Mateo, Calif.)
Book Store (Lewisburg, W.Va.)
Boyson (Brookfield, Conn.)
Brownbag (Rochester, N.Y.)
Brown (Belfast, Maine)
Bullock (Yardley, Pa.)
CGT (College Stn., Texas)
Choctaw (Jackson, Miss.)
Clark's (Spokane, Wash.)
Cobble Crt. (Litchfield, Conn.)
Connolly (Vista, Calif.)
Cragsmoor (Cragsmoor, N.Y.)

Delp (Belding, Mich.)
Dickson St. (Fayetteville, Ark.)
Dolphin (Camden, Maine)
Dust (Cincinnati, Ohio)
Exnowski (Warren, Mich.)
Fessler (Theresa, N.Y.)
Fraser's (Sherman Oaks, Calif.)
Gilbert (Los Angeles, Calif.)
Glassman (Corte Madera, Calif.)
Golden Age (Dix Hills, N.Y.)
Goodman (St. Paul, Minn.)
Gordon (Pasadena, Calif.)
Green Mtn. (Lyndonville, Vt.)
Guerin (Montreal, Que.)
Harrington's (Cos Cob, Conn.)
Haunted (Orleans, Mass.)
Jack's (Mt. Prospect, Ill.)
Jordan (Philadelphia, Pa.)
Knaus (Ft. Bragg, Calif.)
Lawyer (Plains, Mont.)
Lincoln (Foster, R.I.)
Little (U. Montclair, N.J.)
MacLeod's (Vancouver, B.C.)
Marley (Oldwick, N.J.)
Mason (Toronto, Ont.)
Maynard's (Pasadena, Calif.)
McCullough (Los Angeles, Calif.)
McKittrick (Philadelphia, Pa.)
Minnehaha (Minneapolis, Minn.)
Murphy (Iowa City, Iowa)
Myers (Sequim, Wash.)
New Engl. (Bennington, Vt.)

Old Edtns. (Buffalo, N.Y.)
Old #6 (Henniker, N.H.)
O'Neill (Reston, Va.)
Pages (Reading, Mass.)
Palma (Wilmington, Del.)
Pangloss (Cambridge, Mass.)
Parsons (Sonoma, Calif.)
Past (Windsor, Ont.)
Patriot (Lexington, Mass.)
Philosophical (New York, N.Y.)
Pomander (New York, N.Y.)
Poor Richard's (Grand Rapids, Mich.)
Powell's (Chicago, Ill.)
Preservation (Evanston, Ill.)
Rieger (Greenwood, S.C.)
Rostenberg (New York, N.Y.)
Saurus (Bethlehem, Pa.)
2nd Time (Ventura, Calif.)
Shenandoah (Appleton, Wisc.)
Soldier (New York, N.Y.)
Stuart (Yuma, Ariz.)
Swiss (St. Louis, Mo.)
Touchet (New York, N.Y.)
Town (Dutch Flat, Calif.)
Una (St. Johnsbury, Vt.)
Univelt (San Diego, Calif.)
Wade (Cincinnati, Ohio)
Webster's (Milwaukee, Wisc.)
Weston (Weston, Vt.)
Whistles (Rossville, Ga.)
World Of (Willoughby, Ohio)

American History

Abra (Rochester, N.Y.)
Abe. Lincoln (Chicago, Ill.)
Aceto (Sarasota, Fla.)
Amer. Worlds (Hamden, Conn.)
Arthurton (Palmyra, N.Y.)
Austin (Richmond Hill, N.Y.)
Avery (Plymouth, Mass.)
Barn E. (Tivoli, N.Y.)
Barrow (Concord, Mass.)
Book Case (Houston, Texas)
Book Mart (San Antonio, Texas)
Bookstack (Elkhart, Ind.)
Cabin In (Potsdam, N.Y.)
Carolina (Charlotte, N.C.)
Coffman (Cambria, Calif.)
Crofter's (Washington, Conn.)
Dunlap (St. Louis, Mo.)
Estate (Washington, D.C.)

Exnowski (Warren, Mich.)
Graf (Iowa City, Iowa)
Guthman (Westport, Conn.)
Hayman (Carey, Ohio)
Heinoldt (So. Egg, N.J.)
Indian Head (Owego, N.Y.)
JFF (Manhasset, N.Y.)
Johnny (Manchester, Vt.)
Knights (Harwich Port, Mass.)
Leach (Brattleboro, Vt.)
Lien (Minneapolis, Minn.)
Lowe (Boston, Mass.)
Magnalia (No. Amherst, Mass.)
McCosh (Excelsior, Minn.)
Military (New York, N.Y.)
Newman (Chicago, Ill.)
Northeast (Ocean City, N.J.)
Poor Richard's (Grand Rapids,

Mich.)
Powell's (Chicago, Ill.)
Rancho (Santa Monica, Calif.)
Research (Fremont, Neb.)
Rinhart (Colebrook, Conn.)
Rybski (Chicago, Ill.)
Schroeder's (Dickinson, Texas)
Sharp's (No. Hollywood, Calif.)
Shorey (Seattle, Wash.)
Snug Harbor (Wells, Maine)
Stevens (Wake Forest, N.C.)
Stevens (Williamsburg, Va.)
Stone Lion (Ft. Collins, Colo.)
Totty (Lunenburg, Mass.)
Tyson (Providence, R.I.)
Western (Stoughton, Mass.)

Ancient History

Cotswold (Medina, Ohio)

Smith (Mt. Airy, Md.)

Tramp (Jackson, Mich.)

British History

Gallis (Marblehead, Mass.)
Jackson (Weston, Ont.)

Kubik (Dayton, Ohio)
Quechee (Quechee, Vt.)

Stonehill (New Haven, Conn.)

European History

Berliawsky (Camden, Maine)
Book Loft (Solvang, Calif.)

Burbank (Burbank, Calif.)
Dabny (Washington, D.C.)

Hammer Mtn. (Schenectady, N.Y.)
Pearce (Elma, N.Y.)

Local History

Aceto (Sarasota, Fla.)
Antiq. Michiana (Allen, Mich.)
Back Pages (Halifax, N.S.)
Baldwin's (W. Chester, Pa.)
Barn E. (Tivoli, N.Y.)
Berg (Devils Lake, N.D.)
Bookloft (Enterprise, Ore.)
Booklover's (Tucson, Ariz.)
Bookstop (Alexandria, Va.)
Brassers (Seminole, Fla.)
Brauns (Sacramento, Calif.)
Bunkhouse (Gardiner, Maine)
Chamberlin (E. Orleans, Mass.)
Country (Chesterton, Ind.)
Croton (Croton, N.Y.)
Dust (Cincinnati, Ohio)
Elliot Bay (Seattle, Wash.)
Ellis (Queen Charlotte, B.C.)
R E (Fairhope, Ala.)
Forgotten (St. Simon Isl., Ga.)

Fox (Tacoma, Wash.)
Globe (Northampton, Mass.)
Goodson (Vincennes, Ind.)
Grand (Redwood City, Calif.)
Grunder (Ithaca, N.Y.)
Harbor Hill (Harrison, N.Y.)
Heartwood (Charlottesville, Va.)
Henderson (Nashua, N.H.)
Henrietta's (Salisbury, Md.)
Hermit's (Wyoming, Pa.)
Keith (Red Bank, N.J.)
Krause (Warrington, Fla.)
Lewis St. (Lynn, Mass.)
Little (Missoula, Mont.)
Maier (Rockport, Mass.)
Maxwell's (Lima, N.Y.)
McMillen (Staten Isl., N.Y.)
Murphy (Salem, Mass.)
Murphy (Marietta, Ga.)
Necessary (E. Jordan, Mich.)

Nelson's (Albany, N.Y.)
Northingham (Hamilton Sq., N.J.)
Ohio (Cincinnati, Ohio)
Patriot (Lexington, Mass.)
Philatelic (Louisville, Ky.)
Pratt (E. Livermore, Maine)
Publix (Cleveland, Ohio)
Salerno (Hauppauge, N.Y.)
Snowbound (Marquette, Mich.)
Spooner's (Tilton, N.H.)
10 Pound (Gloucester, Mass.)
Thoreau (Concord, Mass.)
Titcomb's (E. Sandwich, Mass.)
Tuttle (Ruthland, Vt.)
Vargo's (Bozeman, Mont.)
Virginia (Berryville, Va.)
Yankee (Plymouth, Mass.)
Ziagos (Lowell, Mass.)

History Of Medicine & Science

Apothecary (New York, N.Y.)
Argosy (New York, N.Y.)
Arkway (New York, N.Y.)
Astronomy (Bernardston, Mass.)
Atticus (Toronto, Ont.)
Biblion (Forest Hills, N.Y.)

Bookcell (Hamden, Conn.)
Bookery (Ithaca, N.Y.)
Books/Buttons (Columbus, Ohio)
Bookstall (San Francisco, Calif.)
Calman (Syracuse, N.Y.)
Chirurgical (Baltimore, Md.)

Dailey (Los Angeles, Calif.)
Dordick (Somerville, Mass.)
Fye (Marshfield, Wisc.)
Gabriel (Northampton, Mass.)
Glaser (Sausalito, Calif.)
Goodrich (Englewood, N.J.)

Heller (Swarthmore, Pa.)
Hist. Tech (Marblehead, Mass.)
Jones (Washington, D.C.)
Key (Baltimore, Md.)
Littlewoods (Waukesha, Wisc.)
Medical (Jenkintown, Pa.)
Metacomet (Providence, R.I.)

19th Cent. (Baltimore, Md.)
Old Hickory (Brinklow, Md.)
Printers' (Arlington, Mass.)
Printers' (Boston, Mass.)
Scientia (Arlington, Mass.)
Significant (Cincinnati, Ohio)
Stern (Chicago, Ill.)

Tesseract (Hastings, N.Y.)
Tweney (Bowling Green, Ohio)
Wehawken (Washington, D.C.)
Wharton (Toronto, Ont.)
Zeitlin (Los Angeles, Calif.)

Military History

Abbey (Los Angeles, Calif.)
Attic (Laurel, Md.)
Bibliomania (Berkeley, Calif.)
Bibliomania (Oakland, Calif.)
B. & J. (Rego Park, N.Y.)
Book-Bird (Anaheim, Calif.)
Booketeria (San Antonio, Texas)
Bookkeepers (Riviera Bch., Fla.)

Book Shoppe (Myrtle Bch., S.C.)
Carduner (Philadelphia, Pa.
Heritage (Columbus, Ohio)
Hunt (Burbank, Calif.)
In #1 (San Francisco, Calif.)
In #2 (San Francisco, Calif.)
Jackson (Weston, Ont.)
Memory (Belfast, Maine)

Mt. Falcon (Greeley, Colo.)
Pearce (Elma, N.Y.)
Stewart's (Camp Spgs., Md.)
Tramp (Jackson, Mich.)
20th Century (Madison, Wisc.)
World War (W. Roxbury, Mass.)

Hobbies

Helmet (W. Islip, N.Y.)
National (Brooklyn, N.Y.)

Reisler (Vienna, Va.)
Schmitt (Rockville, Md.)

Modern Library Publishing Company

Glassman (Corte Madera, Calif.)   NRS (New York, N.Y.)   Wise (Baldwin Pl., N.Y.)

Holistic Health & Nutrition

East West (Hamburg, N.Y.)
Jan-Er (Eureka Spgs., Ark.)

Sophia (Amherst, Mass.)
Vegetarian (Santa Monica, Calif.)

Words (So. Bend, Ind.)

Hollywood

Pantechnicon (1000 Oaks, Calif.)   Stahr (Los Angeles, Calif.)

Sherlock Holmes & A. C. Doyle

DeFreitas (Montreal, Que.)
Edger (Hastings, Mich.)
Evans (Savannah, Ga.)
Greene (Rockville Centre, N.Y.)
Halbach (Santa Barbara, Calif.)

Hess (Brightwaters, N.Y.)
Janus (Tucson, Ariz.)
Joyce (Chicago, Ill.)
Murder (Toronto, Ont.)
Mysteries (Yellow Spgs., Ohio)

Oceanside (Oceanside, N.Y.)
Rue (Boulder, Colo.)
Sleepy (Moraga, Calif.)
221 (Westlake Village, Calif.)

Holocaust

Austin (Kew Gardens, N.Y.)   Morrison (Santa Monica, Calif.)   Seppa (Virginia, Minn.)

Horology (Clocks)

William (Mineola, N.Y.)   Zeitlin (Los Angeles, Calif.)

Horror

Borden (Portsmouth, R. I.)
Daunce (Buffalo, N.Y.)
Drumm (Polk City, Iowa)
Fantasy (New York, N.Y.)

Fantasy (Carmichael, Calif.)
Fantasy (San Francisco, Calif.)
Gavora (Santa Barbara, Calif.)
Hanley's (Chicago, Ill.)

JMD (Groton, N.Y.)
Levin (Los Angeles, Calif.)

Horses & Horse Sports

All Edges (Silver Spg., Md.)
Back Pages (Halifax, N.S.)
Backpocket (Sundance, Wyo.)
Bennett (Southold, N.Y.)
Black Swan (Lexington, Ky.)
Butcher (Youngstown, Ohio)
Elmcress (So. Hamilton, Mass.)
El-Zar (Cedar Rapids, Iowa)

Glover's (Lexington, Ky.)
Harris (Rockville, Md.)
Hooper's (Leesburg, Va.)
Ishtar (Canton, Mass.)
Kimbel (Plant City, Fla.)
Levien (McDowell, Va.)
Lyrical (Saratoga Spgs., N.Y.)
October (Raleigh, N.C.)

Old Favs. (Toronto, Ont.)
Poste (Geneseo, N.Y.)
Schaefer (Ossining, N.Y.)
Smith (Canaan, N.Y.)
Trotting (Morristown, N.J.)
Wilshire (No. Hollywood, Calif.)

Hotels & Inns

Gore (San Gabriel, Calif.)

Radio (New York, N.Y.)

Wine (Ann Arbor, Mich.)

Elbert Hubbard & Roycrofters

Antiq. Archive (Sunnyvale, Calif.)
Backroom (Webster, N.Y.)

Blacher (Branford, Conn.)
Weber (Troy, Minn.)

Hudson River

Book Look (Warwick, N.Y.)
Croton (Croton, N.Y.)
Gobrecht (Kinderhook, N.Y.)

Hope Farm (Cornwallville, N.Y.)
Kreinheder (Warrensburg, N.Y.)
McDonald's (Catskill, N.Y.)

Old Book (Croton, N.Y.)
Pages (Mt. Kisco, N.Y.)
Ridge (Stone Ridge, N.Y.)

Humanism

Gilbert (Los Angeles, Calif.)   Waldo (Rockton, Ill.)

Humanities

Amer. Worlds (Hamden, Conn.)
Armitage (Miamisburg, Ohio)
Bartleby's (Bethesda, Md.)
Bauman (Atlantic City, N.J.)
Bauman (Philadelphia, Pa.)
Book Finder (Geneva, N.Y.)
Darby (Darby, Pa.)
Detering (Houston, Texas)

Farley's (Pensacola, Fla.)
Gabbard (New Boston, Texas)
Good Times (Pt. Jefferson, N.Y.)
Hartmann (Morganton, N.C.)
Hummingbird (Albuquerque, N.M.)
Jaffe (Arlington, Va.)
Johnson (Indianapolis, Ind.)

Lion (Indianapolis, Ind.)
Mason (Phoenix, Ariz.)
Shaman (Ann Arbor, Mich.)
Tuckers (Pittsburgh, Pa.)
Wooden (Ann Arbor, Mich.)
Word (Montreal, Que.)

Humor

Book Chest (New York, N.Y.)
Bridgton (Bridgton, Maine)
Galewitz (Orange, Conn.)

McBride (Hartford, Conn.)
Merkel (Xenia, Ohio)
Old Ver. (Olympia Falls, Ill.)

Photo (Columbus, Ohio)
Robinson (St. Peteersburg, Fla.)

Hunting

*See also
Fishing. Guns*

Bicentennial (Kalamazoo, Mich.)
Butcher (Youngstown, Ohio)
Cabinet/Books (Watertown, Conn.)
Campfire (Evansville, Ind.)
Collector's (Phoenix, Ariz.)
Combs (Great Falls, Mont.)
Cottonwood (Baton Rouge, La.)
Daly (Ridgefield, Conn.)
Delp (Belding, Mich.)
Dorn (Johntown, N.Y.)
Dunn (Dallas, Ore.)

Gallery Of (Bigfork, Mont.)
Gamebag (Twin Lakes, Wisc.)
Gunnerman (Auburn Hgts., Mich.)
Hall (Chambersburg, Pa.)
Highwood (Traverse City, Mich.)
Holsten (Excelsior, Minn.)
Ishii (Seattle, Wash.)
Marcher (Okla. City, Okla.)
McGovern (Berwyn, Ill.)
Memory (Grand Rapids, Mich.)
No. Woods (Duluth, Minn.)

Old Town (Tempe, Ariz.)
Pisces (Albion, Mich.)
Riling (Philadelphia, Pa.)
Sporting (Palmerton, Pa.)
Stewart (Portland, Ore.)
Tayaut (No. Hatley, Que.)
Ten Eyck (Southboro, Mass.)
Tryon (Johnstown, N.Y.)
Webfoot (Portland, Ore.)

Big Game Hunting

Berman (Los Angeles, Calif.)
Collector's (Phoenix, Ariz.)
Drabeck (Tuckahoe, N.Y.)

Dunn (Dallas, Ore.)
Gamebag (Twin Lakes, Wisc.)
Holsten (Excelsior, Minn.)

Terramedia (Wellesley, Mass.)
Trophy (Agoura, Calif.)
World Wide (Long Beach, Calif.)

Hymns & Hymnals

Book Search (Avondale Estates, Ga.)

Fay (Caledonia, N.Y.)

Idaho

Book Shop (Boise, Idaho)
Ex Libris (Sun Valley, Idaho)
Hyde Park (Boise, Idaho)
Judi's (Twin Falls, Idaho)

Market (Idaho Falls, Idaho)
McLaughlin's (Cottage Grove, Ore.)
Nolan (Coeur d'Alene, Idaho)

Ute-Or (W. Jordan, Utah)
West (Provo, Utah)
Yesteryear (Nampa, Idaho)

Illuminated Leaves & Pages

See also Manuscripts, Illuminated

Ferrini (Akron, Ohio)

Rendell (Waban, Mass.)

Rudolph (Portland, Ore.)

Illustrated Books

See also Children's Books

A B I (Santa Barbara, Calif.)
Agranoff (Cincinnati, Ohio)
Albatross II (Tiburon, Calif.)
Aleph-Bet (Valley Cottage, N.Y.)
Alkahest (Evanston, Ill.)
Allen (Baltimore, Md.)

Amer. City (Denver, Colo.)
Amer. Frag. (Escondido, Calif.)
Andover (Andover, Mass.)
Antiq. Book (Toledo, Ohio)
Antiques/Art (Seattle, Wash.)
Arkway (New York, N.Y.)

Arnolds (Contoocook, N.H.)
Arond (Lexington, Mass.)
Ars Libri (Boston, Mass.)
Asendorf (Los Altos Hills, Calif.)
Ashley (Burlington, Vt.)
Barrister (Davie, Fla.)

Bear (W. Brattleboro, Vt.)
Bebbah (Andover, Kan.)
Berry (Kingston, Ont.)
Besnia (Sterling Jctn., Mass.)
Bibelots (Seattle, Wash.)
Bieber (Kenilworth, N.J.)
Black Sun (New York, N.Y.)
Blomgren (San Rafael, Calif.)
Blue Lantern (San Diego, Calif.)
Bonmark (Plainview, N.Y.)
Book Block (Cos Cob, Conn.)
Bookcell (Hamden, Conn.)
Bookdales (Richfield, Minn.)
Book Haven (Lancaster, Pa.)
Book House (Arlington, Va.)
Bookman (Kent, Ohio)
Book Mark (Philadelphia, Pa.)
Book OP (Adrian, Mich.)
Book Pedlars (Cundy's Harbor,
    Maine)
Books/Books (Coral Gables, Fla.)
Book Shop (Beverly Farms, Mass.)
Books In (Turlock, Calif.)
Booksmith (Oak Park, Ill.)
Books Of (New York, N.Y.)
Bookstall (San Francisco, Calif.)
Bowes (Vancouver, B.C.)
Bowie (Seattle, Wash.)
Boyson (Brookfield, Conn.)
Braiterman (Baltimore, Md.)
Breslauer (New York, N.Y.)
Bromer (Boston, Mass.)
Buchanan (New York, N.Y.)
Buck (New York, N.Y.)
Buck (San Francisco, Calif.)
Buddenbrooks (Boston, Mass.)
Caddo (Cartaro, Ariz.)
Califia (San Francisco, Calif.)
Carlitz (Philadelphia, Pa.)
Carousel (Tyler, Texas)
Casavant (Wayland, Mass.)
Chapin (Reading, Pa.)
Cherokee (Hollywood, Calif.)
Chimney (Bridgeport, Conn.)
Choras (Weston, Mass.)
ChoreoGraphica (Boston, Mass.)
Christoffersen (Mamaroneck, N.Y.)
Clare (Getzville, N.Y.)
Cohen (Youngstown, Ohio)

Collectors' (New York, N.Y.)
Collins' (Pottstown, Pa.)
Compulsive (New York, N.Y.)
Culpin's (Denver, Colo.)
Cummins (New York, N.Y.)
Cummins (Pottersville, N.J.)
Curiosity (St. Joseph, Mich.)
Curious Book (E. Lansing, Mich.)
Dailey (Los Angeles, Calif.)
Denver (Stockton, Calif.)
Detering (Houston, Texas)
Diamond (Rochester, N.Y.)
Diva (Coos Bay, Ore.)
Docheff (Berkeley, Calif.)
Doe Run (Cochranville, Pa.)
Dohm's (Olympia, Wash.)
Donaldson's (Knoxville, Tenn.)
Dragon's Lair (Dayton, Ohio)
Drusilla's (Baltimore, Md.)
Dumler (Southport, Conn.)
Duschnes (New York, N.Y.)
Earl (Clarendon, N.Y.)
Eldredge (Vineyard Haven, Mass.)
Ellam (Los Angeles, Calif.)
Enchanted (Brooklyn, N.Y.)
L'Estampe (Saratoga, Calif.)
L'Estampe (New York, N.Y.)
Everard (Santa Barbara, Calif.)
Family Album (Glen Rock, Pa.)
Farnsworth (W. Cornwall, Conn.)
Feiden (Mamaroneck, N.Y.)
Feldman (Cleveland, Ohio)
Fine (Rochester, Mich.)
First (Chicago, Ill.)
First Impressions (Wheaton, Ill.)
Fisher (Williamsport, Pa.)
Flynn (Lake Forest, Ill.)
Forest Park (Ft. Wayne, Ind.)
Forgotten (St. Simon Isl., Ga.)
Frohnsdorff (Gaithersburg, Md.)
Carcia (Turlock, Calif.)
Gilann (Darien, Conn.)
Glenn (Kansas City, Mo.)
Glover (Cambridge, N.Y.)
Golden Age (Dix Hills, N.Y.)
Golden Legend (Los Angeles,
    Calif.)
Grapevine (San Mateo, Calif.)
Grt. Expect. (Staten Isl., N.Y.)

Green (Elkins Park, Pa.)
Green Acre (Wells, Vt.)
Grunewald (Kansas City, Mo.)
Gud (Elmhurst, N.Y.)
Hacker (New York, N.Y.)
Halpern (Flushing, N.Y.)
Hansen (Carlsbad, Calif.)
Harper (New York, N.Y.)
Heller (Cleveland, Ohio)
Heritage (Los Angeles, Calif.)
Hi (Canutillo, Texas)
Hirsch (Hopewell Jctn., N.Y.)
Hirschtritt's (Silver Spg., Md.)
Hoefliger (Buffalo, N.Y.)
Hollander (Santa Monica, Calif.)
Hollywood City (Hollywood,
    Calif.)
Holy Land (Washington, D.C.)
Hooked (Springfield, Mo.)
Hughes (St. Louis, Mo.)
Jaffe (Haverford, Pa.)
Janus (Corea, Maine)
Janus (Hungtinton Stn., N.Y.)
Jense (Los Angeles, Calif.)
Juvelis (Boston, Mass.)
Kane (Santa Cruz, Calif.)
Katz (Los Angeles, Calif.)
Kaufman (New York, N.Y.)
Kaufman (Tempe, Ariz.)
Keller (Overland Park, Kan.)
King (Detroit, Mich.)
Klemm (Apple Valley, Calif.)
Konigsmark (Wayne, Pa.)
Laird (Chicago, Ill.)
Lehr (New York, N.Y.)
Leibowits (New York, N.Y.)
Levinson (Beverly Hills, Calif.)
Littrup (Bay City, Mich.)
Lyrical (Saratoga Spgs., N.Y.)
Macauluso (Kennett Sq., Pa.)
Mahard (Sherborn, Mass.)
Mancevice (Worcester, Mass.)
Mannatt (San Diego, Calif.)
Manning's (San Francisco, Calif.)
Maple St. (New Orleans, La.)
Margolis (Santa Fe, N.M.)
Martignette (Boston, Mass.)
Mawson (New Preston, Conn.)
McManus (Woodbury, Conn.)

Medallion (Wellesley, Mass.)
Memory (Corona Del Mar, Calif.)
Merlin's (Providence, R.I.)
Michaels (Eugene, Ore.)
Midnight (W. Lafayette, Ind.)
Milestone (New York, N.Y.)
Mill (Craftsbury Common, Vt.)
Minkoff (Grt. Barrington, Mass.)
Moye (Putney, Vt.)
Much (Southfield, Mich.)
Nebenzahl (Chicago, Ill.)
Nelson (New Bedford, Mass.)
Nemeroff (Williamstown, Mass.)
Newburyport (Newburyport, Mass.)
Nosegay (Cold Spg. Harbor, N.Y.)
Nudel (New York, N.Y.)
Pan (Catskill, N.Y.)
Pansy (St. Andrews, N.B.)
Paper (Portland, Ore.)
Parmer's (Sarasota, Fla.)
Perata (Oakland, Calif.)
Petersons (Philadelphia, Pa.)
Phillips (New York, N.Y.)
Pinkney (Granby, Conn.)
Plant (Grass Valley, Calif.)
Reisler (Vienna, Va.)
Resnik (Roslyn Hgts., N.Y.)
Rhoads (Richmond, Ind.)

Robbins (Greenville, S.C.)
Roberts (W. Palm Bch., Fla.)
Robinson (Manchester, Maine)
Robinson (New York, N.Y.)
Rockland (Cattaraugus, N.Y.)
Rohr (Byfield, Mass.)
Rush (Baltimore, Md.)
Sackheim (Tucson, Ariz.)
Sail (Newcastle, Maine)
Sail (Lexington, Ky.)
Schaefer (Ossining, N.Y.)
Schiller (New York, N.Y.)
Schlossberg (Newton, Mass.)
Scopazzi (San Francisco, Calif.)
Scott (Stonington, Conn.)
Seluzicki (Portland, Ore.)
Sloat (Flemington, N.J.)
Small (So. Yarmouth, Mass.)
Song Of (Newmarket, N.H.)
Spector (Jackson Hgts., N.Y.)
Starry (Shippensburg, Pa.)
Steigerwald (Bloomington, Ind.)
Sullivan (St. Pete., Fla.)
Sullivan (Coventry, Conn.)
Tamerlane (Havertown, Pa.)
Tamerlis (Mamaroneck, N.Y.)
1023 (Omaha, Neb.)
Terres (Minneapolis, Minn.)
Thomas (San Francisco, Calif.)

1000 Words (Exeter, N.H.)
Time (Sacramento, Calif.)
Tinker (Santa Cruz, Calif.)
Tisza (Chestnut Hill, Mass.)
Titles (Highland Park, Ill.)
Treasure (Oakville, Ont.)
Treehorn (Santa Rosa, Calif.)
Ursus (New York, N.Y.)
Victoria (New York, N.Y.)
Vintage (Wheaton, Ill.)
Waite (Madison, Wisc.)
Warren (Philadelphia, Pa.)
Weintraub #2 (New York, N.Y.)
Weintraub #1 (New York, N.Y.)
Weitz (New York, N.Y.)
West's (Elm Grove, Wisc.)
Willis (Columbus, Ohio)
Wilsey (Olivebridge, N.Y.)
Witten (Southport, Conn.)
Wolf's (Morgantown, W.Va.)
Woodbury (Woodbury, Conn.)
World Of (Willoughby, Ohio)
Yankee (Williamson, N.Y.)
Yankee (Rochester, N.Y.)
Ye Olde (St. Joseph, Mich.)
Yesterdays (Whitman, Mass.)
Young (Dobbs Ferry, N.Y.)
Zita (New York, N.Y.)
Zucker (New York, N.Y.)

Immigration

*See also
Asians in America*

Asian Amer. (New York, N.Y.)
Austin (Kew Gardens, N.Y.)
Austin (Richmond Hill, N.Y.)

Books Amer. (San Francisco, Calif.)
Doi (San Jose, Calif.)

Imprints

Antiquarians (Plainfield, Pa.)   Inner Circle (New York, N.Y.)   Pages (Newton, Conn.)
Family Album (Glen Rock, Pa.)   Lombardo (Shoreham, N.Y.)   Schoen (Northampton, Mass.)

See also
Self-Help

Income Opportunities

Boise Farm (Boise, Idaho)   Wilshire (No. Hollywood, Calif.)

See also
Early Printed Books

Incunabula

Barber (Boston, Mass.)   Harper (New York, N.Y.)   Salloch (Ossining, N.Y.)
Biblion (Forest Hills, N.Y.)   Kraus (New York, N.Y.)   Schreiber (Bronx, N.Y.)
Breslauer (New York, N.Y.)   Levinson (Beverly Hills, Calif.)   Winter (Pittsfield, Maine)
Clare (Getzville, N.Y.)   McKittrick (Philadelphia, Pa.)   Witten (Southport, Conn.)
Family Album (Glen Rock, Pa.)   Pavlov (Dobbs Ferry, N.Y.)
Hamill (Chicago, Ill.)   Pirages (McMinnville, Ore.)

India

Lewis (Seattle, Wash.)   Plain (Arlington Hgts., Ill.)

Indiana

Books/Comics #1 (Indianapolis,   Country (Chesterton, Ind.)   Long (Marietta, Ga.)
   Ind.)   Forest Park (Ft. Wayne, Ind.)   Odds (Indianapolis, Ind.)
Broad Ripple (Indianapolis, Ind.)   Goodson (Vincennes, Ind.)   Used (Dyer, Ind.)
Chanticleer (Ft. Wayne, Ind.)   Hunt (Clayton, Ind.)

Indians & Eskimos

Acoma (Ramona, Calif.)
Allbooks (Colo. Spgs., Colo.)
Ancient (Santa Fe, N.M.)
Arader (Atlanta, Ga.)
Arader (New York, N.Y.)
Arch (Bellows Falls, Vt.)
Arthurton (Palmyra, N.Y.)
Authors (Dundee, Ore.)
Avalon (Hayward, Calif.)
Barjon's (Billings, Mont.)
Blomberg (Rockford, Ill.)
Book Buyers (Houston, Texas)
Book Nook (Yakima, Wash.)
Collins (San Francisco, Calif.)
Dowd (St. Charles, Ill.)
Dupley (Omaha, Neb.)
Ellis (Queen Charlotte, B.C.)
Emerson (Albuquerque, N.M.)
Eshner (Bisbee, Ariz.)

Ethnographic (Mill Valley, Calif.)
Fein (New York, N.Y.)
Grimshaw (Randolph, Mass.)
Guthman (Westport, Conn.)
Hand (Wheeling, W.Va.)
Heinoldt (So. Egg, N.J.)
Hist. Realia (Wooster, Ohio)
Horne (Lakeland, Fla.)
Indian Head (Owego, N.Y.)
Iroqrafts (Ohsweken, Ont.)
Jacobs (Sherman Oaks, Calif.)
Javitch (Montreal, Que.)
Johnson (New York, N.Y.)
La Galeria (Las Vegas, N.M.)
Libros (Redlands, Calif.)
Lien (Minneapolis, Minn.)
Log Cabin (Bigfork, Mont.)
Lopez (Hadley, Mass.)
Lunsford (No. Vancouver, B.C.)

Luther (Taos, N.M.)
Margolis (Monroe, Mich.)
Mason's (Wabash, Ind.)
Ohio (Mansfield, Ohio)
Old Erie (Cleveland, Ohio)
Poste (Geneseo, N.Y.)
Rittenhouse (Albuquerque, N.M.)
Rosetree (Tombstone, Ariz.)
Rybski (Chicago, Ill.)
Shenandoah (Appleton, Wisc.)
Shorey (Seattle, Wash.)
Sloan (Austin, Texas)
Swinford (Paris, Ill.)
3 Geese (Woodstock, N.Y.)
Valley (Galena, Ill.)
Weatherford (Monroe, Wash.)
Wikehgan (Mt. Desert, Maine)

See also
Business, Economics

Industry

Bolerium (San Francisco, Calif.)
Cramer (Kansas City, Mo.)

Fraser (Burlington, Vt.)
Metacomet (Providence, R.I.)

Paulson (Huntington, Mass.)
Southpaw (Roxbury, Mass.)

See also
Hudson River

Inland Waterways

Book Farm (Henniker, N.H.)

Cantrells' (No. East, Pa.)

See also
Limited & Signed Editions

Inscribed Books

Antic Hay (W. Caldwell, N.J.)
Barnes (Philadelphia, Pa.)

Carr (New York, N.Y.)
Dermont (Onset, Mass.)

Koschal (Verona, N.J.)
Lazarus (Ossining, N.Y.)

McCaslin (Ironton, Mo.)
Neville (Santa Barbara, Calif.)
Noble (Greenville, Texas)
Norumbega (Houston, Texas)
Nouveau (Jackson, Miss.)
Pepper/Stern (Sharon, Mass.)

Pepper/Stern (Santa Barbara, Calif.)
Rare Book (Freehold, N.J.)
Richards (Templeton, Mass.)
Sanderson (Stockbridge, Mass.)
Shoebridge (Lafayette, N.Y.)

Signed (Pt. Washington, N.Y.)
Slater (Tarrytown, N.Y.)
Theatrebooks (New York, N.Y.)
Tollett (New York, N.Y.)
Turlington (Pittsboro, N.C.)
Woolmer (Revere, Pa.)

Ireland & The Irish

See also
The Scotch, The Welsh

Arcane (Okla. City, Okla.)
Britannia (New Preston, Conn.)
Cilleyville (Andover, N.H.)
Dickson St. (Fayetteville, Ark.)
Different (Des Moines, Iowa)
Facsimile (New York, N.Y.)
Federation (College St., Texas)

E. C. Gordon (New York, N.Y.)
Harte (Seattle, Wash.)
House (Anaheim, Calif.)
Joyce (Chicago, Ill.)
Keane (State College, Pa.)
Keshcarrigan (New York, N.Y.)
Knaus (Ft. Bragg, Calif.)

Little (U. Montclair, N.J.)
McGahern (Ottawa, Ont.)
Munsell (Newburyport, Mass.)
O'Donoghue (Anoka, Minn.)
O'Malley (Kingston, R.I.)
Sumner (Yarmouth, Maine)
3 Geese (Woodstock, N.Y.)

Islam

see also
Specific Religions, Religious History

Asian Books (Cambridge, Mass.)
Camel (New York, N.Y.)

Sample (Stoneham, Mass.)
Schreyer (New York, N.Y.)

Worldwide (Cambridge, Mass.)

Israel

See also
Hebraica

Biegeleisen (Brooklyn, N.Y.)

Camel (New York, N.Y.)

Holy Land (Washington, D.C.)

Japan

See also
Pacific Region

Asian Amer. (New York, N.Y.)
Asian Rare (New York, N.Y.)
Best (Cambridge, Mass.)
Book Collector (Newton, Mass.)

Gamradt (Minneapolis, Minn.)
Hirschtritt's (Silver Spg., Md.)
Manasek (Hanover, N.H.)
Manasek (Norwich, Vt.)

Oriental (St. Pete., Fla.)
Paragon (New York, N.Y.)
Rare Oriental (Aptos, Calif.)
Sebastopol (Sebastopol, Calif.)

Jazz

See also
Music

Barnstormer (Sacramento, Calif.)
Beasley (Chicago, Ill.)
Bel Canto (Metuchen, N.J.)

City Lights (San Francisco, Calif.)
First Edtns. (Richmond, Va.)
On The (Chambersburg, Pa.)

Quill (Pinellas Park, Fla.)
Rieber (Thomasville, Ga.)
Vanderstoel (El Cerrito, Calif.)

Jehovah's Witnesses & Watchtower

See also Religion

Old Theo. (Minneapolis, Minn.)   Ron Dot (Greensburg, Ohio)

Jewelry

See also
Minerology & Gemology

Cohen (Bronx, N.Y.)
Oceanic (New York, N.Y.)

Peri (San Diego, Calif.)
Poe (Mayaguez, P.R.)

Sisterhood (Los Angeles, Calif.)

Judaica & Hebraica

See also
Israel, Religion

Annie's #1 (Portland, Ore.)
Annie's #2 (Portland, Ore.)
Austin (Kew Gardens, N.Y.)
Austin (Richmond Hill, N.Y.)
Benjamins (Philadelphia, Pa.)
Biegeleisen (Brooklyn, N.Y.)
Bookie Joint (Reseda, Calif.)
Booknook (Evanston, Ill.)
Brill (New York, N.Y.)
Camel (New York, N.Y.)

Celnick (Bronx, N.Y.)
Compulsive (New York, N.Y.)
Fern (New York, N.Y.)
George (Cleveland, Tenn.)
Holy Land (Washington, D.C.)
Ideal (New York, N.Y.)
Jamaica (Jamaica, N.Y.)
Kam (Philadelphia, Pa.)
Kimeldorf (Portland, Ore.)
Loewy (Tallman, N.Y.)

Miranda (Brookline, Mass.)
Moriah (New York, N.Y.)
Morrison (Santa Monica, Calif.)
Raimo (Lancaster, Pa.)
Safir (New York, N.Y.)
Schram (Montclair, N.J.)
Tattered (Denver, Colo.)
Tisza (Chestnut Hill, Mass.)
Under (Shaker Hgts., Ohio)
Wolfe (Pt. Claire, Que.)

Juveniles

See also
Children's, Series Books for Boys & Girls

Aleph-Bet (Valley Cottage, N.Y.)
Assoc. Stu. (Chico, Calif.)

Boardman (Camden, N.Y.)
Book Cellar (Freeport, Maine)

Book Den (Santa Barbara, Calif.)
Book Disp. #1 (Columbia, S.C.)

Book Disp. #3 (Columbia, S.C.)
Books Of (New York, N.Y.)
Bromer (Boston, Mass.)
Burstein (Waltham, Mass.)
Casavant (Wayland, Mass.)
C. Dickens (Atlanta, Ga.)
Cellar (Eugene, Ore.)
Cheap St. (New Castle, Va.)
Country (Chesterton, Ind.)
Cyrano's (Highlands, N.C.)
Deeds (Ellicott City, Md.)
Docheff (Berkeley, Calif.)
Dolphin (Camden, Maine)

Drusilla's (Baltimore, Md.)
Eldredge (Vineyard Haven, Mass.)
Everyday (Burlington, Vt.)
Falls (Farmington Falls, Maine)
Fullam (Babylon, N.Y.)
Halpern (Flushing, N.Y.)
Hamilton's (Williamsburg, Va.)
Henrietta's (Salisbury, Md.)
Herzig-Cohen (Jackson Hgts., N.Y.)
Hopper (Sunnyvale, Calif.)
Howland (New Canaan, Conn.)
Ladner (Orleans, Mass.)

Loose (Jerome, Mich.)
O'Mahony (Clarence Cntr., N.Y.)
Owl (Camden, Maine)
Pendleton (Tiburon, Calif.)
Resnik (Roslyn Hgts., N.Y.)
Rieber (Thomasville, Ga.)
Sackett (Grants Pass, Ore.)
Shadow (Hillsboro, N.H.)
Smith (Amherst, Mass.)
Starratt (Palo Alto, Calif.)
Traveler (Union, Conn.)

Kansas

Dary (Lawrence, Kan.)

Grunewald (Kansas City, Mo.)

Keller (Overland Park, Kan.)

Rockwell Kent

Delle Donne (Ronkonkoma, N.Y.)

Paulson (Huntington, Mass.)

Spector (Jackson Hgts., N.Y.)

Kentucky

Black Swan (Lexington, Ky.)
Borderland (Alvaton, Ky.)

Glover's (Lexington, Ky.)
Pennyroyal (Hopkinsville, Ky.)

Stephen King

*See also
Fantasy, Horror*

Dourgarian (Walnut Creek, Calif.)

Fantasy (New York, N.Y.)

Golden Age (Seattle, Wash.)

Labor & Labor History

Good Times (Pt. Jefferson, N.Y.)   Vol. I (Hillsdale, Mich.)

Languages

See also
Specific Languages

Book Assoc. (Orange, Conn.)   Lawyer (Plains, Mont.)   Wheel (Oak Park, Ill.)
Dragoman (Annapolis, Md.)   Loome (Stillwater, Minn.)
E. C. Gordon (New York, N.Y.)   Lozinski (Westport, Mass.)

Latin America

See also
Central America, South America

Allen (Philadelphia, Pa.)   Foreign (Flushing, N.Y.)   Poe (Mayaguez, P.R.)
Bookery (Farmington, N.H.)   Ginsberg (Sharon, Mass.)   R. Ramer (New York, N.Y.)
Book Search (Brooklyn, N.Y.)   Golder (Collinsville, Conn.)   Ross (Albany, Calif.)
Bromsen (Boston, Mass.)   Hoefliger (Buffalo, N.Y.)   Rybski (Chicago, Ill.)
Carling's (Pomona Park, Fla.)   Jenkins (Austin, Texas)   Scharf (Pittsburgh, Pa.)
Diamond (Burbank, Calif.)   Karno (Santa Monica, Calif.)   Schiefer (Wilton, Conn.)
El Cascajero (New York, N.Y.)   Katz (Los Angeles, Calif.)   Seppa (Virginia, Minn.)
Eshner (Bisbee, Ariz.)   Libros (Redlands, Calif.)   Sloan (Austin, Texas)
Ethnographic (Mill Valley, Calif.)   Lopez (Hadley, Mass.)   Wahrenbrock's (San Diego, Calif.)
Fein (New York, N.Y.)   Marchioness (Laguna Bch., Calif.)   Wright (Waxahachie, Texas)
Ferndale (Ferndale, Calif.)   Phila. Rare (Philadelphia, Pa.)   Zwisohn (Albuquerque, N.M.)

Law

A C (Brooklyn, N.Y.)   Dabny (Washington, D.C.)   Old Book (Kennebunk, Maine)
Amer. SW (Amarillo, Texas)   Heath (Toronto, Ont.)   Phila. Rare (Philadelphia, Pa.)
Arthurton (Palmyra, N.Y.)   Joyce (Chicago, Ill.)   Rubin (Brookline, Mass.)
Austin (Kew Gardens, N.Y.)   Lake (San Francisco, Calif.)   Sadoff (Jenkintown, Pa.)
Austin (Richmond Hill, N.Y.)   Laster (Winston-Salem, N.C.)   Smith (Montclair, N.J.)
Bauman (Philadelphia, Pa.)   Little (Rehobeth, Mass.)   Town (Dutch Flat, Calif.)
Bauman (Atlantic City, N.J.)   Magnalia (No. Amherst, Mass.)   Watson (Buelah, Colo.)
Chicago Law (Chicago, Ill.)   Meyer (San Francisco, Calif.)
Claitor's (Baton Rouge, La.)   Norumbega (Houston, Texas)

Limited Editions Club

*See also
Heritage Press*

Duschnes (New York, N.Y.)
Pinkney (Granby, Conn.)

Sleepy (Moraga, Calif.)
Temares (Plandome, N.Y.)

Limited & Signed Editions

*See also
Association Copies*

Barrister (Davie, Fla.)
Beatific (Schenectady, N.Y.)
Birmingham (Birmingham, Mich.)
City Spirit (Denver, Colo.)
Fisher (Williamsport, Pa.)
Granat (Woodmere, N.Y.)
Grunewald (Kansas City, Mo.)

History (Long Valley, N.J.)
Joe the Pro (Santa Barbara, Calif.)
Keane (State College, Pa.)
Levin (Los Angeles, Calif.)
Magic (Johnson City, Tenn.)
Max Gate (Kankakee, Ill.)
Million (Cambridge, Mass.)

Nisula (Okemos, Mich.)
Ohio (Mansfield, Ohio)
Reprint (Washington, D.C.)
Russell (Montreal, Que.)
Turkey (Westport, Conn.)
Vandoros (Middleton, Wisc.)
Watermark W. (Wichita, Kan.)

Abraham Lincoln

*See also Presidential
Assassinations, Presidents*

Abe. Lincoln (Chicago, Ill.)
Appomatox (Chicago, Ill.)

Barrister (Davie, Fla.)
Hist. News (Skokie, Ill.)

Old Quenzel (Pt. Tobacco, Md.)

Joseph C. Lincoln

Chamberlin (E. Orleans, Mass.)

Morritt (Warwick, R.I.)

Staten (Harwich, Mass.)

Linguistics

Atticus (Toronto, Ont.)
Bolerium (San Francisco, Calif.)

Bond (Reading, Mass.)
Kripke (New York, N.Y.)

White (Granger, Texas)

Literature

Abelard (Toronto, Ont.)
About (Toronto, Ont.)
Academy (New York, N.Y.)
Acorn (San Francisco, Calif.)
Allen (Philadelphia, Pa.)
Allison (No. Bay, Ont.)
Alphabet (Toronto, Ont.)
Amer. Worlds (Hamden, Conn.)
Annex (Toronto, Ont.)
Annie's #1 (Portland, Ore.)
Annie's #2 (Portland, Ore.)
Anson-Cartwright (Toronto, Ont.)
Antic Hay (W. Caldwell, N.J.)
Antiquus (San Francisco, Calif.)
Appelfeld (New York, N.Y.)
Appel (Mt. Vernon, N.Y.)
Armens (Iowa City, Iowa)
Armitage (Miamisburg, Ohio)
Atlanta (Atlanta, Ga.)
Authors (Dundee, Ore.)
Avocet (Corvallis, Ore.)
Barn E. (Tivoli, N.Y.)
Barnes (Evanston, Ill.)
Barrister (Davie, Fla.)
Barrow (Concord, Mass.)
Bartleby's (Bethesda, Md.)
Benjamin (Hunter, N.Y.)
Berliawsky (Camden, Maine)
Bernard (Rockville, Md.)
Biblioctopus (Idyllwild, Calif.)
Bibliomania (Berkeley, Calif.)
Bibliomania (Schenectady, N.Y.)
Bibliomania (Oakland, Calif.)
Biermaier's (Minneapolis, Minn.)
Black Oak (Berkeley, Calif.)
Book Bazaar (Ottawa, Ont.)
Book Cellar (Fullerton, Calif.)
Book Cellar (Brattleboro, Vt.)
Book Cellar (Bethesda, Md.)
Booked Up (Washington, D.C.)
Book End (Monterey, Calif.)
Book Farm (Henniker, N.H.)
Bookie Joint (Reseda, Calif.)
Book Lady (Savannah, Ga.)

Bookman (Tybee Isl., Ga.)
Bookman (Kent, Ohio)
Book Mark (Philadelphia, Pa.)
Books/Books (Coral Gables, Fla.)
Books 'n (New York, N.Y.)
Bookstore (Lenox, Mass.)
Boss (Brookline, Mass.)
Boston Annex (Boston, Mass.)
Bowie (Seattle, Wash.)
Brookline (Brookline, Mass.)
Brown (New London, Conn.)
Burrows (Downers Grove, Ill.)
Burstein (Waltham, Mass.)
Cahan (Narberth, Pa.)
Captain's (Ashville, N.C.)
Carduner (Philadelphia, Pa.)
Cassidy (Sacramento, Calif.)
Chaney (Ossining, N.Y.)
Chimera (Palo Alto, Calif.)
Chip's Search (New York, N.Y.)
Chloe's (Sacramento, Calif.)
ChoreoGraphica (Boston, Mass.)
City Spirit (Denver, Colo.)
Clark's (Spokane, Wash.)
Colburn (Atlanta, Ga.)
Collectabilia (Valley Stream, N.Y.)
Colonial (Pleasantville, N.Y.)
Connolly (Vista, Calif.)
Cotswold (Medina, Ohio)
Cragsmoor (Cragsmoor, N.Y.)
Darby (Darby, Pa.)
Deeds (Ellicott City, Md.)
Desmarais (Palo Alto, Calif.)
Diamond (Burbank, Calif.)
Dickson St. (Fayetteville, Ark.)
Donaldson's (Knoxville, Tenn.)
Donnally (Seattle, Wash.)
Dyment (Ottawa, Ont.)
Elliott (New York, N.Y.)
Else Fine (Dearborn, Mich.)
Emerson (Falls Village, Conn.)
Emerson (Albuquerque, N.M.)
Enchanted (Brooklyn, N.Y.)
Ernest (Ottumwa, Iowa)

Fay (Caledonia, N.Y.)
Feiden (Mamaroneck, N.Y.)
Felcone (Princeton, N.J.)
50,000 (El Cajon, Calif.)
First Edtns. (Richmond, Va.)
Folger (Washington, D.C.)
Footnote (Brooklyn, N.Y.)
Fraser's (Sherman Oaks, Calif.)
George Sand (Los Angeles, Calif.)
Gilbo (Carpinteria, Calif.)
Globe (Northampton, Mass.)
Golden Legend (Los Angeles, Calif.)
Gotham (New York, N.Y.)
Grt. Expect. (Staten Isl., N.Y.)
Griffon (So. Bend, Ind.)
Grimshaw (Randolph, Mass.)
Guerin (Montreal, Que.)
Gull Gall. (Oakland, Calif.)
Hamilton's (Williamsburg, Va.)
Hammer (Santa Barbara, Calif.)
Harris (Northfield, Mass.)
Haunted (Victoria, B.C.)
Headley (St. Catherines, Ont.)
Heartwood (Charlottesville, Va.)
Hermitage (Denver, Colo.)
Hirsch (Hopewell Jctn., N.Y.)
Hoefliger (Buffalo, N.Y.)
Hoffer (Vancouver, B.C.)
Horizon (Seattle, Wash.)
Horne (Lakeland, Fla.)
Hughes (St. Louis, Mo.)
Hummingbird (Albuquerque, N.M.)
Huntley (Claremont, Calif.)
Hyde Park (Tampa, Fla.)
Irene's (So. Gardner, Mass.)
Jaffe (Arlington, Va.)
Jenkins (Austin, Texas)
Johnson's (Los Angeles, Calif.)
Jordan (Philadelphia, Pa.)
Juvelis (Boston, Mass.)
King (Detroit, Mich.)
Konigsmark (Wayne, Pa.)

Kristiansen (Boston, Mass.)
Lambert (Hancock, N.H.)
Leach (Brattleboro, Vt.)
Lemon (Lemon Grove, Calif.)
Lien (Minneapolis, Minn.)
Lighthouse (St. Pete., Fla.)
Lopez (Hadley, Mass.)
Lowe (Eastsound, Wash.)
MacLeod's (Vancouver, B.C.)
MacManus (Philadelphia, Pa.)
Maelstrom (San Francisco, Calif.)
Mahoney (Buffalo, N.Y.)
Maiden (W. Chester, Pa.)
Manor (Huntington Valley, Pa.)
Marley (Oldwick, N.J.)
Marlowe's (Boston, Mass.)
Mason (Toronto, Ont.)
Maxwell's (Lima, N.Y.)
McCosh (Excelsior, Minn.)
Memorable (Stone Mtn., Ga.)
Merlin's (Providence, R.I.)
Michlestreet (E. Lebanon, Maine)
Mill (Craftsbury Common, Vt.)
Minnehaha (Minneapolis, Minn.)
Minters (New York, N.Y.)
M. & M. (E. Northport, N.Y.)
Modern (Huntingdon Valley, Pa.)
Monie (Cooperstown, N.Y.)
Monie Shop (Cooperstown, N.Y.)
Mott (Sheffield, Mass.)
M & S (Weston, Mass.)

Mullins (Encinitas, Calif.)
Nelson's (Albany, N.Y.)
Nelson's (Troy, N.Y.)
Norumbega (Houston, Texas)
Novel (San Luis Obispo, Calif.)
O'Brien (Portland, Maine)
Old Books (Brunswick, Maine)
Old Erie (Cleveland, Ohio)
Old Ver. (Olympia Falls, Ill.)
O'Neal (Boston, Mass.)
Pageant (New York, N.Y.)
Pangloss (Cambridge, Mass.)
Parsons (Sonoma, Calif.)
Perkinson (Deer Isle, Maine)
Philosophical (New York, N.Y.)
Pirages (McMinnville, Ore.)
Pomander (New York, N.Y.)
Potter (Santa Fe, N.M.)
Preservation (Evanston, Ill.)
Prosser (Chicago, Ill.)
Publix (Cleveland, Ohio)
Quill (Pinellas Park, Fla.)
Ray (Baldwin Park, Calif.)
Redding (Sequim, Wash.)
Red Horse (Tampa, Fla.)
Reese (New Haven, Conn.)
Rieger (Greenwood, S.C.)
Rulon-Miller (Minneapolis, Minn.)
Russica (New York, N.Y.)
Sanderson (Stockbridge, Mass.)
Saurus (Bethlehem, Pa.)

Schlossberg (Newton, Mass.)
Schoyer's (Pittsburgh, Pa.)
Seville (Pensacola, Fla.)
Shelton (Tampa, Fla.)
Sherick (Santa Barbara, Calif.)
Sidney's (Missoula, Mont.)
Smith's (Brewster, Mass.)
Stuart (Yuma, Ariz.)
Sylvester (Los Angeles, Calif.)
Talisman (Georgetown, Calif.)
Temple (Toronto, Ont.)
Ten Eyck (Southboro, Mass.)
This Old (Montclair, Calif.)
Thomas (San Francisco, Calif.)
Tisza (Chestnut Hill, Mass.)
Town (Dutch Flat, Calif.)
Transition (San Francisco, Calif.)
Typographeum (Francestown, N.H.)
University (Hull, Mass.)
Valley (Amherst, Mass.)
Waiting (Cambridge, Mass.)
Water Row (Sudbury, Mass.)
Wessex (Menlo Park, Calif.)
West L.A. (Los Angeles, Calif.)
Woolmer (Revere, Pa.)
Word (Montreal, Que.)
Wyatt (San Diego, Calif.)
Ximenes (New York, N.Y.)
Yesterday's (Ashfield, Mass.)
Zubel (Cleveland, Ohio)

American Literature

Alcala (San Diego, Calif.)
Beyer (Stratford, Conn.)
Bookshelf (Ogden, Utah)
Brick Row (San Francisco, Calif.)
Brownstone (New York, N.Y.)
Casavant (Wayland, Mass.)
Colophon (Epping, N.H.)
Different (Des Moines, Iowa)
Dysinger (Brunswick, Maine)
Eldredge (Vineyard Haven, Mass.)
1st Edtn. (Muskegon Hgts., Mich.)
Gilliam (Charlottesville, Va.)

In Our (Cambridge, Mass.)
Joe the Pro (Santa Barbara, Calif.)
Lambeth (San Antonio, Texas)
Laurie (St. Paul, Minn.)
Limestone (Glen Rose, Texas)
Mac Donnell (Austin, Texas)
Magnum (Charlottesville, Va.)
Metacomet (Providence, R.I.)
Minkoff (Grt. Barrington, Mass.)
Nudelman (Seattle, Wash.)
Respess (Durham, N.C.)
Respess (Chapel Hill, N.C.)

Ridge (Stone Ridge, N.Y.)
Robinson (Windsor, Conn.)
Savoy (Lanesborough, Mass.)
2nd Life (Lanesborough, Mass.)
Starr (Boston, Mass.)
Stephens (Hastings, N.Y.)
Watson (Buelah, Colo.)
Wells (Wells, Maine)
Wilder (Hubbardston, Mass.)
Wreden (Palo Alto, Calif.)

Beat Literature

Beatific (Schenectady, N.Y.)
Joslin (Springfield, Mass.)

Margolis (Monroe, Mich.)
Rare Book (New York, N.Y.)

Sample (Stoneham, Mass.)
Water Row (Sudbury, Mass.)

See also
Canada & Canadiana

Canadian Literature

Alphabet (Toronto, Ont.)
Ball (Paris, Ont.)

Donaldson (Nanaimo, B.C.)
Temple (Toronto, Ont.)

Conservative Literature & Authors

See also Radical Politics & Literature

Bolingbroke (Pinnacle, N.C.)

Concord (Kailua-Kona, Haw.)

Sessions (Birmingham, Ala.)

18th Century Literature

Allen (Altadena, Calif.)
Attic (Hodges, S.C.)
Carpenter (Balboa Isl., Calif.)
Cleland's (Portsmouth, N.H.)

Cummings (Stillwater, Minn.)
Hartfield (Ann Arbor, Mich.)
Manor (Huntington Valley, Pa.)
Marley (Oldwick, N.J.)

Martin (La Grange, Ill.)
Pacific (Honolulu, Haw.)
Rose (New York, N.Y.)
Tramp (Jackson, Mich.)

English Literature

Ackerman (Walpole, N.H.)
Ahab (Cambridge, Mass.)
Attic (Hodges, S.C.)
Auerbach (New York, N.Y.)
Berkelouw (Los Angeles, Calif.)
Brick Row (San Francisco, Calif.)
Britannia (New Preston, Conn.)
Brooks (Macon, Ga.)

Chip's Shop (New York, N.Y.)
Cleland's (Portsmouth, N.H.)
Clover (Charlottesville, Va.)
Colophon (Epping, N.H.)
Cummings (Stillwater, Minn.)
Debra (No. Hills, Pa.)
Eldredge (Vineyard Haven, Mass.)
Emerson (Wellsboro, Pa.)

Fern (New York, N.Y.)
Garnett (St. Louis, Mo.)
Gilliam (Charlottesville, Va.)
Green (Philadelphia, Pa.)
Guelker (St. Louis, Mo.)
Hartfield (Ann Arbor, Mich.)
Joe the Pro (Santa Barbara, Calif.)
Lambeth (San Antonio, Texas)

Laurie (St. Paul, Minn.)
Limestone (Glen Rose, Texas)
Link (Redding, Calif.)
Lowe (Eastsound, Wash.)
Mac Donnell (Austin, Texas)
Magnum (Charlottesville, Va.)
Manor (Huntington Valley, Pa.)
Matthews (Ft. Erie, Ont.)
Metacomet (Providence, R.I.)
Minkoff (Grt. Barrington, Mass.)
Modern (Huntingdon Valley, Pa.)

Nudelman (Seattle, Wash.)
Pepper/Stern (Sharon, Mass.)
Pepper/Stern (Santa Barbara, Calif.)
Respess (Durham, N.C.)
Respess (Chapel Hill, N.C.)
Rose (New York, N.Y.)
Ross (Redwood City, Calif.)
Savoy (Lanesborough, Mass.)
Schneeman (Chicago, Ill.)
2nd Life (Lanesborough, Mass.)

Starr (Boston, Mass.)
Stonehill (New Haven, Conn.)
Sumner (Yarmouth, Maine)
Taylor (Austin, Texas)
Trebizond (New Preston, Conn.)
Turlington (Pittsboro, N.C.)
Vandoros (Middleton, Wisc.)
Waite (Madison, Wisc.)
Wreden (Palo Alto, Calif.)

Gay & Lesbian Literature

Elysian (Elmhurst, N.Y.)
Glad Day (Toronto, Ont.)

Lambda (Washington, D.C.)
Paths (New York, N.Y.)

Sisterhood (Los Angeles, Calif.)
Webster's (Milwaukee, Wisc.)

Literature In English Translation

Burbank (Burbank, Calif.)
Hoffer (Vancouver, B.C.)
Maelstrom (San Francisco, Calif.)
McCosh (Excelsior, Minn.)

Scholarly (Los Angeles, Calif.)
Seluzicki (Portland, Ore.)
Stephens (Hastings, N.Y.)
Temple (Toronto, Ont.)

10 O'Clock (Elk Grove, Calif.)
Waiting (Cambridge, Mass.)

19th Century Literature

Auerbach (New York, N.Y.)
Benson (W. Cornwall, Conn.)
Buddenbrooks (Boston, Mass.)
Currey (Elizabethtown, N.Y.)
Elliott (New York, N.Y.)
E. Wharton (Oakton, Va.)
Fullam (Babylon, N.Y.)
Greene (Rockville Centre, N.Y.)
Heartwood (Charlottesville, Va.)
Hirschtritt's (Silver Spg., Md.)
Jack London (Glen Ellen, Calif.)

Mac Donnell (Austin, Texas)
Manor (Huntington Valley, Pa.)
Marley (Oldwick, N.J.)
Martin (La Grange, Ill.)
Mason (Toronto, Ont.)
19th Cent. (Baltimore, Md.)
Old Almanack (Concord, N.H.)
Old Books (New Orleans, La.)
Osgood (Rockport, Mass.)
Pepper/Stern (Sharon, Mass.)
Pepper/Stern (Santa Barbara,

Calif.)
Pharos (New Haven, Conn.)
Pride (Ballston Lake, N.Y.)
Rare Book (New York, N.Y.)
Rose (New York, N.Y.)
Ross (Redwood City, Calif.)
Small (So. Yarmouth, Mass.)
Spooner's (Tilton, N.H.)
12th St. (Santa Monica, Calif.)

20th Century Literature

Ampersand (New York, N.Y.)
Archer's (Kent, Ohio)
Associates (Falls Church, Va.)
Auerbach (New York, N.Y.)
Babcock (Derry, N.H.)
Batta (Toronto, Ont.)
Benson (W. Cornwall, Conn.)
Book Den (Santa Barbara, Calif.)
Book Den E. (Oak Bluffs, Mass.)
Books & Co. (New York, N.Y.)
C. Dickens (Atlanta, Ga.)
Clipper Ship (San Antonio, Texas)
Clover (Charlottesville, Va.)
Davis (Sherman Oaks, Calif.)
Dinkytown (Minneapolis, Minn.)

Elliott (New York, N.Y.)
E. Wharton (Oakton, Va.)
Fugitive (Nashville, Tenn.)
Glover (Cambridge, N.Y.)
Joe the Pro (Santa Barbara, Calif.)
Lemuria (Jackson, Miss.)
Link (Redding, Calif.)
Mac Donnell (Austin, Texas)
Martin (La Grange, Ill.)
Monahan (New York, N.Y.)
Myers (Sequim, Wash.)
Nomland (Los Angeles, Calif.)
Nouveau (Jackson, Miss.)
Old Almanack (Concord, N.H.)
Pepper/Stern (Santa Barbara,

Calif.)
Pharos (New Haven, Conn.)
Pride (Ballston Lake, N.Y.)
Ridge (Stone Ridge, N.Y.)
Riverrun (Hastings, N.Y.)
Ross (Redwood City, Calif.)
Schoen (Northampton, Mass.)
Southpaw (Roxbury, Mass.)
Sullivan (St. Pete., Fla.)
Talisman (Georgetown, Calif.)
Turlington (Pittsboro, N.C.)
Willow (Englewood, Colo.)
Yesterday's (Oak Park, Mich.)

Literary Criticism

Alcala (San Diego, Calif.)
Amer. Worlds (Hamden, Conn.)
Appel (Mt. Vernon, N.Y.)
Arond (Lexington, Mass.)
Atlanta (Atlanta, Ga.)
Atticus (Toronto, Ont.)
Ball (Paris, Ont.)
Bibelots (Seattle, Wash.)
Booked Up (Washington, D.C.)
Chip's Search (New York, N.Y.)
Chip's Shop (New York, N.Y.)
City Lights (San Francisco, Calif.)
Colonial (Pleasantville, N.Y.)
Constant (Milwaukee, Wisc.)

Cragsmoor (Cragsmoor, N.Y.)
Darby (Darby, Pa.)
Diamond (Burbank, Calif.)
Drew's (Santa Barbara, Calif.)
Estate (Washington, D.C.)
Evergreen (Ft. Worth, Texas)
Hood (Lawrence, Kan.)
Horizon (Seattle, Wash.)
Howard (Burlingame, Calif.)
Island (Isleboro, Maine)
Jaffe (Arlington, Va.)
Joslin (Springfield, Mass.)
Library (Dallas, Texas)
Lincoln (Foster, R.I.)

Martin (La Grange, Ill.)
Memorable (Stone Mtn., Ga.)
Merkel (Xenia, Ohio)
Morrell's (Ocean Grove, N.J.)
Murphy (Iowa City, Iowa)
Old N.Y. (Atlanta, Ga.)
Palma (Wilmington, Del.)
Paulson (Huntington, Mass.)
Scott (Portland, Maine)
Stanley (Wilder, Vt.)
Talbothay's (Aurora, N.Y.)
Valley (Amherst, Mass.)
Wooden (Ann Arbor, Mich.)
Zubel (Cleveland, Ohio)

Little Magazines & Literary Small Presses

See also Back Issue Magazines, Back Issue Periodicals, Press Books & Fine Printing

Ampersand (New York, N.Y.)
Ball (Paris, Ont.)
Benjamins (Philadelphia, Pa.)
Bookstore (Lenox, Mass.)
Burgman (Santa Rosa, Calif.)
Canner (Boston, Mass.)
Chloe's (Sacramento, Calif.)

Daedalus (Charlottesville, Va.)
Dermont (Onset, Mass.)
Eldredge (Vineyard Haven, Mass.)
Ex Libris (New York, N.Y.)
George Sand (Los Angeles, Calif.)
Gotham (New York, N.Y.)
Left Bank (Oak Park, Ill.)

Macksey (Baltimore, Md.)
Magazine (New York, N.Y.)
O'Malley (Kingston, R.I.)
Phoenix (New York, N.Y.)
Stockman (Palmyra, N.Y.)
Water Row (Sudbury, Mass.)

Livre d'Artiste

See also Press Books & Fine Printing

A B I (Santa Barbara, Calif.)
Heller (Washington, D.C.)
Herlin (New York, N.Y.)

Juvelis (Boston, Mass.)
Phillips (New York, N.Y.)
Printed (New York, N.Y.)

Reisman (Philadelphia, Pa.)
Saturdays' (Euclid, Ohio)
Zwicker (New York, N.Y.)

Jack London

Chalfin (New York, N.Y.)
Diablo (Walnut Creek, Calif.)
Jack London (Glen Ellen, Calif.)

Noto (Cupertino, Calif.)
Ookkees (Olympia, Wash.)
Perry's (San Jose, Calif.)

Smith (Pleasant Hill, Calif.)
West Side (Ann Arbor, Mich.)

Louisiana

Beckham's (New Orleans, La.)
Clark (Baton Rouge, La.)
Librairie (Chartres) (New Orleans,

La.)
Martin (Atlanta, Ga.)
Old Books (New Orleans, La.)

Samuel (New Orleans, La.)

Back Issue Magazines

See also Little Magazines, Back Issue Periodicals, Small Presses & Fine Printing

Aboud (Stayton, Ore.)
Alsberg (Skokie, Ill.)
Antiq. Book (Portsmouth, N.H.)
Avenue (Boston, Mass.)
Back No. (Danvers, Mass.)
Barber (Boston, Mass.)
Barbier (Seaside, Calif.)
Book Broker (Evansville, Ind.)
Bookery (Fairborn, Ohio)
Bookie Joint (Reseda, Calif.)
Bunker (Spring Valley, Calif.)
City Wide (Brooklyn, N.Y.)
Denver Fair (Denver, Colo.)

1st Edtn. (Muskegon Hgts., Mich.)
4th Estate (New London, Conn.)
Harvard (Stockton, Calif.)
Highwood (Traverse City, Mich.)
Jaeger (Commack, N.Y.)
Kirch (Thornville, Ohio)
Kravette (Jericho, N.Y.)
Magazine (San Francisco, Calif.)
Magazine (New York, N.Y.)
Morrell's (Ocean Grove, N.J.)
Pirtle (Bellevue, Wash.)
Red Horse (Tampa, Fla.)
Reedmor (Philadelphia, Pa.)

Rodden's (Long Bch., Calif.)
Scarlet (New Milford, Conn.)
2nd Time (Ventura, Calif.)
Slater (Bakersfield, Calif.)
Sloat (Flemington, N.J.)
Snyder (Pittsburgh, Pa.)
Staten (Harwich, Mass.)
Taste (Fall River, Mass.)
Tinker (Santa Cruz, Calif.)
Village (Rochester, N.Y.)
Village (Amherst, N.Y.)
Way's (Seattle, Wash.)
Wellfleet (Wellfleet, Mass.)

Maine

Bedford's (Ellsworth, Maine)
Bishop (Corea, Maine)
Book Pedlars (Cundy's Harbor, Maine)
Brown (Belfast, Maine)
Canney (Alfred, Maine)
Cotton Hill (Laconia, N.H.)

Cross Hill (Brunswick, Maine)
deBeurs (Dexter, Maine)
Dolphin (Camden, Maine)
Eastman (Springvale, Maine)
Lobster (Spruce Head, Maine)
Memory (Belfast, Maine)
O'Brien (Portland, Maine)

Ockett (Bryant Pond, Maine)
Pratt (E. Livermore, Maine)
River Oaks (Jay, Maine)
Shaw's (Bath, Maine)
Varney's (Casco, Maine)

Mammalogy

Hahn (Cottonwood, Ariz.)
Huxley (Loudonville, N.Y.)

Johnson (No. Bennington, Vt.)
Tolliver's (Los Angeles, Calif.)

Watkins (Dolgeville, N.Y.)

Manuscripts

See also
Diaries & Narratives, Documents

aGatherin' (Wynantskill, N.Y.)
Ahab (Cambridge, Mass.)
Alford (Springfield, Va.)
Americanist (Pottstown, Pa.)
Apfelbaum (Valley Stream, N.Y.)
Armenian (Pico Rivera, Calif.)
Auerbach (New York, N.Y.)
Barnes (Philadelphia, Pa.)
Batchelder (Ambler, Pa.)
B & B (Randolph, Mass.)
Bean (Biddeford, Maine)
Biblioctopus (Idyllwild, Calif.)
Biegeleisen (Brooklyn, N.Y.)
Black Sun (New York, N.Y.)
Book Block (Cos Cob, Conn.)
Borden (Portsmouth, R. I.)
Breslauer (New York, N.Y.)
Bromsen (Boston, Mass.)
Burger (Pine Grove, Calif.)
Burpee Hill (New London, N.H.)
Carlitz (Philadelphia, Pa.)
Carnegie (New York, N.Y.)
Cohasco (Yonkers, N.Y.)
Craig (Newport, R. I.)

Elliott (New York, N.Y.)
E. Wharton (Oakton, Va.)
Fleming (New York, N.Y.)
Granat (Woodmere, N.Y.)
Grunder (Ithaca, N.Y.)
Gventer (So. Egremont, Mass.)
Harper (New York, N.Y.)
Harris (Los Angeles, Calif.)
Heaston (Austin, Texas)
Hist. News (Skokie, Ill.)
Holmes (Philadelphia, Pa.)
Horowitz (New York, N.Y.)
Joe the Pro (Santa Barbara, Calif.)
Koschal (Verona, N.J.)
Kostman (Glendora, Calif.)
Lehr (New York, N.Y.)
Levin (Los Angeles, Calif.)
Lion (New York, N.Y.)
Lowe (New York, N.Y.)
Lubrano (So. Lee, Mass.)
Magic (Johnson City, Tenn.)
Manuscript (Southampton, Pa.)
Morrow (New York, N.Y.)
Nestler (Waldwick, N.J.)

Newburyport (Newburyport, Mass.)
Newman (Chicago, Ill.)
No. Country (Richmond, N.H.)
Phila. Rare (Philadelphia, Pa.)
Pirages (McMinnville, Ore.)
Rendell (Newton, Mass.)
Rendell (Waban, Mass.)
Resnick (Cazenovia, N.Y.)
Richards (Templeton, Mass.)
Rootenberg (Sherman Oaks, Calif.)
Ross (Medina, N.Y.)
Rubinfine (Pleasantville, N.J.)
Scriptorium (Beverly Hills, Calif.)
Seaport (Stonington, Conn.)
Stephens (Hastings, N.Y.)
Stonehill (New Haven, Conn.)
Valentino (Philadelphia, Pa.)
Virginia (Berryville, Va.)
Wade (Cincinnati, Ohio)
Woolmer (Revere, Pa.)
Wyngate (Bethesda, Md.)
Xerxes (Glen Head, N.Y.)

Illuminated Manuscripts

See also
Illuminated Leaves
& Pages

Duschnes (New York, N.Y.)
Ferrini/Greenberg (Akron, Ohio)

Geraci (Accord, N.Y.)
Katz (Los Angeles, Calif.)

Moriah (New York, N.Y.)
Schiller (New York, N.Y.)

Medieval Manuscripts

See also
Illuminated Leaves
& Pages

Caprio (Revere, Mass.)
Carr (Concord, N.H.)
Glenn (Kansas City, Mo.)

Kraus (New York, N.Y.)
Levinson (Beverly Hills, Calif.)
Rendell (Newton, Mass.)

Witten (Southport, Conn.)
Woods (Yakima, Wash.)

Maps, Atlases, & Cartography

See also Voyages, Travels, & Exploration

Abrams (Atlanta, Ga.)
Adams (Chicago, Ill.)
Alsberg (Skokie, Ill.)
Americana (Coral Gables, Fla.)
Amer. Frag. (Escondido, Calif.)
Amherst (Amherst, Mass.)
Antiquaria (Franklin, Tenn.)
Antique Books (Hamden, Conn.)
Arader (Atlanta, Ga.)
Arader (Houston, Texas)
Arader (King of Prussia, Pa.)
Arader (New York, N.Y.)
Arader (San Francisco, Calif.)
Argosy (New York, N.Y.)
Arkway (New York, N.Y.)
Bagley (Fredericton, N.B.)
Bartfield (New York, N.Y.)
Berry (Kingston, Ont.)
Bill (New York, N.Y.)
Book Barn (So. Sioux City, Neb.)
Book Room (Coral Gables, Fla.)
Branford (Branford, Conn.)
Brattle Book (Boston, Mass.)
Broadfoot's (Wilmington, N.C.)
Camelot (Baltimore, Md.)
Carlitz (Philadelphia, Pa.)
Casten (New York, N.Y.)
Cohasco (Yonkers, N.Y.)
Conn. Book (Fairfield, Conn.)
Drew's (Santa Barbara, Calif.)

Dunlap (St. Louis, Mo.)
Fisher (Cobleskill, N.Y.)
Fitch (Santa Fe, N.M.)
Fortunate Finds (Warwick, R.I.)
Gavin (Leominster, Mass.)
Glaeve (Madison, Wisc.)
Glover's (Lexington, Ky.)
Goodspeed's #1 (Boston, Mass.)
Goodspeed's #2 (Boston, Mass.)
Hallberg (Hartford, Conn.)
Hammer (Santa Barbara, Calif.)
Harder (Los Alamos, N.M.)
Heaston (Austin, Texas)
Hensel (Belle Chasse, La.)
High Ridge (Rye, N.Y.)
Holy Land (Washington, D.C.)
Hudson (Dyersburg, Tenn.)
Jolly (Brookline, Mass.)
Kennedy (Des Moines, Wash.)
Kraus (New York, N.Y.)
Lake (Toronto, Ont.)
Manasek (Hanover, N.H.)
Manasek (Norwich, Vt.)
Manning's (San Francisco, Calif.)
Manuscript (Southampton, Pa.)
Marshall Field (Chicago, Ill.)
Martayan (New York, N.Y.)
Martin (Atlanta, Ga.)
Monckton (Chicago, Ill.)
Mt. Eden (Mt. Eden, Calif.)

Nebenzahl (Chicago, Ill.)
Oblong (Millerton, N.Y.)
Observatory (Sitka, Alk.)
Old Almanack (Concord, N.H.)
Old Book (San Francisco, Calif.)
Old Print (Washington, D.C.)
Old Print (New York, N.Y.)
Pageant (New York, N.Y.)
Palmer (Eugene, Ore.)
Pansy (St. Andrews, N.B.)
Parmer's (Sarasota, Fla.)
Patrick (Toronto, Ont.)
Pavlov (Dobbs Ferry, N.Y.)
Phila. Print (Philadelphia, Pa.)
Ritzlin (Evanston, Ill.)
Robinson (Manchester, Maine)
Robinson (St. Pete., Fla.)
Rogers (Athens, Ga.)
Ross (Woodland Hills, Calif.)
Rudolph (Portland, Ore.)
Slifer (New York, N.Y.)
Spellman (Brick Town, N.J.)
Stern (Chicago, Ill.)
Stevens (Williamsburg, Va.)
Suarez (New York, N.Y.)
Tappin (Atlantic Bch., Fla.)
Tattered (Denver, Colo.)
Urrizola (Los Angeles, Calif.)
Washington (Washington Cr., Pa.)
William (Mineola, N.Y.)

Marine Biology

Nautica (Halifax, N.S.)

Seashell (Bayside, Calif.)

Marine & Maritime

See also
Naval & Nautical

Again (Santa Barbara, Calif.)
Antheil (No. Bellmore, N.Y.)
Articles (Skokie, Ill.)
Bayview (Northport, N.Y.)
Bedford's (Ellsworth, Maine)
Boardwalk (Friday Harbor, Wash.)
Bookery (Farmington, N.H.)
Book Prospector (Littleton, Colo.)
Book Ranger (New York, N.Y.)
Books Unltd. (Nat'l City, Calif.)
Book/Tackle (Chestnut Hill, Mass.)
Burnett (Atlanta, Ga.)
Cape (Mashpec, Mass.)
Caravan-Maritime (Jamaica, N.Y.)
Columbia (Suffern, N.Y.)
Compass (Sitka, Alk.)
Comstock's (Auburn, Wash.)
Coventry (Coventry, Conn.)
Crofter's (Washington, Conn.)
Cross Hill (Brunswick, Maine)
Darvill's Book (Eastsound, Wash.)

Davies (Oak Park, Ill.)
Elmcress (So. Hamilton, Mass.)
R E (Fairhope, Ala.)
Garret (Clinton, N.Y.)
Green Dolphin (Portland, Ore.)
Guthman (Westport, Conn.)
Hall (E. Longmeadow, Mass.)
Homestead (Marlborough, N.H.)
JFF (Manhasset, N.Y.)
Jumping (Hartford, Conn.)
Lefkowicz (Fairhaven, Mass.)
Levine (Savannah, Ga.)
Lowe (Boston, Mass.)
Magnalia (No. Amherst, Mass.)
Maritime (Brewer, Maine)
McCullough (Los Angeles, Calif.)
Mil-Air (Compton, Calif.)
Military (New York, N.Y.)
Miller (Johnstown, N.Y.)
Mill (Craftsbury Common, Vt.)
Moore (Wynnewood, Pa.)

Morrill (Newton Centre, Mass.)
Murray (Wilbraham, Mass.)
Nelson (New Bedford, Mass.)
Owl (Camden, Maine)
Parnassus (Yarmouthport, Mass.)
Pier (Piermont, N.Y.)
Rinaldi (Kennebunkport, Maine)
Scott (Portland, Maine)
Sea (Glen Oaks, N.Y.)
Sky (New York, N.Y.)
Soldier (New York, N.Y.)
Tappin (Atlantic Bch., Fla.)
10 Pound (Gloucester, Mass.)
Thunderbird (Aldergrove, B.C.)
Titcomb's (E. Sandwich, Mass.)
Tupper (Vancouver, B.C.)
Tuttle (Madison, Wisc.)
Wharf (Centreville, Md.)
Wikehgan (Mt. Desert, Maine)
Womrath's (Hempstead, N.Y.)

Maryland

Deeds (Ellicott City, Md.)
Old Quenzel (Pt. Tobacco, Md.)

Unicorn (Trappe, Md.)
Wharf (Centreville, Md.)

Wonder (Frederick, Md.)

Massachusetts

Lewis St. (Lynn, Mass.)
Lowenberg (Lafayette, Calif.)

Maier (Rockport, Mass.)
Melvins (Grt. Barrington, Mass.)

Mathematics

Allen's (Baltimore, Md.)
Book Assoc. (Orange, Conn.)
Bookstall (San Francisco, Calif.)
E. K. (Rego Park, N.Y.)
Elgen (Rockville Centre, N.Y.)

Glaser (Sausalito, Calif.)
Levien (McDowell, Va.)
Lubrecht (Forestburgh, N.Y.)
Maxwell (Elmsford, N.Y.)
Merlin's (Isla Vista, Calif.)

Palinurus (Philadelphia, Pa.)
B. Ramer (New York, N.Y.)
Science (Ann Arbor, Mich.)
2nd Front (San Francisco, Calif.)

Books About Medals

Finn (W. Roxbury, Mass.)

Jackson (Weston, Ont.)

Medical & Medicine

See also
History of Medicine & Science

Adamson (Augusta, Ga.)
Alcala (San Diego, Calif.)
Amdur (Mansfield, Conn.)
Antiq. Book (Winter Park, Fla.)
Antiq. Bookworm (Sharon, Mass.)
Avocet (Sanford, N.C.)
Beattie (Parkesburg, Pa.)
Book Barn (Rochester, Mich.)
Bookmine (Old Scaramento, Calif.)
Book/Tackle (Watch Hill, R.I.)
Brunsell's (Hanson, Mass.)

Burleson (Atlanta, Ga.)
Dartmouth (Hanover, N.H.)
Dordick (Somerville, Mass.)
Fish (Minneapolis, Minn.)
Glaser (Sausalito, Calif.)
Goodrich (Englewood, N.J.)
Hoffman (Rillton, Pa.)
Legacy (Iowa City, Iowa)
Maxwell (Elmsford, N.Y.)
Medical (Jenkintown, Pa.)
Michlestreet (E. Lebanon, Maine)

Oasis (San Deigo, Calif.)
Polyanthos (Huntington, N.Y.)
Printers' (Arlington, Mass.)
Quest (Ft. Worth, Texas)
Raskin (Albertson, N.Y.)
Rittenhouse (Philadelphia, Pa.)
Sadoff (Jenkintown, Pa.)
Schab (New York, N.Y.)
Scientia (Arlington, Mass.)
Wehawken (Washington, D.C.)

Medicine & Science

See also
History of Medicine & Science

Aardvark (San Francisco, Calif.)
Antiq. Scientist (Dracut, Mass.)
Antiquarium (Bethany, Conn.)
Autos (Eliz. City, N.C.)
Book Clearing (Larchmont, N.Y.)
Books Unltd. (Nat'l City, Calif.)
Book/Tackle (Chestnut Hill, Mass.)
Burleson (Atlanta, Ga.)

Carlitz (Philadelphia, Pa.)
Celnick (Bronx, N.Y.)
CGT (College Stn., Texas)
Clare (Getzville, N.Y.)
Dast (Madison, Wisc.)
Elgen (Rockville Centre, N.Y.)
Emerson (Falls Village, Conn.)
Finer (Greenfield, Mass.)

Folkways (Bethesda, Md.)
Fye (Marshfield, Wisc.)
Glaser (Sausalito, Calif.)
Hamill (Chicago, Ill.)
Heller (Swarthmore, Pa.)
Hemlock (Neponsit, N.Y.)
Hill (New York, N.Y.)
Hillman (New York, N.Y.)

Hoffman (Rillton, Pa.)
Int'l. Univ. (New York, N.Y.)
Junius (Fairview, N.J.)
Katz (Los Angeles, Calif.)
Levinson (Beverly Hills, Calif.)
Mashman (Ridgefield, Conn.)
McDuffie's (Portland, Ore.)
McKittrick (Philadelphia, Pa.)
Medical (Jenkintown, Pa.)
M & S (Weston, Mass.)

Newburyport (Newburyport, Mass.)
Norman (San Francisco, Calif.)
Norman (Philadelphia, Pa.)
Oasis (San Deigo, Calif.)
Offenbacher (Kew Gardens, N.Y.)
Old #6 (Henniker, N.H.)
Palinurus (Philadelphia, Pa.)
Printers' (Boston, Mass.)
B. Ramer (New York, N.Y.)

Ramshorn (Albuquerque, N.M.)
Robinson (Manchester, Maine)
Rootenberg (Sherman Oaks, Calif.)
Sadoff (Jenkintown, Pa.)
Schick (Hartsdale, N.Y.)
2nd Front (San Francisco, Calif.)
Trotting (Springfield, Mass.)
Ximenes (New York, N.Y.)

H. L. Mencken

Free Lance (Brooklyn, N.Y.)

Unicorn (Trappe, Md.)

Wharf (Centreville, Md.)

Metaphysics

Abintra (Morris, N.Y.)
Academy (San Francisco, Calif.)
Aide (Cardiff, Calif.)
Blue Dragon (Ashland, Ore.)
Book Gall. (Gainesville, Fla.)
Book Harbor (Fullerton, Calif.)
Book Manifest (Portland, Ore.)
Book Nook (Escondido, Calif.)
Book Nook (Yakima, Wash.)
Bookpost (Cardiff, Calif.)
Catbird (Portland, Ore.)
Chips (Tustin, Calif.)

Clipper Ship (San Antonio, Texas)
Cook (Los Angeles, Calif.)
50,000 (El Cajon, Calif.)
Green Apple (San Francisco, Calif.)
Hubert (Walnut Creek, Calif.)
Iliad (Livingston, Mont.)
James (Lynden, Wash.)
Memory (Grand Rapids, Mich.)
Middle (Sterling Hgts., Mich.)
New Age (Westerly, R.I.)
Phoenix (Santa Monica, Calif.)

Printer's (Milldale, Conn.)
Printer's (Middletown, Conn.)
2nd Time (Ventura, Calif.)
Sophia (Amherst, Mass.)
Soundpeace (Ashland, Ore.)
Together (Denver, Colo.)
Valley (No. Hollywood, Calif.)
Whelan (Newberry, Fla.)
Women's (Contoocook, N.H.)
Words (So. Bend, Ind.)
Ye Olde (San Angelo, Texas)
Yesterday's (San Diego, Calif.)

Methodism

See also
Church History, Religion

Green (Philadelphia, Pa.)

Stroud (Williamsburg, W.Va.)

Mexico

See also
Central America, Latin America

Almagre (Bloomington, Ind.)
Associated (Long Beach, Calif.)
Bookshop (Del Rio, Texas)
Cole's (La Jolla, Calif.)

Davidson (San Diego, Calif.)
Eshner (Bisbee, Ariz.)
Hammer (Santa Barbara, Calif.)
Katz (Los Angeles, Calif.)

Kuehn (Bisbee, Ariz.)
Marchioness (Laguna Bch., Calif.)
Nomland (Los Angeles, Calif.)
Tolliver's (Los Angeles, Calif.)

Michigan

Bicentennial (Kalamazoo, Mich.)
Bookman (Grand Haven, Mich.)
Call Me (Saugatuck, Mich.)
Curious Book (E. Lansing, Mich.)
Edger (Hastings, Mich.)

Exnowski (Warren, Mich.)
1st Edtn. (Muskegon Hgts., Mich.)
Leelanau (Leland, Mich.)
Memory (Battle Creek, Mich.)
Memory (Grand Rapids, Mich.)

Peninsula (Traverse City, Mich.)
Pohrt (Flint, Mich.)
Snowbound (Marquette, Mich.)
Wertz (Flint, Mich.)
West Side (Ann Arbor, Mich.)

Middle Ages

Berkowitz (Chester, N.Y.)
Gabbard (New Boston, Texas)
Powell's (Chicago, Ill.)

Rosenthal (San Francisco, Calif.)
Salloch (Ossining, N.Y.)
Tuckers (Pittsburgh, Pa.)

Woods (Yakima, Wash.)
Zambelli (New York, N.Y.)

Middle East

Asian Books (Cambridge, Mass.)
Asian Rare (New York, N.Y.)
Brennan (Salt Lake City, Utah)
Camel (New York, N.Y.)
Feltus (Berkeley, Calif.)
Hoyt (Rockport, Mass.)

Ideal (New York, N.Y.)
Manor (New York, N.Y.)
McBlain (Hamden, Conn.)
Morrison (Santa Monica, Calif.)
19th Cent. (Baltimore, Md.)
O'Neill (Reston, Va.)

Oriental (Pasadena, Calif.)
Paragon (New York, N.Y.)
Terramedia (Wellesley, Mass.)
Worldwide (Cambridge, Mass.)

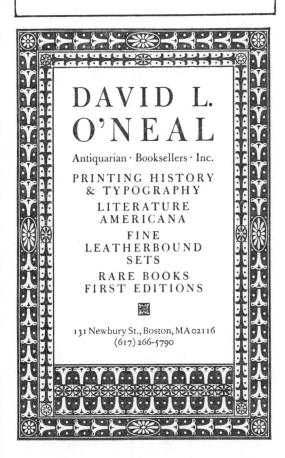

Militaria

Again (Santa Barbara, Calif.)
Air Age (Tollhouse, Calif.)
Allen's (Baltimore, Md.)
Antheil (No. Bellmore, N.Y.)
Articles (Skokie, Ill.)
Ashton (Ottawa, Ont.)
Barber's (Ft. Worth, Texas)
Benson (Ottawa, Ont.)
Bicentennial (Kalamazoo, Mich.)
Book House (Arlington, Va.)
Book Mart (San Antonio, Texas)
Cherokee (Hollywood, Calif.)
Colleen's (Houston, Texas)
Comstock's (Auburn, Wash.)
Croton (Croton, N.Y.)
Dabny (Washington, D.C.)
Delp (Belding, Mich.)

Desch (Wheaton, Md.)
Essential (Centreville, Va.)
Fantasy (San Francisco, Calif.)
Field (Georgetown, Mass.)
Graf (Iowa City, Iowa)
Guthman (Westport, Conn.)
Hall (Chambersburg, Pa.)
Harbar (Casselberry, Fla.)
Harder (Los Alamos, N.M.)
Jackson (Weston, Ont.)
JFF (Manhasset, N.Y.)
Marcher (Okla. City, Okla.)
Mason's (Wabash, Ind.)
Mil-Air (Compton, Calif.)
Military (New York, N.Y.)
Monarski (Syracuse, N.Y.)
Morrill (Newton Centre, Mass.)

Northingham (Hamilton Sq., N.J.)
Ordnance (Madison, Conn.)
Pearson (Chicago, Ill.)
Rutgers (Highland Park, N.J.)
Schmitt (Rockville, Md.)
Shuhi (Morris, Conn.)
Sky (New York, N.Y.)
Snowbound (Norridgeweck, Maine)
Soldier (New York, N.Y.)
Sommer (Niagara Falls, N.Y.)
Talbothay's (Aurora, N.Y.)
Thunderbird (Aldergrove, B.C.)
Womrath's (Hempstead, N.Y.)
Yesteryear (Atlanta, Ga.)

Military

Auslender (Wilton, Conn.)
Battery (Nashville, Tenn.)
Berman (Los Angeles, Calif.)
Book-Bind (Anaheim, Calif.)
Bookseller (Akron, Ohio)
Booksellers (St. Paul, Minn.)
Bullock (Yardley, Pa.)
Curious Book (E. Lansing, Mich.)
Essential (Centreville, Va.)
Filler (Bremerton, Wash.)
Gallis (Marblehead, Mass.)
Gustafson (Chicago, Ill.)
Harold's (St. Paul, Minn.)

Henry (Berwyn, Ill.)
Hunt (Burbank, Calif.)
Jacobs (Sherman Oaks, Calif.)
Kreinheder (Warrensburg, N.Y.)
La Galeria (Las Vegas, N.M.)
Liberty (Concord, Calif.)
McCullough (Los Angeles, Calif.)
Miller (Johnstown, N.Y.)
Monarski (Syracuse, N.Y.)
Old Erie (Cleveland, Ohio)
Old Southport (Southport, Conn.)
Once Upon (W. Hempstead, N.Y.)
Ordnance (Madison, Conn.)

Pandich (Asheville, N.C.)
Reliable (Paterson, N.J.)
Sandys (Albertson, N.Y.)
Schmitt (Rockville, Md.)
Sorrenti (Palatine, Ill.)
Springbook (Springfield, Ohio)
Starr (Boston, Mass.)
Sullivan (New York, N.Y.)
Vogt (Meadow Vista, Calif.)
Weston (Weston, Vt.)
Wolf's (Morgantown, W.Va.)

Minerology & Gemology

See also Jewelry

Geoscience (Yucaipa, Calif.)

Peri (San Diego, Calif.)

12th St. (Santa Monica, Calif.)

Miniature Books

Bromer (Boston, Mass.)
Dawson's (Los Angeles, Calif.)
Feldman (Cleveland, Ohio)
Ford (Lake Worth, Fla.)
Frohnsdorff (Gaithersburg, Md.)
Gregory (New York, N.Y.)
Ha'Penny (Snowville, N.H.)

Herzig-Cohen (Jackson Hgts., N.Y.)
Hurley (Westmoreland, N.H.)
Kapica (New Britain, Conn.)
Kitemaug (Spartanburg, S.C.)
Levien (McDowell, Va.)
Lorson's (Fullerton, Calif.)

Merriam (Conway, Mass.)
Quitzau (Edmeston, N.Y.)
Reisler (Vienna, Va.)
Victoria (New York, N.Y.)
Wake (Ft. Lauderdale, Fla.)
World War (W. Roxbury, Mass.)

Mining & Metallurgy

Argus (Sacramento, Calif.)
Bookmine (Old Scaramento, Calif.)
Earth (Littleton, N.H.)
Geoscience (Yucaipa, Calif.)
Leishman (Menlo Park, Calif.)

Martin's (Fairbanks, Alk.)
McDuffie's (Portland, Ore.)
Mt. Eden (Mt. Eden, Calif.)
Peri (San Diego, Calif.)
Persoff (Alameda, Calif.)

Poe (Mayaguez, P.R.)
Prag (San Francisco, Calif.)
Rails (Rosemead, Calif.)
Research (Fremont, Neb.)
Southwest (Durango, Colo.)

Minnesota

Goodman (St. Paul, Minn.)
Harold's (St. Paul, Minn.)

Laurie (St. Paul, Minn.)
Once Read (Mankato, Minn.)

Mississippi

Grunewald (Kansas City, Mo.)

Lurate (Jackson, Miss.)

Missouri

DC Service (Columbia, Mo.)
Hughes (St. Louis, Mo.)

Keller (Overland Park, Kan.)
Mostly (Carthage, Mo.)

Montana

Chapter 1 (Hamilton, Mont.)
Combs (Great Falls, Mont.)
Gallery Of (Bigfork, Mont.)
Golden Hill (Helena, Mont.)

Graham (Bozeman, Mont.)
Log Cabin (Bigfork, Mont.)
Minckler (Billings, Mont.)
Svoboda (Santa Barbara, Calif.)

Swinford (Paris, Ill.)
Vargo's (Bozeman, Mont.)

Mormons

Brennan (Salt Lake City, Utah)
Cosmic (Salt Lake City, Utah)
Deseret (Salt Lake City, Utah)
Ginsberg (Petersburg, Va.)

Grunder (Ithaca, N.Y.)
Scallawagiana (Salt Lake City, Utah)
Slater (Tarrytown, N.Y.)

Ute-Or (W. Jordan, Utah)
West (Provo, Utah)

Mountaineering

About (Toronto, Ont.)
Aion (Boulder, Colo.)
Anderson (Auburn, Mass.)
Belknap (Boston, Mass.)
Bibliomania (Schenectady, N.Y.)
Book Bin (Kingston, Ont.)
Bookstall (San Francisco, Calif.)

Chessler (New York, N.Y.)
Comstock's (Auburn, Wash.)
Cross (Brunswick, Maine)
Dawson's (Los Angeles, Calif.)
Dunn (Newport, Vt.)
Howard (Burlingame, Calif.)
Hoyt (Rockport, Mass.)

King's (Boulder, Colo.)
Norman (Philadelphia, Pa.)
Rainy (Lexington, Mass.)
Sportsman's (Manotick, Ont.)
Williams (Calgary, Alt.)

Movie & Fan Magazines

Book City (Hollywood, Calif.)

Bradshaw (Chicago, Ill.)

John Muir

Diablo (Walnut Creek, Calif.)

Stickel (Colma, Calif.)

Mushrooms

Gatto (New York, N.Y.)

Ken-L (Newberg, Ore.)

Mycophile (Naples, Fla.)

Music

Allen's (Baltimore, Md.)
Altman (New York, N.Y.)
Artistic (Boston, Mass.)
Bancroft (Newtown, Conn.)
Barnstormer (Sacramento, Calif.)
Bear (W. Brattleboro, Vt.)
Benjamin (Hunter, N.Y.)
Berliawsky (Camden, Maine)
B.J.S. (Forest Hills, N.Y.)
Bond (Reading, Mass.)
Book Bazaar (Ottawa, Ont.)
Book-Bind (Anaheim, Calif.)
Book Cellar (Bethesda, Md.)
Book Search (Avondale Estates, Ga.)
Books With (Concord, Mass.)
Bowling (Rancho Palos Verdes, Calif.)
Broude (New York, N.Y.)
Cadenza (Smithtown, N.Y.)
Cider (Exeter, N.H.)
Clipper Ship (San Antonio, Texas)
Country (Plainfield, Vt.)
Eisenberg (Washington, D.C.)
Footnote (Brooklyn, N.Y.)
Fraser's (Sherman Oaks, Calif.)
Front (Van Nuys, Calif.)
Graham (Forestville, Calif.)
Katt (Los Angeles, Calif.)
Legacy (Hatboro, Pa.)
Lubrano (So. Lee, Mass.)
Mechanical (Darien, Conn.)
Muns (Berkeley, Calif.)
Olde Tyme (Boonton, N.J.)
Old Music (3 Oaks, Mich.)
Organ (Braintree, Mass.)
Pacific (No. Vancouver, B.C.)
Phila. Rare (Philadelphia, Pa.)
Potter (Santa Fe, N.M.)
Rouse (Wattsville, Va.)
Ryan (Rancho Mirage, Calif.)
Schnase (Scarsdale, N.Y.)
7 Roads (San Francisco, Calif.)
Shapiro (Washington, D.C.)
Silver (Santa Barbara, Calif.)
Smith (Pleasant Hill, Calif.)
Sorrenti (Palatine, Ill.)
Sunset (San Francisco, Calif.)
Wellfleet (Wellfleet, Mass.)
Wurlitzer (New York, N.Y.)

Musical Instruments

Bel Canto (Metuchen, N.J.)

Shapiro (Washington, D.C.)

Silver (Santa Barbara, Calif.)

Mechanical Musical Instruments

Bel Canto (Metuchen, N.J.)   Mechanical (Darien, Conn.)   Vi & Si's (Clarence, N.Y.)

See also
Sheet Music
Musical Scores

Gryphon #2 (New York, N.Y.)   Opera Box (Brooklyn, N.Y.)
Magic (Johnson City, Tenn.)   Silver (Santa Barbara, Calif.)

Mystery & Detective Fiction

Aardvarks (Orlando, Fla.)
Abra (Rochester, N.Y.)
Aladdin (Fullerton, Calif.)
Alibi (New Haven, Conn.)
Archer's (Kent, Ohio)
Armens (Iowa City, Iowa)
Attic (Laurel, Md.)
Avenue (Boston, Mass.)
Battersby (Ardmore, Pa.)
Beasley (Chicago, Ill.)
Bernard (Rockville, Md.)
Between (Old Bridge, N.J.)
Biblioctopus (Idyllwild, Calif.)
Blackmer (North Ferrisburg, Vt.)
Blue Lantern (San Diego, Calif.)
Bluestem (Lincoln, Neb.)
Book Baron (Anaheim, Calif.)
Book Carnival (Orange, Calif.)
Bookfinders (Atlanta, Ga.)
Bookie Joint (Reseda, Calif.)
Book Sleuth (Colo. Spgs., Colo.)
Books 'n (El Dorado, Ark.)
Borden (Portsmouth, R. I.)
Boulevard (Topanga, Calif.)
Bunker (Spring Valley, Calif.)
Canford (Freeville, N.Y.)
Chaos (Washington, D.C.)

Chimney (Scotts Valley, Calif.)
Circle West (Annapolis, Md.)
Cornucopia (Syosset, N.Y.)
Dawn (Ann Arbor, Mich.)
Debra (No. Hills, Pa.)
Discher (Castro Valley, Calif.)
Else Fine (Dearborn, Mich.)
Fantasy (San Francisco, Calif.)
Fay (Caledonia, N.Y.)
Fickes (Akron, Ohio)
Fine (Rochester, Mich.)
First Edtns. (Richmond, Va.)
Fithian (Lakewood, Colo.)
Fountain (Indianapolis, Ind.)
Gabbard (New Boston, Texas)
Green Acre (Wells, Vt.)
Green Apple (San Francisco,
   Calif.)
Greene (Rockville Centre, N.Y.)
Hanley's (Chicago, Ill.)
Haunted (Orleans, Mass.)
Hi (Canutillo, Texas)
Hill Haven (Barton, Vt.)
Hooked (Springfield, Mo.)
In #1 (San Francisco, Calif.)
In #2 (San Francisco, Calif.)
Jaffe (Arlington, Va.)

Janus (Tucson, Ariz.)
JMD (Groton, N.Y.)
Krause (Warrington, Fla.)
Kristiansen (Boston, Mass.)
Limestone (Glen Rose, Texas)
Lippincott (Bangor, Maine)
Mainly (No. Hollywood, Calif.)
Mannatt (San Diego, Calif.)
Max Gate (Kankakee, Ill.)
McBride (Hartford, Conn.)
McFarland (Tampa, Fla.)
Mendoza (New York, N.Y.)
Mermaid (Oakland, Calif.)
Meyerson (Brooklyn, N.Y.)
Mitchell (Pasadena, Calif.)
Morgan (Tucson, Ariz.)
Murder (Denver, Colo.)
Murder (Toronto, Ont.)
Murder (Ft. Worth, Texas)
Mysteries (Yellow Spgs., Ohio)
Mystery (Huntingdon Valley, Pa.)
Oceanside (Oceanside, N.Y.)
Old Rare (Jamestown, N.Y.)
Owen (Litchfield, Maine)
Paperback (New York, N.Y.)
Passaic (Passaic, N.J.)
Pepper/Stern (Sharon, Mass.)

Pepper/Stern (Santa Barbara, Calif.)
Pettler (Los Angeles, Calif.)
Powell (Bar Harbor, Maine)
Ransom (Amherst, N.Y.)
Rue (Boulder, Colo.)
Science (Ann Arbor, Mich.)
Sebert (Mt. Nebo, W.Va.)
Shaw (Albany, N.Y.)
Silver (Redondo Bch., Calif.)

Sleepy (Moraga, Calif.)
Sommer (Niagara Falls, N.Y.)
Spade (Seattle, Wash.)
Spenser's (Boston, Mass.)
S & S (St. Paul, Minn.)
Stahr (Los Angeles, Calif.)
Stone House (Elkton, Md.)
Sykes (No. Weare, N.H.)
Sylvester (Los Angeles, Calif.)
Temple (Toronto, Ont.)

Thomolsen (Bayside, N.Y.)
Time (No. Andover, Mass.)
20th Century (Madison, Wisc.)
Ward (Prospect, Ohio)
Webster's (Milwaukee, Wisc.)
West's (Elm Grove, Wisc.)
Wilhite (Clearwater, Fla.)
Willis (Columbus, Ohio)
Woo (Plainview, N.Y.)

Mysticism

Abintra (Morris, N.Y.)

Gateway (Ferndale, Pa.)

Hubert (Walnut Creek, Calif.)

Myths & Mythology

Abintra (Morris, N.Y.)
Fields (San Francisco, Calif.)
E. C. Gordon (New York, N.Y.)
Hanley's (Chicago, Ill.)

Hermeticus (Ashland, Ore.)
Hubert (Walnut Creek, Calif.)
Morrison (Santa Monica, Calif.)
Nemeroff (Williamstown, Mass.)

Scallawagiana (Salt Lake City, Utah)
Sophia (Amherst, Mass.)
3 Geese (Woodstock, N.Y.)

Napoleon

Americana (Coral Gables, Fla.)

Jackson (Weston, Ont.)

"National Geographic" Magazine

Evans (Woodstock, Va.)
Imel (Indianapolis, Ind.)
Johnson's (Springfield, Mass.)

Kennedy (Des Moines, Wash.)
Lutz (Washington C. H., Ohio)
Old Geog. (Sparks, Md.)

Smith (Louisville, Ky.)
Snyder (Pittsburgh, Pa.)
Wellfleet (Wellfleet, Mass.)

Natural History

Adams (W. Medway, Mass.)
Allbooks (Colo. Spgs., Colo.)
All Edges (Silver Spg., Md.)
Amer. Frag. (Escondido, Calif.)
Anderson (Auburn, Mass.)
Antiq. Scientist (Dracut, Mass.)
Antiquarium (Bethany, Conn.)
Arader/Sessler (Philadelphia, Pa.)
Arader (New York, N.Y.)
Arader (Atlanta, Ga.)
Arader (San Francisco, Calif.)
Arader (Houston, Texas)
Arader (King of Prussia, Pa.)
Archer's (Kent, Ohio)
Argus (Sacramento, Calif.)
Avocet (Sanford, N.C.)
Avocet (Corvallis, Ore.)
Bartfield (New York, N.Y.)
Bauman (Atlantic City, N.J.)
Bauman (Philadelphia, Pa.)
Bennett (Southold, N.Y.)
Berman (Los Angeles, Calif.)
Bibby (Gold Hill, Ore.)
Black Swan (Sacramento, Calif.)
Book Barn (Gardner, Mass.)
Book House (Arlington, Va.)
Book Mark (Philadelphia, Pa.)
Book Prospector (Littleton, Colo.)
Books/Buttons (Columbus, Ohio)
Brauns (Sacramento, Calif.)
Buck (New York, N.Y.)
Buck (San Francisco, Calif.)
Buteo (Vermillion, S.D.)
Cabinet/Books (Watertown, Conn.)
Callahan (Peterborough, N.H.)
Calman (Syracuse, N.Y.)
Cassie (Millis, Mass.)
Celnick (Bronx, N.Y.)
Chickadee (Houston, Texas)
Chimney (Bridgeport, Conn.)
Cleland's (Portsmouth, N.H.)
Consolo (Mansfield, Ohio)
Cyrano's (Highlands, N.C.)
Davidson (San Diego, Calif.)

DC Service (Columbia, Mo.)
Debra (No. Hills, Pa.)
Dooling (Middlebury, Conn.)
Dorn (Johntown, N.Y.)
Dunn (Dallas, Ore.)
Dust (Cincinnati, Ohio)
Engard (Tucson, Ariz.)
Fisher (Cobleskill, N.Y.)
Flora (Seattle, Wash.)
Gallery Of (Bigfork, Mont.)
Gamebag (Twin Lakes, Wisc.)
Geological (Falls Village, Conn.)
Glassman (Corte Madera, Calif.)
Glover's (Lexington, Ky.)
Hahn (Cottonwood, Ariz.)
Harder (Los Alamos, N.M.)
Harper (Bristol, Vt.)
Harris (Northfield, Mass.)
Helikon (De Land, Fla.)
Herpetological (Lindenhurst, N.Y.)
Hillman (New York, N.Y.)
Holsten (Excelsior, Minn.)
House (San Diego, Calif.)
Huxley (Loudonville, N.Y.)
Jane Addams (Champaign, Ill.)
Kalanja (Trafford, Pa.)
Ken-L (Newberg, Ore.)
Kreinheder (Warrensburg, N.Y.)
Ledlie (Buckfield, Maine)
Lion's (Salisbury, Conn.)
Lumb (Somersville, Conn.)
Marcher (Okla. City, Okla.)
McLaughlin's (Cottage Grove,
  Ore.)
McQuerry (Jacksonville, Fla.)
Milestone (New York, N.Y.)
Moye (Seattle, Wash.)
Nadolny (Kensington, Conn.)
Natural (Woodland Hills, Calif.)
Natural (Scottsdale, Ariz.)
Nebenzahl (Chicago, Ill.)
New Steamship (El Cajon, Calif.)
Norman (San Francisco, Calif.)
Oklahoma (Yukon, Okla.)

Old Rare (Jamestown, N.Y.)
Owl (Greenwich, N.Y.)
Palmer (Eugene, Ore.)
Persoff (Alameda, Calif.)
Petersen (Davenport, Iowa)
Phila. Print (Philadelphia, Pa.)
Rainy (Lexington, Mass.)
B. Ramer (New York, N.Y.)
Reese (New Haven, Conn.)
Rhoads (Richmond, Ind.)
Rieber (Thomasville, Ga.)
River Oaks (Jay, Maine)
Robertson (Levittown, Pa.)
Rockland (Cattaraugus, N.Y.)
Sail (Newcastle, Maine)
Sail (Lexington, Ky.)
Science (Ann Arbor, Mich.)
Scott (Portland, Maine)
Sebastopol (Sebastopol, Calif.)
2nd Front (San Francisco, Calif.)
Shuhi (Morris, Conn.)
Sidney's (Missoula, Mont.)
Significant (Cincinnati, Ohio)
Small (So. Yarmouth, Mass.)
Smith's (Brewster, Mass.)
Speleobooks (Schoharie, N.Y.)
Sporting (Rancocas, N.J.)
Sporting (Palmerton, Pa.)
Sportsman's (Manotick, Ont.)
Staten (Harwich, Mass.)
Stone House (Elkton, Md.)
Suhm (Westfield, Mass.)
Tamerlane (Havertown, Pa.)
Tayaut (No. Hatley, Que.)
Thoreau (Concord, Mass.)
Tramp (Jackson, Mich.)
Trotting (Springfield, Mass.)
Underhill (Poughkeepsie, N.Y.)
Vargo's (Bozeman, Mont.)
Village (Rumney Village, N.H.)
Vinik (Tucson, Ariz.)
Vogt (Meadow Vista, Calif.)
Watkins (Dolgeville, N.Y.)
Watson (Buelah, Colo.)

Wayner (Ft. Payne, Ala.)
White's (Asbury Park, N.J.)
Wildlife (Gainesville, Fla.)

Wildwood (Old Forge, N.Y.)
Williams (Calgary, Alt.)
Woods (Yakima, Wash.)

Wordsmith (Syracuse, Neb.)
Zaremba (Cambridge, Mass.)
Zucker (New York, N.Y.)

Naval & Nautical

See also
Marine & Maritime

Antiq. Archive (Sunnyvale, Calif.)
Auslender (Wilton, Conn.)
Book/Tackle (Watch Hill, R.I.)
Brisky (Micanopy, Fla.)
Broadfoot's (Wilmington, N.C.)
Brookline (Brookline, Mass.)
Brown (New London, Conn.)
Burnett (Atlanta, Ga.)
Caravan-Maritime (Jamaica, N.Y.)
Columbia (Suffern, N.Y.)
Compass (Sitka, Alk.)
Connecticut (E. Haddam, Conn.)
Coventry (Coventry, Conn.)
Crofter's (Washington, Conn.)

Cross Hill (Brunswick, Maine)
Darvill's Book (Eastsound, Wash.)
Davies (Oak Park, Ill.)
R E (Fairhope, Ala.)
Filler (Bremerton, Wash.)
4th Estate (New London, Conn.)
Gallis (Marblehead, Mass.)
Hamilton's (Williamsburg, Va.)
Helikon (De Land, Fla.)
Hilton Village (Newport News, Va.)
Hist. Tech (Marblehead, Mass.)
History (Ashley Falls, Mass.)
Much (Marblehead, Mass.)

Nautica (Halifax, N.S.)
Northeast (Ocean City, N.J.)
Oar House (Clearwater, Fla.)
Pier (Piermont, N.Y.)
Rulon-Miller (Minneapolis, Minn.)
Seabook (Clinton Corners, N.Y.)
Sea (Glen Oaks, N.Y.)
Stein (Gold Beach, Ore.)
Taste (Fall River, Mass.)
Titcomb's (E. Sandwich, Mass.)
Tona (Grand Isl., N.Y.)
World War (W. Roxbury, Mass.)

Nebraska

Dupley (Omaha, Neb.)

Lee (Lincoln, Neb.)

Wordsmith (Syracuse, Neb.)

Needlework

Brew (New Milford, Conn.)
Clower (Charlottesville, Va.)
Glassman (Corte Madera, Calif.)

Hard-To (Newton, Mass.)
Robertson (Meredith, N.H.)
St. Clair (Van Nuys, Calif.)

Shep (Lopez Isl., Wash.)

Neuroscience

Bookmarx (Roslyn, N.Y.)

Dordick (Somerville, Mass.)

Fye (Marshfield, Wisc.)

Goodrich (Englewood, N.J.)
Mashman (Ridgefield, Conn.)

Printers' (Arlington, Mass.)
Printers' (Boston, Mass.)

Schick (Hartsdale, N.Y.)
Tweney (Bowling Green, Ohio)

New Books

Articles (Skokie, Ill.)
Assoc. Stu. (Chico, Calif.)
Barn Owl (Wellesley, Mass.)
Book Barn (Bend, Ore.)
Bookdales (Richfield, Minn.)
Book Fair (W. Palm Beach, Fla.)
Bookloft (Enterprise, Ore.)
Book Shop (Boise, Idaho)
Book Trader (Naples, Fla.)
Buddenbrooks (Boston, Mass.)
Carmichael's (Louisville, Ky.)
Change (Santa Monica, Calif.)
Chickadee (Houston, Texas)

Federation (College St., Texas)
Fisher (New York, N.Y.)
Golden Gull (Grants Pass, Ore.)
Holmes (Oakland, Calif.)
Homesteader (Wenatchee, Wash.)
Hyde Park (Tampa, Fla.)
Imagine That (Pittsfield, Mass.)
Imagine That (No. Adams, Mass.)
Jeltrups' St. Croix, V.I.)
Jolie's (Stuart, Fla.)
Lift (Brockport, N.Y.)
Lion's (Salisbury, Conn.)
MacBeans (Brunswick, Maine)

Midvale (Portland, Ore.)
Oxford At (Atlanta, Ga.)
Oxford (Atlanta, Ga.)
Oxford Two (Atlanta, Ga.)
Peggatty (Clarkston, Wash.)
Reprint (Washington, D.C.)
Rohe (Chicago, Ill.)
Strand (New York, N.Y.)
Underhill (Poughkeepsie, N.Y.)
Williams (Williamstown, Mass.)
Womanbooks (New York, N.Y.)
Womrath's (Hempstead, N.Y.)

New England

Amer. Eagle (Topsfield, Mass.)
Andover (Andover, Mass.)
Armchair (No. Orange, Mass.)
Barn Loft (Laconia, N.H.)
Bean (Niantic, Conn.)
Bennington (Bennington, Vt.)
Book Bear (W. Brookfield, Mass.)
Book Guild (Portsmouth, N.H.)
Book/Tackle (Watch Hill, R.I.)
Burt (Laconia, N.H.)
Cape Collector (So. Harwich,

Mass.)
Cassie (Millis, Mass.)
Chester (Chester, Conn.)
Cobble Crt. (Litchfield, Conn.)
Cornerstone (Providence, R.I.)
Cotton Hill (Laconia, N.H.)
deBeurs (Dexter, Maine)
Falls (Farmington Falls, Maine)
Globe Crnr. (Boston, Mass.)
Johnson's (Springfield, Mass.)
John Steele (Litchfield, Conn.)

Lord (Marshfield, Mass.)
Maier (Rockport, Mass.)
Melvins (Grt. Barrington, Mass.)
Much (Marblehead, Mass.)
Old #6 (Henniker, N.H.)
Smith (Amherst, Mass.)
Stone Of (Canterbury, Conn.)
Taste (Fall River, Mass.)
Tempest (Waitsville, Vt.)
10 Pound (Gloucester, Mass.)

New Hampshire

Barn Loft (Laconia, N.H.)
Bretton Hall (Bretton Woods, N.H.)

Bretton Hall (Lancaster, N.H.)
Cotton Hill (Laconia, N.H.)
Spooner's (Tilton, N.H.)

Sykes (No. Weare, N.H.)
Village (Rumney Village, N.H.)
Village (Littleton, N.H.)

New Jersey

Escargot (Brielle, N.J.)
Felcone (Princeton, N.J.)

Keith (Red Bank, N.J.)
Much (Southfield, Mich.)

Northeast (Ocean City, N.J.)
Old Book (Morristown, N.J.)

New Mexico

Almagre (Bloomington, Ind.)
Gay (Santa Fe, N.M.)

Grt. Southwest (Santa Fe, N.M.)
Parker (Santa Fe, N.M.)

White (Albuquerque, N.M.)

New Orleans

Librairie (Chartres) (New Orleans, La.)

Old Books (New Orleans, La.)

Newspapers

Aboud (Stayton, Ore.)
Alsberg (Skokie, Ill.)
Barber (Boston, Mass.)
Caren (Nanuet, N.Y.)
Cohasco (Yonkers, N.Y.)
4th Estate (New London, Conn.)

Harrington's (Cos Cob, Conn.)
Hist. News (Skokie, Ill.)
Hughes (Williamsport, Pa.)
Lombardo (Shoreham, N.Y.)
Minckler (Billings, Mont.)
Najarian (Newtown Sq., Pa.)

Richshafer (Cincinnati, Ohio)
Spellman (Brick Town, N.J.)
Totty (Lunenburg, Mass.)
Valentino (Philadelphia, Pa.)

New York City
& Metropolitan Region

Bancroft (Newtown, Conn.)
Bennett (White Plains, N.Y.)
History (Ashley Falls, Mass.)

Keene (Southampton, N.Y.)
Klemperer (New York, N.Y.)
N.Y. Bound (New York, N.Y.)

Old Book (Croton, N.Y.)
Pavlov (Dobbs Ferry, N.Y.)
Roseman (Brooklyn, N.Y.)

New York State

Berry Hill (Deansboro, N.Y.)
Boardman (Camden, N.Y.)
Book-In (Stillwater, N.Y.)
Buffalo (Amherst, N.Y.)
Calhouns' (Geneva, N.Y.)
Fisher (Cobleskill, N.Y.)
Harbor Hill (Harrison, N.Y.)
Hope Farm (Cornwallville, N.Y.)
Jenison's (Canton, N.Y.)

McDonald's (Catskill, N.Y.)
Monarski (Syracuse, N.Y.)
Much (Southfield, Mich.)
Nestler (Waldwick, N.J.)
N.Y. Bound (New York, N.Y.)
Old Book (Croton, N.Y.)
Old Rare (Jamestown, N.Y.)
Pan (Catskill, N.Y.)
Pinkney (Granby, Conn.)

Poste (Geneseo, N.Y.)
Serpent (Oneonta, N.Y.)
Shoebridge (Lafayette, N.Y.)
3 Geese (Woodstock, N.Y.)
Village (Hudson Falls, N.Y.)
Yankee (Williamson, N.Y.)
Yankee (Rochester, N.Y.)

Western New York State

Dorn (Johntown, N.Y.)
Kreinheder (Warrensburg, N.Y.)

Lift (Brockport, N.Y.)
Mahoney (Buffalo, N.Y.)

North Carolina

Avocet (Sanford, N.C.)
Book Mart (Asheville, N.C.)
Book Trader (Fairmont, N.C.)
Captain's (Ashville, N.C.)

Carolina (Charlotte, N.C.)
Cyrano's (Highlands, N.C.)
Grandpa's (Troy, N.C.)
Kearin (Goldens Bridge, N.Y.)

Pandich (Asheville, N.C.)
Patrick (Beaufort, S.C.)
Stevens (Wake Forest, N.C.)

Nostalgic Fiction

Book Cellar (Freeport, Maine)
Hermit's (Wyoming, Pa.)

Kapica (New Britain, Conn.)
Keeler (No. Monmouth, Maine)

People's (Flemington, N.J.)
Zellner's (Easton, Pa.)

Numismatics

Armenian (Pico Rivera, Calif.)
Becker (Acton Centre, Mass.)
Berkowitz (Chester, N.Y.)
Carling's (Pomona Park, Fla.)
Finn (W. Roxbury, Mass.)

Kolbe (Crestline, Calif.)
Lee (Lincoln, Neb.)
Lewis St. (Lynn, Mass.)
San Fernando (San Fernando, Calif.)

Seppa (Virginia, Minn.)
Valentino (Philadelphia, Pa.)
Verde (Winsted, Conn.)

Joyce Carol Oates

Croissant (Athens, Ohio)

Mashman (Ridgefield, Conn.)

Occult & Magic

Aide (Cardiff, Calif.)
Book Bear (W. Brookfield, Mass.)
Book Studio (Atlanta, Ga.)
Circle West (Annapolis, Md.)
East West (Hamburg, N.Y.)
Fields (San Francisco, Calif.)
Gateway (Ferndale, Pa.)
Hermeticus (Ashland, Ore.)
Holmes (Edmonds, Wash.)

Houseman (Yellow Spgs., Ohio)
Hubert (Walnut Creek, Calif.)
James (Lynden, Wash.)
Middle (Sterling Hgts., Mich.)
Minnehaha (Minneapolis, Minn.)
Perry's (San Jose, Calif.)
Scallawagiana (Salt Lake City, Utah)
Sharp's (No. Hollywood, Calif.)

Sullivan (New York, N.Y.)
Thelema (King Bch., Calif.)
U.S. Games (New York, N.Y.)
Walker (San Leandro, Calif.)
Weiser (New York, N.Y.)
Wizard's (San Diego, Calif.)
Woodruff (Grass Lake, Mich.)
Yankee (Plymouth, Mass.)
Ye Olde (San Angelo, Texas)

Ohio

Bibliomania (Delaware, Ohio)
Bookseller (Akron, Ohio)
Old Erie (Cleveland, Ohio)

Paper (So. Euclid, Ohio)
Photo (Columbus, Ohio)
Ron Dot (Greensburg, Ohio)

Roth (Norwalk, Ohio)
Trans (Parkersburg, W.Va.)

Oklahoma (& Indian Territory)

A Points (Okla. City, Okla.)
Bever (Edmond, Okla.)

Carvavan (Stillwater, Okla.)
Dean (Okla. City, Okla.)

Michael's (Okla. City, Okla.)

Olympic Games

Abrams (State College, Pa.)
Iuspa (Newark, N.J.)

Kuo (Atlanta, Ga.)
Tatro (Wethersfield, Conn.)

Opera

Ballet (New York, N.Y.)
Bel Canto (Metuchen, N.J.)
B.J.S. (Forest Hills, N.Y.)

Bond (Reading, Mass.)
Books/Autographs (Eliot, Maine)
Footnote (Brooklyn, N.Y.)

Katt (Los Angeles, Calif.)
Opera Box (Brooklyn, N.Y.)
Silver (Santa Barbara, Calif.)

Optics

Astronomy (Bernardston, Mass.)

Luft (Oakland Gdns., N.Y.)

Tesseract (Hastings, N.Y.)

The Orient & Orientalia

Abbey (Los Angeles, Calif.)
Abbot (Bronx, N.Y.)
Academy (Honolulu, Haw.)
Asian Amer. (New York, N.Y.)
Asian Books (Cambridge, Mass.)
Asian Rare (New York, N.Y.)
Brannan (Garberville, Calif.)
Cheng (Boston, Mass.)
East West (Hamburg, N.Y.)

Hoyt (Rockport, Mass.)
Johnson (Indianapolis, Ind.)
Keramos (Ann Arbor, Mich.)
Lozinski (Westport, Mass.)
Manor (New York, N.Y.)
Nemeroff (Williamstown, Mass.)
Oriental (St. Pete., Fla.)
Oriental (Pasadena, Calif.)
Paragon (New York, N.Y.)

Rare Oriental (Aptos, Calif.)
Rush (Baltimore, Md.)
Scharf (Pittsburgh, Pa.)
Terramedia (Wellesley, Mass.)
Vanderstoel (El Cerrito, Calif.)
Watson (Exeter, N.H.)
Weiser (New York, N.Y.)
Worldwide (Cambridge, Mass.)
Xerxes (Glen Head, N.Y.)

Outlaws & Rangers

See Also
Western Books

Alsberg (Skokie, Ill.)
Arthurton (Palmyra, N.Y.)
Book Mart (San Antonio, Texas)
Book Mart Annex (San Antonio, Tex.)
Dary (Lawrence, Kan.)
Gibbs (State College, Pa.)

Heinoldt (So. Egg, N.J.)
La Galeria (Las Vegas, N.M.)
Princeton (Atlantic City, N.J.)
Reynolds (Willits, Calif.)
Rosetree (Tombstone, Ariz.)
Swinford (Paris, Ill.)
Todd (Cave Creek, Ariz.)

Trackside (Houston, Texas)
Trail (Tucson, Ariz.)
Valley (Galena, Ill.)
Weatherford (Monroe, Wash.)
Wright (Waxahachie, Texas)

Overland Narratives

See also
Diaries

Blomberg (Rockford, Ill.)
Dary (Lawrence, Kan.)
Ginsberg (Sharon, Mass.)
Harris (Los Angeles, Calif.)
Heinoldt (So. Egg, N.J.)

Lunsford (No. Vancouver, B.C.)
Mitch's (Menlo Park, Calif.)
Rancho (Santa Monica, Calif.)
Reynolds (Willits, Calif.)
Rittenhouse (Albuquerque, N.M.)

Tweney (Seattle, Wash.)
Valley (Galena, Ill.)
Weatherford (Monroe, Wash.)

Pacific Region

Academic (No. Vancouver, B.C.)
Academy (Honolulu, Haw.)
Adelson (No. Pomfret, Vt.)
Antipodean (Cold Spg., N.Y.)
Berkelouw (Los Angeles, Calif.)
Best (Cambridge, Mass.)
Book Bin (Corvallis, Ore.)
Cellar (Detroit, Mich.)
Chapman (Los Angeles, Calif.)

Cheng (Boston, Mass.)
Hills (San Francisco, Calif.)
Hoffer (Vancouver, B.C.)
Hopper (Sunnyvale, Calif.)
Jaffe (Arlington, Va.)
Lefkowicz (Fairhaven, Mass.)
Lloyd (Washington, D.C.)
Lunsford (No. Vancouver, B.C.)
Magazine (San Francisco, Calif.)

Orange (Garberville, Calif.)
Oriental (St. Pete., Fla.)
Oriental (Pasadena, Calif.)
Pacificana (Jamestown, N.C.)
Pacific (Honolulu, Haw.)
Reynolds (Willits, Calif.)
Rybski (Chicago, Ill.)
Tusitala (Kailua, Haw.)

Books About Painting

Museum (Fairfield, Conn.)

Olana (Brewster, N.Y.)

Paintings

Adams (Chicago, Ill.)
Artcraft (Baldwin, Md.)
Artistic (Boston, Mass.)
Bartfield Gall. (New York, N.Y.)
Book Store (San Mateo, Calif.)

Burger (Pine Grove, Calif.)
GBI (Smithtown, N.Y.)
Howes (Brewster, Mass.)
Maestro (Bayport, N.Y.)
Old Print (New York, N.Y.)

Reston's (Amsterdam, N.Y.)
Trotting (Morristown, N.J.)
Unique (Putney, Vt.)

Paleontology

Clegg (Eaton Rapids, Mich.)
Geological (Falls Village, Conn.)
Geoscience (Yucaipa, Calif.)

Hahn (Cottonwood, Ariz.)
Leishman (Menlo Park, Calif.)
Mt. Eden (Mt. Eden, Calif.)

Nadolny (Kensington, Conn.)
Zambelli (New York, N.Y.)

Pamphlets

Caren (Nanuet, N.Y.)

Charkoudian (Newton, Mass.)

Early & Collectible Paperbacks

Book Finder (Geneva, N.Y.)
Canford (Freeville, N.Y.)
Carlton (Camino, Calif.)
Cooper's (Decatur, Ga.)
Fantasy (Garden Grove, Calif.)

Katonah (Katonah, N.Y.)
Lippincott (Bangor, Maine)
Lysecki (Winnipeg, Man.)
Mysteries (Yellow Spgs., Ohio)
Pell's (Delray Bch., Fla.)

River Oaks (Jay, Maine)
Robinson (St. Pete., Fla.)
Sommer (Niagara Falls, N.Y.)
Spenser's (Boston, Mass.)

New Paperbacks

All Books (Miami, Fla.)
Annie's (Acton, Mass.)
Attic (London, Ont.)

Attic (London, Ont.)
Bargain (Norfolk, Va.)
Barjon's (Billings, Mont.)

Book Cellar (Temple, Texas)
Book Connect. (Mariposa, Calif.)
Book Exch. (Missoula, Mont.)

Book Fair (W. Palm Beach, Fla.)
Book Mart (Brockton, Mass.)
Book Nook (Ft. Smith, Ark.)
Bookshop (Chapel Hill, N.C.)
Bookstore (Lenox, Mass.)
Book Store (San Mateo, Calif.)
Book Trader (Naples, Fla.)

Change (Santa Monica, Calif.)
City Lights (San Francisco, Calif.)
Dragon's Lair (Dayton, Ohio)
Falls (Farmington Falls, Maine)
50,000 (El Cajon, Calif.)
Imagine That (Pittsfield, Mass.)
Imagine That (No. Adams, Mass.)

Jeltrups' St. Croix, V.I.)
Lighthouse (Rye, N.Y.)
Oblong (Millerton, N.Y.)
Paperback (New York, N.Y.)
Peggatty (Clarkston, Wash.)
Stan's (Brockton, Mass.)
Womrath's (Hempstead, N.Y.)

Used Paperbacks

Abbey (Dearborn, Mich.)
Book Barn (Miami, Fla.)
Book Exch. (Lakewood, Colo.)
Book House (St. Louis, Mo.)
Bookland (Stockton, Calif.)
Books/Advice (Denver, Colo.)
Books/Comics #2 (Indianapolis, Ind.)
Book Stop (Petoskey, Mich.)

Brassers (Seminole, Fla.)
Bridgman (Rome, N.Y.)
Bunker (Spring Valley, Calif.)
City Wide (Brooklyn, N.Y.)
Denver Barter (Denver, Colo.)
Desch (Wheaton, Md.)
Green Acre (Wells, Vt.)
Harvard (Stockton, Calif.)
Oxford At (Atlanta, Ga.)

Oxford Two (Atlanta, Ga.)
Pell's (Delray Bch., Fla.)
Printer's (Milldale, Conn.)
Printer's (Middletown, Conn.)
Sloan's (Wayneville, N.C.)
Snyder (Pittsburgh, Pa.)
Spencer's (Vancouver, Wash.)

Papermaking & Marbling

Battery (Forest Hills, N.Y.)
Busyhaus (Mattapoisett, Mass.)

Chiswick (Sandy Hook, Conn.)
Guelker (St. Louis, Mo.)

Midnight (W. Lafayette, Ind.)

Parenting & Child Care

Eeyore's #1 (New York, N.Y.)

Eeyore's #2 (New York, N.Y.)

Orange (Garberville, Calif.)

Pennsylvania

Baldwin's (W. Chester, Pa.)
Book Haven (Lancaster, Pa.)
Ernst (Selinsgrove, Pa.)

Family Album (Glen Rock, Pa.)
Fisher (Williamsport, Pa.)
Lincoln (Chambersburg, Pa.)

Miller (Warren, Pa.)
Obsolescence (Gettysburg, Pa.)
Otzinachson (Allenwood, Pa.)

Starry (Shippensburg, Pa.)   Thomas (Mechanicsburg, Pa.)   Zellner's (Easton, Pa.)

Western Pennsylvania

Bishop (Steubenville, Ohio)   Trans (Parkersburg, W.Va.)
Erie (Erie, Pa.)   Tuckers (Pittsburgh, Pa.)

Performing Arts

Academy (New York, N.Y.)   Common (New Salem, Mass.)   Old Music (3 Oaks, Mich.)
Allen (Baltimore, Md.)   Galewitz (Orange, Conn.)   Performing (New York, N.Y.)
Armitage (Miamisburg, Ohio)   George Sand (Los Angeles, Calif.)   Silver (Santa Barbara, Calif.)
Backstage (Eugene, Ore.)   Gotham (New York, N.Y.)   Theater (Palo Alto, Calif.)
Bancroft (Newtown, Conn.)   Gryphon #1 (New York, N.Y.)   Theatrebooks (New York, N.Y.)
Bookfinders (Atlanta, Ga.)   In #1 (San Francisco, Calif.)   Theatricana (Athens, Ga.)
Books 'n (New York, N.Y.)   In #2 (San Francisco, Calif.)   Village (Hudson Falls, N.Y.)
Book Store (San Mateo, Calif.)   Katonah (Katonah, N.Y.)   Weintraub #1 (New York, N.Y.)
Bowie (Seattle, Wash.)   Katt (Los Angeles, Calif.)   Weintraub #2 (New York, N.Y.)
Broude (New York, N.Y.)   Laws (Chicago, Ill.)   Words (Cambridge, Mass.)
Buckabest (Palo Alto, Calif.)   Little (U. Montclair, N.J.)   Wurlitzer (New York, N.Y.)
Cadenza (Smithtown, N.Y.)   Lyman (East Otis, Mass.)
Carduner (Philadelphia, Pa.)   Maestro (Bayport, N.Y.)

Back Issue Periodicals

See also Back Issue Magazines, Little Magazines

Aboud (Stayton, Ore.)   Book Stall (Rockford, Ill.)   Info (El Cerrito, Calif.)
Abraham's (New York, N.Y.)   Burgman (Santa Rosa, Calif.)   Int'l. Univ. (New York, N.Y.)
Academic (No. Vancouver, B.C.)   Canner (Boston, Mass.)   Jaeger (Commack, N.Y.)
Alper (Eastchester, N.Y.)   Caren (Nanuet, N.Y.)   Jumping (Hartford, Conn.)
Arrow (Philadelphia, Pa.)   Dragon's Lair (Dayton, Ohio)   Keck (Alexandria, Va.)
Ars Libri (Boston, Mass.)   Educo (Valhalla, N.Y.)   Kennedy (Des Moines, Wash.)
Back No. (Greenbelt, Md.)   Fine (Rochester, Mich.)   Laws (Chicago, Ill.)
Barber (Boston, Mass.)   Fye (Marshfield, Wisc.)   Magazine (San Francisco, Calif.)
Benjamins (Philadelphia, Pa.)   Grandpa's (Troy, N.C.)   Magazine (New York, N.Y.)
Bliss (Middletown, Conn.)   Hansen (Carlsbad, Calif.)   Mason (Phoenix, Ariz.)
Book Exch. (Missoula, Mont.)   Hist. News (Skokie, Ill.)   McDonald's (San Francisco, Calif.)
Book Search (Brooklyn, N.Y.)   Hughes (Williamsport, Pa.)   McGilvery (La Jolla, Calif.)

Merriwell (Islip, N.Y.)
Minters (New York, N.Y.)
Phiebig (White Plains, N.Y.)
Plant (Grass Valley, Calif.)
Resnik (Roslyn Hgts., N.Y.)

Rizzoli (New York, N.Y.)
Rogofsky (Glen Oaks, N.Y.)
Sandys (Albertson, N.Y.)
Schnase (Scarsdale, N.Y.)
Western (Stoughton, Mass.)

Whistles (Rossville, Ga.)
Zeitlin Per. (Los Angeles, Calif.)
Zubel (Cleveland, Ohio)

19th Century Periodicals

Cameron's (Portland, Ore.)

Ross (Woodland Hills, Calif.)

Petroleum

Barbers (Ft. Worth, Texas)
Erie (Erie, Pa.)
Geological (Falls Village, Conn.)

Gibbs (State College, Pa.)
Leishman (Menlo Park, Calif.)
Miller (Warren, Pa.)

Mt. Eden (Mt. Eden, Calif.)
Williams (Calgary, Alt.)

Philately & Philatelic Literature

See also Counterfeit Stamps & Coins

Appletree (Williford, Ark.)
Book Studio (Atlanta, Ga.)
Feltus (Berkeley, Calif.)

Hacker (Rolling Meadows, Ill.)
Hensel (Belle Chasse, La.)
Herst (Boca Raton, Fla.)
Johnson (Waltham, Mass.)

Koerber (Southfield, Mich.)
La Tienda (Conway, N.H.)
Philatelic (Louisville, Ky.)

Philosophy

Abelard (Toronto, Ont.)
Academy (New York, N.Y.)
Academy (San Francisco, Calif.)
A C (Brooklyn, N.Y.)
Atticus (Toronto, Ont.)
Baker (Grand Rapids, Mich.)
Bartleby's (Bethesda, Md.)
Berkley (Berkley, Minn.)
Bibliofile (San Francisco, Calif.)

Bolerium (San Francisco, Calif.)
Book Assoc. (Orange, Conn.)
Bookery (Ithaca, N.Y.)
Book Harbor (Fullerton, Calif.)
Book Nook (Yakima, Wash.)
Booknook (Evanston, Ill.)
Books By (Derby, Conn.)
Books & Co. (New York, N.Y.)
Book Store (Lewisburg, W.Va.)

Brownbag (Rochester, N.Y.)
Chimera (Palo Alto, Calif.)
Dyment (Ottawa, Ont.)
East West (Hamburg, N.Y.)
Edenite (Imlaystown, N.J.)
Epistemologist (Bryn Mawr, Pa.)
Estate (Washington, D.C.)
Folkways (Bethesda, Md.)
Fraser's (Sherman Oaks, Calif.)

Gach (Columbia, Md.)
Gilbert (Los Angeles, Calif.)
Globe (Northampton, Mass.)
Green (Philadelphia, Pa.)
Griffon (So. Bend, Ind.)
Grunewald (Kansas City, Mo.)
House (San Diego, Calif.)
Hubert (Walnut Creek, Calif.)
Hummingbird (Albuquerque, N.M.)
Huntley (Claremont, Calif.)
Ideal (New York, N.Y.)
Jamaica (Jamaica, N.Y.)

Lake (Toronto, Ont.)
Lion (Indianapolis, Ind.)
Loome (Stillwater, Minn.)
Mahoney (Buffalo, N.Y.)
Mandrake (Cambridge, Mass.)
McCullough (Los Angeles, Calif.)
Murphy (Iowa City, Iowa)
Nemeroff (Williamstown, Mass.)
Nisula (Okemos, Mich.)
Phenomenologica (Worcester, Mass.)
Philosophical (New York, N.Y.)
Pomander (New York, N.Y.)

Powell's (Chicago, Ill.)
Rootenberg (Sherman Oaks, Calif.)
Saurus (Bethlehem, Pa.)
Schick (Hartsdale, N.Y.)
Schneeman (Chicago, Ill.)
Tisza (Chestnut Hill, Mass.)
Tweney (Bowling Green, Ohio)
University (Hull, Mass.)
Weiser (New York, N.Y.)
Wilder (Hubbardston, Mass.)
Wizard's (San Diego, Calif.)
Zambelli (New York, N.Y.)

Phonograph Records

Anita's (Manchester, N.H.)
Attic (St. Pete., Fla.)
Book Broker (Evansville, Ind.)
Book Exch. (Plainville, Conn.)
Bryn Mawr (New York, N.Y.)
Gryphon #1 (New York, N.Y.)
Gryphon Record (New York, N.Y.)
Imagine That (Pittsfield, Mass.)
Imagine That (No. Adams, Mass.)

Lansford (Powersville, Ga.)
Lincoln (Chambersburg, Pa.)
Mermaid (Oakland, Calif.)
Olde Tyme (Boonton, N.J.)
Organ (Braintree, Mass.)
People's (Flemington, N.J.)
Pirtle (Bellevue, Wash.)
Quest (Ft. Worth, Texas)
Reader's (Raleigh, N.C.)

2nd Story (Bethesda, Md.)
Silver (Santa Barbara, Calif.)
Terra (Churchville, N.Y.)
Treasure (Oakville, Ont.)
Vi & Si's (Clarence, N.Y.)
Wonder (Frederick, Md.)
Yesteryear (Nampa, Idaho)

Photographically Illustrated Books

Daitz (New York, N.Y.)
de Lellis (New York, N.Y.)

Holden (Pasadena, Calif.)
Phillips (New York, N.Y.)

Photographica (New York, N.Y.)
Zita (New York, N.Y.)

Photographic Manuals

Photo (Columbus, Ohio)

Travis (Hastings, N.Y.)

Photography

Air Age (Tollhouse, Calif.)
All Photog. (Yonkers, N.Y.)
Almagre (Bloomington, Ind.)
Arcana (Santa Monica, Calif.)
Art Cats. (Los Angeles, Calif.)
Backroom (Webster, N.Y.)
Bamberger (San Francisco, Calif.)
Becker (Acton Centre, Mass.)
Bennett (Southold, N.Y.)
Between (Old Bridge, N.J.)
Bibliomania (Schenectady, N.Y.)
Black Oak (Berkeley, Calif.)
Blomgren (San Rafael, Calif.)
Book Cellar (Fullerton, Calif.)
Book City (Hollywood, Calif.)
Brauns (Sacramento, Calif.)
Burpee Hill (New London, N.H.)
Cahan (Narberth, Pa.)
Caren (Nanuet, N.Y.)
Carlitz (Philadelphia, Pa.)
Carry Back (Haverhill, N.H.)
Cinema (Hollywood, Calif.)
Collectors' (New York, N.Y.)
Colorado (Norwood, Colo.)
Curiosity (St. Joseph, Mich.)
Daitz (New York, N.Y.)
Darrah (Gettysburg, Pa.)
de Lellis (New York, N.Y.)
Donnally (Seattle, Wash.)
Ex Libris (New York, N.Y.)
Feldstein (Forest Hills, N.Y.)
Frontier (Bryan, Texas)
G & C (Lafayette, La.)
Ginsberg (Petersburg, Va.)
Grub Street (Detroit, Mich.)
Guarino (De Bary, Fla.)

Hampton (Newberry, S.C.)
Heaston (Austin, Texas)
Heliochrome (Berkeley Hgts., N.J.)
Hess (Andover, Mass.)
Holden (Pasadena, Calif.)
Hollywood City (Hollywood, Calif.)
Jones (Washington, D.C.)
Kaplan (New York, N.Y.)
Landmark (New York, N.Y.)
Legacy (Iowa City, Iowa)
Lehr (New York, N.Y.)
Lion (New York, N.Y.)
Loewenthal (Dover, N.J.)
Lowe (New York, N.Y.)
MacDonald's (Eustis, Maine)
Mandala (Daytona Bch., Fla.)
Manning's (San Francisco, Calif.)
Margolis (Santa Fe, N.M.)
Maxwell's (Lima, N.Y.)
Memory (New York, N.Y.)
Metropolis (Royal Oak, Mich.)
Michaels (Eugene, Ore.)
Minckler (Billings, Mont.)
Minters (New York, N.Y.)
Muns (Berkeley, Calif.)
Necessary (E. Jordan, Mich.)
Nudel (New York, N.Y.)
Old Book (New Haven, Conn.)
Paper (Portland, Ore.)
Photo-Eye (Austin, Texas)
Photographers (New York, N.Y.)
Photographica (New York, N.Y.)
Photo (Columbus, Ohio)
Pollock (Palo Alto, Calif.)
Potter (Santa Fe, N.M.)

Prag (San Francisco, Calif.)
Professional (New York, N.Y.)
Qualman (San Diego, Calif.)
Quill (Pinellas Park, Fla.)
Richshafer (Cincinnati, Ohio)
Rinhart (Colebrook, Conn.)
Rizzoli (New York, N.Y.)
Salerno (Hauppauge, N.Y.)
Southpaw (Roxbury, Mass.)
Southwest (Durango, Colo.)
Spiratone (Flushing, N.Y.)
Spiratone (New York, N.Y.)
Talisman (Georgetown, Calif.)
Testa (No. Newark, N.J.)
Titles (Highland Park, Ill.)
Todd (Cave Creek, Ariz.)
Tollett (New York, N.Y.)
Transition (San Francisco, Calif.)
Travis (Hastings, N.Y.)
Unique (Putney, Vt.)
Untitled II #1 (New York, N.Y.)
Untitled II #2 (New York, N.Y.)
Valley (No. Hollywood, Calif.)
Vasta (New York, N.Y.)
Waiting (Cambridge, Mass.)
Weintraub #1 (New York, N.Y.)
Weintraub #2 (New York, N.Y.)
West Side (Ann Arbor, Mich.)
Williams (Williamstown, Mass.)
Witkin (New York, N.Y.)
Wolf (New York, N.Y.)
Wood (Boston, Mass.)
Wurlitzer (New York, N.Y.)
Xanadu (Bronx, N.Y.)
Xerxes (Glen Head, N.Y.)
Yankee (Williamson, N.Y.)

Physics

Allen's (Baltimore, Md.)
Astronomy (Bernardston, Mass.)
Blake (Fairfield, Conn.)

E. K. (Rego Park, N.Y.)
Manasek (Hanover, N.H.)
Manasek (Norwich, Vt.)

Maxwell (Elmsford, N.Y.)
Merlin's (Isla Vista, Calif.)
White (Granger, Texas)

City & Urban Planning

Anchor (Newport, R.I.) Glaister (New York, N.Y.) Mendelsohn (Cambridge, Mass.)

Plays & Playwrights

Boulevard (Topanga, Calif.) Camelot (Baltimore, Md.) Ridge (Stone Ridge, N.Y.)

Edgar Allan Poe

Caprio (Revere, Mass.) 19th Cent. (Baltimore, Md.)
Lucas (Blandford, Mass.) Weber (Troy, Minn.)

Poetry

All Books (Miami, Fla.)
Alphabet (Toronto, Ont.)
Americanist (Pottstown, Pa.)
Anacapa (Berkeley, Calif.)
Annie's #1 (Portland, Ore.)
Annie's #2 (Portland, Ore.)
Ashton (Ottawa, Ont.)
Authors (Dundee, Ore.)
Backroom (Webster, N.Y.)
Ball (Paris, Ont.)
Bartleby's (Bethesda, Md.)
Bay Side (Soquel, Calif.)
Bibliofile (San Francisco, Calif.)
Bond (Reading, Mass.)
Book Barn (So. Sioux City, Neb.)
Book Cellar (Brattleboro, Vt.)
Book Chest (New York, N.Y.)
Book Farm (Henniker, N.H.)
Bookman (Tybee Isl., Ga.)
Books By (Derby, Conn.)

Books 'n (New York, N.Y.)
Book Store (Lewisburg, W.Va.)
Bookstore (Lenox, Mass.)
Bush (Stonington, Maine)
Campbell (Campbell, Calif.)
Carduner (Philadelphia, Pa.)
Chloe's (Sacramento, Calif.)
City Lights (San Francisco, Calif.)
Clark's (Spokane, Wash.)
Clipper Ship (San Antonio, Texas)
Core Coll. (Great Neck, N.Y.)
Dermont (Onset, Mass.)
Dickson St. (Fayetteville, Ark.)
Different (Des Moines, Iowa)
Facsimile (New York, N.Y.)
Fly Creek (E. Lansing, Mich.)
George Sand (Los Angeles, Calif.)
Globe (Northampton, Mass.)
Gotham (New York, N.Y.)
Graham (Forestville, Calif.)

Grolier (Cambridge, Mass.)
Hobson's (Jenkintown, Pa.)
Hoffer (Vancouver, B.C.)
Invisible (Berkeley, Calif.)
Island (Isleboro, Maine)
Keane (State College, Pa.)
Lambert (Hancock, N.H.)
Library (Dallas, Texas)
Lion (Indianapolis, Ind.)
Loewenthal (Dover, N.J.)
McBride (Hartford, Conn.)
Monahan (New York, N.Y.)
Nomland (Los Angeles, Calif.)
Nosegay (Cold Spg. Harbor, N.Y.)
Nouveau (Jackson, Miss.)
NRS (New York, N.Y.)
Old Benn. (Hancock, N.H.)
Peters (Van Nuys, Calif.)
Pharos (New Haven, Conn.)
Phoenix (New York, N.Y.)

Rouse (Wattsville, Va.)
Sand (Berkeley, Calif.)
Serendipity (Berkeley, Calif.)
Spooner's (Tilton, N.H.)
Sylvester (Los Angeles, Calif.)
Tattered (Denver, Colo.)

Temple (Toronto, Ont.)
Trebizond (New Preston, Conn.)
Turkey (Westport, Conn.)
Wake (Ft. Lauderdale, Fla.)
West L.A. (Los Angeles, Calif.)
Wharf (Centreville, Md.)

Williams (Williamstown, Mass.)
Word (Montreal, Que.)
World Of (Willoughby, Ohio)
Yellin (Northridge, Calif.)

Political Science & Theory

Amer. Pol. (Newtown, Conn.)
Angriff (Hollywood, Calif.)
Bolingbroke (Pinnacle, N.C.)
Book Search (Brooklyn, N.Y.)
Clipper Ship (San Antonio, Texas)
Dee Cee (Nyack, N.Y.)
Dyment (Ottawa, Ont.)

Fraser's (Sherman Oaks, Calif.)
Hive (Easton, Pa.)
Hollywood Service (Hollywood,
  Calif.)
Huntley (Claremont, Calif.)
Lincoln (Foster, R.I.)
Lion (Indianapolis, Ind.)

Little (U. Montclair, N.J.)
McCullough (Los Angeles, Calif.)
Palinurus (Philadelphia, Pa.)
Rostenberg (New York, N.Y.)
Rubin (Brookline, Mass.)
Wordsmith (Syracuse, Neb.)
Words (San Deigo, Calif.)

Political, Social, & Cultural History

Amer. Pol. (Newtown, Conn.)
Angriff (Hollywood, Calif.)
Book Sail (Orange, Calif.)
Book Search (Brooklyn, N.Y.)
Brown (Belfast, Maine)
Dyment (Ottawa, Ont.)
Gutenberg's (Rochester, N.Y.)
Hayman (Carey, Ohio)

Knights (Harwich Port, Mass.)
Last (Williamsport, Pa.)
Mason (Phoenix, Ariz.)
M & S (Weston, Mass.)
Norman (Philadelphia, Pa.)
Old City (St. Augustine, Fla.)
Osgood (Rockport, Mass.)
Pages (Newton, Conn.)

Rubin (Brookline, Mass.)
Ryan (Columbus, Ohio)
Saurus (Bethlehem, Pa.)
Shenandoah (Appleton, Wisc.)
Sun Dance (Hollywood, Calif.)
Vogt (Meadow Vista, Calif.)
Wilder (Hubbardston, Mass.)
Wilson (Kitchener, Ont.)

Gene Stratton Porter

Baumhofer (St. Paul, Minn.)

Devine (Katonah, N.Y.)

Postal History

*See also
Counterfeit Stamps,
Philately*

aGatherin' (Wynantskill, N.Y.)
Branford (Branford, Conn.)

Craig (Newport, R. I.)
Koerber (Southfield, Mich.)

Philatelic (Louisville, Ky.)
Tillinghast (Hancock, N.H.)

Postcards

*See also
Ephemera*

Albatross II (Tiburon, Calif.)
Books 'n (New York, N.Y.)
Bookstop (Alexandria, Va.)
Bradshaw (Chicago, Ill.)
Brunsell's (Hanson, Mass.)
Cameron's (Portland, Ore.)
Carver (Chestnut Hill, Mass.)
Cliffside (Kansas City, Mo.)
Cramer (Media, Pa.)

Dr. Nostalgia (Lynchburg, Va.)
Fortunate Finds (Warwick, R.I.)
Jenison's (Canton, N.Y.)
Jolie's (Stuart, Fla.)
Klemperer (New York, N.Y.)
Merriwell (Islip, N.Y.)
Miranda (Brookline, Mass.)
Old Book (Morristown, N.J.)
Pipkin (Rock Hill, S.C.)

Prag (San Francisco, Calif.)
Red Horse (Tampa, Fla.)
Schmidt (Salem, Ore.)
Taste (Fall River, Mass.)
Terra (Churchville, N.Y.)
Von Blon's (Waco, Texas)
Yesteryear (Nampa, Idaho)

Posters

*See also
Broadsides*

Autobooks (Babylon, N.Y.)
Bookery (Fairborn, Ohio)
Cinema (Hollywood, Calif.)
Collectors' (New York, N.Y.)
L'Estampe (Saratoga, Calif.)
L'Estampe (New York, N.Y.)

Ex Libris (New York, N.Y.)
Herlin (New York, N.Y.)
Leibowits (New York, N.Y.)
Memory (New York, N.Y.)
Miscellaneous (New Freedom, Pa.)
Mobley (Schoharie, N.Y.)

Poster (New York, N.Y.)
Poster (Orangeburg, N.Y.)
Reisman (Philadelphia, Pa.)
Schreyer (New York, N.Y.)
Sisterhood (Los Angeles, Calif.)

Poultry

Norris (Paoli, Pa.)

Zeigler (New Oxford, Pa.)

See also
True Crime
Presidential Assassinations

Gallis (Marblehead, Mass.)

Kalanja (Trafford, Pa.)

Last (Williamsport, Pa.)

President's (Washington, D.C.)

Talvin (Trafford, Pa.)

See also
Specific Presidents
Presidents

Abe. Lincoln (Chicago, Ill.)

Amer. Pol. (Newtown, Conn.)

Barnes (Philadelphia, Pa.)

B & B (Randolph, Mass.)

Bebbah (Andover, Kan.)

Benjamin (Hunter, N.Y.)

Book Shelf (Cleveland, Tenn.)

Cottontail (Bennington, Ind.)

Gallis (Marblehead, Mass.)

Harris (Los Angeles, Calif.)

Hist. News (Skokie, Ill.)

JFF (Manhasset, N.Y.)

Koschal (Verona, N.J.)

Kubik (Dayton, Ohio)

Lazarus (Ossining, N.Y.)

McCaslin (Ironton, Mo.)

Monie Shop (Cooperstown, N.Y.)

Monie (Cooperstown, N.Y.)

Newman (Chicago, Ill.)

President's (Washington, D.C.)

Rinhart (Colebrook, Conn.)

Seaport (Stonington, Conn.)

Stewart (Portland, Ore.)

Press Books & Fine Printing

See also Miniature Books, Little Magazines

Albatross (San Francisco, Calif.)

Andover (Andover, Mass.)

Argonaut (San Francisco, Calif.)

Ashley (Burlington, Vt.)

Balthasar's (Maryknoll, N.Y.)

Bandas (Temple, Texas)

Battery (Forest Hills, N.Y.)

Besnia (Sterling Jctn., Mass.)

Blacher (Branford, Conn.)

Black Sun (New York, N.Y.)

Book Block (Cos Cob, Conn.)

Book Broker (Charlottesville, Va.)

Book Farm (Henniker, N.H.)

Book Mart Annex (San Antonio, Tex.)

Books/Coll. (Encino, Calif.)

Boss (Brookline, Mass.)

Braiterman (Baltimore, Md.)

Brick Row (San Francisco, Calif.)

Bromer (Boston, Mass.)

Cady (Chicago, Ill.)

Califia (San Francisco, Calif.)

Camelot (Baltimore, Md.)

Carlson (Portland, Maine)

Cassidy (Sacramento, Calif.)

Cheap St. (New Castle, Va.)

Chiswick (Sandy Hook, Conn.)

Chloe's (Sacramento, Calif.)

Christoffersen (Mamaroneck, N.Y.)

Collins' (Pottstown, Pa.)

Colophon (Epping, N.H.)

Cummins (Pottersville, N.J.)

Cummins (New York, N.Y.)

Dailey (Los Angeles, Calif.)

Desmarais (Palo Alto, Calif.)

Detering (Houston, Texas)

Diamond (Rochester, N.Y.)

Dobson (Grimsby, Ont.)

Doukas (Kalamazoo, Mich.)

Duschnes (New York, N.Y.)

Elmcress (So. Hamilton, Mass.)

Emerson (Falls Village, Conn.)

Farnsworth (W. Cornwall, Conn.)

Feldman (Cleveland, Ohio)

Fischler (San Jose, Calif.)

Fly Creek (E. Lansing, Mich.)

Folger (Washington, D.C.)

Forgotten (St. Simon Isl., Ga.)

Garnett (St. Louis, Mo.)

Gilann (Darien, Conn.)

Glenn (Kansas City, Mo.)

Graf (Iowa City, Iowa)

Granary (St. Paul, Minn.)

Grt. Southwest (Santa Fe, N.M.)

Greene (Rockville Centre, N.Y.)
Grub Street (Detroit, Mich.)
Gud (Elmhurst, N.Y.)
Guelker (St. Louis, Mo.)
Halloran (St. Louis, Mo.)
Heller (Washington, D.C.)
Heritage (Los Angeles, Calif.)
Hittel (Ft. Lauderdale, Fla.)
Hobson's (Jenkintown, Pa.)
Hooper's (Leesburg, Va.)
Houle (Los Angeles, Calif.)
House (San Diego, Calif.)
Howe (New York, N.Y.)
In Our (Cambridge, Mass.)
Jaffe (Haverford, Pa.)
Karmiole (Santa Monica, Calif.)
Laird (Chicago, Ill.)
Laurie (St. Paul, Minn.)
Leaves (Ann Arbor, Mich.)

Leech (Ormand Bch., Fla.)
Levine (Savannah, Ga.)
Lincoln (Chambersburg, Pa.)
Link (Redding, Calif.)
Lorson's (Fullerton, Calif.)
Mahoney (Buffalo, N.Y.)
McCaslin (Ironton, Mo.)
Michlestreet (E. Lebanon, Maine)
Midnight (W. Lafayette, Ind.)
Minkoff (Grt. Barrington, Mass.)
Morrow (New York, N.Y.)
Much (Southfield, Mich.)
Nudelman (Seattle, Wash.)
Oak Knoll (New Castle, Del.)
Ohio (Mansfield, Ohio)
O'Malley (Kingston, R.I.)
O'Neal (Boston, Mass.)
Parmer's (Sarasota, Fla.)
Perata (Oakland, Calif.)

Peters (Van Nuys, Calif.)
Pirages (McMinnville, Ore.)
Printed (New York, N.Y.)
Printers' (Palo Alto, Calif.)
Rancho (Santa Monica, Calif.)
Randall (Santa Barbara, Calif.)
Ransom (Amherst, N.Y.)
Reynolds (Willits, Calif.)
Scopazzi (San Francisco, Calif.)
Scott (Stonington, Conn.)
Seluzicki (Portland, Ore.)
Serendipity (Berkeley, Calif.)
Shapiro (New York, N.Y.)
Shure (Searsmont, Maine)
Sleepy (Moraga, Calif.)
Small (So. Yarmouth, Mass.)
Steigerwald (Bloomington, Ind.)
Stickel (Colma, Calif.)
Sullivan (St. Pete., Fla.)

Sylvester (Los Angeles, Calif.)
Taylor (Austin, Texas)
1023 (Omaha, Neb.)
Thomas (San Francisco, Calif.)
Tintagel (E. Springfield, N.Y.)
Titles (Highland Park, Ill.)

Truepenny (Tucson, Ariz.)
Typographeum (Francestown, N.H.)
Under (Shaker Hgts., Ohio)
Vandoros (Middleton, Wisc.)
Wilsey (Olivebridge, N.Y.)

Wreden (Palo Alto, Calif.)
Yellin (Northridge, Calif.)
Yerba (San Francisco, Calif.)
Young (Dobbs Ferry, N.Y.)
Zeitlin (Los Angeles, Calif.)
Zwicker (New York, N.Y.)

Primitive & Pre-Columbian Culture

Arcana (Santa Monica, Calif.)
Arte Prim. (New York, N.Y.)
Ethnographic (Mill Valley, Calif.)

Fein (New York, N.Y.)
Fessler (Theresa, N.Y.)
Johnson (New York, N.Y.)

Oceanie (Hillsdale, N.Y.)

See also
Press Books
Printing & Printing History

Battery (Forest Hills, N.Y.)
Books In (Turlock, Calif.)
Brownstone (New York, N.Y.)
Buck (San Francisco, Calif.)
Chiswick (Sandy Hook, Conn.)
Colophon (Epping, N.H.)
Dawson's (Los Angeles, Calif.)
Dobson (Grimsby, Ont.)
Elmcress (So. Hamilton, Mass.)
Emerson (Albuquerque, N.M.)

Feldman (Cleveland, Ohio)
Heller (Washington, D.C.)
Hill (New York, N.Y.)
Homestead (Marlborough, N.H.)
Howe (New York, N.Y.)
Kane (Santa Cruz, Calif.)
Karmiole (Santa Monica, Calif.)
Ladner (Whitneyville, Conn.)
McDermut (Montvale, N.J.)
Miscellaneous (New Freedom, Pa.)

Moye (Putney, Vt.)
Museum (New York, N.Y.)
Oak Knoll (New Castle, Del.)
Offenbacher (Kew Gardens, N.Y.)
O'Neal (Boston, Mass.)
Printers' (Palo Alto, Calif.)
Rancho (Santa Monica, Calif.)
Saifer (W. Orange, N.J.)
Steigerwald (Bloomington, Ind.)
Testa (No. Newark, N.J.)

Prints

Adams (W. Medway, Mass.)
Adams (Chicago, Ill.)
Amer. Frag. (Escondido, Calif.)
Amherst (Amherst, Mass.)
Arader/Sessler (Philadelphia, Pa.)
Arader (Houston, Texas)
Arader (San Francisco, Calif.)
Arader (Chicago, Ill.)
Arader (New York, N.Y.)

Arader (Atlanta, Ga.)
Artistic (Boston, Mass.)
Audubon (Vienna, Va.)
Bankside (Westport, Conn.)
Beatific (Schenectady, N.Y.)
Besnia (Sterling Jctn., Mass.)
Brattle Book (Boston, Mass.)
Broadfoot's (Wilmington, N.C.)
Bromsen (Boston, Mass.)

Buck (New York, N.Y.)
Burger (Pine Grove, Calif.)
Carousel (Tyler, Texas)
Cherokee (Hollywood, Calif.)
Childs (Boston, Mass.)
Cooper's (Decatur, Ga.)
Cronin (Worcester, Mass.)
Cummins (Pottersville, N.J.)
Dailey (Los Angeles, Calif.)

Darvill's Rare(Eastsound, Wash.)	Hallberg (Hartford, Conn.)	Old Print (Washington, D.C.)
Delle Donne (Ronkonkoma, N.Y.)	Jenison's (Canton, N.Y.)	Old Print (New York, N.Y.)
Drew's (Santa Barbara, Calif.)	June 1 (Bethlehem, Conn.)	Pageant (New York, N.Y.)
E. Coast (Wells, Maine)	Kraft (Palm Desert, Calif.)	Pages (Mt. Kisco, N.Y.)
Edenite (Imlaystown, N.J.)	Laurie (St. Paul, Minn.)	Pan (Catskill, N.Y.)
L'Estampe (Saratoga, Calif.)	Leibowits (New York, N.Y.)	Pansy (St. Andrews, N.B.)
L'Estampe (New York, N.Y.)	Lewis (San Rafael, Calif.)	Paulhus (Wells, Maine)
Fitch (Santa Fe, N.M.)	Lloyd (Red Bank, N.J.)	Pavlov (Dobbs Ferry, N.Y.)
Folger (Washington, D.C.)	Manasek (Hanover, N.H.)	Porter (Phoenix, Ariz.)
GBI (Smithtown, N.Y.)	Manasek (Norwich, Vt.)	Resnik (Roslyn Hgts., N.Y.)
Geraci (Accord, N.Y.)	Margolis (Santa Fe, N.M.)	Reston's (Amsterdam, N.Y.)
Glaeve (Madison, Wisc.)	Marshall Field (Chicago, Ill.)	Rohr (Byfield, Mass.)
Golden Legend (Los Angeles, Calif.)	Martayan (New York, N.Y.)	Rudolph (Portland, Ore.)
	Memory (Corona Del Mar, Calif.)	Sackheim (Tucson, Ariz.)
Goodspeed's #1 (Boston, Mass.)	Mobley (Schoharie, N.Y.)	Schab (New York, N.Y.)
Goodspeed's #2 (Boston, Mass.)	Norman (Philadelphia, Pa.)	Scheck (Scarsdale, N.Y.)
M. Gordon (New York, N.Y.)	Old Almanack (Concord, N.H.)	Spellman (Brick Town, N.J.)
Gregory (New York, N.Y.)	Old Book (San Francisco, Calif.)	Stubbs (New York, N.Y.)
Gventer (So. Egremont, Mass.)	Old Edtns. (Buffalo, N.Y.)	Suarez (New York, N.Y.)

Tamerlis (Mamaroneck, N.Y.)
3 Arts (Poughkeepsie, N.Y.)
Toxophilite (Simsbury, Conn.)
Trotting (Morristown, N.J.)

Tunick (New York, N.Y.)
Unique (Putney, Vt.)
Waite (Madison, Wisc.)
Wildwood (Old Forge, N.Y.)

Wilson (New York, N.Y.)
Wortman (New York, N.Y.)
Wurlitzer (New York, N.Y.)
Yerba (San Francisco, Calif.)

Psychiatry, Psychology, & Psychoanalysis

Academy (New York, N.Y.)
Amdur (Mansfield, Conn.)
Atticus (Toronto, Ont.)
Book Bear (W. Brookfield, Mass.)
Booknook (Evanston, Ill.)
Book Stop (Las Vegas, Nev.)
Catbird (Portland, Ore.)
Dordick (Somerville, Mass.)
Dyment (Ottawa, Ont.)
East West (Hamburg, N.Y.)
E. K. (Rego Park, N.Y.)
Epistemologist (Bryn Mawr, Pa.)
Estate (Washington, D.C.)
Fields (San Francisco, Calif.)
50,000 (El Cajon, Calif.)
Folkways (Bethesda, Md.)
Gach (Columbia, Md.)

Gorski (Doylestown, Pa.)
Heller (Swarthmore, Pa.)
Hive (Easton, Pa.)
Hoffman (Rillton, Pa.)
Hood (Lawrence, Kan.)
Jamaica (Jamaica, N.Y.)
King's (Boulder, Colo.)
Mandrake (Cambridge, Mass.)
Moving (Seattle, Wash.)
Oasis (San Deigo, Calif.)
Old #6 (Henniker, N.H.)
Phenomenologica (Worcester,
    Mass.)
Philosophical (New York, N.Y.)
Printers' (Arlington, Mass.)
Printers' (Boston, Mass.)
Quechee (Quechee, Vt.)

Sadoff (Jenkintown, Pa.)
Saurus (Bethlehem, Pa.)
Schick (Hartsdale, N.Y.)
Schoen (Northampton, Mass.)
2nd Front (San Francisco, Calif.)
Shenandoah (Appleton, Wisc.)
Sophia (Amherst, Mass.)
Storeybook (Sycamore, Ill.)
Stormgart (Boston, Mass.)
Sunset (San Francisco, Calif.)
Tattered (Denver, Colo.)
Tweney (Bowling Green, Ohio)
Vinik (Tucson, Ariz.)
Words (So. Bend, Ind.)
Yesterday's (San Diego, Calif.)

Societies & Associations Publications

Bookmart (Gardiner, N.Y.)

Phiebig (White Plains, N.Y.)

Schnase (Scarsdale, N.Y.)

U. S. Government Publications

Bliss (Middletown, Conn.)
Bookmart (Gardiner, N.Y.)
Canner (Boston, Mass.)

Dabny (Washington, D.C.)
Rogers (Athens, Ga.)
Testa (No. Newark, N.J.)

Western (Stoughton, Mass.)

Publishing History

Acoma (Ramona, Calif.)

Lang (Amityville, N.Y.)

Pulps

See also
Movie & Fan Magazines

Avenue (Boston, Mass.)
Book Mart (Brockton, Mass.)
Brown (No. Augusta, S.C.)
Cinema (Hollywood, Calif.)
de la Ree (Saddle River, N.J.)

Fantasy (Garden Grove, Calif.)
Hopper (Sunnyvale, Calif.)
Hughes (Holmes, N.Y.)
Klass (Santa Barbara, Calif.)
Lippincott (Bangor, Maine)

Reedmor (Philadelphia, Pa.)
2nd Time (Ventura, Calif.)
Slater (Bakersfield, Calif.)
Wellfleet (Wellfleet, Mass.)

Puppetry & Marionettes

Allen (Baltimore, Md.)
Backstage (Eugene, Ore.)

Einhorn (New York, N.Y.)
Meyerbooks (Glenwood, Ill.)

Theater (Palo Alto, Calif.)

Radical Politics & Literature

See also Conservative Literature & Authors

Beasley (Chicago, Ill.)
Between (Old Bridge, N.J.)
Burbank (Burbank, Calif.)

Free Lance (Brooklyn, N.Y.)
2nd Life (Lanesborough, Mass.)
Sessions (Birmingham, Ala.)

Southpaw (Roxbury, Mass.)
Treehorn (Santa Rosa, Calif.)
Vol. I (Hillsdale, Mich.)

Railroads

Abbot (Bronx, N.Y.)
Acorn (San Francisco, Calif.)
aGatherin' (Wynantskill, N.Y.)
Antiq. Archive (Sunnyvale, Calif.)
Arden (Noti, Ore.)
Arone (Dobbs Ferry, N.Y.)
Baggage (Wayne, N.J.)
Bohling (Decatur, Mich.)
Book Mart Annex (San Antonio, Tex.)
Bookmine (Old Scaramento, Calif.)
Book Prospector (Littleton, Colo.)
Cliffside (Kansas City, Mo.)

Country (Chesterton, Ind.)
Cramer (Media, Pa.)
Cramer (Kansas City, Mo.)
Crawford's (Cincinnati, Ohio)
Davies (Oak Park, Ill.)
DC Service (Columbia, Mo.)
Diablo (Walnut Creek, Calif.)
Doerres (Wilton, Iowa)
Harbar (Casselberry, Fla.)
High Country (Laramie, Wyo.)
Moore (Wynnewood, Pa.)
Moran (Rocky Point, N.Y.)
Palmer (Eugene, Ore.)

Pearson (Chicago, Ill.)
Poste (Geneseo, N.Y.)
Prag (San Francisco, Calif.)
Rails (Rosemead, Calif.)
Roderick (Medina, Ohio)
Rosenstock (Denver, Colo.)
Southwest (Durango, Colo.)
Talvin (Trafford, Pa.)
Terra (Churchville, N.Y.)
Trackside (Houston, Texas)
Valley (Galena, Ill.)
Von Blon's (Waco, Texas)
Western (Gaston, Ore.)

Rare Books

Aardvark (San Francisco, Calif.)
Amer. City (Denver, Colo.)
Americanist (Pottstown, Pa.)
Antiq. Center (New York, N.Y.)
Antiquarium (Bethany, Conn.)
Appelfeld (New York, N.Y.)
Argonaut (San Francisco, Calif.)
Armchair (No. Orange, Mass.)
Armenian (Pico Rivera, Calif.)
Ashton (Ottawa, Ont.)
Audubon (Vienna, Va.)
Babcock (Derry, N.H.)
Bargain (Norfolk, Va.)
Barnes (Evanston, Ill.)
Bauman (Philadelphia, Pa.)
Bauman (Atlantic City, N.J.)
Biblion (Forest Hills, N.Y.)
Black Ace (Denver, Colo.)
Black Sun (New York, N.Y.)
Blue Dragon (Ashland, Ore.)
Booked Up (Washington, D.C.)
Book Place (Columbia, S.C.)
Book Sail (Orange, Calif.)
Bookseller's (Chicago, Ill.)
Bookstock (So. Orleans, Mass.)

Book Traders (Winter Haven, Fla.)
Brattle Book (Boston, Mass.)
Brookline (Brookline, Mass.)
Burke's (Memphis, Tenn.)
Burrows (Downers Grove, Ill.)
Cady (Chicago, Ill.)
Canney (Alfred, Maine)
Caravan (Los Angeles, Calif.)
Carnegie (New York, N.Y.)
Carr (New York, N.Y.)
Casten (New York, N.Y.)
Chiswick (Sandy Hook, Conn.)
Christoffersen (Mamaroneck, N.Y.)
Clare (Getzville, N.Y.)
Cohen (Youngstown, Ohio)
Crabtree (Signal Mtn., Tenn.)
Curious Raven (Detroit, Mich.)
Dailey (Los Angeles, Calif.)
Detering (Houston, Texas)
Doukas (Kalamazoo, Mich.)
Dragan (Ithaca, N.Y.)
DuPriest (Columbia, S.C.)
E. Coast (Wells, Maine)
Escargot (Brielle, N.J.)
First (Chicago, Ill.)

Firsts (New York, N.Y.)
Fleming (New York, N.Y.)
Ford (Lake Worth, Fla.)
Foster (Corning, Calif.)
Fox (Tacoma, Wash.)
Frohnsdorff (Gaithersburg, Md.)
Gach (Columbia, Md.)
Glenn (Kansas City, Mo.)
Goodspeed's #1 (Boston, Mass.)
Goodspeed's #2 (Boston, Mass.)
Grandpa's (Troy, N.C.)
Grub Street (Detroit, Mich.)
Grunder (Ithaca, N.Y.)
Hamill (Chicago, Ill.)
Harper (Bristol, Vt.)
Hartfield (Ann Arbor, Mich.)
Haunted (Victoria, B.C.)
Havemeyer (Skaneafeles, N.Y.)
Hayman (Carey, Ohio)
Heritage (Los Angeles, Calif.)
Hessel (Calimesa, Calif.)
Hillman (New York, N.Y.)
Hilton Village (Newport News, Va.)
Hirsch (Hopewell Jctn., N.Y.)

Hist. Realia (Wooster, Ohio)
Hoffer (Vancouver, B.C.)
Hollywood City (Hollywood, Calif.)
Holmes (Oakland, Calif.)
Holy Land (Washington, D.C.)
Invisible (Berkeley, Calif.)
Isador (Highland Park, Ill.)
Isaiah (Worcester, Mass.)
Jay's (Marlboro, N.J.)
Johnny (Manchester, Vt.)
Johnson (Syracuse, N.Y.)
Jolie's (Stuart, Fla.)
Joyce (Chicago, Ill.)
Kahn (Montreal, Que.)
Katz (Los Angeles, Calif.)
Keck (Decatur, Ill.)
Keramos (Ann Arbor, Mich.)
Key (Baltimore, Md.)
Koschal (Verona, N.J.)
Kraft (Palm Desert, Calif.)
Kraus (Millwood, N.Y.)
Kripke (New York, N.Y.)
Kristiansen (Boston, Mass.)
Lake (Toronto, Ont.)
Lasley (Berkeley, Ill.)
La Valois (New York, N.Y.)
Leach (Brattleboro, Vt.)
Leaves (Ann Arbor, Mich.)
Legacy (Iowa City, Iowa)
Lemon (Lemon Grove, Calif.)
Lien (Minneapolis, Minn.)

Magic (Johnson City, Tenn.)
Mahoney (Buffalo, N.Y.)
Maiden (W. Chester, Pa.)
Manasek (Hanover, N.H.)
Manasek (Norwich, Vt.)
Manor (New York, N.Y.)
Mason (Toronto, Ont.)
Matthews (Ft. Erie, Ont.)
McGahern (Ottawa, Ont.)
McKittrick (Philadelphia, Pa.)
Midvale (Portland, Ore.)
Milestone (New York, N.Y.)
Monarski (Syracuse, N.Y.)
Mostly (Carthage, Mo.)
Moye (Putney, Vt.)
M & S (Weston, Mass.)
Murray (Wilbraham, Mass.)
Natural (Woodland Hills, Calif.)
Nebenzahl (Chicago, Ill.)
New Age (Westerly, R.I.)
Norman (San Francisco, Calif.)
Norumbega (Houston, Texas)
Offenbacher (Kew Gardens, N.Y.)
Old Mont. (Monterey, Calif.)
Old Oregon (Portland, Ore.)
O'Neal (Boston, Mass.)
O'Neill (Warner, N.H.)
O'Neill (Reston, Va.)
Pageant (New York, N.Y.)
Parmer's (Sarasota, Fla.)
Parsons (Sonoma, Calif.)
Pavlov (Dobbs Ferry, N.Y.)

Peggatty (Clarkston, Wash.)
Pirages (McMinnville, Ore.)
Polyanthos (Huntington, N.Y.)
Publix (Cleveland, Ohio)
Quill (Rockville, Md.)
B. Ramer (New York, N.Y.)
Randall (Santa Barbara, Calif.)
Ravenstree (Yuma, Ariz.)
Ray's (Hartford, Vt.)
Resnick (Cazenovia, N.Y.)
Richshafer (Cincinnati, Ohio)
Rittenhouse (Albuquerque, N.M.)
Roberts (W. Palm Bch., Fla.)
Rohr (Byfield, Mass.)
Rootenberg (Sherman Oaks, Calif.)
Ross (Medina, N.Y.)
Rostenberg (New York, N.Y.)
Rulon-Miller (Minneapolis, Minn.)
Russica (New York, N.Y.)
Sadlon's (De Pere, Wisc.)
Salerno (Hauppauge, N.Y.)
Salloch (Ossining, N.Y.)
Sanderson (Stockbridge, Mass.)
Savoy (Lanesborough, Mass.)
Schick (Hartsdale, N.Y.)
Schreyer (New York, N.Y.)
Sci Fict. (New York, N.Y.)
Scott (Stonington, Conn.)
Sewards' (Providence, R.I.)
Shapiro (New York, N.Y.)
Skeans (Deer Isle, Maine)
Steigerwald (Bloomington, Ind.)

Stern (Chicago, Ill.)
Stevens (Williamsburg, Va.)
Strand Rare (New York, N.Y.)
Tebbetts (Hallowell, Maine)
Thelema (King Bch., Calif.)
Tintagel (E. Springfield, N.Y.)
Titles (Highland Park, Ill.)
Trebizond (New Preston, Conn.)
Tumarkin (New York, N.Y.)

Tumbleweed (Pueblo, Colo.)
Typographeum (Francestown, N.H.)
Una (St. Johnsbury, Vt.)
Urrizola (Los Angeles, Calif.)
Ute-Or (W. Jordan, Utah)
Victoria (New York, N.Y.)
Vintage (Iowa City, Iowa)
Wahrenbrock's (San Diego, Calif.)

Walett (Abington, Mass.)
Wayner (Ft. Payne, Ala.)
Wolfe (Pt. Claire, Que.)
Wreden (Palo Alto, Calif.)
Wurlitzer (New York, N.Y.)
Xerxes (Glen Head, N.Y.)
Yesterday's (Washington, D.C.)
Yesteryear (Atlanta, Ga.)
Ziagos (Lowell, Mass.)

Reference

Academic (Portland, Ore.)
Antiquarium (Bethany, Conn.)
Assoc. Stu. (Chico, Calif.)
Book Clearing (Larchmont, N.Y.)
Book Studio (Atlanta, Ga.)
Bowling (Rancho Palos Verdes, Calif.)
Burstein (Waltham, Mass.)
Canner (Boston, Mass.)
Catholic (Bellingham, Mass.)

Core Coll. (Great Neck, N.Y.)
Discher (Castro Valley, Calif.)
Fitch (Santa Fe, N.M.)
M. Gordon (New York, N.Y.)
Ha'Penny (Snowville, N.H.)
Junius (Fairview, N.J.)
Kaufman (New York, N.Y.)
Lehr (New York, N.Y.)
Library (Dallas, Texas)
McCosh (Excelsior, Minn.)

Minnehaha (Minneapolis, Minn.)
National (Brooklyn, N.Y.)
Nebraska (Lincoln, Neb.)
999 (New York, N.Y.)
Osgood (Rockport, Mass.)
Reference (New York, N.Y.)
Russica (New York, N.Y.)
Univelt (San Diego, Calif.)

Religion & Religious History

ABC Theo. (Springfield, Mo.)
Abelard (Toronto, Ont.)
Academy (San Francisco, Calif.)
A C (Brooklyn, N.Y.)
Aide (Cardiff, Calif.)
All Books (Miami, Fla.)
Allenson (Geneva, Ala.)
Amer. Book (Fresno, Calif.)
Anglican (Saratoga Spgs., N.Y.)
Baker (Grand Rapids, Mich.)
Balthasar's (Maryknoll, N.Y.)
Baptist (Watertown, Wisc.)
Berkley (Berkley, Minn.)
Berkowitz (Chester, N.Y.)
Bever (Edmond, Okla.)
Bibliofile (San Francisco, Calif.)

Boardman (Camden, N.Y.)
Bolerium (San Francisco, Calif.)
Bolingbroke (Pinnacle, N.C.)
Book Bin (Corvallis, Ore.)
Booknook (Evanston, Ill.)
Bookpost (Cardiff, Calif.)
Books By (Derby, Conn.)
Booksellers (St. Paul, Minn.)
Bookstore (Lenox, Mass.)
Burleson (Spartanburg, S.C.)
Catholic (Bellingham, Mass.)
Cellar (Eugene, Ore.)
Celtic (Westmoreland, N.H.)
Chimney (Scotts Valley, Calif.)
Christian (Westminster, Md.)
Constant (Milwaukee, Wisc.)

East West (Hamburg, N.Y.)
Edenite (Imlaystown, N.J.)
Fay (Caledonia, N.Y.)
Fields (San Francisco, Calif.)
Gateway (Ferndale, Pa.)
George (Cleveland, Tenn.)
Gilbert (Los Angeles, Calif.)
Good News (Rossville, Ind.)
Green (Philadelphia, Pa.)
Griffon (So. Bend, Ind.)
Grunder (Ithaca, N.Y.)
Guerrera (Lawrence, Mass.)
Gull Shop (Oakland, Calif.)
Hamilton's (Williamsburg, Va.)
Haslam's (St. Pete., Fla.)
Heritage (Sonora, Calif.)

Hermeticus (Ashland, Ore.)
Holmes (Edmonds, Wash.)
House (Toronto, Ont.)
Huntley (Claremont, Calif.)
Hurley (Westmoreland, N.H.)
Jamaica (Jamaica, N.Y.)
Joyce (Martinez, Calif.)
Kaiser (Santa Cruz, Calif.)
Knaus (Ft. Bragg, Calif.)
Kregel's (Grand Rapids, Mich.)
Left Bank (Oak Park, Ill.)
Little (Rehobeth, Mass.)
Loome (Stillwater, Minn.)
Madonna (Combermere, Ont.)
Margolis (Monroe, Mich.)
Memory (Belfast, Maine)
Monie (Cooperstown, N.Y.)
Monie Shop (Cooperstown, N.Y.)
Morrell's (Ocean Grove, N.J.)

Morrison (Santa Monica, Calif.)
Mt. Zion (Mt. Zion, W.Va.)
New Engl. (Bennington, Vt.)
Noah's (Greenwood, S.C.)
Old Edtns. (Buffalo, N.Y.)
Old N.Y. (Atlanta, Ga.)
Ollie's (Memphis, Tenn.)
Owl Creek (Mt. Vernon, Ohio)
Philosophical (New York, N.Y.)
Plante (St. Cloud, Minn.)
Pomander (New York, N.Y.)
Provident (Bloomington, Ill.)
Rare Book (Freehold, N.J.)
Ravenstree (Yuma, Ariz.)
Roberts (Wheaton, Ill.)
Ryan (Columbus, Ohio)
Sacred (Goffstown, N.H.)
Seminary (Alexandria, Va.)
Sharp's (No. Hollywood, Calif.)

Shenandoah (Appleton, Wisc.)
Shorey (Seattle, Wash.)
Smalley (Columbia, Tenn.)
Stevens (Wake Forest, N.C.)
Stroud (Williamsburg, W.Va.)
Thelema (King Bch., Calif.)
This Old (Montclair, Calif.)
Touchet (New York, N.Y.)
University (Hull, Mass.)
Vinik (Tucson, Ariz.)
Waldo (Rockton, Ill.)
Ward (Prospect, Ohio)
Weiser (New York, N.Y.)
White's (Asbury Park, N.J.)
Wood (Tampa, Fla.)
Ye Olde (San Angelo, Texas)
Yesterday's (Modesto, Calif.)
Yesterday's (San Diego, Calif.)

Eastern Religion

Abintra (Morris, N.Y.)
Book Manifest (Portland, Ore.)

Bookpost (Cardiff, Calif.)
Hermeticus (Ashland, Ore.)

Summers (Pacific, Mo.)
Words (So. Bend, Ind.)

Remainders

Amitin (St. Louis, Mo.)
Book Exch. (Plainville, Conn.)
Books & Co. (San Francisco, Calif.)
Dartmouth (Hanover, N.H.)
Green Apple (San Francisco, Calif.)
Hennessey (Santa Monica, Calif.)

Imagine That (No. Adams, Mass.)
Imagine That (Pittsfield, Mass.)
Jacksonville (Jacksonville, Ore.)
Johnson's (Springfield, Mass.)
John Steele (Litchfield, Conn.)
MacBeans (Brunswick, Maine)
Old Barn (Forsyth, Ill.)
Oriental (Pasadena, Calif.)

Oxford At (Atlanta, Ga.)
Oxford Two (Atlanta, Ga.)
Rohe (Chicago, Ill.)
Ruby's (New York, N.Y.)
Strand (New York, N.Y.)
Tebbetts (Hallowell, Maine)
Vargo's (Bozeman, Mont.)
Wonder (Frederick, Md.)

See also
Middle Ages

Renaissance

Bliss (Middletown, Conn.)
Folger (Washington, D.C.)
Loome (Stillwater, Minn.)
Mancevice (Worcester, Mass.)

McKittrick (Philadelphia, Pa.)
Rosenthal (San Francisco, Calif.)
Rostenberg (New York, N.Y.)
Salloch (Ossining, N.Y.)

Schreiber (Bronx, N.Y.)
Zambelli (New York, N.Y.)

Reprints

Abraham's (New York, N.Y.)
Bliss (Middletown, Conn.)
Darby (Darby, Pa.)

Edenite (Imlaystown, N.J.)
Johnson's (Springfield, Mass.)
Kregel's (Grand Rapids, Mich.)

Lozinski (Westport, Mass.)
Schnase (Scarsdale, N.Y.)
Zeitlin Per. (Los Angeles, Calif.)

Rhode Island

Cellar (Providence, R.I.)
Cornerstone (Providence, R.I.)
Little (Rehobeth, Mass.)

Sewards' (Providence, R.I.)
Theophrastus (Little Compton, R.I.)

Tyson (Providence, R.I.)

Rock 'n Roll

Book City (Hollywood, Calif.)   Quill (Pinellas Park, Fla.)

Russia & Slavic Countries

Dee Cee (Nyack, N.Y.)
Ideal (New York, N.Y.)
Johnson (Indianapolis, Ind.)
Kalanja (Trafford, Pa.)
Lozinski (Westport, Mass.)

Mallahan (Bellevue, Wash.)
McBlain (Hamden, Conn.)
Parnassus (Yarmouthport, Mass.)
Russica (New York, N.Y.)
Slattery (Palo Alto, Calif.)

Szwede (Palo Alto, Calif.)
Talvin (Trafford, Pa.)
Zubel (Cleveland, Ohio)

Sailing & Yachting

Armchair (Newport, R.I.)
Columbia (Suffern, N.Y.)
Compass (Sitka, Alk.)
Cross Hill (Brunswick, Maine)

Glooscap (Pefferlaw, Ont.)
Howland (Jamaica Plain, Mass.)
Lowe (Boston, Mass.)
Nautica (Halifax, N.S.)

Pell's (Delray Bch., Fla.)
Pier (Piermont, N.Y.)

St. Louis Area

Amitin (St. Louis, Mo.)
Hughes (St. Louis, Mo.)

Mandala (Daytona Bch., Fla.)
Swiss (St. Louis, Mo.)

Scholarly Books

About (Toronto, Ont.)
Aion (Boulder, Colo.)
Allen (Philadelphia, Pa.)
Alper (Eastchester, N.Y.)
Amer. City (Denver, Colo.)
Amer. Worlds (Hamden, Conn.)
Ancient (Santa Fe, N.M.)
Antiquarium (Bethany, Conn.)
Askins (New Lebanon, N.Y.)
Avol's (Madison, Wisc.)
Barber (Boston, Mass.)
Barnes (Evanston, Ill.)
Barnstable (New York, N.Y.)
Bear (W. Brattleboro, Vt.)
Ben Franklin (U. Nyack, N.Y.)
Black Oak (Berkeley, Calif.)
Bookcase (Cambridge, Mass.)
Book Forum (Denver, Colo.)
Book Home (Colo. Spgs., Colo.)
Book House (Minneapolis, Minn.)
Bookie Joint (Reseda, Calif.)
Bookseller (Denver, Colo.)
Book Stop (Tucson, Ariz.)
Burrows (Downers Grove, Ill.)
Chimera (Palo Alto, Calif.)
Chip's Shop (New York, N.Y.)
Collins (San Francisco, Calif.)
Collins (Seattle, Wash.)
Compulsive (New York, N.Y.)
Cottonwood (Baton Rouge, La.)
Cragsmoor (Cragsmoor, N.Y.)
Dartmouth (Hanover, N.H.)
De Wit (East Lansing, Mich.)

Dragan (Ithaca, N.Y.)
Edenite (Imlaystown, N.J.)
E. K. (Rego Park, N.Y.)
Elliot's (Northford, Conn.)
Ernest (Ottumwa, Iowa)
Gabriel (Northampton, Mass.)
Good Times (Pt. Jefferson, N.Y.)
Grub Street (Detroit, Mich.)
Gryphon #2 (New York, N.Y.)
Hammer Mtn. (Schenectady, N.Y.)
Heller (Cleveland, Ohio)
Hermitage (Denver, Colo.)
Holmes (San Francisco, Calif.)
Holmes (Edmonds, Wash.)
Hood (Lawrence, Kan.)
Info (El Cerrito, Calif.)
Jaffe (Arlington, Va.)
Johnson's (Los Angeles, Calif.)
Junius (Fairview, N.J.)
Kraus (Millwood, N.Y.)
Kubik (Dayton, Ohio)
Ladner (Whitneyville, Conn.)
Leekley (Winthrop Harbor, Ill.)
Macksey (Baltimore, Md.)
Magus (Seattle, Wash.)
Mandala (Daytona Bch., Fla.)
Marlowe's (Boston, Mass.)
Martin (La Grange, Ill.)
McCosh (Excelsior, Minn.)
Memorable (Stone Mtn., Ga.)
Murphy (Iowa City, Iowa)
Nebraska (Lincoln, Neb.)
Nemeroff (Williamstown, Mass.)

No. Mtn. (Phoenix, Ariz.)
Old Book (Morristown, N.J.)
Old Oregon (Portland, Ore.)
Pangloss (Cambridge, Mass.)
Patrick (Toronto, Ont.)
Patriot (Lexington, Mass.)
Phoenix (Freeville, N.Y.)
Phoenix (San Luis Obispo, Calif.)
Polyanthos (Huntington, N.Y.)
Powell's (Chicago, Ill.)
Princeton (Atlantic City, N.J.)
Quadrant (Easton, Pa.)
Riverow (Owego, N.Y.)
Rosenthal (San Francisco, Calif.)
Ryan (Columbus, Ohio)
Saifer (W. Orange, N.J.)
Schnase (Scarsdale, N.Y.)
Schneeman (Chicago, Ill.)
Schroeder's (Dickinson, Texas)
2nd Story (Washington, D.C.)
Servant's (Atlantic City, N.J.)
Seville (Pensacola, Fla.)
Sewards' (Providence, R.I.)
Shaman (Ann Arbor, Mich.)
This Old (Montclair, Calif.)
Wayner (Ft. Payne, Ala.)
Wessex (Menlo Park, Calif.)
Western (Stoughton, Mass.)
West (Provo, Utah)
Woods (Yakima, Wash.)
Word (Montreal, Que.)

Science

See also
Medicine & Science, History of Medicine & Science

Amer. Book (Fresno, Calif.)
Antiq. Book (Winter Park, Fla.)
Beare (Wilmington, Del.)
Book Assoc. (Orange, Conn.)
Book Barn (Rochester, Mich.)
Book Cellar (Bethesda, Md.)
Book/Tackle (Chestnut Hill, Mass.)
Boyson (Brookfield, Conn.)
Buteo (Vermillion, S.D.)
deBeurs (Dexter, Maine)
Flora (Seattle, Wash.)
Geological (Falls Village, Conn.)
Gilbert (Los Angeles, Calif.)
Gorski (Doylestown, Pa.)
Hale (Washington, D.C.)

Heller (Swarthmore, Pa.)
Hist. Tech (Marblehead, Mass.)
Hoffman (Rillton, Pa.)
Inner Circle (New York, N.Y.)
Key (Baltimore, Md.)
King's (Boulder, Colo.)
Kraus (New York, N.Y.)
Lubrecht (Forestburgh, N.Y.)
Luft (Oakland Gdns., N.Y.)
Macauluso (Kennett Sq., Pa.)
Martayan (New York, N.Y.)
Masi (Montague, Mass.)
Maxwell (Elmsford, N.Y.)
Needle (Chelmsford, Mass.)
Nisula (Okemos, Mich.)

Norman (Philadelphia, Pa.)
No. Mtn. (Phoenix, Ariz.)
Oasis (San Deigo, Calif.)
Old #6 (Henniker, N.H.)
Quechee (Quechee, Vt.)
B. Ramer (New York, N.Y.)
Schab (New York, N.Y.)
Schoen (Northampton, Mass.)
Science (Ann Arbor, Mich.)
Scientia (Arlington, Mass.)
Tolliver's (Los Angeles, Calif.)
Wade (Cincinnati, Ohio)
White (New York, N.Y.)
Wilder (Hubbardston, Mass.)

Science Fiction

See also
Fantasy, Horror

Aladdin (Fullerton, Calif.)
Allbooks (Colo. Spgs., Colo.)
Armens (Iowa City, Iowa)
Atlanta (Atlanta, Ga.)
Attic (Laurel, Md.)
Avalon (Hayward, Calif.)
Avenue (Boston, Mass.)

Avocet (Corvallis, Ore.)
Bakka (Toronto, Ont.)
Bargain (Norfolk, Va.)
Beasley (Chicago, Ill.)
Bernard (Rockville, Md.)
Between (Old Bridge, N.J.)
Biblioctopus (Idyllwild, Calif.)

Bonmark (Plainview, N.Y.)
Book Baron (Anaheim, Calif.)
Book Bin (Kingston, Ont.)
Book Carnival (Orange, Calif.)
Book Case (Houston, Texas)
Bookery (Fairborn, Ohio)
Book Exch. (Plainville, Conn.)

Bookfinders (Atlanta, Ga.)
Bookie (E. Hartford, Conn.)
Bookie Joint (Reseda, Calif.)
Book Mart (Brockton, Mass.)
Books/Comics #2 (Indianapolis, Ind.)
Bookshelf (Ogden, Utah)
Books 'n (El Dorado, Ark.)
Book Stop (Las Vegas, Nev.)
Brownbag (Rochester, N.Y.)
Bunker (Spring Valley, Calif.)
Bunker (Spring Valley, Calif.)
Cabin/Pines (Potsdam, N.Y.)
Campbell (Campbell, Calif.)
Canford (Freeville, N.Y.)
Caravan (Stillwater, Okla.)
Cellar (Providence, R.I.)
Change (Santa Monica, Calif.)
Chaos (Washington, D.C.)
Cheap St. (New Castle, Va.)
Choras (Weston, Mass.)
Circle West (Annapolis, Md.)
Connolly (Vista, Calif.)
Cook (Los Angeles, Calif.)
Cosmic (Salt Lake City, Utah)
Curious Book (E. Lansing, Mich.)
Curious Raven (Detroit, Mich.)
Currey (Elizabethtown, N.Y.)
Dan's (Appleton, Wisc.)
Daunce (Buffalo, N.Y.)
Dawn (Ann Arbor, Mich.)
Debra (No. Hills, Pa.)
de la Ree (Saddle River, N.J.)
Discher (Castro Valley, Calif.)
Dragon's Lair (Dayton, Ohio)
Drümm (Polk City, Iowa)
Dugas (Orlando, Fla.)
Fantasy (New York, N.Y.)
Fantasy (Carmichael, Calif.)
Fantasy (San Francisco, Calif.)
Federation (College St., Texas)
50,000 (El Cajon, Calif.)
Fine (Rochester, Mich.)
Fithian (Lakewood, Colo.)

Ford (Lake Worth, Fla.)
Fountain (Indianapolis, Ind.)
Gabbard (New Boston, Texas)
Gavora (Santa Barbara, Calif.)
George (Cleveland, Tenn.)
Golden Age (Seattle, Wash.)
Gordon (Pasadena, Calif.)
Gorski (Doylestown, Pa.)
Green Apple (San Francisco, Calif.)
Green Mtn. (So. Royalton, Vt.)
Griffon (So. Bend, Ind.)
Gud (Elmhurst, N.Y.)
Hanley's (Chicago, Ill.)
Hittel (Ft. Lauderdale, Fla.)
Hooked (Springfield, Mo.)
Horizon (Seattle, Wash.)
Houseman (Yellow Spgs., Ohio)
Hughes (Holmes, N.Y.)
In #1 (San Francisco, Calif.)
In #2 (San Francisco, Calif.)
Jack's (Mt. Prospect, Ill.)
Janus (Corea, Maine)
Janus (Hungtinton Stn., N.Y.)
JMD (Groton, N.Y.)
Keeler (No. Monmouth, Maine)
Klass (Santa Barbara, Calif.)
Krause (Warrington, Fla.)
Kristiansen (Boston, Mass.)
Lemon (Lemon Grove, Calif.)
Levin (Los Angeles, Calif.)
Lippincott (Bangor, Maine)
Mannatt (San Diego, Calif.)
Matthews (Ft. Erie, Ont.)
Max Gate (Kankakee, Ill.)
McBride (Hartford, Conn.)
McFarland (Tampa, Fla.)
McGovern (Berwyn, Ill.)
Mendoza (New York, N.Y.)
Merlin's (Isla Vista, Calif.)
Merlin's (Providence, R.I.)
Midnight (Marietta, Ga.)
Nelson (New Bedford, Mass.)
O'Donoghue (Anoka, Minn.)

Old Favs. (Richmond, Va.)
O'Leary's (Tacoma, Wash.)
Pantechnicon (1000 Oaks, Calif.)
Passaic (Passaic, N.J.)
Phoenix (San Luis Obispo, Calif.)
Plant (Grass Valley, Calif.)
Printer's (Middletown, Conn.)
Printer's (Milldale, Conn.)
Ralston (Fullerton, Calif.)
Ransom (Amherst, N.Y.)
Reader's (Raleigh, N.C.)
Reedmor (Philadelphia, Pa.)
Reston's (Amsterdam, N.Y.)
Rodden's (Long Bch., Calif.)
Salerno (Hauppauge, N.Y.)
Saurus (Bethlehem, Pa.)
Science (Ann Arbor, Mich.)
Sci Fict. (New York, N.Y.)
Sebert (Mt. Nebo, W.Va.)
2nd Time (Ventura, Calif.)
Slater (Bakersfield, Calif.)
Spectrum (Milwaukee, Wisc.)
Squires (Glendale, Calif.)
S & S (St. Paul, Minn.)
Stan's (Brockton, Mass.)
Stephens (Hastings, N.Y.)
Tauscher (Bristol, Va.)
20th Century (Madison, Wisc.)
Valley (No. Hollywood, Calif.)
West L.A. (Los Angeles, Calif.)
West's (Elm Grove, Wisc.)
White (New York, N.Y.)
Wilhite (Clearwater, Fla.)
Willis (Columbus, Ohio)
Wilson (Bull Shoals, Ark.)
Windsor (Windsor, Conn.)
Woods (Yakima, Wash.)
Words (Cambridge, Mass.)
Wyatt (San Diego, Calif.)
Xanadu (Bronx, N.Y.)
Yellin (Northridge, Calif.)
Ye Olde (Elmhurst, Ill.)
Yesteryear (Nampa, Idaho)

Scientific Instruments

Antiq. Scientist (Dracut, Mass.)   Tesseract (Hastings, N.Y.)

Scotland & The Scotish

Abatis (Springfield, Vt.)   House (Anaheim, Calif.)   Unicorn (Bruceton Mills, W.Va.)
Cider (Exeter, N.H.)   Munsell (Newburyport, Mass.)

Search Service With Stock

Abbies (Temple, N.H.)   Donan (New York, N.Y.)   Reedmor (Philadelphia, Pa.)
Bookbizniz (Atlantic City, N.J.)   Gilfond (Washington, D.C.)   Scanlon-Towers (Shelburne, Vt.)
Buccaneer (Laguna Bch., Calif.)   Kaufman (Tempe, Ariz.)   Shirley's (Springfield, Mo.)
Charing (Hutchinson, Kan.)   Pegram (Sarasota, Fla.)
Continental (New York, N.Y.)   Peninsula (Burlingame, Calif.)

Search Service Without Stock

AlphaBook (Van Nuys, Calif.)   Berman (Atlanta, Ga.)   Buckley (No. Chatham, Mass.)
Avonlea (White Plains, N.Y.)   Bloomsbury (Denver, Colo.)   Egan (Millville, N.J.)
Beardsley (Somerville, N.J.)   Book Search (Petersburg, Va.)   Engle (Cherry Hill, N.J.)

Golden Gull (Grants Pass, Ore.)   Needham (Los Angeles, Calif.)   Powers (Essex Jctn., Vt.)
Murray's (Bridgeport, Conn.)   Phoenix (Plainview, N.J.)   Reed (Birmingham, Ala.)

Self-Help

Grt. Lakes (Ann Arbor, Mich.)   Moving (Seattle, Wash.)   Village (Bellingham, Wash.)

Series Books for Boys & Girls

See also Horatio Alger, Children's Books, Juveniles, Tom Swift

Book Fair (Eugene, Ore.)   Lippincott (Bangor, Maine)   Pendleton (Tiburon, Calif.)
Books Of (Corning, N.Y.)   Littlewoods (Waukesha, Wisc.)   Pipkin (Rock Hill, S.C.)
Dr. Nostalgia (Lynchburg, Va.)   Max Gate (Kankakee, Ill.)   Temares (Plandome, N.Y.)
Downs (Marietta, Ga.)   Merriwell (Islip, N.Y.)   Toy (San Francisco, Calif.)
Eastman (Springvale, Maine)   New Miner (Necedah, Wisc.)   Twyce (Winona, Minn.)
Evans (Savannah, Ga.)   O'Donoghue (Anoka, Minn.)   Varney's (Casco, Maine)
George (Cleveland, Tenn.)   Owen (Litchfield, Maine)   Wise (Lake Delton, Wisc.)
Good News (Rossville, Ind.)   Oz (Kenilworth, N.J.)   Yesterdays (Whitman, Mass.)
Hunt (Clayton, Ind.)   Pages (Reading, Mass.)   Zellner's (Easton, Pa.)

Sets

See also Reference

Appelfeld (New York, N.Y.)   Colebrook (Colebrook, Conn.)   Reference (New York, N.Y.)
Bartfield (New York, N.Y.)   Harris (Little Rock, Ark.)   Sacred (Goffstown, N.H.)
Bliss (Middletown, Conn.)   Hawley (Louisville, Ky.)   Starr (Boston, Mass.)
Booketeria (San Antonio, Texas)   Lewis (San Rafael, Calif.)   Wahrenbrock's (San Diego, Calif.)
Books By (Derby, Conn.)   Midnight (Marietta, Ga.)   Wangner's (Montclair, N.J.)
Caprio (Revere, Mass.)   NRS (New York, N.Y.)   Weitz (New York, N.Y.)
Chicago (Evanston, Ill.)   Prestianni (Penfield, N.Y.)   Wise (Baldwin Pl., N.Y.)

Sexology

See also Curiosa, Erotica

A C (Brooklyn, N.Y.)   Scheiner (Brooklyn, N.Y.)
Elysian (Elmhurst, N.Y.)   Stormgart (Boston, Mass.)

Shakespeare

Backstage (Eugene, Ore.)
Caprio (Revere, Mass.)

Diamond (Burbank, Calif.)
Einhorn (New York, N.Y.)

Folger (Washington, D.C.)

Sheet Music

See also
Musical Scores

Anita's (Manchester, N.H.)
Attic (St. Pete., Fla.)
Boise Farm (Boise, Idaho)
Bookstop (Alexandria, Va.)

Cameron's (Portland, Ore.)
Ellis (Kentfield, Calif.)
Huckleberry (Centralia, Wash.)
Najarian (Newtown Sq., Pa.)

Old Music (3 Oaks, Mich.)
Opera Box (Brooklyn, N.Y.)
Zita (New York, N.Y.)

Ships & The Sea

Antheil (No. Bellmore, N.Y.)
Bankside (Westport, Conn.)
Book Den E. (Oak Bluffs, Mass.)
Cape Collector (So. Harwich, Mass.)
Caravan (Los Angeles, Calif.)
Caravan-Maritime (Jamaica, N.Y.)
Columbia (Suffern, N.Y.)

Compass (Sitka, Alk.)
Copeland (Portland, Maine)
Howland (Jamaica Plain, Mass.)
Jamaica (Jamaica, N.Y.)
Kern (Glendale, Ariz.)
Kionke (Gowanda, N.Y.)
Kitemaug (Spartanburg, S.C.)
Lefkowicz (Fairhaven, Mass.)

Lowe (Boston, Mass.)
Persoff (Alameda, Calif.)
Pier (Piermont, N.Y.)
St. Andrews (Columbia, S.C.)
Seabook (Clinton Corners, N.Y.)
Tuttle (Madison, Wisc.)
West Side (Ann Arbor, Mich.)
Yesterday's (San Diego, Calif.)

Ships & Ship Building

Columbia (Suffern, N.Y.)   Pier (Piermont, N.Y.)

Show Business

Ballet (New York, N.Y.)   Bradshaw (Chicago, Ill.)

Skiing

Ashley (Burlington, Vt.)   Chessler (New York, N.Y.)   Old Tech (Carlisle, Mass.)

See also
Black Studies

Slavery

Conn. Book (Fairfield, Conn.)   Craig (Newport, R. I.)
Cornerstone (Providence, R.I.)   Free Lance (Brooklyn, N.Y.)

Social Science

Book Bear (W. Brookfield, Mass.)   Hartmann (Morganton, N.C.)   Pangloss (Cambridge, Mass.)
Books Amer. (San Francisco,   Hive (Easton, Pa.)   Philosophical (New York, N.Y.)
Calif.)   Int'l. Univ. (New York, N.Y.)   Rubin (Brookline, Mass.)
Book Search (Brooklyn, N.Y.)   Lincoln (Foster, R.I.)   Ryan (Columbus, Ohio)
Dee Cee (Nyack, N.Y.)   Mason (Phoenix, Ariz.)   Sadoff (Jenkintown, Pa.)
Diamond (Burbank, Calif.)   Maxwell (Elmsford, N.Y.)   Smith (Montclair, N.J.)
Epistemologist (Bryn Mawr, Pa.)   Needle (Chelmsford, Mass.)   Town (Dutch Flat, Calif.)
Folkways (Bethesda, Md.)   New Engl. (Bennington, Vt.)   University (Hull, Mass.)
Hammer Mtn. (Schenectady, N.Y.)   Old #6 (Henniker, N.H.)   Village (Hudson Falls, N.Y.)

South America

See also
Latin America

Fein (New York, N.Y.)
Karno (Santa Monica, Calif.)
McBlain (Hamden, Conn.)

R. Ramer (New York, N.Y.)
Ross (Albany, Calif.)
Rulon-Miller (St. Thomas, V.I.)

Schiefer (Wilton, Conn.)

South Carolina

Attic (Hodges, S.C.)
Book Disp. #1 (Columbia, S.C.)
Book Disp. #2 (Columbia, S.C.)
Book Place (Columbia, S.C.)

Book Shoppe (Myrtle Bch., S.C.)
Book Trader (Fairmont, N.C.)
DuPriest (Columbia, S.C.)
Kearin (Goldens Bridge, N.Y.)

Patrick (Beaufort, S.C.)
Pipkin (Rock Hill, S.C.)
St. Andrews (Columbia, S.C.)

Southern Writers

Bond (Roanoke, Va.)
Book Mart (Asheville, N.C.)

Bridges (Sharpsburg, Ga.)
Gilliam (Charlottesville, Va.)

Hampton (Newberry, S.C.)

Spanish Books & Literature

Eshner (Bisbee, Ariz.)
Hamel (Los Angeles, Calif.)

Midwest (Evanston, Ill.)
R. Ramer (New York, N.Y.)

10 O'Clock (Elk Grove, Calif.)

Sporting

See also
Fishing, Hunting

Altau (Waynesboro, Va.)
Amer. Eagle (Topsfield, Mass.)
Anderson (Auburn, Mass.)
Baldwin's (W. Chester, Pa.)
Baseball (Tucson, Ariz.)
Buchanan (New York, N.Y.)

Bunkhouse (Gardiner, Maine)
Cummins (New York, N.Y.)
Felcone (Princeton, N.J.)
Halloran (St. Louis, Mo.)
Hampton (Newberry, S.C.)
Hendsey (Epping, N.H.)

Hennesseys (Saratoga Spgs., N.Y.)
Highwood (Traverse City, Mich.)
Howes (Brewster, Mass.)
Ken-L (Newberg, Ore.)
Kraft (Palm Desert, Calif.)
Lyrical (Saratoga Spgs., N.Y.)

Magazine (San Francisco, Calif.)
Old Southport (Southport, Conn.)
Pan (Catskill, N.Y.)
Pierce (Oroville, Calif.)
Pisces (Albion, Mich.)
Poste (Geneseo, N.Y.)
Respess (Durham, N.C.)

Respess (Chapel Hill, N.C.)
Sidney's (Missoula, Mont.)
Sporting (Rancocas, N.J.)
Sportsman's (Manotick, Ont.)
Sullivan (New York, N.Y.)
Sullivan (Chicago, Ill.)
Tamerlane (Havertown, Pa.)

Tayaut (No. Hatley, Que.)
Watkins (Dolgeville, N.Y.)
Wayner (Ft. Payne, Ala.)
Western (Gaston, Ore.)
Whitlock (Bethany, Conn.)

See also
Specific Sports

Sports

Abrams (State College, Pa.)
Antiquaria (Franklin, Tenn.)
Avocet (Sanford, N.C.)
Book Mart (Brockton, Mass.)
Brassers (Seminole, Fla.)
Carlson (Portland, Maine)
Circle West (Annapolis, Md.)

Golden Age (Dix Hills, N.Y.)
Hall's (Arlington, Mass.)
Hoffman (Rillton, Pa.)
Lloyd (Washington, D.C.)
McGovern (Berwyn, Ill.)
Old Ver. (Olympia Falls, Ill.)
Pell's (Delray Bch., Fla.)

Sandys (Albertson, N.Y.)
Sebastopol (Sebastopol, Calif.)
Sorrenti (Palatine, Ill.)
Taste (Fall River, Mass.)
Tatro (Wethersfield, Conn.)
Valley (Amherst, Mass.)

STC & Wing Books

Bookery (Ithaca, N.Y.)
Clare (Getzville, N.Y.)
Hale (Washington, D.C.)

Levinson (Beverly Hills, Calif.)
Ravenstree (Yuma, Ariz.)
Sanderson (Stockbridge, Mass.)

Stuart (Yuma, Ariz.)
Trebizond (New Preston, Conn.)
Ximenes (New York, N.Y.)

See also
Inland Waterways

Steamboats & River Travel

Autobooks (Babylon, N.Y.)
Cantrells' (No. East, Pa.)

Collins' (Pottstown, Pa.)
Keene (Southampton, N.Y.)

Samuel (New Orleans, La.)
Wooden (Middlebourne, W.Va.)

John Steinbeck

Beyer (Stratford, Conn.)
Book Nest (Los Altos, Calif.)

Dourgarian (Walnut Creek, Calif.)
Mullins (Encinitas, Calif.)

Old Mont. (Monterey, Calif.)

Stereoviews

See also Photography

Fullam (Babylon, N.Y.)
Old Book (New Haven, Conn.)

Photographers (New York, N.Y.)
Talisman (Georgetown, Calif.)

Stock Market & Wall Street

Abbot (Bronx, N.Y.)
Bargain (San Diego, Calif.)
Battersby (Ardmore, Pa.)
Bever (Edmond, Okla.)

Book Clearing (Larchmont, N.Y.)
Fraser (Burlington, Vt.)
Garrison (Williamsburg, Va.)
Guarino (De Bary, Fla.)

Guerrera (Lawrence, Mass.)
Mason (Phoenix, Ariz.)
Wall (Los Angeles, Calif.)
Windsor (Brightwaters, N.Y.)

Submarines

See also Military, Naval

Kitemaug (Spartanburg, S.C.)

Schmitt (Rockville, Md.)

Tom Swift

See also Children's, Juveniles, Series Books

Books Of (Corning, N.Y.)

Pendleton (Tiburon, Calif.)

Tarot

Together (Denver, Colo.)

U.S. Games (New York, N.Y.)

Technical

Academic (Portland, Ore.)

Albatross (San Francisco, Calif.)

Amer. Book (Fresno, Calif.)

Attic (London, Ont.)
Back No. (Greenbelt, Md.)
Book Barn (Gardner, Mass.)
Book Barn (Rochester, Mich.)
Book Bear (W. Brookfield, Mass.)
Book House (St. Louis, Mo.)

Book Nook (Escondido, Calif.)
Dartmouth (Hanover, N.H.)
E. K. (Rego Park, N.Y.)
Fish (Minneapolis, Minn.)
Gustafson (Chicago, Ill.)
Hoffman (Rillton, Pa.)

Kennedy (Des Moines, Wash.)
Nelson's (Troy, N.Y.)
No. Mtn. (Phoenix, Ariz.)
Old Tech (Carlisle, Mass.)
Rainy (Lexington, Mass.)
Univelt (San Diego, Calif.)

See also
Science, Scientific Instruments

Technology

Auslender (Wilton, Conn.)
Beare (Wilmington, Del.)
Book Cellar (Bethesda, Md.)
Bookcell (Hamden, Conn.)
Book Clearing (Larchmont, N.Y.)
Book Stall (Rockford, Ill.)
Books Unltd. (Nat'l City, Calif.)
Bookworm (Wytheville, Va.)
Boyson (Brookfield, Conn.)
Clement (Franklin, N.H.)
Darrah (Gettysburg, Pa.)
deBeurs (Dexter, Maine)
Dictionary (Leeds Point, N.J.)
Elgen (Rockville Centre, N.Y.)
Elwert (Rutland, Vt.)
Farley's (Pensacola, Fla.)
Finer (Greenfield, Mass.)
Geological (Falls Village, Conn.)

Glaser (Sausalito, Calif.)
Gorski (Doylestown, Pa.)
Hall (Chambersburg, Pa.)
Heller (Swarthmore, Pa.)
Hist. Tech (Marblehead, Mass.)
Hive (Easton, Pa.)
Hollander (Santa Monica, Calif.)
Jamaica (Jamaica, N.Y.)
Jay's (Marlboro, N.J.)
Key (Baltimore, Md.)
Knights (Harwich Port, Mass.)
Masi (Montague, Mass.)
McDuffie's (Portland, Ore.)
Mechanical (Darien, Conn.)
Michauds (Iowa City, Iowa)
Needle (Chelmsford, Mass.)
Nestler (Waldwick, N.J.)
Oasis (San Deigo, Calif.)

Offenbacher (Kew Gardens, N.Y.)
Palinurus (Philadelphia, Pa.)
B. Ramer (New York, N.Y.)
Ramshorn (Albuquerque, N.M.)
Reader's (Raleigh, N.C.)
Riverow (Owego, N.Y.)
Roby (San Diego, Calif.)
Saifer (W. Orange, N.J.)
Science (Ann Arbor, Mich.)
Scott (Stonington, Conn.)
Sebastopol (Sebastopol, Calif.)
Significant (Cincinnati, Ohio)
Smith (Montclair, N.J.)
Univelt (San Diego, Calif.)
Vintage (Iowa City, Iowa)
Whistles (Rossville, Ga.)
Wilson (Kitchener, Ont.)
Wood (Boston, Mass.)

Television & Radio

Booklord's (New York, N.Y.)
Dady (Minneapolis, Minn.)
Edmunds (Hollywood, Calif.)
Hampton (Newberry, S.C.)

Lawrence (New York, N.Y.)
Merriwell (Islip, N.Y.)
Morgan (Willowick, Ohio)
Mysteries (Yellow Spgs., Ohio)

Old Tech (Carlisle, Mass.)
Rogofsky (Glen Oaks, N.Y.)

Tennessee

Book Shelf (Cleveland, Tenn.)
Crabtree (Signal Mtn., Tenn.)
Fox (Madison, Tenn.)
Hill (Kingsport, Tenn.)

Texas

Almagre (Bloomington, Ind.)
Amer. SW (Amarillo, Texas)
Arthur (Amarillo, Texas)
Bandas (Temple, Texas)
Barber's (Ft. Worth, Texas)
Book Buyers (Houston, Texas)
Book Cellar (Temple, Texas)
Booketeria (San Antonio, Texas)
Bookshop (Del Rio, Texas)

Evergreen (Ft. Worth, Texas)
Fletcher's (Salado, Texas)
Gibbs (State College, Pa.)
Grossblatt (Dallas, Texas)
Hi (Canutillo, Texas)
Jenkins (Austin, Texas)
Jordan (Philadelphia, Pa.)
Lambeth (San Antonio, Texas)
Parker (Santa Fe, N.M.)

Sayers (Andrews, Texas)
Schroeder's (Dickinson, Texas)
Sloan (Austin, Texas)
Terrapin (Austin, Texas)
Trackside (Houston, Texas)
Trail (Tucson, Ariz.)
Traveller (Laredo, Texas)
Von Blon's (Waco, Texas)
Ye Olde (San Angelo, Texas)

Textiles

Books/Autographs (Eliot, Maine)
Brown (Belfast, Maine)
ChoreoGraphica (Boston, Mass.)
Cohen (Bronx, N.Y.)

East-West (Dresher, Pa.)
Finer (Greenfield, Mass.)
Hard-To (Newton, Mass.)
Lincoln (San Jose, Calif.)

Oceanic (New York, N.Y.)
Shep (Lopez Isl., Wash.)
Starosciak (San Francisco, Calif.)
Wooden (Middlebourne, W.Va.)

Theatre

Ackerman (Walpole, N.H.)
All Edges (Silver Spg., Md.)
Blue Dragon (Ashland, Ore.)
City Lights (San Francisco, Calif.)
Edmunds (Hollywood, Calif.)
Golden Legend (Los Angeles,

Calif.)
Gordon (Pasadena, Calif.)
Limelight (San Francisco, Calif.)
Lubrano (So. Lee, Mass.)
Lyman (East Otis, Mass.)
Mannatt (San Diego, Calif.)

Michlestreet (E. Lebanon, Maine)
Sorrenti (Palatine, Ill.)
Theater (Palo Alto, Calif.)
Theatrebooks (New York, N.Y.)
Theatricana (Athens, Ga.)
Xanadu (Bronx, N.Y.)

Henry David Thoreau

*See also
Transcendentalism*

Books With (Concord, Mass.)   Lucas (Blandford, Mass.)

Tibet

Book Manifest (Portland, Ore.)   Chessler (New York, N.Y.)
Chang Tang (Peekskill, N.Y.)   Gamradt (Minneapolis, Minn.)

Tobacco & Smoking

Abra (Rochester, N.Y.)   Dictionary (Leeds Point, N.J.)   Sullivan (New York, N.Y.)
Antiq. Tobacciana (Fairfax, Va.)   Earthworks (Washington, D.C.)
Burley/Books (Toledo, Ohio)   Edison Hall (Edison, N.J.)

Trade Cards

*See also
Ephemera*

Bookery (Fairborn, Ohio)   Old Music (3 Oaks, Mich.)   Yesteryear (Nampa, Idaho)
Fortunate Finds (Warwick, R.I.)   Roth (Norwalk, Ohio)
Mobley (Schoharie, N.Y.)   Terra (Churchville, N.Y.)

Trade Catalogues

*See also
Ephemera*

aGatherin' (Wynantskill, N.Y.)   Hillcrest (Spg. City, Tenn.)   Saifer (W. Orange, N.J.)
Barilaro (E. Weymouth, Mass.)   Jenison's (Canton, N.Y.)   Schmidt (Salem, Ore.)
Bookworm (Wytheville, Va.)   Kirch (Thornville, Ohio)   Sebastopol (Sebastopol, Calif.)
Broken Kettle (Akron, Iowa)   Maple St. (New Orleans, La.)   Whistles (Rossville, Ga.)
Carlton (Camino, Calif.)   McDuffie's (Portland, Ore.)   Wood (Boston, Mass.)
Collectors' (New York, N.Y.)   Nestler (Waldwick, N.J.)   Wreden (Palo Alto, Calif.)
Finer (Greenfield, Mass.)   Rogers (Athens, Ga.)
Fortunate Finds (Warwick, R.I.)   Roth (Norwalk, Ohio)

Trades

Argus (Sacramento, Calif.)
Beattie (Parkesburg, Pa.)

Bill (Long I. City, N.Y.)
McQuerry (Jacksonville, Fla.)

Transcendentalism

Barrow (Concord, Mass.)
Books With (Concord, Mass.)

Thoreau (Concord, Mass.)
Unicorn (Trappe, Md.)

Transportation

Arden (Noti, Ore.)
Autobooks (Babylon, N.Y.)
Book Harbor (Fullerton, Calif.)

Crawford's (Cincinnati, Ohio)
Old Tech (Carlisle, Mass.)
Pearson (Chicago, Ill.)

Roderick (Medina, Ohio)
Rolls (Rockville Centre, N.Y.)

Travel

Ancient (Santa Fe, N.M.)
Antiquaria (Franklin, Tenn.)
Beattie (Parkesburg, Pa.)
Berk (Studio City, Calif.)
Bill (New York, N.Y.)
Black Swan (Sacramento, Calif.)
Book Barn (So. Sioux City, Neb.)
Bullock (Fargo, N.D.)
Cole's (La Jolla, Calif.)

Dolphin (Camden, Maine)
Globe Crnr. (Boston, Mass.)
Hilton Village (Newport News, Va.)
Huxley (Loudonville, N.Y.)
Inner Circle (New York, N.Y.)
Junction (Peoria, Ill.)
Lloyd (Washington, D.C.)
Memory (Belfast, Maine)

Needle (Chelmsford, Mass.)
Persoff (Alameda, Calif.)
Phila. Print (Philadelphia, Pa.)
Quest (Ft. Worth, Texas)
Rolls (Rockville Centre, N.Y.)
Scholarly (Los Angeles, Calif.)
Shuhi (Morris, Conn.)
Touchet (New York, N.Y.)
Wooden (Ann Arbor, Mich.)

Travel Guides & Baedekers

Abbot (Bronx, N.Y.)
Copeland (Portland, Maine)
Feltus (Berkeley, Calif.)

Halbach (Santa Barbara, Calif.)
Mermaid (Oakland, Calif.)
O'Neill (Reston, Va.)

Rieger (Greenwood, S.C.)
Slattery (Palo Alto, Calif.)

Treasure Hunting

Americana (Coral Gables, Fla.)   Research (Fremont, Neb.)   San Fernando (San Fernando,
Essential (Centreville, Va.)   Calif.)

See also
Law, True Crime

Famous Trials

Chicago Law (Chicago, Ill.)   Pisces (Albion, Mich.)
Meyer (San Francisco, Calif.)   President's (Washington, D.C.)

See also
Transportation

Trolleys

Cliffside (Kansas City, Mo.)   Cramer (Kansas City, Mo.)
Cramer (Media, Pa.)   Moran (Rocky Point, N.Y.)

True Crime

Abra (Rochester, N.Y.)   Hill Haven (Barton, Vt.)   Thomolsen (Bayside, N.Y.)
Attic (London, Ont.)   Powell (Bar Harbor, Maine)   Trotting (Springfield, Mass.)
Cornucopia (Syosset, N.Y.)   President's (Washington, D.C.)   Waite (Madison, Wisc.)
Heath (Toronto, Ont.)   Spade (Seattle, Wash.)

Turn-Of-The-Century Novels

See also Nineteenth-Century Literature, Nostalgic Fiction

Bookseller (Denver, Colo.)   Good News (Rossville, Ind.)
Bridgton (Bridgton, Maine)   Littrup (Bay City, Mich.)

Mark Twain

Bankside (Westport, Conn.)   Bean (Biddeford, Maine)   Becky (Hannibal, Mo.)

Typography & Type Specimens

See also Printing & Printing History

Altman (New York, N.Y.)   Graf (Iowa City, Iowa)   Oak Knoll (New Castle, Del.)
Battery (Forest Hills, N.Y.)   Kane (Santa Cruz, Calif.)   O'Neal (Boston, Mass.)
Books In (Turlock, Calif.)   Klemm (Apple Valley, Calif.)   Printers' (Palo Alto, Calif.)
Broad Ripple (Indianapolis, Ind.)   Kress (Hewitt, N.J.)   Shapiro (New York, N.Y.)
Chiswick (Sandy Hook, Conn.)   Midnight (W. Lafayette, Ind.)   Under (Shaker Hgts., Ohio)
Glasser (Assonet, Mass.)   Miscellaneous (New Freedom, Pa.)

University Press Books

See also Scholarly Books

Academic (Portland, Ore.)   Bookery (Farmington, N.H.)
Bartleby's (Bethesda, Md.)   Wessex (Menlo Park, Calif.)

Utah

Cosmic (Salt Lake City, Utah)   Ute-Or (W. Jordan, Utah)
Deseret (Salt Lake City, Utah)   West (Provo, Utah)

Vegetarianism

Mt. Zion (Mt. Zion, W.Va.)   Vegetarian (Santa Monica, Calif.)

Vermont

Bear (W. Brattleboro, Vt.)
Bennington (Bennington, Vt.)
Bygone (Burlington, Vt.)
Carry Back (Haverhill, N.H.)

Country (Plainfield, Vt.)
Dunn (Newport, Vt.)
Haunted (Cuttingsville, Vt.)
Parkinson (Shelburne, Vt.)

Tempest (Waitsville, Vt.)
Vermont (Middlebury, Vt.)

Veterinary Medicine

Beattie (Parkesburg, Pa.)

Book Shop (Walnut Creek, Calif.)

Trotting (Morristown, N.J.)

Victoriana

Adams (W. Medway, Mass.)

Sherman (Burlington, Ont.)

Videocassettes & Compact Disks

Eeyore's #1 (New York, N.Y.)
Eeyore's #2 (New York, N.Y.)

Grolier (Cambridge, Mass.)
Organ (Braintree, Mass.)

Soundpeace (Ashland, Ore.)
Wonder (Frederick, Md.)

Vietnam War & Literature

Associates (Falls Church, Va.)
Brooks (Macon, Ga.)
Dalley (Christiansburg, Va.)

Glover (Cambridge, N.Y.)
Henry (Berwyn, Ill.)
Hunt (Burbank, Calif.)

Lewis (Seattle, Wash.)
Lopez (Hadley, Mass.)
Waiting (Cambridge, Mass.)

Violins

Bel Canto (Metuchen, N.J.)   Maestro (Bayport, N.Y.)   Shapiro (Washington, D.C.)

Virginia

Altau (Waynesboro, Va.)
Appleland (Winchester, Va.)
Hamilton's (Williamsburg, Va.)
Heartwood (Charlottesville, Va.)

Hilton Village (Newport News, Va.)
Hooper's (Leesburg, Va.)
Lurate (Jackson, Miss.)

Owens (Richmond, Va.)
Traveller (Laredo, Texas)
Virginia (Berryville, Va.)

Voyages, Travels, & Exploration

See also Maps & Atlases, Travel

Abbey (Los Angeles, Calif.)
Academic (No. Vancouver, B.C.)
Adelson (No. Pomfret, Vt.)
Amer. SW (Amarillo, Texas)
Arader/Sessler (Philadelphia, Pa.)
Argonaut (San Francisco, Calif.)
Arkway (New York, N.Y.)
Asian Rare (New York, N.Y.)
Attic (London, Ont.)
Autos (Eliz. City, N.C.)
Avocet (Sanford, N.C.)
Bagley (Fredericton, N.B.)
Bartfield (New York, N.Y.)
Bauman (Philadelphia, Pa.)
Bauman (Atlantic City, N.J.)
Bayview (Northport, N.Y.)
Belknap (Boston, Mass.)
Berk (Studio City, Calif.)
Berry (Kingston, Ont.)
Birmingham (Birmingham, Mich.)
Book Bin (Kingston, Ont.)
Booked Up (Washington, D.C.)
Book Guild (Portsmouth, N.H.)
Bookpress (Williamsburg, Va.)

Book Ranger (New York, N.Y.)
Bowes (Vancouver, B.C.)
Bowie (Seattle, Wash.)
Branford (Branford, Conn.)
Brauns (Sacramento, Calif.)
Bromsen (Boston, Mass.)
Brown (Belfast, Maine)
Burnett (Atlanta, Ga.)
Buteo (Vermillion, S.D.)
Caravan-Maritime (Jamaica, N.Y.)
Casavant (Wayland, Mass.)
CGT (College Stn., Texas)
Chessler (New York, N.Y.)
Cross Hill (Brunswick, Maine)
Cummins (Pottersville, N.J.)
Cummins (New York, N.Y.)
Diablo (Walnut Creek, Calif.)
Diamond (Rochester, N.Y.)
Dooling (Middlebury, Conn.)
Elgen (Rockville Centre, N.Y.)
Emerson (Falls Village, Conn.)
Fitch (Santa Fe, N.M.)
Frontier (Bryan, Texas)
Ginsberg (Sharon, Mass.)

Golder (Collinsville, Conn.)
Grabowski (Ronks, Pa.)
Hand (Wheeling, W.Va.)
Harder (Los Alamos, N.M.)
Harper (Bristol, Vt.)
Helikon (De Land, Fla.)
Heller (Cleveland, Ohio)
Heritage (Los Angeles, Calif.)
High Lat. (Bainbridge, Wash.)
Hill (New York, N.Y.)
Hist. Realia (Wooster, Ohio)
History (Ashley Falls, Mass.)
Hoffer (Vancouver, B.C.)
Hofmann (So. Orleans, Mass.)
Hollander (Santa Monica, Calif.)
Hollyoak (Wilmington, Del.)
Holsten (Excelsior, Minn.)
Holy Land (Washington, D.C.)
House (San Diego, Calif.)
Howard (Burlingame, Calif.)
Hoyt (Rockport, Mass.)
Hudson (Dyersburg, Tenn.)
Janus (Hungtinton Stn., N.Y.)
Johnson (No. Bennington, Vt.)

Johnson (Waltham, Mass.)
Kahn (Montreal, Que.)
Karmiole (Santa Monica, Calif.)
Keramos (Ann Arbor, Mich.)
Kern (Glendale, Ariz.)
Kostman (Glendora, Calif.)
Kostman (Glendora, Calif.)
Lake (Toronto, Ont.)
Lefkowicz (Fairhaven, Mass.)
Lien (Minneapolis, Minn.)
Lowe (Boston, Mass.)
Lucas (Blandford, Mass.)
Mattila (Seattle, Wash.)
McGahern (Ottawa, Ont.)
Morrill (Newton Centre, Mass.)
Moye (Seattle, Wash.)
Nautica (Halifax, N.S.)
Nebenzahl (Chicago, Ill.)
Norman (San Francisco, Calif.)
Observatory (Sitka, Alk.)
Ockett (Bryant Pond, Maine)
Old Harbor (Sitka, Alk.)
Old Rare (Jamestown, N.Y.)
O'Neill (Reston, Va.)
Ordnance (Madison, Conn.)
Otento (San Diego, Calif.)

Pacificana (Jamestown, N.C.)
Palmer (Eugene, Ore.)
Parmer (San Diego, Calif.)
Pettinger (Russell, Iowa)
Phila. Print (Philadelphia, Pa.)
Pollock (Palo Alto, Calif.)
Rainy (Lexington, Mass.)
R. Ramer (New York, N.Y.)
Rancho (Santa Monica, Calif.)
Randall (Santa Barbara, Calif.)
Reese (New Haven, Conn.)
Richardson (Westmont, N.J.)
Richshafer (Cincinnati, Ohio)
Rieger (Greenwood, S.C.)
Rittenhouse (Albuquerque, N.M.)
Robertson (Levittown, Pa.)
Robinson (Alexandria, Va.)
Robinson (Windsor, Conn.)
Robinson (Manchester, Maine)
Ross (Woodland Hills, Calif.)
Ross (Woodland Hills, Calif.)
Rulon-Miller (Minneapolis, Minn.)
Scharf (Pittsburgh, Pa.)
Scopazzi (San Francisco, Calif.)
Seville (Pensacola, Fla.)
Sherman (Burlington, Ont.)

Socolof (Bradenton, Fla.)
Stephenson (Jaffrey, N.H.)
Stern (Chicago, Ill.)
Stevens (Williamsburg, Va.)
Suarez (New York, N.Y.)
Tamerlane (Havertown, Pa.)
Terramedia (Wellesley, Mass.)
Thomas (San Francisco, Calif.)
Totty (Lunenburg, Mass.)
Trebizond (New Preston, Conn.)
Trophy (Agoura, Calif.)
Trotting (Springfield, Mass.)
Tusitala (Kailua, Haw.)
Tweney (Seattle, Wash.)
Viederman (Leonia, N.J.)
Wahrenbrock's (San Diego, Calif.)
Washington (Washington Cr., Pa.)
Weatherford (Monroe, Wash.)
West Side (Ann Arbor, Mich.)
Williams (Calgary, Alt.)
Wolfe (Pt. Claire, Que.)
Xerxes (Glen Head, N.Y.)
Yankee (Plymouth, Mass.)
Yerba (San Francisco, Calif.)
Zaremba (Cambridge, Mass.)
Zwisohn (Albuquerque, N.M.)

Wales & The Welsh

House (Anaheim, Calif.)   Munsell (Newburyport, Mass.)

Minor Wars & Battles

Daunce (Buffalo, N.Y.)   House (Worcester, Mass.)
Free Lance (Brooklyn, N.Y.)   Samuel (New Orleans, La.)

World Wars

Antheil (No. Bellmore, N.Y.)
Antiq. Michiana (Allen, Mich.)
Arch (Bellows Falls, Vt.)
Book Stop (Dearborn Hgts., Mich.)
Brown (No. Augusta, S.C.)
Culpin's (Denver, Colo.)
Grimshaw (Randolph, Mass.)

Hamilton's (Williamsburg, Va.)
Henry (Berwyn, Ill.)
History (Long Valley, N.J.)
Hunt (Burbank, Calif.)
Mallahan (Bellevue, Wash.)
Memory (Battle Creek, Mich.)
Military (New York, N.Y.)

Monarski (Syracuse, N.Y.)
Pearce (Elma, N.Y.)
Quechee (Quechee, Vt.)
Rutgers (Highland Park, N.J.)
Tracery (Dallas, Texas)
Wooden (Ann Arbor, Mich.)
World War (W. Roxbury, Mass.)

Westchester County (New York State)

Old Book (Croton, N.Y.)

Pages (Mt. Kisco, N.Y.)

Western Books

See also
Western Americana

Authors (Dundee, Ore.)
Avenue (Boston, Mass.)
Bever (Edmond, Okla.)
Books/Comics #2 (Indianapolis, Ind.)
Bookshop (Del Rio, Texas)
Books Of (Corning, N.Y.)
Brown (No. Augusta, S.C.)
Canford (Freeville, N.Y.)

Dinkytown (Minneapolis, Minn.)
Fischler (San Jose, Calif.)
Good News (Rossville, Ind.)
High Country (Laramie, Wyo.)
JMD (Groton, N.Y.)
Log Cabin (Bigfork, Mont.)
Minckler (Billings, Mont.)
Myers (Boulder, Colo.)
Owen (Litchfield, Maine)

Pierce (Oroville, Calif.)
Ralston (Fullerton, Calif.)
Ray's (Hartford, Vt.)
Rudolph (Portland, Ore.)
Sebert (Mt. Nebo, W.Va.)
Stan's (Brockton, Mass.)
Starry (Shippensburg, Pa.)
Wilhite (Clearwater, Fla.)
Zellner's (Easton, Pa.)

West Virginia

Bishop (Steubenville, Ohio)

Trans (Parkersburg, W.Va.)

Wolf's (Morgantown, W.Va.)

Whaling

See also
Nautical, Ships & Sea

Bayview (Northport, N.Y.)
B & B (Randolph, Mass.)
Berkelouw (Los Angeles, Calif.)
Bryant's (Provincetown, Mass.)
Burnett (Atlanta, Ga.)

Caravan-Maritime (Jamaica, N.Y.)
Cross Hill (Brunswick, Maine)
Howland (Jamaica Plain, Mass.)
Keene (Southampton, N.Y.)
Lefkowicz (Fairhaven, Mass.)

Lowe (Boston, Mass.)
Lucas (Blandford, Mass.)
Moore (Wynnewood, Pa.)
Nautica (Halifax, N.S.)

White Mountains

Bretton Hall (Lancaster, N.H.)
Bretton Hall (Bretton Woods,

N.H.)
Clement (Franklin, N.H.)

Sykes (No. Weare, N.H.)
Village (Littleton, N.H.)

Wildflowers

St. Andrews (Columbia, S.C.)

Sutley (Centralia, Wash.)

Wines

See also
Beverages

Bookwood (Westwood, N.J.)
G & C (Lafayette, La.)
Gore (San Gabriel, Calif.)

Hillman (New York, N.Y.)
Household (Berkeley, Calif.)
Thomas (Oak Park, Ill.)

Wine (Ann Arbor, Mich.)

Wireless Communication

Copeland (Portland, Maine)
Dady (Minneapolis, Minn.)

Littlewoods (Waukesha, Wisc.)
Old Tech (Carlisle, Mass.)

Wisconsin

Pages #1 (Green Bay, Wisc.)
Shenandoah (Appleton, Wisc.)

Winsted (Spg. Green, Wisc.)
Wise (Lake Delton, Wisc.)

P. G. Wodehouse

*See also
Humor*

Bayshore (Van Nuys, Calif.)

Magazine (New York, N.Y.)

Taylor (Westland, Mich.)

Thomas Wolfe

Cotswold (Medina, Ohio)

Croissant (Athens, Ohio)

Women

Americanist (Pottstown, Pa.)
Annie's #1 (Portland, Ore.)
Annie's #2 (Portland, Ore.)
Antiq. Scientist (Dracut, Mass.)
Asian Books (Cambridge, Mass.)
Austin (Kew Gardens, N.Y.)
Austin (Richmond Hill, N.Y.)
Blackmer (North Ferrisburg, Vt.)
Bolerium (San Francisco, Calif.)
Bookstore (Lenox, Mass.)
Burbank (Burbank, Calif.)
Burgman (Santa Rosa, Calif.)
Carmichael's (Louisville, Ky.)
Catbird (Portland, Ore.)
Common (New Salem, Mass.)
Cragsmoor (Cragsmoor, N.Y.)
Different (Des Moines, Iowa)

E. Wharton (Oakton, Va.)
Hall (San Francisco, Calif.)
Hidden (Kalamazoo, Mich.)
House (Toronto, Ont.)
Hummingbird (Albuquerque, N.M.)
Jane Addams (Champaign, Ill.)
Katz (Seattle, Wash.)
Kern (Glendale, Ariz.)
Metacomet (Providence, R.I.)
Miranda (Brookline, Mass.)
Oblong (Millerton, N.Y.)
Old Rare (Jamestown, N.Y.)
Phoenix (Royal Oak, Mich.)
Pride (Ballston Lake, N.Y.)
Prufrock (Pasadena, Calif.)
Reading (Mexico, Ind.)

Rose (New York, N.Y.)
2nd Life (Lanesborough, Mass.)
Sisterhood (Los Angeles, Calif.)
Sloan (Austin, Texas)
Southpaw (Roxbury, Mass.)
Swiss (St. Louis, Mo.)
Tholin (Evanston, Ill.)
Town (Dutch Flat, Calif.)
Untamed (Waterloo, Wisc.)
Village (Bellingham, Wash.)
Vol. I (Hillsdale, Mich.)
Walzer (Providence, R.I.)
Webster's (Milwaukee, Wisc.)
Womanbooks (New York, N.Y.)
Women's (Contoocook, N.H.)
Words (Cambridge, Mass.)

Woodcut Books

See also
Early Printed Books

Besnia (Sterling Jctn., Mass.)
Books In (Turlock, Calif.)
Buck (San Francisco, Calif.)

Clare (Getzville, N.Y.)
Rare Oriental (Aptos, Calif.)
Scarlet (New Milford, Conn.)

Schab (New York, N.Y.)
Signed (Pt. Washington, N.Y.)
Waite (Madison, Wisc.)

WPA & Federal Writers Project

Book Store (Englewood, N.J.)

Chicago (Evanston, Ill.)

Delle Donne (Ronkonkoma, N.Y.)

World's Fairs

Antiq. Michiana (Allen, Mich.)
Black Swan (Sacramento, Calif.)

Hobby Helpers (Lima, N.Y.)
Laws (Chicago, Ill.)

N.Y. Bound (New York, N.Y.)
Swiss (St. Louis, Mo.)

Howard Bell Wright

ABC Theo. (Springfield, Mo.)

Dabbs (Higginsville, Mo.)

Writing Instruction

Pride (Ballston Lake, N.Y.)

Scribbling (No. Ft. Myers, Fla.)

Wyoming

Backpocket (Sundance, Wyo.)

High Country (Laramie, Wyo.)

Summerhouse (Dayton, Wyo.)

Zeppelins & Dirigibles

Air Age (Tollhouse, Calif.)
Aviation (Glendale, Calif.)

Cramer (Kansas City, Mo.)
Crofter's (Washington, Conn.)

Doerres (Wilton, Iowa)
Mil-Air (Compton, Calif.)

Zoology

See also
Natural History, Science

Buteo (Vermillion, S.D.)
Engard (Tucson, Ariz.)

Fagin (Chicago, Ill.)
Nadolny (Kensington, Conn.)

Oklahoma (Yukon, Okla.)
Zaremba (Cambridge, Mass.)

A

Barbara Aaron—Bryn Mawr (Pittsburgh, Pa.)
Nancy Abe—Tusitala (Kailua, Haw.)
Gerry Aboud—Aboud (Stayton, Ore.)
Harvey Abrams—Abrams (State College, Pa.)
Harvey Dan Abrams—Abrams (Atlanta, Ga.)
Doris E. Abramson—Common Reader (New Salem, Mass.)
G. P. Ackerman—Ackerman (Walpole, N. H.)
Eldora Acott—Eldora's (Newberg, Ore.)
Doris Adams—Goodspeed's #1 (Boston, Mass.)
Marjorie P. Adams—Adams (W. Medway, Mass.)
Robert Adams—Adams (Chicago, Ill.)
Ruth Adams—Buccaneer (Laguna Bch., Calif.)
K. Tilden Adamson—Adamson (Augusta, Ga.)
John K. Addison—Academy (San Francisco, Calif.)
Jane K. Adelson—Adelson (No. Pomfret, Vt.)
Richard H. Adelson—Adelson (No. Pomfret, Vt.)
H. S. Adler—Adobe (Albuquerque, N.M.)
Allan Adrian—Sun Dance (Hollywood, Calif.)
Marilyn Affeldt—Amer. Book (Fresno, Calif.)
Barbara Agranoff—Agranoff (Cincinnati, Ohio)
Joseph Agranoff—Agranoff (Cincinnati, Ohio)
Allen Ahearn—Quill (Rockville, Md.)
Patricia Ahearn—Quill (Rockville, Md.)
Barbara Aikey—Lincoln Hill (Delmar, N.Y.)
Michael Aikey—Lincoln Hill (Delmar, N.Y.)
Jeffrey Akard—A B I (Santa Barbara, Calif.)
Sal Alberti—Lowe (New York, N.Y.)
Jon Aldrich—Aldrich (Groveland, Calif.)
Rita Alexander—Book Store (Englewood, N.J.)
Terry Alford—Alford (Springfield, Va.)
Matthew G. Alfs—Old Theo. (Minneapolis, Minn.)
Emery Allain—Allain (Greenwich, Conn,)
David Allen—Allen (Baltimore, Md.)
D. C. Allen—Old Music (3 Oaks, Mich.)
Edith Allen—Old Music (3 Oaks, Mich.)
Elizabeth Allen—Sleepy (Moraga, Calif.)
Ellie Allen—Allen (Baltimore, Md.)
George Allen—Allen (Philadelphia, Pa.)
Laurie Allen—Book Stop (Tucson, Ariz.)
Priscilla B. Allen—Allen (Altadena, Calif.)
Richard G. Allen—Sleepy (Moraga, Calif.)
Robert Allen—Allen (Altadena, Calif.)
Robert D. Allenson—Allenson (Geneva, Ala.)
G. S. Allison—Allison (No. Bay, Ont.)

Norma Almquist—Scholarly (Los Angeles, Calif.)
Jerry Alper—Alper (Eastchester, N.Y.)
Linda Alsberg—Hist. News (Skokie, Ill.)
Steve Alsberg—Hist. News and Alsberg (both Skokie, Ill.)
Karl Altau—Altau (Waynesboro, Va.)
Si Altman—Vi & Si's (Clarence, N.Y.)
Vi Altman—Vi & Si's (Clarence, N.Y.)
William Altman—Altman (New York, N.Y.)
F. Hampton Alvey—Book Place (Columbia, S.C.)
M. B. Alwan—Worldwide (Cambridge, Mass.)
Sheila B. Amdur—Amdur (Mansfield, Conn.)
Bernard G. Ames—Womrath's (Hempstead, N.Y.)
Lawrence Amitin—Amitin (St. Louis, Mo.)
Betty R. Anderson—Bird's Nest (Missoula, Mont.)
Craig Anderson—Strand Rare (New York, N.Y.)
Diane Anderson—All Edges (Silver Spg., Md.)
Ed Anderson—Cache (Loveland, Colo.)
Frank J. Anderson—Kitemaug (Spartanburg, S.C.)
Kenneth Anderson—Anderson (Auburn, Mass.)
Martha Anderson—Cache (Loveland, Colo.)
Robert R. Anderson—Truepenny (Tucson, Ariz.)
Ronald D. Anderson—Anderson's (Whittier, Calif.)
Steve Anderson—Booksellers (St. Paul, Minn.)
Sylvia Anderson—Book End (Monterey, Calif.)
Warren Anderson—Distinctive (Cedar City, Utah)
Eimi Andrews—Andrews (Niles, Minn.)
J. C. Andrews—La Tienda (Conway, N.H.)
Nicholas Angelo—Stage (Boulder, Colo.)
Charles Annegan—Annegan (San Marcos, Calif.)
Hugh Anson-Cartwright—Anson-Cartwright (Toronto, Ont.)
Charles Anton—Becky (Hannibal, Mo.)
Cecil Antone—Rodden's (Long Bch., Calif.)
Charles Apfelbaum—Apfelbaum (Valley Stream, N.Y.)
Louis Appelfeld—Appelfeld (New York, N.Y.)
Paul P. Appel—Appel (Mt. Vernon, N.Y.)
W. Graham Arader III—Arader (King of Prussia, Pa.)
Scott Arden—Arden (Noti, Ore.)
Richard B. Arkway—Arkway (New York, N.Y.)
Karl Armens—Armens (Iowa City, Iowa)
Glenn Armitage—Armitage (Miamisburg, Ohio)
Claire Arnold—Arnolds (Contoocook, N.H.)

Glenn Armitage—Armitage (Miamisburg, Ohio)
Claire Arnold—Arnolds (Contoocook, N.H.)
Don Arnold—Arnolds (Contoocook, N.H.)
Eva Arond—Arond (Lexington, Mass.)
Frederick Arone—Arone (Dobbs Ferry, N.Y.)
David Aronovitz—Fine (Rochester, Mich.)
Carole Aronson-Plummer—Cape (Mashpec, Mass.)
Norman Arrington—Egg Harbor (Egg
    Harbor, N. J.)
Carmen Arroyo—Seppa (Virginia, Minn.)
Mrs. R. H. Arthur—Arthur (Amarillo, Texas)
K. George Arthurton—Arthurton (Palmyra, N.Y.)
Sylvia Asendorf—Asendorf (Los Altos Hills, Calif.)
Lee Ash—Antiquarium (Bethany, Conn.)
Mrs. A. L. Ashton—Ashton (Ottawa, Ont.)
Grover J. Askins—Askins (New Lebanon, N.Y.)
William Askins—Quixote (Philadelphia, Pa.)

Richard Astle—Garret (Clinton, N.Y.)
Bart Auerbach—Auerbach (New York, N.Y.)
Robert Augustine—Arkway (New York, N.Y.)
Dorthea Augusztiny—Boardwalk (Friday Harbor,
    Wash.)
Stephen Auslender—Auslender (Wilton, Conn.)
Gabriel Austin—Wittenborn (New York, N.Y.)
Gary Austin—Snug Harbor (Wells, Maine)
Karen Austin—Snug Harbor (Wells, Maine)
Kristi Austin—Magus (Seattle, Wash.)
Robert C. Auten—Auten (Bedminster, N.J.)
George F. Avery—Avery (Plymouth, Mass.)
Winifred Avery—Avery (Plymouth, Mass.)
Carol Avol—Avol's (Madison, Wisc.)
Richard Avol—Avol's (Madison, Wisc.)
Bernard Axelrod—12th St. (Santa Monica, Calif.)

B

Bert Babcock—Babcock (Derry, N.H.)
Vaughn Baber—Bicentennial (Kalamazoo, Mich.)
Fernand Baer Jr.—Baer (New York, N.Y.)
David Bagelman—Reedmor (Philadelphia, Pa.)
Harry E. Bagley—Bagley (Fredericton, N.B.)
Al Bai—Curious Raven (Detroit, Mich.)
Brian Bailey—Bailey (New York, N.Y.)
Carrie Bailey—Books/Park (Boulder, Colo.)
Deane Bailey—Vol. I (Greenville, S.C.)
George Bailey—Books/Park (Boulder, Colo.)
Mike Bailey—Vol. I (Greenville, S.C.)
Bob Baird—Book Bin (Corvallis, Ore.)
Newton Baird—Talisman (Georgetown, Calif.)
Gail Baker—Hummingbird (Albuquerque, N.M.)
Henry Karl Baker—Organ (Braintree, Mass.)
Judith A. Baker—Toad (Berkeley, Calif.)
Ken Baker—Yesterday's (San Diego, Calif.)
Kinsey Baker—Book Haven (Lancaster, Pa.)
Bob Baldock—Black Oak (Berkeley, Calif.)
Sarah Baldwin—E. Wharton (Oakton, Va.)
Thomas M. Baldwin—Baldwin's (W. Chester, Pa.)
George Ball—Leelanau (Leland, Mich.)
Nelson Ball—Ball (Paris, Ont.)
Alyce Ballard—Book Disp. #2 (Columbia, S.C.)
Emily Ballinger—Bookpress (Williamsburg, Va.)

John Ballinger—Bookpress (Williamsburg, Va.)
Leon H. Ballon—Dolphin (Camden, Maine)
Mortimer S. Balthasar—Balthasar's (Maryknoll,
    N.Y.)
Alan S. Bamberger—Bamberger (San Francisco,
    Calif.)
Eleanor Bancroft—Bancroft (Newtown, Conn.)
Rick Bandas—Bandas (Temple, Texas)
Jack Banning—Poster (New York, N.Y.)
Phillip J. Barber—Barber (Boston, Mass.)
John Barbier—Barbier (Seaside, Calif.)
James L. Barbour—Old Quenzel (Pt. Tobacco, Md.)
Arbe Bareis—B.J.S. (Forest Hills, N.Y.)
Jim Barilaro—Barilaro (E. Weymouth, Mass.)
Conway Barker—Barker (Dallas, Texas)
Carol Barnes—Gunnerman (Auburn Hgts., Mich.)
Catherine Barnes—Barnes (Philadelphia, Pa.)
Larry Barnes—Gunnerman (Auburn Hgts., Mich.)
Pat Barnes—Barnes (Evanston, Ill.)
Richard Barnes—Barnes (Evanston, Ill.)
Russell Barnes—Boise (Boise, Idaho)
Steve Barnett—Cosmic Aero. (Salt Lake City, Utah)
Rita Barns—Hyde Park (Boise, Idaho)
Russell Barns—Hyde Park (Boise, Idaho)
Frederick Baron—High Ridge (Rye, N.Y.)

Howard Baron—High Ridge (Rye, N.Y.)
Stephen J. Baron—Abraham's (New York, N.Y.)
Joyce Barrow—Broadfoot's (Wendell, N.C.)
Ron Barr—Armchair (Newport, R.I.)
Robert Barry—Stonehill (New Haven, Conn.)
Fred Bass—Strand (New York, N.Y.)
Tom Bass—Seminary (Alexandria, Va.)
Paul Bassinor—University (Hull, Mass.)
Robert Batchelder—Batchelder (Ambler, Pa.)
C. L. Batson—Essential (Centreville, Va.)
Bela Batta—Batta (Toronto, Ont.)
Mark E. Battersby—Battersby (Ardmore, Pa.)
Alfred Bauer—Alcala (San Diego, Calif.)
Paul Bauer—Archer's (Kent, Ohio)
Wallace Bauer—Books/Advice (Denver, Colo.)
Cheryl Baughman—Antiq. Book (Toledo, Ohio)
Pete Baughman—Antiq. Book (Toledo, Ohio)
David L. Bauman—Bauman (Atlantic City, N.J. and
    Philadelphia, Pa.)
Natalie Bauman—Bauman (Atlantic City, N.J. and
    Philadelphia, Pa.)
Wilbur Bauman—Provident (Bloomington, Ill.)
James A. Baumhofer—Baumhofer (St. Paul, Minn.)
Judi Baxter—Judi's (Twin Falls, Idaho)
Fam Bayless—Island (Mercer, Wash.)
Adene Beal—House (Tallahassee, Fla.)
Marshall E. Bean—Bean (Biddeford, Maine)
Samuel Bean—Bean (Niantic, Conn.)
Doug Bearce—Bearce (Salem, Ore.)
Shirley Beard—Murder (Denver, Colo.)
Rosemarie Beardsley—People's (Flemington, N.J.)
Rosemarie Beardsley—Beardsley (Somerville,
    N. J.)
Karen Beare—Beare (Wilmington, Del.)
Steven Beare—Beare (Wilmington, Del.)
James W. Beattie—Beattie (Parkesburg, Pa.)
Terry Beattie—Beattie (Parkesburg, Pa.)
C. Richard Becker—Becker (New York, N.Y.)
Harry W. Becker—Leishman (Menlo Park, Calif.)
J. Richard Becker—Becker (Acton Centre, Mass.)
R. S. Becker—Bay Side (Soquel, Calif.)
Carey Beckham—Librairie (Royal) (New Orleans,
    La.)
Carey Beckham—Old Books (New Orleans, La.)
Carey Beckham—Librairie (Chartres) (New Orleans,
    La.)
Gordon Beckhorn—Beckhorn (Dobbs Ferry, N.Y.)
Gene Beckman—Colorado (Norwood, Colo.)
Marriet Bedard—Tyson (Providence, R.I.)

Harriette M Beeson—Burke's (Memphis, Tenn.)
Margaret H. Behrens—Peggatty (Clarkston, Wash.)
David Belknap—Belknap (Boston, Mass.)
Bill Bell—Thunderbird (Aldergrove, B.C.)
David L. Bell—Magus (Seattle, Wash.)
Hugh F. Bell—Magnalia (No. Amherst, Mass.)
Irving Bell—Abatis (Springfield, Vt.)
Mary Bell—Thunderbird (Aldergrove, B.C.)
Curt Bench—Deseret (Salt Lake City, Utah)
Lori Bender—Book Treasury (Nashville, Tenn.)
Morris Bender—999 (New York, N.Y.)
Doug Benecke—Moving (Seattle, Wash.)
Rosalind C. Benedict—Trebizond (New Preston,
    Conn.)
Williston R Benedict—Trebizond (New Preston,
    Conn.)
Carlos E. Benemann—Ferndale (Ferndale, Calif.)
Marilyn F. Benemann—Ferndale (Ferndale, Calif.)
Mary A. Benjamin—Benjamin (Hunter, N.Y.)
John Benjamins—Benjamins (Philadelphia, Pa.)
Edna Bennett—Bennett (Southold, N.Y.)
James M. Bennett—Lambda (Washington, D.C.)
Marilyn Bennett—House (Anaheim, Calif.)
Michael E. Bennett—Bennett (White Plains, N.Y.)
Virginia B. Bennett—Bryn Mawr (Albany, N. Y.)
W. O. Bennett—House (Anaheim, Calif.)
J. A. Benoit—Benoit (Montreal, Que.)
Bonnie Benrubi—Wolf (New York, N.Y.)
Deborah Benson—Benson (W. Cornwall, Conn.)
Ken Benson—Benson (Ottawa, Ont.)
Lou Bentley—Assoc. Stu. (Chico, Calif.)
Frank Bequaert—Rainy (Lexington, Mass.)
Lucia Bequaert—Rainy (Lexington, Mass.)
Dick Berger—Lutes (Okla. City, Okla.)
Howard O. Berg—Berg (Devils Lake, N.D.)
S. F. Bergstein—Trotting (Morristown, N.J.)
Henry Berkelouw—Berkelouw (Los Angeles, Calif.)
Isidor Berkelouw—Berkelouw (Los Angeles, Calif.)
Fred A. Berk—Berk (Studio City, Calif.)
Carl S. Berkowitz—Berkowitz (Chester, N.Y.)
Paul Berlanga—Bookseller's (Chicago, Ill.)
Lillian Berliawsky—Berliawsky (Camden, Maine)
David Berman—Berman (Los Angeles, Calif.)
David Berman—Abbey (Los Angeles, Calif.)
Gideon Berman—Abbey (Los Angeles, Calif.)
Richard Berman—City Lights (San Francisco, Calif.)
Ruth Berman—Berman (Atlanta, Ga.)
Theodore Berman—Book Collector (Newton, Mass.)
Steven C. Bernard—Bernard (Rockville, Md.)

Peter Bernett—Bernett (Larchmont, N.Y.)
Barry Bernstein—B & B (Randolph, Mass.)
Leonard Bernstein—Caravan (Los Angeles, Calif.)
Lillian E. Bernstein—Caravan (Los Angeles, Calif.)
J. Berry—Kirksco (Ringwood, N.J.)
John Berry—Berry (Kingston, Ont.)
John C. Berry—Book Bin (Kingston, Ont.)
Roger Bertoia—Bishop (Steubenville, Ohio)
A. Berube—A C (Brooklyn, N.Y.)
Howard John Besnia—Besnia (Sterling Jctn., Mass.)
Jim Best—Bookman (Kent, Ohio)
John Best—Best (Cambridge, Mass.)
Linda Best—Bookman (Kent, Ohio)
Jill Bettendorf—St. Andrews (Columbia, S.C.)
Tom Bettendorf—St. Andrews (Columbia, S.C.)
Ron Bever—Bever (Edmond, Okla.)
Elizabeth H. Bevington—Bevington (Terre Haute, Ind.)
Helen Beyer—Beyer (Stratford, Conn.)
Preston C. Beyer—Beyer (Stratford, Conn.)
George Bibby—Bibby (Gold Hill, Ore.)
Judy Bieber—Bieber (Kenilworth, N.J.)
Judy A. Bieber—Oz (Kenilworth, N.J.)
Moses Biegeleisen—Biegeleisen (Brooklyn, N.Y.)
Sol Biegeleisen—Biegeleisen (Brooklyn, N.Y.)
William Biermaier—Biermaier's (Minneapolis, Minn.)
Robert Bijou—Adams (Chicago, Ill.)
Michael Bills—Harvard (Boston, Mass.)
Irving Binkin—Binkin's (Brooklyn, N.Y.)
Sarah Bird—Griffon (So. Bend, Ind.)
Charles Bishop, Jr.—Bishop (Steubenville, Ohio)
Donna Bishop—Bishop (Corea, Maine)
George Bixby—Ampersand (New York, N.Y.)
Susan Bjorkman—Baggage (Wayne, N.J.)
Thomas A. Bjorkman—Baggage (Wayne, N.J.)
Richard Blacher—Blacher (Branford, Conn.)
Pam Blackburn—Links (3 Rivers, Mich.)
Virginia L. Blackburn—Hyman (Los Angeles, Calif.)
Joan Black—Book Search (Petersburg, Va.)
Reading Black—Book Search (Petersburg, Va.)
Anne Blackmer—Blackmer (North Ferrisburg, Vt.)
Joyce Blair—Abelard (Toronto, Ont.)
Robert Blair—Vermont (Middlebury, Vt.)
Warren Blake—Blake (Fairfield, Conn.)
Janet Blakeley—Paper (So. Euclid, Ohio)
Jim Blakely—Old Print (Washington, D.C.)
Judy Blakely—Old Print (Washington, D.C.)

D. H. Blanchard—Antiq. Book (Winter Park, Fla.)
John Blauer—San Marco (Jacksonville, Fla.)
Mike Blauer—San Marco (Jacksonville, Fla.)
Jerry Blaz—Bookie Joint (Reseda, Calif.)
Rose S. Blaz—Bookie Joint (Reseda, Calif.)
Robin Bledsoe—Blue Rider (Cambridge, Mass.)
Mark Blinderman—Bonmark (Plainview, N.Y.)
Rita Blinderman—Bonmark (Plainview, N.Y.)
David M. Block—Book Block (Cos Cob, Conn.)
Grace Block—Block (Thornwood, N.Y.)
Shiu-min Block—Book Block (Cos Cob, Conn.)
Dick Blomberg—Blomberg (Rockford, Ill.)
Carl Blomgren—Blomgren (San Rafael, Calif.)
Betty Blommers—Owl (Bryn Mawr, Pa.)
Myrna Bloom—East-West (Dresher, Pa.)
Peter J. Blum—Soldier (New York, N.Y.)
Crager J. Boardman, Sr.—Boardman (Camden, N.Y.)
Norman F. Boas—Seaport (Stonington, Conn.)
Ray Boas—Boas (Haddonfield, N.J.)
Barbara J. Bogdon—River Oaks (Jay, Maine)
Nicholas J. Bogdon—River Oaks (Jay, Maine)
Chris Bogosian—Maelstrom (San Francisco, Calif.)
Curt Bohling—Bohling (Decatur, Mich.)
Lynette L. Bohling—Bohling (Decatur, Mich.)
John Boisonault—Key (Key West, Fla.)
Keith Bollum—Helikon (De Land, Fla.)
J. Warren Bolotin—Bolotin (Youngstown, Ohio)
Sheila Bolton—Sommer (Niagara Falls, N.Y.)
Harold Bond—Bond (Reading, Mass.)
Nelson Bond—Bond (Roanoke, Va.)
Steve Bond—Plant (Grass Valley, Calif.)
Theresa Bond—Bond (Reading, Mass.)
Betsy Bonin—Book Cellar (Brattleboro, Vt.)
John Boomstra—Book Exch. (Plainville, Conn.)
Bob Borcherdt—Gallery/West (Bigfork, Mont.)
Michael Borden—Borden (Portsmouth, R. I.)
Elizabeth M. Borr—Everyday (Burlington, Vt.)
Joan D. Bossi—Janus (Corea, Maine and Huntington Stn., N.Y.)
Tom Boss—Boss (Brookline, Mass.)
Marla Bottesch—Snowbound (Norridgeweck, Maine)
Gene Bourne—Photographers (New York, N.Y.)
Phyllis Bowersock—Book Place (Richland, Wash.)
Ed Bowes—Bowes (Vancouver, B.C.)
M. Taylor Bowie—Bowie (Seattle, Wash.)
Lance Bowling—Bowling (Rancho Palos Verdes, Calif.)

C

Richard Cady—Cady (Chicago, Ill.)
Andrew Cahan—Cahan (Narberth, Pa.)
Charles Calderone—Northeast (Ocean City, N. J.)
Bill Caldwell—Caldwell (Arkadelphia, Ark.)
Bob Caldwell—Book Shoppe (Myrtle Beach, S.C.)
Henry B. Caldwell—Museum (Fairfield, Conn.)
Douglas Calhoun—Calhouns' (Geneva, N.Y.)
Marlene Calhoun—Calhouns' (Geneva, N.Y.)
Bruce Calkins—Brused (Pullman, Wash.)
Diane Callahan—Callahan (Peterborough, N.H.)
Geraldine Callahan—Iliad (Livingston, Mont.)
Kenneth Callahan—Callahan (Peterborough, N.H.)
Pat Callahan—Boise (Boise, Idaho)
Bruce Calman—Calman (Syracuse, N. Y.)
Fred Campbell—Lowe (Boston, Mass.)
Lee G. Campbell—Joe the Pro (Santa Barbara, Calif.)
Michael Cancellari—Canford (Freeville, N.Y.)
Connie Canney—Canney (Alfred, Maine)
Robert Canney—Canney (Alfred, Maine)
John T. Cannon—Aladdin (Fullerton, Calif.)
Glenn W. Cantrell—Cantrells' (No. East, Pa.)
Kathleen Cantrell—Erie (Erie, Pa.)
Sabra Cantrell—Cantrells' (No. East, Pa.)
Richard R. Caprio—Caprio (Revere, Mass.)
David L. Caraway—La Valois (New York, N.Y.)
Art Carduner—Carduner (Philadelphia, Pa.)
Eric C. Caren—Caren (Nanuet, N. Y.)
James Carey—Books/Wonder (New York, N.Y.)
Barb Carley—Nebraska (Lincoln, Neb.)
Bernard C. Carlitz—Carlitz (Philadelphia, Pa.)
Bob Carlitz—Carlitz (Philadelphia, Pa.)
Norma Carlson—Carlson (Portland, Maine)
John Carlton—Carlton (Camino, Calif.)
Natalie Carlton—Singer (Buena Park, Calif.)
Mike Carnell—C. Dickens (Atlanta, Ga.)
John J. Carney, Jr.—Carney (Oneonta, N.Y.)
Margaret Carney—Carney (Oneonta, N.Y.)
Walter Caron—Mendoza (New York, N.Y.)
David Carpenter—Dee Cee (Nyack, N.Y.)
Glen Carpenter—Carpenter (Barlow, Ohio)
James F. Carr—Carr (New York, N.Y.)
Mary Carr—Book Trader (Muskegon, Mich.)
Robert Carr—Book Trader (Muskegon, Mich.)

Roberta Carr—Carr (Concord, N.H.)
Pat Carrier—Globe Crnr. (Boston, Mass.)
George Carroll—Pacific (No. Vancouver, B.C.)
William Carroll—Carroll (San Marcos, Calif.)
Angela Carter—Keshcarrigan (New York, N.Y.)
John Carter—Shaw's (Bath, Maine)
Franklin Carto—Bookseller (Denver, Colo.)
Sally S. Carver—Carver (Chestnut Hill, Mass.)
Roger F. Casavant—Casavant (Wayland, Mass.)
Doris S. Casperson—Casperson (Niles, Mich.)
Ralph A. Casperson—Casperson (Niles, Mich.)
Barry Cassidy—Cassidy (Sacramento, Calif.)
Brian J. Cassidy—Cramer (Kansas City, Mo.)
Philip T. Cassidy—Cramer (Kansas City, Mo.)
Terence W. Cassidy—Cliffside (Kansas City, Mo.)
Terence W. Cassidy—Cassidy (Kansas City, Mo.)
Terence W. Cassidy—Cramer (Kansas City, Mo.)
Terence W. Cassidy—Cramer (Media, Pa.)
Brian E. Cassie—Cassie (Millis, Mass.)
JoAnn Casten—Casten (New York, N.Y.)
Richard Casten—Casten (New York, N.Y.)
Stephen Casterlin—Hermit's (Wyoming, Pa.)
Connie Castle—Treasures (Rochester, Mich.)
Patricia Castle-Doucet—Allison (No. Bay, Ont.)
Christine Caughren—Household (Berkeley, Calif.)
Harry J. Caughren—Household (Berkeley, Calif.)
Joseph Cavallo—Cavallo (Altadena, Calif.)
Sherry Cavallo—Cavallo (Altadena, Calif.)
Carol Cavat—Zita (New York, N.Y.)
D. D. Cayce, III—Pennyroyal (Hopkinsville, Ky.)
Charles N. Cecere—Educo (Valhalla, N.Y.)
Toby Cedar—Bookstop (Alexandria, Va.)
H. Celnick—Celnick (Bronx, N.Y.)
Barry Cenower—Acanthus (New York, N.Y.)
B. Chaim—Book Search (Brooklyn, N.Y.)
Richard Chalfin—Chalfin (New York, N.Y.)
Robert Chalfin—City Wide (Brooklyn, N.Y.)
Pat Chalmers—Pat's (Salina, Kan.)
Dean Chamberlin—Book Cellar (Freeport, Maine)
Mildred C. Chamberlin—Chamberlin (E. Orleans, Mass.)
Tom Chambers—50,000 (El Cajon, Calif.)
Michael Chandley—Cellar (Providence, R.I.)
Bev Chaney, Jr.—Chaney (Ossining, N.Y.)

Stephanie Chapin—Chapin (Reading, Pa.)
David Chapman—Chapman (Los Angeles, Calif.)
James Chapman—Holmes (Oakland, Calif.)
Joel Chapman—Acorn (San Francisco, Calif.)
"JW" Chapman—Plant (Grass Valley, Calif.)
M. L. Chapman—Book House (Williamsburg, Va.)
Odie Chapman—Old Book (Fairlee, Vt.)
Bethel Charkoudian—Charkoudian (Newton, Mass.)
Tim Chase—Bookshelf (Ogden, Utah)
Ann Cheek—Bolingbroke (Pinnacle, N.C.)
Lee Cheek—Bolingbroke (Pinnacle, N.C.)
John D. Cheesborough—Avocet (Sanford, N.C.)
Pamela S. Chenery—Fugitive (Nashville, Tenn.)
Jill Cheng—Cheng (Boston, Mass.)
Fran Chennells—Bibliomania (Delaware, Ohio)
Estelle Chessid—Book Chest (New York, N.Y.)
Michael Chessler—Chessler (New York, N.Y.)
Gary Chicoine—Book Finder (Geneva, N.Y.)
Johnny Ching—Sharp's (No. Hollywood, Calif.)
David Chmielnicki—Midwest (Evanston, Ill.)
D. Choffel—Dickson St. (Fayetteville, Ark.)
Jane Choras—Choras (Weston, Mass.)
D. M. Christisen—DC Service (Columbia, Mo.)
Jens J. Christoffersen—Harbor Hill (Harrison, N.Y.)
    and Christoffersen (Mamaroneck, N.Y.)
Liz Christopher—Theater (Palo Alto, Calif.)
Philip Ciapponi—Chloe's (Sacramento, Calif.)
Gerald J. Cielec—Cielec (Chicago, Ill.)
David Cioffi—Dartmouth (Hanover, N.H.)
Beryl Claar—Claar (Golden, Colo.)
Rob Claitor—Claitor's (Baton Rouge, La.)
Roy W. Clare—Clare (Getzville, N.Y.)
Keith Clarey—Books & Co. (San Francisco, Calif.)
Arthur H. Clark—Clark (Glendale, Calif.)
David Clark—Burke's (Memphis, Tenn.)
Mary F. Clark—Chanticleer (Ft. Wayne, Ind.)
Paul O. Clark—Bibliolatree (E. Hampton, Conn.)
Ralph W. Clark—Chanticleer (Ft. Wayne, Ind.)
Robert A. Clark—Clark (Glendale, Calif.)
Taylor Clark—Clark (Baton Rouge, La.)
Terry Clark—Bryn Mawr (Pittsburgh, Pa.)
Steve Clay—Granary (St. Paul, Minn.)
Richard E. Clear—Dragon's Lair (Dayton, Ohio)
Albert G. Clegg—Clegg (Eaton Rapids, Mich.)
Evelyn Clement—Clement (Franklin, N.H.)
Julie Clem—Tracery (Dallas, Texas)
Onnie Clem—Tracery (Dallas, Texas)
Chris Cleveland—Book Disp. (Decatur, Ga.)
Cheryl Clevenger—Midvale (Portland, Ore.)

Ron Clevenger—Midvale (Portland, Ore.)
Ron Clewell—Ron Dot (Greensburg, Ohio)
Stanley Clifford—Skeans (Deer Isle, Maine)
B. K. Clinker—Owl Creek (Mt. Vernon, Ohio)
Krista Cliu—Heath (Toronto, Ont.)
Philip R. Cloutier—Borderland (Alvaton, Ky.)
Barbara H. Clower—Clower (Charlottesville, Va.)
Irv Coats—Reader's (Raleigh, N.C.)
Bobbi Cobb—Song (Newmarket, N.H.)
Charles Cockey—Fantasy (San Francisco, Calif.)
David Coffeen—Tesseract (Hastings, N.Y.)
Yola Coffeen—Tesseract (Hastings, N.Y.)
Taylor Coffman—Coffman (Cambria, Calif.)
Aaron L. Cohen—Guidon (Scottsdale, Ariz.)
Albert Cohen—Cohen (Youngstown, Ohio)
Arnold Cohen—Main St. (Brooklyn, N.Y.)
Aveve Cohen—Chiswick (Sandy Hook, Conn.)
Barbara Cohen—N.Y. Bound (New York, N.Y.)
Elaine L. Cohen—Ex Libris (New York, N.Y.)
Herman Cohen—Chiswick (Sandy Hook, Conn.)
Jean Cohen—Cohen (Bonita Springs, Fla.)
Judy M. Cohen—Cohen (New York, N. Y.)
Lillian Cohen—Herzig-Cohen (Jackson Hgts, NY)
Louis Cohen—Argosy (New York, N.Y.)
M. S. Cohen—Cohen (St. Louis, Mo.)
Ruth K. Cohen—Guidon (Scottsdale, Ariz.)
Myron Cohen-Ross—Pantechnicon (1000 Oaks,
    Calif.)
Linda Colarusso—Tunick (New York, N.Y.)
Don Colberg—Willow (Englewood, Colo.)
Nancy Colberg—Willow (Englewood, Colo.)
Chad Colburn—Colburn (Atlanta, Ga.)
Barbara Cole—October (Raleigh, N.C.)
Barbara Cole—Cole's (La Jolla, Calif.)
Lillian Cole—12th St. (Santa Monica, Calif.)
Elspeth Coleman—Weitz (New York, N.Y.)
Louise Coleman—Maple St. (New Orleans, La.)
Gaydell Collier—Backpocket (Sundance, Wyo.)
Paul Collinge—Heartwood (Charlottesville, Va.)
Louis B. Collins, Jr.—Collins (Seattle, Wash.)
Louis Collins—Collins (San Francisco, Calif.)
Reid Collins—Escargot (Brielle, N.J.)
Sue Collins—Collins' (Pottstown, Pa.)
Susan Colman—Wild (Larchmont, N.Y.)
Robert M. Colpitt—Bookery (Farmington, N.H.)
Harris Colt—Military (New York, N.Y.)
Margaret Colt—Military (New York, N.Y.)
Fran Combs—Combs (Great Falls, Mont.)
Jim Combs—Combs (Great Falls, Mont.)

Mrs. C. Comer—Kirksco (Ringwood, N.J.)
Webb T. Comfort—Indian Head (Owego, N.Y.)
Anita Comstock—Comstock's (Auburn, Wash.)
David Comstock—Comstock's (Auburn, Wash.)
Sarah Comstock—Wildwood (Old Forge, N.Y.)
Ted Comstock—Wildwood (Old Forge, N.Y.)
Heidi Congalton—Between (Old Bridge, N.J.)
Thomas Congalton—Between (Old Bridge, N.J.)
Ruth E. Conley—Little (Rehobeth, Mass.)
Duncan Connelly—Arader (Atlanta, Ga.)
Don Conner—Argus (Sacramento, Calif.)
Daniel Connolly—Connolly/Wade (Vista, Calif.)
Peter Connolly—Adler's (Evanston, Ill.)
Paul Conrad—Rainy (Halifax, N.S.)
Elaine Consolo—Consolo (Mansfield, Ohio)
Kelly Constable—Book Haven (Lancaster, Pa.)
Charles Conway—Conway (Attleboro, Mass.)
Alton Cook—Beckham's (New Orleans, La.)
Ruth Cooke—Fields (San Francisco, Calif.)
Grayson D. Cook—Cook (Los Angeles, Calif.)
Richard Cook—Attic (Laurel, Md.)
Rosemarie Coombs—Heritage (Southampton, Mass.)
Marjorie L. Coons—Old Rare (Jamestown, N.Y.)
Carolyn L. Cooper—Key (Baltimore, Md.)
Chris Cooper—2nd Story (Washington, D.C.)
Emily Cooper—Cooper's (Decatur, Ga.)
Raymond D. Cooper—Key (Baltimore, Md.)
Gary Copeland—Comic (New York, N.Y.)
Nathan Copeland—Copeland (Portland, Maine)
Dagny Corcoran—Art Cats. (Los Angeles, Calif.)
Patrick Corcoran—Lighthouse (Rye, N.Y.)
Paul A. Corcoran—Amer. Eagle (Topsfield, Mass.)
Michael V. Cordasco—Junius (Fairview, N.J.)
Ken Corliss—Bartlett St. (Medford, Ore.)
Richard Cormack—Calico Cat (Ventura, Calif.)
David Cormany—Book Cellar (Fullerton, Calif.)
Dianna Cornelius—Easton (Mt. Vernon, Wash.)
Dorothy G. Coslet—Books/Yesterday (Helena, Mont.)
Walter A. Coslet—Books/Yesterday (Helena, Mont.)
Larry Cosner—Heritage (Columbus, Ohio)
Timothy A. Cottrill—Bookery (Fairborn, Ohio)
Harris L. Coulter—Wehawken (Washington, D.C.)
Peter Courmont—Antiq. Center (New York, N.Y.)
J. Courtney—Black Swan (Lexington, Ken.)
Rebecca G. Cowead—Owl (Camden, Maine)
Robert P. Cowell—Cowell (Bridgeport, Conn.)
Ronald L. Cozzi—Old Edtns. (Buffalo, N.Y.)
R. Harry Crabtree—Crabtree (Signal Mtn., Tenn.)

Clayton Craft—Yesterday's (Ashfield, Mass.)
Edward J. Craig—Craig (Newport, R. I.)
Margaret L. Craig—Bradford (Bennington, Vt.)
W. Bradford Craig—Bradford (Bennington, Vt.)
Joyce Crawford—Crawford's (Cedar Rapids, Iowa)
Ken Crawford—Crawford (No. St. Paul, Minn.)
Ken Crawford—High Country (Laramie, Wyo.)
Bill Crawshaw—Book (Stillwater, N.Y.)
Helen Crawshaw—Book (Stillwater, N.Y.)
Donald H. Cresswell—Phila. Print (Philadelphia, Pa.)
A. C. Cressy, Jr.—Elmcress (So. Hamilton, Mass.)
Britta K. Cressy—Elmcress (So. Hamilton, Mass.)
John Crichton—Brick Row (San Francisco, Calif.)
Patricia Crisco—Fithian (Lakewood, Colo.)
Dorothy Crockett—History (Ashley Falls, Mass.)
Howard Crockett—History (Ashley Falls, Mass.)
Barbara L. Croft—Different (Des Moines, Iowa)
A. Crofter—Crofter's (Washington, Conn.)
Frank Crohn—Connecticut (E. Haddam, Conn.)
Paula Cronin—Cronin (Worcester, Mass.)
Dan Cronkhite—Sagebrush (Morongo Valley, Calif.)
Janet Cronkhite—Sagebrush (Morongo Valley, Calif.)
Jim Croom—Bookshop (Del Rio, Texas)
Sue Croom—Bookshop (Del Rio, Texas)
Candace C. Crosby—Clover (Charlottesville, Va.)
Leroy D. Cross—Cross (Brunswick, Maine)
Keith Crotz—Amer. Botanist (Brookfield, Ill.)
Annegret Cukierski—Bedford's (Ellsworth, Maine)
Carol Cullen—Rockland (Cattaraugus, N.Y.)
Thomas Cullen—Rockland (Cattaraugus, N.Y.)
Allan Culpin—Culpin's (Denver, Colo.)
James Cummings—Book House (Minneapolis, Minn.) and Cummings (Stillwater, Minn.)
Kristen Cummings—Book House (Minneapolis, Minn.)
James Cummins—Cummins (New York, N.Y. and Pottersville, N.J.)
Bertha Cunningham—Jerry's (Farmington, Mich.)
Everett V. Cunningham—Gull Shop and Gull Gall. (Oakland, Calif.) and Joyce (Martinez, Calif.)
Kevin Cunningham—Oceanic (New York, N.Y.) and Oceanie (Hillsdale, N.Y.)
Lynda Cunningham—Oceanic (New York, N.Y.) and Oceanie (Hillsdale, N.Y.)
L. W. Currey—Currey (Elizabethtown, N.Y.)
Kit Currie—Kraus (New York, N.Y.)
John R. Curtis, Jr.—Bookpress (Williamsburg, Va.)

Mitchell R. Cutler—Cutler (New York, N.Y.)
Isabel Cymerman—Book Quest (New York, N.Y.)

D

Thomas Dady—Dady (Minneapolis, Minn.)
Robert Dagg—Neville (Santa Barbara, Calif.)
Stan Dahl—Rancho (Santa Monica, Calif.)
Elizabeth Daigle—Stroud (Williamsburg, W.Va.)
Victoria Dailey—Daileys (Los Angeles, Calif.)
William Dailey—Daileys (Los Angeles, Calif.)
Evelyne Daitz—Witkin (New York, N.Y.)
Howard C. Daitz—Daitz (New York, N.Y.)
David Dale—Bookdales (Richfield, Minn.)
Joyce Dale—Bookdales (Richfield, Minn.)
George W. Dalley—Dalley (Christiansburg, Va.)
Katharine Dalton—Papyrus (Chatham, Mass.)
Eleanor DaltonNewfield—Churchilliana
    (Sacramento, Calif.)
James L. Dana—Bookman (Grand Haven, Mich.)
Mary J. Dana—Bookman (Grand Haven, Mich.)
Anita Danello—Anita's (Manchester, N.H.)
Michael Danello—Anita's (Manchester, N.H.)
Stan Darcey—Stan's (Brockton, Mass.)
Benjamin Darling—Blue Lantern (San Diego, Calif.)
Harold Darling—Blue Lantern (San Diego, Calif.)
Kathy Darling—Dog (Larchmont, N.Y.)
W. C. Darrah—Darrah (Gettysburg, Pa.)
David Dary—Dary (Lawrence, Kan.)
Sue Dary—Dary (Lawrence, Kan.)
James C. Dast—Dast (Madison, Wisc.)
Nancy A. Daunce—Daunce (Buffalo, N.Y.)
Robert J. Daunce—Daunce (Buffalo, N.Y.)
Mary A. Davidson—Frontier (Los Angeles, Calif.)
Philip O. Davidson—Frontier (Los Angeles, Calif.)
Rosalie C. Davidson—Davidson (San Diego, Calif.)
Bevan Davies—Untitled II #1 and #2 (both New
    York, N.Y.)
Michele Davies—Untitled II #1 and #2 (both New
    York, N.Y.)
Isaac Davis, Jr.—Bunkhouse (Gardiner, Maine)
Cynthia Davis-Buffington—Phila. Rare
    (Philadelphia, Pa.)
Beverly Davis—Bunkhouse (Gardiner, Maine)

Cal Davis—Davis/Schorr (Sherman Oaks, Calif.)
Charles W. Davis—Concord (Kailua-Kona, Haw.)
Evelyn Davis—Concord (Kailua-Kona, Haw.)
George B. Davis—Cooper Fox (Millbrook, N.Y.)
Jeff Davis—Raintree (Eustis, Fla.)
Lisa Davis—Alibi (New Haven, Conn.)
Lynden Davis—Alibi (New Haven, Conn.)
Claiborne Dawes—Barrow (Concord, Mass.)
Glen Dawson—Dawson's (Los Angeles, Calif.)
James Dawson—Unicorn (Trappe, Md.)
Muir Dawson—Dawson's (Los Angeles, Calif.)
Pat Day—Day's (Quincy, Calif.)
Rod Day—Day's (Quincy, Calif.)
Joanne Deacon—Hawks (Savanna, Ill.)
Ron Deacon—Hawks (Savanna, Ill.)
Bill Dean—Sky (New York, N.Y.)
E. B. Dean—Dean (Oklahoma City, Okla.)
Frederica deBeurs—deBeurs (Dexter, Maine)
Diane DeBlois—aGatherin' (Wynantskill, N.Y.)
Donnis de Camp—Schoyer's (Pittsburgh, Pa.)
Diana De Chene—De Chene (Los Angeles, Calif.)
Gene De Chene—De Chene (Los Angeles, Calif.)
Wilfrid DeFreitas—DeFreitas (Montreal, Que.)
John G. De Graff—Seabook (Clinton Corners, N.Y.)
Eleanor Deines—Deines (Ft. Collins, Colo.)
Harry Deines—Deines (Ft. Collins, Colo.)
Oliver Delaney—Arcane (Okla. City, Okla.)
Gerry de la Ree—de la Ree (Saddle River, N.J.)
Helen de la Ree—de la Ree (Saddle River, N.J.)
Keith de Lellis—de Lellis (New York, N.Y.)
Tom Delle Donne—Delle Donne (Ronkonkoma,
    N.Y.)
William J. Delp—Delp (Belding, Mich.)
Grover DeLuca—Oxford Two (Atlanta, Ga.)
John J. DeMarco—Lyrical (Saratoga Spgs., N.Y.)
Robert Demarest—Mycophile (Naples, Fla.)
Dan Demetriode—Koerber (Southfield, Mich.)
Kieffer Denning—Darvill's (Eastsound, Wash.)
Gertrude Dennis—Weyhe (New York, N.Y.)

Ned Densmore—Village (Littleton, N.H.)
Frank Deodene—Chatham (Madison, N.J.)
Joanne M. Dermont—Dermont (Onset, Mass.)
Joseph A. Dermont—Dermont (Onset, Mass.)
Pam Dernier—Book Mart (Brockton, Mass.)
Patricia Derozier—Pages #1 (Green Bay, Wisc.)
Grace Desch—Desch (Wheaton, Md.)
John A. Desch—Desch (Wheaton, Md.)
Gilles Desmarais—Desmarais (Palo Alto, Calif.)
Rebecca B. Desmarais—Desmarais (Palo Alto, Calif.)
Herman E. Detering III—Detering (Houston, Texas)
Maisie Dethier—Owl (Bryn Mawr, Pa.)
Roy Dethsy—Verde (Winsted, Conn.)
John Detrick—Americana (Coral Gables, Fla.)
Burton Devere—Rosetree (Tombstone, Ariz.)
Robyn DeVilliers—Bearce (Salem, Ore.)
Dalies Devine—Devine (Katonah, N.Y.)
Sean Devlin—Kaufman (New York, N.Y.)
Don Deweber—Checker (Dubuque, Iowa)
Joe Dewey—Williams (Williamstown, Mass.)
Benjamin De Wit—De Wit (East Lansing, Mich.)
Edith Dexter—Lady (Lower Lake, Calif.)
David Deye—Wooden (Ann Arbor, Mich.)
Harold Diamond—Diamond (Burbank, Calif.)
Ray Diamond—Diamond (Rochester, N.Y.)
Douglas Dible—Charing (Hutchinson, Kan.)
Mrs. Fritz Dillmann—Johnny (Manchester, Vt.)
Christine Dimidgian—Front (Van Nuys, Calif.)
Robb Dimmick—Cornerstone (Providence, R.I.)
Larry Dingman—Dinkytown (Minneapolis, Minn.)
Mary Dingman—Dinkytown (Minneapolis, Minn.)
Colleen Dionne—Old Ver. (Olympia Falls, Ill.)
Edward D. Dionne—Old Ver. (Olympia Falls, Ill.)
Don Discher—Discher (Castro Valley, Calif.)
Cheryl Dobbs—Dobbs (Higginsville, Mo.)
Robert Dobbs—Dobbs (Higginsville, Mo.)
Lyndsay Dobson—Dobson (Grimsby, Ont.)
Chester Doby—Book Buyers (Houston, Texas)
Carol Docheff—Docheff (Berkeley, Calif.)
Jerry Dodd—Book Look (Warwick, N.Y.)
Jerry Dodd—New/Used (Warwick, N.Y.)
D. R. Doerres—Doerres (Wilton, Iowa)
Leilani Dogging—MacBeans (Brunswick, Maine)
Janice H. Dohm—Dohm's (Olympia, Wash.)
Stephen Doi—Doi (San Jose, Calif.)
Len Donahue—Olde Tyme (Boonton, N.J.)
Irene Donaldson—Donaldson's (Knoxville, Tenn.)
Morris Donaldson—Donaldson (Nanaimo, B.C.)

Patricia Donaldson—Donaldson (Nanaimo, B.C.)
Elizabeth Donnally—Donnally (Seattle, Wash.)
John Donoghue—Lewis St. (Lynn, Mass.)
Patrick H. Donovan—Donovan (Endicott, N.Y.)
Richard E. Donovan—Donovan (Endicott, N.Y.)
Michael C. Dooling—Dooling (Middlebury, Conn.)
Webb Dordick—Dordick (Somerville, Mass.)
James Dore—Once Upon (W. Hempstead, N.Y.)
Kathleen Dorman—Yesterday's (Modesto, Calif.)
Laurence Dorman—Yesterday's (Modesto, Calif.)
Betty Dorn—Dorn (Johntown, N.Y.)
Charles E. Dornbusch—Hope Farm (Cornwallville, N.Y.)
Merce Dostale—Granary (St. Paul, Minn.)
Jim Doty—JMD (Groton, N. Y.)
Jeanne Douglas—Una (St. Johnsbury, Vt.)
Lee Douglas—Douglas (Sheridan, Wyo.)
John B. Doukas—Doukas (Kalamazoo, Mich.)
John Doull—Schooner (Halifax, N.S.)
James M. Dourgarian—Dourgarian (Walnut Creek, Calif.)
Nancy F. Doutt—Doutt (Big Flats, N. Y.)
Frances Dowd—Dowd (St. Charles, Ill.)
James Dowd—Dowd (St. Charles, Ill.)
Bill Downing—Significant (Cincinnati, Ohio)
Carolyn Downing—Significant (Cincinnati, Ohio)
Katherine Downs—Downs (Marietta, Ga.)
Ellen Doyle—Green Mtn. (Lyndonville, Vt.)
Jim Doyle—Green Mtn. (Lyndonville, Vt.)
Martin Doyle—Traveler (Union, Conn.)
Paul J. Drabeck—Drabeck (Tuckahoe, N.Y.)
Vladimir Dragan—Dragan (Ithaca, N.Y.)
Fred Drake—Dragoman (Annapolis, Md.)
Andrea Drenard—Paper (Portland, Ore.)
Mr. Dreyfuss—Donan (New York, N.Y.)
Howard Dricks—Midnight (Marietta, Ga.)
Barbara Drowne—Book Barn (Gardner, Mass.)
Paul Drowne—Book Barn (Gardner, Mass.)
Ed Drucker—Elysian (Elmhurst, N.Y.)
Chris Drumm—Drumm (Polk City, Iowa)
Tom Drysdale—Old Book (Kennebunk, Maine)
Viola Drysdale—Old Book (Kennebunk, Maine)
Jason Duberman—Free Lance (Brooklyn, N.Y.)
Jason Duberman—Military (New York, N.Y.)
Bonita B. Duck—Duck's (Flagstaff, Ariz.)
John C. Duck—Duck's (Flagstaff, Ariz.)
Gaetan Dufour—Guerin (Montreal, Que.)
Israel Duga—Dugas (Orlando, Fla.)
Paul Duke—Cotswold (Medina, Ohio)

Lore Dulson—Oxford Two (Atlanta, Ga.)
Ann Dumler—Dumler (Southport, Conn.)
Carroll Dunham—Dunham's (Bedford, Mass.)
Grace Dunham—Dunham's (Bedford, Mass.)
Nancy Duniho—Corner-Stone (Plattsburgh, N.Y.)
Elizabeth F Dunlap—Dunlap (St. Louis, Mo.)
Allen A. Dunn—Dunn (Dallas, Ore.)
Michael Dunn—Dunn (Newport, Vt.)
D. N. Dupley—Dupley (Omaha, Neb.)
Serge Dupre—Tayaut (No. Hatley, Que.)
Maggie DuPriest—DuPriest (Columbia, S.C.)
Diane Durante—R. Ramer (New York, N.Y.)
Nancy Durant—Olde Tyme (Boonton, N.J.)

John Durham—Bolerium (San Francisco, Calif.)
Mrs. P. C. Duschnes—Duschnes (New York, N.Y.)
Colleen Dyke—Golden Age (Seattle, Wash.)
Rod Dyke—Golden Age (Seattle, Wash.)
Margaret Dyment—Dyment (Ottawa, Ont.)
Paul Dyment—Dyment (Ottawa, Ont.)
Mary Dysinger—Dysinger (Brunswick, Maine)
Robert Dysinger—Dysinger (Brunswick, Maine)
Bernadine Dziedzic—Chicago Law (Chicago, Ill.)
Alexander A. Dzilvelis—Books/Collector (Encino, Calif.)

E

Hereford Eads—Odds (Indianapolis, Ind.)
Winona Eads—Fountain (Indianapolis, Ind.)
Richard W. Eagleston—Pages (Reading, Mass.)
William B. Earley—Lincoln (Chambersburg, Pa.)
David Eastman—Words (So. Bend, Ind.)
Harland H. Eastman—Eastman (Springvale, Maine)
Richard E. Eckler—Clinton (Clinton, N.Y.)
Julie Ellen Edger—Edger (Hastings, Mich.)
Ernest Ediger—Ediger (Beaverton, Ore.)
Margaret Ediger—Ediger (Beaverton, Ore.)
Adela Edwards—Bookery (Ithaca, N.Y.)
Rose Edwards—Yesterday's (Hot Springs, Ark.)
N. J. Effress—E. K. (Rego Park, N. Y.)
Jesse Effron—3 Arts (Poughkeepsie, N.Y.)
John Egan—Keane (State College, Pa.)
Keith Egan—Egan (Millville, N. J.)
Arnold D. Ehlert—Bible (El Cajon, Calif.)
Tamar Ehlert—Prairie (Springfield, Ill.)
Michael Ehrenthal—Moriah (New York, N.Y.)
Peter Ehrenthal—Moriah (New York, N.Y.)
Marilyn M. Einhorn—Einhorn (New York, N.Y.)
P. Eisenberg—Eisenberg (Washington, D.C.)
R. M. Eisenberg—Stone House (Elkton, Md.)
Joan Eldredge—Eldredge (Vineyard Haven, Mass.)
May Ellam—Ellam (Los Angeles, Calif.)
Fay Elliott—Elliott (New York, N. Y.)
John R. Elliott—Branford (Branford, Conn.)
Anne M. Ellis—Ellis (Kentfield, Calif.)

Bill Ellis—Ellis (Queen Charlotte, B.C.)
Betty Ellsworth—999 (New York, N.Y.)
Charles C. Ellsworth—Crawford's (Cincinnati, Ohio)
Sandra Elm—Poster (New York, N.Y.)
Allan Elsner—Elsner (New York, N.Y.)
Harvey D. Eluto—Bargain (Norfolk, Va.)
Frederic Elwert—Elwert (Rutland, Vt.)
Susan Elzea—Golden Gull (Grants Pass, Ore.)
George Emanuels—Diablo (Walnut Creek, Calif.)
Bob Emerson—Theatrebooks (New York, N.Y.)
Dorothy Emerson—Emerson and Geological (both Falls Village, Conn.)
Ethel Emerson—Falls Barn (Farmington Falls, Maine)
Robert Emerson—Emerson and Geological (both Falls Village, Conn.)
Charles H. Emery, Jr.—Fran's (Philadelphia, Pa.)
Elizabeth Emery—Cotton Hill (Laconia, N.H.)
Francenva Emery—Fran's (Philadelphia, Pa.)
Ron Emery—Emery's (Contoocook, N.H.)
Sherman R. Emery—Books/Autographs (Eliot, Maine)
Dorothy C. Emmert—Book Nook (Yakima, Wash.)
Rodney G. Engard—Engard (Tucson, Ariz.)
Sidney Engelbert—Old Book (San Francisco, Calif.)
Mary Engen—1st Edtn. (Muskegon Hgts., Mich.)
Ruth S. Engle—Engle (Cherry Hill, N. J.)
Ellen Enzler-Herring—Trophy (Agoura, Calif.)

E. Ephraim—Elliot's (Northford, Conn.)
Emma Ephraim—Elliot's (Northford, Conn.)
Harold S. Ephraim—Lincoln (Foster, R.I.)
Linda F. Ephraim—Lincoln (Foster, R.I.)
Kathy Epling—Orange (Garberville, Calif.)
Fred Eppler—Book Nook (Manitowoc, Wisc.)
Judy Eppler—Book Nook (Manitowoc, Wisc.)
Barbara Epstein—Quadrant (Easton, Pa.)
Bill Epstein—Bill (Long Isl. City, N. Y.)
Irma Epstein—Bill (Long Isl. City, N. Y.)
Richard Epstein—Quadrant (Easton, Pa.)
Katharine M Ericson—Lilac Hedge (Norwich, Vt.)
Robert P. Ericson—Lilac Hedge (Norwich, Vt.)
Paul Erling—Nebenzahl (Chicago, Ill.)
Rose Russel Ernest—Ernest (Ottumwa, Iowa)
Donald H. Ernst—Ernst (Selinsgrove, Pa.)
Donald J. Ernst—Ernst (Selinsgrove, Pa.)
David Eshner—Eshner (Bisbee, Ariz.)

Joe Eslick—Log Cabin (Bigfork, Mont.)
Charles Esposito—Carriage (Northford, Conn.)
Marilyn Esposito—Carriage (Northford, Conn.)
John M. Esser—Constant Reader (Milwaukee, Wisc.)
Diane Estep—Carmichael's (Louisville, Ky.)
Emil N. Eusanio—San Fernando (San Fernando, Calif.)
Brent Evans—Basil's (Salt Lake City, Utah)
John Evans—Lemuria (Jackson, Miss.)
Lonnie E. Evans—Evans (Savannah, Ga.)
Mike Evans—Heartwood (Charlottesville, Va.)
Olin O. Evans—Evans (Woodstock, Va.)
Paul Evans—Anglican (Saratoga Spgs., N.Y.)
Edwina Evers—Califia (San Francisco, Calif.)
Bill Ewald—Argus (Sacramento, Calif.)
Eugene Exnowski—Exnowski (Warren, Mich.)

F

T. C. Fabrizio—Terra (Churchville, N.Y.)
Michael Fagin—City Spirit (Denver, Colo.)
Nancy L. Fagin—Fagin (Chicago, Ill.)
Helen Faiella—New Age (Westerly, R.I.)
James Faiella—New Age (Westerly, R.I.)
Anthony Fair—Wilson (New York, N.Y.)
Phyllis Fairchild—Tumbleweed (Pueblo, Colo.)
James Fallon—Ohio (Cincinnati, Ohio)
Flora Faraci—Jane Addams (Champaign, Ill.)
Gilbert Farley—Mendoza (New York, N.Y.)
Moonean Farley—Farley's (Pensacola, Fla.)
Owen Farley—Farley's (Pensacola, Fla.)
Barbara Farnsworth—Farnsworth (W. Cornwall, Conn.)
Rebecca Farnsworth—Trans (Parkersburg, W.Va.)
Eleanor Fasotti—Pasotti (Indianapolis, Ind.)
Virginia Faulkner—Old Book (Morristown, N.J.)
Lois M. Favier—Books End (Syracuse, N. Y.)
Joseph F. Fawls—JFF (Manhasset, N.Y.)
Teresa M. Fawls—JFF (Manhasset, N.Y.)
Don Fay—Fay (Caledonia, N.Y.)
Rose Feick—Book City (Hollywood, Calif.)
Elaine Feiden—Feiden (Mamaroneck, N.Y.)
Todd Feiertag—Poster (Orangeburg, N.Y.)

Jean Feigenbaum—Collector's (Pt. Washington, N.Y.)
Bob Fein—Fein (New York, N.Y.)
Jack Feingold—Gem (New York, N.Y.)
Betty S. Feinstein—Hard-To (Newton, Mass.)
M. C. Feinstein—M. & M. (E. Northport, N.Y.)
M. S. Feinstein—M. & M. (E. Northport, N.Y.)
Joseph J. Felcone—Felcone (Princeton, N.J.)
Arthur L. Feldman—Feldman (Cleveland, Ohio)
Michael Feldman—Buddenbrooks (Boston, Mass.)
Stephen Feldman—Asian Rare (New York, N.Y.)
Henry Feldstein—Feldstein (Forest Hills, N.Y.)
Peter R. Feltus—Feltus (Berkeley, Calif.)
Dolly Fenelon—Oasis (San Deigo, Calif.)
Michael J. Fenelon—Oasis (San Deigo, Calif.)
Kevin Ferguson—Book Shoppe (Myrtle Beach, S.C.)
William Fern—Fern (New York, N.Y.)
Karla Ferrelli—Fraser (Burlington, Vt.)
J. Bruce Ferrier—Treasure (Oakville, Ont.)
Bruce Ferrini—Ferrini and Ferrini/Greenberg (both Akron, Ohio)
Chris Fessler—Fessler (Theresa, N.Y.)
Janet Fetherling—Annex (Toronto, Ont.)
David Ficken—Autobooks (Babylon, N.Y.)

Patricia A. Fickes—Fickes (Akron, Ohio)
Jane Field—Field (Georgetown, Mass.)
Kenneth Field—Field (Georgetown, Mass.)
Darlene Fife—Book Store (Lewisburg, W.Va.)
Russell Filer—Geoscience (Yucaipa, Calif.)
Nancy Filler—Filler (Bremerton, Wash.)
Robert J. Finch—High Lat. (Bainbridge, Wash.)
Steve Finer—Finer (Greenfield, Mass.)
Leonard H. Finn—Finn (W. Roxbury, Mass.)
Al Fischler—Fischler (San Jose, Calif.)
Clifford Fisher—Fisher (Cobleskill, N.Y.)
Dolores Fisher—Fisher (Williamsport, Pa.)
Peter Thomas Fisher—Fisher (New York, N.Y.)
Robert Fisher—Fisher (Williamsport, Pa.)
Gary Fishman—Arader (Houston, Texas)
Clint Fiske—Haunted (Cuttingsville, Vt.)
Lucille Fiske—Haunted (Cuttingsville, Vt.)
Richard Fitch—Fitch (Santa Fe, N.M.)
E. Fithian—Fithian (Lakewood, Colo.)
Ed Fix—Readmore (St. Louis, Mo.)
Johnathan Flaccus—Unique (Putney, Vt.)
W. K. Flaherty—Smith (Pleasant Hill, Calif.)
Richard Flamer—1023 (Omaha, Neb.)
Robert D. Fleck—Oak Knoll (New Castle, Del.)
Don Fleming—Yesterday's (Washington, D.C.)
James T. Fleming—Back No. (Danvers, Mass.)
John F. Fleming—Fleming (New York, N.Y.)
Joseph Fleming—Bargain (Jackson, Mich.)
Thelma R. Fletcher—Fletcher's (Salado, Texas)
Jerry Flokstra—ABC Theo. (Springfield, Mo.)
Gladstone Fluegge—Seville (Pensacola, Fla.)
Andreia Flynn—Printer's (Milldale, Conn. and
     Middletown, Conn.)
Doris Flynn—Flynn (Lake Forest, Ill.)
T. T. Foley—Foley (Bardstown, Ky.)
Jane R. Folger—Hill (New York, N.Y.)
Roland Folter—Kraus (New York, N.Y.)
Edward J. Fontenarosa—Catholic (Bellingham,
     Mass.)
Robert K. Foote—Winter Farm (Pittsfield, Maine)
Richard Force—Bretton Hall (Bretton Woods, N.H.
     and Lancaster, N.H.)
Alla T. Ford—Ford (Lake Worth, Fla.)
Bobby Jo Ford—Book Faire (Woodland, Calif.)
Kent Fordyce—Lambda (Washington, D.C.)
Eleanor Forman—Bryn Mawr (White Plains, N.Y.)
Phyllis M. Forward—Little (Hinsdale, Ill.)
George A. Foster, Jr.—Bookstack (Elkhart, Ind.)
Dorth Foster—Foster (Corning, Calif.)

Henrietta M Foster—Foster (Corning, Calif.)
Jerome Foster—Falmouth (Falmouth, Mass.)
Lavonne Foster—Hooked (Springfield, Mo.)
Mary Foster—Bookstack (Elkhart, Ind.)
Richard W. Foster—Rittenhouse (Philadelphia, Pa.)
Bill Foukes—Big #2 (Detroit, Mich.)
Judi Fouts—Finders (Dallas, Texas)
Barbara Fox—Fox (Tacoma, Wash.)
Richard B. Fox—Fox (Madison, Tenn.)
Vivian P. Fox—Fox (Madison, Tenn.)
Robert Fraker—Savoy (Lanesborough, Mass.)
Ernest Franklin—Little (Detroit, Mich.)
Linda C. Franklin—Franklin (New York, N.Y.)
Mary P. Franklin—Wharf (Centreville, Md.)
Robert Franklin—Allston (Allston, Mass.)
Polly G. Fraser—Yesteryear (Atlanta, Ga.)
Don Frazier—Calderwoods (Long Valley, N.J.)
John Frazier—Urban (New York, N.Y.)
Louise Frazier—Frazier (Gilford, N.H.)
John Freas—Tamerlane (Havertown, Pa.)
Nelson Freck—Chaos (Washington, D.C.)
Frieda Freedman—Wilshire (No. Hollywood, Calif.)
Martha Freedman—2nd Life (Lanesborough, Mass.)
Michael Freedman—Atticus (Toronto, Ont.)
Peg Freedman—Lyman (East Otis, Mass.)
Russell Freedman—2nd Life (Lanesborough, Mass.)
Sam Freedman—Lyman (East Otis, Mass.)
Sandy Freeman—Memory (Corona Del Mar, Calif.)
Barbara French—Visually (Gilford, N.H.)
Charles French—Visually (Gilford, N.H.)
William P. French—University (New York, N.Y.)
Joseph J. Fricelli—Fricelli (Brooklyn, N.Y.)
David Frid—Frid (San Pedro, Calif.)
Henry K. Fried—La Valois (New York, N.Y.)
James T. Friedman—Toy (San Francisco, Calif.)
Janel Frierabend—Folger (Washington, D.C.)
Howard Frisch—Frisch (Livingston, N.Y.)
John Frisk—Frisk/Borodin (Philadelphia, Pa.)
Doris Frohnsdorff—Frohnsdorff (Gaithersburg, Md.)
Theodore Front—Front (Van Nuys, Calif.)
David C. Frost—Footnote (Brooklyn, N.Y.)
Michael Frost—Bartfield Gall. (New York, N.Y.)
M. Frost-Pierson—Mysteries (Yellow Spgs., Ohio)
Carol Fruchter—Collectors' (New York, N.Y.)
J. Fuerst—Wikehgan (Mt. Desert, Maine)
Brandon A. Fullam—Fullam (Babylon, N.Y.)
Marsha Fuller—Books/Such (Springfield, Mass.)
Beverley Furlow—Morgan (Tucson, Ariz.)
Eric Furry—Pro Libris (Bangor, Maine)

Lois B. Fye—Fye (Marshfield, Wisc.) | W. Bruce Fye—Fye (Marshfield, Wisc.)

G

Judith K. Gaarder—Parnassus (Boise, Idaho)
Lorin R. Gaarder—Parnassus (Boise, Idaho)
G. N. Gabbard—Gabbard (New Boston, Texas)
Betty Gach—Gach (Columbia, Md.)
John Gach—Gach (Columbia, Md.)
Jean Gagnon—Gagnon (Quebec, Que.)
Herb Galewitz—Galewitz (Orange, Conn.)
Marge Galicki—Folk (Long Beach, Calif.)
Lorraine Galinsky—Nosegay (Cold Spg. Harbor, N.Y.)
Irving Galis—Gallis (Marblehead, Mass.)
John Gambino—Coventry (Coventry, Conn.)
Beverly N. Gamradt—Gamradt (Minneapolis, Minn.)
Gregory C. Gamradt—Gamradt (Minneapolis, Minn.)
Bob Gardner—Dr. Nostalgia (Lynchburg, Va.)
Mrs. Bob Gardner—Dr. Nostalgia (Lynchburg, Va.)
Judy Gardner—MacBeans (Brunswick, Maine)
Ralph Gardner—Gardner (New York, N.Y.)
Richard Gardner—Battery (Nashville, Tenn.)
Anne Garms—One (Bradenton, Fla.)
Anthony Garnett—Garnett (St. Louis, Mo.)
Elizabeth Garon—Beasley (Chicago, Ill.)
Paul Garon—Beasley (Chicago, Ill.)
George H. Garrison, Jr.—Garrison (Williamsburg, Va.)
Beverly Garst—Carcia-Garst (Turlock, Calif.)
Kenneth Garst—Carcia-Garst (Turlock, Calif.)
Joseph J. Gasior—Chicago Law (Chicago, Ill.)
Brisets M. Gatto—Gatto (New York, N.Y.)
Janet M. Gatto—Gatto (New York, N.Y.)
John Taylor Gatto—Gatto (New York, N.Y.)
R. E. Gauvey—Signed (Pt. Washington, N.Y.)
William T. Gavin—Gavin (Leominster, Mass.)
Robert Gavora—Gavora (Santa Barbara, Calif.)
L. E. Gay—Gay (Santa Fe, N.M.)
Mary R. Gay—Gay (Santa Fe, N.M.)
Seymour Gaynor—Radio (New York, N.Y.)
Thomas Geagen—Geagan (Wareham, Mass.)
E. P. Geauque—Wake (Ft. Lauderdale, Fla.)
H. Jewel Geberth—Cape Collector (So. Harwich, Mass.)

Robert J. Gelink—Otento (San Diego, Calif.)
Esther Geller—Elgen (Rockville Centre, N.Y.)
Leonard Geller—Elgen (Rockville Centre, N.Y.)
Jim Genovese—Bookkeepers (Riviera Bch., Fla.)
Mollyanne George—Rootenberg (Sherman Oaks, Calif.)
Richard D. George—Sporting (Palmerton, Pa.)
R. L. George—George (Cleveland, Tenn.)
Joseph Geraci—Geraci (Accord, N.Y.)
Lois Gereghty—Gereghty (Sepulveda, Calif.)
Victor F. Germack—Professional (New York, N.Y.)
Antoinette Gersdorf—Scribbling (No. Ft. Myers, Fla.)
Joan Gers—999 (New York, N.Y.)
Jay Gertzman—Emerson (Wellsboro, Pa.)
Marina Gerwing—Haunted (Victoria, B.C.)
Garry E. Gibbons—Hist. Realia (Wooster, Ohio)
Michael Gibbs—Gibbs (State College, Pa.)
Peggy Gibbs—Gibbs (State College, Pa.)
Dick Gibson—Alfabooks (Arlington, Va.)
Donna Gibson—Scribe's (Newport, R.I.)
Greg Gibson—10 Pound (Gloucester, Mass.)
Bennett Gilbert—Bennett Gilbert
Richard Gilbo—Gilbo (Carpinteria, Calif.)
Jane Gilbreath—Westport (Kansas City, Mo.)
Duff Gilfond—Gilfond (Washington, D.C.)
Franklin Gilliam—Gilliam (Charlottesville, Va.)
Lynn Gilliam—Webster's (Milwaukee, Wisc.)
William Gillmore—Dawn Treader (Ann Arbor, Mich.)
Stanley Gilman—Gilman (New York, N.Y.)
C. Gilmore—Huntley (Claremont, Calif.)
Milan Gilmore—Book Stop (Lafayette, Calif.)
Betty Ginn—Forgotten (St. Simon Isl., Ga.)
Ed H. Ginn—Forgotten (St. Simon Isl., Ga.)
L. Ginsberg—Ginsberg (Petersburg, Va.)
Michael Ginsberg—Ginsberg (Sharon, Mass.)
Raymond V. Giordano—Antiq. Scientist (Dracut, Mass.)
G. F. Glaeve—Glaeve (Madison, Wisc.)
Nancy S. Glaister—Glaister (New York, N.Y.)

Edwin V. Glaser—Glaser (Sausalito, Calif.)
Peter Glaser—Glaser (Sausalito, Calif.)
Bill Glass—Change (Santa Monica, Calif.)
Howard Glasser—Glasser (Assonet, Mass.)
Peter Glassman—Books/Wonder (New York, N.Y.)
Richard Glassman—Glassman (Corte Madera, Calif.)
Ardis L. Glenn—Glenn (Kansas City, Mo.)
Bob Glick—Columbia (Suffern, N.Y.)
Kenneth Gloss—Brattle Book (Boston, Mass.)
Don Glover—Horizon (Seattle, Wash.)
Ida Glover—Glover (Cambridge, N. Y.)
John T. Glover—Glover's (Lexington, Ky.)
L. E. Gobrecht—Gobrecht (Kinderhook, N.Y.)
Julian Godwin—Bookmonger (Montgomery, Ala.)
Fred Goetz—Cameron's (Portland, Ore.)
C. R. Goez—Pomander (New York, N.Y.)
Brian Gold—Worldwide (Boston, Mass.)
Phillip Gold—221 (Westlake Village, Calif.)
Joan O. Golder—Thomolsen (Bayside, N.Y.)
Lawrence Golder—Golder (Collinsville, Conn.)
Walter E. Golder—Thomolsen (Bayside, N.Y.)
Jack Goldman—Bookery (Ithaca, N.Y.)
Lew Goldmann—Pages (Mt. Kisco, N.Y.)
Chris Gomez—Attic (St. Pete., Fla.)
Osborne Gomez—Attic (St. Pete., Fla.)
Dave C. Gonzales—Yesteryear (Nampa, Idaho)
Stephen Good—Rosenstock (Denver, Colo.)
Gary Goodman—Goodman (St. Paul, Minn.)
Jeanne Goodman—Pinocchio's (Morgantown, W.Va.)
Ruth Goodman—Bookwood (Westwood, N.J.)
James Goodreau—Jacksonville (Jacksonville, Ore.)
James T. Goodrich—Goodrich (Englewood, N.J.)
Dorothy D. Goodrum—Book Case (Houston, Texas)
Richard A. Goodrum—Book Case (Houston, Texas)
Willard Goodson—Goodson (Vincennes, Ind.)
George P. Goodspeed—Goodspeed's #1 (Boston, Mass.)
Carole Goodwin—Left Bank (Oak Park, Ill.)
James Goolsby—Books/Bytes (El Dorado, Ark.)
Andrew Gordon—Archaeologia (Oakland, Calif.)
B. L. Gordon—Book/Tackle (Chestnut Hill, Mass. and Watch Hill, R.I.)
Chandler Gordon—Captain's (Ashville, N.C.)
E. C. Gordon—E. C. Gordon (New York, N.Y.)
Elliot Gordon—E. Gordon (New York, N.Y.)
Jeffrey Gordon—Circle West (Annapolis, Md.)
M. Gordon—Gordon (Pasadena, Calif.)
Martin Gordon—M. Gordon (New York, N.Y.)

Samuel Gordon—Circle West (Annapolis, Md.)
Vesta Lee Gordon—Book Broker (Charlottesville, Va.)
Marian Gore—Gore (San Gabriel, Calif.)
Jeanne Gorham—Gateway (Ferndale, Pa.)
Bill Goring—Nutmeg (Torrington, Conn.)
Debby Goring—Nutmeg (Torrington, Conn.)
Stanley Gorski—Gorski (Doylestown, Pa.)
Michael R. Goth—Phoenix (Santa Monica, Calif.)
Sherry M. Gottlieb—Change (Santa Monica, Calif.)
Ludwig Gottschalk—Biblion (Forest Hills, N.Y.)
Bartlett Gould—Gould (Newburyport, Mass.)
Charles Gould—Webfoot (Portland, Ore.)
Ted Goulden—Oklahoma (Yukon, Okla.)
James Gould—Brownbag (Rochester, N.Y.)
John W. Gould—Cow Country (Prescott, Ariz.)
Margaret Gould—Cow Country (Prescott, Ariz.)
Robert M. Grabowski—Grabowski (Ronks, Penna.)
Mary K. Graf—Graf (Iowa City, Iowa)
William A. Graf—Graf (Iowa City, Iowa)
Jane Graham—Graham (Bozeman, Mont.)
Oscar D. Graham II—Detering (Houston, Texas)
Rebecca Graham—Oxford At (Atlanta, Ga.)
Ron Graham—Graham (Forestville, Calif.)
V. Gramlich—Book-Bind (Anaheim, Calif.)
Anthony Gran—El Cascajero (New York, N.Y.)
Sally Gran—El Cascajero (New York, N.Y.)
Ellen Granat—Granat (Woodmere, N.Y.)
Jerry Granat—Granat (Woodmere, N.Y.)
Michael Grano—Amer. City (Denver, Colo.)
D. Gratz—Gratz (Bluffton, Ohio)
Cliff Graubart—Old N.Y. (Atlanta, Ga.)
Bradford Gray—Folkways (Bethesda, Md.)
Logan Gray—Automobile (Beaverton, Ore.)
Robert O. Greenawalt—Rails (Rosemead, Calif.)
Michael S. Greenbaum—Janus (Tucson, Ariz.)
Carol A. Greenberg—Cornucopia (Syosset, N.Y.)
Chip Greenberg—Chip's Search (New York, N.Y.)
John Greenberg—Bear (W. Brattleboro, Vt.)
Beverly Green—Green (Elkins Park, Pa.)
C. Green—Green (Philadelphia, Pa.)
Denise Greene—Beatific (Schenectady, N.Y.)
Michael Greene—Beatific (Schenectady, N.Y.)
Paulette Greene—Greene (Rockville Centre, N.Y.)
Robert J. Greene—Greene (Rockville Centre, N.Y.)
A. Greenwood—About (Toronto, Ont.)
Robert Greenwood—Talisman (Georgetown, Calif.)
K. Gregory—Gregory (New York, N.Y.)
Daniel Greifenberger—Book Admirer

(Norwalk, Conn.)
J. A. Grenzeback—10 O'Clock (Elk Grove, Calif.)
Carling Gresham—Carling's (Pomona Park, Fla.)
Marian Greswold—Bryn Mawr (Rochester, N.Y.)
E. W. Grieb—Breslauer (New York, N.Y.)
Elizabeth Griffin—Arnolds (Traverse City, Mich.)
Karen Griffin—Bartleby's (Bethesda, Md.)
Mrs. John Grigsby—Coosa Valley (Rome, Ga.)
Johanna Grimes—Old Hickory (Brinklow, Md.)
Ralph Grimes—Old Hickory (Brinklow, Md.)
George Grimshaw—Grimshaw (Randolph, Mass.)
Agnes Grogan—Daly (Ridgefield, Conn.)
Jack L. Grogins—Turkey (Westport, Conn.)
Pauline Grosch—Antiquus (San Francisco, Calif.)
David Grossblatt—Grossblatt (Dallas, Texas)
Patty Grossman—Mainly (No. Hollywood, Calif.)
Sol Grossman—Mainly (No. Hollywood, Calif.)

Rick Grunder—Grunder (Ithaca, N.Y.)
Klaus Grunewald—Grunewald (Kansas City, Mo.)
Frank Guarino—Guarino (De Bary, Fla.)
Ken Guarino—Jamaica (Jamaica, N.Y.)
Anton Gud—Gud (Elmhurst, N.Y.)
Francis T. Guelker—Guelker (St. Louis, Mo.)
Marc-Aime Guerin—Guerin (Montreal, Que.)
Jon Guillot—Magnum (Charlottesville, Va.)
A. Gula—Terrapin (Austin, Texas)
Ken Gustafson—Gustafson (Chicago, Ill.)
William Guthman—Guthman (Westport, Conn.)
Thomas Guthormsen—This Old (Montclair, Calif.)
Andrew Gutterman—Earth (Littleton, N.H.)
Neil Gutterman—Ordnance (Madison, Conn.)
Bruce Gventer—Gventer (So. Egremont, Mass.)
Susan Gventer—Gventer (So. Egremont, Mass.)
Michael Hackenberg—Bolerium (San Francisco,

H

Michael Hackenberg—Bolerium (San Francisco, Calif.)
Carol P. Hacker—Hacker (Rolling Meadows, Ill.)
Seymour Hacker—Hacker (New York, N.Y.)
Lori Hackler—Hill (Kingsport, Tenn.)
Richard Hackney—Fields (San Francisco, Calif.)
Rebecca Haddad—Book Exch. (Missoula, Mont.)
John Hadreas—Aardvark (San Francisco, Calif.)
Donald E. Hahn—Hahn (Cottonwood, Ariz.)
Mrs. Haig—Bookmart (Gardiner, N.Y.)
Robert D. Haines, Jr.—Argonaut (San Francisco, Calif.)
Cindy Haines—Hole (Reedsport, Ore.)
Anne Haisley—Readbeard's (Marion, Ind.)
Helen Halbach—Halbach (Santa Barbara, Calif.)
William Hale—Hale (Washington, D.C.)
Diane Halford—Book Stop (Petoskey, Mich.)
George Hall, Jr.—Hall (Chambersburg, Pa.)
Ann Hall—Matthews (Ft. Erie, Ont.)
Walter E. Hallberg—Hallberg (Hartford, Conn.)
Charles N. Hall—Ye Olde (San Angelo, Texas)
David Hall—Hall's (Arlington, Mass.)
Helen Hall—Hollywood Service (Hollywood, Calif.)
Terry Halliday—Reese (New Haven, Conn.)
Joel Hall—Hall's (Arlington, Mass.)

D. Halloran—Halloran (St. Louis, Mo.)
Walter Hall—Hall's (Arlington, Mass.)
W. D. Hall—Hall (E. Longmeadow, Mass.)
Samuel Halperin—Holy Land (Washington, D.C.)
Michael Halpern—Halpern (Flushing, N.Y.)
Isaac Halsey—Mechanical (Darien, Conn.)
Lisa Halterman—Reisman (Philadelphia, Pa.)
Bernard Hamel—Hamel (Los Angeles, Calif.)
Ben Hamilton—Hampton (Newberry, S.C.)
Elizabeth Hamilton—Wortman (New York, N.Y.)
Jack Hamilton—Hilton Village (Newport News, Va.)
Jack D. Hamilton—Hamilton's (Williamsburg, Va.)
Muriel P. Hamilton—Hampton (Newberry, S.C.)
Jessica Hammer—Hammer (Santa Barbara, Calif.)
Milton Hammer—Hammer (Santa Barbara, Calif.)
Tom Hamm—C. Dickens (Atlanta, Ga.)
Charles F. Hamsa—G & C (Lafayette, La.)
Jeannette Hand—Hand (Wheeling, W.Va.)
Richard Hand—Hand (Wheeling, W.Va.)
Norman R. Hane—Different (Des Moines, Iowa)
Florence Hanley—Hanley's (Chicago, Ill.)
Teri Hannemann—Hollywood City (Hollywood, Calif.)
Clark B. Hansen—Minnehaha (Minneapolis, Minn.)

ames Hansen—Hansen (Carlsbad, Calif.)
George Harder—Antiques/Art (Seattle, Wash.)
ames Harder—Harder (Los Alamos, N.M.)
Douglas Harding—Harding (Wells, Maine)
Dick Harker—Aviation (Glendale, Calif.)
Donn Harman—Tollett (New York, N.Y.)
David Harmon—Alkahest (Evanston, Ill.)
erry Harper—Harper (Bristol, Vt.)
oyce Harrell—Buteo (Vermillion, S.D.)
ee J. Harrer—Midnight (Clearwater, Fla.)
arbara B. Harris—Harris (Northfield, Mass.)
Doris Harris—Harris (Los Angeles, Calif.)
lmer G. Harris—Harris (Oberlin, Ohio)
red Harris—Frisch (Livingston, N.Y.)
redi Harris—Buddenbrooks (Boston, Mass.)
Margaret Harris—Harris (Rockville, Md.)
obert D. Harris—aGatherin' (Wynantskill, N.Y.)
oberta Harris—Harris (Rockville, Md.)
oger D. Harris—New Engl. (Bennington, Vt.)
homas H. Harris—Harris (Little Rock, Ark.)
elen Harte—Harte (Seattle, Wash.)
Martha Hartman—Book Cellar (Bethesda, Md.)
hris Hartmann—Hartmann (Morganton, N.C.)
eonard H. Hartmann—Philatelic (Louisville, Ky.)
lan S. Harvey—No. Country (Richmond, N.H.)
like Harvey—Kugelman (Denver, Colo.)
arol Harwell—Booketeria (San Antonio, Texas)
aul Harwell—Booketeria (San Antonio, Texas)
Marilyn Hasbrouck—Prairie (Chicago, Ill.)
eorge Hassan—Southwest (Durango, Colo.)
nn Hatchell—Carousel (Tyler, Texas)
like Hatchell—Carousel (Tyler, Texas)
D. Hatch—Hatch (Lenox, Mass.)
ennis Hatman—First (Chicago, Ill.)
obert Hauser—Busyhaus (Mattapoisett, Mass.)
ohn Havemeyer—Havemeyer (Skaneafeles, N.Y.)
ancy Havemeyer—Havemeyer (Skaneafeles, N.Y.)
len Havlak—Bennington (Bennington, Vt.)
ichard Havlak—Bennington (Bennington, Vt.)
ith Hawkins—Hawkins (Alpena, Mich.)
obert L. Hawley—Ross (Albany, Calif.)
onald Hawthorne—Attic (Hodges, S.C.)
onald Hawthorne—Noah's (Greenwood, S.C.)
om Hayden—Wessex (Menlo Park, Calif.)
lian Hayes—Old Emery (Derry, N.H.)
rne Hayman—Hayman (Carey, Ohio)
ob Hayman—Hayman (Carey, Ohio)
ick Hazlett—Quill (Pinellas Park, Fla.)
annelore Headley—Headley (St. Catherines, Ont.)

Robert Head—Book Store (Lewisburg, W.Va.)
Bill Healy—Bibliomania (Schenectady, N.Y.)
Robert Hearn—Bel Canto (Metuchen, N.J.)
Michael Heaston—Heaston (Austin, Texas)
Jack Heath—Heath (Toronto, Ont.)
William R. Hecht—Natural (Scottsdale, Ariz.)
Bruce Heckman—Pages (Mt. Kisco, N.Y.)
John L. Heflin, Jr.—Heflin (Brentwood, Tenn.)
Charles Heindl—Heindl (Rochester, N.Y.)
W. S. Heinman—Heinman (New York, N.Y.)
Margaret Heinoldt—Heinoldt (So. Egg, N.J.)
Theodore Heinoldt—Heinoldt (So. Egg, N.J.)
Ron Hein—Backroom (Webster, N.Y.)
Carol Heise—Chicago (Evanston, Ill.)
Martin Held—Book Guild (Portsmouth, N.H.)
Phyllis Held—Book Guild (Portsmouth, N.H.)
John Hellebrand—Palinurus (Philadelphia, Pa.)
Alexandra Heller—Brick House (Morristown Crnrs., Vt.)
Joshua Heller—Heller (Washington, D.C.)
Phyllis Heller—Heller (Washington, D.C.)
Susan Heller—Heller (Cleveland, Ohio)
C. D. Hellyer—Five Quail (Spring Grove, Minn.)
Judith S. Helms—Doe Run (Cochranville, Pa.)
Judith S. Helms—Chadds (Chadds Ford, Pa.)
Allen Hemlock—Else Fine (Dearborn, Mich.)
Judith A. Henault—Hill Haven (Barton, Vt.)
Cliff Henderson—Bookstock (So. Orleans, Mass.)
Kaye Henderson—Book Gallery (Gainesville, Fla.)
Paul Henderson—Henderson (Nashua, N.H.)
John F. Hendsey—Hendsey (Epping, N.H.)
Ellen Hennessey—Hennesseys (Saratoga Spgs., N.Y.)
Helen L. Hennessey—Hennessey (Santa Monica, Calif.)
Marianne Hennessey—Hennessey (Peconic, N.Y.)
Mark P. Hennessey—Hennessey (Santa Monica, Calif.)
Peter Hennessey—Hennessey (Peconic, N.Y.)
Rowena Henry—In #2 (San Francisco, Calif.)
Ted Henry—Harold's (St. Paul, Minn.)
Martha Henschen—Chickadee (Houston, Texas)
Henry C. Hensel—Hensel (Belle Chasse, La.)
Charles Henson—Atlanta (Atlanta, Ga.)
Dave Henson—Henson (Santa Ana, Calif.)
Jean-Noel Herlin—Herlin (New York, N.Y.)
R. Hermans—Oblong (Millerton, N.Y.)
Norma Herndon—Bookshelf (Billings, Mont.)
G. S. Herron—Herron (Rome, Ga.)

Robert Hershoff—Booklover's (Tucson, Ariz.)
Robert Hershoff—Bookmans (Tucson, Ariz.)
Herman Herst, Jr.—Herst (Boca Raton, Fla.)
William H. Hessel—Hessel (Calimesa, Calif.)
John A. Hess—Hess (Andover, Mass.)
Robert C. Hess—Hess (Brightwaters, N.Y.)
H. T. Hicks—Old Cook. (Haddonfield, N.J.)
Kathleen K. Hicks—Kimbel (Plant City, Fla.)
Ann Hill—Hill (Kingsport, Tenn.)
F. Maynard Hill—Hill (Kingsport, Tenn.)
Jonathan A. Hill—Hill (New York, N.Y.)
Herbert R. Hillman, Jr.—Pangloss (Cambridge, Mass.)
Melville C. Hill—Bunker (Spring Valley, Calif.)
N. Hill—Iroqrafts (Ohsweken, Ont.)
Austin D. Hills—Hills (San Francisco, Calif.)
William W. Hill—Cross Hill (Brunswick, Maine)
Herb Hilscher—Hilscher (Anchorage, Alk.)
Linda Hilton—Athena (Kalamazoo, Mich.)
Mark Hime—Biblioctopus (Idyllwild, Calif.)
Melissa A. Hime—Biblioctopus (Idyllwild, Calif.)
James Hinck—Anchor (Newport, R.I.)
C. J. Hinke—Venkatesa (Tofino, B.C.)
Donald R. Hinks—Obsolescence (Gettysburg, Pa.)
Joan Hinks—Obsolescence (Gettysburg, Pa.)
James A. Hinz—Heller (Swarthmore, Pa.)
Daniel Hirsch—Hirsch (Hopewell Jctn., N.Y.)
Ralph Hirschtritt—Hirschtritt's (Silver Spg., Md.)
Robert A. Hittel—Hittel (Ft. Lauderdale, Fla.)
Ella Hoalk—Memorable (Stone Mtn., Ga.)
George Hoalk—Memorable (Stone Mtn., Ga.)
Allen F. Hobbs—Bebbah (Andover, Kan.)
Betsy Hobbs—Bebbah (Andover, Kan.)
Bill Hobson—Book Fair (W. Palm Beach, Fla.)
Ken Hoch—Alper (Eastchester, N.Y.)
Jim Hodgson—Hodgson (Syracuse, N.Y.)
William Hoffer—Hoffer (Vancouver, B.C.)
Ed Hoffman—Photo (Columbus, Ohio)
Ralph Hoffman—Hoffman (Rillton, Pa.)
Tina Hoffman—Photo (Columbus, Ohio)
Nancy W. Hofmann—Hofmann (So. Orleans, Mass.)
Paul Hogan—Robin's (Philadelphia, Pa.)
Ron Hogeland—Bay Window (Florence, Ore.)
Joseph Holden—Holden (Pasadena, Calif.)
Michael S. Hollander—Hollander (Santa Monica, Calif.)
John Holland—Nautica (Halifax, N.S.)

J. R. Hollingsworth—Amer. SW (Amarillo, Texas)
R. D. Hollingsworth—Amer. SW (Amarillo, Texas)
R. R. Hollingsworth—Amer. SW (Amarillo, Texas)
Marilyn Hollinshead—Pinocchio (Pittsburgh, Pa.)
Gordon Hollis—Golden Legend (Los Angeles, Calif.)
Henry Holman—Gryphon #1 (New York, N.Y.)
Megan Holmberg—Book Stop (Poulsbo, Wash.)
Craig B. Holmes—Old Almanack (Concord, N.H.)
David J. Holmes—Holmes (Philadelphia, Pa.)
J. D. Holmes—Holmes (Edmonds, Wash.)
Theodore J. Holsten, Jr.—Holsten (Excelsior, Minn.)
Maxine Hondeman—Memory (Grand Rapids, Mich.)
Chick Hood—Hood (Lawrence, Kan.)
Frank W. Hood—Red Bridge (Kansas City, Mo.)
John Hood—Hood (Lawrence, Kan.)
Betsy Hook—Hook (Sebastopol, Calif.)
Richard Hooper—Hooper's (Leesburg, Va.)
Kathee Hoover—Academy (Honolulu, Haw.)
Norman T. Hopper—Hopper (Sunnyvale, Calif.)
Ginger C. Horne—Horne (Lakeland, Fla.)
Aaron Horowitz—Horowitz (New York, N.Y.)
Glenn Horowitz—Horowitz (New York, N.Y.)
C. W. Horton, Sr.—White (Granger, Texas)
Keith Hotaling—Treehorn (Santa Rosa, Calif.)
C. A. Hough—Science (Ann Arbor, Mich.)
Michael Houghton—Ben Franklin (U. Nyack, N.Y.)
George Houle—Houle (Los Angeles, Calif.)
Norman Houle—Houle (Durham, N.H.)
J. G. House—House (San Diego, Calif.)
Gary Houseman—Houseman (Yellow Spgs., Ohio)
C. J. Houser—Cellar (Eugene, Ore.)
David A. Hovell—Footnote (Brooklyn, N.Y.)
David Howard—Arader (San Francisco, Calif.)
Hank Howard—Owl (Greenwich, N.Y.)
Peter Howard—Serendipity (Berkeley, Calif.)
Vernon Howard—Howard (Burlingame, Calif.)
Ed Howe—Howe (New York, N.Y.)
Claire C. Howell—Old Books (Brunswick, Maine)
Don Howes—Howes (Brewster, Mass.)
Llewellyn Howland III—Howland (Jamaica Plain, Mass.)
David Howland—Howland (New Canaan, Conn.)
D. Roger Howlett—Childs (Boston, Mass.)
Louise Howton—White (La Jolla, Calif.)
George Hoyt—Hoyt (Rockport, Mass.)
Charles G. Hubbell—World Mtn. (Tacoma, Wash.)
Roberta Huber—Paragon (New York, N.Y.)

I

Garret M. Ihler—CGT (College Stn., Texas)
Orval J. Imel—Imel (Indianapolis, Ind.)
David Ince—Bookstore (Valdosta, Ga.)
David K. Ingalls—Hennessey (Santa Monica, Calif.)
Ruth Inglehart—Hartfield (Ann Arbor, Mich.)
Gabor Inke—GBI (Smithtown, N.Y.)
Jim Iraggi—Book Exch. (Corning, N.Y.)

Sally Irving—Book Barn (Bend, Ore.)
Jean Lutz Isador—Isador (Highland Park, Ill.)
Nancy Isakson—A B I (Santa Barbara, Calif.)
Ken Isbell—Beaver (Portland, Ore.)
David Ishii—Ishii (Seattle, Wash.)
Angelo Iuspa—Iuspa (Newark, N.J.)
Linda Ivey—Ivey (Brewton, Ala.)

J

Jean Jacklin—First Impressions (Wheaton, Ill.)
Ian Jackson—Jackson (Berkeley, Calif.)
Margaret Jackson—Red House (Montgomery, Ala.)
Peter L. Jackson—Jackson (Weston, Ont.)
Rosemarie M. Jackson—Jackson (Weston, Ont.)
Arnold Jacobs—Jacobs (Sherman Oaks, Calif.)
H. Jacobs—Univelt (San Diego, Calif.)
Jerry Jacobs—Lost (Santa Barbara, Calif.)
Alf E. Jacobson—Burpee Hill (New London, N.H.)
Sonja Jacobson—Burpee Hill (New London, N.H.)
R. H. Jacobs—Univelt (San Diego, Calif.)
Christopher Jaeckel—Benjamin (Hunter, N.Y.)
Angeline Jaep—Bayshore (Van Nuys, Calif.)
Roger Jaep—Bayshore (Van Nuys, Calif.)
David Jaffe—Jaffe (Arlington, Va.)
James Jaffe—Jaffe (Haverford, Pa.)
Keith Jaggard—Old Books (New Orleans, La.)
Janice M. James—Jeltrups' St. Croix, V.I.)
Stephen M. James—James (Lynden, Wash.)
H. Fred Janson—Pomona (Rockton, Ont.)
Walda Janson—Pomona (Rockton, Ont.)
Lucie Javitch—Javitch (Montreal, Que.)
John M. Jeffrey—Recovery (Greensboro, Vt.)
Mary Anne Jeffrey—Recovery (Greensboro, Vt.)
Dennis E. Jellam—Dennis (Seattle, Wash.)
S. H. Jenike—Dust Jacket (Cincinnati, Ohio)
Thomas Jenison—Jenison's (Canton, N.Y.)
John Jenkins—Jenkins (Austin, Texas)
Matthew Jennett—Pharos (New Haven, Conn.)
Sheila Jennett—Pharos (New Haven, Conn.)
Edgar Jepson—Book Forum (Denver, Colo.)
Lawrence W. Jerome—No. Mtn. (Phoenix, Ariz.)
Jon B. Johansen—Maritime (Brewer, Maine)

Timothy Johns—Cummins (New York, N.Y.)
Ann Johnson—Bonaventura (Evergreen, Colo.)
Betty Johnson—Johnson (No. Bennington, Vt.)
Bruce Johnson—Johnson (Syracuse, N.Y.)
Chris Johnson—Edmunds (Hollywood, Calif.)
Colman C. Johnson—Bookcase (Cambridge, Mass.)
Dale Johnson—Fantasy (Carmichael, Calif.)
Dorothy A. Johnson—Common Reader (New Salem, Mass.)
Greg Johnson—Old Town (Tempe, Ariz.)
Gregory Johnson—Bethlehem (Bethlehem, Conn.)
Harmer Johnson—Johnson (New York, N.Y.)
J. O. Johnson, Jr.—Johnson (Waltham, Mass.)
Lauren Johnson—Burke's (Memphis, Tenn.)
Mary Ellen Johnson—Whistles (Rossville, Ga.)
Robert L. Johnson—Bookcase (Cambridge, Mass.)
Robert L. Johnson—Whistles (Rossville, Ga.)
Roy Johnson—Limelight (San Francisco, Calif.)
Velma Johnson—Johnson (Promise City, Iowa)
Wanda M. Johnson—Bookcase (Cambridge, Mass.)
William S. Johnson—Johnson (Indianapolis, Ind.)
David Jolly—Jolly (Brookline, Mass.)
Bradley Jonas—Powell's (Chicago, Ill.)
Edward Jonas—Berkley (Berkley, Minn.)
Bob Jones—Book Cellar (Temple, Texas)
Charlie Jones—Good News (Rossville, Ind.)
Drusilla P. Jones—Drusilla's (Baltimore, Md.)
Jean C. Jones—Jones (Washington, D.C.)
John Jones—Rancho (Santa Monica, Calif.)
Ken Jones—Good News (Rossville, Ind.)
Laura Jones—Jones (Washington, D.C.)
Florence Jordan—Jordan (Philadelphia, Pa.)
Milton Jordan—Backlot (Oberlin, Ohio)

Jane Jorgensen—Blue Moon (Clearwater, Fla.)
Sher Joseph—Heartwood (Charlottesville, Va.)
Shirley Josephs—Atticus (Toronto, Ont.)
Frank Joslin—Joslin (Springfield, Mass.)
Mary Joyce—Phoenix (Royal Oak, Mich.)
Moira Joyce—3 Geese (Woodstock, N.Y.)

Thomas J. Joyce—Joyce (Chicago, Ill.)
Jesse Judnick—Bolerium (San Francisco, Calif.)
Paul Jung—Baldwin's (W. Chester, Pa.)
Robert Juran—Running (Pittsfield, Mass.)
Hartwin W. Just—Just (Milwaukee, Wisc.)
Priscilla Juvelis—Juvelis (Boston, Mass.)

K

Robert F. Kadlec—Abacus (Santa Fe, N.M.)
Gerald Kahan—Theatricana (Athens, Ga.)
Helen R. Kahn—Kahn (Montreal, Que.)
Lillian Kaiser—Kaiser (Santa Cruz, Calif.)
Lillian Kaiser—Chimney (Scotts Valley, Calif.)
Mary Lou Kalanja—Talvin (Trafford, Pa.)
Robert A. Kalanja—Talvin (Trafford, Pa.)
Robert J. Kalanja—Kalanja (Trafford, Pa.)
Robert J. Kalanja—Talvin (Trafford, Pa.)
Joseph Kaminksy—Appelfeld (New York, N.Y.)
Maxine Kam—Kam (Philadelphia, Pa.)
Michael Kam—Kam (Philadelphia, Pa.)
Robert Kanatous—Binkin's (Brooklyn, N.Y.)
Gary Kane—Americanist (Pottstown, Pa.)
George Robert Kane—Kane (Santa Cruz, Calif.)
Michal Kane—Americanist (Pottstown, Pa.)
Norman Kane—Americanist (Pottstown, Pa.)
Joseph L. Kapica—Kapica (New Britain, Conn.)
Lee Kaplan—Arcana (Santa Monica, Calif.)
Maxine Kaplan—Kaplan (New York, N.Y.)
Mildred F. Kaplan—Arte Prim. (New York, N.Y.)
Stuart R. Kaplan—U.S. Games (New York, N.Y.)
J. Karcz—Pages #1 (Green Bay, Wisc.)
M. Karcz—Pages #1 (Green Bay, Wisc.)
Charlotte Karin—Chirurgical (Baltimore, Md.)
Kenneth Karmiole—Karmiole (Santa Monica, Calif.)
Howard Karno—Karno (Santa Monica, Calif.)
Jason Karp—Earl (Clarendon, N.Y.)
Jeanne Kartz—Pages #2 (Green Bay, Wisc.)
John Kashmanian—Kashmanian (No. Providence, R.I.)
Melvin Katsh—Melvins (Grt. Barrington, Mass.)
Ms. Dudley Katt—Hive (Easton, Pa.)
Elliot M. Katt—Katt (Los Angeles, Calif.)
Adele Katz—Book Barn (Miami, Fla.)
Alvin M. Katz—Continental (New York, N. Y.)
Jane Katzberg—Golden Age (Dix Hills, N.Y.)

Ron Katzberg—Golden Age (Dix Hills, N.Y.)
Elaine Katz—Katz (Seattle, Wash.)
Samuel W. Katz—Katz (Los Angeles, Calif.)
Kim Kaufman—Kaufman (New York, N.Y.)
Ruby D. Kaufman—Kaufman (Tempe, Ariz.)
Edward J. Kearin—Kearin (Goldens Bridge, N.Y.)
Robert Kearney—Anglican (Saratoga Spgs., N.Y.)
Barbara Keck—Keck (Alexandria, Va.)
Dorothy V. Keck—Keck (Decatur, Ill.)
John H. Keck—Traveller (Laredo, Texas)
Mike Keck—Keck (Alexandria, Va.)
Donald J. Keeler—Keeler (No. Monmouth, Maine)
Joyce B. Keeler—Keeler (No. Monmouth, Maine)
Robert Keene—Keene (Southampton, N.Y.)
William Keifer—John Steele (Litchfield, Conn.)
Eileen Keiter—Batchelder (Ambler, Pa.)
Mrs. Edmond Keith—Book Search (Avondale Estates, Ga.)
Edmond D. Keith—Book Search (Avondale Estates, Ga.)
Quentin Keith—Keith (Red Bank, N.J.)
Frank Kellel, Jr.—Book Mart (San Antonio, Texas)
Dr. Frank Kellel—Book Annex (San Antonio, Texas)
Lois M. Kellel—Book Mart (San Antonio, Texas)
Robert F. Kellel—Book Mart (San Antonio, Texas)
George Keller—Keller (Overland Park, Kan.)
Augustus M. Kelley—Theophrastus (Little Compton, R.I.)
Doreen Kelley—Book Vault (Beaverton, Ore.)
Eric Kelley—Book Den (Santa Barbara, Calif.)
Susan C. Kelley—Chamberlin (E. Orleans, Mass.)
Cesi Kellinger—Kellinger (Chambersburg, Pa.)
Helen Kelly—Boston Annex (Boston, Mass.)
Irene Kelly—Lion (Indianapolis, Ind.)
Lowell Kelly—Blue Moon (Clearwater, Fla.)
Martha Kelly—Gutenberg's (Rochester, N.Y.)
Aubyn Kendall—Limestone (Glen Rose, Texas)

Lyle Harris Kendall, Jr.—Limestone (Glen Rose, Texas)
George Kennedy—Maxwell's (Lima, N.Y.)
Richard T. Kennedy—Kennedy (Des Moines, Wash.)
Ruth Kennedy—Maxwell's (Lima, N.Y.)
Kristin Kennell—Elliot Bay (Seattle, Wash.)
Harry E. Kenney, Jr.—Homestead (Marlborough, N.H.)
Constance Kenney—Homestead (Marlborough, N.H.)
Ed Kenney—Audubon (Vienna, Va.)
Robert J. Kenney—Homestead (Marlborough, N.H.)
Ann S. Kent—Village (Rumney Village, N.H.)
George N. Kent—Village (Rumney Village, N.H.)
Robert Kent—Pell's (Delray Bch., Fla.)
Ellyn Kern—Cottontail (Bennington, Ind.)
Ruth Kern—Kern (Glendale, Ariz.)
Cory Kerns—Bookery (Ithaca, N.Y.)
Alton Ketchum—Harrington's (Cos Cob, Conn.)
Craig H. Keyston—Holmes (Oakland, Calif.)
David Kherdian—Abintra (Morris, N.Y.)
Ann Kidd—Norman (San Francisco, Calif.)
M. Kilen—No. Woods (Duluth, Minn.)
Clark Kimball—Grt. Southwest (Santa Fe, N.M.)
Raymond Kimeldorf—Kimeldorf (Portland, Ore.)
Larry Kimmich—Book Shop (Walnut Creek, Calif.)
David M. King—Rolls (Rockville Centre, N.Y.)
John King—Bygone (Dearborn, Mich.)
John K. King—King (Detroit, Mich.)
Adrian King-Edwards—Word (Montreal, Que.)
Russ Kingman—Jack London (Glen Ellen, Calif.)
Winnie Kingman—Jack London (Glen Ellen, Calif.)
Ebba Kingstrom—Kingstrom (Sacred Heart, Minn.)
Virginia King—Book Barn (Rochester, Mich.)
Harold E. Kinney—The Bookie (E. Hartford, Conn.)
Ernest J. Kionke—Kionke (Gowanda, N.Y.)
Lee Kionke—Kionke (Gowanda, N.Y.)
Steve Kirch—Kirch (Thornville, Ohio)
Leland H. Kirk—Cabinet/Books (Watertown, Conn.)
Suzanne H. Kirk—Cabinet/Books (Watertown, Conn.)
David Kirschenbaum—Carnegie (New York, N.Y.)
Yoshio Kishi—Asian Amer. (New York, N.Y.)
Yoshio Kishi—Kishi (New York, N.Y.)
Judy Kisling—Wildlife (Gainesville, Fla.)
Vernon Kisling—Wildlife (Gainesville, Fla.)
Paul Kisselberg—Harold's (St. Paul, Minn.)
James A. Kissko—Camelot (Baltimore, Md.)
Dr. David Klappholz—Heliochrome (Berkeley Hgts., N.J.)
Lance J. Klass—Klass (Santa Barbara, Calif.)
Bernie Klay—Sea (Glen Oaks, N.Y.)
Barbara Kleckley—C. Dickens (Atlanta, Ga.)
Anne Klein—Caravan-Maritime (Jamaica, N.Y.)
Frank S. Klein—Bookseller (Akron, Ohio)
Joyce Klein—Klein (Oak Park, Ill.)
R. G. Klein—Wall (Los Angeles, Calif.)
Robert E. Klein—Johnson's (Los Angeles, Calif.)
Gail Klemm—Klemm (Apple Valley, Calif.)
Judith Klemperer—Klemperer (New York, N.Y.)
Peter Klemperer—Klemperer (New York, N.Y.)
Frances Klenett—Klenett (Brooklyn, N.Y.)
Eric Chaim Kline—Morrison (Santa Monica, Calif.)
Joyce Knauer—Tattered Cover (Denver, Colo.)
Terence M. Knaus—Knaus (Ft. Bragg, Calif.)
Peter B. Knights—Knights (Harwich Port, Mass.)
Yvonne Knight—St. Nicholas (Toronto, Ont.)
Ron Knox—Books/Falls (Derby, Conn.)
Patrick Knupp—Ramshorn (Albuquerque, N.M.)
Jo Koch—Calderwoods (Long Valley, N.J.)
John Koelbel—Little (Missoula, Mont.)
Alexandra Koenig—Country (Plainfield, Vt.)
Benjamin Koenig—Country (Plainfield, Vt.)
Dixie Koenig—Bookmark (Prosser, Wash.)
Duronda Koenig—Book Room (Coral Gables, Fla.)
Glenn Koenig—Bookmark (Prosser, Wash.)
Pat Koerber—Abstract (Indianapolis, Ind.)
Roger Koerber—Koerber (Southfield, Mich.)
Michael M. Kohler—On The (Chambersburg, Pa.)
Louis Kohn—Arrow (Philadelphia, Pa.)
George F. Kolbe—Kolbe (Crestline, Calif.)
Anatole Kondratieff—Inner Circle (New York, N.Y.)
Jocelyn Konigsmark—Konigsmark (Wayne, Pa.)
Pam Konschu—Western (Gaston, Ore.)
Jeanne Kontoleon—Fourth Estate (New London, Conn.)
Howard Kopelson—Kaplan (New York, N.Y.)
Bruce Kopet—Book-O-Rama (Queens Vill., N.Y.)
Stephen Koschal—Koschal (Verona, N.J.)
Laurie Koselke—Bookworm (Wanatah, Ind.)
Nicole Kostean—Museum (New York, N.Y.)
Wayne G. Kostman—Kostman (Glendora, Calif.)
Malcolm Kottler—Scientia (Arlington, Mass.)
June Kraeft—June 1 (Bethlehem, Conn.)
Norman Kraeft—June 1 (Bethlehem, Conn.)
Valerie Kraft—Kraft (Palm Desert, Calif.)
Eric Kramer—Fantasy (New York, N.Y.)
Linda Kramer—Paragon (New York, N.Y.)

Melvin Krapola—Cummins (New York, N.Y.)
E. Krastin—Barnstable (New York, N.Y.)
Charlotte Krause—Krause (Warrington, Fla.)
Evelyn Kraus—Ursus Prints (New York, N.Y.)
Hans P. Kraus—Kraus (New York, N.Y.)
T. Peter Kraus—Ursus (New York, N.Y.)
Ruth Kravette—Kravette (Jericho, N.Y.)
Kenneth L. Kregel—Kregel's (Grand Rapids, Mich.)
Robert L. Kregel—Kregel's (Grand Rapids, Mich.)
Edward L. Kreinheder—Kreinheder (Warrensburg, N.Y.)
Pearl Kreinheder—Kreinheder (Warrensburg, N.Y.)
Lillian Krelove—Legacy (Hatboro, Pa.)
Bernhard J. Kress—Kress (Hewitt, N.J.)
Richard Krieg—Blitz (Weaverville, Calif.)
Madeline Kripke—Kripke (New York, N.Y.)

Cummings Kristen—Cummings (Stillwater, Minn.)
Ralph Kristiansen—Kristiansen (Boston, Mass.)
Leni J. Kroul—Cragsmoor (Cragsmoor, N.Y.)
Genevieve Krueger—Krueger (Sunland, Calif.)
Philip Krumm—Clipper Ship (San Antonio, Texas)
Owen D. Kubik—Kubik (Dayton, Ohio)
John W. Kuehn—Kuehn (Bisbee, Ariz.)
Irena Kuharets—Russica (New York, N.Y.)
W. Kunz—Merriwell (Islip, N.Y.)
Tom Kuo—Kuo (Atlanta, Ga.)
Sheldon Kurland—Barrister (Davie, Fla.)
Dorothy Kuslan—Bookcell (Hamden, Conn.)
Louis Kuslan—Bookcell (Hamden, Conn.)
A. Kutz—Lift (Brockport, N.Y.)
C. S. Kuzbik—Reliable (Paterson, N.J.)

L

Elizabeth Labandwski—Norumbega (Houston, Texas)
Louise Lachapelle—Guerin (Montreal, Que.)
Annette S. Ladner—Ladner (Whitneyville, Conn.)
David Ladner—Ladner (Whitneyville, Conn.)
Franc Ladner—Ladner (Orleans, Mass.)
Nan Laird—Laird (Chicago, Ill.)
Donald Lake—Lake (Toronto, Ont.)
Elaine Lake—Lake (Toronto, Ont.)
Joan Lake—Bloomsbury (Denver, Colo.)
Margaret Lake—Bloomsbury (Denver, Colo.)
Sandra Lake—Lake (Toronto, Ont.)
Mary Lak—Johnson's (Springfield, Mass.)
Alan Lambert—Old Benn. (Hancock, N.H.)
Alan Lambert—Lambert (Hancock, N.H.)
Carol Lambert—Lambert (Mission Hills, Calif.)
Deece Lambert—Lambert (Hancock, N.H.)
Deece Lambert—Old Benn. (Hancock, N.H.)
Maggie Lambeth—Lambeth (San Antonio, Texas)
Dick Lamoureux—Oriole (Fremont, Calif.)
April LaMoy—Village (Hudson Falls, N.Y.)
Richard Lan—Martayan (New York, N. Y.)
Jim Lance—Amer. Frag. (Escondido, Calif.)
Joseph Landau—Jamaica (Jamaica, N.Y.)
Claudia Landfried—Aardvarks (Orlando, Fla.)
Paul Landfried—Aardvarks (Orlando, Fla.)
Christopher Lane—Phila. Print (Philadelphia, Pa.)
Jerry Lane—Emerson-Lane (Albuquerque, N.M.)

Kenneth Lang—Lang (Amityville, N.Y.)
Anne M. Lange—Katonah (Katonah, N.Y.)
Martin Langer—Marlowe's (Boston, Mass.)
Nanci Langley—Associates (Falls Church, Va.)
Robert C. Langmuir, Jr.—Book Mark (Philadelphia, Pa.)
Richard M. Langworth—Churchill (Contoocook, N.H.)
Lucille Lansford—Lansford (Powersville, Ga.)
O. G. Lansford—Lansford (Powersville, Ga.)
Karen La Porte—Silver (Redondo Bch., Calif.)
Jean A. Larkin—Storeybook (Sycamore, Ill.)
Jennifer S. Larson—Yerba (San Francisco, Calif.)
John Larson—Old Book (Fairlee, Vt.)
James L. Lasley—Lasley (Berkeley, Ill.)
Rose Ann Lasley—Lasley (Berkeley, Ill.)
Larry D. Laster—Laster (Winston-Salem, N.C.)
Susan G. Laster—Laster (Winston-Salem, N.C.)
Martin Last—Sci Fict. (New York, N.Y.)
Salvatore M Latona—East West (Hamburg, N.Y.)
Valerie Latona—East West (Hamburg, N.Y.)
Louis Laub—Laub (Berkeley, Calif.)
Louis Laub—Invisible (Berkeley, Calif.)
Karen Laughlin—El-Zar (Cedar Rapids, Iowa)
James Laurie—Laurie (St. Paul, Minn.)
Mary Laurie—Laurie (St. Paul, Minn.)
Larry Lawrence—Lawrence (New York, N.Y.)
Russ Lawrence—Chapter 1 (Hamilton, Mont.)

Larry Laws—Laws (Chicago, Ill.)
William Laws—Truepenny (Tucson, Ariz.)
James L. Lawton—Brookline (Brookline, Mass.)
David A. Lawyer—Lawyer (Plains, Mont.)
Kathleen Lazare—Pansy (St. Andrews, N.B.) and
    Scarlet Letter (New Milford, Conn.)
Michael Lazare—Pansy (St. Andrews, N.B.) and
    Scarlet Letter (New Milford, Conn.)
Carole Lazarus—Paper (So. Euclid, Ohio)
Herb Lazarus—Lazarus (Ossining, N.Y.)
Kenneth Leach—Leach (Brattleboro, Vt.)
Shirley Lebo—Lebo (Washington, D.C.)
Michael Lebowitz—Mt. Zion (Mt. Zion, W.Va.)
Linda Lebsack—Rosenstock (Denver, Colo.)
Rupert LeCraw—Oxford (Atlanta, Ga.)
Mary Lederer—Constant Reader (Denver, Colo.)
Patricia Ledlie—Ledlie (Buckfield, Maine)
Al Ledoux—All Books (Miami, Fla.)
Nguy Lee—Michael's (Okla. City, Okla.)
Jerry Leedy—Book Fair (Eugene, Ore.)
Brian Leekley—Leekley (Winthrop Harbor, Ill.)
Evelyn Leekley—Leekley (Winthrop Harbor, Ill.)
Edward J. Lefkowicz—Lefkowicz (Fairhaven, Mass.)
Marion Legsdin—Rainy (Fitzwilliam, N.H.)
Janet Lehr—Lehr (New York, N.Y.)
T. Leibovitz—Ballet (New York, N.Y.)
Barbara Leibowits—Leibowits (New York, N.Y.)
James G. Leishman—Leishman (Menlo Park, Calif.)
David Lemmo—Holmes (San Francisco, Calif.)
Charles Lenteria—Link (Redding, Calif.)
Evelyn Lenz—Evlen (Centerport, N.Y.)
George R. Lenz—Evlen (Centerport, N.Y.)
Lawrence A. Leo—Leo (Toledo, Ohio)
Blanche Leonardo—Vegetarian (Santa Monica,
    Calif.)
Jennifer Lerew—Edmunds (Hollywood, Calif.)
Herb Levart—Levart (Hartsdale, N.Y.)
Jack R. Levien—Levien (McDowell, Va.)
Barry R. Levin—Levin (Los Angeles, Calif.)
Sally Ann Levin—Levin (Los Angeles, Calif.)
Sylvia Levin—Janus (Corea, Maine and Huntington
    Stn., N.Y.)
Jacqueline Levine—Levine (Savannah, Ga.)
Joan Levine—Levine's (Shokan, N.Y.) and Editions
    (Boiceville, N.Y.)
Norman Levine—Levine's (Shokan, N.Y.) and Edi-
    tions (Boiceville, N.Y.)
Sonja Levinger—Theater (Palo Alto, Calif.)
Harry Levinson—Levinson (Beverly Hills, Calif.)

Ruth Lew—Battery (Forest Hills, N.Y.)
George Lewis—Lewis (Mamaroneck, N.Y.)
Kenneth M. Lewis—Ken-L (Newberg, Ore.)
Nancy Lewis—Mill (Craftsbury Common, Vt.)
Ralph Lewis—Mill (Craftsbury Common, Vt.)
R. E. Lewis—Lewis (San Rafael, Calif.)
Wright Lewis—Green Dolphin (Portland, Ore.)
Susan W. Liebegott—Enchanted (Brooklyn, N.Y.)
Ronald Lieberman—Family Album (Glen Rock,
    Pa.)
Leland N. Lien—Lien (Minneapolis, Minn.)
Rae T. Lien—Lien (Minneapolis, Minn.)
Valerie D. Lien—Lien (Minneapolis, Minn.)
Joe Lihach—Comic (New York, N.Y.)
Cathy Lilburne—Antipodean (Cold Spg., N.Y.)
David Lilburne—Antipodean (Cold Spg., N.Y.)
Sandy Lillydahl—Sophia (Amherst, Mass.)
Wade Lillywhite—Deseret (Salt Lake City, Utah)
Charlotte Lindsey—Poor Farm (W. Cornwall, Conn.)
Dick Lindsey—Poor Farm (W. Cornwall, Conn.)
Jim Lindstrom—Bargain (San Diego, Calif.)
Nancy Lindstrom—Bargain (San Diego, Calif.)
Joyce Link—Lincoln (San Jose, Calif.)
Robert Loren Link—Link (Redding, Calif.)
George Linthicum—Linthicum (Tacoma, Wash.)
Bill Lippincott—Lippincott (Bangor, Maine)
Sharon S. Lips—Librarium (E. Chatham, N.Y.)
Beverly Lishner—Karno (Santa Monica, Calif.)
Kathy Lisiewski—Traveler (Union, Conn.)
Christine Liska—Colophon (Epping, N.H.)
Robert Liska—Colophon (Epping, N.H.)
Marion Littlewood—Littlewoods (Waukesha, Wisc.)
William Littlewood—Littlewoods (Waukesha, Wisc.)
Nancy Littrup—Littrup (Bay City, Mich.)
Charles Lloyd—Lloyd (Red Bank, N.J.) and
    Washington (Washington Cr., Pa.)
Stacy B. Lloyd—Lloyd (Washington, D.C.)
Tod Loberg—Badger (Appleton, Wisc.)
Paul Lockwood—Abelard (Toronto, Ont.)
Bill Loeser—Bookshop (Chapel Hill, N. C.)
Leo Loewenthal—Loewenthal (Dover, N.J.)
Stephen Loewentheil—19th Cent. (Baltimore, Md.)
William Loewy—Loewy (Tallman, N.Y.)
Sal Lombardo—Lombardo (Shoreham, N.Y.)
Dee Longenbaugh—Observatory (Sitka, Alk.)
Judith R. Long—Long (Marietta, Ga.)
M. Sally Long—Seashell (Bayside, Calif.)
Steven J. Long—Seashell (Bayside, Calif.)
Jan Longons—Wine (Ann Arbor, Mich.)

Karen Loome—Loome (Stillwater, Minn.)
Thomas Loome—Loome (Stillwater, Minn.)
Richard S. Loomis, Jr.—Sumner (Yarmouth, Maine)
Ken Lopez—Lopez (Hadley, Mass.)
Michael W. Lora—Burley/Books (Toledo, Ohio)
Bill Lorenz—Associated (Long Beach, Calif.)
Edna Lorenz—Associated (Long Beach, Calif.)
James Lorson—Lorson's (Fullerton, Calif.)
Joan Lorson—Lorson's (Fullerton, Calif.)
Arthur Louis—Phoenix (Plainview, N.J.)
Jean Louis—Phoenix (Plainview, N.J.)
George Loukides—Old Mill (Alexandria, Va.)
Charles Lovett—Lovett (Winston-Salem, N.C.)
David A. Lovett—President's (Washington, D.C.)
Stephanie Lovett—Lovett (Winston-Salem, N.C.)
Derek Lowe—Lowe (Eastsound, Wash.)
James Lowe—Lowe (New York, N.Y.)
Samuel L. Lowe, Jr.—Lowe (Boston, Mass.)
Carlton Lowenberg—Lowenberg (Lafayette, Calif.)
David H. Lowenherz—Lion (New York, N.Y.)
Richard A. Lowenstein—Bankside (Westport, Conn.)
Matt Lowman—Brick Row (San Francisco, Calif.)
Judith Lowry—Argosy (New York, N.Y.)
Philip Lozinski—Lozinski (Westport, Mass.)
Phil Luboviski—Edmunds (Hollywood, Calif.)
John Lubrano—Lubrano (So. Lee, Mass.)
Jude Lubrano—Lubrano (So. Lee, Mass.)
Anne Lubrecht—Lubrecht (Forestburgh, N.Y.)

Harry Lubrecht—Lubrecht (Forestburgh, N.Y.)
Alexander Lucas—Lucas (Fairfield, Conn.)
Bonnie Lucas—Mermaid (Oakland, Calif.)
Kathleen P. Lucas—Lucas (Fairfield, Conn.)
Robert F. Lucas—Lucas (Blandford, Mass.)
Edna Luckman—Gambler's (Las Vegas, Nev.)
Al Luckton—Poe (Mayaguez, P.R.)
Maria Luckton—Poe (Mayaguez, P.R.)
Herbert A. Luft—Luft (Oakland Gdns., N.Y.)
Phyllis M. Lumb—Lumb (Somersville, Conn.)
Stephen C. Lunsford—Lunsford (No. Vancouver, B.C.)
Bob Lurate—Lurate (Jackson, Miss.)
Carol Lurate—Lurate (Jackson, Miss.)
Paul W. Luther—Astronomy (Bernardston, Mass.)
Talmage N. Luther—Luther (Taos, N.M.)
Hank Luttrell—20th Century (Madison, Wisc.)
Jordan D. Luttrell—Meyer (San Francisco, Calif.)
A. Lutwak—Ideal (New York, N. Y.)
Bob Lutz—Lutz (Washington C. H., Ohio)
Doris Lutz—Lutz (Washington C. H., Ohio)
Philip Lyman—Gotham (New York, N.Y.)
Bonita Lynch—Lynch (Sepulveda, Calif.)
P. J. Lynch—Sackheim (Tucson, Ariz.)
Austin Lynn—Lynn (Worthington, Ohio)
Jean Lynn—Lynn (Worthington, Ohio)
Burton Lysecki—Lysecki (Winnipeg, Man.)

M

Kevin Mac Donnell—Mac Donnell (Austin, Texas)
Thomas P. Macaluso—Macaluso (Kennett Sq., Pa.)
L. Page MacCubbin—Earthworks (Washington, D.C.)
Andrew MacDonald—2nd Story (Washington, D.C.)
Elinor MacDonald—Island (Mercer, Wash.)
Mary Lee MacDonald—Schooner (Halifax, N.S.)
Thomas L. MacDonald—MacDonald's (Eustis, Maine)
Thomas P. MacDonnell—Stevens (Williamsburg, Va.)
Amy MacEwen—Victorian (Stockton Spgs., Maine)
Andrew MacEwen—Book Barn (Stockton Spgs., Maine)
Mark Maciag—Books/Falls (Derby, Conn.)

Russel MacKendrick—MacKendrick (Manchester, Conn.)
Mary Mackensen—Mackensen (Lake San Marcos, Calif.)
Carolyn R. Mackie—Old Geog. (Sparks, Md.)
Jerry Mack—Info (San Angelo, Texas)
Dick Macksey—Macksey (Baltimore, Md.)
Jinnee Macomber—Barn Owl (Wellesley, Mass.)
Jerry Madden—Campfire (Evansville, Ind.)
Lawrence E. Madole—Trackside (Houston, Texas)
Jack Magune—House (Worcester, Mass.)
Francis Mahard—Mahard (Sherborn, Mass.)
James J. Mahoney—Liberty (Sloatsburg, N.Y.)
Ron Mahoney—Air Age (Tollhouse, Calif.)
Virginia M. Mahoney—Liberty (Sloatsburg, N.Y.)
John F. Mahony—Wise (Baldwin Pl., N.Y.)

Robert Maier—Maier (Rockport, Mass.)

Virginia Malbin—Invisible (Berkeley, Calif.)

Patrick Mallahan—Mallahan (Bellevue, Wash.)

E. H. Mallory—Mallory (Van Nuys, Calif.)

Carol Maltby—Wilsey (Olivebridge, N.Y.)

F. J. Manasek—Manasek (Hanover, N.H.) and Manasek (Norwich, Vt.)

Jeffrey Mancevice—Mancevice (Worcester, Mass.)

Margaret Manlove—Owl (Bryn Mawr, Pa.)

Margaret Mannatt—Mannatt (San Diego, Calif.)

Kathleen Manning—Manning's (San Francisco, Calif.)

Melvin Marcher—Marcher (Okla. City, Okla.)

Liz Marcucci—Hillman (New York, N.Y.)

Glenn Marcus—Dragon's Lair (Dayton, Ohio)

Bente Margenat—Calico Cat (Ventura, Calif.)

Bernard A. Margolis—Margolis (Monroe, Mich.)

David Margolis—Margolis (Santa Fe, N.M.)

Victor Margolis—Words (San Deigo, Calif.)

Robert Mariardi—Magazine (San Francisco, Calif.)

Elizabeth Marks—Waldo (Rockton, Ill.)

Jeffrey H. Marks—Marks (Rochester, N.Y.)

Robb Marks—Waldo (Rockton, Ill.)

Mark Marlow—Valley (No. Hollywood, Calif.)

Joe Marshall—Ballet (New York, N.Y.)

Sheila Marshall—Shire (Franklin, Mass.)

Wayne Marshall—Shire (Franklin, Mass.)

M. L. Marston—Guerrera (Lawrence, Mass.)

Seyla Martayan—Martayan (New York, N. Y.)

Charles Martignette—Martignette (Boston, Mass.)

Patricia Martinak-Harmon—Alkahest (Evanston, Ill.)

Dolores Martin—Bargain (Long Beach, Calif.)

Carlos Martinez—Cinema (Hollywood, Calif.)

Joe Martinez—Cinema (Hollywood, Calif.)

Jessie Martin—Village (Amherst, N.Y.)

John Wm. Martin—Martin (La Grange, Ill.)

Kenneth Martin—Martin's (Fairbanks, Alk.)

Marie Martin—Martin's (Fairbanks, Alk.)

Robert J. Martin—Martin (Atlanta, Ga.)

Walter Martin—Chimera (Palo Alto, Calif.)

Mary J. Mart—Good Times (Pt. Jefferson, N.Y.)

Michael A. Mart—Good Times (Pt. Jefferson, N.Y.)

Jessie Marvin—Village (Rochester, N.Y.)

Evan Marx—Bookmarx (Roslyn, N.Y.)

Stan Marx—Bookmarx (Roslyn, N.Y.)

Jan Mashman—Mashman (Ridgefield, Conn.)

Peter L. Masi—Masi (Montague, Mass.)

David Mason—Mason (Toronto, Ont.)

Harold J. Mason—Mason (Phoenix, Ariz.)

Jon Mason—Mason's (Wabash, Ind.)

Karl Matsushita—Books America (San Francisco, Calif.)

Jean Mattern—Deeds (Ellicott City, Md.)

Alta Matthews—Alta's (Sonora, Calif.)

Jean Matthews—Chapter 1 (Hamilton, Mont.)

William Matthews—Matthews (Ft. Erie, Ont.)

Robert W. Mattila—Mattila (Seattle, Wash.)

Leslie Mauck—Tin Can (Arcata, Calif.)

William Mauck—Tin Can (Arcata, Calif.)

Rosemary Maurice—Cover/Cover (Ft. Myers, Fla.)

Timothy Mawson—Mawson (New Preston, Conn.)

Lawrence R. Maxwell—Einhorn (New York, N.Y.)

Wendi Maxwell—Maxwell's (Stockton, Calif.)

William Maxwell—Maxwell's (Stockton, Calif.)

Charles Mayer—New Miner (Necedah, Wisc.)

Fran Mayer—Mechanical (Darien, Conn.)

I. Y. Mayer—Hive (Easton, Pa.)

Marie Mayer—Bookmine (Old Scaramento, Calif.)

Oliver Mayer—Hive (Easton, Pa.)

Steve Mayer—Bookmine (Old Scaramento, Calif.)

Lou Maynard—Maynard's (Pasadena, Calif.)

Jon H. Mayo—Tuttle (Ruthland, Vt.)

Howard McAbee—Old N.Y. (Atlanta, Ga.)

Sandy McAdams—Daedalus (Charlottesville, Va.)

Philip McBlain—McBlain (Hamden, Conn.)

Sharon McBlain—McBlain (Hamden, Conn.)

Bill McBride—Jumping and McBride (both Hartford, Conn.)

Mike McCabe—Lion's (Salisbury, Conn.)

Vincent McCaffrey—Avenue (Boston, Mass.)

Clifford McCarty—Boulevard (Topanga, Calif.)

Jean McCarty—Griffith (Griffith, Ind.)

Romilda McCarty—McCarty (Cincinnati, Ohio)

Albert McCasey—Used (Dyer, Ind.)

William D. McCaskie—Staten (Harwich, Mass.)

Boyce E. McCaslin—McCaslin (Ironton, Mo.)

K. H. McClure—Sportsman's (Manotick, Ont.)

W. A. McClure—Sportsman's (Manotick, Ont.)

Philip C. McComish—Watermark (Wichita, Kan.)

Shirley McCormick—Booksville (Montrose, Calif.)

Della Kay McCulloch—First Edtn. (Tulsa, Okla.)

Larry McCullough—McCullough (Los Angeles, Calif.)

Whitney McDermut—McDermut (Montvale, N.J.)

Francis J. McDonald—McDonald's (Catskill, N.Y.)

Viola McDonald—Rodden's (Long Bch., Calif.)

William McDonnell—Sebastopol (Sebastopol, Calif.)

Cassandra McDonough—Federation (College St.,

Texas)
Nancy McDougall—Book Den (Ft. Myers, Fla.)
Kevin T. McEneaney—Facsimile (New York, N.Y.)
C. S. McFarland—McFarland (Tampa, Fla.)
Patrick McGahern—McGahern (Ottawa, Ont.)
Ollie McGarrh—Ollie's (Memphis, Tenn.)
Pat McGarvey—Manuscript (Southampton, Pa.), Medical (Jenkintown, Pa.), and Manor, Mystery, and Modern (all Huntington Valley, Pa.)
Lawrence McGill—McGill (New City, N.Y.)
Geraldine McGilvery—McGilvery (La Jolla, Calif.)
Laurence McGilvery—McGilvery (La Jolla, Calif.)
James McGovern—McGovern (Berwyn, Ill.)
Robert D. McGrath Sr.—World War (W. Roxbury, Mass.)
Sean P. McGrath—World War (W. Roxbury, Mass.)
Mrs. Thomas McGrath—Thoreau (Concord, Mass.)
Robert McGuire—Wild (Larchmont, N.Y.)
John J. McHale—Christian (Westminster, Md.)
Katherine T McHale—Christian (Westminster, Md.)
Ann McKee—Booksellers (St. Paul, Minn.)
Harper McKee—Booksellers (St. Paul, Minn.)
Jim McKee—Lee (Lincoln, Neb.)
James F. McKenna—Taste (Fall River, Mass.)
James S. McKenna—Taste (Fall River, Mass.)
Jean S. McKenna—Book Shop (Beverly Farms, Mass.)
Mary McKenna—Taste (Fall River, Mass.)
Paul McKenna—Tona (Grand Isl., N.Y.)
Peggy McKissick—Twice-Loved (Youngstown, Ohio)
Bruce McKittrick—McKittrick (Philadelphia, Pa.)
John McLaughlin—Book Sail (Orange, Calif.)
Robert F. McLaughlin—McLaughlin's (Cottage Grove, Ore.)
Tom McLaughlin—Arader (New York, N.Y.)
Virginia McLean—Country (Chesterton, Ind.)
Beryl McLeod—Book Bazaar (Ottawa, Ont.)
Vicki McLeod—Unicorn (Bruceton Mills, W. Va.)
W. R. McLeod—Unicorn (Bruceton Mills, W. Va.)
Preston McMann—Old Oregon (Portland, Ore.)
Bernie McManus—Woodbury (Woodbury, Conn.)
Bernie McManus—McManus (Woodbury, Conn.)
Bob McMaster—Book Bin (Albany, Ore.)
William McMasters—Kirksco (Ringwood, N.J.)
Mary McMichael—Ritzlin (Evanston, Ill.)
Harlow McMillen—McMillen (Staten Isl., N.Y.)
Larry McMurtry—Booked Up (Washington, D.C.)
Carol McNally—Gamebag (Twin Lakes, Wisc.)
Chris McPhee—Murder (Denver, Colo.)

Jack W. McQuerry—McQuerry (Jacksonville, Fla.)
Mary N. McQuerry—McQuerry (Jacksonville, Fla.)
Patricia McTague—Denning (Salisbury Mills, N.Y.)
Prudy Mead—Leelanau (Leland, Mich.)
Betty Means—Means (Charlotte, N.C.)
Drucilla Meary—Haunted (Orleans, Mass.)
Sawyer E. Medbury—Bridgton (Bridgton, Maine)
Harold Medjuck—House (Thornhill, Ont.)
Ami Megiddo—Compulsive (New York, N.Y.)
Cindy Megiddo—Compulsive (New York, N.Y.)
Paul Meilin—Ute-Or (W. Jordan, Utah)
Cynthia Meisner—Book Den East (Oak Bluffs, Mass.)
Andrew Melhato—Village (New York, N.Y.)
Andrew Melhato—Comic (New York, N.Y.)
Dennis Melhouse—First (Chicago, Ill.)
Frances E. Memoe—Bland's (Sharon, Mass.)
Harvey L. Mendelsohn—Mendelsohn (Cambridge, Mass.)
Hubert Mengin—Midwest (Evanston, Ill.)
Barbara Meredith—Shadow (Hillsboro, N.H.)
Lois Meredith—Shadow (Hillsboro, N.H.)
Michael Merims—Yesterday's (Larchmont, N.Y.)
Jerry Merkel—Merkel (Xenia, Ohio)
Arnold Merkitch—Helmet (W. Islip, N.Y.)
Kathleen Mero—Liberty (Concord, Calif.)
Robert L. Merriam—Merriam (Conway, Mass.)
Harold P. Merry—Books/Autographs (Eliot, Maine)
Linda Metaxas—Tinker (Santa Cruz, Calif.)
P. V. Metz—Dust Jacket (Cincinnati, Ohio)
Bern Meyer—Booklord's (New York, N.Y.)
David Meyer—Meyerbooks (Glenwood, Ill.)
Arthur Meyerfeld—Meyerfeld (San Carlos, Calif.)
Jeffrey Meyerson—Meyerson (Brooklyn, N.Y.)
Alan Meyrowitz—Especially (Burke, Va.)
Barbara Meyrowitz—Especially (Burke, Va.)
William Michalski—Marley (Oldwick, N.J.)
Joe Michaud—Michauds (Iowa City, Iowa)
Joe Michaud—Vintage (Iowa City, Iowa)
Frank Michelli—Michelli (Ogunquit, Maine)
Harold Mick—Lewis (Seattle, Wash.)
Georgine Mickler—Mickler's (Chuluota, Fla.)
Thomas Mickler—Mickler's (Chuluota, Fla.)
Martita Midence—Womanbooks (New York, N.Y.)
Marjorie Miele—Miele (New York, N.Y.)
Linda Millemann—Tattered Cover (Denver, Colo.)
Bruce W. Miller III—Phoenix (San Luis Obispo, Calif.)
Ernest C. Miller—Miller (Warren, Pa.)
Gene Miller—Appleland (Winchester, Va.)

Harold N. Miller—Mil-Air (Compton, Calif.)
Karl Miller—Miller (Johnstown, N.Y.)
Matthew Miller—Tattered Cover (Denver, Colo.)
Peter Miller—Miller (Seattle, Wash.)
Richard Miller—Hermeticus (Ashland, Ore.)
Russell W. Miller—Pioneer (Seattle, Wash.)
Shirley Miller—Book Place (Richland, Wash.)
Walter Miller—Miller (Syracuse, N.Y.)
Howard Mills—Avocet (Corvallis, Ore.)
R. C. Mills—Dictionary (Leeds Point, N.J.)
Saundra A. Mills—Avocet (Corvallis, Ore.)
Thomas Minckler—Minckler (Billings, Mont.)
George Robert Minkoff—Minkoff (Grt. Barrington, Mass.)
Arthur H. Minters—Minters (New York, N.Y.)
Dan Miranda—Miranda (Brookline, Mass.)
Jo Mish—Serpent (Oneonta, N.Y.)
John Mitchell—Mitchell (Pasadena, Calif.)
Paul Mitchell—Talbothay's (Aurora, N.Y.)
Emily Mobley—Speleobooks (Schoharie, N.Y.)
William F. Mobley—Mobley (Schoharie, N.Y.)
C. Moebius—Moebius (Westbury, N.Y.)
Karl Moehling—Book Stall (Rockford, Ill.)
Bill Moeller—Huckleberry (Centralia, Wash.)
Bibi Mohamed—Bartfield (New York, N.Y.)
Bibi Mohamed—Bartfield Gall. (New York, N.Y.)
Leo Mohl—Book Home (Colo. Spgs., Colo.)
Henry Moises—Bookstall (San Francisco, Calif.)
Louise Moises—Bookstall (San Francisco, Calif.)
Jearld Moldenhauer—Glad Day (Toronto, Ont.)
Matthew Monahan—Gotham and Monahan (both New York, N.Y.)
Ed Monarski—Monarski (Syracuse, N.Y.)
John T. Monckton—Monckton (Chicago, Ill.)
Marvin Mondlin—Strand Rare (New York, N.Y.)
Willis Monie—Monie Shop (Cooperstown, N.Y.)
Willis Monie—Monie (Cooperstown, N.Y.)
Alice Montgomery—Tryon (Johnstown, N.Y.)
Roger Montgomery—Tryon (Johnstown, N.Y.)
Gloria Montlack—Montlack (Old Bethpage, N.Y.)
Gil Moody—Magic (Johnson City, Tenn.)
Gil Moody—Moody (Johnson City, Tenn.)
Linda Moody—Magic (Johnson City, Tenn.)
Earl E. Moore—Moore (Wynnewood, Pa.)
Frederick Moore—Holmes (Oakland, Calif.)
Henrietta J Moore—Henrietta's (Salisbury, Md.)
Mel Moore—Book Prospector (Littleton, Colo.)
Ed Moran—Moran (Rocky Point, N.Y.)
Kitty Moran—Oxford (Atlanta, Ga.)
Elizabeth Morath—Medallion (Wellesley, Mass.)

Don Moreland—Lewis (Seattle, Wash.)
Constance Morelle—Morelle (Haverhill, Mass.)
Dan Morgan—Book Gallery (Gainesville, Fla.)
Michele Morgan—Morgan (Willowick, Ohio)
Robert E. Morgan—Morgan (Willowick, Ohio)
William M. Moroney—Hill Haven (Barton, Vt.)
Benjamin C. Morrell—Morrell's (Ocean Grove, N.J.)
Ernest Morrell—ChoreoGraphica (Boston, Mass.)
Lillian G. Morrell—Morrell's (Ocean Grove, N.J.)
Samuel R. Morrill—Morrill (Newton Centre, Mass.)
Hugh S. Morris—Michlestreet (E. Lebanon, Maine)
John B. Morris—Burnett (Atlanta, Ga.)
J. W. Morris—Forest Park (Ft. Wayne, Ind.)
Lois Morris—Forest Park (Ft. Wayne, Ind.)
David Morrison—Morrison (Santa Monica, Calif.)
Elizabeth Morrison—Phoenix (Freeville, N.Y.)
Helen Morrison—Old #6 (Henniker, N.H.)
Ian Morrison—Old #6 (Henniker, N.H.)
Ian Morrison—Quechee (Quechee, Vt.)
William Morrison—Angriff (Hollywood, Calif.)
Viola Morris—Michlestreet (E. Lebanon, Maine)
B. O. Morritt—Morritt (Warwick, R.I.)
J. W. Morritt—Morritt (Warwick, R.I.)
Bradford Morrow—Morrow (New York, N.Y.)
C. W. Mortenson—Attic (Newark, Del.)
Frank Mosher—Oriental (Pasadena, Calif.)
Frank E. Mosher—British (No. Weymouth, Mass.)
Dick Moskowitz—Abra (Rochester, N.Y.)
Larry Moskowitz—Joe the Pro (Santa Barbara, Calif.)
Saul Moskowitz—Hist. Tech (Marblehead, Mass.)
Jean Moss—Margolis (Santa Fe, N.M.)
Wendy Moss—Scottsdale (Scottsdale, Ariz.)
Donald N. Mott—Mott (Sheffield, Mass.)
Howard S. Mott—Mott (Sheffield, Mass.)
Jo Mott—Novel (San Luis Obispo, Calif.)
Phyllis Mott—Mott (Sheffield, Mass.)
Francis Moul—Wordsmith (Syracuse, Neb.)
Linda Moulton—Tattersalls (Conyers, Ga.)
Sean Moye—Moye (Putney, Vt.)
Wayne Moye—Moye (Seattle, Wash.)
Frank C. Mrouse—Mrouse (New Orleans, La.)
Zucker Mrs.—Milestone (New York, N.Y.)
Frank Muccie, Jr.—Edenite (Imlaystown, N.J.)
Bill Mueller—Wooden (Middlebourne, W.Va.)
Lois Mueller—Wooden (Middlebourne, W.Va.)
Robert Mueller—Bookseller's (Chicago, Ill.)
John Mullen—Legacy (Iowa City, Iowa)
Gary Mullens—Book Loft (Solvang, Calif.)

Lois Mueller—Wooden (Middlebourne, W.Va.)
Robert Mueller—Bookseller's (Chicago, Ill.)
John Mullen—Legacy (Iowa City, Iowa)
Gary Mullens—Book Loft (Solvang, Calif.)
Don Muller—Old Harbor (Sitka, Alk.)
Paul F. Mullins—Mullins (Encinitas, Calif.)
Roslyn Mullins—Mullins (Encinitas, Calif.)
Capria Munro—Hoffer (Vancouver, B.C.)
Grace Munsell—Munsell (Newburyport, Mass.)
J. B. Muns—Muns (Berkeley, Calif.)
Anne R. Munson—Munson (Mattoon, Ill.)
Clare M. Murphy—Payson (Belmont, Mass.)
Jane Murphy—Murphy (Iowa City, Iowa)
Robert Murphy—Murphy (Salem, Mass.)
Robert Murphy—Murphy (Marietta, Ga.)
Terrence V. Murphy—Mt. Sterling (Mt. Sterling, Ky.)
Robinson Murray III—Marray (Melrose, Mass.)

George Murray—Bartfield (New York, N.Y.)
George Murray—Bartfield Gall. (New York, N.Y.)
Paul Murray—Murray (Wilbraham, Mass.)
Paula Murray—Stone Lion (Ft. Collins, Colo.)
Samuel Murray—Murray (Wilbraham, Mass.)
Owen R. Murtagh—Curious Raven (Detroit, Mich.)
Benjamin Muse, Jr.—Parnassus (Yarmouthport, Mass.)
Eugene Musiel—Buffalo (Amherst, N.Y.)
Rita Musumeci—Guerrera (Lawrence, Mass.)
Samuel Musumeci—Guerrera (Lawrence, Mass.)
Carol Myers—Myers (Boulder, Colo.)
Lawrence Myers—Myers (Sequim, Wash.)
Lawrence D. Myers—Johnson's (Los Angeles, Calif.)
Mrs. Myers—Virginia (Berryville, Va.)

N

Lois Nadel—Chester (Chester, Conn.)
Julian J. Nadolny—Nadolny (Kensington, Conn.)
James Nagel—Peninsula (Burlingame, Calif.)
Terry Nagel—Peninsula (Burlingame, Calif.)
Paul Naiditch—Zeitlin (Los Angeles, Calif.)
Barbara E. Nailler—Wolf's (Morgantown, W.Va.)
Chris Najarian—Najarian (Newtown Sq., Pa.)
Steve Najarian—Najarian (Newtown Sq., Pa.)
Al Nanitski—Book Bear (W. Brookfield, Mass.)
Grayce Nash—Authors (Dundee, Ore.)
Lee Nash—Authors (Dundee, Ore.)
Karen Nathan—Arader/Sessler (Philadelphia, Pa.)
Karl Neary—Colonial (W. Lebanon, N.H.)
Kathleen Neary—Colonial (W. Lebanon, N.H.)
Kenneth Nebenzahl—Nebenzahl (Chicago, Ill.)
Matthew Needee—Newburyport (Newburyport, Mass.)
Nancy Needham—Women's (Contoocook, N.H.)
Cheryl Needle—Needle (Chelmsford, Mass.)
Ellis H. Neel, Jr.—Holmes (Philadelphia, Pa.)
Marjorie Neikrug—Photographica (New York, N.Y.)
Martin Neil—Mermaid (Oakland, Calif.)
Mayrene Nelms—Book Nook (Fort Smith, Ark.)

Audrey Nelson—Nelson (Goshen, N.H.)
David R. Nelson—Nelson (New Bedford, Mass.)
John L. Nelson, Sr.—Nelson's (Albany, N.Y.)
John Nelson, Jr.—Nelson's (Troy, N.Y.)
Joyce C. Nelson—Nelson (New Bedford, Mass.)
Seth Nemeroff—Nemeroff (Williamstown, Mass.)
Y. T. Nercessian—Armenian (Pico Rivera, Calif.)
H. Nestler—Nestler (Waldwick, N.J.)
Petra F. Netzorg—Cellar (Detroit, Mich.)
Robert E. Neutrelle—Acoma (Ramona, Calif.)
S. Dale Neutrelle—Acoma (Ramona, Calif.)
Maurice F. Neville—Neville (Santa Barbara, Calif.)
Harry Newman—Old Print (New York, N.Y.)
Julia S. Newman—Newman (Battle Creek, Mich.)
Kenneth Newman—Old Print (New York, N.Y.)
Patricia L. Newman—Newman (Chicago, Ill.)
Ralph Geoffrey Newman—Appomatox, London, and Newman (all Chicago, Ill.)
Richard Newman—Lambeth (New York, N.Y.)
Robert Newman—Old Print (New York, N.Y.)
Victor Newman—Mandala (Daytona Bch., Fla.)
Tom Nicely—Leaves (Ann Arbor, Mich.)
Chris Nickle—Burbank (Burbank, Calif.)

Gertrude Nie—Nie (Chicago, Ill.)
Joseph Nie—Nie (Chicago, Ill.)
Donna Nieves—Munson (Mattoon, Ill.)
Jeremy Nissel—Michaels (Eugene, Ore.)
Einer Nisula—Nisula (Okemos, Mich.)
Donnell Noble—Noble (Greenville, Texas)
Alice Nolan—Book OP (Adrian, Mich.)
George Nolan—Nolan (Coeur d'Alene, Idaho)
John Nolan—Book OP (Adrian, Mich.)
John Nomland—Nomland (Los Angeles, Calif.)
James Noonan—In #1 (San Francisco, Calif.)
Jeremy Norman—Norman (San Francisco, Calif.)
Wilbur Norman—Norman (Philadelphia, Pa.)
John E. Norris—Norris (Paoli, Pa.)
James Neil Northe—A Points (Okla. City, Okla.)
Frank North—Becky (Hannibal, Mo.)
Jane Northshield—Old Book (Croton, N.Y.)

Russell Norton—Old Book (New Haven, Conn.)
Sal Noto—Noto (Cupertino, Calif.)
Andrew Nottman—Polyanthos (Huntington, N.Y.)
David Nottman—Polyanthos (Huntington, N.Y.)
Murray Novick—Murray's (Bridgeport, Conn.)
Alex Novitzsky—Book Barn (Rochester, Mich.)
Claudia Novitzsky—Book Barn (Rochester, Mich.)
Judith Noyes—Chinook (Colo. Spgs., Colo.)
Richard Noyes—Chinook (Colo. Spgs., Colo.)
Harry Nudel—Nudel (New York, N.Y.)
Edward D. Nudelman—Nudelman (Seattle, Wash.)
Ray E. Nugent—Book Trader (Naples, Fla.)
Zena A. Nugent—Book Trader (Naples, Fla.)
James B. Nunley—Quest (Ft. Worth, Texas)
Pauline Nunley—Quest (Ft. Worth, Texas)
Ray Nurmi—Snowbound (Marquette, Mich.)
D. W. Nyback—Spade (Seattle, Wash.)

O

Louise Oberschmidt—Else Fine (Dearborn, Mich.)
Anne O'Brien—Cummins (Pottersville, N.J.)
F. M. O'Brien—O'Brien (Portland, Maine)
Laura M. O'Brien—Book Pedlars (Cundy's Harbor, Maine)
Lucy O'Brien—Red Horse (Tampa, Fla.)
Thomas O'Brien—Booksmith (Oak Park, Ill.)
Walter A. O'Brien, Jr.—Book Pedlars (Cundy's Harbor, Maine)
Peter J. O'Connell—Communications (New Haven, Conn.)
John O'Connor—Bonners (Bonners Ferry, Ind.)
Roger O'Connor—Mostly (Carthage, Mo.)
Bernadine O'Donnell—Mystic (Mystic, Conn.)
Bernadine O'Donnell—Wayside (Westerly, R.I.)
C. O'Donnell—Dickson St. (Fayetteville, Ark.)
Ed O'Donnell—Johnson (Syracuse, N.Y.)
Jean O'Donoghue—O'Donoghue (Anoka, Minn.)
Emil Offenbacher—Offenbacher (Kew Gardens, N.Y.)
David B. Ogle—Antiq. Archive (Sunnyvale, Calif.)
William L. Ohm—Bill's (Stevens Point, Vis
Barbara L. Oldford—Harbar (Casselberry, Fla.)
Harry J. Oldford—Harbar (Casselberry, Fla.)
Gary Oleson—Waiting (Cambridge, Mass.)

Janet Olinkiewicz—Olinkiewicz (Shelter Isl., N.Y.)
Paul Olinkiewicz—Olinkiewicz (Shelter Isl., N.Y.)
Bill Olsen—Old City (St. Augustine, Fla.)
Carolyn T. Olsen—Old City (St. Augustine, Fla.)
Cate Olson—Much (Marblehead, Mass.)
Deirdre O'Mahony—O'Mahony (Clarence Cntr., N.Y.)
William T. O'Malley—O'Malley (Kingston, R.I.)
George O'Nale—Cheap St. (New Castle, Va.)
Jan O'Nale—Cheap St. (New Castle, Va.)
David L. O'Neal—O'Neal (Boston, Mass.)
Gary O'Neal—Old Favs. (Richmond, Va.)
Mary T. O'Neal—O'Neal (Boston, Mass.)
Eugene O'Neil—In Our (Cambridge, Mass.)
Robert M. O'Neill—O'Neill (Warner, N.H.)
Stathis Orphanos—Sylvester (Los Angeles, Calif.)
Marcia Orr—History (Long Valley, N.J.)
Marcia Orr—Back Pages (Halifax, N.S.)
Ronald Orr—History (Long Valley, N.J.)
Ronald Orr—Back Pages (Halifax, N.S.)
Paricio Ortega—Bookshelf (Ogden, Utah)
Michael Osborne—Reprint (Washington, D.C.)
G. R. Osgood—Osgood (Rockport, Mass.)
Simon Ottenberg—Ottenberg (Seattle, Wash.)
Gabriele Ouellette—Ars Libri (Boston, Mass.)

Maurice E. Owen—Owen (Litchfield, Maine)
McDuffie Owen—McDuffie's (Portland, Ore.)
Thomas Owen—Avenue (Boston, Mass.)
Linda Owens—Owens (Richmond, Va.)

Michael Owens—Owens (Richmond, Va.)
Ken Owings, Jr.—Antiques (No. Abington, Mass.)
Felix Oyens—Harper (New York, N.Y.)

P

Jim Pagliasotti—Black Ace (Denver, Colo.)
Thomas Paine—Bookfinders (Atlanta, Ga.)
Theodore W. Palmer—Palmer (Eugene, Ore.)
Richard A. Pandich—Pandich (Asheville, N.C.)
Ellie Panos—Yesterdays (Whitman, Mass.)
Nicolaas Pansegrouw—Town (Dutch Flat, Calif.)
Bob Paolone—Assoc. Stu. (Chico, Calif.)
Betty Parker—Parker (Santa Fe, N.M.)
Riley Parker—Parker (Santa Fe, N.M.)
Wyman Parker—Parker (Middlebury, Vt.)
John C. Parkhurst—Jan-Er (Eureka Spgs., Ark.)
Phyllis J. Parkinson—Peacock (Littleton, Mass.)
William L. Parkinson—Parkinson (Shelburne, Vt.)
Albert L. Parks—Grandpa's (Troy, N.C.)
Mary R. Parks—Grandpa's (Troy, N.C.)
Sandy Parks—Armchair (Newport, R.I.)
Jean Parmer—Parmer (San Diego, Calif.)
Jerry Parmer—Parmer (San Diego, Calif.)
Michael Parrish—Jenkins (Austin, Texas)
Gilman Parsons—Parsons (Sonoma, Calif.)
Georgini Paskuly—Marshall Field (Chicago, Ill.)
Joel Patrick—Patrick (Beaufort, S.C.)
John R. Paul—Prairie (Springfield, Ill.)
A. David Paulhus—Wells (Wells, Maine)
A. David Paulhus—Paulhus (Wells, Maine)
Lee Pauline—Book Fair (W. Palm Beach, Fla.)
Barbara Paulson—Paulson (Huntington, Mass.)
Robert Paulson—Paulson (Huntington, Mass.)
Nicolai Pavlov—Pavlov (Dobbs Ferry, N.Y.)
Nina Pavlov—Pavlov (Dobbs Ferry, N.Y.)
Bud Pearce—Pearce (Elma, N.Y.)
Emily Pearlman—Chip's Shop (New York, N.Y.)
Becky Pearson—Book Disp. #1 and #3 (both
    Columbia, S.C.)
J. E. Pearson—Pearson (Chicago, Ill.)
Teresa R. Pearson—Pearson (Chicago, Ill.)
Ken Peczkowski—Griffon (So. Bend, Ind.)
Catherine Pederson—Darvill's (Eastsound, Wash.)

Dale Pederson—Darvill's (Eastsound, Wash.)
Christine Pegram—Pegram (Sarasota, Fla.)
William Pencelly—Antiq. Michiana (Allen, Mich.)
David Pendleton—Twyce (Winona, Minn.)
John Pendleton—Twyce (Winona, Minn.)
Mary Pendleton—Twyce (Winona, Minn.)
Charles Penrose—Cabin/Pines (Potsdam, N.Y.)
James Pepper—Pepper/Stern (Santa Barbara, Calif.)
Paul Peranteau—Benjamins (Philadelphia, Pa.)
Robert Perata—Perata (Oakland, Calif.)
J. C. Percell—Baseball (Tucson, Ariz.)
Brian Perkins—Barber's (Ft. Worth, Texas)
Larue Perkins—Barber's (Ft. Worth, Texas)
Grace Perkinson—Perkinson (Deer Isle, Maine)
Angela Perko—Lost (Santa Barbara, Calif.)
Frank Perry—Perry's (San Jose, Calif.)
Damon Persiani—First Edtns. (Richmond, Va.)
Richard Persoff—Persoff (Alameda, Calif.)
Jack M. Perz—Monroe (Fresno, Calif.)
John M. Perz—Monroe (Fresno, Calif.)
Nancy Peters—City Lights (San Francisco, Calif.)
Steven Peters—Peters (Van Nuys, Calif.)
John Petersen—Abe. Lincoln (Chicago, Ill.)
Mary Lou Petersen—Petersen (Davenport, Iowa)
Peter C. Petersen—Petersen (Davenport, Iowa)
Bob Peterson—Blue Dragon (Ashland, Ore.)
Jack Peterson—Twice-Loved (Youngstown, Ohio)
John Peterson—Book Stall (Rockford, Ill.)
Marcia Peterson—Fish (Minneapolis, Minn.)
Mary T. Peterson—Books In (Turlock, Calif.)
Murray Peterson—Petersons (Philadelphia, Pa.)
Richard Peterson—Book Bin (Kingston, Ont.)
Richard Peterson—Berry (Kingston, Ont.)
Selma Peterson—Petersons (Philadelphia, Pa.)
Robert Petrilla—Petrilla (Roosevelt, N.J.)
Gerald Pettinger—Pettinger (Russell, Iowa)
Robert H. Pettit—Viewpoint (New York, N.Y.)
Robert Pettler—Pettler (Los Angeles, Calif.)

Elsie Phalen—Phalen (Chicago, Ill.)
Albert J. Phiebig—Phiebig (White Plains, N.Y.)
Peter Philbrook—Books & Co. (New York, N.Y.)
Claude Phillips—Hidden (Kalamazoo, Mich.)
Elizabeth Phillips—Phillips (New York, N.Y.)
Kathy Phillips—Time (No. Andover, Mass.)
Nancy Phillips—Hidden (Kalamazoo, Mich.)
Walter J. Phillips—Paths (New York, N.Y.)
Leonard E. Piasecki—Carr (New York, N.Y.)
Bill Pic—Kensington (Kensington, Md.)
Joan Pickard—Cunningham (Portland, Maine)
Ken Pierce—Pierce (Park Forest, Ill.)
Wayne Pierce—Pierce (Oroville, Calif.)
Lois Pinkney—Pinkney (Granby, Conn.)
William Pinkney—Pinkney (Granby, Conn.)
James S. Pipkin—Pipkin (Rock Hill, S.C.)
Phillip J. Pirages—Pirages (McMinnville, Ore.)
Steven L. Pirtle—Pirtle (Bellevue, Wash.)
A. J. Pischl—Dance Mart (Brooklyn, N.Y.)
Mary L. Pitblado—Murder (Toronto, Ont.)
Danny Plaisance—Cottonwood (Baton Rouge, La.)
Julian Plante—Plante (St. Cloud, Minn.)
R. Plapinger—Plapinger (Ashland, Ore.)
Jay Platt—West Side (Ann Arbor, Mich.)
Sheri Plummer-Raphael—Argus and Barnstormer
   (both Sacramento, Calif.)
Anne Plunkett—Royal (Charlemont, Mass.)
A. Jo Poersch—Academy (Denver, Colo.)
Marion D. Pohrt—Pohrt (Flint, Mich.)
Valerie J. Polin—Book Mark (Philadelphia, Pa.)
Edward T. Pollack—Pollack (Boston, Mass.)
George W. Pollen—Estate (Washington, D.C.)
John L. Polley—Seattle (Seattle, Wash.)
James W. Pollock—Pollock (Palo Alto, Calif.)
E. J. Polonsky—Literary (Pittsburgh, Pa.)
Sarah Polonsky—Literary (Pittsburgh, Pa.)
Norma Ponard—Manor (New York, N.Y.)
Al Pond—Jolie's (Stuart, Fla.)
Jolie Pond—Jolie's (Stuart, Fla.)
William Poole—Dobson (Grimsby, Ont.)
Richard L. Pope—Books/Marvel (Corning, N.Y.)
H. J. Popinski—Henry (Berwyn, Ill.)
Gary Popma—Baker (Grand Rapids, Mich.)

Dick Port—Shaman (Ann Arbor, Mich.)
Karl Port—Shaman (Ann Arbor, Mich.)
Bonita Porter—Porter (Phoenix, Ariz.)
Paul Porter—Porter (Phoenix, Ariz.)
Renee Porter—Bargain (Norfolk, Va.)
Arnold Porterfield—Appalachia (Bluefield, W.Va.)
Edwin D. Posey—Midnight (W. Lafayette, Ind.)
Marvin Post—Attic (London, Ont.)
Les Poste—Poste (Geneseo, N.Y.)
Frederica Postman—Printers' (Palo Alto, Calif.)
Nicholas Potter—Potter (Santa Fe, N.M.)
Eugene Povirk—Southpaw (Roxbury, Mass.)
Mary Powell—Ancient (Santa Fe, N.M.)
Steve Powell—Powell (Bar Harbor, Maine)
Jed Power—Cape Ann (Peabody, Mass.)
Melvin Powers—Wilshire (No. Hollywood, Calif.)
Polly Powers—Bookshelf (Concord, N.H.)
Thomas Powers—Green Mtn. (So. Royalton, Vt.)
Virginia Powers—Powers (Essex Jctn., Vt.)
Richard Q. Praeger—Transition (San Francisco,
   Calif.)
Ken Prag—Prag (San Francisco, Calif.)
Alden B. Pratt—Pratt (E. Livermore, Maine)
Betty W. Presgraves—Bookworm (Wytheville, Va.)
James S. Presgraves—Bookworm (Wytheville, Va.)
Jerome Pressler—Mt. Eden (Mt. Eden, Calif.)
Susanne S. Prestianni—Prestianni (Penfield, N.Y.)
Vincent Prestianni—Prestianni (Penfield, N.Y.)
Don Pretari—Black Oak (Berkeley, Calif.)
Doug Price—West Side (Ann Arbor, Mich.)
John Prior—Wreden (Palo Alto, Calif.)
Elizabeth Proper—Joslin (Concord, Mass.)
Forrest Proper—Joslin (Concord, Mass.)
Andrew C. Prosser—Prosser (Chicago, Ill.)
Helen Protasewicz—Jaeger (Commack, N.Y.)
Charmagne Pruner—Valley (Amherst, Mass.)
Jerry Pruner—Valley (Amherst, Mass.)
Ellebeth Pugh—Bookshelf (Miller, S. D.)
John Pugh—Bookshelf (Miller, S. D.)
Robert Pugh—Trail (Tucson, Ariz.)
Gennaro Pugliese—Paperback (New York, N.Y.)
Charles F. Purro—Yankee (Plymouth, Mass.)
John Wm. Pye—Bromer (Boston, Mass.)

Q

Jack Qualman—Qualman (San Diego, Calif.)
Michael Qualman—Qualman (San Diego, Calif.)
Richard Quartaroli—Grand (Redwood City, Calif.)
Ron Querry—Taos (Taos, N.M.)

Gloria Quinn—Patriot (Lexington, Mass.)
Howard Quinn—Patriot (Lexington, Mass.)
Ingeborg Quitzau—Quitzau (Edmeston, N.Y.)
H. B. Quoyoon—Magazine (New York, N.Y.)

R

Antonio Raimo—Raimo (Lancaster, Penna.)
Al Ralston—Ralston (Fullerton, Calif.)
Al Ralston—Book Harbor (Fullerton, Calif.)
Bruce J. Ramer—B. Ramer (New York, N.Y.)
Richard C. Ramer—R. Ramer (New York, N.Y.)
Howard L. Ramey—Backstage (Eugene, Ore.)
James Randall—Ahab (Cambridge, Mass.)
Ronald R. Randall—Randall (Santa Barbara, Calif.)
Katharine Ransom—Books By (Albuquerque, N.M.)
Kevin T. Ransom—Ransom (Amherst, N.Y.)
E. J. Ransome—Past (Windsor, Ont.)
W. R. Ransome—Past (Windsor, Ont.)
Benjamin Rapaport—Antiq. Tobacciana (Fairfax, Va.)
Otto Rapp—Maxwell (Elmsford, N.Y.)
Anita Raskin—Book Lady (Savannah, Ga.)
Martin B. Raskin—Raskin (Albertson, N.Y.)
B. Ratner-Gantscher—Artistic (Boston, Mass.)
G. J. Rausch—Rausch (Bloomington, Ind.)
David Ray—Allen's (Baltimore, Md.)
Jack Ray—Ray (Baldwin Park, Calif.)
Leslie Ray—Ray's (Hartford, Vt.)
Rick Rayfield—Tempest (Waitsville, Vt.)
Lewis L. Razek—Highwood (Traverse City, Mich.)
A. N. Real—Apothecary (New York, N.Y.)
I. C. Reaveni—Booknook (Evanston, Ill.)
Adrienne Redd—Saurus (Bethlehem, Pa.)
Jeanine Reddaway—Pirtle (Bellevue, Wash.)
Charles A. Redding—Book Broker (Evansville, Ind.)
Robert Redding—Redding (Sequim, Wash.)
Jim Reed—Reed (Birmingham, Ala.)
Rixon Reed—Photo-Eye (Austin, Texas)
William Reese—Reese (New Haven, Conn.)

Lee Reeve—Tusitala (Kailua, Haw.)
Kelly Rego—Harvard (Stockton, Calif.)
Joy Regula—Burton's (Greenport, N.Y.)
Dick Reiber—Rieber (Thomasville, Ga.)
Francis J. Reich—Webster's (Milwaukee, Wisc.)
Susan Reigler—Hawley (Louisville, Ky.)
Donald Reisler—Reisler (Vienna, Va.)
JoAnn Reisler—Reisler (Vienna, Va.)
Frank Reiss—Acorn (San Francisco, Calif.)
Milton Reissman—Victoria (New York, N.Y.)
Diana J. Rendell—Rendell (Waban, Mass.)
Kenneth Rendell—Rendell (Newton, Mass.)
John Renjilian—Pages (Newton, Conn.)
Carol Resnick—Resnick (Cazenovia, N.Y.)
Stephen Resnick—Resnick (Cazenovia, N.Y.)
Blossom Resnik—Resnik (Roslyn Hgts., N.Y.)
Lin Respess—Respess (Chapel Hill and Durham, N.C.)
Donna Reston—Reston's (Amsterdam, N.Y.)
J. E. Reynolds—Reynolds (Willits, Calif.)
Phyllis Rhoades—R E (Fairhope, Ala.)
R. E. Rhoades—R E (Fairhope, Ala.)
Robert A. Rhoads—Rhoads (Richmond, Ind.)
Jane Rhodes—Bryn Mawr (New York, N.Y.)
Mark Ricci—Memory (New York, N.Y.)
Irvine Richards—Rare Book (New York, N.Y.)
Janet Richards—Books Unltd. (Nat'l City, Calif.)
Christine Richardson—Richardson (Westmont, N.J.)
Herbert Richardson—Richardson (Westmont, N.J.)
Paul C. Richards—Richards (Templeton, Mass.)
Roger Richards—Rare Book (New York, N.Y.)
Daniel Rich—Vathek (Ft. Lee, N.J.)
William Richert—Richert (Fresno, Calif.)

Robert Richshafer—Richshafer (Cincinnati, Ohio)
Stacy Richshafer—Richshafer (Cincinnati, Ohio)
Arthur Richter—Archaeologia (Oakland, Calif.)
Ray Rickman—Cornerstone (Providence, R.I.)
Jacques Ricux—Stone Lion (Ft. Collins, Colo.)
Joanne Riddle—Annie's (Acton, Mass.)
Branimir M. Rieger—Rieger (Greenwood, S.C.)
Lance Rieker—Aion (Boulder, Colo.)
John Riley—Gabriel (Northampton, Mass.)
Joseph Riling—Riling (Philadelphia, Pa.)
John F. Rinaldi—Rinaldi (Kennebunkport, Maine)
Nate Rind—Antheil (No. Bellmore, N.Y.)
Sheila Rind—Antheil (No. Bellmore, N.Y.)
Sonny Rinen—Rinen (New York, N.Y.)
Dana Ringlein—Plant (Grass Valley, Calif.)
George Rinhart—Rinhart (Colebrook, Conn.)
Edward Ripley-Duggan—Wilsey (Olivebridge, N.Y.)
R. T. Risk—Typographeum (Francestown, N.H.)
Jack D. Rittenhouse—Rittenhouse (Albuquerque, N.M.)
George Ritzlin—Ritzlin (Evanston, Ill.)
David C. Roach—Pier (Piermont, N.Y.)
E. Leslie Robart—Cilleyville (Andover, N.H.)
Sands B. Robart—Cilleyville (Andover, N.H.)
Doug Robbins—Denver Barter (Denver, Colo.)
Hilda Robbins—Bayview (Northport, N.Y.)
LeRoy Robbins—Robbins (Greenville, S.C.)
Nash Robbins—Much (Marblehead, Mass.)
Norman V. Robbins—Bayview (Northport, N.Y.)
Debra Robboy—Catbird (Portland, Ore.)
Richard Robb—Wizard's (San Diego, Calif.)
Roland Roberge—Roberge (Princeton, N.J.)
Roger Roberton—Robertson (Levittown, Pa.)
Barbara Roberts—Island (Isleboro, Maine)
Charles Roberts—Wonder (Frederick, Md.)
Don Roberts—Island (Isleboro, Maine)
James W. Roberts—Oriental (St. Pete., Fla.)
Mark Roberts—Phenomenologica (Worcester, Mass.)
Robert Owen Roberts—Roberts (Wheaton, Ill.)
Stanley Roberts—Roberts (W. Palm Bch., Fla.)
Mary Robertson—Robertson (Meredith, N.H.)
Henry A. Robidoux—Green Acre (Wells, Vt.)
Sheila A. Robidoux—Green Acre (Wells, Vt.)
Jane W. Robie—Landscape (Exeter, N.H.)
Jerry Robinette—Denver Fair (Denver, Colo.)
John Robinette—Ivey (Brewton, Ala.)
Charles J. Robinove—Allbooks (Colo. Spgs., Colo.)
Ben Robinson—Robinson (Alexandria, Va.)
Cedric L. Robinson—Robinson (Windsor, Conn.)

Charles Robinson—Robinson (Manchester, Maine)
Chuck Robinson—Village (Bellingham, Wash.)
Connie Robinson—Robinson (Yucca Valley, Calif.)
Dee Robinson—Village (Bellingham, Wash.)
Louise Robinson—Book Revue (Clearwater, Fla.)
Lynn Robinson—World Of (Willoughby, Ohio)
Michael F. Robinson—Robinson (New York, N.Y.)
Robbie Robinson—Robinson (Yucca Valley, Calif.)
Ruth E. Robinson—Robinson (Morgantown, W.Va.)
Stuart Robinson—Carpenter (Balboa Isl., Calif.)
Wallace Robinson—Robinson (St. Pete., Fla.)
Walter Robinson—Book Farm (Henniker, N.H.)
Joan Robles—Robles (Tucson, Ariz.)
Hulda Robuck—Bookshop (Warner Robins, Ga.)
John Roby—Roby (San Diego, Calif.)
Bette Roden—Ha'Penny (Snowville, N.H.)
Tom Roden—Ha'Penny (Snowville, N.H.)
Jack Roderick—Roderick (Medina, Ohio)
Nancy Roderick—Roderick (Medina, Ohio)
V. David Rodger—Andover (Andover, Mass.)
Paula Rodman—Green Apple (San Francisco, Calif.)
Gil Rodriguez—Gilann (Darien, Conn.)
Bernard Rogers—Rogers (Athens, Ga.)
Ted Rogers—Bookpost (Cardiff, Calif.)
Ted Rogers—Aide (Cardiff, Calif.)
Bernard Rogge—Artcraft (Baldwin, Md.)
Gloria E. Rogge—Artcraft (Baldwin, Md.)
Arnold M. Rogoff—Ethnographic (Mill Valley, Calif.)
Gail Rogofsky—Rogofsky (Glen Oaks, N.Y.)
Howard Rogofsky—Rogofsky (Glen Oaks, N.Y.)
Arnold A. Rogow—Firsts (New York, N.Y.)
Christopher Rohe—Rohe (Chicago, Ill.)
Paul Rohe—Rohe (Chicago, Ill.)
Hans E. Rohr—Rohr (Byfield, Mass.)
Craig Rohrer—Rohrer (Downers Grove, Ill.)
Bill Romero—Abbey (Dearborn, Mich.)
Wray Romingen—Purple (Fleischmanns, N.Y.)
Paul Ronning—Krickett's (Battle Creek, Mich.)
Alida Roochvarg—Collectrix (W. Hempstead, N.Y.)
Michael D. Brooks—Brooks (Macon, Ga.)
Mary Clark Roone—Collectors' (Richmond, Va.)
Barbara Rootenberg—Rootenberg (Sherman Oaks, Calif.)
Leon Rootenberg—Rootenberg (Sherman Oaks, Calif.)
Vicki Roper—Gierspeck/Roper (Conroe, Texas)
David Rose—Book Exch. (Plainville, Conn.)
Dorothy Rose—Rose (Sparta, Mich.)

Jim Rose—Andrews and Michiana (both Niles, Minn.)

Jim Rose—Coachman (La Porte, Ind.)

John Rose—Bakka (Toronto, Ont.)

Paula Rose—Book Exch. (Plainville, Conn.)

Paulette Rose—Rose (New York, N.Y.)

H. G. Roseman—Roseman (Brooklyn, N.Y.)

Bernard Rosenberg—Olana (Brewster, N.Y.)

Edward L. Rosenberry—Antiquarians (Plainfield, Pa.)

Linda K. Rosenberry—Antiquarians (Plainfield, Pa.)

Mort Rosenblatt—Hollyoak (Wilmington, Del.)

Ruth Rosenblatt—Brown Bag (Dobbs Ferry, N.Y.)

Bernard Rosenthal—Rosenthal (San Francisco, Calif.)

Jon K. Rosenthal—Amherst (Amherst, Mass.)

Ruth Rosenthal—Rosenthal (San Francisco, Calif.)

Allen Ross—Ross (Redwood City, Calif.)

Craig W. Ross—Ross (Medina, N.Y.)

Laurie M. Ross—Metropolis (Royal Oak, Mich.)

Robert Ross—Ross (Woodland Hills, Calif.)

Antonio Rossas—Ballet (New York, N.Y.)

Fred Rosselot—Rosselot (Grand View, N. Y.)

Leona Rostenberg—Rostenberg (New York, N.Y.)

Irving M. Roth—Roth (Norwalk, Ohio)

Irene Rouse—Rouse (Wattsville, Va.)

B. Rowell—Academic (No. Vancouver, B.C.)

Donald E. Roy—Chang Tang (Peekskill, N.Y.)

Ernest Roy—Book Rack (Aurora, Colo.)

Bob Rozandovich—Yesterday's (Kalamazoo, Mich.)

Sue Rozandovich—Yesterday's (Kalamazoo, Mich.)

Beth Rozier—Spade (Seattle, Wash.)

Marie Rozier—Truepenny (Tucson, Ariz.)

Robert H. Rubin—Rubin (Brookline, Mass.)

Joseph Rubinfine—Rubinfine (Pleasantville, N.J.)

Joel Rudikoff—Rudikoff (New York, N.Y.)

Emanuel D. Rudolph—Books/Buttons (Columbus, Ohio)

Robert E. Rudolph—Rudolph (Portland, Ore.)

Joel R. Ruduloff—Art (Purchase, N.Y.)

Robert E. Ruffolo II—Princeton and Servant's (both Atlantic City, N.J.)

Barbara J. Rule—Rule (Rochester, Mich.)

Robert Rulon-Miller Sr.—Rulon-Miller (St. Thomas, V.I.)

Rob Rulon-Miller—Rulon-Miller (Minneapolis, Minn.)

Robert Ruman—Articles (Skokie, Ill.)

Ed Rumrill—Armchair (No. Orange, Mass.)

Pat Rumrill—Armchair (No. Orange, Mass.)

Rose Runes—Philosophical (New York, N.Y.)

Ilene Ruppert—Obsolescence (Gettysburg, Pa.)

Tom Rusch—Stahr (Los Angeles, Calif.)

Wilma Ruscio—Book Exch. (Lakewood, Colo.)

Betty Rush—Rush (Baltimore, Md.)

Cecil A. Rush—Rush (Baltimore, Md.)

John Rush—Rush (Hamilton, Ont.)

Niall Russell—Russell (Montreal, Que.)

Reg Russell—Russell (Montreal, Que.)

Robert R. Russo—Hoosier (Indianapolis, Ind.)

Aileen H. Rutherford—Junction (Peoria, Ill.)

Bonnie D. Ruttan—Denver (Stockton, Calif.)

Irma Ryan—Novel (Fairfax, Va.)

Louis J. Ryan—Ryan (Columbus, Ohio)

R. M. Ryan—Ryan (Rancho Mirage, Calif.)

John Rybski—Rybski (Chicago, Ill.)

S

Julianna Saad—Terramedia (Wellesley, Mass.)

Linda Saaremaa—Bookshop (Chapel Hill, N. C.)

Irene M. Sabbot—Natural (Woodland Hills, Calif.)

Rudolph Wm. Sabbot—Natural (Woodland Hills, Calif.)

Charles W. Sachs—Scriptorium (Beverly Hills, Calif.)

Anthony Sackett—Many (Lake Hill, N.Y.)

Ernest L. Sackett—Sackett (Grants Pass, Ore.)

Ben Sackheim—Sackheim (Tucson, Ariz.)

Ramona J. Sadlon—Sadlon's (De Pere, Wisc.)

Robert L. Sadoff—Sadoff (Jenkintown, Pa.)

Martin Sadofsky—Ruby's (New York, N.Y.)

Roberta Sadofsky—Ruby's (New York, N.Y.)

Arnold Sadow—All Photog. (Yonkers, N.Y.)

Charlotte F Safir—Safir (New York, N.Y.)

Bill Safka—B.J.S. (Forest Hills, N.Y.)

Sandra Safris—L'Estampe (New York, N.Y. and Saratoga, Calif.)

Albert Saifer—Saifer (W. Orange, N.J.)

Mark Sailor—Book Co. (Pasadena, Calif.)

Lois St. Clair—St. Clair (Van Nuys, Calif.)

Donald St. John—Carry Back (Haverhill, N.H.)

Ruth St. John—Carry Back (Haverhill, N.H.)

M. Lenora Salandi—Bks./Begonias (Columbia, Mont.)

Hank Salerno—Salerno (Hauppauge, N.Y.)

Rose Salerno—Salerno (Hauppauge, N.Y.)

Gil Salk—Books/Birds (Vernon, Conn.)

William Salloch—Salloch (Ossining, N.Y.)

Jimmy Saloom—R E (Fairhope, Ala.)

Alan Sample—Sample (Stoneham, Mass.)

Ray Samuel—Samuel (New Orleans, La.)

Jeanne Sanders—Reading (Mexico, Ind.)

John R. Sanderson—Sanderson (Stockbridge, Mass.)

Doris Sandys—Sandys (Albertson, N.Y.)

Norman Sandys—Sandys (Albertson, N.Y.)

James Sanford—Metacomet (Providence, R.I.)

Mildred E. Santille—Fortunate Finds (Warwick, R.I.)

Peter R. Sarra—Ishtar (Canton, Mass.)

K. E. Saunders—Old Favs. (Toronto, Ont.)

Heidi Savage—Calliope (Pittsburgh, Pa.)

Jack Saviano—Jamaica (Jamaica, N.Y.)

Carol Savoy—Sunset (San Francisco, Calif.)

Phillip Sax—Compass Rose (Sitka, Alk.)

R. J. Sayers—Sayers (Andrews, Texas)

R. J. Sayers, Jr.—Sayers (Andrews, Texas)

Robert C. Scace—Scace (Calgary, Alt.)

Sheila Scanlon-Towers—Scanlon-Towers (Shelburne, Vt.)

Frederick G Schab—Schab (New York, N.Y.)

Mary B. Schaefer—Schaefer (Ossining, N.Y.)

Elizabeth M Schaffer—Paper (Ft. Lauderdale, Fla.)

Enid Schantz—Rue (Boulder, Colo.)

Tom Schantz—Rue (Boulder, Colo.)

Arthur Scharf—Scharf (Pittsburgh, Pa.)

Bob Schatz—Academic (Portland, Ore.)

Richard Schaubeck—Phoenix (New York, N.Y.)

Nancy Scheck—Scheck (Scarsdale, N.Y.)

Al Scheinbaum—Colonial (Pleasantville, N.Y.)

C. J. Scheiner—Scheiner (Brooklyn, N.Y.)

Ralph C. Schemp—Cranbury (Cranbury, N.J.)

Karl Schick—Schick (Hartsdale, N.Y.)

Wolfgang Schiefer—Schiefer (Wilton, Conn.)

Justin G. Schiller—Schiller (New York, N.Y.)

Robert Schlesinger—Bookmans (Tucson, Ariz.)

Don Schlitten—Xanadu (Bronx, N.Y.)

Suzanne Schlossberg—Schlossberg (Newton, Mass.)

David H. Schlottmann—Ookkees (Olympia, Wash.)

Betty Schmid—Schmid (Pittsburgh, Pa.)

Earl Schmid—Schmid (Pittsburgh, Pa.)

Anthony C. Schmidt—Schmidt (Collingswood, N.J.)

Dale C. Schmidt—Schmidt (Salem, Ore.)

Jeff Schmidt—Windsor (Brightwaters, N.Y.)

Stephen Schmidt—Windsor (Brightwaters, N.Y.)

J.R. Crittenden Schmitt—Schmitt (Rockville, Md.)

Edwin Schmitz—Book Nest (Los Altos, Calif.)

Annemarie Schnase—Schnase (Scarsdale, N.Y.)

Walter R. Schneemann—Schneeman (Chicago, Ill.)

Duane Schneider—Croissant (Athens, Ohio)

Reba Schneider—Bibelots (Seattle, Wash.)

Shirley Schneider—Bibelots (Seattle, Wash.)

Michael E. Schnitter—Dabny (Washington, D.C.)

Kenneth N. Schoen—Kraus (Millwood, N.Y.) and Schoen (Northampton, Mass.)

Seth Schoen—Schoen (Northampton, Mass.)

Lissa Schorr—Davis (Sherman Oaks, Calif.)

Abner Schram—Schram (Montclair, N.J.)

Marlow Schram—Book Fair (Ft. Lauderdale, Fla.)

Ellen Schreiber—Schreiber (Bronx, N.Y.)

Fred Schreiber—Schreiber (Bronx, N.Y.)

Michael Schreiber—Koerber (Southfield, Mich.)

Robert N. Schreiner—Foreign (Flushing, N.Y.)

Dr. Oscar Schreyer—Schreyer (New York, N.Y.)

Bert Schroeder—Schroeder's (Dickinson, Texas)

Faye Schroeder—Schroeder's (Dickinson, Texas)

J. H. Schrooten—J. & L. (Mesa, Ariz.)

David Schulson—Schulson (New York, N.Y.)

Betty Schulte—Woods (Yakima, Wash.)

Catherine Schultz—Ancramdale (Ancramdale, N.Y.)

John Schultz—Ancramdale (Ancramdale, N.Y.)

Terry Schultz—Trident (Boulder, Colo.)

Mr. Clair A Schulz—Decline/Fall (Clinton, Wisc.)

Tom Schuppe—Bookland (Stockton, Calif.)

Eugene L. Schwaab, Jr.—Western (Stoughton, Mass.)

Mariam Schwab—Soundpeace (Ashland, Ore.)

Howard Schwartz—Gambler's (Las Vegas, Nev.)

Richard Schwarz—Stage (Boulder, Colo.)

Merlin D. Schwegman—Merlin's (Isla Vista, Calif.)

Bruno H. Schwegmann—Monckton (Chicago, Ill.)
Gertrude F. Schweibish—GFS (Great River, N.Y.)
Mary Schwertz—Bryn Mawr (Rochester, N.Y.)
Frank Scioscia—Riverrun (Hastings, N.Y.)
Jeffery A. Scoggins—Detering (Houston, Texas)
John Scopazzi—Scopazzi (San Francisco, Calif.)
Allen Scott—Scott (Portland, Maine)
Barry Scott—Scott (Stonington, Conn.)
Edith U. Scott—Croton (Croton, N.Y.)
Peter E. Scott—Ridge (Stone Ridge, N.Y.)
Robert Scott—Croton (Croton, N.Y.)
Alison Seaman—Glooscap (Pefferlaw, Ont.)
R. T. Seaman—Glooscap (Pefferlaw, Ont.)
Percy H. Seamans—Wise (Lake Delton, Wisc.)
Claudia Seaton—Birmingham (Birmingham, Mich.)
Elvin Sebert—Sebert (Mt. Nebo, W.Va.)
Ralph Secord—Green Mtn. (Lyndonville, Vt.)
John Segal—1000 Words (Exeter, N.H.)
Edward Se Gall—Books/Things (Boca Raton, Fla.)
Gini Segedi—Book Stop (Las Vegas, Nev.)
Basil Segun—Ockett (Bryant Pond, Maine)
Elmar W. Seibel—Ars Libri (Boston, Mass.)
Michael Seidenberg—Brazenhead (New York, N.Y.)
R. William Selander—Associates (Falls Church, Va.)
John T. Selawsky—Bibliofile (San Francisco, Calif.)
Charles Seluzicki—Seluzicki (Portland, Ore.)
Marc Selvaggio—Schoyer's (Pittsburgh, Pa.)
M. Sempliner—Library (Ferndale, Mich.)
Dale Seppa—Seppa (Virginia, Minn.)
Julius Ser—Books/Books (Coral Gables, Fla.)
Lana Servies—King (Pensacola, Fla.)
Lewe H. Sessions—Sessions (Birmingham, Ala.)
J. Peterkin Seward—Sewards' (Providence, R.I.)
Schuyler Seward—Sewards' (Providence, R.I.)
John Sexton—Stone Mtn. (Stone Mountain, Ga.)
Robert Seymour—Colebrook (Colebrook, Conn.)
Randolph P. Shaffner—Cyrano's (Highlands, N.C.)
Norman Shaftel—Hemlock (Neponsit, N.Y.)
Sheila Shaftel—Hemlock (Neponsit, N.Y.)
Oscar Shapiro—Shapiro (Washington, D.C.)
S. R. Shapiro—Shapiro (New York, N.Y.)
Gail Shariff—Tintagel (E. Springfield, N.Y.)
Rabic Shariff—Tintagel (E. Springfield, N.Y.)
Rose Sharp—Albatross II (Tiburon, Calif.)
Rose H. Sharp—Albatross (San Francisco, Calif.)
Robert Sharrard—City Lights (San Francisco, Calif.)
Peter Sharrer—Johnson (New York, N.Y.)

Esther Shaver—Shaver (Savannah, Ga.)
Thomas W. Shaw—Shaw (Albany, N.Y.)
Florence Shay—Titles (Highland Park, Ill.)
Juanita Shearer—Renaisscance (Lincolnshire, Ill.)
Robert Sheeby—Rizzoli (New York, N.Y.)
W. Michael Sheehe—Ex Libris (New York, N.Y.)
Dee Shelley—Landmark (New York, N.Y.)
Henry Shelley—Landmark (New York, N.Y.)
Jim Shelton—Hyde Park (Tampa, Fla.)
Jim Shelton—Shelton (Tampa, Fla.)
Vivian Shelton—Hyde Park (Tampa, Fla.)
Daniel K. Shenan—Dan's (Appleton, Wisc.)
Barbara Shenkel—Barjon's (Billings, Mont.)
Jack Sheomaker—Sand (Berkeley, Calif.)
R. L. Shep—Shep (Lopez Isl., Wash.)
Michael J. Sherick—Sherick (Santa Barbara, Calif.)
J. G. Sherlock—Patrick (Toronto, Ont.)
Lewis Sherman—Sherman (Burlington, Ont.)
Ruth Sherman—Sherman (Burlington, Ont.)
Margery Shine—Reference (New York, N.Y.)
Saul Shine—Reference (New York, N.Y.)
Jerome Shochet—Shochet (Sykesville, Md.)
Harold J. Shoebridge—Shoebridge (Lafayette, N.Y.)
Victoria Shoemaker—Sand (Berkeley, Calif.)
Lillian Sholin—Bryn Mawr (New York, N.Y.)
Elliot Kay Shorter—Merlin's (Providence, R.I.)
Hudson Shotwell—Trident (Boulder, Colo.)
C. R. Shuey—Shuey (Elk Grove, Calif.)
Richard Shuh—Alphabet (Toronto, Ont.)
Bob Shuhi—Shuhi (Morris, Conn.)
Pat Shuhi—Shuhi (Morris, Conn.)
Nate Shulimson—Book Shoppe (Myrtle Beach, S.C.)
Betty Shultz—Bookseller (Evansville, Ind.)
Kenneth N. Shure—Shure (Searsmont, Maine)
Alan Siegel—Hollywood City (Hollywood, Calif.)
Daniel G. Siegel—M & S (Weston, Mass.)
Frances Siegel—Hollywood City (Hollywood, Calif.)
Henry A. Siegel—Anglers (Goshen, Conn.)
Marci Siegel—Book City (Hollywood, Calif.)
Mitch Siegel—Book City (Hollywood, Calif.)
Maestro Signorelli—Maestro (Bayport, N.Y.)
Stephen Silberman—Nouveau (Jackson, Miss.)
Martin A. Silver—Silver (Santa Barbara, Calif.)
Arnold Silverman—Goodspeed's #2 (Boston, Mass.)
M. Simmons—Buckabest (Palo Alto, Calif.)
Bobbie Simms—Evergreen (Ft. Worth, Texas)
Irene Simon—Clark's (Spokane, Wash.)
James R. Simon—Clark's (Spokane, Wash.)

Stanley Simon—Stan's (Oceanside, N.Y.)
Rick Simonson—Elliot Bay (Seattle, Wash.)
Barry Singer—Chartwell (New York, N.Y.)
George C. Singer—Ashley (Burlington, Vt.)
Gloria B. Singer—Ashley (Burlington, Vt.)
Kurt Singer—Singer (Buena Park, Calif.)
John Sinkankas—Peri (San Diego, Calif.)
Marjorie J. Sinkankas—Peri (San Diego, Calif.)
Ralph B. Sipper—Joe the Pro (Santa Barbara, Calif.)
Christoper Skagen—Book Manifest (Portland, Ore.)
Marcia Skalnik—Worldwide (Boston, Mass.)
Paul A. Skenadors—Shenandoah (Appleton, Wisc.)
Barry Skolnick—B. & J. (Rego Park, N.Y.)
Y. J. Skutel—Conn. Book (Fairfield, Conn.)
Bill Slater—Slater (Bakersfield, Calif.)
Kathleen Slater—Slater (Bakersfield, Calif.)
Milton Slater—Slater (Tarrytown, N.Y.)
John Slattery—Slattery (Palo Alto, Calif.)
Madeleine Slattery—Slattery (Palo Alto, Calif.)
Gay N. Slavsky—Pacific (Honolulu, Haw.)
Catherine Slicker—Lighthouse (St. Pete., Fla.)
Michael Slicker—Lighthouse (St. Pete., Fla.)
Rosejeanne Slifer—Slifer (New York, N.Y.)
Ann Sloan—Again (Santa Barbara, Calif.)
Charles Sloan—Sloan's (Wayneville, N. C.)
Dorothy Sloan—Sloan (Austin, Texas)
John M. Sloan—Again (Santa Barbara, Calif.)
Julie Sloan—Sloan (Austin, Texas)
Peter S. Sloat—Sloat (Flemington, N.J.)
Kaye Slotnick—E. Coast (Wells, Maine)
Merv Slotnick—E. Coast (Wells, Maine)
Gary F. Smalley—Smalley (Columbia, Tenn.)
Ted Small—Small (So. Yarmouth, Mass.)
Barbara Smith—Smith (Amherst, Mass.)
Camila P. Smith—Smith (Canaan, N.Y.)
Dave Smith—Fantasy (Garden Grove, Calif.)
Don Smith—Smith (Louisville, Ky.)
Donald Smith—Atticus (Toronto, Ont.)
Fred C. Smith—Choctaw (Jackson, Miss.)
Fred W. Smith—Smith (Pleasant Hill, Calif.)
Mrs. H. P. Smith—Thelema (King Bch., Calif.)
Isabel Smith—Marchioness (Laguna Bch., Calif.)
Kathleen Smith—Choctaw (Jackson, Miss.)
Kempton J. C. Smith—Smith (Boxborough, Mass.)
Marie Smith—Book Fair (W. Palm Beach, Fla.)
Nolan E. Smith—Amer. Worlds (Hamden, Conn.)
Patricia S. Smith—Old Book (Bethel, Vt.)
Patterson Smith—Smith (Montclair, N.J.)

P. W. Smith—Smith (Pleasant Hill, Calif.)
Stephen B. Smith—Civil War (So. Miami, Fla.)
Terry Smith—Golden Age (Seattle, Wash.)
V. O. Smith—Smith (Waynesville, N.C.)
Wendell Smith—Smith's (Brewster, Mass.)
William G. Smith—Bill (New York, N.Y.)
William P. Smith—Smith (Mt. Airy, Md.)
Arnold Smoller—Book Clearing (Larchmont, N.Y.)
Nancy Smoller—Book Clearing (Larchmont, N.Y.)
Jeff Smull—Toadstool (Keene, N.H.)
Elaine Smyth—Taylor (Austin, Texas)
Bob Snell—Book Assoc. (Orange, Conn.)
William R. Snell—Book Shelf (Cleveland, Tenn.)
Robert H. Snider—Cohasco (Yonkers, N.Y.)
Dorothy J. Snyder—Springbook (Springfield, Ohio)
Irene Snyder—Bargain (Norfolk, Va.)
Olga Snyder—Snyder (Pittsburgh, Pa.)
Philip D. Snyder—Springbook (Springfield, Ohio)
Jan Sobota—Saturdays' (Euclid, Ohio)
Jarmila Sobota—Saturdays' (Euclid, Ohio)
Ross Socolof—Socolof (Bradenton, Fla.)
James R. Soladay—Diva (Coos Bay, Ore.)
Louisa Solano—Grolier (Cambridge, Mass.)
Paul Solano—NRS (New York, N.Y.)
Shirley Solomon—Pageant (New York, N.Y.)
Wayne Somers—Hammer Mtn. (Schenectady, N.Y.)
Marv Sommer—Sommer (Niagara Falls, N.Y.)
Oscar Sorge—Grandview (Hudson, N.Y.)
Peter G. Sorrenti—Sorrenti (Palatine, Ill.)
R. Sorsky—Sorsky (Fresno, Calif.)
Philip T. Soucy—Peggatty (Clarkston, Wash.)
Harry Soul, Jr.—Pleasant St. (Woodstock, Vt.)
Judy Soule—Homesteader (Wenatchee, Wash.)
Constance R. Spande—Wyngate (Bethesda, Md.)
Thomas F. Spande—Wyngate (Bethesda, Md.)
Esther Sparks—Arader (Chicago, Ill.)
Julie Spears—Reading (Mexico, Ind.)
George Spector—Spector (Jackson Hgts., N.Y.)
Gladys Spector—Spector (Jackson Hgts., N.Y.)
Michael Speer—Europe (Staten Isl., N.Y.)
Michael F. Speers—Weston (Weston, Vt.)
J. R. Speirs—Amer. Pol. (Newtown, Conn.)
Richard W. Spellman—Spellman (Brick Town, N.J.)
Darwin Spencer—Spencer's (Vancouver, Wash.)
John D. Spencer—Riverow (Owego, N.Y.)
Ann Spigler—Out-Of (San Clemente, Calif.)
Sharalyn Spiteri—Grapevine (San Mateo, Calif.)
W. G. Spittal—Iroqrafts (Ohsweken, Ont.)

Bertrand L. Spooner, Jr.—Spooner's (Tilton, N.H.)

Virginia I. Spooner—Spooner's (Tilton, N.H.)

Roy A. Squires—Squires (Glendale, Calif.)

Mike Stafford—Books/Comics #1 and #2 (both Indianapolis, Ind.)

James Staley—2nd Time (Ventura, Calif.)

Peter Stalker II—Everard (Santa Barbara, Calif.)

Robert M. Stamp—Heritage (Toronto, Ont.)

Mark Stanfield—Clark (Baton Rouge, La.)

David Stang—Ars Libri (Boston, Mass.)

Florence Stang—Edison Hall (Edison, N.J.)

George Stang—Edison Hall (Edison, N.J.)

Kathleen Stanley—Stanley (Wilder, Vt.)

Thomas Stanley—Stanley (Wilder, Vt.)

Jerrold G. Stanoff—Rare Oriental (Aptos, Calif.)

John Stark—Ohio (Mansfield, Ohio)

K. Starosciak—Starosciak (San Francisco, Calif.)

Jan Starratt—Starratt (Palo Alto, Calif.)

Ernest Starr—Starr (Boston, Mass.)

Norman Starr—Starr (Boston, Mass.)

Dale W. Starry, Sr.—Starry (Shippensburg, Pa.)

Sheldon Stedolsky—Baroque (Hollywood, Calif.)

Craig Steele—Together (Denver, Colo.)

Gary Steele—Cinema (Hollywood, Calif.)

Geoffrey Steele—Steele (Lumberville, Pa.)

Helen Steele—Winsted (Spg. Green, Wisc.)

Virgil Steele—Winsted (Spg. Green, Wisc.)

Gary Steigerwald—Steigerwald (Bloomington, Ind.)

Mary Ann Steimle—Busy Hermit (Niles, Mich.)

Diana G. Stein—La Galeria (Las Vegas, N.M.)

John G. Stein—Stein (Gold Beach, Ore.)

Joseph W. Stein—La Galeria (Las Vegas, N.M.)

Robert Stein—Spectrum (Milwaukee, Wisc.)

Marjorie O. Steininger—Otzinachson (Allenwood, Pa.)

Bob Stenard—William (Mineola, N.Y.)

Christopher Stephens—Stephens (Hastings, N.Y.)

John Stephens—Book Cellar (Bethesda, Md.)

Michael Stephens—Treehorn (Santa Rosa, Calif.)

Robert B. Stephenson—Stephenson (Jaffrey, N.H.)

David C. Sterling—Toxophilite (Simsbury, Conn.)

Carol Stern—Sidney's (Missoula, Mont.)

Harry Stern—Stern (Chicago, Ill.)

Madeleine B. Stern—Rostenberg (New York, N.Y.)

Peter L. Stern—Pepper/Stern (Sharon, Mass.)

Diane Stevens—Book Sleuth (Colorado Spgs., Colo.)

Richard L. Stevens—Stevens (Wake Forest, N.C.)

James G. Stevenson—Stevensons (Euless, Texas)

Roger P. Steward—Attic (Torrington, Conn.)

Bee Stewart—Judi's (Twin Falls, Idaho)

Don Stewart—MacLeod's (Vancouver, B.C.)

Frances M. Stewart—Stewart's (Camp Spgs., Md.)

Jennifer Stewart—Browsers' (Olympia, Wash.)

Tom Stewart—Stewart (Portland, Ore.)

William F. Stewart—Stewart's (Camp Spgs., Md.)

Jack Sticha—S & S (St. Paul, Minn.)

Pat Sticha—S & S (St. Paul, Minn.)

Christophe Stickel—Stickel (Colma, Calif.)

Vivian Stidham—Readbeard's (Marion, Ind.)

Margaret Stilwell—Stilwell (Morgantown, W.Va.)

Don Stine—Antic Hay (W. Caldwell, N.J.)

Annette Stith—Book Sleuth (Colorado Spgs., Colo.)

Olympia T. Stitt—7 Roads (San Francisco, Calif.)

Robert B. Stitt—7 Roads (San Francisco, Calif.)

Katina Stockbridge—Yesterday's (Washington, D.C.)

Peter Stockman—Stockman (Palmyra, N.Y.)

Richard Stoddard—Performing (New York, N.Y.)

Gerard Stodolski—Richards (Templeton, Mass.)

D'Ann Stone—Bay Window (Florence, Ore.)

David L. Stone—Stone (Huntsville, Ala.)

John Stone—Bay Window (Florence, Ore.)

Don Stonestreet—Mad (Maumee, Ohio)

Sandra Stonestreet—Mad (Maumee, Ohio)

Ivan Stormgart—Stormgart (Boston, Mass.)

Jack Stouten—Bookpeople (Wadena, Minn.)

Linda Stouten—Bookpeople (Wadena, Minn.)

Steven W. Strange—Murder (Ft. Worth, Texas)

Elaine Stratton—Swiss (St. Louis, Mo.)

Jan Stratton—Stone Of (Canterbury, Conn.)

Tom Stratton—Stone Of (Canterbury, Conn.)

John Nathan Stroud—Stroud (Williamsburg, W.Va.)

T. G. Stryker—Stryker's (Montreal, Que.)

G. W. Stuart, Jr.—Ravenstree and Stuart (both Yuma, Ariz.)

Harry M. Stuart—Palma (Wilmington, Del.)

Lenore Stuart—Cookbooks (Yuma, Ariz.)

Jane Stubbs—Stubbs (New York, N.Y.)

John H. Stubbs—Stubbs (New York, N.Y.)

Mark Stueve—Old Erie (Cleveland, Ohio)

Ron Stump—Mt. Falcon (Greeley, Colo.)

Allan Stypeck—2nd Story (Bethesda, Md.)

Ahngsana Suarez—Suarez (New York, N.Y.)

Thomas Suarez—Suarez (New York, N.Y.)

June Sublett—Broad Ripple (Indianapolis, Ind.)

Gustave H. Suhm—Suhm (Westfield, Mass.)

Dorothy Sullivan—Sullivan (St. Pete., Fla.)

John Sullivan—Sullivan (Chicago, Ill.)
Kathleen T. Sullivan—Sullivan (Coventry, Conn.)
Bonita Summers—Summers (Pacific, Mo.)
Margaret Summers—Golden Hill (Helena, Mont.)
William Summers—National (Brooklyn, N.Y.)
C. Sussman—Chapter/Verse (Maywood, N.J.)
Jane Sutley—Sutley (Centralia, Wash.)
Henry Suzuki—Weiser (New York, N.Y.)
Mary Swanson—Catbird (Portland, Ore.)
D. L. Swarthout—Berry Hill (Deansboro, N.Y.)

Gary Swartzburg—Books & Co. (San Francisco, Calif.)
Tom A. Swinford—Swinford (Paris, Ill.)
Tonya Y. Swinford—Swinford (Paris, Ill.)
Wally Swist—Globe (Northampton, Mass.)
Bonnie Switzer—Summerhouse (Dayton, Wyo.)
Mary F. Sykes—Sykes (No. Weare, N.H.)
Richard L. Sykes—Sykes (No. Weare, N.H.)
Ralph Sylvester—Sylvester (Los Angeles, Calif.)
David Szewczyk—Phila. Rare (Philadelphia, Pa.)

T

Fran Taber—Homesteader (Wenatchee, Wash.)
Joan Tainter—Research (Fremont, Neb.)
Olga Tainter—Tainters (Temple, N.H.)
Olga E. Tainter—Abbies (Temple, N.H.)
Paul Tainter—Research (Fremont, Neb.)
Alan Taksler—New Steamship (El Cajon, Calif.)
Victor Tamerlis—Tamerlis (Mamaroneck, N.Y.)
Melvin Tanditash—Tanditash (New York, N.Y.)
Matthew Tannenbaum—Bookstore (Lenox, Mass.)
Terence Tanner—Hamill (Chicago, Ill.)
Douglas C. Tappin—Tappin (Atlantic Bch., Fla.)
F. Donald Tappin—Tappin (Atlantic Bch., Fla.)
Mary Tardiff—House (Toronto, Ont.)
E. Tatro—Tatro (Wethersfield, Conn.)
Mimi Taube—Cadenza (Smithtown, N.Y.)
Bill Tauscher—Tauscher (Bristol, Va.)
Aileen T. Taylor—Taylor (Kerrville, Texas)
Frederic Taylor—Johnny (Manchester, Vt.)
James R. Taylor—Grub Street (Detroit, Mich.)
Mary C. Taylor—Grub Street (Detroit, Mich.)
Pegi Taylor—Webster's (Milwaukee, Wisc.)
Richard C. Taylor—Fox Hill (Palmer, Mass.)
Tom Taylor—Taylor (Austin, Texas)
Tom Taylor—Taylor (Westland, Mich.)
Leon Tebbetts—Tebbetts (Hallowell, Maine)
Howard Tedder—Northampton (Hamilton Sq., N.J.)
Lee Temares—Temares (Plandome, N.Y.)
Mike Temares—Temares (Plandome, N.Y.)
Steve Temple—Temple (Toronto, Ont.)
Arthur Ten Eyck—Ten Eyck (Southboro, Mass.)
Catherine Ten Eyck—Ten Eyck (Southboro, Mass.)

Gene Terres—Terres (Minneapolis, Minn.)
John V. Terrey—Old Tech (Carlisle, Mass.)
D. Testa—Testa (No. Newark, N.J.)
Albert Tetreault—Elm St. (Lancaster, N.H.)
George Theofiles—Miscellaneous (New Freedom, Pa.)
Lote Thistlethwaite—Eeyore (Cotati, Calif.)
Phyllis Tholin—Tholin (Evanston, Ill.)
Anne Thomas—Thomas (Oak Park, Ill.)
Della Thomas—Caravan (Stillwater, Okla.)
Ed Thomas—Book Carnival (Orange, Calif.)
Jeffrey Thomas—Thomas (San Francisco, Calif.)
John E. Thomas—Caravan (Stillwater, Okla.)
Kathy Thompson—Book Attic (San Bernardino, Calif.)
Ken Thompson—In #1 (San Francisco, Calif.)
Richard D. Thompson—Book Attic (San Bernardino, Calif.)
William Thompson—Cleland's (Portsmouth, N. H.)
George Thomson—Book Barrel (Los Angeles, Calif.)
John Thomson—Bartleby's (Bethesda, Md.)
Andrew Thurnauer—Spenser's (Boston, Mass.)
Roberta Tichenor—Annie's #1 (Portland, Ore.)
Roberta Tichenor—Annie's #2 (Portland, Ore.)
James C. Tillinghast—Tillinghast (Hancock, N.H.)
Gloria Timmel—Vintage (Wheaton, Ill.)
Richard Timmel—Vintage (Wheaton, Ill.)
Don Tinker—Tinker (Santa Cruz, Calif.)
Barbara Tippin—Britannia (New Preston, Conn.)
Magda Tisza—Tisza (Chestnut Hill, Mass.)
Nancy E. Titcomb—Titcomb's (E. Sandwich, Mass.)

Ralph M. Titcomb—Titcomb's (E. Sandwich, Mass.)
Bernard Titowsky—Austin (Kew Gardens, N.Y.)
Bernard Titowsky—Austin (Richmond Hill, N.Y.)
Joanne Titus—Memory (Battle Creek, Mich.)
James Todd—Shorey (Seattle, Wash.)
J. W. Todd, Jr.—Shorey (Seattle, Wash.)
Russ Todd—Todd (Cave Creek, Ariz.) and Scottsdale (Scottsdale, Ariz.)
Marian Todish—Poor Richard's (Grand Rapids, Mich.)
Terrence S. Todish—Poor Richard's (Grand Rapids, Mich.)
Robert Tollett—Tollett (New York, N.Y.)
James D. Tolliver, Jr.—Tolliver's (Los Angeles, Calif.)
Barry Tominik—Jay's (Marlboro, N.J.)
Jay Tominik—Jay's (Marlboro, N.J.)
Phyllis Tominik—Jay's (Marlboro, N.J.)
Sam Tomlin—Old Mill (Alexandria, Va.)
Jan Tonnesen—Wahrenbrock's (San Diego, Calif.)
Walter Toop—Cheshire (Yakima, Wash.)
Deborah B. Topliff—Grt. Lakes (Ann Arbor, Mich.)
Tom Torbert—Collector's (Phoenix, Ariz.)
Jane Tormey—Bygone (Burlington, Vt.)
Gordon Totty—Totty (Lunenburg, Mass.)
Dr. Francis Touchet—Touchet (New York, N.Y.)
Charles D. Townsend—Aceto (Sarasota, Fla.)
John Townsend—Schooner (Halifax, N.S.)
Elizabeth Trace—Trace (Peekskill, N.Y.)
Roberta Tracy—Tempest (Waitsville, Vt.)

T. Trafton—Max Gate (Kankakee, Ill.)
George Tramp—Tramp (Jackson, Mich.)
Carol Travis—Xerxes (Glen Head, N.Y.)
Dennis Travis—Xerxes (Glen Head, N.Y.)
Adelaide M. Trigg—Far Corners (Mobile, Ala.)
Ron Trimble—O'Leary's (Tacoma, Wash.)
Rita Trote—Printed (Savannah, Ga.)
Esther J. Tucker—Tuckers (Pittsburgh, Pa.)
Harvey Tucker—Black Sun (New York, N.Y.)
Linda Tucker—Black Sun (New York, N.Y.)
Susan C. Tucker—Books With (Concord, Mass.)
Anthony M. Tufts—Cider (Exeter, N.H.)
Peter Tumarkin—Tumarkin (New York, N.Y.)
Bob Tune—Antiquaria (Franklin, Tenn.)
Linda Tune—Antiquaria (Franklin, Tenn.)
David Tunick—Tunick (New York, N.Y.)
C. H. Tupper—Tupper (Vancouver, B.C.)
Henry Turlington—Turlington (Pittsboro, N.C.)
Breck Turner—With (Lake Placid, N.Y.)
David Turner—Carlson (Portland, Maine)
Joel Turner—Under (Shaker Hgts., Ohio)
Julie Turner—With (Lake Placid, N.Y.)
Phyllis Turner—Pirages (McMinnville, Ore.)
Charles E. Tuttle—Tuttle (Ruthland, Vt.)
Judith A. Tuttle—Tuttle (Madison, Wisc.)
Katherine Tuttle—Chaos (Washington, D.C.)
Robert P. Tuttle—Tuttle (Madison, Wisc.)
George H. Tweney—Tweney (Seattle, Wash.)
Maxine R. Tweney—Tweney (Seattle, Wash.)
Ryan D. Tweney—Tweney (Bowling Green, Ohio)

U

Clarke Uhler—Old Barn (Forsyth, Ill.)
Sue Ujlaki—Book Traders (Winter Haven, Fla.)
Robert E. Underhill—Underhill (Poughkeepsie, N.Y.)
Willis D. Underwood—Antique Books (Hamden, Conn.)
Ira Unschuld—Abbot (Bronx, N.Y.)

Colleen Urbanek—Colleen's (Houston, Texas)
Marjorie E. Uren—Keramos (Ann Arbor, Mich.)
Manuel Urrizola—Urrizola (Los Angeles, Calif.)
Bryant Urstadt—Green Mtn. (So. Royalton, Vt.)
Gordon Usticke—Pan (Catskill, N.Y.)

V

Carmen D. Valentino—Valentino (Philadelphia, Pa.)
C. A. Valverde—Wahrenbrock's (San Diego, Calif.)
Robert Vance—Heritage (Sonora, Calif.)
Karen Van De Loop—Madonna (Combermere, Ont.)
James Vanderberg—Viewpoint (New York, N.Y.)
Eve Vanderstoel—Vanderstoel (El Cerrito, Calif.)
Graeme Vanderstoel—Vanderstoel (El Cerrito, Calif.)
Takis Vandoros—Vandoros (Middleton, Wisc.)
Daryl Van Fleet—Bibliomania (Berkeley and Oakland, Calif.)
Elizabeth Van Treuren—Bookfinder (Eureka, Calif.)
P. Van Zoeren—Asian Books (Cambridge, Mass.)
Cindy Vargo—Vargo's (Bozeman, Mont.)
Fran Vargo—Vargo's (Bozeman, Mont.)
David Varner—Varner (Belton, Mo.)
A. Lois Varney—Varney's (Casco, Maine)
Betty Vasin—AlphaBook (Van Nuys, Calif.)
Ray Vasin—AlphaBook (Van Nuys, Calif.)
Joseph Vasta—Vasta (New York, N.Y.)
Charles Vercoutere—Black Swan (Sacramento, Calif.)
Barbara Verrilli—Trotting (Springfield, Mass.)

Rocco Verrilli—Trotting (Springfield, Mass.)
Stephen Viederman—Viederman (Leonia, N.J.)
Alfonso Vijil—Libros (Redlands, Calif.)
Robert Villegas—Lion (Indianapolis, Ind.)
Charles Vilnis—Sebastopol (Sebastopol, Calif.)
J. C. Vincent—Buccaneer (Laguna Bch., Calif.)
Kathleen Vincent—East West (Hamburg, N.Y.)
Patricia G. Vinge—Call Me Ishmael (Saugatuck, Mich.)
Gene Vinik—Vinik (Tucson, Ariz.)
Joanne Vinik—Vinik (Tucson, Ariz.)
Jim Visbeck—Isaiah (Worcester, Mass.)
Rose Mary Vissage—Heinoldt (So. Egg, N.J.)
Molly Vogel—Old Southport (Southport, Conn.)
Isabel Vogt—Vogt (Meadow Vista, Calif.)
Itzhak Volansky—McDonald's (San Francisco, Calif.)
Darleen Volkert—Book Barn (S. Sioux City, Neb.)
A. F. Von Blon, Jr.—Von Blon's (Waco, Texas)
Richard A. Vorpe—Dragon's Lair (Dayton, Ohio)
Suzanne Vuillet—Chartwell (New York, N.Y.)

W

Peter Wackell—Phenomenologica (Worcester, Mass.)
Glory Wade—Connolly/Wade (Vista, Calif.)
John Wade—Wade (Cincinnati, Ohio)
Barbara Wadhams—Bygone (Burlington, Vt.)
Olga Wagensonner—Hoefliger (Buffalo, N.Y.)
Cecil M. Wahle—Old Mont. (Monterey, Calif.)
Paul Waite—Waite (Madison, Wisc.)
Irene Walet—Irene's (So. Gardner, Mass.)
Francis G. Walett—Walett (Abington, Mass.)
Kent Walgren—Scallawagiana (Salt Lake City, Utah)
Byron Walker—Walker (San Leandro, Calif.)
Jane Hobson Walker—Hobson's (Jenkintown, Pa.)
K. H. Walker—Jense (Los Angeles, Calif.)
Ruth Walker—Sebastopol (Sebastopol, Calif.)

Ann Marie Wall—Anchor (Newport, R.I.)
Simone Wallace—Sisterhood (Los Angeles, Calif.)
Pat Wallesir—Book Connection (Mariposa, Calif.)
L. A. Wallrich—About (Toronto, Ont.)
Sherlu R. Walpole—Shirley's (Springfield, Mo.)
Frank O. Walsh III—Yesteryear (Atlanta, Ga.)
Ray Walsh—Curious Book (E. Lansing, Mich.)
Mrs. William Walsh—Bookcase (Greenfield, N.H.)
Barbara Walzer—Walzer (Providence, R.I.)
Rich Wandschneider—Bookloft (Enterprise, Ore.)
Victor E. Wangner—Wangner's (Montclair, N.J.)
Raymond M. Wapner—Schiller and Schiller-Wapner (both New York, N.Y.)
Lois H. Ward—Ward (Prospect, Ohio)
Rita Wardo—Auten (Bedminster, N.J.)

James Ware—Books/Comics #1 (Indianapolis, Ind.)
Robert C. Warner—Loose (Jerome, Mich.)
John F. Warren—Warren (Philadelphia, Pa.)
Lawrence Washington—Breadloaf (E. Middlebury, Vt.)
Andrew Washton—Washton (New York, N.Y.)
Larry C. Watkins—Watkins (Dolgeville, N.Y.)
Barrie D. Watson—Watson (Buelah, Colo.)
Jenny Watson—Watson (Exeter, N.H.)
Jack Way—Way's (Seattle, Wash.)
Robert Wayne—King's (Boulder, Colo.)
Gary Wayner—Wayner (Ft. Payne, Ala.)
R. M. Weatherford—Weatherford (Monroe, Wash.)
Dale A. Weber—Weber (Troy, Minn.)
E. L. Weber—Beaver (Daly City, Calif.)
Jeff Weber—Zeitlin (Los Angeles, Calif.)
Phyllis Weber—Weber (Troy, Minn.)
Pamela W. Webster—Bibliofile (San Francisco, Calif.)
John W. Weekly—Mahoney (Buffalo, N.Y.)
Dr. Richard Weeks—Baptist (Watertown, Wisc.)
Hassie Weiman—Darby (Darby, Pa.)
Jerry Weiman—Darby (Darby, Pa.)
Daniel R. Weinberg—Abe. Lincoln (Chicago, Ill.)
Jeffrey H. Weinberg—Water Row (Sudbury, Mass.)
Barbara Weindling—Weindling (Danbury, Conn.)
Alan Weiner—Academy (New York, N.Y.)
Richard Weiner—Escargot (Brielle, N.J.)
Steven Weinkselbaum—Bay Shore (Bay Shore, N.Y.) and Herpetological (Lindenhurst, N.Y.)
Ben Weinstein—Heritage (Los Angeles, Calif.)
Bob Weinstein—Book Baron (Anaheim, Calif.)
Louis Weinstein—Heritage (Los Angeles, Calif.)
Michael Weintraub—Weintraub #1 and #2 (both New York, N.Y.)
Stephen Weisman—Ximenes (New York, N.Y.)
Laura Weiss—Book Nook (Escondido, Calif.)
Philip R. Weiss—Collectabilia (Valley Stream, N.Y.)
Herbert Weitz—Weitz (New York, N.Y.)
Elizabeth Wells—Imagine That (No. Adams and Pittsfield, Mass.)
Priscilla Welsh—Bygone (Burlington, Vt.)
Pat Wendt—Bluestem (Lincoln, Neb.)
Scott Wendt—Bluestem (Lincoln, Neb.)
Sam Wenger—3 Geese (Woodstock, N.Y.)
Martin Wenkle—Buddenbrooks (Boston, Mass.)
Irene Werner—Caddo (Cartaro, Ariz.)
Nora C. Wertz—Little (U. Montclair, N.J.)
R. Wertz—Wertz (Flint, Mich.)

B. C. West, Jr.—Autos (Eliz. City, N.C.)
Richard West—West's (Elm Grove, Wisc.)
Walt West—West (Provo, Utah)
Douglas Westerberg—Yankee (Rochester and Williamson, N.Y.)
Janet Westerberg—Yankee (Rochester, N.Y.)
John Westerberg—Yankee (Rochester and Williamson, N.Y.)
A. Westlake—Ye Olde (St. Joseph, Mich.)
Arthur Westlake—Curiosity (St. Joseph, Mich.)
Roslyn Westlake—Curiosity (St. Joseph, Mich.)
Billie Wetall—Antiq. Bookworm (Sharon, Mass.)
Jim Weyant—Scribe's (Newport, R.I.)
Arthur Wharton—Wharton (Toronto, Ont.)
Bern Wheel—Wheel (Oak Park, Ill.)
Bill Wheeler—Oar House (Clearwater, Fla.)
Caroline C. Wheeler—Little (Hinsdale, Ill.)
Joy A. Wheeler—Wheeler (Elgin, Ore.)
Susan Wheeler—Printed (New York, N.Y.)
Dennis E. Whelan—Whelan (Newberry, Fla.)
Diane Whitburn—Pride (Ballston Lake, N.Y.)
Merrill Whitburn—Pride (Ballston Lake, N.Y.)
Barbara White—Geraci (Accord, N.Y.)
Bill White—Earthworks (Washington, D.C.)
Evelyn White—White's (Asbury Park, N.J.)
Fred White, Jr.—Frontier (Bryan, Texas)
Gary L. White—Arcana (Santa Monica, Calif.)
John W. White—Book Studio (Atlanta, Ga.)
Jonathan White—White (New York, N.Y.)
Robert R. White—White (Albuquerque, N.M.)
Barbara Whitehead—Arch (Bellows Falls, Vt.)
Barbara Whitehead—Quechee (Quechee, Vt.)
Duane Whitehead—Arch (Bellows Falls, Vt.)
Duane Whitehead—Quechee (Quechee, Vt.)
Everett Whitlock—Whitlock (Bethany, Conn.)
Gilbert Whitlock—Whitlock (Bethany, Conn.)
Reverdy Whitlock—Whitlock's (New Haven, Conn.)
Billy Whitted—Book Trader (Fairmont, N.C.)
Roger Wicker—Transition (San Francisco, Calif.)
Barbara Widdoes—Bryn Mawr (Pittsburgh, Pa.)
Anne Wiedenkeller—Printers' (Boston and Arlington, Mass.)
Barry Wiedenkeller—Printers' (Boston and Arlington, Mass.)
L. M. Wiggin—Cobble Crt. (Litchfield, Conn.)
Claire G. Wilcox—Pisces (Albion, Mich.)
Joe Wilcox—Pisces (Albion, Mich.)
Ann Wilder—Wilder (Brookline, Mass.)
Tim Wilder—Wilder (Hubbardston, Mass.)

Tennessee Wilde—Opera Box (Brooklyn, N.Y.)

Effie Wildman—Market (Idaho Falls, Idaho)

Richard Wiles—Barn E. (Tivoli, N.Y.)

W. Wiles—Patrick (Toronto, Ont.)

Dave Wilhelm—Preservation (Evanston, Ill.)

Colleen Wilhite—Wilhite (Clearwater, Fla.)

Virgil Wilhite—Wilhite (Clearwater, Fla.)

Robert L. Wilkerson—Prufrock (Pasadena, Calif.)

Robin Wilkerson—Wilkerson (Lincoln, Mass.)

Lillian Wilkins—Rodden's (Long Bch., Calif.)

George F. Wilkinson—Albatross (San Francisco, Calif.)

A. A. Williams—Sporting (Rancocas, N.J.)

Adrienne Williams—Oceanside (Oceanside, N.Y.)

Bleecker Williams—Ordnance (Madison, Conn.)

Diane F. Williams—Williams (Bethany, Conn.)

Harriet Williams—Sail (Newcastle, Maine and Lexington, Ky.)

Robert B. Williams—Williams (Bethany, Conn.)

Ruth Williams—Fortuna (Kirkland, Wash.)

Tom Williams—Williams (Calgary, Alt.)

Wesley C. Williams—Publix (Cleveland, Ohio)

Steve Willins—Wellfleet (Wellfleet, Mass.)

Roy Willis—Willis (Columbus, Ohio)

Marjory E. Willkins—Island (Mercer, Wash.)

Gail Wills—Lord (Marshfield, Mass.)

Jane Willsea—Anacapa (Berkeley, Calif.)

Eric Wilska—Bookloft (Grt. Barrington, Mass.)

Gail Wilson—Wilson (Kitchener, Ont.)

James Wilson—Wilson (New York, N.Y.)

Jean Wilson—Book Shop (Boise, Idaho)

Robert A. Wilson—Phoenix (New York, N.Y.)

Sarah Wilson—Wilson (Bull Shoals, Ark.)

Steve Wilson—Amer. City (Denver, Colo.)

Andrew Winiarczyk—Last (Williamsport, Pa.)

Linda Winiarczyk—Last (Williamsport, Pa.)

Michael Winne—About (Moline, Ill.)

Walt Winner—Aviation (Glendale, Calif.)

David S. Wirshup—Anacapa (Berkeley, Calif.)

Andrew Wittenborn—Wittenborn (Pleasantville, N.Y.)

Laurence Witten—Witten (Southport, Conn.)

Michael Witter—2nd Front (San Francisco, Calif.)

Lois Wodika—Yesterday's (Oak Park, Mich.)

Al Woebcke—Chimney (Bridgeport, Conn.)

Alan Wofsy—Wofsy (San Francisco, Calif.)

Clarence Wolf—MacManus (Philadelphia, Pa.)

Daniel Wolf—Wolf (New York, N.Y.)

Harvey J. Wolf—Wolf's (Morgantown, W.Va.)

Kenneth L. Wolf—Wolf (Orcutt, Calif.)

Christopher Wolfe—Heller (Swarthmore, Pa.)

R. Chris Wolff—Old Book (Morristown, N.J.)

Janet Wolney—Summerhouse (Dayton, Wyo.)

Bengta Woo—Woo (Plainview, N.Y.)

Charles Wood—Wood (Boston, Mass.)

Guy A. Wood—Peninsula (Traverse City, Mich.)

James Wood—Wood (Tampa, Fla.)

Elisabeth Woodburn—Woodburn (Hopewell, N.J.)

Peter A. Woodruff—Woodruff (Grass Lake, Mich.)

Jay Woods—Woods (Yakima, Wash.)

Amelia Woolf—Woolf's (Atlanta, Ga.)

Gene Woolf—Woolf's (Atlanta, Ga.)

Linda Woolley—Alphabet (Toronto, Ont.)

Grant Woolmer—Woolmer (Montreal, Que.)

J. Howard Woolmer—Woolmer (Revere, Pa.)

Deborah K. Woolverton—Chirurgical (Baltimore, Md.)

Jeffrey Wortman—Wortman (New York, N.Y.)

Lynn Wozniak—Epistemologist (Bryn Mawr, Pa.)

Rob Wozniak—Epistemologist (Bryn Mawr, Pa.)

H. Donley Wray—Sacred (Goffstown, N.H.)

William P. Wreden—Wreden (Palo Alto, Calif.)

William P. Wreden, Jr.—Wreden (Palo Alto, Calif.)

Bessie L. Wright—Wright (Waxahachie, Texas)

Hugh M. Wright—Wright (Waxahachie, Texas)

Nancy Wright—Snowbound (Norridgeweck, Maine)

William Wroth—Almagre (Bloomington, Ind.)

Emily Wunsch—Vol. I (Hillsdale, Mich.)

Richard Wunsch—Vol. I (Hillsdale, Mich.)

Ludo J. Wurfbain—World Wide (Long Beach, Calif.)

Mareanne Wurlitzer—Wurlitzer (New York, N.Y.)

Carl Wurtzel—Camel (New York

Faith Wurtzel—Camel (New York

Charles E. Wyatt—Wyatt (San Diego, Calif.)

William Wyer—Ursus (New York, N.Y.)

Ann Wyllie—Windsor (Windsor, Conn.)

Arthur Wyllie—Windsor (Windsor, Conn.)

Y

Edmund Yankov—Witkin (New York, N.Y.)
Rhett R. Yap—Bookbizniz (Atlantic City, N.J.)
William Yeago—Lake (San Francisco, Calif.)
Herb Yellin—Yellin (Northridge, Calif.)
G. A. Yeomans—Andover Sq. (Knoxville, Tenn.)
Vivian York—Lobster (Spruce Head, Maine)

Morris N. Young—Young (New York, N.Y.)
Roy Young—Young (Dobbs Ferry, N.Y.)
Bob Younger—Morningside (Dayton, Ohio)
Helen Younger—Aleph-Bet (Valley Cottage, N.Y.)
Mary Younger—Morningside (Dayton, Ohio)
Ruth L. Yule—Fly Creek (E. Lansing, Mich.)

Z

Fred Zaharoff—Bookcase (St. Clair Shores, Mich.)
Alfred F. Zambelli—Zambelli (New York, N.Y.)
Maria D. Zambelli—Zambelli (New York, N.Y.)
Ric Zank—Pan (Catskill, N.Y.)
Bohdan Zaremba—Zaremba (Cambridge, Mass.)
Suzanne Zavrian—Pomander (New York, N.Y.)
Giampiero Zazzera—Hillman (New York, N.Y.)
G. Zeehandelaar—Cat (New Rochelle, N.Y.)
W. L. Zeigler—Zeigler (New Oxford, Pa.)
Jacob Zeitlin—Zeitlin (Los Angeles, Calif.)
Stanley Zeitlin—Zeitlin Per. (Los Angeles, Calif.)
Mary Zeller—Bookman (Tybee Isl., Ga.)
Geraldine C Zellner—Zellner's (Easton, Pa.)
Maurice A. Zellner—Zellner's (Easton, Pa.)
Anthony Ziagos—Ziagos (Lowell, Mass.)

Carol Zientek—Left Bank (Oak Park, Ill.)
Carol Zimmer—Book Stop (Dearborn Hgts., Mich.)
Thomas Zimmerman—Plain (Arlington Hgts., Ill.)
Marlene Znoy—Southpaw (Roxbury, Mass.)
Josephine Zollinger—Dakota (Eugene, Ore.)
John Zollner—Traveler (Union, Conn.)
John Zubel—Zubel (Cleveland, Ohio)
Michael Zubel—Zubel (Cleveland, Ohio)
Harvey Zucker—Photographers (New York, N.Y.)
Irving Zucker—Milestone and Zucker (both New York, N.Y.)
Mrs. Zucker—Milestone (New York, N.Y.)
Tony Zwicker—Zwicker (New York, N.Y.)
Jane Zwisohn—Zwisohn (Albuquerque, N.M.)

Index
of
All Dealers
Listed

A

Bayshore (Van Nuys, Calif.)
Bay Side (Soquel, Calif.)
Bayview (Northport, N.Y.)
Bay Window (Florence, Ore.)
B & B (Randolph, Mass.)
Bean (Biddeford, Maine)
Bean (Niantic, Conn.)
Bear (W. Brattleboro, Vt.)
Bearce (Salem, Ore.)
Beardsley (Somerville, N.J.)
Beare (Wilmington, Del.)
Beasley (Chicago, Ill.)
Beatific (Schenectady, N.Y.)
Beattie (Parkesburg, Pa.)
Beaver (Daly City, Calif.)
Beaver (Portland, Ore.)
Bebbah (Andover, Kan.)
Becker (Acton Centre, Mass.)
Becker (New York, N.Y.)
Beckham's (New Orleans, La.)
Beckhorn (Dobbs Ferry, N.Y.)
Becky (Hannibal, Mo.)
Bedford's (Ellsworth, Maine)
Bel Canto (Metuchen, N.J.)
Belknap (Boston, Mass.)
Ben Franklin (U. Nyack, N.Y.)
Benjamin (Hunter, N.Y.)
Benjamins (Philadelphia, Pa.)
Bennett (Southold, N.Y.)
Bennett (White Plains, N.Y.)
Bennington (Bennington, Vt.)
Benoit (Montreal, Que.)
Benson (W. Cornwall, Conn.)
Benson (Ottawa, Ont.)
Berg (Devils Lake, N.D.)
Berk (Studio City, Calif.)
Berkelouw (Los Angeles, Calif.)
Berkley (Berkley, Minn.)
Berkowitz (Chester, N.Y.)
Berliawsky (Camden, Maine)
Berman (Los Angeles, Calif.)
Berman (Atlanta, Ga.)
Bernard (Rockville, Md.)
Bernett (Larchmont, N.Y.)
Berry Hill (Deansboro, N.Y.)
Berry (Kingston, Ont.)
Besnia (Sterling Jctn., Mass.)
Best (Cambridge, Mass.)
Bethlehem (Bethlehem, Conn.)

Between (Old Bridge, N.J.)
Bever (Edmond, Okla.)
Bevington (Terre Haute, Ind.)
Beyer (Stratford, Conn.)
Bibby (Gold Hill, Ore.)
Bibelots (Seattle, Wash.)
Bible (El Cajon, Calif.)
Biblioctopus (Idyllwild, Calif.)
Bibliofile (San Francisco, Calif.)
Bibliolatree (E. Hampton, Conn.)
Bibliomania (Delaware, Ohio)
Bibliomania (Berkeley, Calif.)
Bibliomania (Schenectady, N.Y.)
Bibliomania (Oakland, Calif.)
Biblion (Forest Hills, N.Y.)
Bicentennial (Kalamazoo, Mich.)
Bieber (Kenilworth, N.J.)
Biegeleisen (Brooklyn, N.Y.)
Biermaier's (Minneapolis, Minn.)
Big #2 (Detroit, Mich.)
Big #1 (Detroit, Mich.)
Bill (Long I. City, N.Y.)
Bill (New York, N.Y.)
Bill's (Stevens Pt., Wisc.)
Binkin's (Brooklyn, N.Y.)
Bird's Nest (Missoula, Mont.)
Birmingham (Birmingham, Mich.)
Bishop (Steubenville, Ohio)
Bishop (Corea, Maine)
B. & J. (Rego Park, N.Y.)
B.J.S. (Forest Hills, N.Y.)
Blacher (Branford, Conn.)
Black Ace (Denver, Colo.)
Blackmer (North Ferrisburg, Vt.)
Black Oak (Berkeley, Calif.)
Black Sun (New York, N.Y.)
Black Swan (Sacramento, Calif.)
Black Swan (Lexington, Ky.)
Blake (Fairfield, Conn.)
Bland's (Sharon, Mass.)
Bliss (Middletown, Conn.)
Blitz (Weaverville, Calif.)
Block (Thornwood, N.Y.)
Blomberg (Rockford, Ill.)
Blomgren (San Rafael, Calif.)
Bloomsbury (Denver, Colo.)
Blue Dragon (Ashland, Ore.)
Blue Lantern (San Diego, Calif.)
Blue Moon (Clearwater, Fla.)

Blue Rider (Cambridge, Mass.)
Bluestem (Lincoln, Neb.)
Boardman (Camden, N.Y.)
Boardwalk (Friday Harbor, Wash.)
Boas (Haddonfield, N.J.)
Bohling (Decatur, Mich.)
Boise Farm (Boise, Idaho)
Boise Mart (Boise, Idaho)
Bolerium (San Francisco, Calif.)
Bolingbroke (Pinnacle, N.C.)
Bolotin (Youngstown, Ohio)
Bonaventura (Evergreen, Colo.)
Bond (Reading, Mass.)
Bond (Roanoke, Va.)
Bonmark (Plainview, N.Y.)
Bonners (Bonners Ferry, Ind.)
Book Admirer (Norwalk, Conn.)
Book/Art (Dothan, Ala.)
Book Assoc. (Orange, Conn.)
Book Attic (San Bernardino, Calif.)
Book Barn (So. Sioux City, Neb.)
Book Barn (Miami, Fla.)
Book Barn (Gardner, Mass.)
Book Barn (Bend, Ore.)
Book Barn (Stockton Spgs., Maine)
Book Barn (Rochester, Mich.)
Book Baron (Anaheim, Calif.)
Book Barrel (Los Angeles, Calif.)
Book Bazaar (Ottawa, Ont.)
Book Bear (W. Brookfield, Mass.)
Book Bin (Kingston, Ont.)
Book Bin (Albany, Ore.)
Book Bin (Corvallis, Ore.)
Book-Bind (Anaheim, Calif.)
Bookbizniz (Atlantic City, N.J.)
Book Block (Cos Cob, Conn.)
Book Broker (Evansville, Ind.)
Book Broker (Charlottesville, Va.)
Book Buyers (Houston, Texas)
Book Carnival (Orange, Calif.)
Book Case (Houston, Texas)
Bookcase (Cambridge, Mass.)
Bookcase (St. Clair Shores, Mich.)
Bookcase (Greenfield, N.H.)
Book Cellar (Freeport, Maine)
Book Cellar (Brattleboro, Vt.)
Book Cellar (Fullerton, Calif.)
Book Cellar (Temple, Texas)
Book Cellar (Bethesda, Md.)

Book Stall (Rockford, Ill.)
Books/Things (Boca Raton, Fla.)
Bookstock (So. Orleans, Mass.)
Book Stop (Petoskey, Mich.)
Book Stop (Lafayette, Calif.)
Book Stop (Tucson, Ariz.)
Bookstop (Alexandria, Va.)
Book Stop (Poulsbo, Wash.)
Book Stop (Dearborn Hgts., Mich.)
Book Stop (Las Vegas, Nev.)
Book Store (Lewisburg, W.Va.)
Bookstore (Lenox, Mass.)
Book Store (San Mateo, Calif.)
Bookstore (Valdosta, Ga.)
Book Store (Englewood, N.J.)
Book Studio (Atlanta, Ga.)
Books Unltd. (Nat'l City, Calif.)
Booksville (Montrose, Calif.)
Books With (Concord, Mass.)
Book/Tackle (Chestnut Hill, Mass.)
Book/Tackle (Watch Hill, R.I.)
Book Trader (Naples, Fla.)
Book Trader (Fairmont, N.C.)
Book Trader (Muskegon, Mich.)
Book Traders (Winter Haven, Fla.)
Book Treasury (Nashville, Tenn.)
Book Vault (Beaverton, Ore.)
Bookwood (Westwood, N.J.)
Bookworm (Wytheville, Va.)
Bookworm (Wanatah, Ind.)
Borden (Portsmouth, R. I.)
Borderland (Alvaton, Ky.)
Boss (Brookline, Mass.)
Boston Annex (Boston, Mass.)
Boulevard (Topanga, Calif.)
Bowes (Vancouver, B.C.)
Bowie (Seattle, Wash.)
Bowling (Rancho Palos Verdes, Calif.)
Bowman (Bedford, N.Y.)
Boyce (Carmel, N.Y.)
Boyson (Brookfield, Conn.)
Bradford (Bennington, Vt.)
Bradshaw (Chicago, Ill.)
Brady (Assonet, Mass.)
Braiterman (Baltimore, Md.)
Branford (Branford, Conn.)
Brannan (Garberville, Calif.)
Brassers (Seminole, Fla.)

Brattle Book (Boston, Mass.)
Brauns (Sacramento, Calif.)
Brazenhead (New York, N.Y.)
Breadloaf (E. Middlebury, Vt.)
Brennan (Salt Lake City, Utah)
Breslauer (New York, N.Y.)
Bretton Hall (Bretton Woods, N.H.)
Bretton Hall (Lancaster, N.H.)
Brew (New Milford, Conn.)
Brick House (Morristown Crnrs., Vt.)
Brick Row (San Francisco, Calif.)
Bridges (Sharpsburg, Ga.)
Bridgman (Rome, N.Y.)
Bridgton (Bridgton, Maine)
Brill (New York, N.Y.)
Brisky (Micanopy, Fla.)
Britannia (New Preston, Conn.)
British (No. Weymouth, Mass.)
Broadfoot's (Wilmington, N.C.)
Broadfoot's (Wendell, N.C.)
Broad Ripple (Indianapolis, Ind.)
Broken Kettle (Akron, Iowa)
Bromer (Boston, Mass.)
Bromsen (Boston, Mass.)
Brookline (Brookline, Mass.)
Brooks (Macon, Ga.)
Broude (New York, N.Y.)
Brown (Toledo, Ohio)
Brownbag (Rochester, N.Y.)
Brown Bag (Dobbs Ferry, N.Y.)
Brown (Belfast, Maine)
Brown (New London, Conn.)
Brown (No. Augusta, S.C.)
Brownstone (New York, N.Y.)
Browsers' (Olympia, Wash.)
Brubacher (Stevens, Pa.)
Brunsell's (Hanson, Mass.)
Brused (Pullman, Wash.)
Bryant's (Provincetown, Mass.)
Bryn Mawr (White Plains, N.Y.)
Bryn Mawr (New York, N.Y.)
Bryn Mawr (Rochester, N.Y.)
Bryn Mawr (New Haven, Conn.)
Bryn Mawr (Albany, N.Y.)
Bryn Mawr (Pittsburgh, Pa.)
Buccaneer (Laguna Bch., Calif.)
Buchanan (New York, N.Y.)

Buckabest (Palo Alto, Calif.)
Buckingham (New Canton, Va.)
Buck (New York, N.Y.)
Buck (San Francisco, Calif.)
Buckley (No. Chatham, Mass.)
Buddenbrooks (Boston, Mass.)
Buffalo (Amherst, N.Y.)
Bullock (Yardley, Pa.)
Bullock (Fargo, N.D.)
Bunker (Spring Valley, Calif.)
Bunkhouse (Gardiner, Maine)
Burbank (Burbank, Calif.)
Burger (Pine Grove, Calif.)
Burgman (Santa Rosa, Calif.)
Burke's (Memphis, Tenn.)
Burleson (Atlanta, Ga.)
Burleson (Spartanburg, S.C.)
Burley/Books (Toledo, Ohio)
Burnett (Atlanta, Ga.)
Burpee Hill (New London, N.H.)
Burrows (Downers Grove, Ill.)
Burstein (Waltham, Mass.)
Burt (Laconia, N.H.)
Burton's (Greenport, N.Y.)
Bush (Stonington, Maine)
Busyhaus (Mattapoisett, Mass.)
Busy Hermit (Niles, Mich.)
Butcher (Youngstown, Ohio)
Buteo (Vermillion, S.D.)
Butterworth (Claremont, Calif.)
Bygone (Dearborn, Mich.)
Bygone (Burlington, Vt.)

C

Cabin In (Potsdam, N.Y.)
Cabinet of (Watertown, Conn.)
Cache (Loveland, Colo.)
Caddo (Cartaro, Ariz.)
Cadenza (Smithtown, N.Y.)
Cady (Chicago, Ill.)
Cahan (Narberth, Pa.)
Calderwoods (Long Valley, N.J.)
Caldwell (Arkadelphia, Ark.)
Calhouns' (Geneva, N.Y.)

Calico Cat (Ventura, Calif.)
Califia (San Francisco, Calif.)
Callahan (Peterborough, N.H.)
Calliope (Pittsburgh, Pa.)
Call Me Ishmael (Saugatuck, Mich.)
Calman (Syracuse, N.Y.)
Camel (New York, N.Y.)
Camelot (Baltimore, Md.)
Cameron's (Portland, Ore.)
Campbell (Campbell, Calif.)
Campfire (Evansville, Ind.)
Canford (Freeville, N.Y.)
Canner (Boston, Mass.)
Canney (Alfred, Maine)
Cantrells' (No. East, Pa.)
Cape (Mashpec, Mass.)
Cape Ann (Peabody, Mass.)
Cape Collector (So. Harwich, Mass.)
Caprio (Revere, Mass.)
Captain's (Ashville, N.C.)
Caravan (Los Angeles, Calif.)
Caravan (Stillwater, Okla.)
Caravan (Jamaica, N.Y.)
Carduner (Philadelphia, Pa.)
Caren (Nanuet, N.Y.)
Carling's (Pomona Park, Fla.)
Carlitz (Philadelphia, Pa.)
Carlson (Portland, Maine)
Carlton (Camino, Calif.)
Carmichael's (Louisville, Ky.)
Carnegie (New York, N.Y.)
Carney (Oneonta, N.Y.)
Carolina (Charlotte, N.C.)
Carousel (Tyler, Texas)
Carpenter (Balboa Isl., Calif.)
Carpenter (Barlow, Ohio)
Carr (Concord, N.H.)
Carr (New York, N.Y.)
Carriage (Northford, Conn.)
Carroll (San Marcos, Calif.)
Carry Back (Haverhill, N.H.)
Carver (Chestnut Hill, Mass.)
Casavant (Wayland, Mass.)
Casperson (Niles, Mich.)

Cassidy (Kansas City, Mo.)
Cassidy (Sacramento, Calif.)
Cassie (Millis, Mass.)
Casten (New York, N.Y.)
Cat (New Rochelle, N.Y.)
Catbird (Portland, Ore.)
Cather (Birmingham, Ala.)
Catholic (Bellingham, Mass.)
Cavallo (Altadena, Calif.)
C. Dickens (Atlanta, Ga.)
Cellar (Detroit, Mich.)
Cellar (Eugene, Ore.)
Cellar (Providence, R.I.)
Celnick (Bronx, N.Y.)
Celtic (Westmoreland, N.H.)
CGT (College Stn., Texas)
Chadds (Chadds Ford, Pa.)
Chalfin (New York, N.Y.)
Chamberlin (E. Orleans, Mass.)
Chaney (Ossining, N.Y.)
Change (Santa Monica, Calif.)
Chang Tang (Peekskill, N.Y.)
Chanticleer (Ft. Wayne, Ind.)
Chaos (Washington, D.C.)
Chapin (Reading, Pa.)
Chapman (Los Angeles, Calif.)
Chapter 1 (Hamilton, Mont.)
Chapter/Verse (Maywood, N.J.)
Charing (Hutchinson, Kan.)
Charkoudian (Newton, Mass.)
Chartwell (New York, N.Y.)
Chatham (Madison, N.J.)
Cheap St. (New Castle, Va.)
Checker (Dubuque, Iowa)
Cheng (Boston, Mass.)
Cherokee (Hollywood, Calif.)
Cheshire (Yakima, Wash.)
Chessler (New York, N.Y.)
Chester (Chester, Conn.)
Chicago (Evanston, Ill.)
Chicago Law (Chicago, Ill.)
Chickadee (Houston, Texas)
Childs (Boston, Mass.)
Chimera (Palo Alto, Calif.)
Chimney (Bridgeport, Conn.)
Chimney (Scotts Valley, Calif.)

Chinook (Colo. Spgs., Colo.)
Chip's Search (New York, N.Y.)
Chip's Shop (New York, N.Y.)
Chips (Tustin, Calif.)
Chirurgical (Baltimore, Md.)
Chiswick (Sandy Hook, Conn.)
Chloe's (Sacramento, Calif.)
Choctaw (Jackson, Miss.)
Choras (Weston, Mass.)
ChoreoGraphica (Boston, Mass.)
Christian (Westminster, Md.)
Christoffersen (Mamaroneck, N.Y.)
Churchill (Contoocook, N.H.)
Churchilliana (Sacramento, Calif.)
Cider (Exeter, N.H.)
Cielec (Chicago, Ill.)
Cilleyville (Andover, N.H.)
Cinema (Hollywood, Calif.)
Cinemabilia (New York, N.Y.)
Circle West (Annapolis, Md.)
City Lights (San Francisco, Calif.)
City Spirit (Denver, Colo.)
City Wide (Brooklyn, N.Y.)
Civil War (So. Miami, Fla.)
Claar (Golden, Colo.)
Claitor's (Baton Rouge, La.)
Clare (Getzville, N.Y.)
Clark (Baton Rouge, La.)
Clark (Glendale, Calif.)
Clark's (Spokane, Wash.)
Clegg (Eaton Rapids, Mich.)
Cleland's (Portsmouth, N.H.)
Clement (Franklin, N.H.)
Cliffside (Kansas City, Mo.)
Clinton (Clinton, N.Y.)
Clipper Ship (San Antonio, Texas)
Clover (Charlottesville, Va.)
Clower (Charlottesville, Va.)
Coachman (La Porte, Ind.)
Cobble Crt. (Litchfield, Conn.)
Coffman (Cambria, Calif.)
Cohasco (Yonkers, N.Y.)
Cohen (Bonita Springs, Fla.)
Cohen (Bronx, N.Y.)
Cohen (St. Louis, Mo.)
Cohen (Youngstown, Ohio)

Herzig-Cohen (Jackson Hgts, NY)
Colburn (Atlanta, Ga.)
Colebrook (Colebrook, Conn.)
Cole's (La Jolla, Calif.)
Collectabilia (Valley Stream, N.Y.)
Collector's (Phoenix, Ariz.)
Collector's (Pt. Washington, N.Y.)
Collectors' (New York, N.Y.)
Collectors' (Richmond, Va.)
Collectrix (W. Hempstead, N.Y.)
Colleen's (Houston, Texas)
Collins (San Francisco, Calif.)
Collins (Seattle, Wash.)
Collins' (Pottstown, Pa.)
Colonial (Pleasantville, N.Y.)
Colonial (W. Lebanon, N.H.)
Colophon (Epping, N.H.)
Colorado (Norwood, Colo.)
Columbia (Suffern, N.Y.)
Columbus (San Francisco, Calif.)
Combs (Great Falls, Mont.)
Comic (New York, N.Y.)
Common (New Salem, Mass.)
Communications (New Haven, Conn.)
Compass (Sitka, Alk.)
Compulsive (New York, N.Y.)
Comstock's (Auburn, Wash.)
Concord (Kailua-Kona, Haw.)
Connecticut (E. Haddam, Conn.)
Conn. Book (Fairfield, Conn.)
Connolly (Vista, Calif.)
Consolo (Mansfield, Ohio)
Constant (Denver, Colo.)
Constant (Milwaukee, Wisc.)
Continental (New York, N.Y.)
Conway (Attleboro, Mass.)
Cook (Los Angeles, Calif.)
Cookbooks (Yuma, Ariz.)
Cooper Fox (Millbrook, N.Y.)
Cooper's (Decatur, Ga.)
Coosa Valley (Rome, Ga.)
Copeland (Portland, Maine)
Core Coll. (Great Neck, N.Y.)
Corner-Stone (Plattsburgh, N.Y.)
Cornerstone (Providence, R.I.)
Cornucopia (Syosset, N.Y.)
Cosmic (Salt Lake City, Utah)
Cotswold (Medina, Ohio)

Cotton Hill (Laconia, N.H.)
Cottontail (Bennington, Ind.)
Cottonwood (Baton Rouge, La.)
Country (Chesterton, Ind.)
Country (Plainfield, Vt.)
Coventry (Coventry, Conn.)
Cover (Ft. Myers, Fla.)
Cow Country (Prescott, Ariz.)
Cowell (Bridgeport, Conn.)
Crabtree (Signal Mtn., Tenn.)
Cragsmoor (Cragsmoor, N.Y.)
Craig (Newport, R. I.)
Cramer (Kansas City, Mo.)
Cramer (Media, Pa.)
Cranbury (Cranbury, N.J.)
Crawford (No. St. Paul, Minn.)
Crawford's (Cedar Rapids, Iowa)
Crawford's (Cincinnati, Ohio)
Crofter's (Washington, Conn.)
Croissant (Athens, Ohio)
Cronin (Worcester, Mass.)
Cross (Brunswick, Maine)
Cross Hill (Brunswick, Maine)
Croton (Croton, N.Y.)
Culpin's (Denver, Colo.)
Cummings (Stillwater, Minn.)
Cummins (New York, N.Y.)
Cummins (Pottersville, N.J.)
Cunningham (Portland, Maine)
Curiosity (St. Joseph, Mich.)
Curious Book (E. Lansing, Mich.)
Curious Raven (Detroit, Mich.)
Currey (Elizabethtown, N.Y.)
Cutler (New York, N.Y.)
Cyrano's (Highlands, N.C.)

D

Dabbs (Higginsville, Mo.)
Dabny (Washington, D.C.)
Dady (Minneapolis, Minn.)
Daedalus (Charlottesville, Va.)
Dailey (Los Angeles, Calif.)
Daitz (New York, N.Y.)

Dakota (Eugene, Ore.)
Dalley (Christiansburg, Va.)
Daly (Ridgefield, Conn.)
Dance Mart (Brooklyn, N.Y.)
Dan's (Appleton, Wisc.)
Darby (Darby, Pa.)
Darrah (Gettysburg, Pa.)
Dartmouth (Hanover, N.H.)
Darvill's Book (Eastsound, Wash.)
Darvill's Rare(Eastsound, Wash.)
Dary (Lawrence, Kan.)
Dast (Madison, Wisc.)
Daunce (Buffalo, N.Y.)
Davidson (San Diego, Calif.)
Davies (Oak Park, Ill.)
Davis (Sherman Oaks, Calif.)
Dawn (Ann Arbor, Mich.)
Dawson's (Los Angeles, Calif.)
Day's (Quincy, Calif.)
DC Service (Columbia, Mo.)
Dean (Oklahoma City, Okla.)
deBeurs (Dexter, Maine)
Debra (No. Hills, Pa.)
De Chene (Los Angeles, Calif.)
Decline (Clinton, Wisc.)
Dee Cee (Nyack, N.Y.)
Deeds (Ellicott City, Md.)
DeFreitas (Montreal, Que.)
Deines (Ft. Collins, Colo.)
de la Ree (Saddle River, N.J.)
de Lellis (New York, N.Y.)
Delle Donne (Ronkonkoma, N.Y.)
Delp (Belding, Mich.)
Denning (Salisbury Mills, N.Y.)
Dennis (Seattle, Wash.)
Denver (Stockton, Calif.)
Denver Barter (Denver, Colo.)
Denver Fair (Denver, Colo.)
Dermont (Onset, Mass.)
Desch (Wheaton, Md.)
Deseret (Salt Lake City, Utah)
Desmarais (Palo Alto, Calif.)
Detering (Houston, Texas)
Devine (Katonah, N.Y.)
De Wit (East Lansing, Mich.)
Diablo (Walnut Creek, Calif.)
Diamond (Burbank, Calif.)
Diamond (Rochester, N.Y.)
Dickson St. (Fayetteville, Ark.)

E

F

Farley's (Pensacola, Fla.)
Farnsworth (W. Cornwall, Conn.)
Fay (Caledonia, N.Y.)
Federation (College St., Texas)
Feiden (Mamaroneck, N.Y.)
Fein (New York, N.Y.)
Felcone (Princeton, N.J.)
Feldman (Cleveland, Ohio)
Feldstein (Forest Hills, N.Y.)
Feltus (Berkeley, Calif.)
Fern (New York, N.Y.)
Ferndale (Ferndale, Calif.)
Ferrini (Akron, Ohio)
Ferrini/Greenberg (Akron, Ohio)
Fessler (Theresa, N.Y.)
Fickes (Akron, Ohio)
Field (Georgetown, Mass.)
Fields (San Francisco, Calif.)
50,000 (El Cajon, Calif.)
Filler (Bremerton, Wash.)
Finders (Dallas, Texas)
Fine (Rochester, Mich.)
Finer (Greenfield, Mass.)
Finn (W. Roxbury, Mass.)
First (Chicago, Ill.)
1st Edtn. (Muskegon Hgts., Mich.)
1st Edtn. (Tulsa, Okla.)
First Edtns. (Richmond, Va.)
First Impressions (Wheaton, Ill.)
Firsts (New York, N.Y.)
Fischler (San Jose, Calif.)
Fish (Minneapolis, Minn.)
Fisher (Cobleskill, N.Y.)
Fisher (New York, N.Y.)
Fisher (Williamsport, Pa.)
Fitch (Santa Fe, N.M.)
Fithian (Lakewood, Colo.)
5 Quail (Spg. Grove, Minn.)
Fleming (New York, N.Y.)
Fletcher's (Salado, Texas)
Flora (Seattle, Wash.)
Fly Creek (E. Lansing, Mich.)
Flynn (Lake Forest, Ill.)
Foley (Bardstown, Ky.)
Folger (Washington, D.C.)
Folk (Long Beach, Calif.)
Folkways (Bethesda, Md.)
Footnote (Brooklyn, N.Y.)
Ford (Lake Worth, Fla.)

Foreign (Flushing, N.Y.)
Forest Park (Ft. Wayne, Ind.)
Forgotten (St. Simon Isl., Ga.)
Fortuna (Kirkland, Wash.)
Fortunate Finds (Warwick, R.I.)
Foster (Corning, Calif.)
Fountain (Indianapolis, Ind.)
4th Estate (New London, Conn.)
Fox (Madison, Tenn.)
Fox (Tacoma, Wash.)
Fox Hill (Palmer, Mass.)
Franklin (New York, N.Y.)
Fran's (Philadelphia, Pa.)
Fraser (Burlington, Vt.)
Fraser's (Sherman Oaks, Calif.)
Frazier (Gilford, N.H.)
Free Lance (Brooklyn, N.Y.)
Fricelli (Brooklyn, N.Y.)
Frid (San Pedro, Calif.)
Frisch (Livingston, N.Y.)
Frisk (Philadelphia, Pa.)
Frohnsdorf (Gaithersburg, Md.)
Front (Van Nuys, Calif.)
Frontier (Bryan, Texas)
Frontier (Los Angeles, Calif.)
Fugitive (Nashville, Tenn.)
Fullam (Babylon, N.Y.)
Fye (Marshfield, Wisc.)

G

Gabbard (New Boston, Texas)
Gabriel (Northampton, Mass.)
Gach (Columbia, Md.)
Gagnon (Quebec, Que.)
Galewitz (Orange, Conn.)
Gallery Of (Bigfork, Mont.)
Gallis (Marblehead, Mass.)
Gambler's (Las Vegas, Nev.)
Gamebag (Twin Lakes, Wisc.)
Gamradt (Minneapolis, Minn.)
Carcia (Turlock, Calif.)
Gardner (New York, N.Y.)
Garnett (St. Louis, Mo.)
Garret (Clinton, N.Y.)

Garrison (Williamsburg, Va.)
Gateway (Ferndale, Pa.)
Gatto (New York, N.Y.)
Gavin (Leominster, Mass.)
Gavora (Santa Barbara, Calif.)
Gay (Santa Fe, N.M.)
GBI (Smithtown, N.Y.)
G & C (Lafayette, La.)
Geagan (Wareham, Mass.)
Gem (New York, N.Y.)
Geological (Falls Village, Conn.)
George (Cleveland, Tenn.)
George Sand (Los Angeles, Calif.)
Geoscience (Yucaipa, Calif.)
Geraci (Accord, N.Y.)
Gereghty (Sepulveda, Calif.)
GFS (Great River, N.Y.)
Gibbs (State College, Pa.)
Gierspeck (Conroe, Texas)
Gilann (Darien, Conn.)
Gilbert (Los Angeles, Calif.)
Gilbo (Carpinteria, Calif.)
Gilfond (Washington, D.C.)
Gilliam (Charlottesville, Va.)
Gilman (New York, N.Y.)
Ginsberg (Petersburg, Va.)
Ginsberg (Sharon, Mass.)
Glad Day (Toronto, Ont.)
Glaeve (Madison, Wisc.)
Glaister (New York, N.Y.)
Glaser (Sausalito, Calif.)
Glasser (Assonet, Mass.)
Glassman (Corte Madera, Calif.)
Glenn (Kansas City, Mo.)
Globe (Northampton, Mass.)
Globe Crnr. (Boston, Mass.)
Glooscap (Pefferlaw, Ont.)
Glover (Cambridge, N.Y.)
Glover's (Lexington, Ky.)
Gobrecht (Kinderhook, N.Y.)
Golden Age (Dix Hills, N.Y.)
Golden Age (Seattle, Wash.)
Golden Gull (Grants Pass, Ore.)
Golden Hill (Helena, Mont.)
Golden Legend (Los Angeles,
  Calif.)
Golder (Collinsville, Conn.)
Good News (Rossville, Ind.)
Good Times (Pt. Jefferson, N.Y.)

H

Heritage (Los Angeles, Calif.)
Heritage (Sonora, Calif.)
Heritage (Southampton, Mass.)
Heritage (Toronto, Ont.)
Herlin (New York, N.Y.)
Hermeticus (Ashland, Ore.)
Hermitage (Denver, Colo.)
Hermit's (Wyoming, Pa.)
Herpetological (Lindenhurst, N.Y.)
Herron (Rome, Ga.)
Herst (Boca Raton, Fla.)
Hessel (Calimesa, Calif.)
Hess (Andover, Mass.)
Hess (Brightwaters, N.Y.)
Hi (Canutillo, Texas)
Hidden (Kalamazoo, Mich.)
High Country (Laramie, Wyo.)
High Lat. (Bainbridge, Wash.)
High Ridge (Rye, N.Y.)
Highwood (Traverse City, Mich.)
Hill (Kingsport, Tenn.)
Hill (New York, N.Y.)
Hill Haven (Barton, Vt.)
Hillcrest (Spg. City, Tenn.)
Hillman (New York, N.Y.)
Hills (San Francisco, Calif.)
Hilscher (Anchorage, Alk.)
Hilton Village (Newport News, Va.)
Hirsch (Hopewell Jctn., N.Y.)
Hirschtritt's (Silver Spg., Md.)
Hist. News (Skokie, Ill.)
Hist. Realia (Wooster, Ohio)
Hist. Tech (Marblehead, Mass.)
History (Long Valley, N.J.)
History (Ashley Falls, Mass.)
Hittel (Ft. Lauderdale, Fla.)
Hive (Easton, Pa.)
Hobbit (Westfield, N.J.)
Hobby Helpers (Lima, N.Y.)
Hobson's (Jenkintown, Pa.)
Hodgson (Syracuse, N.Y.)
Hoefliger (Buffalo, N.Y.)
Hoffer (Vancouver, B.C.)
Hoffman (Rillton, Pa.)
Hofmann (So. Orleans, Mass.)
Holden (Pasadena, Calif.)
Hole (Reedsport, Ore.)
Hollander (Santa Monica, Calif.)

Hollyoak (Wilmington, Del.)
Hollywood City (Hollywood, Calif.)
Hollywood Service (Hollywood, Calif.)
Holmes (Edmonds, Wash.)
Holmes (Oakland, Calif.)
Holmes (Philadelphia, Pa.)
Holmes (San Francisco, Calif.)
Holsten (Excelsior, Minn.)
Holy Land (Washington, D.C.)
Homestead (Marlborough, N.H.)
Homesteader (Wenatchee, Wash.)
Hood (Lawrence, Kan.)
Hook (Sebastopol, Calif.)
Hooked (Springfield, Mo.)
Hooper's (Leesburg, Va.)
Hoosier (Indianapolis, Ind.)
Hope Farm (Cornwallville, N.Y.)
Hopper (Sunnyvale, Calif.)
Horizon (Seattle, Wash.)
Horne (Lakeland, Fla.)
Horowitz (New York, N.Y.)
Houle (Durham, N.H.)
Houle (Los Angeles, Calif.)
House (Anaheim, Calif.)
House (San Diego, Calif.)
House (Tallahassee, Fla.)
House (Thornhill, Ont.)
House (Toronto, Ont.)
House (Worcester, Mass.)
Household (Berkeley, Calif.)
Houseman (Yellow Spgs., Ohio)
Howard (Burlingame, Calif.)
Howe (New York, N.Y.)
Howes (Brewster, Mass.)
Howland (Jamaica Plain, Mass.)
Howland (New Canaan, Conn.)
Hoyt (Rockport, Mass.)
Hubert (Walnut Creek, Calif.)
Huckleberry (Centralia, Wash.)
Hudson (Dyersburg, Tenn.)
Hughes (Holmes, N.Y.)
Hughes (St. Louis, Mo.)
Hughes (Williamsport, Pa.)
Hummingbird (Albuquerque, N.M.)
Hunter (Harriman, N.Y.)
Hunt (Clayton, Ind.)

Huntley (Claremont, Calif.)
Hunt (Burbank, Calif.)
Huxley (Loudonville, N.Y.)
Hurley (Westmoreland, N.H.)
Hyde Park (Boise, Idaho)
Hyde Park (Tampa, Fla.)
Hyman (Los Angeles, Calif.)

I

Ideal (New York, N.Y.)
Iliad (Livingston, Mont.)
Imagine That (No. Adams, Mass.)
Imagine That (Pittsfield, Mass.)
Imel (Indianapolis, Ind.)
Indian Head (Owego, N.Y.)
Info (El Cerrito, Calif.)
Info (San Angelo, Texas)
Inner Circle (New York, N.Y.)
In #1 (San Francisco, Calif.)
In #2 (San Francisco, Calif.)
In Our (Cambridge, Mass.)
Int'l. Univ. (New York, N.Y.)
Invisible (Berkeley, Calif.)
Irene's (So. Gardner, Mass.)
Iroqrafts (Ohsweken, Ont.)
Isador (Highland Park, Ill.)
Isaiah (Worcester, Mass.)
Ishii (Seattle, Wash.)
Ishtar (Canton, Mass.)
Island (Isleboro, Maine)
Island (Mercer, Wash.)
Iuspa (Newark, N.J.)
Ivey (Brewton, Ala.)

J

Jack London (Glen Ellen, Calif.)
Jack's (Mt. Prospect, Ill.)
Jackson (Berkeley, Calif.)
Jackson (Weston, Ont.)
Jacksonville (Jacksonville, Ore.)

Lang (Amityville, N.Y.)
Lansford (Powersville, Ga.)
Lasley (Berkeley, Ill.)
Laster (Winston-Salem, N.C.)
Last (Williamsport, Pa.)
La Tienda (Conway, N.H.)
Laub (Berkeley, Calif.)
Laurie (St. Paul, Minn.)
La Valois (New York, N.Y.)
Lawrence (New York, N.Y.)
Laws (Chicago, Ill.)
Lawyer (Plains, Mont.)
Lazarus (Ossining, N.Y.)
Leach (Brattleboro, Vt.)
Leaves (Ann Arbor, Mich.)
Lebo (Washington, D.C.)
Ledlie (Buckfield, Maine)
Lee (Lincoln, Neb.)
Leech (Ormand Bch., Fla.)
Leekley (Winthrop Harbor, Ill.)
Leelanau (Leland, Mich.)
Lefkowicz (Fairhaven, Mass.)
Left Bank (Oak Park, Ill.)
Legacy (Hatboro, Pa.)
Legacy (Iowa City, Iowa)
Lehr (New York, N.Y.)
Leibowits (New York, N.Y.)
Leishman (Menlo Park, Calif.)
Lemon (Lemon Grove, Calif.)
Lemuria (Jackson, Miss.)
Leo (Toledo, Ohio)
Levart (Hartsdale, N.Y.)
Levien (McDowell, Va.)
Levin (Los Angeles, Calif.)
Levine (Savannah, Ga.)
Levine's (Shokan, N.Y.)
Levinson (Beverly Hills, Calif.)
Lewis (Mamaroneck, N.Y.)
Lewis (San Rafael, Calif.)
Lewis (Seattle, Wash.)
Lewis St. (Lynn, Mass.)
Liberty (Concord, Calif.)
Liberty (Sloatsburg, N.Y.)
Librairie (Chartres) (New Orleans, La.)
Librairie (Royal) (New Orleans, La.)
Librarium (E. Chatham, N.Y.)
Library (Dallas, Texas)

Library (Ferndale, Mich.)
Libros (Redlands, Calif.)
Lien (Minneapolis, Minn.)
Lift (Brockport, N.Y.)
Lighthouse (Rye, N.Y.)
Lighthouse (St. Pete., Fla.)
Lilac Hedge (Norwich, Vt.)
Limelight (San Francisco, Calif.)
Limestone (Glen Rose, Texas)
Lincoln (Chambersburg, Pa.)
Lincoln (Delmar, N.Y.)
Lincoln (Foster, R.I.)
Lincoln (San Jose, Calif.)
Link (Redding, Calif.)
Links (3 Rivers, Mich.)
Linthicum (Tacoma, Wash.)
Lion (Indianapolis, Ind.)
Lion (New York, N.Y.)
Lion's (Salisbury, Conn.)
Lippincott (Bangor, Maine)
Literary (Pittsburgh, Pa.)
Little (Detroit, Mich.)
Little (Hinsdale, Ill.)
Little (Missoula, Mont.)
Little (Rehobeth, Mass.)
Little (U. Montclair, N.J.)
Littlewoods (Waukesha, Wisc.)
Littrup (Bay City, Mich.)
Lloyd (Red Bank, N.J.)
Lloyd (Washington, D.C.)
Lobster (Spruce Head, Maine)
Loewenthal (Dover, N.J.)
Loewy (Tallman, N.Y.)
Log Cabin (Bigfork, Mont.)
Lombardo (Shoreham, N.Y.)
London (Chicago, Ill.)
Lonesome (Eugene, Ore.)
Long (Marietta, Ga.)
Loome (Stillwater, Minn.)
Loose (Jerome, Mich.)
Lopez (Hadley, Mass.)
Lord (Marshfield, Mass.)
Lorson's (Fullerton, Calif.)
Lost (Santa Barbara, Calif.)
Lovett (Winston-Salem, N.C.)
Lowe (Eastsound, Wash.)
Lowe (New York, N.Y.)
Lowe (Boston, Mass.)
Lowenberg (Lafayette, Calif.)

Lozinski (Westport, Mass.)
Lubrano (So. Lee, Mass.)
Lubrecht (Forestburgh, N.Y.)
Lucas (Fairfield, Conn.)
Lucas (Blandford, Mass.)
Luft (Oakland Gdns., N.Y.)
Lumb (Somersville, Conn.)
Lunsford (No. Vancouver, B.C.)
Lurate (Jackson, Miss.)
Lutes (Okla. City, Okla.)
Luther (Taos, N.M.)
Lutz (Washington C. H., Ohio)
Lyman (East Otis, Mass.)
Lynch (Sepulveda, Calif.)
Lynn (Worthington, Ohio)
Lyrical (Saratoga Spgs., N.Y.)
Lysecki (Winnipeg, Man.)

M

Macauluso (Kennett Sq., Pa.)
MacBeans (Brunswick, Maine)
MacDonald's (Eustis, Maine)
Mac Donnell (Austin, Texas)
MacKendrick (Manchester, Conn.)
Mackensen (Lake San Marcos, Calif.)
Macksey (Baltimore, Md.)
MacLeod's (Vancouver, B.C.)
MacManus (Philadelphia, Pa.)
Mad (Maumee, Ohio)
Madonna (Combermere, Ont.)
Maelstrom (San Francisco, Calif.)
Maestro (Bayport, N.Y.)
Magazine (San Francisco, Calif.)
Magazine (New York, N.Y.)
Magic (Johnson City, Tenn.)
Magnalia (No. Amherst, Mass.)
Magnum (Charlottesville, Va.)
Magus (Seattle, Wash.)
Mahard (Sherborn, Mass.)
Mahoney (Buffalo, N.Y.)
Maiden (W. Chester, Pa.)
Maier (Rockport, Mass.)
Main St. (Brooklyn, N.Y.)
Mainly (No. Hollywood, Calif.)

Mallahan (Bellevue, Wash.)
Mallory (Van Nuys, Calif.)
Manasek (Hanover, N.H.)
Manasek (Norwich, Vt.)
Mancevice (Worcester, Mass.)
Mandala (Daytona Bch., Fla.)
Mandrake (Cambridge, Mass.)
Mannatt (San Diego, Calif.)
Manning's (San Francisco, Calif.)
Manor (Huntington Valley, Pa.)
Manor (New York, N.Y.)
Manuscript (Southampton, Pa.)
Many (Lake Hill, N.Y.)
Maple St. (New Orleans, La.)
Marcher (Okla. City, Okla.)
Marchioness (Laguna Bch., Calif.)
Margolis (Monroe, Mich.)
Margolis (Santa Fe, N.M.)
Marion (Auburn Hills, Mich.)
Maritime (Brewer, Maine)
Market (Idaho Falls, Idaho)
Marks (Rochester, N.Y.)
Marley (Oldwick, N.J.)
Marlowe's (Boston, Mass.)
Marshall Field (Chicago, Ill.)
Martayan (New York, N.Y.)
Martignette (Boston, Mass.)
Martin (Atlanta, Ga.)
Martin (La Grange, Ill.)
Martin's (Fairbanks, Alk.)
Mashman (Ridgefield, Conn.)
Masi (Montague, Mass.)
Mason (Phoenix, Ariz.)
Mason (Toronto, Ont.)
Mason's (Wabash, Ind.)
Matthews (Ft. Erie, Ont.)
Mattila (Seattle, Wash.)
Mawson (New Preston, Conn.)
Max Gate (Kankakee, Ill.)
Maxwell (Elmsford, N.Y.)
Maxwell's (Stockton, Calif.)
Maxwell's (Lima, N.Y.)
Maynard's (Pasadena, Calif.)
McBlain (Hamden, Conn.)
McBride (Hartford, Conn.)
McCarty (Cincinnati, Ohio)
McCaslin (Ironton, Mo.)
McCosh (Excelsior, Minn.)
McCullough (Los Angeles, Calif.)

McDermut (Montvale, N.J.)
McDonald's (Catskill, N.Y.)
McDonald's (San Francisco, Calif.)
McDuffie's (Portland, Ore.)
McFarland (Tampa, Fla.)
McGahern (Ottawa, Ont.)
McGill (New City, N.Y.)
McGilvery (La Jolla, Calif.)
McGovern (Berwyn, Ill.)
McKittrick (Philadelphia, Pa.)
McLaughlin's (Cottage Grove,
   Ore.)
McManus (Woodbury, Conn.)
McMillen (Staten Isl., N.Y.)
McQuerry (Jacksonville, Fla.)
Means (Charlotte, N.C.)
Mechanical (Darien, Conn.)
Medallion (Wellesley, Mass.)
Medical (Jenkintown, Pa.)
Melvins (Grt. Barrington, Mass.)
Memorable (Stone Mtn., Ga.)
Memory (Battle Creek, Mich.)
Memory (Belfast, Maine)
Memory (Corona Del Mar, Calif.)
Memory (Grand Rapids, Mich.)
Memory (New York, N.Y.)
Mendelsohn (Cambridge, Mass.)
Mendoza (New York, N.Y.)
Merkel (Xenia, Ohio)
Merlin's (Isla Vista, Calif.)
Merlin's (Providence, R.I.)
Mermaid (Oakland, Calif.)
Merriam (Conway, Mass.)
Merriwell (Islip, N.Y.)
Metacomet (Providence, R.I.)
Metropolis (Royal Oak, Mich.)
Meyerbooks (Glenwood, Ill.)
Meyer (San Francisco, Calif.)
Meyerfeld (San Carlos, Calif.)
Meyerson (Brooklyn, N.Y.)
Michaels (Eugene, Ore.)
Michael's (Okla. City, Okla.)
Michauds (Iowa City, Iowa)
Michelli (Ogunquit, Maine)
Michiana (Niles, Mich.)
Michlestreet (E. Lebanon, Maine)
Mickler's (Chuluota, Fla.)
Middle (Sterling Hgts., Mich.)
Midnight (Clearwater, Fla.)

Midnight (Marietta, Ga.)
Midnight (W. Lafayette, Ind.)
Midvale (Portland, Ore.)
Midwest (Evanston, Ill.)
Miele (New York, N.Y.)
Mil-Air (Compton, Calif.)
Milestone (New York, N.Y.)
Military (New York, N.Y.)
Mill (Craftsbury Common, Vt.)
Miller (Johnstown, N.Y.)
Miller (Seattle, Wash.)
Miller (Syracuse, N.Y.)
Miller (Warren, Pa.)
Million (Cambridge, Mass.)
Minckler (Billings, Mont.)
Minkoff (Grt. Barrington, Mass.)
Minnehaha (Minneapolis, Minn.)
Minters (New York, N.Y.)
Miranda (Brookline, Mass.)
Miscellaneous (New Freedom, Pa.)
Mitchell (Pasadena, Calif.)
Mitch's (Menlo Park, Calif.)
M. & M. (E. Northport, N.Y.)
Mobley (Schoharie, N.Y.)
Modern (Huntingdon Valley, Pa.)
Moebius (Westbury, N.Y.)
Monahan (New York, N.Y.)
Monarski (Syracuse, N.Y.)
Monckton (Chicago, Ill.)
Monie (Cooperstown, N.Y.)
Monie Shop (Cooperstown, N.Y.)
Monroe (Fresno, Calif.)
Montclair (Montclair, N.J.)
Montlack (Old Bethpage, N.Y.)
Moody (Johnson City, Tenn.)
Moore (Wynnewood, Pa.)
Moran (Rocky Point, N.Y.)
Morelle (Haverhill, Mass.)
Morgan (Tucson, Ariz.)
Morgan (Willowick, Ohio)
Moriah (New York, N.Y.)
Morningside (Dayton, Ohio)
Morrell's (Ocean Grove, N.J.)
Morrill (Newton Centre, Mass.)
Morrison (Santa Monica, Calif.)
Morritt (Warwick, R.I.)
Morrow (New York, N.Y.)
Mostly (Carthage, Mo.)
Mott (Sheffield, Mass.)

Mt. Eden (Mt. Eden, Calif.)
Mt. Falcon (Greeley, Colo.)
Mt. Sterling (Mt. Sterling, Ky.)
Mt. Zion (Mt. Zion, W.Va.)
Moving (Seattle, Wash.)
Moye (Putney, Vt.)
Moye (Seattle, Wash.)
Mrouse (New Orleans, La.)
M & S (Weston, Mass.)
Much (Marblehead, Mass.)
Much (Southfield, Mich.)
Mullins (Encinitas, Calif.)
Munsell (Newburyport, Mass.)
Muns (Berkeley, Calif.)
Munson (Mattoon, Ill.)
Murder (Denver, Colo.)
Murder (Ft. Worth, Texas)
Murder (Toronto, Ont.)
Murphy (Iowa City, Iowa)
Murphy (Marietta, Ga.)
Murphy (Salem, Mass.)
Marray (Melrose, Mass.)
Murray (Wilbraham, Mass.)
Murray's (Bridgeport, Conn.)
Museum (Fairfield, Conn.)
Museum (New York, N.Y.)
Mycophile (Naples, Fla.)
Myers (Boulder, Colo.)
Myers (Sequim, Wash.)
Mysteries (Yellow Spgs., Ohio)
Mystery (Huntingdon Valley, Pa.)
Mystic (Mystic, Conn.)

N

Nadolny (Kensington, Conn.)
Najarian (Newtown Sq., Pa.)
National (Brooklyn, N.Y.)
Natural (Scottsdale, Ariz.)
Natural (Woodland Hills, Calif.)
Nautica (Halifax, N.S.)
Nebenzahl (Chicago, Ill.)
Nebraska (Lincoln, Neb.)
Necessary (E. Jordan, Mich.)
Needham (Los Angeles, Calif.)
Needle (Chelmsford, Mass.)

Nelson (Goshen, N.H.)
Nelson (New Bedford, Mass.)
Nelson's (Albany, N.Y.)
Nelson's (Schenectady, N.Y.)
Nelson's (Troy, N.Y.)
Nemeroff (Williamstown, Mass.)
Nestler (Waldwick, N.J.)
Neville (Santa Barbara, Calif.)
New Age (Westerly, R.I.)
Newburyport (Newburyport, Mass.)
New Engl. (Bennington, Vt.)
Newman (Battle Creek, Mich.)
Newman (Chicago, Ill.)
New Miner (Necedah, Wisc.)
New Steamship (El Cajon, Calif.)
New/Used (Warwick, N.Y.)
N.Y. Bound (New York, N.Y.)
Nie (Chicago, Ill.)
999 (New York, N.Y.)
19th Cent. (Baltimore, Md.)
Nisula (Okemos, Mich.)
Noah's (Greenwood, S.C.)
Noble (Greenville, Texas)
Nolan (Coeur d'Alene, Idaho)
Nomland (Los Angeles, Calif.)
Norman (Philadelphia, Pa.)
Norman (San Francisco, Calif.)
Norris (Paoli, Pa.)
No. Country (Richmond, N.H.)
No. Mtn. (Phoenix, Ariz.)
No. Woods (Duluth, Minn.)
Northeast (Ocean City, N.J.)
Norumbega (Houston, Texas)
Nosegay (Cold Spg. Harbor, N.Y.)
Northingham (Hamilton Sq., N.J.)
Noto (Cupertino, Calif.)
Nouveau (Jackson, Miss.)
Novel (Fairfax, Va.)
Novel (San Luis Obispo, Calif.)
NRS (New York, N.Y.)
Nudel (New York, N.Y.)
Nudelman (Seattle, Wash.)
Nutmeg (Torrington, Conn.)

O

Oak Knoll (New Castle, Del.)
Oar House (Clearwater, Fla.)
Oasis (San Deigo, Calif.)
Oblong (Millerton, N.Y.)
O'Brien (Portland, Maine)
Observatory (Sitka, Alk.)
Obsolescence (Gettysburg, Pa.)
Oceanic (New York, N.Y.)
Oceanie (Hillsdale, N.Y.)
Oceanside (Oceanside, N.Y.)
Ockett (Bryant Pond, Maine)
October (Raleigh, N.C.)
Odds (Indianapolis, Ind.)
O'Donoghue (Anoka, Minn.)
Offenbacher (Kew Gardens, N.Y.)
Ohio (Mansfield, Ohio)
Ohio (Cincinnati, Ohio)
Oklahoma (Yukon, Okla.)
Olana (Brewster, N.Y.)
Old Almanack (Concord, N.H.)
Old Barn (Forsyth, Ill.)
Old Benn. (Hancock, N.H.)
Old Book (Bethel, Vt.)
Old Book (Croton, N.Y.)
Old Book (Fairlee, Vt.)
Old Book (Kennebunk, Maine)
Old Book (Morristown, N.J.)
Old Book (New Haven, Conn.)
Old Book (San Francisco, Calif.)
Old Books (Brunswick, Maine)
Old Books (New Orleans, La.)
Old City (St. Augustine, Fla.)
Old Cook. (Haddonfield, N.J.)
Old Edtns. (Buffalo, N.Y.)
Old Emery (Derry, N.H.)
Old Erie (Cleveland, Ohio)
Old Eugene (Eugene, Ore.)
Old Favs. (Toronto, Ont.)
Old Favs. (Richmond, Va.)
Old Geog. (Sparks, Md.)
Old Harbor (Sitka, Alk.)
Old Hickory (Brinklow, Md.)
Old Mill (Alexandria, Va.)

P

Pierce (Oroville, Calif.)
Pierce (Park Forest, Ill.)
Pinkney (Granby, Conn.)
Pinocchio (Pittsburgh, Pa.)
Pinocchio's (Morgantown, W.Va.)
Pioneer (Seattle, Wash.)
Pipkin (Rock Hill, S.C.)
Pirages (McMinnville, Ore.)
Pirtle (Bellevue, Wash.)
Pisces (Albion, Mich.)
Plain (Arlington Hgts., Ill.)
Plant (Grass Valley, Calif.)
Plante (St. Cloud, Minn.)
Plapinger (Ashland, Ore.)
Pleasant St. (Woodstock, Vt.)
Poe (Mayaguez, P.R.)
Pohrt (Flint, Mich.)
Pollack (Boston, Mass.)
Pollock (Palo Alto, Calif.)
Polyanthos (Huntington, N.Y.)
Pomander (New York, N.Y.)
Pomona (Rockton, Ont.)
Poor Farm (W. Cornwall, Conn.)
Poor Richard's (Grand Rapids, Mich.)
Porter (Phoenix, Ariz.)
Poste (Geneseo, N.Y.)
Poster (New York, N.Y.)
Poster (Orangeburg, N.Y.)
Potter (Santa Fe, N.M.)
Powell (Bar Harbor, Maine)
Powell's (Chicago, Ill.)
Powers (Essex Jctn., Vt.)
Prag (San Francisco, Calif.)
Prairie (Chicago, Ill.)
Prairie (Springfield, Ill.)
Pratt (E. Livermore, Maine)
Preservation (Evanston, Ill.)
President's (Washington, D.C.)
Prestianni (Penfield, N.Y.)
Pride (Ballston Lake, N.Y.)
Princeton (Atlantic City, N.J.)
Printed (New York, N.Y.)
Printed (Savannah, Ga.)
Printers' (Arlington, Mass.)
Printers' (Boston, Mass.)
Printer's (Middletown, Conn.)
Printer's (Milldale, Conn.)
Printers' (Palo Alto, Calif.)

Professional (New York, N.Y.)
Pro Libris (Bangor, Maine)
Prosser (Chicago, Ill.)
Provident (Bloomington, Ill.)
Prufrock (Pasadena, Calif.)
Publix (Cleveland, Ohio)
Purple (Fleischmanns, N.Y.)

Q

Quadrant (Easton, Pa.)
Qualman (San Diego, Calif.)
Quebecoise (Montral, Que.)
Quechee (Quechee, Vt.)
Quest (Ft. Worth, Texas)
Quill (Pinellas Park, Fla.)
Quill (Rockville, Md.)
Quitzau (Edmeston, N.Y.)
Quixote (Philadelphia, Pa.)

R

Radio (New York, N.Y.)
Rails (Rosemead, Calif.)
Raimo (Lancaster, Pa.)
Raintree (Eustis, Fla.)
Rainy (Fitzwilliam, N.H.)
Rainy (Halifax, N.S.)
Rainy (Lexington, Mass.)
Ralston (Fullerton, Calif.)
B. Ramer (New York, N.Y.)
R. Ramer (New York, N.Y.)
Ramshorn (Albuquerque, N.M.)
Rancho (Santa Monica, Calif.)
Randall (Santa Barbara, Calif.)
Ransom (Amherst, N.Y.)
Rare Book (Freehold, N.J.)
Rare Book (New York, N.Y.)
Rare Oriental (Aptos, Calif.)
Raskin (Albertson, N.Y.)
Rausch (Bloomington, Ind.)
Ravenstree (Yuma, Ariz.)
Ray (Baldwin Park, Calif.)
Ray's (Hartford, Vt.)

Readbeard's (Marion, Ind.)
Reader's (Raleigh, N.C.)
Reading (Mexico, Ind.)
Readmore (St. Louis, Mo.)
Recovery (Greensboro, Vt.)
Red Bridge (Kansas City, Mo.)
Red Horse (Tampa, Fla.)
Red House (Montgomery, Ala.)
Redding (Sequim, Wash.)
Reed (Birmingham, Ala.)
Reedmor (Philadelphia, Pa.)
Reese (New Haven, Conn.)
Reference (New York, N.Y.)
Reisler (Vienna, Va.)
Reisman (Philadelphia, Pa.)
Reliable (Paterson, N.J.)
Renaisscance (Lincolnshire, Ill.)
Rendell (Waban, Mass.)
Rendell (Newton, Mass.)
Reprint (Washington, D.C.)
Research (Fremont, Neb.)
Resnick (Cazenovia, N.Y.)
Resnik (Roslyn Hgts., N.Y.)
Respess (Chapel Hill, N.C.)
Respess (Durham, N.C.)
Reston's (Amsterdam, N.Y.)
Reynolds (Willits, Calif.)
Rhoads (Richmond, Ind.)
Richards (Templeton, Mass.)
Richardson (Westmont, N.J.)
Richert (Fresno, Calif.)
Richshafer (Cincinnati, Ohio)
Ridge (Stone Ridge, N.Y.)
Rieber (Thomasville, Ga.)
Rieger (Greenwood, S.C.)
Riling (Philadelphia, Pa.)
Rinaldi (Kennebunkport, Maine)
Rinen (New York, N.Y.)
Rinhart (Colebrook, Conn.)
Rittenhouse (Albuquerque, N.M.)
Rittenhouse (Philadelphia, Pa.)
Ritzlin (Evanston, Ill.)
River Oaks (Jay, Maine)
Riverow (Owego, N.Y.)
Riverrun (Hastings, N.Y.)
Rizzoli (New York, N.Y.)
Robbins (Greenville, S.C.)
Roberge (Princeton, N.J.)
Robertson (Levittown, Pa.)

S

T

Tainters (Temple, N.H.)
Talbothay's (Aurora, N.Y.)
Talisman (Georgetown, Calif.)
Talvin (Trafford, Pa.)
Tamerlane (Havertown, Pa.)
Tamerlis (Mamaroneck, N.Y.)
Tanditash (New York, N.Y.)
Taos (Taos, N.M.)
Tappin (Atlantic Bch., Fla.)
Taste (Fall River, Mass.)
Tatro (Wethersfield, Conn.)
Tattered (Denver, Colo.)
Tattersalls (Conyers, Ga.)
Tauscher (Bristol, Va.)
Tayaut (No. Hatley, Que.)
Taylor (Austin, Texas)
Taylor (Kerrville, Texas)
Taylor (Westland, Mich.)
Tebbetts (Hallowell, Maine)
Temares (Plandome, N.Y.)
Tempest (Waitsville, Vt.)
Temple (Toronto, Ont.)
Ten Eyck (Southboro, Mass.)
10 O'Clock (Elk Grove, Calif.)
10 Pound (Gloucester, Mass.)
1023 (Omaha, Neb.)
Terra (Churchville, N.Y.)
Terramedia (Wellesley, Mass.)
Terrapin (Austin, Texas)
Terres (Minneapolis, Minn.)
Tesseract (Hastings, N.Y.)
Testa (No. Newark, N.J.)
Theater (Palo Alto, Calif.)
Theatrebooks (New York, N.Y.)
Theatricana (Athens, Ga.)
Thelema (King Bch., Calif.)
Theophrastus (Little Compton, R.I.)
This Old (Montclair, Calif.)
Tholin (Evanston, Ill.)
Thomas (Mechanicsburg, Pa.)
Thomas (Oak Park, Ill.)
Thomas (San Francisco, Calif.)
Thomolsen (Bayside, N.Y.)

Thoreau (Concord, Mass.)
Those Were (Tempe, Ariz.)
1000 Words (Exeter, N.H.)
3 Arts (Poughkeepsie, N.Y.)
3 Geese (Woodstock, N.Y.)
Thunderbird (Aldergrove, B.C.)
Tillinghast (Hancock, N.H.)
Time (No. Andover, Mass.)
Time (Sacramento, Calif.)
Tin Can (Arcata, Calif.)
Tinker (Santa Cruz, Calif.)
Tintagel (E. Springfield, N.Y.)
Tisza (Chestnut Hill, Mass.)
Titcomb's (E. Sandwich, Mass.)
Titles (Highland Park, Ill.)
Toad (Berkeley, Calif.)
Toadstool (Keene, N.H.)
Todd (Cave Creek, Ariz.)
Together (Denver, Colo.)
Tollett (New York, N.Y.)
Tolliver's (Los Angeles, Calif.)
Tona (Grand Isl., N.Y.)
Totty (Lunenburg, Mass.)
Touchet (New York, N.Y.)
Town (Dutch Flat, Calif.)
Toxophilite (Simsbury, Conn.)
Toy (San Francisco, Calif.)
Tracery (Dallas, Texas)
Trace (Peekskill, N.Y.)
Trackside (Houston, Texas)
Trail (Tucson, Ariz.)
Tramp (Jackson, Mich.)
Trans (Parkersburg, W.Va.)
Transition (San Francisco, Calif.)
Traveler (Union, Conn.)
Traveller (Laredo, Texas)
Travis (Hastings, N.Y.)
Treasure (Oakville, Ont.)
Treasures (Rochester, Mich.)
Trebizond (New Preston, Conn.)
Treehorn (Santa Rosa, Calif.)
Trident (Boulder, Colo.)
Trophy (Agoura, Calif.)
Trotting (Morristown, N.J.)
Trotting (Springfield, Mass.)
Truepenny (Tucson, Ariz.)
Tryon (Johnstown, N.Y.)
Tuckers (Pittsburgh, Pa.)
Tumarkin (New York, N.Y.)

Tumbleweed (Pueblo, Colo.)
Tunick (New York, N.Y.)
Tupper (Vancouver, B.C.)
Turkey (Westport, Conn.)
Turlington (Pittsboro, N.C.)
Tusitala (Kailua, Haw.)
Tuttle (Madison, Wisc.)
Tuttle (Ruthland, Vt.)
12th St. (Santa Monica, Calif.)
Tweney (Seattle, Wash.)
Tweney (Bowling Green, Ohio)
20th Century (Madison, Wisc.)
Twice-Loved (Youngstown, Ohio)
221 (Westlake Village, Calif.)
Twyce (Winona, Minn.)
Typographeum (Francestown, N.H.)
Tyson (Providence, R.I.)

U

Una (St. Johnsbury, Vt.)
Under (Shaker Hgts., Ohio)
Underhill (Poughkeepsie, N.Y.)
Unicorn (Bruceton Mills, W. Va.)
Unicorn (Trappe, Md.)
Unique (Putney, Vt.)
Univelt (San Diego, Calif.)
University (Hull, Mass.)
University (New York, N.Y.)
Untamed (Waterloo, Wisc.)
Untitled II #1 (New York, N.Y.)
Untitled II #2 (New York, N.Y.)
Urban (New York, N.Y.)
Urrizola (Los Angeles, Calif.)
Ursus (New York, N.Y.)
Ursus Prints (New York, N.Y.)
Used (Dyer, Ind.)
U.S. Games (New York, N.Y.)
Ute-Or (W. Jordan, Utah)

V

alentino (Philadelphia, Pa.)
alley (Amherst, Mass.)
alley (Galena, Ill.)
alley (No. Hollywood, Calif.)
anderstoel (El Cerrito, Calif.)
andoros (Middleton, Wisc.)
argo's (Bozeman, Mont.)
arner (Belton, Mo.)
arney's (Casco, Maine)
asta (New York, N.Y.)
athek (Ft. Lee, N.J.)
egetarian (Santa Monica, Calif.)
enkatesa (Tofino, B.C.)
erde (Winsted, Conn.)
ermont (Middlebury, Vt.)
ictoria (New York, N.Y.)
ictorian (Stockton Spgs., Maine)
iederman (Leonia, N.J.)
iewpoint (New York, N.Y.)
illage (Amherst, N.Y.)
illage (Bellingham, Wash.)
illage (Hudson Falls, N.Y.)
illage (Littleton, N.H.)
illage (New York, N.Y.)
illage (Rochester, N.Y.)
illage (Rumney Village, N.H.)
inik (Tucson, Ariz.)
intage (Iowa City, Iowa)
intage (Wheaton, Ill.)
irginia (Berryville, Va.)
i & Si's (Clarence, N.Y.)
isually (Gilford, N.H.)
ogt (Meadow Vista, Calif.)
ol. I (Greenville, S.C.)
ol. I (Hillsdale, Mich.)
on Blon's (Waco, Texas)

W

ade (Cincinnati, Ohio)
ahrenbrock's (San Diego, Calif.)
aite (Madison, Wisc.)

Waiting (Cambridge, Mass.)
Wake (Ft. Lauderdale, Fla.)
Waldo (Rockton, Ill.)
Walett (Abington, Mass.)
Walker (San Leandro, Calif.)
Wall (Los Angeles, Calif.)
Walzer (Providence, R.I.)
Wangner's (Montclair, N.J.)
Ward (Prospect, Ohio)
Warren (Philadelphia, Pa.)
Washington (Washington Cr., Pa.)
Washton (New York, N.Y.)
Watermark (Wichita, Kan.)
Water Row (Sudbury, Mass.)
Watkins (Dolgeville, N.Y.)
Watson (Buelah, Colo.)
Watson (Exeter, N.H.)
Wayner (Ft. Payne, Ala.)
Wayside (Westerly, R.I.)
Way's (Seattle, Wash.)
Weatherford (Monroe, Wash.)
Weber (Troy, Minn.)
Webfoot (Portland, Ore.)
Webster's (Milwaukee, Wisc.)
Wehawken (Washington, D.C.)
Weindling (Danbury, Conn.)
Weintraub #1 (New York, N.Y.)
Weintraub #2 (New York, N.Y.)
Weiser (New York, N.Y.)
Weitz (New York, N.Y.)
Wellfleet (Wellfleet, Mass.)
Wells (Wells, Maine)
Wertz (Flint, Mich.)
Wessex (Menlo Park, Calif.)
West (Provo, Utah)
West L.A. (Los Angeles, Calif.)
West's (Elm Grove, Wisc.)
West Side (Ann Arbor, Mich.)
Western (Gaston, Ore.)
Western (Stoughton, Mass.)
Weston (Weston, Vt.)
Westport (Kansas City, Mo.)
Weyhe (New York, N.Y.)
Wharf (Centreville, Md.)
Wharton (Toronto, Ont.)
Wheel (Oak Park, Ill.)
Wheeler (Elgin, Ore.)
Whelan (Newberry, Fla.)
Whistles (Rossville, Ga.)

White (Granger, Texas)
White (La Jolla, Calif.)
White (New York, N.Y.)
White (Albuquerque, N.M.)
White's (Asbury Park, N.J.)
Whitlock (Bethany, Conn.)
Whitlock's (New Haven, Conn.)
Wikehgan (Mt. Desert, Maine)
Wilder (Brookline, Mass.)
Wilder (Hubbardston, Mass.)
Wildlife (Gainesville, Fla.)
Wild (Larchmont, N.Y.)
Wildwood (Old Forge, N.Y.)
Wilhite (Clearwater, Fla.)
Wilkerson (Lincoln, Mass.)
William (Mineola, N.Y.)
Williams (Bethany, Conn.)
Williams (Calgary, Alt.)
Williams (Williamstown, Mass.)
Willis (Columbus, Ohio)
Willow (Englewood, Colo.)
Wilsey (Olivebridge, N.Y.)
Wilshire (No. Hollywood, Calif.)
Wilson (Bull Shoals, Ark.)
Wilson (Kitchener, Ont.)
Wilson (New York, N.Y.)
Windsor (Brightwaters, N.Y.)
Windsor (Windsor, Conn.)
Wine (Ann Arbor, Mich.)
Winsted (Spg. Green, Wisc.)
Winter (Pittsfield, Maine)
Wise (Baldwin Pl., N.Y.)
Wise (Lake Delton, Wisc.)
With (Lake Placid, N.Y.)
Witkin (New York, N.Y.)
Witten (Southport, Conn.)
Wittenborn (New York, N.Y.)
Wittenborn (Pleasantville, N.Y.)
Wizard's (San Diego, Calif.)
Wofsy (San Francisco, Calif.)
Wolf (New York, N.Y.)
Wolf (Orcutt, Calif.)
Wolf's (Morgantown, W.Va.)
Wolfe (Pt. Claire, Que.)
Womanbooks (New York, N.Y.)
Women's (Contoocook, N.H.)
Womrath's (Hempstead, N.Y.)
Wonder (Frederick, Md.)
Woo (Plainview, N.Y.)

Wood (Boston, Mass.)
Wood (Tampa, Fla.)
Woods (Yakima, Wash.)
Woodburn (Hopewell, N.J.)
Woodbury (Woodbury, Conn.)
Wooden (Ann Arbor, Mich.)
Wooden (Middlebourne, W.Va.)
Woodruff (Grass Lake, Mich.)
Woolf's (Atlanta, Ga.)
Woolmer (Montreal, Que.)
Woolmer (Revere, Pa.)
Word (Montreal, Que.)
Words (Cambridge, Mass.)
Words (San Deigo, Calif.)
Words (So. Bend, Ind.)
Wordsmith (Syracuse, Neb.)
World Mtn. (Tacoma, Wash.)
World Of (Willoughby, Ohio)
World War (W. Roxbury, Mass.)
Worldwide (Boston, Mass.)
Worldwide (Cambridge, Mass.)
World Wide (Long Beach, Calif.)
Wortman (New York, N.Y.)
Wreden (Palo Alto, Calif.)
Wright (Waxahachie, Texas)
Wurlitzer (New York, N.Y.)
Wyatt (San Diego, Calif.)
Wyngate (Bethesda, Md.)

X

Xanadu (Bronx, N.Y.)
Xerxes (Glen Head, N.Y.)
Ximenes (New York, N.Y.)

Y

Yankee (Plymouth, Mass.)
Yankee (Rochester, N.Y.)
Yankee (Williamson, N.Y.)
Yellin (Northridge, Calif.)
Ye Olde (Elmhurst, Ill.)
Ye Olde (St. Joseph, Mich.)
Ye Olde (San Angelo, Texas)
Yerba (San Francisco, Calif.)
Yesterday's (Ashfield, Mass.)
Yesterday's (Hot Springs, Ark.)
Yesterday's (Kalamazoo, Mich.)
Yesterday's (Larchmont, N.Y.)
Yesterday's (Modesto, Calif.)

Yesterday's (Oak Park, Mich.)
Yesterday's (San Diego, Calif.)
Yesterday's (Washington, D.C.)
Yesterdays (Whitman, Mass.)
Yesteryear (Atlanta, Ga.)
Yesteryear (Nampa, Idaho)
Young (New York, N.Y.)
Young (Dobbs Ferry, N.Y.)

Z

Zambelli (New York, N.Y.)
Zaremba (Cambridge, Mass.)
Zeigler (New Oxford, Pa.)
Zeitlin (Los Angeles, Calif.)
Zeitlin Per. (Los Angeles, Calif.)
Zellner's (Easton, Pa.)
Ziagos (Lowell, Mass.)
Zita (New York, N.Y.)
Zubel (Cleveland, Ohio)
Zucker (New York, N.Y.)
Zwicker (New York, N.Y.)
Zwisohn (Albuquerque, N.M.)